TEACHING
SECONDARY SCHOOL SCIENCE

EIGHTH EDITION

TEACHING
SECONDARY SCHOOL SCIENCE

STRATEGIES FOR
DEVELOPING
SCIENTIFIC LITERACY

LESLIE W. TROWBRIDGE

Professor Emeritus of Science Education
University of Northern Colorado

RODGER W. BYBEE

Executive Director, Biological Science Curriculum Study (BSCS)

JANET CARLSON POWELL

Associate Director, Biological Sciences Curriculum Study (BSCS)

Upper Saddle River, New Jersey
Columbus, Ohio

Library of Congress Cataloging in Publication Data
Trowbridge, Leslie W.
   Teaching secondary school science: strategies for developing scientific literacy.–8th ed.
  / Leslie W. Trowbridge, Rodger W. Bybee, Janet Carlson Powell.
      p. cm.
   Includes bibliographical references and index.
   ISBN 0-13-099234-8
   1. Science–Study and teaching (Secondary)–United States. 2. Science teachers-United
States. I. Bybee, Rodger W. II. Carlson Powell, Janet. III. Title.
Q183.3.A1T76 2004
507'.1'2—dc21   2003054128

Vice President and Executive Publisher: Jeffery W. Johnston
Senior Editor: Linda Ashe Montgomery
Associate Editor: Ben M. Stephen
Editorial Assistant: Laura Weaver
Production Editor: Mary M. Irvin
Production Coordination: Lea Baranowski, Carlisle Publishers Services
Design Coordinator: Diane C. Lorenzo
Photo Coordinator: Cynthia Cassidy
Cover Designer: Jason Moore
Cover Image: NASA, Life Cycle of Stars, Hubble Space Telescope Center
Production Manager: Pamela D. Bennett
Director of Marketing: Ann Castel Davis
Marketing Manager: Darcy Betts Prybella
Marketing Coordinator: Tyra Poole

Photo Credits: Anthony Magnacca/Merrill, pp. 11, 93, 99, 156, 160, 170, 181, 342, 343; Library of Congress, p. 44; Laima Druskis/PH College, p. 146; Pearson Learning, p. 144; Scott Cunningham/Merrill, pp. 151, 195, 322, 354, 357; David Mager/Pearson Learning, p. 205; Anne Vega/Merrill, pp. 212, 362; Merrill Education, p. 229; NASA/John F. Kennedy Space Center, p. 234; Pearson Learning, p. 237; Robert Vega/Merrill, p. 257; Laimute Druskis/PH College, p. 324; Rick Singer/PH College, p. 326; Kathy Kirtland/Merrill, p. 359.

This book was set in Berkley by Carlisle Communications, Ltd., and was printed and bound by Banta Book Group. The cover was printed by The Lehigh Press, Inc.

Pearson Education Ltd.
Pearson Education Singapore Pte. Ltd.
Pearson Education Canada, Ltd.
Pearson Education—Japan

Pearson Education Australia Pty. Limited
Pearson Education North Asia Ltd.
Pearson Educación de Mexico, S.A. de C.V.
Pearson Education Malaysia Pte. Ltd

10 9 8 7 6 5 4 3 2 1
ISBN: 0-13-099234-8

PREFACE

The authors have designed the eighth edition of *Teaching Secondary School Science: Strategies for Developing Scientific Literacy* primarily for use by undergraduate preservice teachers of science. The text provides information and suggestions for teaching physical, biological, and earth sciences in the middle school, junior high school, and high school grades. It is also useful for graduate students whose undergraduate majors were outside the field of education, but for whom teaching middle and secondary school science is now a primary career goal. This book is also an important resource for graduate students and experienced teachers in courses concerned with assessment in science classes, curriculum development and reform, instructional problems, and current trends in science teaching. It may also be used as a guide and reference in workshops and institutes for teachers emphasizing strategies for inquiry teaching. The current emphases on science education standards are fully explained and brought to the foreground for science programs in this new edition.

The eighth edition retains the strong features of previous editions. Among these features are emphasis on active pupil involvement in learning, use of inquiry and investigative teaching strategies to provide experiences in solving real problems, gathering data to support hypotheses, discussion of the constructivist approach to teaching, and use of the learning cycle strategy. Many practical examples of successful teaching strategies are provided, based on the extensive science teaching experience of the authors.

Throughout the textbook, the theme of developing scientific literacy among science students is stressed. Included are suggestions for fostering the effective reading of science materials, developing the vocabulary of science, and raising the level of awareness of the interrelationships among science, technology, and society.

ORGANIZATION

The eighth edition has been newly organized to encompass seven units:

- Introduction
- Historical Perspectives and Contemporary Trends
- Goals and Objectives
- Curriculum Perspectives
- Planning for Instruction and Assessment
- Understanding and Working with Students
- Induction and Professional Development

These units have been reorganized not only to provide prospective secondary science teachers with the tools and resources they need to teach science effectively on a day-to-day basis, but also to help them to develop a holistic view of the career in science teaching that they have chosen and to promote enthusiasm and a desire to succeed at the tasks they encounter.

NEW AND UNIQUE FEATURES IN THIS EDITION

- **Teaching science activity features,** including *Investigating Science Teaching, Engaging in Action*

Research, and *Experiencing Ethical Analysis,* are located at the end of each chapter and provide an opportunity for students to experience science.

♦ **Icons highlight new integrated technology resources.** Discussions of technology have been updated and woven throughout the text, including *Technology margin notes* that encourage students to visit the text's new website at www.prenhall.com/ trowbridge for further research and supplemental science activities.

♦ **Guest Editorials** that showcase actual preservice and inservice science teachers appear throughout the text to help illustrate concepts and provide some real-world context for students.

♦ **Two Resource Sections: Appendix A** provides additional *Teaching Science Activities* in biology, chemistry, earth sciences, physics, problem solving, science fair projects, technology, and mathematics, as well as activities for gifted students. *Appendix B* provides sample daily lesson plans that offer practice in using the five-step *learning cycle strategy* for inquiry teaching and learning in physical, life, and earth/ environmental sciences.

ACKNOWLEDGMENTS

The authors wish to acknowledge the many people who assisted in the preparation of this eighth edition of *Teaching Secondary School Science,* including our editors at Merrill/Prentice Hall, Linda Ashe Montgomery and Ben M. Stephen, our project editor at Carlisle Communications, Lea Baranowski, and our many colleagues who helped with the review process: Hans O. Anderson, Indiana University; Richard L. Benoit, University of Novston–Clear Lake; John R. Cannon, University of Nevada, Reno; John Dunkhase, University of Iowa; Linda Cronin Jones, University of Florida; Terrie L. Kielborn, State University of West Georgia; Michael Odell, University of Idaho; Thomas G. Teates, Virginia Tech, Emeritus; Rita K. Voltmer, Miami University; and Robert A. Warren, Dakota State University.

Special recognition is given to the late Dr. Robert B. Sund, whose foresight regarding the philosophy and teaching methods in the first three editions of this text have strongly influenced subsequent editions, including this one. In particular, the current emphasis on inquiry teaching, recommended by the National Research Council in its publication "National Science Education Standards," reflects a teaching strategy that was embodied in all of Dr. Sund's teaching and subsequently became a fundamental part of the philosophy of this book.

DISCOVER THE COMPANION WEBSITE ACCOMPANYING THIS BOOK

THE PRENTICE HALL COMPANION WEBSITE: A VIRTUAL LEARNING ENVIRONMENT

Technology is a constantly growing and changing aspect of our field that is creating a need for content and resources. To address this emerging need, Prentice Hall has developed an online learning environment for students and professors alike—Companion Websites—to support our textbooks.

In creating a Companion Website, our goal is to build on and enhance what the textbook already offers. For this reason, the content for each user-friendly website is organized by topic and provides the professor and student with a variety of meaningful resources. Common features of a Companion Website include:

For the Professor—

Every Companion Website integrates **Syllabus Manager**™, an online syllabus creation and management utility.

- **Syllabus Manager**™ provides you, the instructor, with an easy, step-by-step process to create and revise syllabi, with direct links into Companion Website and other online content without having to learn HTML.
- Students may log on to your syllabus during any study session. All they need to know is the web address for the Companion Website and the password you've assigned to your syllabus.
- After you have created a syllabus using **Syllabus Manager**™, students may enter the syllabus for their course section from any point in the Companion Website.
- Clicking on a date, the student is shown the list of activities for the assignment. The activities for each assignment are linked directly to actual content, saving time for students.
- Adding assignments consists of clicking on the desired due date, then filling in the details of the assignment—name of the assignment, instructions, and whether or not it is a one-time or repeating assignment.
- In addition, links to other activities can be created easily. If the activity is online, a URL can be entered in the space provided, and it will be linked automatically in the final syllabus.
- Your completed syllabus is hosted on our servers, allowing convenient updates from any computer on the Internet. Changes you make to your syllabus are immediately available to your students at their next logon.

For the Student—

- **Topic Overviews**—Outline key concepts in topic areas.
- **Activities and Lesson Plans**—A collection of annotated links to a variety of meaningful science lessons and activities available on the Web. This module also includes useful web links related to national science teaching standards.
- **Web Links**—Topic-specific lists of links to websites that feature current information and resources for educators.
- **Electronic Bluebook**—Send homework or essays directly to your instructor's email with this paperless form.
- **Message Board**—Virtual bulletin board to post or respond to questions or comments from a national audience.
- **Chat**—Real-time chat with anyone who is using the text anywhere in the country—ideal for discussion and study groups, class projects, etc.

To take advantage of the many available resources, please visit the *Teaching Secondary School Science: Strategies for Developing Scientific Literacy, Eighth Edition,* Companion Website at

www.prenhall.com/trowbridge

EDUCATOR LEARNING CENTER:
AN INVALUABLE ONLINE RESOURCE

Merrill Education and the Association for Supervision and Curriculum Development (ASCD) invite you to take advantage of a new online resource, one that provides access to the top research and proven strategies associated with ASCD and Merrill—the Educator Learning Center. At www.EducatorLearningCenter.com you will find resources that will enhance your students' understanding of course topics and of current educational issues, in addition to being invaluable for further research.

HOW THE EDUCATOR LEARNING CENTER WILL HELP YOUR STUDENTS BECOME BETTER TEACHERS

With the combined resources of Merrill Education and ASCD, you and your students will find a wealth of tools and materials to better prepare them for the classroom.

Research

- More than 600 articles from the ASCD journal *Educational Leadership* discuss everyday issues faced by practicing teachers.
- A direct link on the site to Research Navigator™ gives students access to many of the leading education journals, as well as extensive content detailing the research process.
- Excerpts from Merrill Education texts give your students insights on important topics of instructional methods, diverse populations, assessment, classroom management, technology, and refining classroom practice.

- *Classroom Practice*
- Hundreds of lesson plans and teaching strategies are categorized by content area and age range.
- Case studies and classroom video footage provide virtual field experience for student reflection.
- Computer simulations and other electronic tools keep your students abreast of today's classrooms and current technologies.

LOOK INTO THE VALUE OF EDUCATOR LEARNING CENTER YOURSELF

Preview the value of this educational environment by visiting www.EducatorLearningCenter.com and clicking on "Demo." For a free 4-month subscription to the Educator Learning Center in conjunction with this text, simply contact your Merrill/Prentice Hall sales representative.

CONTENTS

SPECIAL FEATURES CONTENTS

INTRODUCTION

As she worked late into the night on her first lesson, Maria Romero wondered about her effectiveness as a science teacher. The next day, Ms. Romero began her lesson by asking the students to describe some genetic concepts: *genes, chromosomes,* and *mutations.* Because Ms. Romero assumed students had learned these concepts in elementary school, she was surprised when they expressed a range of responses, mostly incorrect. She recognized that most students identified the terms as scientific, even biological, but that they consistently responded incorrectly. For example, students indicated that genes were different layers of skin, something in one's blood, things that indicate one's age, and a reproductive part of the body. They also thought chromosomes were either things that clogged one's arteries, or plant-eating animals. Finally, they had the idea that mutations were changes that occurred as one got older, sicknesses caused by bacteria, or structures in plants.

Maria knew that elementary teachers had taught biology and even introduced some of these same ideas about genetics, but the students had little understanding of the information, and the terms had no meaning or importance to them. Maria wondered about her role in helping students develop scientific literacy, especially in connection with teaching secondary school science.

After a little research on the Internet, Ms. Romero discovered that the students displayed what contemporary learning theorists referred to as *misconceptions* or *naive theories.* As she investigated further, she found that psychologists had proposed explanations for student misconceptions and the learning process. Ms. Romero discovered that the model of learning was referred to as *constructivism,* a term that expresses a dynamic and interactive view of learning. In the constructivist view of learning, students continually revise, redefine, and reorganize concepts through interactions among themselves, natural phenomena, science lessons, discussions with other individuals, and the introduction of information from other sources, such as textbooks and science teachers. Students first interpret objects and events in terms of their prior experiences, which, from the perspective of the science teacher, may be incorrect or a misconception. In order to change the misconceptions, someone (for example, a teacher or another student) or an experience (for example, observations of natural phenomena, textbooks, or laboratory experiences) has to challenge the students' misconceptions by showing them that their current ideas are inadequate. Further, students must have time and additional experiences to reconstruct a more adequate and scientifically accurate conception.

The results of this brief review of research provided Maria with insights about teaching secondary school science and strategies for developing scientific literacy. When science teachers discover new and better ways to teach, they experience the excitement of education, and the extension of these insights to students' learning science can be the most exhilarating of a teacher's career.

A life in science teaching can entail frustrations and disappointments; but it also involves satisfactions and achievements that promise to outweigh the problems. This unit introduces some of the ideas and issues that you will have to consider as a science teacher. Ms. Romero's story about the connections between student learning and science teaching is only one of many that could be told, but more importantly, the stories reflect ones you will experience as you become a science teacher and pursue the goal of developing scientific literacy for your students.

BECOMING A SCIENCE TEACHER

If you are reading this sentence, you are in the process of becoming a science teacher. As with other important issues in your life, you no doubt struggled with this decision. While deciding, you probably gathered information on the options—you might have explored the science major, talked to friends and parents, conferred with your college advisor, and even visited your high school science teacher. With all the facts in mind, you decided to become a science teacher. Thinking all was settled, you went to work on your science major and began taking education courses. For a time, most aspects of your career choice seemed resolved. Now you are taking a course to learn about science teaching; soon you will be student teaching; in the foreseeable future, you will have your first job as a science teacher.

All of this is exciting. But now you have an entirely new set of questions about your career. "How do I teach science?" "Am I qualified to teach science?" "What do I need to know about science and technology?" "What science do I teach to middle school or high school students?" "What is science teaching like?" "What are the problems facing science teachers today?" Constantly emerging questions and concerns regarding science teaching are part of becoming a science teacher.

Some of your questions have answers; others depend on your specific talents, personality, knowledge, enthusiasm, and other important, but elusive, qualities. Obviously, we cannot answer all of these questions in this chapter or in this book. However, we can provide some information and direction and can suggest activities to help clarify your strengths and weaknesses and the realities and possibilities of science teaching. The best way you can begin is by completing Activity 1-1, How I See Myself As a Science Teacher, at the end of this chapter.

Visit http://www.prenhall.com/trowbridge and select Topic 6—Professional Development. Select "Web Links," and find the link to the "National Science Teachers Association." Information on this link will give you an introduction to the world's greatest professional science teaching organization, where you will find answers to your questions on choice of a career in science teaching. Write a brief synopsis of your thoughts and decision points on selecting a career to your instructor using the Electronic Bluebook module.

AM I QUALIFIED TO TEACH SCIENCE?

This question is difficult to answer with a simple "yes" or "no" because of the adjective *qualified*. Traditionally, persons have qualified as science teachers by completing a set of educational requirements. In this sense, most individuals can be qualified for teaching. However, there is more to teaching science than fulfilling a set of requirements and more to teaching science than being able to talk about science. Some of the dimensions of science teaching addressed in Activity 1-1 are identifiable in the following discussion.

Understanding Science and Technology

Technology

Link

You should have a background in science, including a broad general knowledge of science and specific knowledge of science in your major. These statements seem obvious. In today's world, however, you also will need an understanding of technology because our society and the experiences of your students are extensively based on technology. You should be aware of the many relationships between science and technology. In the past, science teachers and textbooks presented technology as *applied science;* that is, the enterprise of science resulted in knowledge that was applied to human problems. Although this statement is partially accurate, in some cases scientific advances must wait until technology is developed. Technology can also be viewed as an area of study. As with science, technology also has products and processes that form the basis of study.

In addition to having scientific and technological knowledge, you should apply this knowledge in new situations, use basic science concepts to analyze problems presented by students and synthesize knowledge so that you can answer questions accurately.

Understanding the Purposes of Science Teaching

You have already encountered the term *scientific literacy.* Most individuals in the science education community use this term to express the major purposes of science education. The term also refers to your role in advancing individual development of students and achieving society's aspirations within the context of your classroom. While scientific literacy expresses the highest and most admirable purposes of science teaching, as science teachers, we must be a little more concrete and practical.

What do you think the scientifically and technologically literate person should know, value, and do—as a citizen? As you think about this question, recognize that the final phrase—*as a citizen*—is an important orientation for your answer. An answer that focuses on acquiring knowledge about biology, chemistry, physics, and the earth sciences should be mediated by the question, "What is it about the knowledge from these disciplines that is important for citizens?" How do you justify that knowledge in terms of your student's future role as a citizen? What about values and skills? What values, attitudes, and habits of mind does your teaching of science and technology help students develop?

A very close connection exists between the purpose of developing scientific literacy and various books you will encounter. Both the *National Science Education Standards*[1] and the *Benchmarks for Science Literacy*[2] address the question of exactly what is meant by scientific literacy. We discuss these and other reports in later chapters. For now, think about the following statement on the purpose of science teaching:

> Science teaching should facilitate students' learning about science and technology as they need to understand and use them in their personal lives and as future citizens. Science teaching should sustain students' natural curiosity; develop their skills in inquiry and design; improve their scientific explanations; help them develop an understanding and use of technology; contribute to their understanding of the role, limits, and possibilities of science and technology in society; and inform the choices they must make in their personal and social lives.

Indeed this statement about science teaching is tightly packed with ideas. As you proceed through this book, we will provide many ideas for you as a science teacher.

Visit http://www.prenhall.com/trowbridge and select Topic 1—Science Teaching Standards. Select "National Science Teaching Standards," and find the link to review the standards for personal and social perspectives. This link will provide perspectives on how students connect with their social and personal world and how you as a teacher may understand and fit into their needs. Write and submit your responses to your instructor using the Electronic Bluebook module.

Organizing Science Instruction

You should be well-prepared, thoroughly organized, and have a clear direction in your teaching. There is no substitute for a well-prepared lesson. At one time or another, most science teachers have tried to teach without preparation. More often than not, the lesson was less than effective. As you begin organizing your science program, try to establish the "big picture" by determining the sequence of your program for the year. You may wish to divide the year into units and the units into individual lessons. This simple procedure will give you an overall organization. However, there is more to teaching than organization.

Effective science teachers have a variety of instructional methods, choosing the best for each lesson. Keep in mind the following simple questions: "What do I want my students to learn? How will I know when my students have learned? What experience will best help my students learn?" The answers to these questions will direct you to different teaching methods. We recommend completing Activity 1-2, The What and How of Science Lessons, at the end of this chapter.

Understanding Student Learning

Imagine that you are ready to begin your first science lesson. The students are sitting at their desks, waiting for you to teach them. Do the students in front of you already understand any science concepts? The answer is most probably yes. The students you will be teaching have lived 12 to 16 years. Through formal and informal experiences, the students already have developed ideas about the natural and designed world. They also have placed labels on many of the events, objects, and organisms in the world. In this regard, three points will help you: (1) students have explanations and concepts about their world, (2) many of these concepts are inadequate when compared to scientific explanations or concepts, and (3) students' current concepts of the natural world influence what and how they learn science.[3] David Ausubel summarized this when he wrote: "If I had to reduce all of educational psychology to just one principle, I would say this: The most important single factor influencing learning is what the learner already knows. Ascertain this and teach him accordingly."[4]

Many science teachers approach instruction as though students are empty vessels to be filled with facts, information, and concepts about the world. This perception of how students learn generally is inaccurate. Perhaps a different metaphor is appropriate. Students have packed a suitcase for a trip, but many garments are out of fashion, inappropriate for the climate, and inadequate because the student has grown. The science teacher's task is to help students improve their "intellectual wardrobe." A formal statement of this process would be that students construct their explanations of the world through a personal process in which sensory data are given meaning in terms of prior knowledge. In order for learning to occur, the adequacy of students' current conceptions must be challenged, and appropriate time and opportunities must be provided so students can reconstruct newer and more adequate explanations. Ways to facilitate this learning process will be explored in later chapters. How is this process of learning different from what you currently understand about student learning? Review your response to Activity 1-2, The What and How of Science Lessons, at the end of this chapter.

Recognizing Personal Meaning in Teaching and Learning

Imagine two middle school lessons about the life cycles of organisms. In the first lesson, the students individually read about mealworms. In the second, a container of mealworms is given to small groups of students, and they are allowed to observe the tiny organisms. There are numerous exclamations of "Ooh," "Ahh," "I can't touch this," "It squirmed," "Look at my worm back up!" and other utterances that indicate the students' feelings about the experience.

The second lesson provides an experience that is physically close, is less abstract, and is emotionally connected to the subject. This exercise easily could be ex-

tended into areas such as designing experiments, reaction to stimuli, and the life cycle of mealworms. Both lessons convey the material; however, the second probably would be more effective in teaching the concepts because it offers physical and psychological involvement and social interactions, all of which contribute to personal meaning for the students.

Many contemporary science curricula are inquiry-oriented. For the most part, the inquiry centers on science facts and concepts; physical involvement with materials through laboratory activities provides the primary teaching method for presenting these facts and concepts. The next step in the teaching task is discovery of the personal meaning of these facts and concepts. Obviously, learning science is easier when students are interested and involved. For example, you have been motivated to read this chapter because it has some personal meaning. You are becoming a science teacher and you want to be as effective as possible. What is said in this book likely has personal meaning for you.

Personal meaning has three aspects: (1) the physical closeness of the materials, (2) the psychological interest the individual has in the materials, and (3) the social relevancy of the material or topic. To state this idea succinctly: learning science is enhanced when students have personal involvement with materials and organisms that have some direct importance to them. Usually, science teachers have started lessons with content and assumed that personal meaning would emerge. This progression, as it turns out, may or may not occur. It also is possible to begin with interest, motivation, and personal meaning, and structure the content on these experiences while still teaching scientific concepts.

Personalizing Science Teaching

The effective science teacher realizes the importance of interpersonal relations. One of the important findings in regard to helping others is that objectivity has a negative correlation with effectiveness; that is, if students are treated as objects, the teacher is less successful with students. No one becomes significant to someone else, whether student, fellow teacher, or friend by making the other person feel insignificant. You become significant to others by treating them with integrity, sincerity, and openness.[5] Some of the best science teachers make a conscious effort to regard all students positively, to understand them as human beings, and to help them grow in every way possible. In these situations, students learn science; in fact, they probably learn more science because of the interpersonal rapport. If you become a significant person to your students, the final reward is yours.

Personalizing your relationship with students can include many things, such as, a greater understanding of the pupils, devising different tasks for different students, individual assessment, varied questioning, or the use of different materials and equipment. The idea of effective communication covers, in one way or another, most of the important aspects of personalizing science teaching.

Talking and listening to students is a subtle and important way of recognizing adolescents' growing need for identity. It also enhances the learning relationship and increases the teacher's efficiency in facilitating students' understanding of science.

Managing the Classroom and Maintaining Discipline

When beginning teachers talk about managing the classroom, they usually mean managing students in various activities of science teaching. For example: How will students form groups for laboratory? How will they handle materials and equipment safety? How do you get students to change from one type of activity to another? Such concerns are realistic, but soon you will find that most students respond to directions. Several chapters include detailed information that will help you manage the classroom. The following is some initial advice.

◆ *Preparation will resolve many problems.* For example, having materials ready, knowing the size of groups and how you want to form them, understanding what you expect in the way of behavior and learning outcomes, and giving clear and simple directions all will contribute to effective classroom management.

◆ *Recognize the need for transition between activities.* Making a transition, for instance, from laboratory work to a class discussion, will take several minutes. The students will have to adjust to the different class structure. Plan for the transition time. It should not be long, but this is a time when some students are apt to cause a conflict, and some teachers expect the new norms of behavior to emerge instantly. Sometimes a visible signal, such as turning on an overhead projector, helps complete the transition.

◆ *Try not to panic in nonpanic situations.* Things happen in science classrooms. We cannot tell you what they will be, only that something unexpected will happen. Our advice: stay calm, quickly think about the situation, and act decisively on a proposed solution. And if it doesn't work, try another.

The second topic of the section concerns discipline. This is a concern of most teachers; so if you have this concern, you are not alone. Conflicts between your goals and some student behaviors are inevitable. You should know that most conflicts in science classrooms are resolved quickly and with little difficulty. We prefer the term *conflict* instead of *discipline problem* because its definition—the activities or behaviors of two (or more) individuals are incompatible—suggests that you, as a teacher, have goals, and that part of your duty is to achieve those goals. Avoiding or resolving educational conflicts is the key to maintaining discipline. It is more productive to think and act in ways to avoid or resolve conflicts rather than to engage in discussions of the appropriateness or fairness of rules, policies, or expectations of behavior. Chapter 24 discusses classroom conflicts and their resolution. The following are a few initial suggestions:

◆ Center attention on avoiding or resolving the conflict, as opposed to defining who is right or wrong.
◆ Establish clear communication and agreement on the issues, rules, or expectations that define the conflict.
◆ Use cooperative problem solving. Because of your position as a science teacher, you have the responsibility for resolving classroom conflicts cooperatively and constructively.

Realizing That Your Decisions Determine Effective Science Teaching

Imagine that you are about to begin a chemistry lesson on pollution. Your plan is to demonstrate how the common air pollutants sulfur dioxide (SO_2) and sulfur trioxide (SO_3) are produced when coal and oil containing sulfur are burned. You then plan to show how sulfur trioxide can react with water vapor (H_2O) to form sulfuric acid. You have some sulfuric acid on the demonstration desk so that you can show the students the corrosive power of this acid. As you begin your demonstration, you accidentally knock over the beaker containing the acid, which spills onto papers and books. Take a moment and think about the situation. What would you do?

Suppose you have just finished an activity investigating the effects of continental glaciers. You begin a video on the subject. As soon as you turn off the lights, you hear funny noises and muffled comments. You are fairly (but not absolutely) certain that Melvin, the class clown, is the one making the noise. Take a moment to think about this situation. What would you do?

You could consult this textbook for answers. You could call your methods teacher for answers. You could ask the science supervisor in your district for answers. You could do any number of things, most of which would help only in the unlikely event that the same situation recurred. The one certainty in these and all other real classroom situations is that you will have to decide what to do and respond in the best way possible. Your role as a science teacher will be to combine your knowledge and perceptions of classroom situations with your understanding of the students and then to decide on appropriate action. Many science teachers do not realize this central role of decision making. You must adapt the textbook, the curriculum, and the inquiry method to the events that occur in actual teaching situations.

Look back to the opening question, "Am I qualified to teach science?" This question still cannot be answered with a simple "yes" or "no." But you have begun thinking about what it means to become a science teacher. How well do you understand science? How do you incorporate the purposes of science education? How are you at organizing instruction in science? What ideas do you have about student learning? Can you personalize science teaching? How can you include personal meaning as a part of science lessons? Do you realize what your role will be as manager and conflict resolver in the science classroom? These questions and many more will emerge as you continue the process of becoming a science teacher.

WHAT IS SCIENCE TEACHING REALLY LIKE?

Most individuals entering the teaching profession are concerned about daily happenings in the school. In one form or another they inquire, "What is science teaching like?" When asked to further clarify the question, they want to know what the science programs are like, what teachers talk about, what it is like actually being in front of a class, and the concerns of other science teachers. If you complete Activity 1-3, A First Lesson, at the end of this chapter, some of these questions will be answered. In addition, the next sections give glimpses into different schools, science programs, and science teachers. We have adapted these vignettes from case studies funded by the National Science Foundation (NSF) and completed as part of a larger evaluation of science education. The case studies were completed by individuals who spent time at different schools, observing and participating in the various activities of science teachers.[6] Our adaptations have maintained themes from the original case studies while updating some of the ideas, language, and issues of contemporary science teaching. Although we realize that schools, science programs, and teachers differ, the case studies present some perspectives of actual science programs, some glimpses of teacher conversations, and some insights about science teaching.

Middle School Science Programs

This section characterizes two middle school science programs from the same science district. The district is located in central California (Western City is the name used in the case study), a region where much of the

population is involved in agriculture. Due to the large African American and Hispanic American populations student backgrounds and interests are diverse. This comparison of middle school science programs points out how differently science can be taught at the same grade level and within the same district.[7]

Case Study 1

Science instruction at both schools is offered at the discretion of the building principal. If the principal had no interest in science, the science program at either school would fail to exist. As a consequence, the science program at both schools is a minimal program and is only as complete and thorough as the teachers who instruct in the program. The following observations (made during site visits) tell the story.

> At Middle School I, the "science room" is almost bare. There are some bulletin boards, but they, too, have only a few items about earth tacked on them. The storeroom is badly supplied. There are three microscopes that are in semioperable condition, a few unlabeled chemicals, a few pieces of broken glassware (thistle tubes, test tubes), a Fisher burner, and a Bunsen burner. There is no evidence of any packaged kits (such as Introductory Physical Science [IPS]) or other pieces of equipment that would indicate that the students would have some experience with hands-on equipment. The desks and only a few tables are available in the room. The principal is making a great effort to upgrade this area.
>
> The "science room" at Middle School II is not in the same condition as the science room at Middle School I. Although the walls are still relatively bare, the closets are filled with old, unused materials. There are ample supplies of glassware, hardware, and chemicals normally used in a middle school science class. The collection of rocks and minerals is minimal, as is the preserved animal collection. Relatively speaking, the science room is much better supplied and organized at Middle School II than the science room at Middle School I.

The science program at Middle School II has been well-established by the instructor, who has been at Middle School II for three years. He follows a course of study that he has developed over the years, and he continues to modify it. His counterpart at Middle School I appears to flounder in the science area. At Middle School I, a considerable amount of time is spent studying earthquakes. ("Since we live in an area that is earthquake-prone, I feel the students should spend some time studying earthquakes.") Besides earthquakes, there is not much evidence of other science topics being discussed, nor is there any evidence of students having an opportunity to get their hands on any equipment.

Because the science program at the middle school level is left up to the individual school and the respective science teachers, a wide range of areas and approaches are used by the science teachers. A great number of science teachers in the district are not aware of contemporary science curricula and their packaged equipment and, as a consequence, do not use them.

The teachers, when asked about their major concerns about the science program at their respective schools, responded accordingly:

Middle School I

The students lack discipline. They make little or no effort to learn. They would rather talk and delay the teaching process. They are the ones that will suffer the most.

Middle School II

The biggest problem at the school is absences. The students don't seem to care. They would much rather be somewhere else. Discipline is not as much of a problem here as is the lack of supplies and equipment. I always have to be on the lookout for equipment.

Other teachers in the same schools have voiced concern about such things as

- lack of administrative support,
- lack of supplies and equipment,
- use of outdated books,
- large classes,
- lack of student motivation,
- lack of parental interest, and
- lack of adequate facilities.

When the science teachers were asked to describe a typical day in their science classes, they replied with this summary:

The kids come into class as soon as the bell rings. We check their homework (this is done for purposes of reinforcement). We present a short lecture (at least 20 minutes) on a given topic. We make an assignment for the following day. On Fridays, we schedule quizzes based on the last four days of work.

High School Science Programs

This case study was completed in a small city on the plains east of the Rocky Mountains. The name used for the school was Fall River.[8]

Case Study 2

The high school science program consists of 18 courses. Despite lenient graduation requirements, enrollments are high. The courses are staffed with an impressive group of teachers, most of whom have advanced degrees in the disciplines and have attended summer programs.

The biology program has the largest enrollment and staff. All students who elect biology take a one-semester introductory course, after which they can choose one or more follow-up courses in ecology, plant structure and function, social biology, microbiology, heredity, and animal anatomy. Some students fail or opt out of biology after the introductory course. An advanced placement course in biology is also offered.

The content of the introductory course is largely the same, regardless of who teaches it. The text used is from the Biology Sciences Curriculum Study (BSCS). The instructional methods are largely lectures, laboratory investigations, review sheets, and occasionally films and guest speakers. Although the BSCS text emphasizes developing students' interest and heuristic inquiry, the classroom instruction at Fall River High tends to be formal, didactic, and organized. Almost the entire text is covered. This is a large quantity of material for one semester, but it provides the background needed for the more specialized follow-up courses. In the ecology course, for example, the students review the relevant BSCS chapters and then go on to more specialized texts. They participate in simulations designed to show the relationship between values and environmental processes. Topics covered include ecology and the law, mountain ecosystems, and the food chain. Laboratory investigations are conducted on photosynthesis and chromatography, as are field investigations in small ecosystems near the school building. The students conduct independent research on biomes.

Although the other follow-up courses are not so directly related to the environment, a strong environmental consciousness pervades the entire department and has been adopted by many of the students. When asked about the principles behind the program, three teachers made the following statements:

The purpose is to make them better citizens, help them understand the issues in society that are related to science, help them make better decisions. For example, I ask them how much longer they're going to be able to drive up and down Main Street. I don't try to impose my own view on them, but I do try to make them think.

You can't separate our values and science anymore. When we talk about population growth or genetics, issues come in. I tell them they should learn the material, if only so they can determine their own future.

A person just can't be an effective citizen unless he can read and understand political issues that have scientific overtones. . . . The average citizen must have the awareness and appreciation of how his actions affect the environment and what is likely to happen, depending on the choices he makes now.

In addition to the idea of developing environmental consciousness, the teachers believe their purpose is to provide a strong and diverse academic experience that puts the students in touch with the

GUEST EDITORIAL ◆ LAUREL HALL

Science Education Student
Geology Carleton College, Northfield, Minnesota

WHO ME?! A SCIENCE TEACHER?

"Teaching science? Me? You've got to be nuts." This would have been my reaction a few months ago; however, today my response is just the opposite: science teaching is a plausible career for me. Why the change of opinion in such a short time? The answer is simple: After seriously evaluating my interests and goals, with respect to possible careers, I found that teaching would allow me to incorporate and use more of them. The next step was to discover what education is and what methods are used. This step was achieved through a science methods course where I actually observed and participated in various teaching activities of a class at a local school. The career experience in this field has had an important positive effect on my knowledge and opinions of the educational system, besides showing me some of the realities of science teaching.

I have always been interested in helping people learn; my past working experience as a camp counselor, recreational leader, and YMCA swimming instructor and coach is evidence of this interest. However, teaching in the educational system did not appeal to me; I felt that I would become very bored with teaching the same thing to several classes year after year. Yet, with my recent finding that education was a career possibility and that many of my goals and interests could be combined with it, I began to take a new look at education and saw it as a challenge as long as I could eradicate my adolescent biases toward the educational system.

I entered the education program still unsure of what teaching science entailed. I soon found out that my preconceived biases toward the educational system, based on my own public school experiences, were not universally true. The elimination of these biases was the major factor in altering my opinion of the system. Now, instead of looking at the system as hopeless, I see myself as an agent of change: I can set an example and hope others will follow. I can challenge myself to improve, change, and alter lessons, activities, and methods to counteract any boredom in myself and in the students and to communicate with more students.

Through a science methods course, I learned about education, the variety of methods that can be used to attain objectives, and some of the realities of teaching. From these new views, I can see that teaching can be a much tougher occupation than I had previously expected. It involves many time-consuming activities, such as developing new units, changing lesson plans, improving activities, keeping up to date on recent developments in the specific area of science, and keeping enthusiasm at a high level. Yet, it is through these same time-consuming processes that the rewards of teaching are to be found: for example, communicating with those who previously did not understand or care, introducing students to new and interesting ideas and techniques, developing within the students an enthusiasm for continued learning, and watching them develop as individuals.

major body of knowledge in biology and the processes used to gain the knowledge. One teacher reported, "Any systematized body of knowledge is part of the foundation of civilization. It's part of their responsibilities as citizens to be aware of it. Science has applications in all their lives."

The biology program is not without its rough edges. Students in the introductory course fail in higher proportions than in other courses. Most teachers are determined to hold to their standards, however. Based on previous experience, teachers are convinced that students will take the easiest possible path, dilute the content of the course, and make the follow-up course

structure impossible. The teachers feel that any student who makes the effort can pass.

Another serious problem is lack of space and facilities. There are two well-equipped laboratories, but sometimes four sections must share them in a single class period. Therefore, the teachers have to coordinate classes so that while one section is doing lab work, the other teacher must lecture in a classroom designed for physics. No space is available for advanced laboratory preparations. They look back wistfully on the year they had a teacher's aide. *"Not having the facilities lowers my interest and energy and influences what I teach. The situation has discouraged every bit of open-ended inquiry I've got. A question comes up from the class and I think of an investigation that would be related, but there we are in the physics room, so I lecture."*

About 40 percent of each graduating class go to college. A greater proportion of students follow a traditional college-preparatory course of study. Most of this group take chemistry in the junior year. The chemistry classes are packed, but whether the high enrollment is due to students' scientific curiosity, the genial personality and showmanship of the teacher, or the abundance of A grades is unclear. Although some of the best students complained that the class "wasn't tough enough . . . didn't go too deep into chemistry," the instructor primarily wants *"them to be interested in science and to master the basic material in the field. I feel like anybody can learn at the level I teach them. The kids who are really interested then can go off on their own and learn more."*

The text *Modern Chemistry* is used, and the approach is traditional. The greatest amount of class time is spent in lectures and laboratory experiments. The laboratory areas are well equipped for a basic program, but the teacher longs for materials that would support more advanced work. The laboratories are terribly overcrowded, and the teacher worries that someone will be injured in an accident.

The physics course is taught by a man with experience and impressive credentials—advanced degrees in physics and math. His laboratory is well equipped, and under his leadership the science program has always received a healthy share of the school budget.

In answering a question about the purpose of science education, the physics teacher spoke of his own philosophy:

> In recent years, I've wondered if you could justify it. Earlier I would have said that physics was a part of cultural knowledge, something enormously practical, like all science having something philosophically to offer the public, and intellectual integrity which would carry over into politics and society.
>
> Now I don't know. We live in a technological society, so it is necessary to propagate information to some parts of the society. But for the general person in high school who will eventually go into business or become a homemaker they really don't need to know about physics, except in a very superficial way. If you want a kid to know how to change a tire, you teach him about levers. . . . I'm a good sailor and I apply my knowledge of physics, but other people are better sailors and have no physics background.
>
> That is too pessimistic. Let me state it this way. Everyone deals with nature. Every high school student knows a great deal of physics, and the teacher merely encourages him to abstract his knowledge to form more general and sometimes more useful patterns of thought. If the student can deal with ideas in the abstract, he learns this before going to college and can thereby make a sounder choice of careers. He may not do better than another competent college student, but he has had the benefit of guidance and

proven academic discipline. Finally, and this is important for all ability ranges of students, a sense of being at home in the universe must be transmitted. The physical world and the technology of man must be dealt with as an important part of the total culture he is to inherit.

In addition to the more traditional track of three courses, the science program includes a great variety of offerings: astronomy, archaeology, geology, conceptual physics, electronics (less mathematical than the physics course), introduction to chemistry (a student-centered laboratory program using discovery techniques and emphasizing the process of science), and space science (a rather easy course for students who have a previous failure or little interest in science).

The man responsible for several of these courses is a former geologist who runs his classes very informally, trying to structure each one around the interests and questions of the students. Environmental consciousness appears to be a strong focus in his course as well. In the course description for geology, he wrote:

> Our study of geology will be centered around the following concepts. Geology, the study of the earth, is essentially an environmental science. . . . Man . . . must learn to function in harmony with the earth environment. . . . Citizen roles dictate an understanding of the environmental problems confronting man, solutions to these problems, and the responsibilities of citizens and government to work toward their solutions.

These objectives are not mere educational cant. During his classes this philosophy is never far off, injected even into a presentation on the physical properties of minerals.

In his courses, perhaps more than those of others, scientific methods are given prominent attention. One of his science courses centers on the following objectives:

> Demonstrates an understanding of the process of identifying and defining a scientific problem or question to be investigated . . . of proposing a logical test of a hypothesis . . . of testing the effects of variables and controlling relevant variables . . . the ability to synthesize data from several sources to arrive at generalizations or conclusions . . . withhold judgments or conclusions until adequate information has been validated.

The following is a second view of high school science. This program is from a large high school in a major city in the Pacific Northwest. The name used to identify the school is Hardy.[9]

> The natural science program at Hardy is strong. It is paced by an active biology program team-taught by three full-time and one part-time teacher. Currently 472 students (93 percent of the sophomore enrollment)[10] are enrolled in a laboratory course led by the department chairman. The classrooms are filled with science artifacts (birds, weather maps, rocks, specimens, snakes, etc.), and the

An experienced science teacher uses interesting examples of natural phenomena to engage student interest.

spirit of the group can be portrayed by two episodes: an open session with students one day after school to discuss the implications for science of the presidential election and a weekend assault on the walls separating the three biology rooms, resulting in open portals that central administration had stalled on for nearly two years.

Probably 80 percent of the class time is spent by students working on experiments, and three tracks (developed locally) are provided, depending on student ability. The course is patterned after college science courses and seems difficult for many of the students. However, teacher enthusiasm and interest seem to rub off on students, and they rate the course as very good. Marine biology, human physiology, mushrooms, and wildflowers are other courses offered as part of this strong program. Exactly which courses will be offered during a given semester depends a great deal on student interest. A college-style registration procedure is used, and if a given course doesn't fill (i.e., isn't selected by more than 25 students), then it may not be offered. Conversely, sections are added if student interest is high.

During the semester following the site visit, the life science enrollment was as follows:

Biology II 250
Molecular Biology 29
Marine Biology 53
Wild Flowers/Edibles 34
Human Physiology 53

Apparently, some of those students in the first semester of biology opt for more specialized courses the second semester.

The first year of chemistry is currently taken by 146 students (27 percent of the junior enrollment) and is taught as a laboratory science. The five sections of chemistry are handled by the physics teacher and a chemistry

teacher who also teaches biology. The course is viewed by students and teachers as primarily a college-preparatory course. A third semester of general chemistry and a semester of organic chemistry are offered if enough students register for these courses.

Physics may be taken in either the junior or senior year, and currently 68 students (13 percent of the senior enrollment) are enrolled. About half of the group are girls, which is seen by students and teachers as a result of changing female roles. Counselors, parents, and friends are relaxing their attitude that advanced science is only for males. The course has some laboratory components, but in general is taught more like a mathematics class—that is, explain concepts, assign problems, correct problems, discuss difficulties. This routine is interrupted occasionally by exams or experiments, but the doing of problems is predominant over the doing of science found in the other classes. The class is clearly for the academically elite, and the teacher sees no need to try to increase enrollments.

An adjunct to the science program is a popular horticulture program offered in the technology education department. In a temporary building and greenhouse located about two blocks from the main building, 113 students were enrolled in environmental horticulture. The course meets the state requirements for a laboratory science, but although it is considered a strong program by the science teachers, there seems to be very little interaction between it and the rest of the science program. It has grown through the efforts of an active teacher whose academic home is technology education.

The science program is strong and surviving, but it is being subjected to many challenges: transfer of teachers, declining budgets for texts and equipment, and competition from the basics. It may be seriously affected if subjected to many more problems.

Conversations with Science Teachers

In this section, comments from the teachers' lounge are used to point out some issues in science education. The observations are from a case study made in a greater Boston high school.[11]

The Role of the Experiment in Science Teaching

STEVE (Looking through a workbook of experiments David has been using in his class): The trouble with a lot of this stuff is that it is so obvious. Even when you have done the experiment, you only know what you knew already.

DAVID: Maybe it's obvious to you, but it isn't always obvious to these kids. To some of them maybe, but not to all of them. Sometimes they do know what is going to happen in the experiment, but they only know it vaguely; they haven't really thought it out. Like this morning we were talking about that experiment where you float a cork in water, then push an upturned glass down on top of it. They did the experiment and saw what happened. When I asked why the cork went down, one girl just said "gravity." Well, you can see what she means; it does involve gravity, but that's not an explanation of what you see happening.

STEVE: Yes, but you can't say that's exciting. Floating corks in water. I want to get these kids interested in science. I want experiments you can do that set them all off saying, "Wow! How did that happen?" Something that really challenges and excites them. (Looking at the book) Finding out 20 percent of the air is oxygen, that's no challenge. Why not just tell them. You shouldn't just have to do an experiment for everybody, only if it excites them or triggers them off.

DAVID: But before you can work on these dramatic experiments they have got to know scientific procedures and appreciate the methods. All this week I've been emphasizing the five stages of writing a lab report and getting them to appreciate the difference between observation and explanation. You have to do it several times, and it takes practice. And for most of them, writing a scientific report is not something they are used to doing; in fact, some of them have gotten so used to multiple-choice tests that it is an effort for them to write complete sentences.

STEVE: Maybe you are right. I think teaching them rigor and method is a useful thing to do. The danger, though, is that you end up just pacifying them. The science that is going to affect their lives isn't the five stages of writing a lab report. It is nuclear power, pollution, recombinant DNA research. Those are the things I want them to know about, and I want them to be able to pursue things for themselves, not just because they are in a course or a textbook.

The Strategies and Methods of Science Teaching

CIVICS TEACHER: I feel constrained by the forty-minute period and the pressures of working in a building that is really only a heap of classrooms. I'd like to be able to get out more with the students and get to do more things.

SCIENCE TEACHER: I don't agree. I think almost the most important thing for the students to learn is the discipline of working in the classroom. When they come here at the beginning of the year, they are all up in the air and we have got to bring them down. You've got to get order and discipline before you can give it up.

CIVICS TEACHER: By this time of year [March], they should have learned some sort of classroom discipline. The problem is that enforcing it starts to become an end in itself. You begin to forget about what you are trying to teach and just think about keeping a neat, orderly class.

SCIENCE TEACHER: I don't just think of discipline as keeping an island of sanity in my class, whatever happens in the rest of the school. I don't think you can separate discipline in class from the discipline of the subject. In science especially, where you have expensive equipment and valuable things around, you have to learn certain ways of behaving, and learning those ways of behaving are [sic] part of learning the subject.

SECOND SCIENCE TEACHER: I'd like to get out of the classroom more because there are a lot of things I want to do that you can't very easily do in school. I think really the only way to get students to appreciate the significance of things like environmental pollution is to get them out of the classroom [and] looking at it.

ENGLISH TEACHER: My classroom is important to me. I can't imagine a better place for doing the kind of teaching I want to do. Going outside the classroom on some occasions might have advantages. I'd like to have students going out to interview people, for example. But what they do in the classroom (which is mainly writing) has got to remain at the center of everything else for me.

CIVICS TEACHER: Sometimes I feel limited by the expectations the students have of me as their teacher. For most of them, the range of things they will allow in a teacher is very limited, and this makes it very hard to start anything new or different. The experience I have had in the past of working a lot outside school has shown me that you can have quite a different kind of relationship with students once you get them out of the school building.

ENGLISH TEACHER: I don't want a different kind of relationship. I want to be the kind of teacher I am.

Visit http://www.prenhall.com/trowbridge and select Topic 1—Science Teaching Standards. Select "National Science Teaching Standards" and find the link to review the "National Science Education Standards" for Physical, Life, and Earth and Space Science standards. This subject focuses on science concepts, principles, and theories that are fundamental for all students. You can then assess your own competencies for teaching the content.

A Conclusion About Science Teaching

People in schools are conscientiously doing the jobs they have defined: tutor, scholar, but also at times, counselor, steward, custodian, and social director.

Teachers must juggle the expectations of the invisible, distant, and mostly impersonal profession of science education and the local, powerful, and relentless demands of teaching. The two roles do not necessarily conflict, but the latter usually overpowers and preempts the former.[12]

We recommend completing Activity 1-4, An Interview with a Science Teacher.

HOW CAN YOU BECOME AN EFFECTIVE SCIENCE TEACHER?

We assume that you have the normal concerns of beginning teachers. We also assume that you are motivated to become an effective science teacher. Three things that will help reduce these concerns and increase effectiveness are time, experience, and preparation. Remember that this is only the beginning of your career as a science teacher and you cannot accomplish everything you wish, learn everything you need, or do everything you would like during the science methods course or even during the first year of teaching. Becoming an effective science teacher and comfortable in your role takes time.

The corollary to time is experience. There is no substitute for the actual experience of teaching science. It is the one sure way that you will detect strengths and weaknesses in yourself as a teacher. You will learn more about yourself and science teaching in the first year than you can now imagine. It will not be easy, but it will be interesting and challenging. Every day will involve you in experiences that contribute to your effectiveness.

You can do something specific and immediate to help reduce your concerns and develop your effectiveness. *Be prepared.* This message is crucial. Some teach-

ers equate preparation with knowledge of their scientific discipline. Although this is essential, we imply much more by the words "Be prepared." We have mentioned some ideas, such as understanding the purposes of science teaching, organizing science instruction, understanding student learning, and managing the classroom. Many of these are the other topics of this book. For now, one thing we can do is turn to you and ask about your concerns, apprehensions, and needs concerning science teaching, as in Activity 1–5, My Concerns, at the end of this chapter.

BECOMING A SCIENCE TEACHER: SOME CLOSING REFLECTIONS

One premise in this chapter (and of this book) is that you can become a better science teacher. Students entering science teaching and those already in the profession are concerned about improving the quality of instruction in science and increasing student learning. Your own concerns and activities in studying this book and taking the methods course have already demonstrated your willingness to learn more about science teaching. Once you obtain a teaching position, professional development in the form of workshops, curriculum revision, and continuing education courses will be available. Participation in all of these programs indicates a desire to become a better science teacher.

A second premise is that you are the one person who best knows what is necessary for you to become an effective teacher. This is the reason for the self-evaluation exercises. Your college supervisor, methods professor, and perhaps classroom teachers also will provide you with feedback. This feedback will help, especially when you combine it with your own insights and act on the information. In other words, you have many personal choices in the process of becoming a science teacher.

The responsibility for becoming an effective science instructor is yours. Many individuals and an abundance of programs are available to aid you. Ultimately, however, you are the person who must combine all of the elements to facilitate science education for your students.

The following are several goals that are related to your professional growth. Becoming a science teacher means continually:

♦ Demonstrating an adequate understanding of scientific knowledge. This goal includes an in-depth understanding of specific disciplines, as well as a broad understanding of science in general. It also includes a comprehension of the role of science in our society.

- Demonstrating an adequate understanding of scientific inquiry. Specifically, this understanding includes the attitudes and abilities of inquiry and the application of scientific philosophies to classroom instruction.
- Demonstrating an adequate awareness of educational foundations and the place of science education as a discipline in the larger realm of education.
- Demonstrating an adequate understanding of and ability to use teaching methods. This goal includes the ability to plan and organize activities for the classroom, to carry out standard classroom procedures, to use a variety of techniques and equipment in teaching science lessons, and to assess student progress.
- Demonstrating adequate interpersonal relations and an enthusiasm for working with all students.
- Demonstrating the synthesis of these five goals into the practice of teaching science in the secondary school.

Summary

The experience of becoming a science teacher is identifiable through the questions one asks. Here we assumed you might ask, "Am I qualified to teach science?" Although this is impossible to answer, several activities were presented, each allowing you to investigate the question. We also described several attributes essential for science teaching: understanding science, understanding students, organizing materials for science instruction, personalizing your interaction with students, recognizing personal meaning as a part of learning, managing the classroom and maintaining discipline, and very important, realizing your own role as decision maker in the science classroom.

After discussing the first question, we turned to a second: "What is science teaching like?" To answer this we used a variety of vignettes drawn from case studies of schools from all over the country.

Next, we turned to the question of becoming an effective science teacher. The question seems to be a part of the natural sequence of questions asked by students as they enter teaching. Once the initial anxiety of becoming a science teacher is overcome, individuals turn to the problem of becoming a better teacher. Time, experience, and preparation contribute to the increasing effectiveness of the beginning teacher. One way of helping to overcome apprehension is to identify concerns and act on reducing them. We recommended completing a self-examination by responding to the question, "What are my concerns?"

The chapter ends with some goals related to the process of becoming a science teacher. The goals are summarized as demonstrating an understanding of scientific knowledge and inquiry, of science education as a discipline, and of teaching methods; forming adequate interpersonal relationships with students; and synthesizing these goals into the teaching of science in the secondary school.

◆

References

1. National Research Council, *National Science Education Standards* (Washington, DC: Author, 1996).
2. American Association for the Advancement of Science, *Benchmarks for Science Literacy* (Washington, DC: Author, 1993).
3. Joseph D. Novak, "Learning Science and the Science of Learning," *Studies in Science Education*, 15 (1988): 77–101.
4. David Ausubel, *The Psychology of Meaningful Verbal Learning* (New York: Grune & Stratton, 1963).
5. Arthur W. Combs, Donald L. Avila, and William W. Purkey, *Helping Relationships: Basic/Concepts for the Helping Professions* (Boston: Allyn and Bacon, 1978).
6. The project, titled "Case Studies in Science Education," was directed by Robert Stake and Jack Easley at the Center for Instructional Research and Curriculum Evaluation at the University of Illinois at Urbana-Champaign, in 1977.
7. Rodolfo G. Serrano, *The Status of Science, Mathematics, and Social Science in Western City, U. S. A., Case Studies in Science Education,* Booklet 7 (Urbana-Champaign: University of Illinois, June 1977), pp. 10–13.
8. Mary Lee Smith, *Teaching and Science Education in Fall River, Case Studies in Science Education,* Booklet 2 (Urbana-Champaign: University of Illinois, May 1977), pp. 5–9.
9. Wayne Welch, *Science Education in Urbanville: A Case Study, Case Studies in Science Education,* Booklet 5 (Urbana-Champaign: University of Illinois, April 1977), pp. 4–5.
10. This figure is obtained by dividing the total biology enrollment by the number of sophomores. Some juniors and seniors, however, take biology, and some sophomores take other sciences.
11. Rob Walker, *Case Studies in Science Education: Boston,* Booklet 11 (Urbana-Champaign: University of Illinois, April 1977), pp. 6, 7, 15, 25.
12. Smith, *Fall River,* p. 23.

◆ ———————— INVESTIGATING SCIENCE TEACHING ———————— ◆

ACTIVITY 1–1
HOW I SEE MYSELF AS A SCIENCE TEACHER

The statements in this exercise allow you to examine your perceptions about yourself as a science teacher. The exercise is designed for your personal knowledge and need not be shared with others. Read the statement and decide if you strongly agree, moderately agree, agree, are neutral, slightly disagree, moderately disagree, or strongly disagree. Then place the appropriate number in the space to the left of the statement.

Strongly agree 7	*Moderately* agree 6	*Slightly* agree 5	*Neutral* 4	*Slightly* disagree 3	*Moderately* disagree 2	*Strongly* disagree 1

_____ 1. I am well informed about science and technology.

_____ 2. Students can generally take care of themselves.

_____ 3. I identify with people.

_____ 4. My task as a science teacher is one of assisting students to learn.

_____ 5. The meaning of science and technology for our society is more important than the facts and events of science and technology.

_____ 6. Science and technology are meaningful in my personal life.

_____ 7. For the most part, other people are friendly.

_____ 8. Basically, I am an adequate science teacher.

_____ 9. I see my purpose as concerned with larger issues of science, technology, and society.

_____ 10. I try to understand how my students perceive things.

_____ 11. I have a commitment to the field of science and technology.

_____ 12. Students have their own worth and integrity.

_____ 13. I am a dependable and reliable science teacher.

_____ 14. I usually do not conceal my personal feelings and shortcomings from students.

_____ 15. Teaching science is best done by encouraging personal development of students.

_____ 16. Science and technology are essential in our society.

_____ 17. People are basically trustworthy and dependable.

_____ 18. Students generally see me as personable and likable.

_____ 19. I am personally involved with my students.

_____ 20. I am accepting of individual differences in my students.

_____ 21. My understanding of science and technology is adequate.

_____ 22. Students are important sources of personal and professional satisfaction for me.

_____ 23. As a science teacher, I am worthy of respect.

_____ 24. The process of learning science is important for our culture.

_____ 25. My orientation is toward people more than things.

The items in this list are keyed to five important dimensions of science teaching as a helping profession. If you would like to see how you perceive yourself on these dimensions, complete the following section. Add your response for the items in the left column. Divide that number by five. The result should be a number between seven and one for each of the dimensions of science teaching listed. The numbers give some indication of your perceptions of yourself as related to the different categories.

Items	Average		Dimensions of Science Teaching
1, 6, 11, 16, 21	÷ 5	_____	Perceptions about science subject matter
2, 7, 12, 17, 22	÷ 5	_____	Perceptions of students
3, 8, 13, 18, 23	÷ 5	_____	Perceptions of yourself as a science teacher
4, 9, 14, 19, 24	÷ 5	_____	Perceptions of your purpose as a science teacher
5, 10, 15, 20, 25	÷ 5	_____	Perceptions of the teaching task

ACTIVITY 1–2
THE WHAT AND HOW OF SCIENCE LESSONS

In this activity you are presented with a teaching situation on the left and asked to match a method from the right to achieve your teaching goal. In each case you should give a rationale for your choice of method. Complete the activity alone. Then share your responses with several other students in the class.

What you want to accomplish—the goal	How you would accomplish your goal—the method	Methods of teaching
1. Introduce the concept of acids and bases	_____	A Bulletin board
2. Clarify the effects of air pollution	_____	B Demonstration
3. Summarize the effects of erosion	_____	C Discussion
4. Show the interrelationships of organisms in a community	_____	D Field Trip / E Video
5. Evaluate the students' understandings of pulleys	_____	F Internet / G CD-ROM
6. Differentiate the phylum Echinodermata from the phylum Chordata	_____	H Guest speaker / I Laboratory investigation
7. Realize the ethical decisions involved in scientific research	_____	J Library research / K Lecture
8. Introduce the structure of DNA	_____	L Projects / M Questioning
9. Show the dynamic qualities of weather	_____	N Quiz / O Analyzing data
10. Expand the students' understanding of the systems concept	_____	P Role playing / Q Presentation using video images
11. Review the concept of force	_____	R Simulation game / S Television
12. Teach students to handle the microscope correctly	_____	T Test / U Chalkboard

Additional methods:
V Computer simulation
W Calculator (hand-held)
X Records

13. Outline safety procedures for the chemistry laboratory   _____

14. Introduce students to careers in science   _____

15. Help students understand the role of science and   _____
    technology in society

ACTIVITY 1–3
A FIRST LESSON

It is strongly recommended that you teach a short science lesson early in the methods course. Preferably, this lesson should be taught in a local science class; however, it may be taught to your peers in the methods class. An important objective of this lesson is to help you answer two questions: "Can I teach science?" and "What is science teaching like?" There is no better way to answer these questions than to actually teach a science lesson.

Here are some guidelines to help you prepare your first lesson.

1. Keep the lesson simple. Try to present a single concept, single process, or single skill.
2. What do you hope to accomplish by the end of the lesson? What should the students know or be able to do that they could not do before the lesson?
3. What experiences will best achieve the goals and be interesting and motivating for the students?
4. What is the most effective way to organize the materials or experiences of the lesson? What is its conceptual structure and instructional sequence?
5. Use the following format as the basis of your lesson plan.

Title of Lesson

Goal of lesson (See item 2 above.)

Procedures (Outline the progress and methods of the lesson.)

What do you want to teach?	*How* do you plan to teach it?	*How* will you know the students learned?
1.	1.	1.
2.	2.	2.
3.	3.	3.
4.	4.	4.
5.	5.	5.
6.	6.	6.

What is your plan for starting the lesson?

What is your plan for ending the lesson?

Materials needed for lesson:

Length of lesson in minutes:

SELF-CRITIQUE OF YOUR FIRST LESSON

1. Rate the following:

	Poor	Fair	Good	Excellent	Comments
Voice quality and articulation	_____	_____	_____	_____	_____
Poise	_____	_____	_____	_____	_____
Adaptability and flexibility	_____	_____	_____	_____	_____
Use of English	_____	_____	_____	_____	_____
Procedure	_____	_____	_____	_____	_____
Enthusiasm	_____	_____	_____	_____	_____
Continuity	_____	_____	_____	_____	_____
Maintenance of good class control	_____	_____	_____	_____	_____
Provision for individual differences	_____	_____	_____	_____	_____
Ability to interest students	_____	_____	_____	_____	_____
Ability to involve students	_____	_____	_____	_____	_____
Ability to ask questions	_____	_____	_____	_____	_____
Ability to answer questions	_____	_____	_____	_____	_____
Use of instructional methods	_____	_____	_____	_____	_____
Provision of adequate summaries	_____	_____	_____	_____	_____
Budgeting of time	_____	_____	_____	_____	_____
Organization of the lesson	_____	_____	_____	_____	_____
Knowledge of subject	_____	_____	_____	_____	_____

2. Did you achieve your goals?
3. What were the strengths of the presentation?
4. What were the weaknesses of the presentation?
5. What would you change if you were to teach this lesson again?

ACTIVITY 1–4
AN INTERVIEW WITH A SCIENCE TEACHER

One way to find out what science teaching is like is to interview a science teacher. Tell the teacher the reason for the meeting and the general topics of discussion. If at all possible, make arrangements to observe a class period before the interview. This visit will give you some insights concerning the teacher's style and approach to science instruction. It will also provide some bases of discussion. You may wish to ask the following questions to get the conversation started:

1. What is the science program in your school?
   How many courses are offered?
   What is the enrollment in life science? Earth science? Physical science? What textbook is used?
   How does the science program in your school relate to the rest of the science program in the district?
   Do you offer any special science courses?
   Has the science program changed in the last five years?
2. What do you see as the important trends and issues in science teaching?

Have enrollments in science increased? Decreased? Has the science budget increased? Decreased? How much do you use the laboratory in science teaching? Do you introduce any science-related social issues?

3. What are your concerns as a science teacher? Are your facilities adequate? Do you have materials for your program? Is student interest high? Low? Is maintaining discipline a problem?

4. What are your greatest rewards as a science teacher? Seeing students learn? Helping other people? Working with interesting and exciting colleagues? Contributing to the public's scientific literacy?

5. Why is science important?

ACTIVITY 1–5
MY CONCERNS

Listed below are several statements that are commonly expressed by students entering teaching. Indicate your present concern about the problem by placing an "X" in a space provided on the continuum: Number 1 indicates little concern, whereas number 9 indicates a high degree of concern.

1. Developing short- and long-term purposes, goals, and objectives for science instruction 1 2 3 4 5 6 7 8 9
2. Understanding scientific inquiry 1 2 3 4 5 6 7 8 9
3. Motivating students to learn science 1 2 3 4 5 6 7 8 9
4. Designing programs to increase the learning of science 1 2 3 4 5 6 7 8 9
5. Recognizing and responding to different developmental levels of students 1 2 3 4 5 6 7 8 9
6. Understanding the dynamics of student groups 1 2 3 4 5 6 7 8 9
7. Adapting to the special needs and abilities of pupils 1 2 3 4 5 6 7 8 9
8. Designing programs for the individual needs of students 1 2 3 4 5 6 7 8 9
9. Knowing about science-curriculum programs and instructional materials 1 2 3 4 5 6 7 8 9
10. Incorporating other disciplines, such as mathematics or social science, into the science program 1 2 3 4 5 6 7 8 9
11. Understanding and using different instructional strategies 1 2 3 4 5 6 7 8 9
12. Planning and organizing science activities 1 2 3 4 5 6 7 8 9
13. Evaluating student progress 1 2 3 4 5 6 7 8 9
14. Handling problems of classroom management, pupil control, and student misbehavior 1 2 3 4 5 6 7 8 9
15. Preparing for practice teaching 1 2 3 4 5 6 7 8 9
16. Budgeting time and judging the flow of science lessons 1 2 3 4 5 6 7 8 9
17. Handling routines such as making out reports, attendance, and keeping records 1 2 3 4 5 6 7 8 9
18. Lack of an adequate background in science 1 2 3 4 5 6 7 8 9
19. Lack of self-confidence to teach science 1 2 3 4 5 6 7 8 9
20. Presenting science demonstrations, questioning, and guiding student discussions 1 2 3 4 5 6 7 8 9
21. Adapting to the unique problems of school facilities, materials, and equipment 1 2 3 4 5 6 7 8 9
22. Understanding and using special school services such as counseling and testing 1 2 3 4 5 6 7 8 9
23. Knowing how to obtain a science teaching job 1 2 3 4 5 6 7 8 9
24. Understanding the place and importance of science education 1 2 3 4 5 6 7 8 9
25. Other concerns 1 2 3 4 5 6 7 8 9

These statements constitute a personal inventory of concerns. Many of them are addressed in this book and will be included as part of the methods course. Identifying and clarifying your concerns will better enable you to direct your work, study, and activities during this preparation for science teaching.

BEGINNING YOUR INSTRUCTIONAL THEORY

In this chapter we introduce some practical aspects of science teaching. Chapter 1 focused on questions, such as, "Am I qualified to teach science?" and "What is science teaching like?" The questions for this chapter include: "What do I have to know in order to teach science?" "What do I have to be able to do to teach science?" and "How do I put it all together for effective science teaching?" To answer these questions, we use the idea of an *instructional theory* to help you formulate some ideas about science teaching. Further, we have you begin developing an approach to science teaching.

Teaching science requires continual decision making. One way to characterize the decision-making process is through questions. How do I respond to students' misconceptions in science? The light burned out on the overhead projector—what should I do? Where should I use this new piece of software? How can I use the Internet with my class? Is this laboratory safe? Indeed, you will have to consider many variables from moment to moment and day to day. Effective science teachers act efficiently and respond constructively to numerous classroom situations. Before continuing in this chapter, you should complete Activity 2–1, What Would You Do?

WHY DEVELOP AN INSTRUCTIONAL THEORY?

Scientists use theories to guide their research and to help them develop new insights into the intricacies of nature. A theory is an effective intellectual tool that integrates many concepts. Recall that in science a theory is a well-substantiated explanation of some aspect of the natural world. A theory is based on evidence and it incorporates facts, inferences, tested knowledge, and laws. Through knowing relatively little—a theory—the individual actually knows a great deal. A theory has several fundamental attributes. It (1) guides scientific inquiries, (2) organizes observations and data, (3) provides explanations for phenomena, and (4) helps predict events and therefore provides direction.

An instructional theory should provide well-substantiated explanations for aspects of teaching and learning in science classrooms. Your instructional theory should be based on evidence—observations and research—and not prevailing myths about students and teaching. As a science teacher your effectiveness can be enhanced by your ability to organize observations of students, explain behaviors, and predict what will happen as a result of your activities and actions in the classroom. Although an instructional theory may not have the power and utility of a scientific theory, it will certainly help you bring consistency to the variety of decisions you make in the process of teaching.

WHAT ARE THE FOUNDATIONS OF AN INSTRUCTIONAL THEORY?

One essential foundation is your understanding of the purposes for science education. Other foundational elements include principles of learning, motivation, development, and social psychology, as well as attitudes and values of the scientific enterprise, curriculum ma-

GUEST EDITORIAL ◆ MARY MCMILLAN

Science Education Student
Geology Carleton College, Northfield, Minnesota

ANTICIPATING STUDENT TEACHING

As I anticipate my student teaching placement in the fall, I am beginning to formulate my definition of a successful teacher. The ideal teacher is organized, energetic, and confident. He or she uses subject matter as a means of helping students to develop an appreciation of themselves, others, and society. During my student teaching placement, I hope to develop the skills of an "ideal" teacher. As I work toward my goal, student teaching will have a dual purpose for me. I want to help my students appreciate their own abilities, and I hope to learn more about myself as a science teacher.

To recognize students' abilities, I will need to become acquainted with them and their interests. As I search for topics that interest them, I will hope for interesting moments and sparks of thoughtful questions. It will be necessary to appreciate diversity. Some students will have trouble with analytical skills, but they may demonstrate the ability to lead others, to communicate, or to be creative. To provide each student with the opportunity for success and enthusiasm, I will have to include a broad range of activities.

As I envision activities for students, I recognize one of the causes of my own enthusiasm. I believe that science classes provide a means of understanding the earth and its resources. Such understanding is essential if we hope to protect and improve the environment. The science courses I most enjoyed were those that increased my awareness of the environment and my perceptions of change. As a teacher, the opportunity to select materials and topics will be very important to me. I hope to teach about general principles by providing a background of specific examples. I plan to infuse a good deal of environmental education in my classes, and I hope that my enthusiasm for science will be shared.

As I try to share my interests and concerns with others, I also will be learning about myself. A cooperating teacher will probably provide both criticism and praise. Students' actions and reactions in the classroom will challenge my assumptions as well as my creativity. There will be times when I cannot select the exact subject matter I would like to teach. Unless I demonstrate my willingness to take risks and correct mistakes, however, I will not learn the ways in which I need to change. To succeed as a student teacher, I will need to be persistent, open, and energetic. I want to help others value their own abilities and, by doing so, I hope to become better acquainted with myself.

terials, and instructional techniques. Individual science teachers combine all of these elements in unique ways.

CHARACTERISTICS OF AN INSTRUCTIONAL THEORY

Some years ago, Jerome Bruner outlined the characteristics of an instructional theory in a book entitled *Toward a Theory of Instruction*.[1] According to Bruner, a theory of instruction is *prescriptive*. It gives direction and provides guidelines for effective instruction and enables the teacher to evaluate teaching techniques and procedures. A theory of instruction also is *normative*; it is general rather than specific. For example, a theory of instruction would give some criteria for a chemistry lesson on acids and bases but would not give specific guidelines for the lesson.

What help does a theory of instruction provide? What questions will it answer? An instructional theory has four important characteristics. It should help you specify the following:

1. *The most effective experiences to enhance learning.* An instructional theory helps you answer the question, "What activities will encourage learning?"
2. *The most effective way in which knowledge can be structured to enhance learning.* An instructional theory helps you answer the question, "What is the best way to structure the knowledge and skills of my lesson?"
3. *The most effective sequence in which to present material.* An instructional theory helps you answer the

question, "How do I present the lesson so all students will develop their understandings of science?"

4. *The most effective processes for feedback and evaluation.* An instructional theory helps you answer the questions, "How and when should I give feedback?" "When should instruction be assessed?" "What is the most appropriate form to obtain and return feedback?" "How should I modify instruction?"

One of the most important conditions for learning is *active participation by students.* Science teachers often ask, "How can I motivate students?" You will slowly accumulate ideas and activities that encourage a predisposition toward learning. Engaging the learner is difficult for even the most experienced science teacher. Consider your own response to the problems in Activity 2–1, What Would You Do? Ideally, the problems engaged your interest. One response you could have made was the exploration of alternative solutions to the problem. Another was a curiosity concerning details of the situation. Both of these responses originated in the uncertainty and the ambiguity of the problems. There is an optimal level of uncertainty and ambiguity: too little and the problem is easily resolved; too much and there is confusion, anxiety, and lack of resolution. Part of your task as a science teacher is to help learners stay within the optimal range of their interest and curiosity.

Once you have engaged the learners, they must continue to work on the problem. To stimulate continued interest, the rewards of the exploration must be greater than the risks. Was this true with your work on the problems in What Would You Do? Giving or receiving instruction should increase the rewards and decrease risks; if such is not the case, your instruction is not as effective as it should be.

Finally, you need a direction or goal. From the alternatives provided you were asked to resolve the classroom problems in the best way that you could. The question—What would you do?—helped define the direction and goal.

A second condition for effective instruction is the *optimal structure of the knowledge.* In most cases this condition is provided by the instructional materials and the teaching sequence. The body of knowledge should be presented in a form simple enough to be understood by the learner. The fact that the material is in a textbook means that the science teacher will have to adapt the structure of knowledge to accommodate the needs and interests of students.

A third condition for learning is the *optimal sequence of knowledge.* As science instruction progresses, teachers present and draw students' attention to relationships among ideas, processes, and skills. The instructional sequence should increase the probability that at each step the learner understands, transforms, and applies these ideas, processes, and skills. Here again you may encounter the problem of steps that are too small, resulting in students' boredom, or steps that are too large, resulting in frustration. In part, the purpose of your instructional theory is to help you bridge the gap between the structural and sequential logic of the curriculum and the social and psychological needs of the students.

A fourth condition essential to the earlier three is your ability to receive, respond, and give *feedback in the teaching environment.* Motivating, structuring, and sequencing of instruction are contingent on your ability to receive and respond to cues from the students. Student feedback should in turn influence your instruction and your response to student achievement.

PURPOSE, GOALS, AND OBJECTIVES

Like any journey, in science teaching you have to know where you are going. What is it that you perceive as the destination for your students? What do you see as the stops along the way to this final destination? In the first chapter we suggested that the term *scientific literacy* expresses the destination for all students. Translating scientific literacy into concrete goals of knowledge, skills, and values of curriculum and instruction is an important process for science teachers because the translation has to be fairly consistent with the overall purpose. Finally, the specific objectives of lessons have to be consistent with the purpose of developing scientific literacy. Separate chapters are devoted to these topics. Before continuing, complete Activity 2–3, My Aims and Preferences. You should review your responses on this investigation after completing the chapter.

The *National Science Education Standards*[2] also provide purpose, goals, and objectives for science teaching. They give a valuable description of your destination, and they outline the territory for your travels. But they do not have specific, detailed maps for the trip. You will have to create your own maps for curriculum, instruction, and assessment. Your instructional theory will be invaluable for this process.

LEARNING AND TEACHING

Research on student learning has long been an important factor in any teacher's instructional theory. In the 1960s and 1970s, science teachers looked to Jean Piaget's theory of cognitive development.[3] The research focused on two major features of Piagetian theory. First, Piaget proposed that learning occurs through an individual's interaction with the environment. This interaction is described as a student assimilating new information and ideas from various educational experiences and the accommodation of the new information with previously held information, thus establishing a consistency between the individual's cognitive structure and everyday experience. Second, each individual passes through different stages of development, each characterized by the ability to perform various cognitive tasks.

The most relevant stages for science education are concrete reasoning and formal reasoning. Simply put, a concrete reasoner requires tangible objects and experiences and their observable relations in order to reason logically, and a formal reasoner can manipulate abstract ideas.

Piaget's notion of learning as an interaction with the environment has been generally supported[4,5] and, in fact, was a foundation for contemporary constructivist explanations of students' conceptual understanding and change. The concept of stages of concrete and formal reasoning, however, has been criticized and revised. Several studies[6,7,8] have demonstrated that, as measured by performance on cognitive tasks, the majority of secondary students are at the concrete stage of reasoning. There is also evidence that performance on such tasks is strongly influenced by context, mode, and language of task presentation, and subject matter.[9,10] Other studies have demonstrated that even young children are capable of abstract thought in certain situations.[11]

Because most secondary students engage primarily in concrete reasoning, you should be careful about introducing tasks that primarily require formal, abstract thought. For example, most texts of secondary science implicitly assume that the reader can reason at the formal level. A statement about where students *are* in their reasoning ability does not, however, mean they cannot learn and develop more sophisticated levels of reasoning. Students much younger than secondary students are capable of reasoning and logical thought under certain conditions. Appropriate contexts and experiences that progress from concrete to abstract could foster the reasoning abilities necessary for understanding many science concepts.

In recent years science educators have used a model termed *constructivism* to help understand students' learning. The theoretical basis for constructivist research comes from several sources, including David Ausubel.[12] We have introduced the essence of Ausubelian theory[13] earlier: a learner's prior knowledge is an important factor in determining what is learned in a given situation. L. S. Vygotsky[14] is a second important source for constructivism. He wrote of student conceptions and teacher conceptions, and how students and teachers might use similar words to describe concepts, yet have different personal interpretations of those concepts. Vygotsky's work implies that science instruction should take into account the differences between teacher and student conceptions and should provide a great deal of student-student interaction so that learners can develop concepts from those whose understandings and interpretations are closer to their own.

Early work in constructivist research focused on identifying students' conceptions about scientific phenomena and how those student conceptions differ from accepted scientific conceptions. These student conceptions have been referred to by various unfortunate labels, such as misconceptions, alternative conceptions, alternative frameworks, and naive theories. We think it is much more useful to simply recognize students' *current* conceptions and emphasize your role in changing those conceptions so they are more aligned with those recognized as scientific. Several good reviews of this research exist.[15,16,17] We especially recommend that you review *How People Learn: Brain, Mind, Experiences, and School* published by the National Research Council.[18]

In the constructivist model, students construct knowledge by interpreting new experiences in the context of their prior knowledge, experiences, episodes, and images. Students' construction of knowledge begins at an early age so that by the time students encounter formalized study of science, they have developed stable and highly personal conceptions for many natural phenomena. Given this view, one goal of your approach to instruction must be to facilitate change in students' conceptions of the world. Some researchers[19,20] have likened this process of conceptual change to the process by which scientific theories undergo change and restructuring. In fact, studies have demonstrated that student beliefs and conceptions often parallel early scientific theories, dating back to Aristotle and Lamarck.[21,22,23] However, other research cautions against drawing too strong a parallel between student conceptions and the history of science, largely because student conceptions are not nearly as comprehensive as, say, Aristotelian theories.

G. J. Posner and others[24] have proposed four conditions for conceptual change that should be recognized as you formulate your instructional theory. First, in order for students to change their conceptions of a given phenomenon, they must be *dissatisfied* with their current conception. This dissatisfaction presumably comes about through repeated exposure to experiences they cannot explain by using current conceptions. Second, the new conception must be *intelligible* in terms of prior experiences and knowledge. Third, the new conception must be *plausible* in that it can explain a number of prior experiences and observations. Finally, the new conception must be *fruitful* in that it opens up new areas of inquiry, primarily through predictions about future events.

Constructivist research also suggests other strategies to promote conceptual change. You should be aware that students have conceptions of the world and that they often do not differentiate concepts.[25] Students need time to make their ideas explicit, and they should have a chance to apply their conceptions of the world in different contexts.[26]

Contemporary research associated with cognitive sciences and constructivism has had an important influence on science teaching. We recommend reviewing *Learning*

TABLE 2–1   Science Educator's Grand Mean Ranking Compared with Other Population's Data Reported by Rank

Category	Science Educators N = 172	In-Service Teachers N = 76	Preservice Elementary Majors N = 58	High School Students Average N = 44	High School Students Disad-vantaged N = 106	High School Students Advantaged N = 31	Elementary School Children Grade 6 N = 25	Elementary School Children Grades 4, 5, 6 N = 18
Knowledge of subject matter	4	4	4	3	4	3	3	3
Adequate personal relations with students	1	1	1	1	1	2	1	1
Adequate planning and organization	5	5	5	4	3	4	5	4
Enthusiasm in working with students	2	2	2	2	2	1	2	2
Adequate teaching methods and class procedures	3	3	3	5	5	5	4	5

Science and the Science of Learning, a publication prepared specifically for science teachers.[27, 28]

When considering your approach to instruction, you should recognize that your students probably already have explanations or conceptions for many objects, events, and phenomena. Stated another way, your students are not empty vessels into which you can pour scientific facts, information, and concepts. Your challenge as a science teacher is to help students realize the inadequacy of their current conceptions and provide the time and opportunity for them to construct more scientifically-accurate concepts. In later chapters, we will return to the theme of constructivism and your role in providing linkages between students' explanations and scientific explanations.

 Visit http://www.prenhall.com/trowbridge and select Topic 2—Constructivism and Learning in Science. Select "Web Links" and find "The Constructivist Zone." This link will help you follow the development of constructivism from an historical perspective. Summarize the main points of this development and submit your response to your instructor using the Electronic Bluebook module.

EFFECTIVE RELATIONSHIPS WITH STUDENTS

For many years psychologists have investigated the characteristics of effective helping relationships, including teaching. Their research indicates that a teacher's perceptions of self, students, and the teaching task are critical to effective instruction.

Effective teachers perceive other people, particularly their students, as able, friendly, worthy, intrinsically motivated, dependable, and helpful. In the same manner, effective teachers see themselves as good teachers who are needed and trustworthy, and who relate well to other people.

Better teachers see themselves assisting and facilitating rather than coercing and controlling. They identify with larger issues, are personally involved with issues, problems, and other people, and view the whole process of education as important. In addition, they tend to be altruistic and self-revealing. Effective teachers see their task as helping people rather than dealing with objects. And, generally, they try to understand the perceptions and backgrounds of their students.

These studies delineated the perceptions of effective teachers. What about the students' perceptions of the science teacher? One author (Bybee) conducted research on the perceptions of the ideal science teacher.[29,30,31] The results of these studies are summarized in Table 2–1, which shows that adequate personal relations with students, and enthusiasm in working with them, consistently rank as the most important characteristics for science teachers. With only one exception, these two categories were ranked first or second by all the groups studied. Although this research indicates that personal qualities are perceived as important dimensions of science instruction, knowledge, personal relations, planning, enthusiasm, and methods are all important for effective science teaching. An instructional theory should incorporate these elements, adapting them individually and *in toto* to the situation in the science classroom.

EFFECTIVE INSTRUCTION

Lee Shulman of Stanford University reported the role and development of teachers' knowledge in relation to teaching.[32] Shulman identified three categories of content knowledge: (1) subject matter, (2) pedagogical, and (3) curricular.

For science teachers *subject matter* is more than information and facts about a discipline. Content knowledge of a subject includes what Joseph Schwab called the "substantive and syntactic structures" of a discipline. That is, substantial knowledge is an understanding of the different ways the basic concepts and principles of a discipline are organized. What are the major conceptual schemes in your discipline? If you had to organize the information and facts of physics, chemistry, biology, or the earth sciences, what major ideas would you identify as basic structures of these disciplines? In biology, for example, one can use the levels of organization approach, studying biology from the smallest particles to larger domains, and explaining living processes in terms of molecular activities. One also can use an ecological approach in which the ecosystem is the basic level of study and individual activities are studied in terms of the systems in which they live and interact. Using either of these structures you can develop basic conceptual schemes of biology, such as energetics, genetics, diversity, and evolution.

The syntax of a discipline is the set of ways scientists establish the truth or falsehood, validity or invalidity, of new or extant knowledge claims. Science teachers' use of inquiry introduces students to the processes of obtaining new knowledge, such as observation, hypothesis, and experimentation. Students also gain the understanding that knowledge must be evaluated. By what criteria do biologists, geologists, or astronomers evaluate the worth of different theories?

Pedagogical content knowledge describes the depth and breadth of knowledge a teacher has about teaching a particular subject. Pedagogical content knowledge is the capacity to formulate and represent science in ways that make it comprehensible to learners. Examples of pedagogical knowledge include forms of representing concepts such as use of analogies, examples, illustrations, and demonstrations. Effective science teachers have a variety of ways and means of representing such ideas as ionic bonding, density, recombination of DNA, or stellar evolution.

Another dimension of pedagogical content knowledge is the understanding of what makes a concept easy or difficult for a learner to grasp. What misconceptions might students have about phenomena, such as heat and temperature, position and velocity, or living and nonliving? What preconceptions do students have for objects and events in the natural world? The science teacher's instructional theory helps establish links between new concepts and the students' current understanding.

Next we consider *curricular knowledge*. One goal of this book is to introduce you to the many methods and materials used in science teaching. The science curriculum includes a full range of materials with which science teachers should be familiar. Materials are designed for a particular subject, at a particular level, to be used with particular students. Each discipline has its own textbooks, kinds of laboratory equipment, and educational software.

In addition to knowledge of curricular materials and how best to use them, curricular knowledge extends to science teachers' abilities to relate topics of study to the curricula their students may be studying in other disciplines.

INSTRUCTIONAL DECISIONS

The discussion of teacher knowledge as it relates to content, pedagogy, and curriculum is obviously important, even essential, but you will need more than an adequate knowledge base for your instructional theory; as we have mentioned, you will also have to make many instructional decisions. David Berliner reviewed research on teaching and provided some valuable insights about these decisions, using the categories of preinstructional decisions, instructional decisions, and postinstructional decisions.[33]

First, we introduce *preinstructional decisions*. Before you begin teaching a science lesson, you should be aware of the effect of certain decisions on student achievement, attitudes, and behaviors. You must make *content decisions*. What is the content of your science lesson? You must consider not only national standards and state and local standards and assessments, but also your judgments about issues, such as the effort required to teach a subject and the problems that you perceive the students will have with the subject. Finally, you must take into account the subjects you enjoy teaching. Which are the areas within your discipline that you really like? Are you excited about introducing students to the nature and history of science? Do you think it most important to have students recognize science-related social issues?

Science teaching involves groups of students. *Grouping decisions* are part of your preparation for a lesson. What is the best size of a group? How much laboratory equipment do you have? Who should (or should not) work together? Should you use cooperative groups? What criteria do you have for forming a particular group? Whether you lecture to the entire class or work in the laboratory, you will usually make grouping decisions. Even when assigning individual work on projects, experiments, and tests, a group in some sense still exists.

Finally, you will have to make *decisions about activities*. Laboratory work, for example, has specific functions; that is, it is used to achieve certain goals. In a laboratory students may learn to design an experiment, manipulate equipment, and use computers. Operations—the rules or norms of conduct for the activity—are also important. Is it okay to be out of one's seat? What type of conversation is acceptable? What rules *must* be followed for safety reasons?

The importance of these kinds of decisions cannot be overstated. Just reading this section should make you aware of the many and varied decisions you must make *before you begin teaching even the simplest lesson.*

Next is the importance of *instructional decisions*. Once you begin teaching a lesson, numerous factors determine what your students learn. The amount of time students spend on a task—*engaged time*—is directly related to how much students will learn. You should recognize that *engaged* can mean physically (hands-on), mentally (minds-on), or both. Although this seems obvious, the amount of engaged time varies from student to student and class to class. You should be aware of the amount of time students are actually working. Engaged time is especially important for underachieving and low-ability students. These students will benefit most from time *on task*, and they also are the students who are most likely to be *off task*.

The *success rate* of students is related to continued achievement. Success in the early stages of learning new concepts or skills is especially important for unsuccessful and low-ability students. If students do not experience some success in the early stages of lessons, their frustration and lack of understanding can contribute to low achievement.

Decisions you make about *questioning* will also influence your teaching effectiveness. Science teachers in particular should ask many questions—questions about the natural world are the foundation of science. The first thing to consider is the cognitive level of the question. Most teachers ask low-level questions, such

as, "What do the letters DNA stand for?" "What is the second law of thermodynamics?" or "What is a silicon oxygen tetrahedron?" Although questions of this nature have some benefit, remember that higher-level questions facilitate thinking and learning. Questions that require students to analyze and synthesize will produce higher levels of student achievement. You could, for example, provide data in graph form and ask the students to analyze the results and form an explanation based on the evidence. Or, you could provide information from two separate but related experiments and ask students for their predictions of possible outcomes.

Another point about questioning concerns the importance of *waiting* after you have asked a question. Research by Mary Budd Rowe[34] confirms the importance of wait time. Longer waits (most teachers wait less than one second after asking a question) result in increases in the appropriateness, confidence, variety, and cognitive level of responses. A two- to three-second adjustment in your teaching style can result in a much higher return for you and your students.

Finally, there are *postinstructional* decisions. Now that the lesson unit or semester is over, how much did the students learn? Science teachers usually arrive at an answer through the assessments, grades, and feedback given to students.

Assessment is not the central issue. In fact, we propose that planning the assessment should exactly correlate with your aims and should have been designed *before* developing the instructional sequence and providing students opportunities to learn. Although this may seem backwards, it is designing school science instruction so it is coherent.[35]

Grades do motivate students to achieve. However, the overuse of grades or their use as coercion can have detrimental effects. Corrective feedback, if properly given, results in positive achievement and attitudes on the part of students. Your decisions to give praise for correct work, recognition for proper behavior, and personally neutral criticism (as opposed to sarcasm) for incorrect responses all can influence student learning.

It is easy to feel overwhelmed at the number of decisions that go into science teaching. We think the early introduction of these ideas will prepare you for the topics and activities to come. For the time being, only an awareness of these decisions is necessary.

RESEARCH ON EFFECTIVE TEACHING

Research on good teaching provides some insights that may help you synthesize the ideas in this section. After reviewing the research on good teaching, Andrew Porter and Jere Brophy concluded that the concept of good teaching is changing.[36] In the past, teachers sometimes were viewed as technicians who had to apply how-to lessons, or as weak links in the education system who had to be circumvented with a teacher-proof curriculum. Such approaches did not work. The current concept of effective teaching deals with empowering teachers. How are teachers empowered? A brief answer is through the application of research on teaching, and a longer answer involves the continuous development of an instructional theory. Our discussion assumes that student learning within science classes requires good teaching, and good teaching requires science teachers who make appropriate decisions about how to educate students.

A contemporary image of the good teacher is that of a thoughtful professional who works purposefully toward educational goals. According to Porter and Brophy:

♦ Effective teachers are clear about their instructional goals. They inform their students of these goals and keep them in mind as they design lessons and communicate with students.

♦ Effective instruction provides students with strategies they can use for their own learning.

♦ Effective instruction creates learning situations in which students are expected to learn information, solve problems, and organize that information in new ways.

♦ Effective teachers continually monitor student understanding and adjust instruction accordingly.

♦ Effective teachers frequently integrate other subjects and skills into their lessons.

♦ Effective teachers design instruction so that what is learned can be used in the future.

♦ Effective teachers are thoughtful and reflective about their instruction.

Figure 2–1 summarizes these points.

Science teachers have been depicted as individuals who can do almost everything or practically nothing. In reality, science teachers are continually developing and improving their approach to instruction—what we call an instructional theory. The feature that mediates the instructional theory and teaching practice is decision-making as it applies to different teaching situations.

 Visit http://www.prenhall.com/trowbridge and select Topic 6—Professional Development. Select "Web Links" and find the "National Center for Improving Student Learning and Achievement in Mathematics and Science (NCISLA)," which will provide you with research-based information on developing math and science education. Review the main areas of research and submit a paper to your instructor using the Electronic Bluebook module.

Good teaching is fundamental to effective schooling. From the studies of the Institute for Research on Teaching and from other studies conducted over the last 10 years, there is a picture of effective teachers as semiautonomous professionals who

■ are clear about their instructional goals,
■ are knowledgeable about lesson content and strategies for teaching it,
■ communicate to their students what is expected of them—and why,
■ make expert use of existing instructional materials in order to devote more time to practices that enrich and clarify lesson content,
■ teach students metacognitive strategies and give them opportunities to master them,
■ address higher- as well as lower-level cognitive objectives,
■ monitor students' understandings by offering regular and appropriate feedback,
■ integrate their instruction with that of other subject areas,
■ accept responsibility for student outcomes, and
■ are thoughtful and reflective about their practice.

FIGURE 2–1 Highlights of Research on Good Teaching (Source: Andrew Porter and Jere Brophy, "Synthesis of Research on Good Teaching: Insights from the Work of the Institute for Research on Teaching," *Educational Leadership* [May 1988]: 75.)

SOME METHODS TO CONSIDER IN FORMING YOUR INSTRUCTIONAL THEORY

When science teachers use the Internet, show a video, take a field trip, have students work in the laboratory, or guide a discussion, they are using instructional methods that they assume will develop understanding, skills, or values relative to science and technology. The assumption underlying an instructional method is that it is the most effective, efficient, and appropriate means of facilitating learning.

In this section, we introduce a variety of teaching methods. They are listed in alphabetical order along with a brief description and guides for effective use.

Assessment

Purpose: to provide feedback to both the students and teacher about student understanding of concepts and ability to use skills
Predominant Learning Modes: visual and kinesthetic
Group Size: individual, occasionally small

Tests, quizzes, performance-based assessments, and portfolios used frequently in science classes should be designed to provide accurate feedback concerning student progress. Appropriate and effective use of assessment includes the following:

- Assess the opportunities students have had to learn science.
- Use performance-based assessments to evaluate the processes of scientific inquiry and technological design.
- Provide students feedback about their understanding of concepts.
- Use questions and situations that require critical thinking and problem solving at different cognitive levels; that is, recall, comprehension, application, analysis, synthesis, and evaluation.

Chalkboard/Marker Board

Purpose: to illustrate, outline, or underscore ideas in written or graphic form
Predominant Learning Mode: visual
Group Size: small to large

Chalkboards/marker boards are used extensively in science classrooms. Most science teachers use the chalkboard/marker board with some skill. Here are a few helpful hints:

- Say what you are going to write before writing it.
- Use key words or concepts.
- Write legibly and spell correctly.
- Stand to the side of the material so the students can see the board and you can see the students.
- Erase the board before writing a new concept, idea, or diagram.

Debate

Purpose: to allow students to gain information, discuss different sides of an issue, and resolve conflicts
Predominant Learning Mode: auditory
Group Size: medium—10 to 15 students

Debate is an effective way to introduce different sides of science-related issues. The debate can continue over several days and involve several teams in various aspects of a topic. Students will have to understand information concerning their position and develop the skills of analysis and evaluation concerning their opponent's position. Here are some guidelines for using debate:

- Be sure the debate topic has clear pro/con sides.

- Use teams of 3 to 4 students per side for an issue.
- Set clear time limits for opening statements, rebuttals, and closing statements.
- Make it clear that there are to be no interruptions while a speaker has the floor.

Demonstrations

Purpose: to provide students the opportunity to see a phenomenon or event that they otherwise would not observe
Predominant Learning Modes: visual, auditory
Group Size: medium to large

Demonstrations can be used to teach concepts or skills directly, or to prepare students for work in the laboratory. Demonstrations are often used due to safety concerns or lack of equipment. The best demonstrations have a dramatic quality and usually deal with something that is puzzling to the students. Here are a few helpful hints:

- Present demonstrations so students can see them and hear you.
- Do the demonstration *before* trying it in class.
- Take all necessary safety precautions.
- Plan your demonstration so it clearly shows the intended concepts or skills.

Discussion

Purpose: to promote an exchange of information and ideas among members of a group or class
Predominant Learning Mode: auditory
Group Size: small to medium—2 to 8 students

Discussions are used frequently in science instruction. The teacher must plan the discussion so that information is accurate and students stay on the topic. Some suggestions follow:

- Think carefully about the initial questions.
- Prepare students for the discussion through reading or a laboratory experience.
- Provide a sheet of topics and/or questions that help guide the discussion.
- Facilitate discussions through planning, questioning, and summarizing.

Educational Software/Computers

Technology

Link

Purpose: to allow students the opportunity to review, record, model, and acquire concepts and skills

Predominant Learning Modes: visual and auditory

Group Size: individual to small—2 to 4 students

Examples of this technology in the science classroom include word processing, computer-assisted instruction, microcomputer-based laboratories, HyperCard, simulations, and modeling. Suggestions for use of software include the following:

◆ Select software aligned with the learning task
◆ Use the software as part of the planned instruction.

Field Trips

Purpose: to provide a learning experience that is unique and cannot be accomplished in the classroom

Predominant Learning Modes: kinesthetic, visual, auditory

Group Size: large

Field trips can be an exciting complement to the science program. They also can be a disaster. The difference between a learning experience and a disaster lies in the preparation for and appropriateness of the trip. As a science teacher, you will have to decide the appropriateness of the timing, destination, and place of the trip in the instructional sequence. Concerning preparation, here are some guidelines:

◆ Take the trip yourself before making the trip with students.
◆ Prepare the students for the trip by informing them of the objectives, activities, and expected behaviors.
◆ Make sure transportation arrangements have been made and are safe and adequate.
◆ Confirm any prior arrangements for admission and guides at your destination.
◆ Obtain permission slips from parents.
◆ Arrange for additional adults (teachers and/or parents) to go on the trip.

Video/CD-ROM

Purpose: to present information in an interesting and efficient manner

Predominant Learning Modes: auditory and visual

Group Size: small to large

Most students are interested in video. Science teachers need to use media in a manner that will attain the established objectives. Placement of a video in the instructional sequence is critical. These are some recommendations for effective use of films and videos:

◆ Preview the video before showing it.
◆ Decide where the video can best fit in the curriculum.
◆ Prepare and distribute questions to the students.
◆ Identify one or two places to stop the video and have a discussion.
◆ Conduct a discussion after the video. You can evaluate the students' understanding of key concepts. Answer questions and make connections between the content presented and students' knowledge.

Games

Purpose: to give the students an opportunity to learn in an enjoyable, stimulating manner

Predominant Learning Mode: kinesthetic

Group Size: small to medium

If used wisely, they can be valuable for developing concepts and ideas not generally conveyed by other methods. Here are some guides to the use of the games:

◆ Consider the difficulty of the game.
◆ Consider the appropriateness of the game for your objectives.
◆ Provide clear rules for the game.
◆ Conduct pre- and postgame discussions.

Inquiry/Design

Purpose: to give students experience so they develop knowledge, skills, and values related to science (inquiry) and technology (design)

Predominant Learning Mode: kinesthetic

Group Size: individual to small

Methods related to use of inquiry and design include asking questions, using technology, designing experiments, analyzing data, formulating explanations, thinking about the relationship between evidence and explanation, and communicating explanations and methods. Here are some introductory guides:

◆ Select the inquiry activity that best illustrates the concepts or skills you have as objectives.
◆ Be sure materials are available and functional.
◆ Check any equipment to be sure it works.
◆ Give clear, succinct directions including safety precautions, how to handle equipment, where to obtain materials, assignment of groups, and your expectations of conduct and reporting.

Internet

Purpose: to provide students with opportunities to gather information from a wide range of sources

Predominant Learning Mode: visual

Group Size: individual to small—2 to 4 students

The Internet is an effective educational resource. Students can access the Internet for data and information about various topics.

- Connect use of the Internet with current activities and topics.
- Review the quality of information.

Laboratory Report

Purpose: to have students formalize their experiences and make connections between prior and present knowledge

Predominant Learning Mode: visual

Group Size: individual to small

Laboratory reports can be valuable means to bring different ideas into focus, to have students consider the context of concepts, and to reflect on the meaning of the laboratory experience. In order for the laboratory report to be effective, we recommend the following guidelines:

- Provide a purpose for the report.
- Outline your expectations in terms of content, length, and format.
- Have all members of groups sign the report, indicating they contributed.

Lecture

Purpose: to present a large body of information in an efficient manner

Predominant Learning Mode: auditory

Group Size: large

Unfortunately, lecture is used more often than it is effective, especially for middle school students. Here are some suggestions for effective lecturing.

- Use an outline and either distribute it before the lecture or place it on the overhead projector.
- Supplement the lecture with slides, overheads, or charts to illustrate concepts and ideas.
- Monitor student attention and understanding.
- Talk clearly and in a manner that identifies key points and facilitates note taking.

Oral Reports

Purpose: to allow students to demonstrate their understanding of a subject

Predominant Learning Mode: auditory

Group Size: individual to small

Oral reports are the students' equivalent of the teacher's lectures. Students, individually or in small groups, research information, organize material, and present a report. In effect, students teach other students. Here are some helpful hints:

- Presentations should align with the science program objectives.
- Allow students to report on topics of interest to them.
- Organize presentations as if they were to take place at a professional scientific meeting.
- Help students with audiovisual aids.
- Set clear time limits for the preparation and presentation of reports.
- Provide a formal evaluation in advance.

Problem Solving

Purpose: to give students experience in identifying and resolving a problem

Predominant Learning Mode: visual

Group Size: individual to small

Basically, the method is to place the students in a situation where they must take some action that is not immediately obvious. Problem solving provides opportunities for students to encounter concepts such as criteria, constraints, costs, risks, benefits, and trade-offs. Since students usually have not had much experience in problem solving, it is helpful to do some of the following:

- Identify general problems for study and resolution.
- Help students narrow their problems.
- Provide an opportunity to brainstorm possible solutions to the problem.
- Select and test reasonable solutions for the problem.
- Evaluate the tested solutions.
- Prepare a formal report using the protocol of professional papers.

Projects

Purpose: to give students knowledge, skills, and understanding related to a unique problem

Predominant Learning Mode: kinesthetic

Group Size: individual to small

Many science teachers like to have students work on projects and participate in local or regional science fairs. We believe projects are a wonderful way to give students a real sense of science. Here are some things to consider:

- Develop a list of project ideas for students.

♦ Provide written guidelines concerning the purpose and nature of the project and the final product.

♦ Provide time and assistance as the students work on their projects, particularly in locating resources.

Multimedia Projects

Technology
Link

Purpose: to provide an opportunity to demonstrate understanding of a concept visually to a large group

Predominant Learning Mode: visual, kinesthetic

Group Size: individual to small

Multimedia techniques such as the use of slide show, hypermedia, and video clips provide means for students to put together in creative ways their ideas about a science concept. The use of computers with multimedia capabilities, including presentation software has been shown to positively influence student achievement.[37] If considering the inclusion of multimedia projects in your classroom consider the following:

♦ Make sure you have provided options so that all students have access to appropriate technology and software, not just those with equipment at home.

♦ Provide a non-technology alternative for completing the project so that the mechanism for demonstrating understanding doesn't overshadow the actual concept learned.

Questioning

Purpose: to stimulate thinking by engaging the learner

Predominant Learning Mode: auditory

Group Size: individual, or small, medium, and large

Questioning is one of the primary means teachers use to engage learners. Asking questions can be one of the most effective and efficient means of stimulating students to think about the topic. Here are some suggestions on questioning:

♦ Use both convergent and divergent questions.

♦ Provide time for students to think about the answer.

♦ Use questions that require thinking at different levels; that is, recall, comprehension, application, analysis, synthesis, and evaluation.

Reading

Purpose: to present information that is uniform and consistent

Predominant Learning Mode: visual

Group Size: individual

Reading is central to effective instruction. Though reading should be used in science classes, it should not be the exclusive learning method. We also encourage reading of materials other than the textbook. Some guidelines follow:

♦ Use reading materials that are appropriate to the students' abilities and your program objectives.

♦ Assign a variety of readings (for example, textbook, science books, popular magazines, and articles or tracts of historical significance).

Simulations

Purpose: to increase students' abilities to apply concepts, analyze situations, solve problems, and understand different points of view

Predominant Learning Modes: visual and auditory

Group Size: small to medium—5 to 15 students

Simulations provide teachers with a means of presenting situations, concepts, and issues in a condensed and simplified form. Simulations are especially useful for involving students in science-related social issues. Use of simulations can be enhanced by doing the following:

♦ Select a problem or issue of interest to the students.

♦ Include key issues and concepts in a realistic way.

♦ Make procedures clear, including expected behaviors, roles to be played, and time limits.

♦ Use lifelike materials and situations.

♦ Conclude the simulation with a discussion of different perceptions of the issue, how the students felt about the issue, how the conflict was resolved, and what actions might be taken in the future.

Computer-based Learning

Technology
Link

Purpose: to provide course content and interactive instruction in a variety of forms using the computer.

Predominant Learning Mode: visual kinesthetic

Group size: individual, small group, whole class

Drill and practice a repetitive approach emphasizing rote memory, was one of the earliest forms of computer-based learning. Through enhanced motivation and ample practice afforded by drill and practice programs, learners improve their abilities to solve the type problems presented. Software design has now gone well beyond the drill and practice stage; this form of computer-based learning is rarely emphasized today. Many curriculum programs include software—see Chapters 8 and 9 for examples.

Programming advances and the use of the Internet have greatly changed the face of computer-based learning options for the science classroom. Simulations provide a computer model of the attributes, concepts, and relationships in the real world. In simulations the student plays an active role in manipulating various factors in the computer simulation to better understand real-world phenomena. Through the variation of various factors the computer generates creative, perhaps even impossible, environments. The computer may for example, permit time compression by condensing a great amount of data into a very short time frame or it may expand the time base to allow longer looks at changes that take place within a short time span. It can produce graphic displays of processes at work and the effects of different variable factors on the processes. Simulations allow the effects of changes to be seen in a model before irrevocable changes are made in the real system. In this sense, minor or hypothetical risks can be taken without the cost or danger of carrying out the experiment in real life. Students using simulations are often forced to make decisions on the basis of incomplete data, and the results of these decisions can be seen quickly. This is excellent practice for the real world in which important decisions frequently need to be made on the basis of meager information. There are many examples of simulations available for teaching secondary science. One interesting example combined the use of genetics databases and bioinformatics software to help students seek answers to questions about evolutionary relationships. Maier reports that students are able to build genetic distance matrices and phylogenetic trees based on molecular sequence data using web-based resources.[37]

Technology

Link

Probeware

Purpose: to collect real-time data
Predominant Learning Mode: kinesthetic
Group Size: small

Probeware refers to equipment that can be attached to a computer or hand-held device for collecting data on physical phenomena in real time, and special software for recording and displaying the results.[38] For instance, temperature data might be collected with a temperature-sensing probe over a fixed time sequence, such as every five minutes and the data converted into line graphs and data tables.

Powerful MBL tools for investigation have been available to students at the secondary level only since the mid-1980s. The Technical Education Research Center (TERC) in Cambridge Massachusetts has played a pivotal role in their development. Probes are available for measuring a wide variety of phenomena

including the following: temperature sound, light, intensity, motion, atmospheric pressure, pH, EKG, EMG, heart rate, brain waves; humidity, wind speed, and wind direction. Commercial packages for computer-based laboratories are marketed by a variety of companies.

A goal of using probeware in your instruction should be to increase students intuitive feel for events and to build causal links between external events and the graphs.[39,40,41] Time for exploring the probes and finding out what they can tell us about the world is necessary in developing a general sense about what to expect for certain natural phenomena, such as temperature changes over time. Writing about all aspects of an experiment and telling the story of the graph is a good way to help students build correlations between the world and the graph and to reveal what students are seeing and thinking. Used in this way computer-based laboratories represent another way to help bridge the gap between the concrete physical world and abstract conceptualizations.

This description of methods is intentionally brief; complete chapters are devoted to some of them later in this book. Use the methods described in this section in Activity 2–2, Applying the Best Method.

Visit http://www.prenhall.com/trowbridge and select Topic 6—Professional Development. Select "Web Links" and find the "Office of Educational Research and Improvement," which provides national leadership for educational research and statistics. Obtain relevant research on topics you are concerned with in developing a theory of instruction and highlight the main points. Submit your response to your instructor using the Electronic Bluebook module.

A FINAL NOTE

Developing your personal instructional theory will be one of the most helpful and rewarding accomplishments of your preparation for science teaching. Over time, education has fractionated, divided, and isolated many of the important components of successful teaching. Unfortunately, many teacher preparation programs emphasize these *ad hoc* components: "If you are well planned. . . ," "If you use this curriculum. . . ," "If you understand the students' misconceptions. . . ," and "If you know your subject. . . ," Planning, classroom procedures, methods, and subject matter are obviously important, but they are means, not ends. This educational view has shifted the emphasis of programs

GUEST EDITORIAL ◆ CARYL E. BUCHWALD
Professor of Geology and Director of the Arboretum
Carleton College, Northfield, Minnesota

TEACHING SCIENCE

Science is important to all of us. The world is in desperate need of more and better science precisely because it has been one of the dominant forces in our lives and the life of the world for several hundred years. Science and its derivative, technology, have increased the life expectancy and material well-being of Western people but at the same time have led us to the brink of disaster through ecological catastrophe or nuclear war. Science raises the hope that we can truly progress to a higher understanding of ourselves and our interrelationships with nature.

There can scarcely be a higher calling or more honorable occupation than teaching science to young people. It is important because, when well taught, science leads us to discover two characteristics that are important not only to our own lives but to the future of humanity. Science should help us to discover humility on the one hand and the ability to affect our own futures on the other.

Humility comes from studying science, for the obvious reason that we learn about our own place in nature. That we are minuscule in the universe, but domineering in the biosphere, is a position not always easy to grasp. That we are a part of the very biosphere that we dominate should lead us to realize that we cannot deny the integration of our own lives with nature.

Science is often portrayed as possessing facts and laws. Yet, when we attempt explanation in our own research, most of the time we discover that facts are contextual in time and place. Because science is really explanation and not discovery, the explanations change as we learn more or see causal relations that were previously unsuspected. When reflecting on my own career as a teacher, I am constantly amazed by how the so-called facts have changed. What has not changed is the search for data and their meaning, the use of logic, the need for verification, and the consequences of knowledge.

The consequences of knowing are important. They lead us to moral dilemmas time and time again. Atomic research has given us improved medical treatment but also nuclear bombs. Better medical treatment has eased human suffering, extended our lifetimes, and contributed to the population explosion. It is hard to do one thing at a time. The reality remains: knowledge requires action.

What can we do with and for our students to improve their understanding of science? It seems to me that the best teachers possess two essential attributes: enthusiasm and patience. Enthusiasm stems from a love of what is being done, a belief that science is important and worth doing. Patience is needed because science is a process that must be internalized. Science is not a set of operating procedures that goes one, two, three . . . conclusions. Often it is difficult to figure out the steps that were actually taken in framing a question and seeking an explanation. To require a lock-step progression from data gathering through hypothesis to conclusion not only denies the reality of scientific activity but is likely to make students seek preconceived answers rather than to invent their own explanations.

Patience means letting students seek the relationships and explanations that fit their experience. If we insist that they hunt for the right answers, we end up teaching them the wrong thing; that is, that science is discovering the hidden. We want to teach them that science is a way to perceive nature. Seeking right answers also leads to the conclusion that science has answers entrusted to an elite and that is counter to the democratic idea.

So, we must be enthusiastic. This enthusiasm will flow from belief in what we are doing and our confidence with our subject. We must be patient because science is a complex way of thinking, and it takes time for it to develop and mature.

Science teachers should consider their perceptions of themselves, students, the teaching task, and the subject before starting an instructional theory. Once this is done, they can begin to formulate such a theory by clarifying goals and preferences, understanding the theories and methods of science teaching, analyzing similarities and differences of theories and methods, and synthesizing their goals and preferences with appropriate theories and methods. Above all, science teachers should realize that they are the most important aspect of the instructional theory.

away from the primary and crucial variable in the classroom—the teacher. Science teachers with an adequate instructional theory have knowledge, plans, methods, and curricular materials. In addition, they have larger goals for their interaction with students and the added dimension of a personalized approach to education.

When the goals, theories, techniques, plans, and materials are combined, you are ready to interact with students. The *way* in which science teachers combine these elements and build a helping relationship with students is crucial. An instructional theory will help provide the needed direction. Science teaching is characterized by situations that require the teacher to react immediately. The creative, insightful, and prepared science teacher will effectively respond to the immediate needs of the students and school.

SUMMARY

An instructional theory helps the science teacher make predictions, explain different strategies that will enhance learning, and organize instruction. It increases instructional effectiveness by prescribing motivation, structure, sequence, and feedback.

Research indicates that knowledge of subject matter, pedagogical content knowledge, and curricular knowledge are all important to effective teaching. This knowledge can be applied to specific decisions relative to preinstruction (content, time allocation, pacing, grouping activities), instruction (engaged time, success rate, questioning), and postinstruction (tests, grades, feedback). All these ideas contribute to the goal of good teaching. Characteristics of good teachers include the following:

- clarity of instructional goals,
- knowledge of content and strategies to teach it,
- adequate communication with students,
- expert use of extant materials,
- knowledge of student needs and development,
- development of lower and higher order thinking in students,
- monitoring of student learning with appropriate feedback,
- integration of science instruction with other disciplines, and
- thought and reflection about their teaching.

◆

REFERENCES

1. Jerome S. Bruner, *Toward a Theory of Instruction* (New York: W. W. Norton, 1968).
2. National Research Council, *National Science Education Standards* (Washington, DC: Author, 1996) (www.nas.edu).
3. Rodger W. Bybee and Robert Sund, *Piaget for Educators* (Columbus, OH: Merrill, 1982).
4. E. A. Luzner, "Cognitive Development: Learning and the Development of Change," in *Cognitive Classroom Learning*, G. D. Phye and T. Andre, eds. (New York: Academic Press, 1986).
5. J. W. Renner, M. R. Abraham, and H. H. Birnie, "The Importance of the Form of Student Acquisition of Data in Physics Learning Cycles," *Journal of Research in Science Teaching*, 23 (2) (1986): 121–143.
6. E. L. Chiapetta, "A Review of Piagetian Studies Relevant to Science Instruction at the Secondary and College Level," *Science Education*, 60 (2) (1976): 253–261.
7. J. W. Renner, R. M. Grant, and P. Sutherland, "Content and Concrete Thought," *Science Education*, 62 (2) (1978): 215–221.
8. M. J. Wavering, B. Perry, and D. Birdd, "Performance of Students in Grades 6, 9, and 12 on Five Logical, Spatial, and Formal Tasks," *Journal of Research in Science Teaching*, 23 (1986): 321–333.
9. S. L. Golbeck, "The Role of Physical Content in Piagetian Spatial Tasks: Sex Differences in Spatial Knowledge," *Journal of Research in Science Teaching*, 23 (1986): 321–333.
10. Paul Brandwein, "A General Theory of Instruction," *Science Education*, 63 (3) (1979): 291.
11. M. T. H. Chi and R. D. Koeske, "Network Representation of a Child's Dinosaur Knowledge," *Development Psychology*, 19 (1983): 29–39.
12. David P. Ausubel, *Educational Psychology: A Cognitive View* (New York: Academic Press, 1968).
13. David P. Ausubel, J. D. Novak, and H. Hanesian, *Educational Psychology: A Cognitive View*, 2d ed. (New York: Holt, Rinehart, and Winston, 1978).
14. L. S. Vygotsky, *Thought and Language*, trans. and ed. A. Kozulin (Cambridge, MA: MIT Press, 1968).
15. R. Driver, E. Guesne, and A. Tiberghien, eds., *Children's Ideas in Science* (Philadelphia, PA: Open University Press, 1985).
16. R. J. Osborne and P. Freyberg, eds., "Concepts, Misconceptions, and Alternative Conceptions: Changing Perspectives in Science Education," *Studies in Science Education*, 10 (1983): 61–98.
17. R. Duit, "Research on Students' Alternative Frameworks in Science: Topics, Theoretical Frameworks, Consequences for Science Teaching," *Proceedings of the Second International Seminar on Misconceptions and Educational Strategies in Science and Mathematics* (Ithaca, NY: 1987).

18. J. Bransford, A. Brown, and R. Cocking, eds., *How People Learn: Brain, Mind, Experience, and School* (Washington, DC: National Academy Press, 2000).

19. G. J. Posner, K. A. Strike, P. W. Hewson, and W. A. Gertzog, "Accommodation of a Scientific Conception: Toward a Theory of Conceptual Change," *Science Education,* 66 (2) (1982): 211–227.

20. C. Smith, S. Carey, and M. Wiser, "On Differentiation: A Case Study of the Development of the Concepts of Size, Weight, and Density," *Cognition,* (1985): 177–237.

21. A. Caramazza, M. McCloskey, and B. Green, "Naive Beliefs in 'Sophisticated' Subjects: Misconceptions about Trajectories of Objects," *Cognition,* 9 (1981): 117–123.

22. A. B. Champagne, L. E. Klopfer, and R. F. Gunstone, "Cognitive Research and the Design of Science Instruction," *Educational Psychologist,* 17 (1) (1982): 31–53.

23. J. H. Wandersee, "Can the History of Science Help Science Educators Anticipate Students' Misconceptions?" *Journal of Research in Science Teaching,* 23 (1986): 581–597.

24. G. J. Posner, K. A. Strike, P. W. Hewson, and W. A. Gertzog, "Accommodation of a Scientific Conception: Toward a Theory of Conceptual Change," *Science Education,* 66 (2) (1982): 211–227.

25. D. E. Trowbridge and L. C. McDermott, "Investigation of Student Understanding of the Concept of Acceleration in One Dimension," *American Journal of Physics,* 49 (1981): 242–253.

26. J. A. Minstrell, "Teaching Science for Understanding," in *Toward the Thinking Curriculum: Current Cognitive Research, 1989 Yearbook of the ASCD,* L. Resnick and L. Klopfer, eds. (Alexandria, VA: Association for Supervision and Curriculum Development, 1989).

27. Rodger, W. Bybee, ed., *Learning Science and the Science of Learning* (Arlington, VA: NSTA Press, 2002).

28. Kate McGilly, ed, *Classroom Lessons: Integrating Cognitive Theory and Classroom Practice,* (Cambridge, MA: MIT Press, 1995).

29. R. W. Bybee, "The Teacher I Like Best: Perceptions of Advantaged, Average, and Disadvantaged Science Students," *School Science and Mathematics,* 73 (5) (May 1973): 384–390.

30. R. W. Bybee, "The Ideal Elementary Science Teacher: Perceptions of Children, Pre-service and In-service Elementary Science Teachers," *School Science and Mathematics,* 75 (3) (March 1975): 229–235.

31. R. W. Bybee, "Science Educators' Perceptions of the Ideal Science Teacher," *School Science and Mathematics,* 78 (1) (January 1978): 13–22.

32. Lee S. Shulman, "Those Who Understand: Knowledge Growth in Teaching," *Educational Researcher,* 15 (2) (February 1986): 4–14.

33. David Berliner, "The Half-Full Glass: A Review of Research on Teaching," in *Using What We Know about Teaching,* Philip Hosford, ed. (Alexandria, VA: Association for Supervision and Curriculum Development, 1984).

34. Mary Budd Rowe, "Wait Time and Rewards As Instructional Variables: Their Influence on Language, Logic, and Fate Control. Part One. Wait Time," *Journal of Research in Science Teaching,* 11 (1974): 81–94.

35. Grant Wiggins and Jay McTighe, *Understanding by Design* (Alexandria, VA: Association for Supervision and Curriculum Development, 1998).

36. Andrew Porter and Jere Brophy, "Synthesis of Research on Good Teaching: Insights from the Work of the Institute for Research on Teaching," *Educational Leadership* (May 1988): 74–85.

37. Del Siegle and Theresa Foster. Laptop Computers and Multimedia and Presentation Software: Their Effects on Student Achievement in Anatomy and Physiology. *Journal of Research on Technology in Education,* 34(1) (Fall 2001): 29–37.

38. Caroline Alexandra Maier, Building Phylogenetic Trees from DNA Sequence Data: Investigating Polar Bear and Giant Panda Ancestry. *American Biology Teacher,* 63(9) (Nov–Dec 2001): 642–46.

39. Nathan Kimball, "Essential Elements of MBLs," in *LabNet,* pp. 257–262.

40. Richard Ruopp and Sarah Haavind, "From Current Practices to Projects," in *LabNet,* pp. 21–57.

41. Barbara Means, William R. Penuel, and Christine Padilla, *The Connected School: Technology and Learning in High School* (New York: John Wiley, 2001).

◆ —————————————— **INVESTIGATING SCIENCE TEACHING** —————————— ◆

ACTIVITY 2–1
WHAT WOULD YOU DO?

When you become a science teacher, you will be required to make decisions continually. An instructional theory helps you to make those decisions. This investigation directs your attention to sample situations that require decisions. It is Monday morning. You have planned a lesson examining life in pond water. Over the weekend, the heating system failed and there is no life in your pond. What would you do? (Select the answer closest to what you think you would do. Then prepare a brief justification of your answer.)

1. Omit the section on "life in a pond."
2. Tell the students to read the section in their text entitled "life in a pond."
3. Have the students find other life to examine.
4. Say nothing, ask the students to find life in the water, and when they discover that there is none, have them determine what could have happened.

Justification:

As part of an environmental studies unit, the class is to examine the possibility that a local mining operation is polluting the environment. A group of parents asks you to describe your science program at the next PTA meeting. Their primary concern is that you are going to cause trouble for the community's major economic support. What would you do? (Select the answer closest to what you think you would do. Then prepare a brief justification of your answer.)

1. Decline the invitation.
2. Accept the invitation, take samples of the lesson, data sheets, and questions the students will be answering, and be prepared to explain your goals.
3. Accept the invitation on the condition that the parents come to class and complete the lesson with their sons and daughters.
4. Accept the invitation and plan the lesson in cooperation with the PTA.

Justification:

You are in the middle of a class discussion. You have noticed that for 20 minutes one student has not only paid no attention, but he has also been creating a disturbance. You reprimand him. The student merely looks at you then continues to talk and disturb the class. What would you do? (Select the answer closest to what you think you would do. Then prepare a brief justification for your answer.)

1. Demand that the student stop talking.
2. Request that the student conform to the class rules.
3. Tell the other students that you cannot expect much more from such a person (hoping that public ridicule will terminate the disruptive behavior).
4. Tell the student that "we have a problem" and we will have to work it out. Then, ask the student to leave the room temporarily.

Justification:

All of the materials are ready for your first lesson in physical science. The lesson is on density. As you explain the procedures, you notice that the students are sending nonverbal messages of "Oh, no—boring!" Then, several students say, "We did this same lesson last year—the answer is $D = m/v$." What would you do? (Select the answer closest to what you think you would do. Then prepare a brief justification of your answer.)

1. Have the students describe what they did in the experiment last year.

2. Skip this lesson and go on to the next, where students apply the concepts of density.

3. Do the activity as planned and try to extend each student's understanding of density through personal discussion.

4. At the end of the investigation, have the students answer questions to see if they understand density.

Justification:

ACTIVITY 2–2
APPLYING THE BEST METHOD

When planning a lesson, it is important to have in mind a variety of teaching methods to complement the many classroom situations you might encounter. In this activity you meet various situations or aims of instruction, suggest a teaching method to accomplish your goal, and provide a short justification for the method you select. Your teacher may assign different situations to individuals or groups. The line to the left of the number is provided for you to indicate the suggested teaching method. The methods described in this chapter are listed below. Even if your teacher does not assign these, we recommend that you complete at least one situation in each category.

Situation	Method	Justification
Assessment		
Video/CD-ROM	Problem Solving	
Chalkboards/Marker Board	Games	Projects
Debate/Dispute Resolution	Inquiry/Design	Questioning
Demonstrations	Internet	Reading
Discussion	Laboratory Report	Simulations
Educational Software	Lecture	
Field Trip	Oral Report	

Applications

_____ 1. A student has brought to class a newspaper clipping of a current scientific event.

_____ 2. You wish to use an everyday application as a review.

_____ 3. You wish to make your course particularly functional by relating it to a "do-it-yourself" experience.

Appreciations

_____ 4. You wish to bring about the realization that we have not exhausted the unsolved problems in science. On the contrary, the more we know the more we realize how much is still to be learned.

_____ 5. You wish to develop an appreciation for the work of scientists in the past.

_____ 6. You wish to apply scientific concepts just acquired to the home situation with particular emphasis on how lack of knowledge often leads to inadequate solutions.

_____ 7. You wish to relate scientific knowledge developed in class to intelligent consumer buying.

_____ 8. You decide to try to develop an appreciation for a truly unusual scientific phenomenon.

_____ 9. You decide to try to orient the group to an appreciation for the rapid advances of scientific knowledge through consideration of what new things the text might contain for students taking the course ten years from now.

Attitudes

_____ 10. You wish to develop the proper attitude toward thorough observation and proper interpretation of what is observed.

_____ 11. You wish to guide the group in developing a sensible attitude toward those scientific problems or situations for which there is not, as yet, a definite answer.

Demonstrations

_____ 12. A demonstration experiment has just failed to produce the desired scientific results.

_____ 13. You wish to teach the proper method to use a scientific device.

_____ 14. You wish to demonstrate how the proper problem-solving approach can be used to answer a "why does it work" type of question.

_____ 15. You wish to make the teaching of a scientific principle more functional by demonstrating several everyday applications.

_____ 16. You wish to demonstrate a new scientific principle in a simple manner that the students themselves can try out at home.

Individual Differences

_____ 17. You wish to make a genuine effort in adjusting to differences by teaching one concept so that the slowest person will understand it and the most capable one will not be bored.

_____ 18. You wish to familiarize students with new vocabulary at the beginning of a unit and convince them of the need for correct knowledge of new words.

_____ 19. You wish to emphasize the opportunities available in science careers in a manner that will appeal to students.

Knowledge

_____ 20. You wish to orient the students to the first unit of the course.

_____ 21. You wish to correct a prevalent misconception.

_____ 22. You wish to place a complex concept in a more concrete setting.

_____ 23. You wish to develop an understanding that our idea of what is "true" changes as we gain more knowledge.

_____ 24. You wish to bring about the realization that, through functional knowledge of a principle, we can group together many everyday applications.

Methods

_____ 25. You wish to emphasize the dangers of making quick decisions without enough supporting evidence.

_____ 26. You wish to use the inductive approach to teach a scientific principle.

Review

_____ 27. You wish to conduct a drill experience but at the same time use a technique that will be enjoyable for the students.

_____ 28. You wish to use an instructional game as a means of developing new learning or review, or to lend variety to the class instruction.

_____ 29. You wish to give a demonstration using "common gadgets" as a means of reviewing material previously taught.*

You may wish to share your responses with other members of the class. These situations form a good basis for discussion.

---

*The original list of situations was provided courtesy of Lawrence Conrey, "Instructional Techniques," unpublished work. University of Michigan, Ann Arbor, Mich.

ACTIVITY 2–3
MY AIMS AND PREFERENCES

1. What do you wish to accomplish as a science teacher?
2. Which goals do you see as important outcomes of science instruction? Rank the following in order of importance.

   _____ Develop an understanding of fundamental knowledge of science.

   _____ Develop an understanding of and an ability to use the methods of science.

   _____ Prepare students to make responsible decisions concerning science-related social issues.

   _____ Fulfill the personal needs and development of students.

   _____ Inform students about careers in science.

3. What do you think is important for effective instruction in science? Rank the following in order of importance.

   _____ Knowledge of subject matter.

   _____ Adequacy of personal relations with students.

   _____ Planning and organization of classroom procedures.

   _____ Enthusiasm in working with students.

   _____ Adequacy of teaching methods and strategies.

HISTORICAL PERSPECTIVES AND CONTEMPORARY TRENDS

If you have not already heard, contemporary science education is in the process of reform. We have established goals for all of education, and national, state, and local school districts are implementing standards to help guide the reform and assessments to help determine how well we have met our goals. Who determines why, when, and if science education should change? Are these decisions determined at the national level, or are they decided by the local school personnel? Teaching science in your classroom represents one small component of a larger system of science education. That system has a history that shows how it changes due to new scientific discoveries, new insights about students' development and learning, and new issues in society.

Although your primary responsibility as a science teacher rests in the daily organization and introduction of productive learning experiences in your classroom, you also have a professional responsibility to understand the larger domain of science education. In order to appreciate contemporary reform, it is best to develop some historical perspective of the discipline. In this unit, we present such information and offer a view on scientific literacy that you will find helpful as you design lessons and find strategies for teaching science and developing higher levels of scientific literacy among your students.

Developing students' scientific literacy means, in part, helping them to realize that throughout history philosophers and scientists have tried to clarify the process by which scientists generate scientific knowledge. In the seventeenth century, for example, individuals argued that the fundamental source of scientific knowledge was pure observations of nature. Scientists had the obligation to cleanse their minds of any ideas that might interfere with their observations. Thus, if scientists gathered facts and information without bias, they would eventually develop a correct theory. This may sound good until one asks if it is at all possible to observe nature with absolutely no preconceptions, no ideas, and no possible explanation for what is observed. The answer is no.

Over the years, philosophers, scientists, and science educators have proposed other formulations of the *scientific method*. For instance, there is the method often outlined in science textbooks. This method usually includes (1) stating the problem, (2) forming a hypothesis, (3) designing an experiment, (4) collecting data, and (5) forming a conclusion. Scientists generally view such a formula with suspicion. Perhaps this method helps organize the results of scientific investigation, but it does not express the actual process of doing science, which is, in fact, not as neat and orderly.

You can see that science teaching is more than the process of designing learning experiences about life, earth, and physical science. It requires perspectives on science education, on science and technology, and on science and technology in society. Chapter 3 reviews the history of science education, and Chapter 4 presents an introduction to the national standards for science education and an overview of scientific literacy.

HISTORICAL PERSPECTIVES ON SCIENCE EDUCATION

As society continues to change, so too must science education. The need for change is underscored by the widespread concern about social policies—debates over national security, economic stability, health and welfare; environment and cities; affluence and poverty. Weaving through these issues one identifies the recurrent themes of science and technology, ethics and values, education and learning. Present social conditions mandate a rethinking and reformulation of science education policies, programs, and practices. The changes that must occur in the early decades of the 21st century will be made by those who are entering the teaching profession as well as those already teaching science. Decisions you will make as a science teacher should be grounded in an understanding of the various forms and functions of science education in society. That is, you should be aware of the history of science education and the present situation in science, society, and science education. Realize also that the decisions you make about your science curricula, instruction, classroom, and students help define the future.

This chapter has three parts. The first has sections on science teaching in our first and second centuries. In the second section, we review the golden age of science curriculum. In the third, the view is toward the future and the role of science education in our changing national and global society.

THE FIRST TWO CENTURIES OF SCIENCE TEACHING

The First Century: 1776–1875, an Age of National Development

Even before the Declaration of Independence, the social institutions directed major efforts toward developing a nation. Ours was an agricultural society that later was to experience the tremors of industrial and civil revolutions.

In the decades after independence was declared, public education slowly was recognized as a necessary force for socialization. Education at this time was primarily religious and private. In 1779, Thomas Jefferson introduced a bill for educational reform in Virginia. The bill called for free public education for those of "worth and genius." At its base, however, in the Jeffersonian conception, education was designed to maintain social distinctions and a natural aristocracy between "the labour and the learned." In the late 18th and early 19th centuries, the government began granting land to each new state for public schools and to encourage universal free education. Although each state, county, and township had land, it generally lacked the necessary economic support and public enthusiasm to develop an adequate educational system.

Between 1820 and 1850, in the spirit of Jacksonian democracy, public schools received new support. By 1850, most elementary school children were receiving publicly supported education. The development of public high schools soon followed, so that, with the Jacksonian era, the social institution of public education was established. Later, the 1874 *Kalamazoo* decision set the precedent for tax-supported public high schools.

During the late 18th and early 19th centuries, religious indoctrination decreased and utilitarian objectives increased in schools. With this change science education slowly gained a prominent place in American education.

The earliest forms of science instruction for children have been traced to the stories and didactic literature designed for home tutoring. These materials were based on the theories of John Locke and Jean Jacques Rousseau and emphasized the firsthand study of "things and phenomena" as well as Christian doctrine. Originating about 1750, these materials reached their peak from 1800–1825. With the rise of group instruction, books for home use evolved into textbooks designed for school use. Science was included in many of the lessons, all of which stressed the memorization of factual knowledge, usually supporting theological concepts.[1]

Object teaching, from approximately 1860 to 1880, was a prominent movement in elementary science education. The primary aim of object lessons was personal development; science subject matter was of secondary importance. A method of teaching based primarily on the ideas of Johann Pestalozzi, this movement has had some impact on American education, but from its inception, it was strongly criticized for not emphasizing subject matter and was seldom fully implemented.

The mid 18th to early 19th century marked the period of the academy in secondary level education. As religion ceased to dominate the instructional program, it was replaced with a more practical curriculum, which included science, such as agriculture and navigation.

Next came the early high schools (circa 1820–1870). The principal objectives of science education included learning practical arts and duties of citizenship. Sciences were firmly established in the curriculum during this period, although they were listed as natural philosophy (such as physics and chemistry) and natural history (such as biology and Earth science).

After the Depression of 1873, American schools were severely criticized by citizens asking a question common to such periods: "What are we getting for our money?" As social and economic patterns changed, educators followed with clear demands for more science in the classroom. The aim of science education was to give the public greater understanding of science and technology, the foundation of the emerging Industrial Revolution.

The Second Century: 1876–1976, an Age of Industrial Progress

In the first 100 years of our nation, there were immense changes in the rate and direction of growth in American society. With the transition from an agricultural to an industrial economy, America became an industrial society. After World War II there was the further technological-industrial development of an atomic age. However, as social development continued, negative trade-offs of technological development emerged. Suburban development influenced urban decay; corporate conglomerates increased while small businesses decreased; and society became affluent with new minorities of organizational men, lonely crowds, and other Americans. By the 1960s, almost every aspect of public policy—both domestic and foreign—was being severely criticized

while basic institutions, including education, were being called to reform.

Periodically, throughout the century 1876–1976, schools were asked to make changes that more accurately reflected the realities of our developing society. Committee reports often reveal the nature of these reformations; several from this period will serve as examples of the suggested changes in education.

In 1893, the Committee of Ten[2] stated that all students should be taught the same curriculum whether or not they planned to attend college. The committee detailed such matters as the subjects to be taught and the hours per week and weeks per year to be devoted to each subject. This report helped reduce the domination of colleges over high school programs and formed a stronger connection between high school and elementary school programs. It also stressed academic or intellectual goals.

The slow but steady recognition of the role of science and technology in developing an industrial society inevitably resulted in a popular interest in science and subsequently in science education. Laboratory instruction was very popular because it contributed to a primary objective of the period: development of reasoning, observation, and concentration.

By 1915, the emphasis in science education shifted to goals broader than those for college entrance. A report of the Central Association of Science and Mathematics Teachers Committee on Unified High School Science Courses[3] suggested that science should (1) give pupils such a knowledge of nature as will help them get along better in everyday life, (2) stimulate people to more direct purposeful activity, (3) help them choose intelligently for future occupations, (4) give students methods of obtaining accurate knowledge, and (5) enable students to achieve a greater, clearer, and more intelligent enjoyment of life.

In 1918, the Commission on the Reorganization of Secondary Education completed its work by publishing "The Cardinal Principles of Secondary Education."[4] This report called for a shift in the goal of education from the narrower intellectual indoctrination to a broadened socialization of the student. The seven cardinal principles were health, command of fundamental processes, worthy home membership, vocation, civic education, worthy use of leisure, and ethics. School subjects were to be reorganized so that students would more effectively attain these objectives.

College domination of the high school science program was further eroded by the 1918 publication of the Cardinal Principles by the National Education Association. A report on the reorganization of science in the secondary schools was also published by a subcommittee of the original commission. This report discussed the contributions that science teaching could make to the cardinal principles of secondary education.

Early science laboratories emphasized performance and reenactment of historical discoveries and breakthroughs in science.

In general, it stressed the importance of organization and sequencing of secondary science, but it also pointed out social goals beyond the traditional knowledge goals usually stressed in secondary school science.

By 1924, science teachers used the scientific process as a means to help students learn scientific knowledge. The Committee on the Place of Science in Education of the American Association for the Advancement of Science reported a study on the problems of science teaching. The report underscored the importance of scientific thinking as an objective of teaching. Science instruction, according to the committee, should be founded on scientific observation and experimentation for "a factual basis worthy of the spirit of science."[5]

In 1932, a national survey of secondary education reported on science teaching guides, courses of study, and syllabi. In general, the report stated that the knowledge taught lacked a coherent theoretical structure, that grade-level placement of courses was confusing, and that teaching methods were inconsistent. The report also indicated a variety of innovative practices to be considered when constructing new programs. Such considerations included problem methods of teaching, interpretation of the environment, use of illustrative materials, use of demonstrations, coordination of laboratory and textbook work, and greater use of visual aids.

These reports represent the change in values, as seen in science education, from the high ideals and social unity following World War I to the disillusionment of the economic depression of the late 1920s and 1930s.

The Great Depression raised doubts and questions concerning science education. There were two impor-

tant publications in this period. The National Society for the Study of Education book, *A Program for Science Teaching*,[6] emphasized the importance of broad scientific principles that aid students in a fundamental understanding of nature. The Progressive Education Association publication, *Science in General Education*,[7] stressed progressive goals, such as personal-social relationships, personal living, economic relations, and reflective thinking. The general orientation of science programs was toward the more immediate needs of students; the content was of personal and social significance; and recommendations included programs in health, vocation, and consumerism. The greatest changes were in biology and general science courses, while physics and chemistry courses changed very little.

The period after the Depression was a relatively calm one for science education. The National Society for the Study of Education published *Science Education in American Schools*,[8] with general objectives for science teaching, such as functional information, concepts and principles, skills and attitudes aligned with the scientific method, and the recreational and social values of science. With World War II, America recovered a sense of national purpose, which was reflected in the literature of science education.

After World War II, reports on the American school system stressed life-adjustment education. Examples included the Educational Policies Commission's *Education for All American Youth*,[9] the Department of Secondary School Principals' *Planning for American Youth*,[10] and *Life Adjustment Education for Every Youth*, published by the Office of Education.[11]

In the 1950s, during another economic recession, schools were again criticized for lacking adequate academic goals.[12,13] The demand was for a return to the basics, emphasis on traditional subjects, and special attention to the gifted. This tide of criticism was aided by the October 1957 launching of Sputnik I, which became the symbol for a major reform in science education. The movement led to the most extensive period of curriculum revision and teacher education in American history. Reform of science curricula strongly influenced a model described by Jerome Bruner in *The Process of Education*.[14] Scientific knowledge was the dominant aim, and students used inquiry as a process to acquire knowledge. In Bruner's model, knowledge involved the concepts that formed the structure of a science discipline.

By the middle of the 1960s, however, a new group of social critics appealed for a greater understanding of student alienation, identity, and self-concept. The focus in education shifted from the space race to urban disgrace, and by 1976 the science education community felt tremors of a new reform.

THE GOLDEN AGE: SCIENCE CURRICULUM: 1958–1988

In the late 1950s, society focused attention on the cold war. One aspect included direct competition with the Soviet Union, especially in areas strongly associated with science and technology, for example, nuclear weapons and space exploration.

Although reform of the science curriculum began in the late 1950s, the movement was supported as a result of the Soviet Union's launch of Sputnik I in October 1957. Several years later, in 1961, President John F. Kennedy articulated a national goal when, in a special message to a joint session of Congress, he stated, "I believe that this nation should commit itself to achieving the goal, before this decade is out, of landing a man on the moon and returning him safely to the earth." From the president, the symbol and purpose of this goal was translated into support for science programs that encouraged students to enter careers in science and engineering. The curriculum materials developed and implemented in this period have had tremendous influences on education in general and science education in particular. In the next sections we examine many of the programs developed for junior and senior high schools.

Science Curriculum for the Junior High School

EARTH SCIENCE

Early in 1963, the American Geological Institute received a grant to implement the Earth Science Curriculum Project (ESCP) in the ninth grade. This course was interdisciplinary, involving geology, meteorology, astronomy, and oceanography. Its emphasis was on laboratory and field study.

ESCP materials included a textbook, *Investigating the Earth;* the laboratory was augmented by the text, teacher's guide, films, laboratory equipment, maps, and a pamphlet series. After three years of testing and preparation of materials, the course was published commercially.

The table of contents from the first edition (1967) included the following chapters:

1. The Changing Earth
2. Earth Materials
3. Earth Measurement
4. Earth Motions
5. Fields and Forces
6. Energy Flow
7. Energy and Air Motions
8. Water in the Air
9. Waters of the Land
10. Water in the Sea
11. Energy, Moisture, and Climate
12. The Land Wears Away
13. Sediments in the Sea
14. Mountains from the Sea
15. Rocks within Mountains
16. Interior of the Earth
17. Time and Its Measurement
18. The Record in Rocks
19. Life—Present and Past
20. Development of a Continent
21. Evolution of Landscapes
22. The Moon: A Natural Satellite
23. The Solar System
24. Stars as Other Suns
25. Stellar Evolution and Galaxies
26. The Universe and Its Origin

The project continued its programs until 1969, when two offshoots, Environmental Studies (ES) and Earth Science Teacher Preparation Project (ESTPP), were initiated to deal specifically with the environmental problems and issues of teacher preparation in the earth sciences.

A serious problem that first faced ESCP was the preparation of persons qualified to teach the course, but continued efforts in teacher preparation have narrowed the gap between supply and demand. The advances made in the design and implementation of *Investigating the Earth* were commendable. The text design, integration of concepts from life and physical sciences, and the careful presentation of knowledge, process, and skills were unprecedented. Subsequent revisions of the text have replaced many innovative topics and realigned the book with older, traditional earth science texts.

PHYSICAL SCIENCE

Another program developed for the junior high school was the Introductory Physical Science (IPS) program of Educational Services, Incorporated. This project, supported by the NSF, was to develop a one-year course in physical science. Laboratory work and equipment were designed in such a way that students performed the experiments in ordinary classrooms. The table of contents of the Introductory Physical Science course included the following:

1. Introduction
2. Quantity of Matter: Mass
3. Characteristic Properties
4. Solubility and Solvents
5. The Separation of Substances
6. Compounds and Elements
7. Radioactivity
8. The Atomic Model of Matter
9. Sizes and Masses of Atoms and Molecules
10. Molecular Motion
11. Heat

The IPS course was tested in several centers throughout the United States, and the materials, which included textbooks, teachers' guides, laboratory notebooks, and comprehensive apparatus kits, were eventually published commercially.

The attractiveness of the IPS course to better-than-average junior high school students was made clear in the results of a test survey of representative IPS students in the 1965–1966 school year. "In that year, 1,005 ninth-grade IPS students and 400 eighth-grade IPS students took the School and College Abilities Test (SCAT) Survey Form, a test of verbal and mathematical ability. The results made it clear that the IPS students were more scholastically able on the average than typical junior high school students in the nation."[15]

As the success of a new course depends on well-qualified teachers, the National Science Foundation supported a program to locate qualified science teachers and to prepare them to instruct other teachers in the use of IPS. The program was quite successful; in IPS workshops, teachers were trained by their peers in the local environment.

INTEGRATED SCIENCE

Among junior high school courses was the Intermediate Science Curriculum Study (ISCS) financed by the United States Office of Education and National Science Foundation. "The fundamental assumption underlying the ISCS plan is that science at the junior high school level serves essentially a general education function."[16] Three levels were prepared, corresponding to the junior high school grades 7, 8, and 9. Level I for seventh grade was tightly structured. Its title, *Energy, Its Forms and Characteristics,* permitted students to delve into

physical science principles by dealing with science in their environment. Level II put the students more on their own in designing experiments and recording and interpreting data. This level dealt with *Matter and Its Composition and Model Building.* Level III for the ninth grade dealt with biological concepts and was designed to use laboratory blocks six to eight weeks long as its basic plan of operation. The ninth grade student was expected to use the concepts and investigative skills acquired in the seventh and eighth grades. All of the class activity in the ISCS course was planned for individualized work, and the teacher's task was assisting students. No formal lectures or information-dispensing sessions were planned for the course, unless needed on a short-term basis by a small group of students.

An innovative feature of the ISCS course was the production of a complete course on Computer-Assisted Instruction (CAI). Using behavioral objectives and a system of computer feedback, it was possible to obtain detailed information on the progress and problems encountered by each student. This information was used to modify and revise the trial versions of the course.

There were other smaller scale projects for revising junior high school science. Among them were the Interaction Science Curriculum Project (ISCP), Ideas and Investigations in Science (IIS), and a BSCS program, *Patterns and Processes in Science.* Each was extensively field tested and met with certain elements of success. The field of science teaching in the junior high school received an impetus similar to that enjoyed by senior high school teaching.

Science Curriculum for the High School

At the high school level, advances in science and technology have traditionally exerted the greatest influence on programs. In this section, we review traditional disciplines for school science—physics, chemistry, and biology.

Visit http://www.prenhall.com/ trowbridge and select Topic 1—Science Teaching Standards. Select "National Science Teaching Standards," click on the link for the science content standards, and find the link to review the standards for "History and Nature of Science." This link will complement the material on historical perspective and allow you to make comparisons on changes over recent years. Write and submit your response about your perceptions to your instructor using the Electronic Bluebook module.

PHYSICS

Physics was first known as *natural philosophy* and appeared in the academies of the early 1700s. Content was organized into topics similar to those of many courses today. Mechanics, fluids, heat, light, sound, magnetism, and electricity were taught, mainly by recitation. The Civil War and the advent of land-grant colleges in the 1860s placed emphasis on military and vocational aspects of science, and the course became known as physics. Laboratory instruction was emphasized. A list of standard experiments, called *The Descriptive List*, was circulated by Harvard in 1886 for use by the high schools. Candidates for admission to Harvard who had taken physics as a prerequisite were then tested by use of these experiments.

PHYSICAL SCIENCE STUDY COMMITTEE

In 1956, a group of university physicists at Cambridge, Massachusetts, looked at the secondary school physics curriculum and found that it did not present the content or spirit of modern physics. From this group, the Physical Science Study Committee (PSSC) was formed, with the objective of producing a new physics course for the high school level.

In four years this group developed a textbook, a laboratory guide, a teacher's guide, a set of apparatus, monographs, and films. All of these aids were correlated closely with one another to produce an effective curriculum package. In addition, there were many summer institutes for upgrading teachers in physics and in the philosophy of the new course.

Some of the important differences between the PSSC physics course and other high school physics became apparent:

- fewer topics covered at greater depth,
- greater emphasis on laboratory work,
- more emphasis on basic physics,
- less attention to technological applications,
- development approach showing origins of basic ideas of physics, and
- increased difficulty and rigor of the course.

Teachers and administrators had conflicting opinions about the merits of the PSSC course. There was general agreement that it was a definite improvement over traditional courses, especially for better-than-average college-bound students. For average or below-average students, its merit was questionable.

In a 1971 study by John Wasik, PSSC students showed significantly higher performance than non-PSSC students in the process skills of application and analysis.[17] However, non-PSSC students performed at a higher level on the taxonomic process measure of knowledge. Wasik concluded that the results supported the position of new curriculum writers that the PSSC instructional materials were most effective in developing higher cognitive-process skills.

A 1983 analysis of the effects of new science curricula on student performance revealed that the physics curricula was second only to the biology curricula in terms of overall advances in student performances. Studies of achievement and analytic skills showed that students participating in the new physics courses gained at least a half-year more than students in traditional courses.[18] This result indicates that the new physics curricula was partially successful in achieving its stated goals. The goal generally not assessed was the students' perceptions of physics. This omission is unfortunate because it could have given some insights to help slow the long and steady decline in physics enrollments.

PROJECT PHYSICS

Project Physics, a course designed for the average student and produced at Harvard University, attempted to treat physics as a lively and fundamental science, closely related to achievements both in and outside the discipline itself.[19]

Financial support for the project was provided by the Carnegie Corporation of New York, the Ford Foundation, the National Science Foundation, the Alfred P. Sloan Foundation, the United States Office of Education, and Harvard University. Several hundred participating schools throughout the United States tested the course as it went through several revisions.

The philosophy of this course is emphasized in eight points:[20]

1. Physics is for everyone.
2. A coherent selection within physics is possible.
3. Doing physics goes beyond physics.
4. Individuals require a flexible course.
5. A multimedia system stimulates better learning.
6. The time has come to teach science as one of the humanities.
7. A physics course should be rewarding to take.
8. A physics course should be rewarding to teach.

Materials of Project Physics included a textbook, teacher's guide, student guide, experiments, films, transparencies, tests, film loops, readers, and other items. The chapter headings for the Project Physics course were[21]

Unit 1: Concepts of Motion

Unit 2: Motion in the Heavens

Unit 3: The Triumph of Mechanics

Unit 4: Light and Electromagnetism

Unit 5: Models of the Atom

Unit 6: The Nucleus

Several studies attempted to find reasons for the decreasing enrollments in high school physics. In a questionnaire sent by Raymond Thompson to 1,382 high school physics teachers, 79 percent believed that students stayed away because the course was too difficult.[22] Of these students, 40 percent ascribed their reluctance to fear of jeopardizing their grade average, and 16 percent attributed it to fear of mathematics.

In a study of 450 physics students enrolled in Project Physics in 1966–1967, Wayne Welch concluded that students received lower grades in physics than in their other courses.[23] In the sample studied, the median IQ was at the 82nd percentile, but the average grade received by these bright students was in the C+ to B− range. Thus, the students were dissatisfied with their experience.

The course was extensively evaluated during its development. Results were encouraging, both with respect to the performance of Project Physics students on standard tests such as the College Board Examinations and with respect to attracting increasing numbers of high school students to elect physics in their junior or senior years. The percentage of girls taking the course also appeared to have increased over PSSC or traditional physics courses.

Chemistry

The teaching of high school chemistry began in the early 1800s in girls' academies, while the Civil War years provided a stimulus to the course because of military and industrial applications. Laboratory work increased during the late 1800s, and efforts were made to reproduce many of the classical experiments of early chemists such as Joseph Priestly and Antoine-Laurent Lavoisier. As with physics, Harvard in 1886 placed chemistry on the optional list for college entrance and controlled the quality of entering students by publishing *The Pamphlet,* containing 60 experiments, on which the prospective enrollee was tested in the laboratory. Influence of *The Pamphlet* was profound, and the high school chemistry course became highly standardized. Laboratory workbooks were developed, containing experiments that were mainly exercises in observation and manipulation of chemical reactions.

CHEMICAL BOND APPROACH

In 1957, a summer conference of chemistry teachers at Reed College in Portland, Oregon, produced a plan for a new type of chemistry course and initiated the Chemical Bond Approach (CBA) Project. There followed a series of writing conferences, use of the new materials by trial schools, and the production of a commercial textbook in 1963. The major theme of this course was the chemical bond, and particular attention was given to *mental models* (conceptual schemes) of structure, kinetic theory, and energy.

The laboratory program and textbook paralleled and reinforced each other. No unusual chemicals or equipment were required, and the cost of conducting the CBA chemistry course was not significantly different from that of conducting conventional courses.

CHEMICAL EDUCATION MATERIALS STUDY

A second course-improvement project in chemistry was initiated at Harvey Mudd College in Claremont, California, in 1959. Called the Chemical Education Materials Study (CHEM), the project developed a course that was strongly based on experiment and included a text and laboratory manual, a teacher's guide, a score of excellent films, and a series of wall charts.

Both the CBA and CHEM Study chemistry programs received grants from the National Science Foundation, which supported numerous in-service and summer institutes for teachers.

Enrollment in CBA and CHEM chemistry classes increased initially. In 1968, approximately 40 percent of high school chemistry taught in the United States was the CHEM Study course.[24] Approximately 10 percent of the schools were using CBA.[25] At this time the CHEM project terminated its work, and commercial publishers were invited to prepare courses based on the philosophy and materials of the CHEM Study course. Several publishers produced high school chemistry textbooks influenced by the philosophies and pedagogies of the CHEM and CBA programs.

In a survey by Frank Fornhoff in 1970, in which 2,395 students were queried, the most widely used high school chemistry textbook was *Modern Chemistry; Chemistry—An Experimental Science* was second; and *Chemical Systems* was third.[26] The latter two texts were CHEM Study and CBA chemistry, respectively. Other information obtained in the study showed that most chemistry classes met five times per week for 40 to 59 minutes, and 13 percent of students reported taking a college-level chemistry course in high school.

In a 1978 report it was estimated that fewer than 25 percent of chemistry teachers were using either CHEM Study, a CBA approach, or a combination of the two.[27] The same study found that CHEM Study was used in 15 percent of school districts; yet, neither textbook appeared on the list of most commonly used textbooks. A 1983 report on the effects of new curricula found that the new chemistry curricula, both CBA and CHEM Study, produced the least impact in terms of student cognitive achievement and process skills.[28]

INTERDISCIPLINARY APPROACHES TO CHEMISTRY

In March 1972, a new chemistry course was developed by the University of Maryland: the Interdisciplinary Approaches to Chemistry (IAC). The IAC course approached the teaching of chemistry somewhat differently by using a group of modules dealing with special topics of an interdisciplinary nature. The titles of the modules were

- Reactions and Reason (Introductory)
- Diversity and Periodicity (Inorganic)
- Form and Function (Organic)
- Molecules in Living Systems (Biochemistry)
- The Heart of the Matter (Nuclear)
- Earth and Its Neighbors (Geochemistry)
- The Delicate Balance (Environmental)
- Communities of Molecules (Physical)

Among the goals of IAC was the

> realization that a student's attitudes or feelings about chemistry are just as important in the long run as his acquisition of special chemical concepts.
>
> Thus, in molding the IAC program, equal emphasis has been placed on providing the student with a sound background in those basic skills and concepts normally found in an introductory high school chemistry course as well as on developing the attitude that chemistry is not a dry, unrealistic science, but an exciting, relevant, human activity that can be enjoyable to study.[29]

Several characteristics made the IAC chemistry different from traditional chemistry courses or previous curriculum projects, with an emphasis on making chemistry more relevant and successful for the student. The program is modular, instead of being a single, structured text. Each module is devoted to a different aspect of chemistry and its relationship to the other sciences and society. This format allows for many degrees of flexibility within the program.

A module consists of chemistry content and laboratory experiments integrated into a unified whole. The program includes suggested readings for students, problems and activities, safety precautions, and relevant chemical data, such as periodic tables and charts. Each module deals with a specific area of chemistry as indicated in the titles, relating chemistry to other sciences and phenomena encountered in the natural world.

IAC was revised in 1979 to update its content and its teaching techniques in concepts and in laboratory experiments. It was well received by chemistry teachers who enjoy the freedom to experiment with different modules in their classes and to rearrange content in accordance with student and teacher interests.

Research by Robert Stevenson in 1977–1978 on the use of IAC chemistry in high school indicated that age, sex, and attitude had no effect on the achievement level of students; that cognitive-reasoning ability and grade-point averages were highly correlated with achievement success; and that achievement success on the introductory module tests could be used to predict success on subsequent modules.[30]

Biology

In school science programs, biology began in botany, physiology, and zoology courses and in the nineteenth century was patterned after college courses in these subjects. A course of study in biology appeared in New York in 1905, and the College Entrance Examination Board prepared an examination for the course in 1913. Biology was placed either in the ninth or tenth grade.

Of all the high school sciences, biology had the largest enrollment, due to a combination of factors. Placement in the ninth or tenth grade where the effect of school dropouts is less pronounced, the effect of compulsory education laws, the nonmathematical nature of the course, and the general requirement of a minimum of one science course for graduation from high school all combined to increase enrollments over the years. In 1958, approximately 68 percent of tenth grade students enrolled in the biology course.[31]

BIOLOGICAL SCIENCES CURRICULUM STUDY

The American Institute of Biological Science organized the Biological Sciences Curriculum Study (BSCS) at the University of Colorado in 1958, with Arnold B. Grobman as director. In discussing the design of the course, he said:

> A realistic general biology program must take into account a wider range of student ability, interests, and potential than exists in other high school science courses. It must be a course that most tenth-grade students can handle and at the same time prove challenging to the above-average student. For these reasons, the committee thought it undesirable to limit the course to a single design.[32]

Three courses were developed, based on a molecular approach, a cellular approach, and an ecological approach. Although the courses differ in emphasis, nine common themes run through them:

1. change of living things through time—evolution,
2. diversity of type and unity of pattern of living things,
3. genetic continuity of life,
4. biological roots of behavior,
5. complementarity of organisms and environment,
6. complementarity of structure and function,
7. regulation and homeostasis: the maintenance of life in the face of change,
8. science as inquiry, and
9. intellectual history of biological concepts.[33]

Among the course materials were textbooks, laboratory guides, supplementary readings, and tests. Innovations include laboratory blocks consisting of a series of interlocking and correlated experiments on a special topic of biology. Eleven laboratory blocks were developed, including Plant Growth and Development; Microbes: Their Growth and Development; and Interdependence of Structure and Function. A second-level course was prepared for advanced biology, and a course called Patterns and Processes in Science was designed for unsuccessful learners.

Other supplementary materials included excerpts from historical papers, BSCS Invitations to Inquiry, discussion outlines for the laboratory, films on laboratory techniques, the *Biology Teacher's Handbook,* and the BSCS Pamphlet Series.

The BSCS biology courses received a generally favorable response throughout the country. Two versions of the course are still available, and it has been found that different versions are chosen in different regions. Several foreign countries are also using the course.

Several researchers have studied the effects of BSCS biology in the schools. In one study, Kenneth George found that students taking Blue Version scored significantly higher on critical thinking, as measured by the Watson Glaser Critical Thinking Appraisal Form ZM, than did students taking conventional biology.[34] B. J. Adams found no difference in the retention of biological information between BSCS students and those taking traditional biology.[35] However, there were significant relationships between retention and intelligence, reading scores, and teacher grading, with the BSCS students generally scoring higher. Charles Granger and Robert Yager[36] found no significant difference between students experiencing BSCS and non-BSCS backgrounds with respect to achievement in either high school or college-level biology. However, a significantly larger percentage of BSCS students felt their background was better in meeting individual needs, as well as preparing them for college level biology.[37] Jack Carter and Alan Nakosteen, in a study with 8,500 college freshmen, found that BSCS students scored higher on inquiry and recall items on the BSCS Comprehensive Biology Tests than did students who enrolled in a non-BSCS course in high school.[38]

In a 1983 report, BSCS fared very well in the major review of curricula developed in the 1960s and 1970s. Biology curricula showed the greatest effect on student performance, particularly in the area of developing analytic skills. In a 1984 report on the BSCS programs, James Shymansky had this to say:

> We found the new science programs to be consistently more effective than their traditional counterparts. Moreover, we found Biological Sciences Curriculum Study (BSCS) to be the most effective of all the new high school programs.[39]

COMMON ELEMENTS OF GOLDEN AGE COURSES

A survey of various course materials developed in secondary school science during the 1960s and 1970s shows close similarity both in types of materials offered and in general objectives. The following common elements can be discerned:

- less emphasis on social and personal applications of science and technology than in the traditional courses;
- more emphasis on abstractions, theory, and basic science—the structure of scientific disciplines;
- increased emphasis on discovery—the modes of inquiry used by scientists;
- frequent use of quantitative techniques;
- newer concepts in subject matter;
- an upgrading of teacher competency in both subject matter and pedagogical skills;
- well integrated and designed teaching aids to supplement the courses;
- little emphasis on career awareness as a goal of science teaching;
- primarily an orientation toward college-bound students; and
- similarities in emphasis and structure in the high school and junior high school programs.

AN ERA OF EDUCATIONAL REFORM: SCIENCE EDUCATION IN SECONDARY SCHOOLS: 1980–?

Beginning in the early 1980s, science education entered a new era of reform. In 1981, Norris Harms and Robert Yager published the results of Project Synthesis, a major effort to evaluate the status of, and make recommendations for, science education. In a larger context, the publication of *A Nation at Risk* in 1983 symbolized a wider and deeper national effort to reform education. Though varied in approach and recommendations, the national reports on education in the United States consistently identified science and technology as a vital area with a pressing need for reform. What brought about this national concern with science and technology education were a number of disturbing trends, including declines in the following:

- science enrollments in secondary schools,
- science education in elementary schools,
- achievement test scores,
- students entering science and engineering careers,
- qualified science teachers,
- public attitudes toward science education, and
- the quality and quantity of American science education compared to that of other countries.[40,41,42]

The history of American education had never witnessed such widespread calls for educational reform. By the late 1980s, more than 300 reports admonished those within the educational system to improve. Depending on who published the report, recommendations emphasized such issues as updating scientific and technological knowledge, applying learning theory and new teaching strategies, improving approaches to achieve equity, and providing better preparation for the workplace. Various calls for reform continued into the 1990s and 2000. The need to improve continues in the 21st century.

For science education at the secondary school level, there are significant differences between the 1960s and 1990s reforms. The 1960s reform began at the secondary level and progressed to the elementary level. In the 1990s, reports have generally addressed all levels, K–12, but the specific curriculum reform began at the elementary school level and progressed to secondary schools. The impetus for this sequential reform was initiated by funding from the NSF for new elementary and middle school programs. In the early 21st century educators can anticipate curricular changes at the secondary school level. The important point is that school science programs structured from the top down, from twelfth grade physics to elementary programs, are quite different from school science programs that are structured from the bottom up, or when the science curriculum is viewed more holistically as a total K–12 program.

A second difference between these two decades is that in the late 1990s and early 21st century there are fewer curriculum projects at the national level. Reform efforts are being initiated through national standards and benchmarks, as well as state-level frameworks and guidelines, but they are being completed through local development of materials. Such efforts have the advantage of higher levels of implementation and the disadvantage of lower levels of actual program reform. These lower levels of reform result from a lack of time and money to develop new materials, so, subsequently, school districts adopt textbooks. Additionally, staff development programs to update teachers in science and technology content and innovative teaching strategies are not implemented as a complement to the instructional materials. The result is a nationwide low level of reform in both quantity and quality.

REVIEWING THE GOALS OF SCIENCE EDUCATION

As soon as discussions of reform in science education began, so did talk of rethinking goals. Obviously the direction of reform had to be guided by new goals. Anna Harrison called attention to the inadequacy of science education goals in an editorial in *Science*.[43] And Ronald Anderson asked the rhetorical question, "Are Yesterday's Goals Adequate for Tomorrow?"[44] He, too, called attention to the inadequacy of contemporary goals. In the 1980s these were only two instances in which peo-

ple began directing science educators toward the reform of goals for science teaching.

Others began addressing the need and substance for new goals in more detail. In a short monograph entitled *Reforming Science Education: The Search for a New Vision*, Paul DeHart Hurd summarized the emerging vision of goals. "The rationale and goals are derived from a consideration of how science and technology influenced social well-being and human affairs. The goals for teaching science are based on scientific and technological systems in social, cultural, and individual contexts."[45]

A major report issued by the National Science Board (NSB) in 1983 was titled *Educating Americans for the 21st Century*.[46] This report was quite comprehensive, including a section on goals for science and technology education. The report very clearly describes a vision that would eventually be set in place by the *Standards* and *Benchmarks*. The list of general outcomes recommended by this report were

- ability to formulate questions about nature and seek answers from observation and interpretation of natural phenomena;
- development of students' capacities for problem solving and critical thinking in all areas of learning;
- development of particular talents for innovative and creative thinking;
- awareness of the nature and scope of a wide variety of science- and technology-related careers open to students of varying aptitudes and interests;
- the basic academic knowledge necessary for advanced study by students who are likely to pursue science professionally;
- scientific and technical knowledge needed to fulfill civic responsibilities, improve the student's own health and life, and ability to cope with an increasingly technological world; and
- means for judging the worth of articles presenting scientific conclusions.

The NSB report continues by saying that materials to achieve these outcomes must be developed and tests must be devised to measure the degree to which these goals are met. The section then concludes with a summary statement of the goals:

In summary, students who have progressed through the Nation's school systems should be able to use both the knowledge and products of science, mathematics and technology in their thinking, their lives and their work. They should be able to make informed choices regarding their own health and lifestyles based on evidence and reasonable personal preferences, after taking into consideration short- and long-term risks and benefits of different decisions. They should also be prepared to make similarly informed choices in the social and political arenas. (p. 45)

The goal statement is finally extended to the curriculum:

New science curricula that incorporate appropriate scientific and technological knowledge and are oriented toward practical issues are needed. They also will provide an excellent way of fostering traditional basic skills. The introduction of practical problems which require the collection of data, the communication of results and ideas and the formulation and testing of solutions or improvement would: (1) improve the use and understanding of calculation and mathematical analysis; (2) sharpen the student's ability to communicate verbally and to write precisely; (3) develop problem-solving skills; (4) impart scientific concepts and facts that can be related to practical applications; (5) develop a respect for science and technology and more generally for quantitative observation and thinking; and (6) stimulate an interest in many to enter scientific, engineering, and technical careers. (p. 45)

The need to develop a new reform for goals is based on the national standards that education in science and technology should be grounded on recent advances in scientific and technologic disciplines, needs and aspirations of society, and the interrelationship of science, technology, and society.

First and foremost is the need to develop a contemporary perspective of goals for science and technology education. There have been tremendous advances in science, changes in social needs, and new-recognized interactions between science and society. These changes have been generally recognized in the goals expressed in the *National Science Education Standards* and *Benchmarks for Science Literacy*.

Visit http://www.prenhall.com/trowbridge and select Topic 1—Science Teaching Standards. Select "Web Links" and find the link to "History of Standards." This link will offer an excellent historical perspective and allow you to make comparisons on changes over recent years. Write and submit your response about your perceptions to your instructor using the Electronic Bluebook module.

Science Education in Secondary Science

The science curriculum in secondary schools is largely determined at the state and local levels by science teachers, science supervisors, administrators, and school boards.[47] Research studies supported by the NSF have shown that even with significant autonomy there is considerable uniformity of science programs nation-wide, and curriculum and methods of instruction have not changed significantly.[48,49,50]

SCIENCE COURSES

Typically, the science curriculum is general or earth science at the ninth grade, biology at the tenth grade, and chemistry and physics at the eleventh and twelfth grades, respectively. In 1978, the largest science enrollment in junior high schools was general science, with approximately five million students. Another two million students in schools with grades 7–12 or 9–12 were also enrolled in general science. Earth science enrollments were approximately 1.25 million. Enrollments did not change substantially in a decade, although they are currently changing more due to the emergence of middle schools.[51] General biology is offered to all students and enrolls approximately three million students each year. About 80 percent of graduating seniors have taken high school biology. However, this statistic is misleading and has an important bearing on reform of science education at the secondary level. For 50 percent of high school students who graduate each year, biology is their last experience with any science course. High school chemistry and physics courses are generally perceived as college preparatory, as are the majority of other courses offered in the high school curriculum. As a result, many students lack an understanding of physical science. This observation is supported by results from the Third International Mathematics and Science Study.[52]

TEXTBOOKS

The nature of the high school science curriculum can be determined by examining textbooks for the respective disciplines. The similarity among textbooks for a discipline— and even among textbooks for different disciplines—is remarkable. These characteristics include presenting a significant number of facts in simple and condensed form and an emphasis on extensive vocabulary and technical terms. In addition to being encyclopedic, science texts currently in use implicitly suggest a pedagogy of *inform*, *verify*, and *practice*. The NSF materials developed in the 1960s and 1970s espoused goals of understanding conceptual schemes (the structure of disciplines) and using scientific processes (the modes of inquiry); changes in textbooks and, subsequently, teaching evolved in different directions. For example, recent reviews of the inquiry goal in science teaching found that teachers give little attention to inquiry and associated skills.[53]

STUDENT ACHIEVEMENT

The need for contemporary reform is supported by poor student achievement in science that was first recorded in the 1960s. In 1988 Ina Mullis and Lynn Jenkins summarized two decades of results from the National Assessment of Educational Progress (NAEP) in the *Science Report Card.* Following are summaries of achievement for 17-year-olds, that is, those students leaving high school.

1. At age 17, students' science achievement was well below those of students graduating in 1969. Steady declines occurred throughout the 1970s, followed by an upturn in performance between 1982 and 1986.
2. More than half of the nation's 17-year-olds were inadequately prepared for jobs that require technical skills or for specialized on-the-job training. The thinking skills and science knowledge possessed by high school students in the 1980s were inadequate for participation in the nation's civic affairs.
3. Only 7 percent of the nation's 17-year-olds had the prerequisite knowledge and skills to perform well in college-level science courses.

The National Assessment of Educational Progress completed assessments in 1996 and the year 2000. The national results present achievement levels for students in grades 4, 8, and 12. The National Assessment Governing Board (NAGB) set student performance standards.[54,55] The levels of student performance are reported as *basic, proficient,* and *advanced.*

How did American students do? In 1996, 3 percent of the nation's students reached the *advanced* level at all three grades—4, 8, and 12. In the year 2000, 3 percent of the nation's fourth and eighth graders reached the *advanced* level. Only 2 percent of twelfth graders reached *advanced* levels.

Twenty-six percent of fourth and eighth grade students and 18 percent of twelfth grade students performed within the *proficient* level. Again, in 2000 fourth graders remained the same—26 percent were *proficient.* Eighth graders had 28 percent proficiency in 2000 compared to 26 percent in 1996. The percent of twelfth graders who were *proficient* dropped from 19 percent in 1996 to 16 percent in 2000. Thirty-eight percent, 32 percent, and 36 percent performed within the *basic* level for grades 4, 8, and 12, respectively. In 2000, these percentages were 37 percent, 29 percent, and 34 percent, respectively. Concerning the results at the *basic* level, we can look at these results another way; namely how many students were *below basic levels.* The answer is both disappointing and a challenge for science teachers. Respectively, 33 percent, 39 percent, and 43 percent of fourth, eighth, and twelfth grade students were *below basic levels* of achievement in 1996. In the year 2000, these percentages were 34 percent, 39 percent, and 47 percent for grades 4, 8, and 12 respectively. These results are summarized in Figure 3–1.

Nationally, what percentages of males and females reached the three achievement levels? Results for males and females were the same at grade 8. At grade 4, greater percentages of males than females were at or above the *proficient* level. At grade 12, males outperformed females at all three levels—*basic, proficient,* and *advanced.*

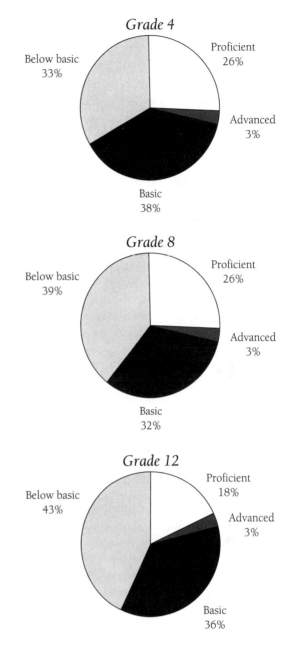

FIGURE 3–1   National Science Achievement-Level Results

Source: *The Nation's Report Card: Science Highlights 2000.*

Based on these results current programs do not seem to be contributing to the two primary goals of science education: developing informed citizenship and developing future scientists and engineers.

ACHIEVEMENT OF UNDERREPRESENTED GROUPS

Social and economic realities have influences that far exceed the effect of school in general or a science program in particular. Still, the science program should contribute, in some small measure, to the future opportunities of all students. The NAEP data indicate continued and substantial disparities in science proficiency among groups of differing race, ethnicity, and gender.

The NAEP results for 1996 indicated differences in achievement levels by various racial and ethnic groups at the three grade levels. The report states:

> Significant differences in attainment of achievement levels by racial and ethnic groups were evident at all grade levels, especially in comparisons of Whites with Hispanics and Whites with Blacks. (p. 37)

Causes of these disparities are many and varied; most are beyond the control of school science programs. At a minimum, science programs in secondary schools should not perpetuate initial inequities, and—ideally—curriculum, instruction, and assessment in science should ameliorate inequities. Reform in textbook design, increased participation in hands-on activities, and use of cooperative learning strategies are three recommendations to improve achievement in underrepresented groups.

International comparisons of student achievement have also been made. In particular, the science education community has been, and will be, influenced by results from the Third International Mathematics and Science Study, usually referred to by the acronym, TIMSS. TIMSS was the largest and most comprehensive comparative international study of education that has ever been undertaken. The study reported results for eighth grade students in November 1996, for fourth grade students in June 1997, and for twelfth grade students in February 1998. In all, the study assessed a half million students from 41 countries in 30 languages to compare their mathematics and science achievement. In addition to achievement results, TIMSS also included thorough reviews of curriculum materials and instructional methods in the countries. A brief summary of 1996 achievement levels for students in the United States: At fourth grade, our students are above the international average and among the best in the world. At eighth grade, our students are just above average in science and just below average in mathematics. At twelfth grade, U.S. students' performance was among the lowest of the participating countries in mathematics and science general knowledge, physics, and advanced mathematics. These results indicate a steady decline in U.S. students' achievement during their school years.

In 1999, the Third International Mathematics and Science Study (TIMSS) was replicated at the eighth grade. Involving 41 countries and testing at five grade levels, TIMSS was originally conducted in 1995 to provide a base from which policy makers, curriculum specialists, and researchers could better understand the performance of their educational systems. Conducted under the auspices of the International Association for the Evaluation of Educational Achievement (IEA), TIMSS was the first

step in a long-term strategy, with further assessments in mathematics and science planned for 2003, and beyond.

TIMSS 1999, also known as TIMSS-Repeat or TIMSS-R, was designed to provide trends in eighth-grade mathematics and science achievement in an international context. Thirty-eight countries participated in TIMSS 1999. Of these, 26 countries also participated in TIMSS 1995 at the eighth grade and have trend data included in this report. Also, 1999 represents four years since the first TIMSS, and the population of students originally assessed as fourth-graders had advanced to the eighth grade. Thus, for 17 of the 26 countries that participated in TIMSS 1995 at the fourth grade, TIMSS 1999 also provides information about whether the relative performance of these students has changed in the intervening years.

Six content areas were covered in the TIMSS 1999 science test: earth science; life science; physics; chemistry; environmental and resource issues; and scientific inquiry and the nature of science. About one-fourth of the questions were in the free-response format, requiring students to generate and write their answers. The achievement data are accompanied by extensive questionnaire data about the home, classroom, school, and national contexts within which science learning takes place.[56]

U.S. students scored above the international average in both mathematics and science at the fourth-grade level. At the eighth-grade level, U.S. students performed above the international average in science and below the international average in mathematics. In the final year of secondary school (twelfth grade in the U.S.), U.S. performance was among the lowest in both science and mathematics, including among our most advanced students.[57]

It is also important to be aware of the Programs for International Student Assessment (PISA). Although not as popular as TIMSS in the U.S., PISA is having an international impact.

The results of NAEP, TIMSS, and PISA provide substantial evidence that our educational system is not attaining the goal of scientific literacy. Indeed, it is failing to provide our students an adequate science education. The twelfth grade students who did most poorly on TIMSS entered school in the late 1980s. Their science education consisted of traditional textbooks and instructional methods, and their achievement is dismal. Indeed, it was the worst in the world. The national and international results show that American science education needs improvement. Further, the TIMSS results also provide some indications of how we should reform curriculum, instruction, and assessments.[58,59,60,61]

Trends in Secondary School Science

There is widespread support for reform of the educational system. Scientific and technological literacy is the main purpose of science education in K–12. This goal is for all students, not just for those individuals destined for careers in science and engineering.

As we begin the 21st century, the curriculum for science education at the secondary school level is inadequate to the challenge of achieving scientific and technological literacy. Many scientists and science educators are urging a review of school science programs, a review that would affect millions of school personnel in thousands of autonomous school districts, but one that is necessary. Increasing the scientific and technological literacy of students also requires several fundamental changes in science curricula at the secondary school level. First, the information presented must be balanced with key conceptual themes that are learned in some depth. Second, the rigid disciplinary boundaries of earth science, biology, chemistry, and physics should be softened; greater emphasis should also be placed on connections among the sciences and among disciplines generally thought of as outside of school science, such as technology, mathematics, ethics, and social studies.[62,63]

Achieving the goal of scientific and technological literacy requires more than understanding concepts and processes of science and technology. Indeed, there is some need for citizens to understand science and technology as an integral part of society. Science and technology are enterprises that shape, and are shaped by, human thought and social actions.[64,65] Our recommendation includes some understanding of the nature and history of science and technology. There is recent and substantial support for this recommendation, though few curriculum materials. Including the nature and history of science and technology provides opportunities to focus on topics that blur disciplinary boundaries and show connections between such fields as science and social studies.

The substantial body of research on learning should be the basis for making instruction more effective.[66] This research suggests that students learn by constructing their own meaning of the experiences they have.[67,68,69,70,71] A constructivist approach requires very different methods of science instruction in the secondary school.[72]

Related to the implications of research on learning theory is the recommendation that science teaching should consist of experiences exemplifying the spirit, character, and nature of science and technology. Students should begin with questions about the natural world (science) and problems about human beings adapting (technology). They should be actively involved in the processes of inquiry and design. They should have opportunities to present their explanations for phenomena and solutions to problems and to compare their explanations and solutions to those concepts of science and technology. And, they should have a chance to apply their understandings in new situations. In short, the inquiry-oriented laboratory is an infrequent experience for secondary school students, but it should be a central part of their experience in science education. Extensive use of the inquiry-oriented laboratory is consistent with the other recommendations made in this section, and it has widespread support.

The issue of equity must be addressed in science programs and by school personnel. For the past several decades, science educators at all levels have discussed the importance of changing science programs to enhance opportunities for historically underrepresented groups. Calls for scientific and technological literacy assume the inclusion of *all* Americans. Other justifications—if any are needed for this position—include the supply of future scientists and engineers, changing demographics, and prerequisites for work. Research results, curricula recommendations, and practical suggestions are available to those developing science curricula for the secondary school.[73,74,75,76]

Science education in middle schools is a special concern as educators look toward achieving higher levels of scientific literacy. Numerous reports and commissions have addressed the need for educational reform for high school science education, but few have specifically recognized the emergence of middle schools in the 1980s. The movement toward implementing middle schools, and phasing out junior high schools, is a significant trend in education. Yet, thus far, the middle school reform has not thoroughly addressed the particular issues of subject-matter disciplines—in this case, science and technology. Contemporary reform must not allow the science education of early adolescents to be overlooked or assumed to be part of either the elementary school or secondary school curriculum.

Improving curriculum and instruction will be a hollow gesture without concomitant changes in assessment at all levels, from the local classroom to the national and international levels. In general, the changes in assessment practices must reflect the changes described earlier for curriculum and instruction. Incongruities, such as teaching fewer concepts in greater depth but testing for numerous facts in fine detail, will undermine the reform of science education. New forms of assessment are available and being recommended by researchers, policymakers, and practitioners.[77,78,79,80]

Reform of science education at the secondary school level must be viewed as part of the general reform of education. Approaching the improvement of science education by changing textbooks, buying new computers, or adding new courses simply will not work. Fortunately, widespread educational reform, which includes science education, is under way. The improvement of science education in the secondary school must be part of the reconstruction of science education for K–12 and must include all courses and students, a staff development program, reform of science teacher preparation, and support from school administrators. This comprehensive or systemic recommendation is based on the research on implementation[81,82] and research literature on school change and restructuring.[83,84,85,86]

As we begin the 21st century we think the improvement of science education is a national mandate. You will be a part of that process. Although the challenge is large, we have clear guidance in national standards and benchmarks. These guidelines will be followed through changes in instructional materials and increased support of professional development to help science teachers improve. We have all the tools for the job; now we need commitment at the local, state, and national levels.

 Visit http://www.prenhall.com/trowbridge and select Topic 1—Science Teaching Standards. Select "Web Links" and find the link to the "History of Standards." This link will offer an excellent historical overview of the standards movement in the U.S. Write and submit a concise account of this topic to your instructor using the Electronic Bluebook module.

SUMMARY

The need for changes in high school science programs became increasingly evident midway through the 20th century. A number of forces produced conditions that affected the curriculum. The rapid increase in scientific knowledge, the competitive nature of the race for space, technological advancements in teaching tools, a gradual dissatisfaction with the encyclopedic approach to the teaching of science, and new understandings of student learning and development combined to encourage changes.

In the 1950s and 1960s, the first secondary science curriculum course to react to these pressures was physics, followed by chemistry, biology, and junior high science, in that order. New courses for all these subjects appeared, stimulated by massive financial support from the National Science Foundation and other agencies.

Students of the investigative sciences were given opportunities for increased laboratory work and application of inquiry methods for learning. They were directed to better understandings of how scientists work and how knowledge is obtained.

The reform reached further than the materials developed under National Science Foundation grants. Authors of popular science textbooks incorporated many aspects of the new science materials.

In the late 1960s and early 1970s, problems in urban environments began to influence science programs. By the middle 1970s, a new set of social forces redirected the attention of science educators: population growth, pollution, economic problems, and energy and resource shortages.

The 1980s witnessed increasing support for educational reform, including science education. By the 1990s, general calls for reform had become more focused on national, state, and local standards. The *National Science Education Standards* and *Benchmarks for Science Literacy* established a solid foundation for achieving higher levels of science literacy.

This historical survey has shown the changes in science education resulting from the needs and demands of society. It seems that there is a clear relationship between social needs and the type of curricula and instruction that science educators are called on to provide in our schools. The major social pressures have been the early development of a nation, growth of an industrial-technological society, demands of a depressed economy, emergence of an atomic age, start of the space race, and the recent appearance of alienation and anxiety.

◆

REFERENCES

1. O. E. Underhill, *The Origins and Development of Elementary-School Science* (New York: Scott Foresman, 1941).
2. Committee on Secondary School Studies, *Report of the Committee of Ten on Secondary Studies* (Washington, DC: National Education Association, 1983).
3. "Report of the Central Association of Science and Mathematics Teachers Committee on the Unified High School Science Course," *School Science and Mathematics,* 15 (4) (1915): 334.
4. Commission on the Reorganization of Secondary Education, "Cardinal Principals of Secondary Education,"

U.S. Bureau of Education Bulletin, 35 (Washington, DC: U.S. Bureau of Education, 1918).
5. O. Caldwell, "Report of the American Association for the Advancement of Science, Committee on the Place of the Sciences in Education," *Science,* 60 (1924): 536.
6. National Society for the Study of Education, *A Program for Science Teaching* (Chicago: University of Chicago Press, 1932).
7. Progressive Education Association, *Science in General Education* (New York: Appleton-Century-Crofts, 1938).

8. National Society for the Study of Education, *Science Education in American Schools* (Chicago: University of Chicago Press, 1947).

9. Educational Policies Commission, *Education for All American Youth: A Further Look* (Washington, DC: National Education Association and the American Association of School Administrators, 1952).

10. Department of Secondary School Principals, *Planning for American Youth* (Washington, DC: National Education Association, 1946).

11. United States Office of Education, *Life Adjustment Education for Every Youth* (Washington, DC: U.S. Government Printing Office, 1951).

12. A. Bestor, *Educational Wastelands: A Retreat from Learning in Our Public Schools* (Urbana: University of Illinois Press, 1953).

13. H. Rickover, *Education and Freedom* (New York: Random House, 1970).

14. Jerome Bruner, *The Process of Education* (New York: Vintage, 1960).

15. *Introductory Physical Science—Physical Science II: A Progress Report* (Newton, MA: IPS Group, Education Development Center, 1968), p. 16.

16. David D. Redfield and Stewart P. Darrow, *Physics Teacher,* 8 (April 1970): 170–180.

17. John L. Wasik, "A Comparison of Cognitive Performance of PSSC and Non-PSSC Students," *Journal of Research in Science Teaching,* 8 (1) (1971): 85–90.

18. James A. Shymansky, William Kyle, and Jennifer Alport, "The Effects of New Science Curricula on Student Performance," *Journal of Research in Science Teaching,* 20 (5) (1983): 387–404.

19. Harvard Project Physics, Newsletter no. 1 (Cambridge: Harvard University Press).

20. Harvard Project Physics, Newsletter no. 7 (Cambridge: Harvard University Press).

21. Harvard Project Physics, Newsletter no. 10 (Cambridge: Harvard University Press).

22. Raymond E. Thompson, "A Survey of the Teaching of Physics in Secondary Schools," *School and Society,* 98 (1970): 243–244.

23. Wayne W. Welch, "Correlates of Course Satisfaction in High School Physics," *Journal of Research in Science Teaching,* 6 (1969): 54–58.

24. J. David Lockard, ed., *Seventh Report of the International Clearinghouse on Science and Mathematics Curricular Developments* (College Park: Science Teaching Center, University of Maryland, 1970), p. 305.

25. Gordon Cawelti, "Innovative Practices in High Schools: Who Does What—and Why—and How," *Nation's Schools,* 79 (1968): 36–41.

26. Frank J. Fornoff, "Survey of the Teaching of Chemistry in Secondary Schools," *School and Society,* 98 (1970): 242–243.

27. Iris Weiss, *Report of the 1977 National Survey of Science, Mathematics and Social Studies Education* (Washington, DC: U.S. Government Printing Office, March 1978).

28. Shymansky et al., "The Effects of New Science Curricula," pp. 387–404.

29. *IAC Newsletter* (College Park: Chemistry Department, University of Maryland) 2 (1) (January 1973): 3.

30. Robert Stephenson, "Relationships between the Intellectual Level of the Learner and Student Achievement in High School Chemistry" (Ph.D. dissertation, University of Northern Colorado, 1978).

31. Kenneth Brown and Ellsworth Obourn, *Offerings and Enrollments in Science and Mathematics in Public High Schools, 1958* (Washington, DC: U.S. Government Printing Office, 1961).

32. Quoted in American Association for the Advancement of Science, *The New School Science: A Report to School Administrators on Regional Orientation Conferences in Science,* Publication no. 63–6 (Washington, DC: 1963), p. 27.

33. *The New School Science,* p. 29.

34. Kenneth D. George, "The Effect of BSCS and Conventional Biology in Critical Thinking," *Journal of Research in Science Teaching,* 3 (1965): 293–299.

35. B. J. Adams, "A Study of the Retention of Biological Information by BSCS Students and Traditional Biology Students" (Ed.D. dissertation, Colorado State College, 1968).

36. Charles R. Granger and Robert E. Yager, "Type of High School Biology Program and Its Effect on Student Attitude and Achievement in College Life Science," *Journal of Research in Science Teaching,* 7 (1970): 383–389.

37. James Shymansky, "BSCS Programs: Just How Effective Were They?" *American Biology Teacher,* 4 (4) (1984): 54–57.

38. Jack L. Carter and Alan R. Nakosteen, "Summer: A BSCS Evaluation Study," *The Biological Sciences Curriculum Study,* 42 (February, 1971).

39. Shymansky et al., "The Effects of New Science Curricula," pp. 387–404.

40. Bill Aldridge and Karen Johnston, "Trends and Issues in Science Education," in *Redesigning Science and Technology Education, 1984 NSTA Yearbook,* Rodger Bybee, Janet Carlson, and Alan McCormack, eds. (Washington, DC: National Science Teachers Association, 1984).

41. Paul DeHart Hurd, "State of Precollege Education in Mathematics and Science," *Science Education,* 67 (1) (January 1983): 57–67.

42. Marjorie Gardner and Robert Yager, "How Does the U.S. Stack Up?" *Science Teacher* (October 1983): 22–25.

43. Anna Harrison, "Goals of Science Education," *Science,* 217 (455) (July 1982): 109.

44. Ronald Anderson, "Are Yesterday's Goals Adequate For Tomorrow?" *Science Education,* 67 (2) (1983): 171–176.

45. Paul DeHart Hurd, *Reforming Science Education: The Search For A New Vision* (Washington, DC: Council for Basic Education, 1984), p. 17.

46. The National Science Board Commission on Precollege Education in Mathematics, Science and Technology, *Educating Americans for the 21st Century* (Washington, DC: National Science Board, 1983).

47. Council of Chief State School Officers, *Key State Education Policies on K–12 Education: 2000* (Washington, DC: Author, 2000).

48. Ina V. Mullis and Lynn B. Jenkins, *The Science Report Card: Elements of Risk and Recovery* (Princeton, NJ: Education Testing Service, September 1988).

49. Iris Weiss, *Report of the 1977 National Survey of Science, Mathematics, and Social Studies Education* (Washington, DC: U.S. Government Printing Office, March, 1977).

50. Iris Weiss, *Report of the 1985–86 National Survey of Science and Mathematics Education* (Research Triangle Park, NC: Research Triangle Institute, 1987).

51. R. W. Bybee, C. E. Buchwald, S. Crissman, D. R. Heil, P. J. Kuerbis, C. Matsumoto, and J. D. McInerney, *Science and Technology Education for the Middle Years: Frameworks for Curriculum and Instruction* (Washington, DC: The National Center for Improving Science Education, 1990).

52. U.S. Department of Education, National Center for Education Statistics, *Pursuing Excellence* (Washington, DC: U.S. Government Printing Office, 1996).

53. K. Costenson and A. Lawson, "Why Isn't Inquiry Used in More Classrooms?" *American Biology Teacher,* 48 (3) (1986): 150–158.

54. Mary Lyn Bourque, Audrey Champagne, and Sally Crissman, *1996 Science Performance Standards: Achievement Results for the Nation and States* (Washington, DC: National Assessment Governing Board, 1997).

55. U.S. Department of Education. Office of Educational Research and Improvement. National Center for Education Statistics. *The Nation's Report Card: Science Highlights 2000* (NCES 2002-452) (Washington, DC: National Center for Education Statistics, 2001).

56. Michael O. Martin, Ina V. S. Mullis, et al., *Executive Summary: TIMSS 1999 International Science Report* (Chestnut Hill, MA: Boston College, 2000).

57. A more detailed discussion of the achievement results from TIMSS appears in: Patrick Gonzales, Christopher Calsyn, et al., *Highlights from the Third International Math and Science Study-Repeat (TIMSS-R)*(NCES 2001-027) (Washington, DC: National Center for Education Statistics, 2000).

58. William Schmidt, Curtis McKnight, and Senta Raizen, *A Splintered Vision: An Investigation of U.S. Science and Mathematics Education* (Dordrecht/Boston/London: Kluwer Academic Publishers, 1997).

59. William Schmidt et al., *Facing the Consequences. Using TIMSS for a Closer Look at United States Mathematics and Science Education* (Dordrecht/Boston/London: Kluwer Academic Publishers, 1998).

60. Gilbert Valverde and William Schmidt, "Refocusing U.S. Math and Science Education," *Issues in Science and Technology,* (2) (1997–98): 60–66.

61. William Schmidt et al., *Characterizing Pedagogical Flow: An Investigation of Mathematics and Science Teaching in Six Countries* (Dordrecht/Boston/London: Kluwer Academic Publishers, 1996).

62. J. Confrey, "A Review of the Research on Student Conceptions in Mathematics, Science, and Programming," in *Review of Research in Education,* C. B. Cazden, ed. (Washington, DC: The American Educational Research Association, 1990): pp. 3–56.

63. F. M. Newmann, "Can Depth Replace Coverage in the High School Curriculum?" *Phi Delta Kappan,* 69 (5) (1988): 345–348.

64. R. W. Bybee, "Science Education and the Science-Technology-Society (STS) Theme," *Science Education,* 71 (5) (1987): 667–783.

65. Robert Yager, ed., Science/Technology/Society As Reform in Science Education (Albany: State University of New York Press, 1996).

66. Kenneth Tobin, Deborah Tippins, and Alejandro Jose Gallard, "Research on Instructional Strategies for Teaching Science," in *Handbook of Research on Science Teaching and Learning,* D. Gabel, ed. (New York: MacMillan Publishing Company, 1994).

67. R. Driver and V. Oldham, "A Constructivist Approach to Curriculum Development in Science," *Studies in Science Education,* 13 (1986): 105–122.

68. T. P. Sachse, "Making Science Happen," *Educational Leadership,* 47 (3) (1989): 18–21.

69. B. Watson and R. Konicek, "Teaching for Conceptual Change: Confronting Children's Experience," *Phi Delta Kappan,* 71 (9) (1990): 680–685.

70. John Bruer, *Schools for Thought* (Cambridge, MA: The MIT Press, 1994).

71. Kate McGilly, ed., *Classroom Lessons* (Cambridge, MA: The MIT Press, 1995).

72. John Bransford, Ann Brown, and Rodney Cocking, eds., *How People Learn: Brain, Mind, Experience, and School* (Washington, DC: National Academy Press, 2000).

73. A. L. Gardner, C. L. Mason, and M. L. Matyas, "Equity, Excellence, and 'Just Plain Good Teaching,' " *American Biology Teacher,* 51 (2) (1989): 72–77.

74. M. C. Linn and J. S. Hyde, "Gender, Mathematics, and Science," *Educational Researcher,* 18 (8) (1989): 17–19, 22–27.

75. S. M. Malcom, "Who Will Do Science in the Next Century?" *Scientific American,* 262 (2) (1990): 112.

76. J. Oakes and the Rand Corporation, "Opportunities, Achievement, and Choice: Women and Minority Students in Science and Mathematics," in *Review of Research in Education,* C. B. Cazden, ed. (Washington, DC: The American Educational Research Association, 1990): pp. 153–222.

77. J. R. Frederiksen and A. Collins, "A Systems Approach to Educational Testing," *Educational Researcher,* 18 (9) (1989): 27–32.

78. R. Murnane and S. Raizen, Improving Indicators of the Quality of Science and Mathematics Education in Grades K–12 (Washington, DC: National Academy Press, 1988).

79. L. Roueche III, N. Sorensen, and C. Roueche, "Strategies to Verify the Essential Elements in Secondary Science: An Alternative Approach to Involve Students," *The Clearing House,* 62 (2) (1988): 65–73.

80. R. J. Shavelson, N. B. Carey, and N. M. Webb, "Indicators of Science Achievement: Options for a Powerful Policy Instrument," *Phi Delta Kappan,* 71 (9) (1990): 692–697.

81. M. Fullan, *The Meaning of Educational Change* (New York: Teachers College Press, Columbia University, 1982).

82. G. E. Hall, "Changing Practice in High School: A Process Not an Event," in *High School Biology: Today and Tomorrow,* W. G. Rosen, ed. (Washington, DC: National Academy Press).

83. P. Kloosterman, J. Matkin, and P. C. Ault, "Preparation and Certification of Teachers in Mathematics and Science," *Contemporary Education,* 59 (3) (1988): 146–149.

84. D. A. Roberts and A. M. Chastko, "Absorption, Refraction, Reflection: An Exploration of Beginning Science Teacher Thinking," *Science Education,* 74 (2) (1990): 197–224.

85. K. Tobin and M. Espinet, "Impediments to Change: Applications of Coaching in High School Science Teaching," *Journal of Research in Science Teaching,* 26 (2) (1989): 105–120.

86. H. Yeany and M. J. Padilla, "Training Science Teachers to Utilize Better Teaching Strategies: A Research Synthesis," *Journal of Research in Science Teaching,* 23 (2) (1986): 85–95.

CHAPTER

4

NATIONAL STANDARDS AND SCIENTIFIC LITERACY

In this chapter we introduce the *National Science Education Standards*.[1] We begin with background on the project and then review the project's major goals through a discussion of scientific literacy and the social orientation of national standards. We then summarize the components of the *National Science Education Standards*. Next, we review Project 2061 and reports on *Science for All Americans*[2] and *Benchmarks for Science Literacy*.[3] Both the *Standards* and *Benchmarks* have had, and will continue to have, a major influence on science education at national, state, and local levels.

BACKGROUND ON NATIONAL STANDARDS

The National Council of Teachers of Mathematics (NCTM) introduced the word *standards* into the public dialogue on education when they published the *Curriculum and Evaluation Standards for School Mathematics* in 1989. This statement of a profession's vision for what students should know and be able to do as a result of their mathematics education identified educational goals and provided a means of helping teachers of mathematics achieve them.

In the late 1980s and 1990s, politicians in the United States expressed their intense interest in improving education. This was symbolized by the *National Education Goals* created by President George Bush and the nation's governors, with leadership from then-governor Bill Clinton, in their unprecedented summit in 1989. The *National Education Goals Panel* established the idea of subject-matter standards and performance-based assessments. These bipartisan *National Education Goals* were the basis for the Goals 2000: Educate Amer-

ica Act signed by President Clinton in 1994 (see Figure 4–1 for a summary of these goals).

National standards define expectations and minimal competencies; they set focus and direction. From the beginning of this discussion it is important to understand that *Standards* for science education are policies, not a curriculum; they are national, not federal; they are voluntary, not mandatory; and they are dynamic, not static.

Visit http://www.prenhall.com/trowbridge and select Topic 1—Science Teaching Standards. Select "Web Links" and find "The National Science Education Standards," which gives information as to why the Standards are so important. Briefly summarize the reasons given and submit your response to your instructor using the Electronic Bluebook module.

The National Science Education Standards Project

In the spring of 1991, Dr. Bonnie Brunkhorst, the President of the National Science Teachers Association (NSTA), acting on the basis of a unanimous vote of the NSTA Board, wrote to the Chairman of the National Research Council (NRC) requesting the NRC to convene and coordinate a process leading to national science education standards, K–12. This was seconded by the presidents of several leading science and science education

60

The Goals state that by the year 2000:

1. All children in America will start school ready to learn.
2. The school graduation rate will increase to at least 90 percent.
3. All students will leave grades 4, 8, and 12 having demonstrated competency over challenging subject matter, including English, mathematics, science, foreign languages, civics and government, economics, arts, history, and geography; and every school in America will ensure that all students learn to use their minds well, so they may be prepared for responsible citizenship, further learning, and productive employment in our nation's modern economy.
4. The nation's teaching force will have access to programs for the continued improvement of their professional skills and the opportunity to acquire the knowledge and skills needed to instruct and prepare all American students for the next century.
5. United States students will be the first in the world in mathematics and science achievement.
6. Every adult American will be literate and will possess the knowledge and skills necessary to compete in a global economy and exercise the rights and responsibilities of citizenship.
7. Every school in the United States will be free of drugs, violence, and the unauthorized presence of firearms and alcohol and will offer a disciplined environment conducive to learning.
8. Every school will promote partnerships that will increase parental involvement and participation in promoting the social, emotional, and academic growth of children.

FIGURE 4–1   The National Education Goals
In stressing quality education from early childhood through lifelong learning, the President and the Governors adopted the National Education Goals, which became law in 1994 when Congress passed the Goals 2000: Educate America Act

associations, as well as the U. S. Secretary of Education, the Assistant Director of Education and Human Resources at the NSF, and the cochairs of the National Education Goals Panel. The NRC agreed to take the lead, and the U.S. Department of Education provided initial funding. Throughout that autumn the NRC developed a general design and time line for the project, and Dr. James Ebert, Vice President of the National Academy of Sciences, was designated Chair of a National Committee on Science Education Standards and Assessment (NCSESA). His job was to oversee both development of science education standards and a nationwide critique and consensus process. In early 1994, Dr. Richard Klausner of the National Institutes of Health assumed Dr. Ebert's responsibilities.

As 1992 began, a chair's advisory committee was formed. Consisting of representatives of several national science education organizations, it worked to assist in planning and directing the project. This group participated directly in the process of identifying and recruiting staff.

Early in the project, staff and committee members decided to develop an integrated volume containing content, teaching, and assessment standards, all displayed in mutually reinforcing ways. Another decision involved a serious and extensive critique and consensus process, which would issue frequent updates on the project and materials suitable for intense critique by teachers, educators in colleges and universities, scientists, engineers, policymakers, and others interested in science educa-

tion. The project released discussion and working papers in October and December of 1992, February 1993, and June 1993. In spring 1994, the NRC prepared a draft copy of standards for internal review. The first integrated draft of content, teaching, assessment, program, and system standards appeared for extensive national review in late 1994, and the *National Science Education Standards* were released in December 1995 with a 1996 copyright.[4]

NATIONAL SCIENCE EDUCATION STANDARDS: AN OVERVIEW

National standards in science education have several functions, depending on who is using them and the purpose for which they are being used. For example, standards can serve as vision, aspiration, and attainment; they also can be used as measures to judge the quality of current science education and criteria to design school science programs.

The *National Science Education Standards* offer a coherent vision of what it means to be scientifically literate. The standards describe what *all* students must understand and be able to do as a result of their cumulative learning experiences. The standards also provide criteria for judgments regarding programs, teaching, assessment, policies, and initiatives that can provide opportunities for all students to learn in ways that are aligned with the standards. Use of the adjective *national* means a nationwide agreement, not a federal mandate, on what defines successful science learning and the school practices that support the learning. National standards neither define a national curriculum nor are they a form of national standardization.

The eight categories of content standards are displayed in Figure 4–2. The first seven categories have standards for grade levels K–4, 5–8, and 9–12. The final category (Unifying Concepts and Processes) crosses all grade levels. Within each of the areas represented in Figure 4–2, there are fundamental understandings. The content described in the standards does *not* represent a science curriculum. Curriculum includes not only the content but also the structure, organization, balance, and presentation of the content. The selection of the fundamental concepts in these standards was based on the following criteria: it represents scientific ideas; it has rich explanatory power; it guides fruitful investigations; it applies to situations and contexts common to everyday experiences; it can be linked to meaningful learning experiences; and it is developmentally appropriate for students at the grade level specified.

Science As Inquiry should be recognized as a basic in curriculum organization and in students' science education experiences. This standard highlights the ability to *do* inquiry and the fundamental concepts *about* scientific inquiry that students should develop. The emphasis on inquiry moves beyond the processes of science and emphasizes the students' cognitive development based on critical thinking and scientific reasoning required in the use of evidence and information to construct scientific explanations.

Physical, Life, and *Earth and Space Science* standards express the traditional subject matter of science. This subject matter focuses on those science concepts, principles, and theories that are fundamental for all students.

The *Science and Technology* standard establishes useful connections between the natural world and the designed world and offers essential decision-making abilities. This standard has two components. One emphasizes the development of abilities associated with technological design and problem solving. The second centers on developing understanding about the similar-ities and differences between science and technology, and their respective influences within society.

The standard on *Science in Personal and Social Perspectives* connects the students with their social and personal world. It helps students understand health, populations, resources, environments, and natural hazards that will enable them to fulfill their obligations as citizens.

The standard on the *History and Nature of Science* includes an understanding of the nature of science and uses history in school science programs to clarify different aspects of science in society, the human aspects of science, and how scientific advances occur.

The *Unifying Concepts and Processes* standard provides students with powerful ideas that help them understand the natural world. These conceptual and procedural schemes are integral to any school science program and students' learning experiences in science. The understanding and abilities associated with this standard should be developed over the entire K–12 continuum.

Science Teaching Standards identify the characteristics of and provide a vision for good science teaching. Those standards center on the practice of teaching and are criteria for judging the quality of teaching in the science classroom. They describe roles and responsibilities in the areas listed in Figure 4–3.

The *Professional Development Standards* underscore the idea that becoming an effective science teacher is a continuous process, beginning with your current experiences and stretching throughout your career (see Figure 4–4).

Science Assessment Standards identify essential characteristics of fair and accurate student assessments and provide criteria for judging the quality of assessment at the classroom, district, state, and national levels. The definition of assessment includes not only familiar tests but also a range of strategies for collecting and interpreting information about student attainment, teacher performance; and the work of educational institutions. Very important, the *Science Assessment Standards* include an evaluation of the opportunities that all students have to learn science. Assessment standards are not tests, and they do not describe strategies to judge student learning or a school science program. Figure 4–5 displays standards for assessment in science.

Program Standards describe how content, teaching, and assessment are coordinated in school practice over a range of school experience to provide all students the opportunity to learn science. They describe criteria for judging the quality of a K–12 science program.

System Standards for science education guide the policies that must be implemented and the alignments

Science As Inquiry
Physical Science
Life Science
Earth and Space Science
Science and Technology
Science in Personal and Social Perspectives
History and Nature of Science
Unifying Concepts and Processes

FIGURE 4–2 *National Science Education Standards:* Science Content

FIGURE 4–3 Standards for Science Teachers

Teachers of science plan an inquiry-based science program for their students. In doing this, they

- develop a framework of year-long and short-term goals for students;
- select science content and adapt and design curricula to meet the interests, knowledge, understanding, ability, and experiences of students;
- select teaching and assessment strategies that support the development of student understanding and nurture a community of science learners; and
- work together as colleagues within and across disciplines and grade levels.

Teachers of science guide and facilitate science learning. In doing this, they

- focus and support inquiries as they interact with their students;
- orchestrate discourse among students about scientific ideas;
- challenge students to accept and share responsibility for their own learning;
- recognize and respond to student diversity and encourage all students to participate fully in science learning; and
- encourage and model the skills of scientific inquiry as well as the curiosity, openness to new ideas and data, and skepticism that characterize science.

Teachers of science should engage in ongoing assessment of their teaching and of student learning. In doing this, they

- use multiple methods to systematically gather data about student understanding and ability;
- analyze assessment data to guide teaching;
- guide students in self-assessment;
- use student data, observations of teaching, and interactions with colleagues to reflect on and improve teaching practice; and
- use student data, observations of teaching, and interactions with colleagues to report student achievement and opportunities to learn to students, teachers, parents, policymakers, and the general public.

Teachers of science should design and manage learning environments that provide students with the time, space, and resources needed for learning science. In doing this, they

- structure the time available so that students are able to engage in extended investigations;
- create a setting for student work that is flexible and supportive of science inquiry;
- ensure a safe working environment;
- make the available science tools, materials, print, media, and technological resources accessible to students;
- identify and use resources outside the school; and
- engage students in designing the learning environment.

Teachers of science develop communities of science learners that reflect the intellectual rigor of scientific inquiry and the attitudes and social values conducive to science learning. In doing this, they

- display and demand respect for the diverse ideas, skills, and experiences of all students;
- enable students to have a significant voice in decisions about the content and context of their work, and require students to take responsibility for the learning of all members of the community;
- nurture a collaboration among students;
- structure and facilitate ongoing formal and informal discussion based on a shared understanding of rules of scientific discourse; and
- model and emphasize the skills, attitudes, and values of scientific inquiry.

Teachers of science actively participate in the ongoing planning and development of the school science program. In doing this, they

- plan and develop the school science program;
- participate in decisions concerning the allocation of time and other resources to the science program; and
- plan and implement professional growth and development strategies for themselves and their colleagues.

Professional development for teachers of science requires learning essential science content through the perspectives and methods of inquiry. Science learning experiences for teachers must
- involve teachers in actively investigating phenomena that can be studied scientifically, interpreting results, and making sense of findings consistent with currently accepted scientific understanding;
- address issues, events, problems, or topics significant in science and of interest to participants;
- introduce teachers to scientific literature, media, and technological resources that expand their ability to access further knowledge;
- build on the teacher's current science understanding, ability, and attitudes;
- incorporate ongoing reflection on the process and outcomes of understanding science through inquiry; and
- encourage and support teachers in efforts to collaborate.

Professional development for teachers of science requires integrating knowledge of science, learning, pedagogy, and students; it also requires applying that knowledge to science teaching. Learning experiences for teachers of science must
- connect and integrate all pertinent aspects of science and science education;
- occur in a variety of places where effective science teaching can be illustrated and modeled, permitting teachers to struggle with real situations and expand their knowledge and skills in appropriate contexts;
- address teacher needs as learners and build on their current knowledge of science content, teaching, and learning; and
- use inquiry, reflection, interpretation of research, modeling, and guided practice to build understanding and skill in science teaching.

Professional development for teachers of science requires building understanding and abilities for lifelong learning. Professional development activities must
- provide regular, frequent opportunities for individual and collegial examination and reflection on classroom and instructional practice;
- provide opportunities for teachers to receive feedback about their teaching and to understand, analyze, and apply that feedback to improve their practice;
- provide opportunities for teachers to learn and use various tools and techniques for self-reflection and collegial reflection, such as peer coaching, portfolios, and journals;
- support the sharing of teacher expertise by preparing and using mentors, teacher advisors, coaches, lead teachers, and resource teachers to provide professional development opportunities;
- provide opportunities to know and have access to existing research and experiential knowledge; and
- provide opportunities to learn and use the skills of research to generate new knowledge about science and the teaching and learning of science.

FIGURE 4–4 Standards for Professional Development for Teachers of Science

Assessments are consistent with the decisions they are designed to inform.
- Assessments are deliberately designed.
- Assessments have explicitly stated purposes.
- The relationship between the decisions and the data should be clear.
- Assessments procedures are internally consistent.

Science achievement and opportunity to learn science must both be assessed.
- Achievement data collected focus on the science content that is most important for students to learn.
- Opportunity-to-learn data collected focus on the most powerful indicators of the students' opportunity to learn.
- Equal attention must be given to the assessment of opportunity to learn and to the assessment of student achievement.

The technical quality of the data collected is well matched to the consequences of the decisions and actions taken on the basis of their interpretation.
- The feature that is claimed to be measured is actually measured.
- Assessment tasks are authentic.
- An individual student's performance is similar on two or more tasks that claim to measure the same aspect of student achievement.
- Students have adequate opportunity to demonstrate their achievements.
- Assessment tasks and methods of presenting them provide data that are sufficiently stable to lead to the same decisions if used at different times.

Assessment practices must be fair.
- Assessment tasks must be reviewed for the use of stereotypes, for assumptions that reflect the perspectives or experiences of a particular group, for language that might be offensive to a particular group, and for other features that might distract students from the intended task.
- Large-scale assessments must use statistical techniques to identify differential performance among subgroups that signal potential bias.
- Assessment tasks must be appropriately modified to accommodate the needs of the students with physical disabilities, learning disabilities, or limited English proficiency.
- Assessment tasks must be set in a variety of contexts, engaging to students with different interests and experiences, and must not assume the perspective or experience of a particular gender, racial, or ethnic group.

The inferences made from assessments about student achievement and opportunity to learn must be sound.
- When making inferences from assessment data about student achievement and opportunity to learn science, explicit reference needs to be made to the assumptions on which the inferences are based.

FIGURE 4–5 Standards for Assessment in Science

that must be pursued by policymakers and others in order to support science learning described in the standards. System standards also address the essential functions that serve to build and sustain the capacities demanded by the standards of teachers and school communities.

Visit http://www.prenhall.com/trowbridge and select Topic 1—Science Teaching Standards. Select "National Science Education Standards," then click on the link for Science Teaching Standards, and find "Planning inquiry-based programs" (ST1). A variety of links found there will provide much information on planning inquiry lessons for the science classroom. The Standards put "Inquiry" at the top of the list on teaching science. Choose one activity organized around inquiry and submit it to your instructor using the Electronic Bluebook module.

NATIONAL STANDARDS, SOCIAL COMMITMENTS, AND SCIENTIFIC LITERACY

The *National Science Education Standards* define the level of understanding of science that all students should develop, regardless of background, future aspirations, or interest in science. The standards embody the belief that all students can learn science. These standards encourage all students—including members of populations defined by race, ethnicity, economic status, gender, and physical and intellectual capacity—to study science throughout their school years and to pursue careers in science. By adopting the goal of science for all, the standards will promote the participation of all students in challenging opportunities to learn science.

The *Standards* forcefully advocate the inclusion of those who traditionally have not received encouragement and opportunities to learn science—women and girls, all racial and ethnic groups, the physically and educationally challenged, and those with limited proficiency in English—as well as those who have traditionally made achievements in science: the gifted and talented students.

Various methods of learning and different sources of motivation are accommodated because the curriculum, teaching, and assessment standards take into account the diversity of the student population, disparate interests, motivation, experience, and ways of understanding science. The standards define criteria for high-quality instructional experiences that engage all students in the full range of science content. These experiences teach the nature and processes of science. In addition to the subject matter they will reinforce the belief that people of diverse backgrounds can engage and participate in science. They will uphold the premise that all students have a claim on understanding science as a common human heritage.

The *National Science Education Standards* present an explicit definition of scientific literacy. School science education contributes to the broader goals of education by providing students with a scientific understanding of the natural world through knowledge of the basic concepts of science, scientific modes of inquiry, the nature of the scientific endeavor, and the historical, social, and intellectual contexts within which science is practiced. The ability to apply such scientific knowledge to aspects of one's personal and civic life is referred to as *scientific literacy.*

The goals of school science education include the preparation of students who understand

- a limited number of the basic concepts of science and the fundamental principles, laws, and theories that organize the body of scientific knowledge and can apply them;
- the modes of reasoning embodied in scientific inquiry and can use them;
- the nature of the scientific endeavor and its ways of knowing, laws, and theories; and
- the history of scientific development, the relationship between science and technology, and the historical, cultural, and social contexts in which this relationship is embedded.

In order to support and develop the broad social goals of education, school science must attend to students' understanding of scientific knowledge and provide opportunities for them to practice using that knowledge. Therefore, school science programs must provide experiences that

- are personally and socially relevant;
- call for a wide range of knowledge, methods, and approaches to analyze personal and societal issues critically;
- encourage students to act in ways that reflect their understanding of the impact of scientific knowledge on their lives, society, and the world;
- encourage students' appreciation of the scientific endeavor and their excitement and pleasure in its pursuit; and
- develop in students an appreciation of the beauty and order of the natural world.

Notice that these statements both identify goals and provide recommendations for achieving those goals, while allowing for a diversity in approaches and teaching styles. Eventually, science teachers will transform these general policies into actual curriculum materials and teaching practices.

DEVELOPING SCIENTIFIC LITERACY

Your goal as a science teacher is to help individuals achieve higher levels of scientific literacy. Most directly, this goal applies to your students, but it also applies to professional colleagues, parents, and community. In this section, we first elaborate the idea of scientific literacy and then establish the connection between the general idea of scientific literacy and your specific need to teach students science in a manner that helps them to become more scientifically literate. One author of this textbook, Rodger Bybee, has written *Achieving Scientific Literacy: From Purposes to Practices.*[5] You may wish to refer to this book for a more detailed discussion of scientific literacy.

Background on Scientific Literacy

In Chapter 1, we introduced *scientific literacy* as the term used to express the major purposes of science education. In fact, we went a step beyond this definition and suggested that you could define some aspects of scientific literacy by answering the question, "What should the scientifically and technologically literate person know, value, and do—as a citizen?" In answering this question you should note several things. First, the question includes both science and technology. Second, the question includes knowledge, values, and skills. Third, and very important, the question asks to justify the answer in terms of citizenship.

In the history of science education, many individuals have addressed the goals of science teaching and the idea of scientific literacy.[6,7] In Tables 4–1, 4–2, and 4–3, we present discussions of scientific literacy so you can see what others have included in the translation of the idea to actual topics or themes for school science programs. These tables summarize various views of scientific literacy over the 30-year period from the 1960s to the 1990s.

Scientific literacy expresses general education purposes of a science education. The goal represents an orientation of the science curriculum and instructional practices that includes experiences and outcomes for all students. You should contrast the general education orientation with a specific or vocational education that would orient school science programs toward the knowledge, values, and skills required in scientific and technologic careers.

Note the domains of scientific literacy described in Table 4–3. These domains parallel content in the

National Science Education Standards and the *Benchmarks for Science Literacy.* In Table 4–4, we summarize the content from these two documents. This summary of two reports provides a contemporary description of the domains of scientific literacy.

The Domains of Scientific Literacy

Clearly, scientific literacy includes *more* than the knowledge, values, and skills associated with a specific discipline such as biology or chemistry. Concepts associated with scientific disciplines must be included, but students also should develop understandings and abilities associated with scientific inquiry and technological design, as well as understandings associated with personal and social aspects of science, the history and nature of science, and major unifying ideas of the sciences. In later chapters we provide more specific details of the *Standards* and *Benchmarks,* including content information. Table 4–5 should help clarify the different domains of content associated with scientific literacy. We adapted the model for this framework from original work of Mortimer Adler and the *Paideia Proposal.*[8] Also note that the content parallels the *National Science Education Standards* and, with some modification of titles, *Benchmarks for Science Literacy.*

The framework for scientific literacy (see Table 4–5) depicts three columns, each with a distinctive orientation for content. As the elements of this framework might be translated to curriculum and instruction, you should recognize that all three columns are essential to the development of scientific literacy. You might also note the parallel between the earlier question—"What should the scientifically and technologically literate person know, value, and do—as a citizen?"—and the three different columns. We suggest that the development of scientific literacy includes the acquisition of organized knowledge, the development of intellectual abilities and manipulative skills, and the enlarged understanding of ideas and values.

Column one centers on the acquisition of knowledge in five domains—physical sciences, life sciences, earth sciences, unifying concepts in the sciences, and the nature of science and technology. It is important to note that these are domains of knowledge and not necessarily the curriculum or courses of study for middle and high school science. In fact, the science curriculum should include content from all three columns and may have an emphasis on social challenges, inquiry, or an integrated approach to science content.[9]

Why these five domains of science content? There are several reasons. First, these domains, especially the physical, life, and earth sciences, have a tradition as branches of the sciences. These are generic in that more

TABLE 4–1   Some Characteristics of Scientific Literacy: The 1960s

National Science Teachers Association Theory into Practice (1964) Conceptual Schemes	National Science Teachers Association Theory into Practice (1964) Processes of Science	Milton Pella (1967)
(1) All matter is composed of units called *fundamental particles;* under certain conditions these particles can be transformed into energy and vice versa. (2) Matter exists in the form of units that can be classified into hierarchies of organizational levels. (3) The behavior of matter in the universe can be described on a statistical basis. (4) Units of matter interact. The basis of all ordinary interactions are electro-magnetic, gravitational, and nuclear forces. (5) All interacting units of matter tend toward equilibrium states in which the energy content (enthalpy) is a minimum and the energy distribution (entropy) is most random. In the process of attaining equilibrium, energy transformations or matter transformations occur; nevertheless, the sum of energy and matter in the universe remains constant. (6) One of the forms of energy is the motion of units of matter. Such motion is responsible for heat and temperature and for the states of matter: solid, liquid, and gaseous. (7) All matter exists in time and space, and since interactions occur among its units, matter is subject in some degree to changes with time. Such changes may occur at various rates and in various patterns.	(1) Science proceeds on the assumption, based on centuries-old experience, that the universe is not capricious. (2) Scientific knowledge is based on observation of samples of matter that are accessible to public investigation in contrast to purely private inspection. (3) Science proceeds in a piecemeal manner, even though it also aims at achieving a systematic and comprehensive understanding of various sectors or aspects of nature. (4) Science is not, and will probably never be, a finished enterprise, and there remains much more to be discovered about how things in the universe behave and how they are interrelated. (5) Measurement is an important feature of most branches of modern science because the formulation, as well as the establishment, of laws are facilitated through the development of quantitative distinctions.	(1) Interrelationships between science and society (2) Ethics of science (3) Nature of science (4) Conceptual knowledge (5) Science and technology (6) Science in the humanities

TABLE 4–2   Some Characteristics of Scientific Literacy: The 1970s

Michael Agin (1974)	Victor Showalter (1974)	Benjamin Shen (1974)
(1) Science and Society (2) Ethics of Science (3) Nature of Science (4) Knowledge of the Concepts of Science (5) Science and Technology (6) Science and the Humanities	(1) Nature of Science (2) Concepts in Science (3) Processes of Science (4) Values of Science (5) Science and Society (6) Interest in Science (7) Skills Associated with Science	(1) Practical Science Literacy (2) Civic Science Literacy (3) Cultural Science Literacy

TABLE 4–3　Some Characteristics of Scientific Literacy: The 1980s

National Science Teachers Association, Science-Technology-Society: Science Education for the 1980s (NSTA, 1982)	National Commission on Excellence in Education, A Nation at Risk (NCEE, 1983)	Improving Indicators of the Quality of Science and Mathematics Education in Grades K–12, (Murnane & Raizen, 1988)	American Association for the Advancement of Science, Science for All Americans (AAAS, 1989)
(1) Scientific and technological process and inquiry skills (2) Scientific and technological knowledge (3) Skills and knowledge of science and technology in personal and social decisions (4) Attitudes, values, and appreciation of science and technology (5) Interactions among science-technology-society via context of science-related societal issues	(1) Concepts, laws, and processes of physical and biological sciences (2) Methods of scientific inquiry and reasoning (3) Applications of knowledge to everyday life (4) Social and environmental implications of scientific and technological development	(1) The nature of the scientific worldview (2) The nature of the scientific enterprise (3) Scientific habits of mind (4) Science and human affairs	(1) The nature of science (2) The nature of mathematics (3) The nature of technology (4) The physical setting (5) The living environment (6) The human organism (7) Human society (8) The designed world (9) The mathematical world (10) Historical perspectives (11) Common themes (12) Habits of mind

TABLE 4–4　Content Summary for the National Science Education Standards and Benchmarks for Science Literacy

National Science Education Standards	Benchmarks for Science Literacy
Unifying Concepts and Processes Science As Inquiry Physical Science Life Science Earth and Space Science Science and Technology Science in Personal and Social Perspectives History and Nature of Science	The Nature of Science The Nature of Mathematics The Nature of Technology The Physical Setting The Living Environment The Human Organism Human Society The Designed World The Mathematical World Historical Perspectives Common Themes Habits of Mind

TABLE 4–5　A Framework for the Content of Scientific Literacy

Goal	Acquisition of Organized Knowledge	Development of Intellectual Abilities and Manipulative Skills	Enlarged Understanding of Ideas and Values
Domains of Content	*In the Subject Matter of* Physical Science Life Science Earth Science Unifying Concepts Nature of Science and Technology	*In the Processes of* Scientific Inquiry and Technological Design	*In the Contexts of* Personal Matters Social Challenges Historical Perspectives Cultural Perspectives

specific branches, such as particle physics and molecular biology, could be included but are not emphasized for educational purposes. Unifying concepts include scientific ideas, such as Isaac Newton's laws of force and motion, the laws of thermodynamics governing energy and entropy, and the atomic structure of matter, that can provide connection among the traditional subject-matter domains. Science teachers can use the unifying concepts to show the interconnectedness and interdependence among the sciences and to develop understanding of the larger theories of science. Unifying concepts become especially useful in many research studies and in developing explanations for such things as social challenges and health issues. Science education programs traditionally have not done very much to help students understand the nature of science and technology, yet this understanding (or lack of it) relates to many discussions of the role, limits, and possibilities of science and technology in society.

Second, you will notice that these domains provide linkage between the national standards and benchmarks. Finally, it is important to see students acquiring scientific knowledge as a part of developing scientific literacy. Some educators have interpreted the constructivist approach as acceptance of students' explanations as scientific. This view fails to recognize the body of knowledge recognized as science and to view scientific literacy as the students' development of explanations more closely aligned with those we recognize as scientific.

Column two emphasizes the development of skills and abilities associated with scientific inquiry and technological design. If you examine the national standards for *Science As Inquiry* and *Science and Technology,* you will notice the specific cognitive abilities related to inquiry and design (see Figure 4–6 and 4–7).

Using science as the example, abilities include applying science processes (observing, inferring, experimenting, classifying, controlling variables), constructing scientific explanations (interpreting data, using critical thinking and logic to link evidence to explanation, formulating models, defining operationally), recognizing alternative explanations (maintaining an open mind, accepting the tentative nature of explanations, being skeptical), and communicating (reading, writing, speaking, listening).

If column one is know-about, column two is know-how. In column two, the learning outcomes indicate that students know how to do scientific investigations and technologic problem solving. The skills and abilities proposed in column two have very close connections with the domains of science outlined in column one. Developing scientific literacy includes developing the intellectual skills and abilities outlined in column two. If we wish students to acquire and use these skills, they must have experience doing investigations in science classrooms. That is to say, these skills must be practiced as a part of the students' science education. The method of teaching these skills cannot be lecture; rather, students must be engaged in investigations, and the science teacher should act as a coach, helping students to acquire the best techniques, pointing out strengths and weaknesses, giving directions, demonstrating the right moves, and sequencing actions to achieve a goal.

The innovative aspect of this domain consists of having students engage in inquiry and design. Most evidence indicates that students do not have many such experiences in their science education.[10] From your point of view as a science teacher, implementing the standards implies innovations through combinations of such teaching strategies and good coaching.

The content in column three provides important contexts for teaching and learning science. While column one is know-about and column two is know-how, column three is know-why. Recall that scientific literacy places science in the context of history, society, and individual decisions. The content of column three engages students in content that provides meaning for science knowledge and intellectual skills. It is here, as students encounter the personal and social contexts of science, that they will recognize the ideas and values of science and further develop their own ideas and values. The development of understanding occurs because students have to use their knowledge and skills to respond to the proposed challenges of understanding science and technology in their own lives, in societal problems, in historical contexts, and in different cultures.

The content of column three serves the purpose of developing scientific literacy, because the topics require students to use their intellectual skills and scientific knowledge as they examine and analyze various positions. Sometimes those positions present a marked difference from their own. They become aware of their own ideas and values of science and technology. In order to help fulfill the requirements of citizenship, the content of column three requires students to correct misconceptions and improve their understanding of science and technology.

In this discussion we have tried to show how the three columns represent an integrated approach to the development of scientific literacy. As you translate the content outlined in the framework to curriculum and instruction, you should implement the information in all three columns.

The Dimensions of Scientific Literacy

Developing scientific literacy is a lifelong goal for all individuals. Many discussions of scientific literacy use the terms and various domains we have described as a goal

- **Identify questions and concepts that guide scientific investigations.** Students should formulate a testable hypothesis and demonstrate the logical connections between the scientific concepts guiding a hypothesis and the design of an experiment. They should demonstrate procedures, a knowledge base, and conceptual understanding of scientific investigations.

- **Design and conduct scientific investigations.** This requires an introduction to conceptual areas of investigation, proper equipment, safety precautions, assistance with methodological problems, recommendations for use of technologies, clarification of ideas that guide the inquiry, and scientific knowledge obtained from sources other than the actual investigation. The investigation may also include such abilities as identification and clarification of the question, method, controls, and variables; the organization and display of data; the revision of methods and explanations; and the public presentation of the results and the critical response from peers. Regardless of the scientific investigations and procedures, students must use evidence, apply logic, and construct an argument for their proposed explanation.

- **Use technology and mathematics to improve investigations and communications.** Students' ability to use a variety of technologies, such as hand tools, measuring instruments, and calculators, should be an integral component of scientific investigations. The use of computers for the collection, analysis, and display of data is also a part of this standard. Mathematics plays an essential role in all aspects of an inquiry. For example, measurement is used for posing questions, formulas are used for developing explanations, and charts and graphs are used for communicating results.

- **Formulate and revise scientific explanations and models using logic and evidence.** Student inquiries should culminate in formulating an explanation or model. In the process of answering the questions, students should engage in discussions and arguments that result in the revision of their explanations. These discussions should be based on scientific knowledge, the use of logic, and evidence from their investigation.

- **Recognize and analyze alternative explanations and models.** This standard emphasizes the critical abilities of analyzing an argument by reviewing current scientific understanding, weighing the evidence, and examining the logic, thus revealing which explanations and models are better and showing that although there may be several plausible explanations, they do not all have equal weight. Students should appeal to criteria for scientific explanations in order to determine which explanations are best.

- **Communicate and defend a scientific argument.** Students in school science programs should develop the abilities associated with accurate and effective communication, including writing and following procedures, expression concepts, reviewing information, summarizing data, using language appropriately, developing diagrams and charts, explaining statistical analysis, speaking clearly and logically, constructing a reasoned argument, and responding to critical comments through the use of current data, past scientific knowledge, and present reasoning.

FIGURE 4–6   Abilities of Scientific Inquiry

- **Identify a problem or design an opportunity.** Students should be able to identify new problems or needs and have the ability to change and improve current technological designs.

- **Propose designs and choose between alternative solutions.** Students should demonstrate thoughtful planning for a piece of technology or technique.

- **Implement a proposed solution.** A variety of skills can be needed depending on the type of technology that is involved. The construction of artifacts can require the skills of cutting, shaping, or forming; treating; and joining common materials, such as wood, metal, plastics, and textiles.

- **Evaluate the solution and its consequences.** Students should test any solution against the needs or criteria it was designed to meet. At this stage students may review new criteria not originally considered.

- **Communicate the problem, process, and solution.** Students should present their results in a variety of ways, such as orally to other students, in writing, and in a variety of forms, including models, diagrams, and demonstrations.

FIGURE 4–7   Abilities of Technological Design

that one achieves or does not. It is the either/or, all-or-none position one often hears. It is much more helpful to recognize that all of your students occupy positions somewhere on a continuum of literacy for various scientific concepts. It also seems clear that one can associate different levels of understanding with scientific concepts. For example, students might correctly spell and use the word *cell* in a simple sentence. However, the same students might not recognize several other important concepts about cells, for example that they convey information and reproduce. Further, what if you asked these students about the function of cells in cancer and they indicated that they had no idea about the relationship? Well, what would you say—are these students scientifically literate? If you look at the situation using a strict definition of literacy, one would have to say they are scientifically literate for this life science topic. What about the fact that the same students did not understand the structure and function of cells or the fact that cells have a role in cancer? It might be easier to use the either/or approach to scientific literacy, but it will probably not be very helpful in deciding what to do to further these students' understanding of cells and other domains of science.

As a science teacher you should help students advance their scientific understandings and abilities. In order to help you, we provide a model of different dimensions of scientific literacy. In the following descriptions note that these dimensions are not developmental levels, nor are they intended to suggest that they represent a teaching sequence. These are different dimensions of scientific literacy that you should be aware of, as they relate to your decisions about how to structure lessons and units for your classes and how to respond to individual students who indicate a lack of understanding.

Visit http://www.prenhall.com/trowbridge and select Topic 1—Science Teaching Standards. Select "National Science Teaching Standards," click on Science Teaching Standards and find "Actions to Guide and Facilitate Student Learning" (ST2). Here, you will find many examples of inquiry teaching strategies to help develop scientific literacy. Choose one, write it as a lesson plan, and submit it to your instructor using the Electronic Bluebook module.

Scientific Illiteracy

In this model, some individuals may be scientifically illiterate because of age, stage of development, or impaired cognitive abilities. These students are small in number and for various reasons will probably not be in your science classroom. The indicator of scientific illiteracy is the fact that they cannot relate to or respond to a reasonable question about science. They do not have the vocabulary, concepts, contexts, or cognitive capacity to identify the question as scientific.

Nominal Scientific Literacy

Suppose you begin a lesson on force and soon discover that students' statements about force indicate that they think force is a property of the moving object. They make statements such as, "A moving object has a force inside it; that is what makes it move." You try to introduce the idea that force is not a property of an object, but forces are characteristics of action between objects. Still, the students' ideas persist. These students exemplify nominal scientific literacy for the concept of force. (The example comes from *Making Sense of Secondary Science*.[11]) The students understood the topic as scientific, but the level of understanding clearly indicates a misconception. You should recognize that such examples will be evident in your class and that they will usually express the students' current understanding.

Functional Scientific Literacy

Students may know scientific terms through other science classes, television, or reading. Students can memorize appropriate definitions of terms, and in this sense have some scientific knowledge, but they have limited knowledge and lack a full scientific understanding. Science textbooks and programs that exclusively emphasize rote memorization lead to functional levels of scientific literacy. Unfortunately, this has been the emphasis of many science textbooks and classrooms, and the result is emphasis on only one dimension of scientific literacy. Teaching that emphasizes functional scientific literacy leaves students with little or no understanding of the discipline, no experience with the excitement of inquiry, and probably little interest in science.

Conceptual and Procedural Scientific Literacy

In this dimension, students develop some understanding of the conceptual schemes of a discipline related to the whole discipline. They begin to understand central ideas such as matter, energy, and motion in physical sciences and evolution in biological sciences.

Procedural abilities and understandings include the processes of scientific inquiry and technological design. Students actually have ability and understand that scientific inquiry includes asking questions, designing scientific investigations, using appropriate tools and techniques, developing explanations and models using evidence, thinking critically and logically about the relationship between evidence and explanation, recognizing alternative explanations, and communicating scientific procedures and explanations.

Multidimensional Scientific Literacy

This perspective of scientific literacy incorporates an understanding of science that extends beyond the concepts of scientific disciplines and procedures of scientific investigation. It includes philosophical, historical, and social dimensions of science and technology. Here students develop some understanding and appreciation of science and technology as they have been and are a part of the culture. Students begin to make connections within scientific disciplines, between science and technology, and between science and technology and the larger issues of social challenges.

Although a number of individuals have presented frameworks for scientific literacy that incorporate the dimensions just described,[12, 13, 14, 15] two examples dominate the contemporary scene in science education, the *National Science Education Standards* and the *Benchmarks for Science Literacy*. Figure 4–8 summarizes the dimensions of scientific literacy.

SUMMARY

National Science Education Standards provide the qualitative criteria and framework for judging science programs (content, teaching, and assessment) and the policies necessary to support them. Among other ob-

jectives, the *Standards* and *Benchmarks* (1) define the understanding of science that all students—without regard to background, future aspirations, or prior interest in science—should develop; (2) present criteria for judging science education content and programs at the K–4, 5–8, and 9–12 levels, including learning goals, design features, instructional approaches, and assessment characteristics; (3) include all natural sciences and their interrelationships, as well as the connections with technology, social science, and history; (4) provide criteria for judging models, benchmarks, curricula, and learning experiences developed under the guidelines of ongoing national projects, under state frameworks, or under local district, school, or teacher-designed initiatives; and (5) provide criteria for judging teaching, the provision of opportunities to learn (including such resources as instructional materials and assessment methods), and science education programs at all levels.

The national standards provide a broad view of scientific literacy, one that includes all students. Although the effort encompasses the entire nation, the *National Science Education Standards* honors the diversity of school districts, schools, and science teachers. Science teachers such as you can use many means to achieve the standards and the primary goals of developing higher levels of scientific literacy for all citizens.

FIGURE 4–8 Dimensions of Scientific Literacy

Nominal Scientific Literacy

- Identifies terms, questions, as scientific but demonstrates incorrect topics, issues, information, knowledge, or understanding.
- Has misconceptions of scientific concepts and processes.
- Gives inadequate and inappropriate explanations of scientific phenomena.
- Expresses scientific principles in a naive manner.

Functional Scientific Literacy

- Uses scientific vocabulary.
- Defines scientific terms correctly.
- Memorizes technical words.

Conceptual and Procedural Scientific Literacy

- Understands conceptual schemes of science.
- Understands procedural knowledge and skills of science.
- Understands relationships among the parts of a science discipline and the conceptual structure of the discipline.
- Understands organizing principles and processes of science.

Multidimensional Scientific Literacy

- Understands the unique qualities of science.
- Differentiates science from other disciplines.
- Knows the history and nature of science disciplines.
- Understands science in a social context.

◆
REFERENCES

1. National Research Council (NRC), *National Science Education Standards* (Washington, DC: Author, 1996).

2. American Association for the Advancement of Science, *Science for All Americans: A Project 2061 Report on Goals in Science, Mathematics, and Technology* (Washington, DC: Author, 1989).

3. American Association for the Advancement of Science, *Benchmarks for Science Literacy* (Washington, DC: Author, 1993).

4. Angelo Collins, "National Science Education Standards in the United States: A Process and a Product," *Studies in Science Education,* 26 (1) (1995): 7–37.

5. Rodger Bybee, *Achieving Scientific Literacy: From Purposes to Practices* (Portsmouth, NH: Heinemann, 1997).

6. G. E. DeBoer, *A History of Ideas in Science Education* (New York: Teachers College Press, 1991).

7. R. W. Bybee and G. E. DeBoer, "Goals and the Science Curriculum," in *A Handbook of Research on Science Teaching and Learning,* Dorothy Gabel, ed. (Washington, DC: National Science Teachers Association, 1993).

8. Mortimer Adler, *The Paideia Proposal: An Educational Manifesto* (New York: Macmillan, 1982).

9. D. Roberts, "Developing the Concept of 'Curriculum Emphasis' in Science Education." *Science Education,* 66 (2) (1982): 243–260.

10. K. Costenson and A. E. Lawson, "Why Isn't Inquiry Used in More Classrooms?" *American Biology Teacher,* 48 (3) (1986): 150–158.

11. R. Driver, A. Squires, P. Rushworth, and V. Wood-Robinson, *Making Sense of Secondary Science: Research into Children's Ideas* (New York: Routledge, 1994).

12. M. O. Pella, G. T. O'Hearn and C. W. Gale, "Referrents to Scientific Literacy," *Journal of Research in Science Teaching,* 4 (1966): 199–208.

13. M. Agin, "Education for Scientific Literacy: A Conceptual Frame of Reference and Some Applications," *Science Education,* 58 (1974): 3.

14. V. Showalter, "What Is Unified Science Education? Program Objectives and Scientific Literacy," *Prism* 2 (2) (1974): 1–6.

15. R. J. Murname and S. A. Raizen, eds., *Improving Indicators of the Quality of Science and Mathematics Education in Grades K–12* (Washington, DC: National Academy Press, 1988).

UNIT 3

GOALS AND OBJECTIVES

A 30-year veteran science teacher, Jim Jefferson continually demonstrated the characteristics of effective teaching. He knew the content of science, he used different instructional strategies, he efficiently managed the classroom, he was enthusiastic, and he had a good rapport with students. Jim's activity as a science teacher impressed everyone. He used discussions with students and gently challenged their ideas, he directed them to science knowledge, he helped them formulate new ideas, and he always asked them to justify their ideas. Jim's teaching revealed a consistency that enhanced student learning. Recognizing Jim's effectiveness required extended observations in a variety of classrooms for even the careful observer to see the patterns.

We asked Jim about his approach to science teaching.

I think of science education as consisting of knowledge and abilities related to science and the application of science to personal and social issues. These might be the big goals. I also think of scientific literacy as having several different dimensions. These goals provide frameworks that help me make decisions about the structure and content of my interaction with students. In teaching biology I keep major conceptual schemes from the *National Science Education Standards* and *Benchmarks for Science Literacy* in mind; for example, I try to keep ideas like evolution of living systems, genetic continuity, energetics, biosphere and interdependence in mind. I also know that students have to develop

more specific terms and ideas, such as carrying capacity and limiting factors, gene regulation, DNA, and metabolism. Students need to know the terms *and* they need to see how the terms relate to big ideas in biology. Not only that, they need to see how the whole discipline of biology connects to other sciences and the student's life and social issues. I realize this is a lot, but you don't have to teach all of this at once, you teach a little at a time by making sure the students have meaningful experiences.

Let me say that the same ideas apply when I emphasize scientific inquiry. I try to get students to clarify their questions, obtain data using the best methods they can, and then develop their answer to the question. I know this emphasis is different from just teaching biological knowledge. I cannot emphasize the importance of inquiry enough. Students should be able to formulate a testable hypothesis and demonstrate the connections between the science concepts that guide the investigation. At some time in a student's experience in secondary school science, students should design and conduct a full scientific investigation. Every lesson does not have to be a full investigation, but I really think this is the best way to develop both the abilities of scientific inquiry and the understandings about scientific inquiry. In other lessons I try to incorporate different aspects of the inquiry goal. Sometimes it is as simple as asking a question about another student's explanation, sometimes it involves asking students to explain the connection between evidence and explorations, sometimes I ask students to explain what scientists have said about the topic. I think all of this contributes to students' understanding, and, for me, this emphasis on inquiry is one of the most exciting goals of science teaching.

Jim used this framework to help organize his science program and to guide his daily interactions with students. He also let the students know when he was emphasizing concepts or inquiry and when he was try-ing to get them to understand the nature of science or interaction between science and society. Whatever the goals, Jim seemed to know how to organize, emphasize, and present science. Even when students would take him off track, he returned to his goals and objectives.

Jim's teaching demonstrated constant variation, but there also was a consistent structure. He knew his goals and what he was trying to accomplish with any individual student. Jim responded to the difficulty of concepts and the current conception of students with his repertoire of teaching strategies. We would say that, among other things, Jim Jefferson had a clear view of the goals of science education and the objectives of particular science lessons.

CHAPTER 5

THE GOALS OF SCIENCE TEACHING

Begin this chapter by completing an activity concerning the goals of science teaching. Do Activity 5-1, Goals of Science Teaching, at the end of this chapter.

Science teachers continuously reexamine the goals and objectives of their programs. "Which units will I teach this year?" "What new topics shall I introduce?" Questions such as these, and the answers, are the bases of revised goals and changes in science programs. Only the individual science teacher knows the variables that must be evaluated in the decision-making process. "What is my budget?" "What are the abilities and attitudes of my students?" "What are my interests?" "What was the students' response to last year's units?" "What new ideas did I get from the NSTA convention I attended?" There are, of course, other questions, but these examples illustrate how goals are revised by individual science teachers.

In the next two chapters we are not using the terms *goals* and *objectives* synonymously. There is a clear distinction. Goals are broad statements that give a general direction to a science curriculum and classroom instruction. Broad goals have the advantage of relating to many aspects of science, society, and education, and, simultaneously, of giving some direction to classroom planning and instruction. The disadvantage of goals is precisely that they are too broad for specific direction concerning grade levels, science subjects, and personal aims and preferences of science teachers. It is necessary to reformulate goals into objectives that are appropriate for each science teacher. Although goals and objectives differ, they are logically related because objectives are derived from goals.

BASIC GOALS OF SCIENCE EDUCATION

As you found in the introductory activity, there are many goals of science teaching. By using the following simple criteria, most goals can be summarized into a few categories.

- ◆ Goals should be comprehensive enough to include the generally accepted aims and objectives of science teaching.
- ◆ Goals should be understandable for other teachers, administrators, and parents.
- ◆ Goals should be neutral; that is, free of bias and not oriented toward any particular view of science teaching.
- ◆ Goals should be few in number.
- ◆ Goals should differentiate concepts and abilities.
- ◆ Goals should be easily applicable to instructional and learning objectives.

Science teachers use a small number of goals when they construct lessons or design curricula. If you are interested in the role of goals in the history of science education, you may wish to read George DeBoer's *A History of Ideas in Science Education*[1] and "Research on Goals for the Science Curriculum" by Rodger Bybee and George DeBoer in *Handbook of Research on Science Teaching and Learning*.[2]

Using the aforementioned criteria, we can identify the following goals of science education: scientific knowledge, scientific methods, social issues, personal needs, and career awareness. You probably recognize many of the goals in the introductory activity as relating to these categories. Many objectives can be deduced from these goals, but keep in mind that at any time all of the goals are not equally important. Still, they have been the goals underlying science curriculum and instruction.

1. *Scientific Knowledge.* There is a body of knowledge concerning biological, physical, and earth systems. For over 200 years, our science education programs have aimed toward informing students of these natural systems. This goal has been, and will continue to be, of significant importance for science teachers. Stated formally, this goal is: *Science education should develop fundamental understandings of natural systems.*

2. *Scientific Methods.* A second goal has centered on the abilities and understandings of the methods of scientific investigation. Descriptions of the goal have changed; for example, the terms *inquiry* and *discovery* have been used to describe the scientific methods goal. The goal can be stated as: *Science education should develop a fundamental understanding of, and ability to use, the methods of scientific inquiry.*

3. *Societal Issues.* Science education exists in society and should contribute to the maintenance and aspirations of the culture. This goal is especially important when there are social challenges directly related to science. This goal is: *Science education should prepare citizens to make responsible decisions concerning science-related social issues.*

4. *Personal Needs.* All individuals have needs related to their own biological/psychological systems. Briefly stated, this goal is: *Science education should contribute to an understanding and fulfillment of personal needs, thus contributing to personal development.*

5. *Career Awareness.* Scientific research, development, and application continue through the work of individuals within science and technology and through the support of those not directly involved in scientific work. Therefore, one important goal has been: *Science education should inform students about careers in the sciences.*

SCIENCE EDUCATION GOALS AND PROGRAMS: PRELUDE TO REFORM

In the late 1970s, three national surveys assessed the status of science education: *The Status of Pre-College Science, Mathematics, and Social Science Education;*[3] *Report of the 1977 National Survey of Science, Mathematics, and Social Studies Education;*[4] and *Case Studies in Science Education.*[5] The following discussion is based on an extensive review of these studies.[6] In addition, we used Paul DeHart Hurd's review, "The Golden Age of Biological Education: 1960–1975," in *Biology Teachers Hand-*

book (3rd Edition)[7] and the *1976–1977 National Assessment of Education Progress—Science.*[8,9]

This review of goals is especially important because it is a landmark in the history of science education. These studies present the first major national assessment of science education. We shall first give a general review of science education and then discuss the specific goals outlined earlier.[10]

AN OVERVIEW OF GOALS FOR SCIENCE EDUCATION

You can gain a better understanding of science education by examining the long-standing goals described earlier: scientific knowledge, scientific methods, societal issues, personal needs, and career awareness. In the period 1955–1975, these goals were in transition. Between 1975 and approximately 1995, the science education community reformed the goals. The publication of *Science for All Americans,*[11] *Benchmarks for Science Literacy,*[12] and the *National Science Education Standards*[13] clearly set new goals for science education. The following discussion describes the status of goals in 1975–2005 and suggests the direction of change.[14]

Scientific Knowledge

Science programs are primarily oriented toward knowledge of the academic disciplines. In the classroom, knowledge goals become the scientific facts, concepts, and principles that reflect the structure of science. Science teachers report that they want their students to understand the subject matter of science. For example, they want the students to know scientific concepts and definitions of scientific words, and to develop inquiry abilities and critical thinking skills. Understanding science is generally interpreted as passing a test.

Scientific Method

There is little effort by science teachers to realize the goal of understanding and using the methods of science. For example, teachers do not use questioning techniques or instructional procedures that facilitate the cognitive abilities of scientific inquiry.

However, evidence indicates that students can attain an understanding of scientific inquiry as a process, develop essential inquiry skills, and are able to use these skills to improve their ability to think critically about science-related problems.[15]

Several factors hinder the implementation of the scientific methods goal. First, science teachers are neither *model inquirers* for their students nor have they been educated in methodologies of scientific research. Second, most science teachers lecture for more than 75 percent of the class time, leaving students few opportunities to ask questions. Third, inquiry as a goal of science teaching is generally not seen as productive and is not accepted by most science teachers. Fourth, teachers who are aware of scientific methods as a goal of teaching feel that only bright, highly motivated students can profit from inquiry teaching. Fifth, inquiry teaching is seen by teachers as time-consuming, thus reducing the time available for basics, that is, learning facts and getting so-called "right" answers. The current improvement of science education and national support for the goal of scientific inquiry should change the lack of emphasis on this goal.

Societal Issues

Increasing interest in science literacy and societal goals is evident in science programs. Science teachers are including these goals to make science relevant to the concerns of all students.

The goals for teaching science indicate more emphasis on environmental concepts, world problems, decision making, and interdisciplinary studies—all areas related to the goal of teaching students how to deal with societal issues. *National Science Education Standards* are having a direct impact on state and local frameworks for science education. State departments of education are influencing changes in goals through their legislative and regulatory powers, such as specific requirements to include energy conservation, environmental problems, and health, alcohol, and drugs in educational programs.

Personal Needs

School personnel and parents express their concerns about meeting the personal needs of students through science education. This rhetoric takes the form of life-and-work and school-to-work skills related to science, the preparation ethic, and vocational or career education. In response, science courses often emphasize content that is seen as useful in everyday living.

Attempts to meet personal needs are made primarily through health or advanced placement courses. Some of the other goals, such as career awareness, overlap with these courses. Sometimes personal needs are met as a secondary effect of another goal. A socially relevant course on environmental science may provide fundamental knowledge that stimulates students to examine the life worth living.

The goal of meeting personal needs has always been subordinate in science education programs, especially when compared to goals such as knowledge. In the past three decades, the goal of fulfilling students' personal

needs has become increasingly important. This goal is closely related to both career and societal goals.

Career Awareness

One of the currently important goals of science education is to provide information and training that will be useful in future employment. Recent increased emphasis on this goal is due in part to public opinion. The career awareness goal was found consistently across science programs, although it was not the primary goal of science education. What mattered most was the scientific and technological knowledge needed for the next course and whether all the courses were eventually related to one's future job.

There is some resistance to implementing the career goal in science education. Several issues emerge: teachers and communities have questioned whether the school should serve labor needs; that is, whether the school should help prepare for work. They have questioned the apparent conflict between work of the school and the world of work. Science teachers are reluctant to sacrifice the scholastic program to help youth prepare for jobs. When teachers, parents, and science coordinators were asked about vocational goals of science courses, they all agreed that these goals should be included—however, the majority selected general education goals over vocational goals.

In recent decades, the inclusion of career goals in science programs has been increasingly important. Although the career goal has been emphasized and is important, it probably will not become a primary goal of science education in the 21st century. This is an excellent place to stop and complete Activity 5–2, The Status of Goals and Programs, at the end of this chapter.

SCIENCE EDUCATION GOALS FOR THE 21ST CENTURY: NATIONAL STANDARDS AND BENCHMARKS

In contemporary reform, the configuration of goals for science education should relate to the overall purpose of achieving scientific literacy. Thus, any review of national standards should assess the degree to which the standards incorporate the acquisition of scientific knowledge, development of inquiry abilities and understandings, and understanding of the applications of science (especially personal and social aspects of science, and the history and nature of science and technology). Further, those implementing the *Standards, Benchmarks,* and state and local frameworks should review the priorities and emphases suggested for the different goals. To what degree and in what form are the goals expressed? Do the standards suggest one orientation for the structuring of the goals, or do they suggest variations? Do the standards allow for a variety of curriculum materials and instructional approaches in order to achieve the goals? These questions should help focus your review of the national standards and the following discussion of science content in the standards.

The science content presented in the *National Science Education Standards* describes major concepts as well as fundamental concepts and abilities for all students. Content only represents one component of a comprehensive view of science education expressed by the national standards. This comprehensive view includes teaching *and* assessment. As we mentioned in Chapter 4, the *National Science Education Standards* organize science content into eight categories, displayed in Figure 5–1.

 Visit http://www.prenhall.com/trowbridge and select Topic 1—Science Teaching Standards. Select "Web Links" and find the link to review the "National Science Education Standards" for using inquiry learning strategies. This can be found in the Youth Learn website and offers a series of strategies for using inquiry learning in science classrooms. Determine how that goal could be met. Suggest a plan and submit it to your instructor using the Electronic Bluebook module.

Scientific Methods

The standard *Science As Inquiry* represents the goal we have discussed under Scientific Methods. The standard on inquiry has two features, the ability to *do* inquiry and the development of understandings *about* scientific inquiry. The inquiry standard emphasizes the students' ability to ask scientific questions; plan and conduct investigations; use appropriate tools, techniques, and educational technologies; think critically and logically about the relationship between evidences and explanations; construct and analyze alternative explanations; and communicate scientific investigations and explanations.

Science As Inquiry
Physical Science
Life Science
Earth and Space Science
Science and Technology
Science in Personal and Social Perspectives
History and Nature of Science
Unifying Concepts and Processes

FIGURE 5–1   National Science Education Standards: Science Content

Understandings about scientific inquiry generally parallel abilities. For example, the national standards encourage the students' development of knowledge about the types of questions scientists ask, the various reasons for conducting investigations, technology's role in inquiry, criteria for acceptable scientific explanations, and the results and use of scientific inquiry.

The inquiry standard emphasizes the students' ability to think critically and to use observations and knowledge to construct scientific explanations. The *Standards* have moved science education a step beyond the traditional *processes of science,* which centered on students engaging in activities emphasizing skills such as observing, inferring, hypothesizing, experimenting, and controlling variables. These processes of science are obviously included in *Science As Inquiry,* but the *Standards* require students to use the processes, combined with existing knowledge, as a means to gather evidence used in their analysis, reasoning, and construction of other scientific understanding.

The *Standards* include *Science and Technology,* in which students would develop abilities of technological design as well as greater understanding of science and technology. The standard intentionally parallels the *abilities* outlined in *Science As Inquiry.* The difference between the standards is based in the difference between scientific inquiry and technological design. The latter includes identifying a problem; proposing designs and selecting from alternative solutions; implementing a solution; evaluating the solution; and communicating the problem, process, and solution.

In the *National Science Education Standards,* inquiry and design serve to (1) assist students in the development of their understanding of scientific concepts, (2) help students answer the question "How do we know what we know in science?" (3) introduce one aspect of the nature of science, (4) develop abilities of critical thinking, scientific reasoning, and critical analysis, and (5) acquire the habits of mind associated with science and technology.

Scientific Knowledge

The *Standards* and *Benchmarks* have defined a wide range of scientific knowledge and emphasize that the content of secondary school science programs is not strictly confined to the *Physical, Life,* and *Earth Sciences.* However, three standards outline major concepts and fundamental understandings of *Physical, Life,* and *Earth Sciences,* three major divisions of the scientific disciplines. Figures 5–2, 5–3, and 5–4 present the conceptual organizers for these major divisions of science. Although the focus of this book is on secondary schools, we thought it important to present the conceptual organizers for grades K–4 so that you can review the overall development of concepts.

In the section on Scientific Methods, we discussed the standards on *Science As Inquiry* and portions of the

Physical Science K–4	Physical Science 5–8	Physical Science 9–12

Properties of Objectives
Position and Motion of Objects
Light, Heat, Electricity, and
   Magnetism
	Properties and Changes in Properties
	   of Matter
	Motions and Forces
	Transfer of Energy
		The Structure of Atoms and Materials
		Structure and Properties of Matter
		Chemical Reactions
		Motion and Force
		Conservation of Energy and
		   the Increase in Disorder
		Interactions of Energy and Matter

FIGURE 5–2   Conceptual Organizers for Physical Science Standards

Life Science K–4	Life Science 5–8	Life Science 9–12

Characteristics of Organisms
Life Cycles of Organisms
Organisms and Environments
	Structure and Function in Living
	   Systems
	Reproduction and Heredity
	Regulation and Behavior
	Populations and Ecosystems
	Diversity and Adaptations of
	   Organisms
		The Cell
		The Molecular Basis of Heredity
		Biological Evolution
		The Interdependence of Organisms
		Matter, Energy, and Organization in
		   Living Systems
		The Behavior of Organisms

FIGURE 5–3   Conceptual Organizers for Life Science Standards

Earth and Space Science K–4	Earth and Space Science 5–8	Earth and Space Science 9–12

Properties of Earth Materials
Objects in the Sky
Changes in Earth and Sky
	Structure of the Earth System
	Earth's History
	Earth in the Solar System
		Energy in the Earth System
		Geochemical Cycles
		The Origin and Evolution of the
		   Earth System
		The Origin and Evolution of the
		   Universe

FIGURE 5–4   Conceptual Organizers for Earth and Space Science Standards

standard on *Science and Technology.* Both of these standards also elaborate fundamental understandings for their respective areas. These understandings extend the goal of scientific knowledge from a narrow focus on the disciplines to a broader view that includes understanding scientific inquiry, science and technology, and the history and nature of science. We discussed some examples from understanding scientific inquiry in an earlier section. Generally, these understandings elaborate various aspects of scientific investigations. For example, scientific concepts guide investigations; technology enhances accuracy of data; scientific explanations use evidence, logically consistent arguments, and propose, modify, or elaborate principles, models, and theories in science; and science advances through legitimate skepticism.

In the standards on *Science and Technology,* understandings highlight the connections between science and technology and maintain a view of the scientific and technologic enterprise (for example, a larger and external view of science and technology in society). Examples of understandings include the similarities and differences between science and technology; the contributions of science to technology and technology to science; and the understanding that different people in different cultures have made, and continue to make, contributions to science and technology.

The scientific knowledge outlined in the *Standards* also includes the *History and Nature of Science* (see Figure 5–5). This standard does not imply that students develop understandings of a complete history of science. Rather, science teachers can present history to clarify

History and Nature of Science K–4	History and Nature of Science 5–8	History and Nature of Science 9–12
Science As a Human Endeavor	Science As a Human Endeavor Nature of Science History of Science	Science As a Human Endeavor Nature of Scientific Knowledge Historical Perspectives

FIGURE 5–5   Overview of the History and Nature of Science Standards

Unifying Concepts and Processes K–12
Systems, Order, and Organization Evidence, Models, and Explanation Constancy, Change, and Measurement Evolution and Equilibrium Form and Function

FIGURE 5–6   Overview of Unifying Concepts and Processors

various aspects of scientific inquiry, the human dimensions of science, and the various roles science has played in Western and non-Western cultures. Science teachers might use case studies from history, classical experiments, and perspectives of normal and revolutionary science in order to provide students with opportunities to develop the understandings described in this standard.

The *National Science Education Standards* also include *Unifying Concepts and Processes* within the goal of scientific knowledge. These standards present major conceptual and procedural schemes that unify science disciplines and, when understood, provide students with very powerful ways of understanding the natural and designed world (see Figure 5–6). *Unifying Concepts and Processes* do not have specific grade-level designations; rather, science teachers should continually bring these ideas to awareness in appropriate contexts, based on students' experiences. Specific understandings included in this standard are

- Systems, Order, and Organization—levels of organization, systems, prediction, and a statistical view of nature
- Evidence, Models, and Explanation—observations, data, models, hypothesis, law, and theory
- Constancy, Change, and Measurement—interactions, rate, scale, patterns, quantitative aspects of change, conservation of energy and matter
- Evolution and Equilibrium—gradual changes, present as connected to the past, descent from common ancestors, homeostasis, and energy content and distribution
- Form and Function—complimentarity, natural and designed world, and systems and subsystems

Personal Needs and Societal Issues

As mentioned in the first section describing goals, one fundamental purpose of science teaching is to help students understand and act on various issues and challenges they will confront as individuals and as citizens. The *Standards* recognize this goal through inclusion of *Science in Personal and Social Perspectives* (see Figure 5–7).

These standards provide a context and topics for science curriculum and instructions. You should notice that the national standards include different aspects of health at each grade level, and that there is the implied development of understanding about population, resources, and environments at all grade levels. The standards at grades 5–8 and 9–12 include natural hazards, such as earthquakes, volcanoes, floods, and hurricanes. Finally, this standard recommends that students come to understand and act on science and technology challenges at local (grades K–4), social (grades 5–8), and global (grades 9–12) levels.

Career Awareness

The *Standards* do have an explicit goal supporting career awareness; however, they do not have a standard emphasizing careers. It should be clear that the experience implied by the understandings and abilities outlined in the *Standards* would have a positive benefit on students' attitudes and inclinations toward careers in, for example, science, engineering, and the health professions.

The *National Science Education Standards* present a fairly balanced approach to the goals of science education, with career awareness as the exception. Further, the *Standards* align quite well with the dimensions of

Visit http://www.prenhall.com/trowbridge and select Topic 1—Science Teaching Standards. Select "Web Links" and find the link on "Benchmarks for Science Literacy." This link gives recommendations at each grade level for making progress toward adult science literacy goals. Evaluate the recommendations for the grade level you will teach and submit your evaluation to your instructor using the Electronic Bluebook module.

Science in Personal and Social Perspectives K–4	Science in Personal and Social Perspectives 5–8	Science in Personal and Social Perspectives 9–12
Personal Health	Personal Health	Personal and Community Health
Characteristics and Changes in Populations	Populations, Resources, and Environment	Population Growth
Types of Resources	Natural Hazards	Natural Resources
Changes in Environments	Risks and Benefits	Environmental Quality
Science and Technology in Local Challenges	Science and Technology in Society	Natural and Human-Induced Hazards
		Science and Technology in Local, National, and Global Challenges

FIGURE 5–7 Conceptual Organizers for Science in Personal and Social Perspectives

scientific literacy described in Chapter 4. The content standards form a complete set of outcomes for students. Development of students' understandings, attitudes, and abilities are grounded in scientific investigations, and they form a solid foundation in life, earth, and physical sciences and apply fundamental understanding and ability within various personal, social, and historical perspectives. Although balanced, thorough, and clearly aligned with long-standing goals of science education, the *National Science Education Standards* must be transformed in curriculum materials, instructional practices, and assessment strategies, all topics discussed in later chapters. Complete Activity 5–3, Goals of Science Textbooks, and Activity 5–4, Reforming Goals to Align with National Standards and Benchmarks.

SUMMARY

This chapter provided an overview of five enduring goals of science education: scientific knowledge, scientific methods, societal issues, personal needs, and career awareness. We reviewed the status and changes of these goals in light of reports assessing science education for the period 1955–1975 and reform efforts of the 1980s.

Entering the 21st century, national standards have had, and will continue to have, a profound influence on the goals of science education. *National Science Education Standards* incorporate the enduring goals. Scientific knowledge includes the major divisions of *Physical, Life,* and *Earth Science* and other areas such as *Science and Technology,* the *History and Nature of Science,* and *Unifying Concepts and Processes.* The goal of scientific methods is expressed as the standard on scientific inquiry, which includes both abilities and understandings associated with inquiry. Personal needs and societal issues are consolidated in the standard on *Science in Personal and Social Perspectives.*

The national standards provide a balanced and fairly thorough expression of traditional goals. It is clear that some areas, such as technology, personal and societal perspectives, the history and nature of science, and the unifying concepts and processes, will require science teachers to broaden their understanding on content. It is significant that the aforementioned areas have the status of national standards.

◆

REFERENCES

1. George E. DeBoer, *A History of Ideas in Science Education* (New York: Teachers College Press, 1991).
2. Rodger Bybee and George DeBoer, "Research on Goals for the Science Curriculum," in Dorothy Gabel, ed., *Handbook of Research on Science Teaching and Learning* (Washington, DC: National Science Teachers Association, 1993).
3. Stanley L. Helgeson, Patricia E. Blosser, and Robert W. Howe, *The Status of Pre-College Science, Mathematics,* *and Social Science Education: 1955–1975,* vol. 1, Science Education (SE 78–73 Vol. 1, Center for Science and Mathematics Education, Ohio State University, NSF Contract C762067) (Washington, DC: U.S. Government Printing Office, 1977).
4. Iris R. Weiss, *Report of the 1977 National Survey of Science, Mathematics, and Social Studies Education* (SE 78–72, Center for Educational Research and Evaluation, Research

Triangle Institute, NSF Contract C7619848) (Washington, DC: U.S. Government Printing Office, 1978).

5. Robert E. Stake, Jack Easley, et al., *Case Studies in Science Education, Vol. 1: The Case Reports* and *Vol. 2: Design, Overview and General Findings* (SE 78–74 Vol. 1 and SE 78–74 Vol. 2, Center for Instructional Research and Curriculum Evaluation, University of Illinois at Urbana-Champaign, NSF Contract C7621134) (Washington, DC: U.S. Government Printing Office, 1978).

6. Work on this review was completed as part of one author's (Rodger W. Bybee) participation on the National Science Foundation's "Project Synthesis," Dr. Norris Harms, director. Dr. Paul DeHart Hurd, Dr. Jane Kahle, and Dr. Robert Yager also worked on the project. We wish to thank them for their comments, criticism, and discussion.

7. Paul DeHart Hurd, "The Golden Age of Biological Education: 1960–1975," in *Biology Teachers Handbook,* 3rd ed., William Mayer, ed. (New York: Wiley & Sons, 1978).

8. National Assessment of Educational Progress, Science Achievement in the Schools, *A Summary of Results from the 1976–1977 National Assessment of Science* (Science Report No. 08–01) (Denver, CO: Education Commission of the States, 1978).

9. National Assessment of Educational Progress, *Three National Assessments of Science: Changes in Achievement, 1969–1977* (Denver, CO: Education Commission of the States, 1978).

10. We have not footnoted each statement, fact, and statistic in this discussion in order to make reading the summary easier. All material is supported by the studies and reviews cited at the beginning of this section.

11. American Association for the Advancement of Science, *Science for All Americans: A Project 2061 Report on Goals in Science, Mathematics, and Technology* (Washington, DC: Author, 1989).

12. American Association for the Advancement of Science, *Benchmarks for Science Literacy* (Washington, DC: Author, 1994).

13. National Research Council, *National Science Education Standards* (Washington, DC: Author, 1996).

14. See The National Commission on Excellence in Education, *A Nation At Risk* (Washington, DC: U.S. Department of Education, April, 1983); Task Force on Education for Economic Growth, *Action for Excellence* (Denver, CO: Education Commission of the States, June 1983); John Goodlad, *A Place Called School* (New York: McGraw-Hill, 1984); Mortimer Adler, *The Paideia Proposal* (New York: Macmillan, 1982); Ernest Boyer, *High School* (New York: Harper and Row, 1983); and Theodore Sizer, *Horace's Compromise* (Boston: Houghton Mifflin Co., 1984).

15. Susan Loucks-Horsley and Steve Olson, *Inquiry and the National Science Education Standards: A Guide for Teaching and Learning* (Washington, DC: National Academy Press, 2000)

◆ ────────────── INVESTIGATING SCIENCE TEACHING ────────── ◆

ACTIVITY 5–1
GOALS OF SCIENCE TEACHING

Directions:

1. In the blank in front of the goal statements, indicate whether you agree (A) or disagree (D) with the goal or have no opinion (NO).
2. Review and discuss your individual responses in a group of three or four persons. At this point you can add new goals, combine, modify, or omit goals. As a group you should agree on the goal statements.
3. Compile the goals from the small groups into a class set of goals for science teaching.

GOALS. SCIENCE TEACHING SHOULD:

_____ 1. Make students aware of good health practices.

_____ 2. Include contemporary social problems and solutions for those problems.

_____ 3. Emphasize analytic skills more than the skills of synthesis.

_____ 4. Prepare students for careers in science-related fields.

_____ 5. Help individuals cope with their environment.

_____ 6. Provide students with an understanding of the crucial role of science and technology in our society.

_____ 7. Provide students with the ability to form a hypothesis and plan an experiment to test the hypothesis. obj

_____ 8. Be more concerned with scientific facts than with broad generalizations since students cannot comprehend the generalizations.

_____ 9. Develop skills basic to technical occupations and professions.

_____ 10. Be related to and clarify individual beliefs, attitudes, and values.

_____ 11. Make students aware of the fact that science is the only answer to our many social problems.

_____ 12. Help students organize concepts into broad conceptual schemes.

_____ 13. Make students aware of science-related careers.

_____ 14. Enable students to use the scientific method to solve daily problems.

_____ 15. Present fundamental knowledge and not contemporary, relevant information. If students understand the fundamentals, they can deal responsibly with personal and social issues.

_____ 16. Be future-oriented; the past and present should receive marginal emphasis.

_____ 17. Place more emphasis on the methods and processes of scientific investigation.

_____ 18. Train the intuitive, inventive, creative talents more than the rational, logical, and methodological; the former more than the latter talents are responsible for new knowledge.

_____ 19. Actually involve students in science activities.

_____ 20. Develop the following abilities: creative thinking, effective communication, and decision making.

_____ 21. Demonstrate the aesthetic and ethical values of science.

_____ 22. Place great emphasis on recognizing the moral obligation of science and technology to the individual and to society.

_____ 23. Deal with broad, encompassing knowledge, since it is impossible to determine the best specific knowledge that most students will need.

_____ 24. Focus on the nature of scientific inquiry since this is the one aspect of the scientific enterprise that does not change.

_____ 25. Help students differentiate between facts and opinion and determine which is the best information available concerning problems.

Activity 5–2
The Status of Goals and Programs

As you enter this profession, it is important to reflect on your goals of science teaching in comparison with our best estimate of what is actually happening in the field. To assist you in this process, you might answer the following questions.

1. Why did the goals of science remain unchanged for approximately 20 years (1955–1975), then go into a period of transition?
2. What is your position on teaching science by inquiry?
3. What do you think are the important goals of science teaching?
4. What is the best way of achieving those goals?
5. What is your reaction to the teaching of science as "a body of information to be learned as dogma and accepted on faith"?

Activity 5–3
Goals of Science Textbooks

You have seen that the goals of textbooks are, essentially, the goals for science programs. In this activity you will first compare the goals of three textbooks or curriculum programs in your discipline. In the second part of the activity you will observe a science class for several days to see if goals are recognizable aspects of daily science teaching.

    First, select three textbooks in your discipline (e.g., physics, chemistry, biology, or earth science) at the level at which you plan to teach (e.g., junior high, middle, or high school). Next, examine the textbooks and teacher guides carefully and identify the goals of the program. Are they stated clearly? Did you have to derive the goals from the text materials? Complete the following information about goals:

	Text 1	Text 2	Text 3
1. Which goals were present and recognizable? (Y = yes, N = no, or M = marginal)			
Scientific knowledge	_____	_____	_____
Scientific methods	_____	_____	_____
Societal issues	_____	_____	_____
Personal needs	_____	_____	_____
Career awareness	_____	_____	_____
2. Rank the importance of goals presented in the text.			
(1 = very important, 2 = important, 3 = somewhat important, 4 = marginally important, 5 = not important)			
Scientific knowledge	_____	_____	_____
Scientific methods	_____	_____	_____
Societal issues	_____	_____	_____
Personal needs	_____	_____	_____
Career awareness	_____	_____	_____
3. Were the goals: (Y = yes, N = no, M = marginal)			
Comprehensive enough to include the generally accepted objectives of science teaching?	_____	_____	_____
Understandable to other teachers, administrators, and parents?	_____	_____	_____
Free of bias toward a particular philosophy of science teaching?	_____	_____	_____
Few in number?	_____	_____	_____
Conceptually different?	_____	_____	_____
Applicable to teaching and learning objectives?	_____	_____	_____

Now that you have reviewed the goals of three texts:

1. Which text do you prefer?
2. How does the text reflect your own goals for science teaching?
3. What did you learn about the transfer of goals to the science classroom?

ACTIVITY 5–4
REFORMING GOALS TO ALIGN WITH NATIONAL STANDARDS AND BENCHMARKS

The initial task of redesigning science programs is to identify what it is about science and technology that has significance for students. This statement applies to national curriculum reform or the local development of a science program. Take a few minutes to answer the following questions.

1. What knowledge, values, skills, and sensibilities relative to science and technology are important for citizens in the 21st century?
2. What scientific and technologic knowledge do you think is important? Why?
3. What values of science and technology would you emphasize? Why?
4. What skills and abilities are important? Why?
5. What are the sensibilities required of citizens?

CHAPTER

6

THE OBJECTIVES OF SCIENCE TEACHING

Teachers often talk about "teaching objectives." What is meant by this term? Are they really necessary in one's day-to day teaching? How can they help you? Might they stifle your creative impulses? Most science teachers would agree that some form and recognition of teaching objectives are necessary to become an effective teacher.

As Robert Mager, in "Preparing Instructional Objectives" (1962) once said, "If you don't know where you are going, you might end up someplace else." Do objectives help you determine where you are going? This chapter may help you get a clearer picture of "where you are going" with your class. There are at least two different aspects of this. Certainly you have certain objectives you wish to accomplish with respect to your own teaching progress. Then there are certain objectives you wish to have your students achieve. It is the latter group we shall concentrate on in this chapter.

As a teacher your purpose is to make it possible for students to develop an understanding of what their objectives should be. Is it factual knowledge? Is it changes in attitude? Is it recognition of their own potential as lifelong learners? Most teachers would subscribe to all of these, plus many more. This chapter will help you think about all of these possibilities.

One of the best ways to learn is to be actively involved in and with the material to be studied. To apply this principle, start by completing Activity 6–1, Objectives of Science Teaching, at the end of this chapter. In the previous chapter, we described some of the larger purposes and directions of science education; now we will discuss some of the specific objectives for science teaching. General goals are related to specific objectives, and both types of goals should be related to your

purposes as a science teacher. Be sure you have the most appropriate objectives for your purposes.

NEW THRUST IN TEACHING OBJECTIVES

Today, emphasis is put on the development of scientific literacy, for a scientifically literate citizenry is essential in a highly technological society such as ours. Students in secondary schools form a preferred target group for developing this objective.

To realize success in their efforts to develop scientifically literate students, science teachers must have a clear idea of what comprises scientific literacy and proceed to formulate classroom objectives that emphasize appropriate activities and foster the desired learning and skill development. The BSCS (Biological Sciences Curriculum Study) has detailed various levels of scientific literacy as they apply to biology. These levels have relevance to other areas of science teaching and are discussed below.

The lowest level of literacy is the *nominal level*. Students may enter a class with minimal recognition of science terms but may not be able to give adequate or correct explanations of the scientific phenomena under discussion and may have misconceptions about them. A common problem in middle school classes is that students, when presented with a new topic to study, may believe they have already covered the material, thus diminishing their enthusiasm for the task ahead. In fact, they may have only name recognition of the topic and little or no understanding of the depth of the subject being proposed. A teacher's objective in this situation might be to develop a realization of the breadth and depth of the topic under consideration.

At a higher functional level students may be able to define science terms correctly from memory but have little understanding of purpose, interrelationships between parts, or organizational hierarchy of terms. Teachers may want to consider objectives that emphasize the role scientific terms play in classification, in organization, and in delineating scientific usage from everyday usage of some words.

Students may have reached *structural literacy* if they can construct appropriate explanations based on their experiences in class or out of school and can explain concepts in their own terms. Objectives and activities at this level should emphasize development of interrelationships between parts, applications of scientific phenomena to everyday experiences, and personal relevance of the newly learned material.

At the *multidimensional level* students can apply the knowledge they have gained and the skills they have developed to solve authentic problems that may require integration from other related disciplines, such as social studies, reading, and language arts. Objectives and activities at this level should provide many opportunities to work on real problems with alternate solutions that bring out the trade-offs that frequently are needed to make progress in the solutions of real-life problems.

OBJECTIVES FOR CONSTRUCTIVIST TEACHING

What is the main purpose of teaching? What is the science teacher attempting to do? What is the teacher's role as he or she faces a roomful of eager (or perhaps apathetic) students? Unfortunately, there exists a residual belief that teaching is like filling a bucket—pouring knowledge in like water or sand until the child's mind (the bucket) is overflowing. A study by Aguirre, Haggerty, and Linder (quoted in Hewson)[1] used an open-ended questionnaire to elicit preservice science teachers' conceptions of teaching science. They found students entering preservice education programs "possessed a variety of views about science teaching and learning. For example, almost half of 74 prospective science teachers believed that teaching is a matter of knowledge transfer from teacher to the 'empty' minds of children, in contrast to about a third who believed that for learning to occur, new information should be related to existing understanding." Perhaps the encouraging feature is that as many as a third of the preservice teachers viewed teaching in a quasi-constructivist manner.

Appleton[2] has described a constructivist-based model used during science classes. He points out that "Constructivist ideas have had a major influence on science educators over the last decade. . . . This study

has resulted in a model for science lessons which allows the identification and description of students' cognitive progress through the lessons." He also asserts that "The main tenet of constructivist theories is that existing ideas which learners may hold are used to make sense of new experiences and new information. Learning therefore occurs when there is a change in the learner's existing ideas, either by adding some new information or by reorganizing what is already known."

Methods for conducting science classes frequently focus on use of discrepant events. These seem to generate "cognitive conflict" or "disequilibrium" in Piaget's terms. Examples of three useful approaches are a) teacher demonstrations to present the discrepant event, b) teacher discussion including questioning and identifying examples drawn from students' experiences, and c) students' conduct of the discrepant event followed by small group discussion of possible explanations. Such discrepant events as the Cartesian diver and the double pendulum were cited as examples.

The recent emphasis on hands-on science has put constructivism in the middle of learning theories relevant for teaching and learning science. The basic premise of constructivism is that learners receive sensory input, compare it to existing ideas of what appears to be similar events, modify, if necessary, and construct explanations that seem to make sense.[3] What learners actually construct from a given learning experience varies from student to student and often deviates from what the teacher had intended. According to George Bodner of Purdue University, "There is no conduit from one brain to another. All teachers can do is disturb the environment. Effective instruction depends on our ability to understand how students make sense of our disturbances (stimuli) rather than how we make sense of those stimuli ourselves. Knowledge is constructed by the learner."[4]

Appleton and Asoko have outlined the characteristics of constructivist teaching as follows: a) A prior awareness of the ideas which children bring to the learning situation, and/or attempts to elicit such ideas, b) Clearly defined conceptual goals for the learners and an understanding of how learners might progress toward the (ideas), c) Use of teaching strategies which involve challenge to or development of the initial ideas of the learners and ways of making new ideas accessible to them, d) Provision of opportunities for the learners to utilize new ideas in a range of contexts, and e) Provision of a classroom atmosphere which encourages children to put forward and discuss ideas.[5]

Considering these factors, it becomes necessary to develop and refine classroom objectives in science. A highly effective instructional model based on constructivism is the Learning Cycle. Jay Hackett's modification of the learning cycle[6] as revised by Bybee in the late

1980[7] (see Chapter 15), employs five phases: Engagement, Exploration, Explanation, Elaboration, and Evaluation. Working objectives for each of these phases are:

- Engagement: Mentally engage students in the big ideas or concepts of the lesson. Access prior knowledge and understandings. Whet interest and curiosity.
- Exploration: Investigate and explore ideas together to establish a common experience base and share prior understandings.
- Explanation: Put forth explanations based upon prior knowledge. Develop vocabulary. Provide experiences to reinforce and strengthen understandings.
- Elaboration: Challenge and extend students' conceptual understanding and skills. Transfer and apply understandings of concepts to different situations. Make connections to other curriculum areas.
- Evaluation: Encourage students to assess their understandings and abilities and provide opportunities for teachers to evaluate progress toward achieving the educational objectives.

SELECTING OBJECTIVES FOR SCIENCE TEACHING

As you probably discovered during the introductory activity, there are many objectives for science teaching. Rather than giving our answers to your questions about objectives, we will clarify different types of science objectives and then discuss the preparation of objectives for science teaching. First, we examine six criteria that will help differentiate objectives from goals and give you a guide to selecting objectives for science teaching.

Science objectives:

1. should be general enough to be identifiably related to science goals and specific enough to give clear direction for planning and evaluating science instruction.
2. should be understandable for students, teachers, administrators, and parents.
3. should be few in number but comprehensive for any lesson, unit, or program.
4. should be challenging yet attainable for your students.
5. should differ conceptually from each other.
6. should be appropriate for the subject you are teaching.

TYPES OF OBJECTIVES FOR SCIENCE TEACHING

Objectives can be stated in terms of instructional or learning results. In the first example, the emphasis is on what the teacher does; in the second example, it is on what the student does.

"To demonstrate to students how to use a barometer"
"Students should be able to describe correct procedures in the use of a barometer"

The advantage of stating objectives as instructional results is that it gives you direction. The disadvantage is that you may not be clear as to whether the students learned anything. In general, we suggest that you concentrate on learning results when forming objectives. Doing so will help define the instruction sequence and set the stage for evaluation.

Objectives can be classified as either behavioral or nonbehavioral. Behavioral objectives state how the student will behave as a result of instruction. Behaviors are an observable indication that learning has occurred. Examples of behavioral objectives are:
The student should be able to

- identify symbols on a weather map,
- describe predator and prey relationships, and
- define the term energy.

For contrast, examples of nonbehavioral objectives are: the student should be able to

- learn scientific names for common animals,
- comprehend the concept of work,
- know how to use the scientific method, and
- note the action verb in each stated objective.

All seven of these examples could be objectives for science lessons, and they are all stated in terms of learning results for students. In the first set, the specific behaviors have been stated: if students can identify . . . , describe . . . , and define . . . , then they have learned. The second set is a little less clear as to how you will know whether or not students have learned . . . , do comprehend . . . , or do know. Are behavioral objectives better than nonbehavioral? Here are some advantages and disadvantages of behavioral objectives.

Some of the advantages of behavioral objectives are:

1. They help the science teacher become more precise in her or his teaching.
2. They clarify exactly what is expected.
3. They provide performance criteria for student achievement and accountability for the teacher.
4. The teacher plans more carefully because she or he knows what performance the students should display after finishing a science lesson, unit, or course of study.
5. The teacher knows what materials are needed and is able to give more specific help to students in directing them to outside sources of information.
6. The teacher who prepares behavioral objectives finds them very helpful in evaluation. When preparing paper and pencil tests, the questions can be matched to the objectives and, by deciding on certain criteria of performance, questions can be phrased in such a way that the teacher has precise

knowledge of the ability of the student to perform certain tasks.

Some disadvantages of behavioral objectives are:

1. They may tend toward an emphasis on trivial behaviors and ignore important objectives that are too difficult to define behaviorally.
2. They may inhibit the teacher's spontaneity and flexibility.
3. They may provide a precise measurement of less important behaviors, leaving more important outcomes unevaluated.
4. They may be used against teachers who are held accountable for the performance of students who do not learn.
5. They tend to focus the teacher's attention on the small, less-significant aspects of teaching, leaving the larger picture unattended.
6. They represent only one particular psychology and philosophy of education (namely behaviorism).

DOMAINS OF OBJECTIVES FOR SCIENCE TEACHING

It is customary to think of objectives in three aspects: *cognitive, affective,* and *psychomotor.* These terms come from the work of Benjamin Bloom and others who developed taxonomies of educational objectives.[8,9,10] Cognitive objectives deal with intellectual results, knowledge, concepts, and understanding. Affective objectives include the feelings, interests, attitudes, and appreciations that may result from science instruction. The psychomotor domain includes objectives that stress motor development, muscular coordination, and physical skills.

Traditionally, cognitive objectives have received far more attention over the years than affective or psychomotor objectives. With increased attention to behavioral objectives and performance competencies, the cognitive area becomes fertile ground for writing objectives that stress performance in science knowledge and conceptual understanding. Still, science teachers should not omit important learning results in the affective and psychomotor domains.

Your understanding of the three domains will be one of the most helpful aids in formulating objectives for science teaching. We have used categories from the cognitive, affective, and psychomotor domains as the basis for tables summarizing instructional objectives in science (see Tables 6–1 through 6–6). The tables are based on the original work of Bloom et al., Krathwohl et al., and Norman Gronlund.[11] The domains are arranged in a hierarchical order, from simple to complex learning results.

TABLE 6–1   Cognitive Domain for Science Teaching

Knowing

Knowledge represents the lowest level of science objectives. The definition of knowledge for this level is remembering previously learned scientific material. The requirement is to simply recall, i.e., bring to mind appropriate information. The range of information may vary from simple facts to complex theories, but all that is required is to remember the information.

Comprehending

Comprehension is the first step beyond simple recall. It is the first level, demonstrating and understanding of scientific information. It is the ability to apprehend, grasp, and understand the meaning of scientific material. Comprehension is shown in three ways: (1) translation of scientific knowledge into forms, (2) interpretation of science knowledge by reordering and showing interrelationships and summarizing material, and (3) extrapolation and interpolation of science knowledge. Here the students can estimate or predict future trends or infer consequences between two points or items of data.

Applying

Application is the ability to show the pertinence of scientific principles to different situations. At this level students may apply scientific concepts, methods, laws, or theories to actual concrete problems.

Analyzing

Analysis requires more than knowledge, comprehension, and application. It also requires an understanding of the underlying structure of the material. Analysis is the ability to break down material to its fundamental elements for better understanding of the organization. Analysis may include identifying parts, clarifying relationships among parts, and recognizing organizational principles of scientific systems.

Synthesizing

Synthesis requires the formulation of new understandings of scientific systems. If analysis stresses the parts, synthesis stresses the whole. Components of scientific systems may be reorganized into new patterns and new wholes. A bringing together of scientific ideas to form a unique idea, place, or pattern could be a learning result at this level.

Evaluating

Evaluation is the highest level of learning results in the hierarchy. It includes all the other levels plus the ability to make value judgments based on internal evidence and consistency and/or clearly defined external criteria.

GUEST EDITORIAL ◆ JEFF MOW

Science Education Student
Environmental Education
Carleton College, Northfield, Minnesota

ENVIRONMENTAL EDUCATION AND SCIENCE TEACHING

As a junior at Carleton College, I am just beginning my career in science education. Originally a Geology major, later I changed to Environmental Education. As I completed a science methods course, I realized that the informal teaching and educational opportunities found outdoors have the most meaning for me. I would like to be an outdoor educator or perhaps a visiting teacher and curriculum developer. One reason for this choice is that I have a strong interest in geology and would like to explore the career opportunities in this field. Another reason is that I have been teaching and developing curriculum materials for the U.S. Geological Survey. Because of this opportunity, I have already been exposed to some novel approaches to environmental education. This experience, in conjunction with my own personal education and teacher training, has made me think about issues in environmental education.

The first question I have is, "What is environmental education?" A common conception of environmental education is that it is recreationally oriented. Also, environmental programs often offer such a different subject matter focus that students are unable to relate the environmental activity to an everyday experience such as going to school. This lack of integration often results in an ineffective environmental program. Is environmental education going hiking in the woods, viewing a film on pollution, or hugging a tree? Or is environmental education calculating the rate of erosion on a poorly-managed farm field or making physical measurements of the forest regeneration process? I think that environmental education should take the latter form, as it allows students to integrate concepts learned in the classroom with an actual life experience. I also

think that it is important that the outdoor experience can and should be used as a laboratory; that is, "a classroom without walls." I have developed and taught a map unit of the U.S. Geological Survey in which I have secondary students make detailed maps of their local environment. When I first taught this course, many of the students took the opportunity to run off. Since then, I have learned that for the exercise to be successful, I have to lay down some initial ground rules. The result of outlining my expectations of them is that I am able to focus the students' activity despite the loss of the classroom's physical constraints. I have found that the environmental activities I have taught have been successful, and I would hope that you might also try this approach.

A much larger issue is the role of science education in our society. My own education and what I have seen in the schools indicate a distinct gap or void between the science taught in the classroom and that encountered in life. As a future science educator, how can I help bridge this gap? For example, in your high school physics course, how much exposure did you have to daily scientific issues such as nuclear technology and electronic technology? A poll of my peers has revealed that these issues were not dealt with and I realized that, in hindsight, they should have been. I believe it is important that, as a future science teacher, I try to relate classroom material to everyday science applications. I think that it is clear that science and technology will be an important factor in solving many of our world's problems and that, as a science teacher, I have the responsibility of creating an increased awareness of the importance of science in our society.

The Cognitive Domain

The cognitive domain starts with acquiring simple knowledge about science and proceeds through increasingly difficult levels: comprehension, application, analysis, synthesis, and evaluation. The categories are inclusive because higher-level results incorporate

the lower levels. For example, students must know a science concept before they can apply it. Science teachers usually have concentrated on the cognitive domain and the lower levels of learning within the domain. Understanding the hierarchical nature of this and other domains increases your awareness of higher levels of science objectives and, subsequently, higher levels of

A science teacher and her supervisor review objectives for science lessons.

student achievement. (See Tables 6–1 and 6–2 for a summary of the cognitive domain and examples of general and specific instructional objectives in science.)

WRITING COGNITIVE OBJECTIVES

Much of science learning in the past has been concerned with gaining knowledge of factual or conceptual nature on science topics. This is still true, but it now comes with some recent recognition that the volume of such knowledge has become overwhelming with the rapid advancements in science. The information overload for science students has become intolerable. What is a realistic solution to this problem?

One solution is to make appropriate selections within the topical field and reduce the number of topics taught. Judicious use of well-defined cognitive objectives can help in this process. To do this, prepare a short list of cognitive objectives that progress from simple to more complex levels. For example, suppose the topic you plan to teach is "weather" with a subtopic of "severe storms."

It is not necessary to spell out in detail every cognitive objective that might seem necessary to learn about severe storms. Instead, use Bloom's taxonomy of educational objectives as a guide and prepare one objective for each level (knowledge, comprehension, application, analysis, synthesis, and evaluation). As illustration, under knowledge, you might have, "Student should be able to describe several differences between tornadoes and hurricanes." Or, under evaluation, you might have, "Student should be able to assess the probable damage to beach-side residences as a result of a close passage of a moderate hurricane on the East Coast of the United States."

Keep in mind that every objective should contain an action verb that describes what the student should be able to do as a result of studying the particular topic under concern. In the two previous examples the words "describe" and "assess" are the action verbs.

Visit http://www.prenhall.com/trowbridge and select Topic 1—Science Teaching Standards. Select "Web Links" and find the link on "National Science Education Standards" (SC1). When you open the page for the National Academy Press, click "access now" to review the table of contents for the standards. Review the standards for your content area and grade level. Choose one standard and determine three or more ideas students should know before you teach the chosen standard. Submit those to your instructor using the Electronic Bluebook module.

The Affective Domain

Affective objectives deal with feelings, interests, and attitudes. Science teachers are becoming increasingly concerned with this area in our schools today. Neglect or lack of attention to attitudes has produced some unexpected results. Often students are losing interest in science at a time when scientific advances are unparalleled in the history of humanity. Greater numbers of students and adults are questioning science, perhaps

TABLE 6–2   Examples of General Objectives, Behavioral Objectives, and Terms for Specifying Objectives for Science Instruction in the Cognitive Domain

	General Objectives	Behavioral Objectives	Terms for Objectives
Knowing	Knows scientific facts Knows scientific methods Knows basic principles of earth science, biology, chemistry, physics Knows the conceptual schemes of science	To label the parts of a frog To list the steps in the scientific method To state the second law of thermodynamics	Define, describe, identify, label, list, name, select, state
Comprehending	Understands scientific facts Interprets scientific principles Translates formulas to verbal statements Estimates the consequences of data Justifies procedures of scientific investigation	To distinguish between scientific facts and theories To explain Newton's laws To give examples of density To infer the results of continued population growth To defend procedures in problem solving	Convert, defend, interpolate, estimate, explain, extrapolate, generalize, infer, predict, summarize
Applying	Applies scientific concepts to new situations Applies theories to practical events Constructs graphs from data Uses scientific procedures correctly	To apply the theory of natural selection to new data To predict the results of fossil fuel depletion To prepare a graph of temperature changes of ascending and descending air masses	Apply, compute, discover, modify, operate, predict, prepare, relate, show, use
Analyzing	Identifies stated and unstated assumptions of a scientific theory Recognizes logical fallacies in arguments Differentiates between facts and inferences Evaluates the appropriateness of data Analyzes the structure of a scientific inquiry	To identify the assumptions of Newtonian physics To point out logical connections in the reasoning of scientific principles applied to practice To distinguish fact from assertion To select relevant data for the solution of a problem	Analyze, diagram, differentiate, discriminate, divide, identify, illustrate, infer, relate, select
Synthesizing	Gives an organized account of two theories applied to a problem Proposes procedures for solving a problem Integrates principles from meteorology, biology, and chemistry in a discussion of pollution Formulates a scheme for resolving an interdisciplinary problem	To combine the second law of thermodynamics and principles of supply and demand in discussing energy To solve an original scientific problem To relate different scientific principles To design procedures for classifying unrelated objects	Arrange, combine, compile, compose, construct, devise, design, generate, organize, plan, relate, reorganize, summarize, synthesize
Evaluating	Judges the adequacy of a theory to explain actual phenomena Judges the value of a solution by use of internal and external criteria	To criticize the theory of continental drift To evaluate the Green Revolution as a solution to world food problems	Appraise, compare, conclude, contrast, discriminate, explain, evaluate, interpret, relate, summarize

TABLE 6–3   Affective Domain for Science Teaching

Receiving

Receiving or attending to stimuli related to science is the lowest level of learning result in the affective domain. Receiving means that students are aware of the existence of and willing to attend to scientific phenomena. When students are paying attention in science class, they are probably behaving at this level. The three levels of receiving are (1) awareness that science-related topics and issues exist, (2) willingness to receive information about science, and (3) selective attention to science topics.

Responding

Responding means that the learner does something with or about scientific phenomena. The student not only attends to but also reacts to science-related materials. Learning results can have three levels of responses: (1) acquiescence, meaning that the student does what is assigned or required, (2) willingness, meaning that the student does science study above and beyond requirements, and (3) satisfaction, meaning that the student studies science for pleasure and enjoyment.

Valuing

Valuing refers to consistent behavior that indicates the student's preference for science. The valuing level is based on

internalized values related to science. Again, valuing includes three levels: (1) acceptance of scientific values, (2) preference for scientific values, and (3) commitment to scientific values. Instructional objectives related to attitudes and appreciation would be included at this level of the affective hierarchy.

Organizing

Organizing means that the student brings together different scientific values and builds a consistent value system. Learning results include the conceptualization of scientific values and the organization of a personal value system based on science. The student is organizing a philosophy of life based on scientific values.

Characterizing

Characterizing means that, in effect, the individual has developed a lifestyle based on the preferred value system, in this case science. The individual's behavior is consistently and predictably related to scientific values. Learning results related to general patterns of behavior would be aligned with this level.

---

because of a poor understanding of its role in society or because of confusion over the relationships between science and technology.

Writing affective objectives usually is more difficult than writing those in the cognitive area. It requires more care to formulate criteria for feelings, interests, and attitudes. It is impossible to peer inside the student's head and determine what attitudes are there. However, certain behaviors are indicative of students' attitudes or interests. And students do have attitudes and values toward the scientific enterprise, an enterprise that is, of course, valuable in itself.

As science teachers we are as much obligated to present scientific attitudes and values as we are to present scientific facts and concepts. What are some of these attitudes and values? In Chapter 3 we described some scientific values. Others are curiosity, openness to different ideas, objectivity, precision, accuracy in reporting, perseverance in work, and questioning of ideas. Tables 6–3 and 6–4 should further clarify science objectives for the affective domain.

WRITING AFFECTIVE OBJECTIVES

Turning the student objectives in the affective domain into behavioral objectives requires attention to the use of action verbs that describe behavioral changes in such things as interest development, changes in attitudes, appreciations, and development of values. These are all le-

gitimate objectives and important in the growth of understanding the essence of science and technology in society today.

Because the observation and evaluation of behavioral changes among students in the affective areas is somewhat more difficult than in cognitive and psychomotor domains, it is important to design objectives that are carefully thought out and stated with precision. The teacher can observe many affective changes in behavior during the course of instruction. These might be called overt behavioral changes. Others, more subtle, may not be directly observable and, therefore, can be called covert.

Here are some examples of overt and covert behavioral objectives in the affective domain.

> overt: Students should be able to give evidence of behavioral change in the development of interest in the study of crystals by voluntarily selecting three or more books from the library and reading them for their own understanding of crystals.

Note that in the statement of this behavioral objective, the word *voluntarily* is included. This is important because evidence of behavioral change in interest development can only be credible if the student shows a voluntary response. If it is in the form of a teacher assignment, extra credit, or some other structured request, there is doubt about whether the response represents a true behavioral change.

TABLE 6–4 Examples of General Objectives, Behavioral Objectives, and Terms for Specifying Objectives for Science Instruction in the Affective Domain

	General Objectives	Behavioral Objectives	Terms for Objectives
Receiving	Attention to activities in science Awareness of the importance of science Sensitivity toward science-related social issues	To listen during chemistry class To ask questions about physics To select a book on geology to read	Ask, attend, choose, follow, identify, listen, locate, look, select, tell
Responding	Completes assignments in science Participates in science class Discusses science Shows an interest in science Helps other students with science	To respond to questions related to photosynthesis To complete a report on glaciers To discuss the limitations and potential of science in social issues	Answer, assist, complete, discuss, do help, perform, practice, read, recite, report, select, tell, watch, write
Valuing	Demonstrates confidence in science and technology Appreciates the role of science and technology Demonstrates the values of scientific problem solving Prefers science over other subjects	To initiate further study in ecology To work on community projects relating to recycling To complete a science project To accept leadership in the science club	Accept, argue, complete, commit, describe, do, explain, follow, initiate, invite, join, prefer, propose, read, report, study, work
Organizing	Recognizes the responsibility of science and technology to society Develops a rationale for the place of science in society Bases judgments on evidence Accepts scientific values as personal values	To present scientific values as one's own To defend the right of scientists to do research To argue using fact, evidence, and data	Adhere, alter, argue, combine, defend, explain, integrate, modify, organize, synthesize
Characterizing	Uses problem solving for daily problems in work Displays scientific values Shows a consistent philosophy of life based on scientific values	To solve problems objectively To verify knowledge To display scientific attitudes	Act, confirm, display, influence, perform, practice, propose, question, refute, serve, solve, use, verify

covert: Students will give evidence of behavioral change in development of a set of values in classroom demeanor by voluntarily self-reporting that they plan to assist other students to improve their skills of sharing with other classmates.

In this statement, note the addition of the words *self-reporting*. In a covert objective there can be no outward sign of the behavioral change, although such change may have taken place in the student. Therefore, the teacher must rely on the student's own statement of intent. While this may not insure complete validity, it is an improvement over complete lack of observable evidence. Many covert objectives involving feelings, likes and dislikes, and valuing fall into this category.

The Psychomotor Domain

In science, psychomotor objectives concern learning results which involve physical manipulation of apparatus, skill development, and proficiency in using tools, such as scientific instruments and devices. Many of these desired behaviors are not ends in themselves but are means for cognitive and affective learning. This observation points out the interrelation of the three domains and stresses the importance of total learning by the individual. Since one of the goals of education is to produce fully competent individuals who are self-reliant and capable of pursuing learning on their own throughout their lives, the psychomotor objectives occupy an important place in the overall educational endeavor. Although psychomotor ob-

TABLE 6–5 Alternative View of Psychomotor Domain for Science Teaching – Skill development

Simple

This initial state of psychomotor behavior is one which confirms positive readiness and mental set for the learner's further development in this skill area. It is not to be viewed as an objective in "performance" terms. Learner objectives need not be written at this level. However, if the teacher is keenly observing the learner's imitative activity, and reads the learner's need accurately, the teacher can, at this point, identify appropriate objectives(s) to move the learner through the succeeding stages (manipulation, etc.).

Imitation

Imitation refers to perceptual readiness (eyes, touch, muscle sense, etc.) When learners are exposed to an observable action they begin to make covert imitation of that action. Such covert behavior appears to be the starting point in the growth of psychomotor skill. This is then followed by overt performance of an act and capacity to repeat it. The performance, however, lacks neuromuscular coordination or control and hence is generally in a crude and imperfect form. This level is characterized by impulse, crude reproduction, and repetition, as well as a low degree of learner control, accuracy, and confidence.

Manipulation

This domain emphasizes the development of skill in following directions, performing selected actions, and fixation of performance through necessary practice. At this level learners are capable of performing an act according to instruction rather than just on the basis of observation as is the case at the level of imitation. They are able to follow directions, give attention to form, and begin to integrate their motor responses.

Precision

The proficiency of performance reaches a higher level of refinement in reproducing a given act. Here, accuracy, proportion and exactness in performance become significant. The actions are characterized by minimal errors, higher degree of control and increased self-confidence.

Articulation

Articulation involves the coordination of a series of acts by establishing appropriate sequence and accomplishing harmony or internal consistency among different acts. There is accurate, controlled performance that incorporates elements of speed and time. Learners' responses become habitual, yet are capable of being modified.

Naturalization

A high level of proficiency in the skill or performance of a single act is required. The behavior is performed with the least expenditure of psychic energy. At this level, the performance is smooth and natural. It is routinized, automatic, and spontaneous, and performed with a high degree of learner confidence.

---

jectives play a major role in physical activities, their importance in science classes should not be overlooked, especially since much of science instruction involves laboratory work requiring the physical handling and manipulation of materials. In Tables 6–5 and 6–7, we have relied on our own experience and understanding of psychomotor skills required for learning science. Table 6–5 represents a view used in music education and may be applicable in science education as well.

WRITING PSYCHOMOTOR OBJECTIVES

In science teaching, one is particularly concerned that objectives include developing the types of behaviors involving physical movement relating to the use of equipment in laboratories, field observations, and investigative activities that require careful and precise measurements. The skills that are to be developed are those that will be used repeatedly in all science classes and will form the basis for good scientific study as students progress to higher class levels in high school and college.

As with cognitive and affective objectives, keep in mind the use of action verbs that designate clearly what the student should do or perform to satisfy the objective.

Repeated attention to this will develop habits that automatically will insure the performance outcomes to be desired. The cognitive, affective, and psychomotor domains have been outlined for your use in preparing instructional objectives for science teaching. Each domain has a hierarchical order that goes from simple to complex learning results. As you prepare objectives for science teaching, we suggest that you use Tables 6–1 to 6–6 as guides to the levels of learning and the formulation of general and specific objectives. The tables should help you:

1. Clarify objectives for an instructional unit.
2. Identify appropriate levels for instructional objectives.
3. Define objectives in meaningful terms.
4. Prepare comprehensive lists of objectives for instruction.
5. Integrate the cognitive, affective, and psychomotor domains in your teaching.
6. Communicate intentions, levels, and nature of learning, relative to your instructional unit.

Don't be a slave to the classification systems. You may have some objectives that do not fit in any domains and others that fit all three. Be less concerned about classifying your objectives and more concerned about how

TABLE 6–6 Examples of General Objectives, Behavioral Objectives, and Terms for Specifying Objectives for Science Instruction in the Psychomotor Domain

	General Objectives	Behavioral Objectives	Terms for Objectives
Moving	Walking smoothly in science class Moving around the science class without problems Keeping up with the class on science field trips	To clean and replace science materials To carry a microscope properly To obtain and carry materials for laboratory activities	Adjust, carry, clean, follow, locate, move, obtain, store, walk
Manipulating	Manipulating science materials without damaging them Coordinating several activities during laboratory periods Performing skillfully in the science laboratory Operating science equipment safely	To set up science laboratory equipment quickly To adjust a microscope so that the image is clear To dissect with precision To operate scientific instruments correctly To assemble science apparatus To pour chemicals safely	Adjust, assemble, build, calibrate, change, clean, connect, construct, dismantle, fasten, handle, heat, make, mix, repair, set, stir, weigh
Communicating	Informing the teacher of problems Communicating results of science activities Drawing accurate reproductions of microscopic images Talking and writing clearly and logically Explaining science information clearly	To communicate problems in handling equipment To ask questions about problems To listen to other students To write legibly To report data accurately To graph data accurately	Ask, analyze, describe, discuss, compose, draw, explain, graph, label, listen, record, sketch, write
Creating	Creating new scientific apparatus for solving problems Designing new scientific devices Inventing different techniques	To create different ways of solving problems To combine different pieces of equipment to form a new science instrument or device To plan ways to solve problems	Analyze, construct, create, design, invent, plan, synthesize

they will contribute to making you more effective as a science teacher so that your students will become better learners.

PREPARING OBJECTIVES FOR SCIENCE TEACHING

The task of writing objectives can be simplified by following these steps.

1. *Have your overall instructional objectives in mind.* What are your general objectives for the lesson or unit you are going to teach? Is it improvement of a skill? Developing the understanding of a concept?

Stimulating interest in a new area of science? A combination of these objectives? Are your objectives cognitive? Affective? Psychomotor? Is there congruence between the levels of objectives and your instructional aims? For example, your instructional objective may be: To teach problem solving.

2. *Select the content desired to achieve the objectives of the unit.* In many teaching situations, unit goals may depend on the sequence of topics found in a science textbook or curriculum guide. However, the presence of a topical outline should not influence your teaching objectives. After all, you are trying to achieve certain objectives for a unique group of students. The topics chosen should be vehicles to achieve these objectives. Usually, several

Students and teachers work together to establish appropriate teaching and learning objectives.

subject-matter topics can be used to accomplish the task. Select those that are appropriate in terms of student interests and needs, your interest, suitability to the background of the students, and other factors. If you live in a mountainous area, use mountain terrain and topography to teach about variations of weather in different locations. Adapt your teaching to local situations. If brachiopods and trilobites can be found in a local limestone quarry, use that resource to teach about fossils rather than discussing forms that can be found only as pictures in books or in exotic collections from laboratory supply houses. Selection of content is very important. Try to find content that is both appropriate to your objectives and personally meaningful to your students.

3. *Write general statements describing how the student should perform.* Begin these statements with a verb (knows, defines, responds, calibrates, etc.), and then state what it is you intend to accomplish. It is helpful to write these statements in terms of learning results for the students. Be sure you have stated only one learning result per objective. Three or four general objectives should be sufficient for any lesson and six to eight for sets of lessons or units. When the general objectives are completed, you should be able to relate them to the general goals of science education and to identify an instructional plan or sequence for your lesson. (See the first column of Tables 6–2, 6–4, and 6–6.)

4. *Write specific objectives under the general statements.* Again, the objective should start with a verb and state a learning result that is related to the general objective. Usually two or three specific objectives will be sufficient to describe the specific learning

results. You may wish to change general and/or specific objectives after the closer analysis provided by this step. (See the second and third columns of Tables 6–2, 6–4, and 6–6.) Following is an example using the general objective stated in step 3 "Interprets scientific principles":

a. defends procedures in problem solving
b. distinguishes between scientific facts and theories
c. identifies correct and incorrect problem-solving procedures in the work of others

Note that the conditions for good objectives are clear in the example; that is, both the general and specific objectives are clear, since they use a verb and they define observable learning results. Satisfactory performance of the task can be shown by the student's ability to apply the inquiry process to his or her own problem, to summarize the process, and to identify correct and incorrect procedures in the work of other students. Certainly there could be other learning results for this problem, but this one should serve as an example.

5. *Review and evaluate objectives in terms of their comprehensiveness, coherence, and contribution to the science lesson unit or program.* The evaluation should identify any imbalance between levels of objectives or domains. Are all your objectives at the lower levels of the cognitive domain? We hope not. (Use Tables 6–2, 6–4, and 6–6 to help in the review.)

SUMMARY

It is important to have good objectives for science teaching. Without objectives, teaching becomes a confused and directionless experience, frustrating to the teacher, and ineffective for the students. Recent decades saw increased attention to stating objectives in performance terms. Good objectives include a statement that uses action verbs, signifies learning results in observable or measurable terms, describes the conditions under which the performance can be expected, and indicates the level of attainment needed to satisfy the objective. Objectives often are divided into cognitive, affective, and psychomotor types. The first pertains to conceptual understandings or knowledge objectives. The second refers to attitudes, feelings, interests, and appreciations. Psychomotor objectives refer to skills and competencies that involve manipulation, muscular coordination, or sensory achievements.

The steps in preparing objectives are as follows: (1) review your general intentions; (2) select the content; (3) write general objectives; (4) write specific objectives; and (5) review your objectives for comprehensiveness, coherence, and contribution to the lesson.

The use of clearly stated objectives in science teaching is significant. Although critics have cited certain pitfalls to be avoided, the overall effect of good objectives appears to be beneficial. Science teachers are more conscious of the performance they expect from their students. Evaluation becomes more precise. Progress toward the attainment of goals is more easily measurable. Science teaching assumes a quality that is more satisfying and defensible.

◆

REFERENCES

1. Peter W. Hewson and others, Determining the Conceptions of Teaching Science Held by Experienced High School Science Teachers, JRST, 32 (5) (1995): 503–520.
2. Ken Appleton, "Analysis and Description of Students' Learning During Science Classes Using a Constructivist-Based Model," *Journal of Research in Science Teaching,* 34 (3) (1997): 303–318.
3. Ken Appleton and Hilary Asoko, "A Case Study of a Teacher's Progress Toward Using a Constructivist View of Learning to Improve Teaching in Elementary Science," Science Education 80 (2) (1996): 165–180.
4. Jay K. Hackett, "Constructivism: Hands On and Minds On," *Science Matters* (Staff Development Series, Macmillan-McGraw Hill, 1992).
5. *Ibid.*
6. *Ibid.*
7. Biological Sciences Curriculum Study, "Innovative Science Education" (Colorado College, Colorado Springs, CO, September, 1992).
8. Benjamin Bloom et al., *A Taxonomy of Educational Objectives: Handbook, 1, The Cognitive Domain* (New York: David McKay, 1950).
9. David Krathwohl and others, *Taxonomy of Educational Objectives: Handbook 2, Affective Domain* (New York: David McKay, 1965).
10. R. Kibler and others, *Behavioral Objective and Instruction* (Boston: Allyn & Bacon, 1970).
11. Norman Gronlund, *Stating Behavioral Objectives for Classroom Instruction* (New York: Macmillan, 1970).

1) G   Cognitive   Know + Comprehending
2) G   psychomotor
3) NO
*4) G   Affective
5) F   emphasis on teacher
6) NO -
7) G to F Cognitive - Knowing
8) G   - psychomotor - manipulating
9) G   ## psychomotor - communicating
10) G - Cognitive - Applying
11) NO - Affective domain - actions
12) no I don't think one - more Affective domain - actions
13) P - psycomotor
14) *P - cognitive n affective
15) F - Affective - Characterizing
16) P - Cognitive - Know
17) * P - emphasis on teacher
18) NO - Affective domain - Actions
19) F - Cognitive - Knowing
20) P - Cognitive -
21) No - affective - actions
22) NO
23) NO
24) P
25) G + F - Cognitive - ?

◆ ———————————— **INVESTIGATING SCIENCE TEACHING** ———————————— ◆

ACTIVITY 6–1
OBJECTIVES OF SCIENCE TEACHING

Directions:

1. In the blank provided before each statement of objectives, indicate your evaluation of each. Is it excellent (E), good (G), fair (F), poor (P), or not an objective (NO)? Complete this portion individually.

2. Review your individual responses in a small group of three or four persons. At this point you should discuss why you evaluated the objectives the way you did.

3. As a class, review the strengths and weaknesses of the objectives as you presently understand them.

Objectives:

_____ 1. Describe the relationship between pressure and volume of an enclosed gas and predict either variable when the other is changed independently.

_____ 2. Demonstrate skill in setting up science laboratory materials.

_____ 3. Know science.

_____ 4. Appreciate the nature of scientific inquiry.

_____ 5. Teach students the concept of density.

_____ 6. Enjoy interacting with friends in science class.

_____ 7. Given a scientific problem, define variables, formulate hypotheses, and test the hypotheses.

_____ 8. Handle a microscope properly.

_____ 9. Record data appropriately.

_____ 10. At the completion of the lesson, prepare a growth curve showing the relationship of the age of a bacterial culture to the density of organisms and predict the results of continued growth.

_____ 11. Really show curiosity.

_____ 12. Show scientific attitudes (for example, openness, reality testing, risk-taking, objectivity, precision, perseverance).

_____ 13. Perform skillfully while working in the laboratory.

_____ 14. Judge the logical consistency of a scientific theory.

_____ 15. Display habits of safety.

_____ 16. Know common scientific terms.

_____ 17. To demonstrate to the students different geologic processes.

_____ 18. Having fun in science.

_____ 19. To identify energy chains in a community.

_____ 20. Is able, upon completion of the lesson, to draw, label, and explain it.

_____ 21. Science teaching should make students aware of the relationship between the scientific enterprise and society.

_____ 22. At the completion of this lesson the student should understand the meaning of science as it relates to the good life.

_____ 23. Operational definition of scientific truth.

_____ 24. The student shows the scientific attitude of perseverance by pursuing a problem to its solution.

_____ 25. Understands the basic principle of density.

    a. States the principle in his or her own words.

    b. Give an example of the principle from life, physical, and earth science.

    c. Distinguish between correct and incorrect applications of the principle.

CURRICULUM PERSPECTIVES

When you think of the science curriculum, what do you think of? Is it expressions of what students *should learn;* that is, the content of district guidelines, course syllabi, and science textbooks? Is this curriculum made up of the *experiences* students have with laboratory investigations, computer programs, readings, and discussions that science teachers present to students? Or is the science curriculum the knowledge, values, and skills that students actually *learn* as a result of all the varied experiences in a school science program? The science curriculum may consist of all of these. Certainly, you can find examples of them in any school system or science classroom. The three perspectives just mentioned—the *intended* science curriculum, the *taught* science curriculum, and the *learned* science curriculum—all contribute to an understanding of what we mean by the science curriculum.

Think of other questions. What should be emphasized in the students' experiences with science? Should the emphasis be on science principles and concepts? Should the curriculum emphasize scientific inquiry and processes of science? Should science teachers orient the curriculum toward science- and technology-related social issues? How would you justify answers to these questions?

Should you consider different orientations for science curricula at middle schools and high schools? You can see that an answer to the lead question of this section—When you think of the science curriculum, what do you think of?—involves much more than the science textbook. The science curriculum consists of the science content, your expected actions and teaching behaviors, the students' experiences, the educational technologies, the laboratories, and the textbook. As a science teacher you have the responsibility of organizing and orchestrating the curriculum for students.

Your career as a science teacher will include improving the science curriculum in your school. The chapters in this section on Curriculum Perspectives provide you with information and understanding about the science curriculum and help you answer some of the questions we posed in this introduction. Beyond background information on middle and high school curriculum, we have included examples of instructional materials originally supported by the NSF and generally aligned with national standards.

By now you probably recognize that curriculum is really more than content. Your curriculum includes science content, manipulative skills, attitudes you wish students to develop, the context or environment of the classroom, various teaching strategies, and the means you use to assess student progress. There will be a difference between the science curriculum represented in your school district syllabus, the national standards, state and local frameworks, science textbooks, and what your students learn. Discussing the curriculum is more complex than it may seem. Rather than resolve all the issues surrounding curriculum, in these chapters we direct attention to the national standards and benchmarks, instructional materials representing different courses of study you may encounter, and a general process for the design and development of curriculum.

CHAPTER

7

DESIGNING SCHOOL SCIENCE CURRICULUM

In this chapter we first provide some background on middle and high school curriculum reform. Second, we introduce contemporary curriculum frameworks: *Science for All Americans*,[1] *Benchmarks for Science Literacy*[2], and the *National Science Education Standards*.[3] Finally, in the latter part of the chapter, we discuss processes for designing a school science curriculum.

A BACKGROUND ON CURRICULUM REFORM

Adolescence is a period of significant physical, intellectual, social, and emotional development. The fact that adolescence generally spans the years of secondary education makes understanding this period generally important, but of particular importance is the period of middle school. Education during the middle school years, generally from ages 10 to 14, must extend the experiences of elementary school. The goals, curriculum, and instruction for science should be conceptualized and implemented as unique and congruent with the particular needs of the developing adolescent.

History of the Junior High

In the latter part of the nineteenth century, most elementary schools included grades 1 through 8 while high schools included grades 9 through 12. By 1920, about 80 percent of students graduating from high school had experienced eight years of elementary school and four years of high school. Although the schools were actually structured in this eight-four plan,

leading educators continually debated school organization for three decades beginning in the 1890s. Junior high schools, or school systems with six years of elementary school, three years of junior high school, and three years of high school, emerged in the early 1900s. Not until the 1918 Commission on the Reorganization of Secondary Education (CRSE) did the junior high become firmly established in the American educational system. The 1918 CRSE report, *Cardinal Principles of Secondary Education*, stated:

> We, therefore, recommend a reorganization of the school system whereby the first six years shall be devoted to elementary education designed to meet the needs of pupils approximately 6 to 12 years of age, and the second six years to secondary education designed to meet the needs of pupils approximately 12 to 18 years of age. The six years to be devoted to secondary education may well be divided into two periods which may be designated as the junior and senior periods.[4]

With the CRSE report, the concept of junior high schools was established. Their numbers grew, from an estimated 800 junior high schools in the United States in 1920 to 1,787 by 1930. The reasons for the rapid increase of junior high schools included shortages of facilities and economic restraints placed on schools between World War I and World War II. Justifications for junior high programs cited the needs of adolescents, the transition to high school, the elimination of dropouts, and vocational preparation. By 1940, prominent educators had developed a rationale for the junior high school. W. T. Gruhn and N. R. Douglas summarize the essential functions of junior high schools as:

104

◆ *Integration*. Basic skills, attitudes, and understanding learned previously should be coordinated into effective behaviors.

◆ *Exploration*. Individuals should explore special interests, aptitudes, and abilities for educational opportunities, vocational decisions, and recreational choices.

◆ *Guidance*. Assistance should be provided for students making decisions regarding education, careers, and social adjustment.

◆ *Differentiation*. Educational opportunities and facilities should provide for varying backgrounds, interests, and needs of the students.

◆ *Socialization*. Education should prepare early adolescents for participation in a complex democratic society.

◆ *Articulation*. Orientation of the program should provide a gradual transition from preadolescent (elementary) education to a program suited to the needs of adolescents.[5]

In reality, most science teachers were trained for the high school and had little desire to teach in junior high schools. A junior high school teaching job was perceived as a stepping stone to a high school position. Most educators forgot or ignored the important goals of education for early adolescents, and education in grades 7, 8, and 9 became scaled-down versions of grades 10, 11, and 12.

Science Curriculum in Junior High Schools

General science was the course offered in the ninth grade of eighty-four schools when the first junior high schools came into existence. Begun in the decade 1910–1920, the course was designed to satisfy the needs and interests of students in early adolescence. The first course was established through research and was designed to fill a perceived need.

Junior high school science encountered several difficulties. For one, there was a shortage of well-trained general science teachers. Many teachers at this level were physics, chemistry, and biology teachers whose primary interest was not the problems of junior high school science. Second, teachers in other disciplines, such as English, mathematics, and physical education, were recruited to teach science. For these reasons, the general science texts for these grades were written in an effort to relieve these problems, but the variations in school and grade-level organization, such as six-three-three, eight-two-two, and eight-four, necessitated much repetition of science topics to produce universally saleable textbooks.

Deficiencies also existed in equipment and facilities for teaching science. Many science classes were taught in ordinary classrooms without water or gas outlets and without adequate facilities for demonstrations and experiments. Further, there was no clear knowledge of what junior high school science should actually accomplish. Objectives ranged from "preparation for the rigorous science courses in the senior high school" to "general education for good citizenship." Science educators and teachers gave considerable thought to development of attitudes and interests. Some felt that general science should be exploratory in nature. Courses designed on this premise became rapid surveys of chemistry, physics, astronomy, meteorology, biology, and geology. Others believed that students should study the applications of science in the world around them. Courses of this kind centered on home appliances, transportation, communication, health problems, and natural resources.

Enrollments in general science grew to about 65 percent of the ninth-grade classes by 1956 then declined as new courses began to permeate the ninth grade and as the seventh and eighth grades took over more of the general science offerings.[6]

Usually junior high school science is organized in one of three patterns: (1) a one-, two-, or three-year program called general science; (2) a three-year program in which life, physical, and earth sciences are taught individually for a year each; (3) a one-, two-, or three-year program of integrated or thematically organized science. One of the first two patterns is found in the majority of schools.[7] Revision of junior high school science courses through national curriculum studies of the 1960s did not occur until late in the reform movement. Attention centered on the senior high school courses. The reform movement of the 1960s and 1970s made no effort to improve general science. In fact, many educators hoped that by implementing new life, earth, and physical science programs, the traditional general science program would eventually be replaced. This did not occur.

Emergence of Middle Schools

During the 1960s, several factors contributed to the emergence of middle schools as an alternative to junior high schools. Those factors included general criticisms of the schools and a need to increase the quality of education; an emphasis on curriculum improvement in science, mathematics, and foreign language; renewed interest in preparation for college; recognition of Jean Piaget's work in developmental psychology; the need to eliminate *de facto* racial segregation; the need to restructure schools due to overcrowding; and a general desire to improve education. These and other factors contributed to an increase from 100 middle schools in 1960 to over 5,000 in 1980. In 1988, there were 12,000 separate middle schools with an estimated enrollment of 8,000,000 students.

The middle school represents an important conceptual and physical change in the American educational system. Some of the important characteristics of the middle school were described in *The Status of Middle School and Junior High School Sciences:*[8]

♦ a program specifically designed for pre- and early adolescents;
♦ a program that encourages exploration and personal development;
♦ a positive and active learning environment;
♦ a schedule that is flexible with respect to time and grouping;
♦ a staff that recognizes students' needs, motivations, fears, and goals;
♦ an instructional approach that is varied;
♦ an emphasis on acquiring essential knowledge, skills, and attitudes in a sequential and individual manner;
♦ an emphasis on developing decision-making and problem-solving skills; and
♦ interdisciplinary learning and team teaching.

Middle schools, in structure and function, have many advantages, as follows:

♦ The middle school has a unique status; the school and program are not junior to another program.
♦ Specific subjects, like science and mathematics, can be introduced at lower grades by specialists.
♦ Developing new middle schools provides the impetus for redesigning goals, curriculum, and instruction for the early adolescent learner.
♦ Developing of middle schools can facilitate changes in teacher certification standards, and subsequently teacher education programs.
♦ Some discipline problems can be eliminated through different groupings of students, primarily the inclusion of some younger students.
♦ Middle schools can be designed to provide greater guidance and counseling at the time it is needed.

High School Science Curriculum in Transition

In an earlier chapter we reviewed the history and major programs developed during the Golden Age of science education. We now turn attention to the present era of reform.

We should first note that in about half of the states in the United States, the high school science curriculum is selected at the local level by science teachers, administrators, and school boards. In making their decisions, they use suggestions and guidelines from national frameworks and policies (such as the national standards) and state departments of education. Even with

significant autonomy, recent NSF studies have shown two things: there is considerable uniformity of programs, and the curriculum has not changed significantly in recent history.

Typically, the senior high school science curriculum is biology at the tenth grade and chemistry and physics at the eleventh and twelfth grade levels, respectively. In 2000, Horizon Research conducted a study funded by NSF that indicated that approximately 30 percent of the science courses offered in grades 9–12 are first-year biology courses. Nineteen percent of the courses are first-year chemistry, 10 percent are first-year physics, and physical science and earth science account for 7 percent each. The remaining courses fall out with 9 percent of high school offerings covering general, integrated, or coordinated science and 11 percent including advanced courses in biology, chemistry, or physics.[9]

By nature of the traditional emphasis on science facts and vocabulary, little attention is paid to the goals of scientific inquiry, investigation, or analytical thinking. A recent review of the inquiry goal in science teaching found that teachers gave little attention to the aim of inquiry and associated skills.[10] Despite the research[11] supporting the effectiveness of the NSF-funded programs from the Golden Age (see Chapter 3), school curricula are dominated by basic science concepts with less emphasis on the nature of science and the conducting of scientific inquiries.[12] Subsequently, in the early 1990s, the NSF began funding proposals to develop a new generation of programs for high school science.

FRAMEWORKS FOR SCIENCE CURRICULUM

Several frameworks for curriculum have significantly influenced state and local reform of middle school and high school science programs. Those frameworks include the AAAS reports *Science for All Americans and Benchmarks for Science Literacy,*[13] and the *National Science Education Standards.*[14]

Science for All Americans

Late in the 1980s, F. James Rutherford established Project 2061 at AAAS. He designed Project 2061 to take a long-term, large-scale view of education reform in the sciences. This reform is based on the goal of scientific literacy. The core of *Science for All Americans* and in 1993 the subsequent publication *Benchmarks for Science Literacy* consist of recommendations by a distinguished group of scientists and educators about what understandings and habits of mind are essential for all citizens in a scientifically literate society.

Project 2061 staff used the reports of five independent scientific panels. In addition, Project 2061 staff sought the advice of a large and diverse array of consultants and reviewers—scientists, engineers, mathematicians, historians, and educators. The process took more than three years, involved hundreds of individuals, and culminated in the publication of *Science for All Americans* and the characterization of scientific literacy. Thus, the project's recommendations are presented in the form of basic learning goals for American students. A premise of Project 2061 is that science teachers do not need to teach more; they should teach less so that content can be taught better.

Science for All Americans covers an array of topics. Many already are common in school curricula (for example, the structure of matter, the basic functions of cells, prevention of disease, communications technology, and different uses of numbers). However, the treatment of such topics differs from traditional approaches in two ways. One difference is that boundaries between traditional subject-matter categories are softened and connections are emphasized through the use of important conceptual themes, such as systems, evolution, cycles, and energy. Transformations of energy, for example, occur in physical, biological, and technological systems; and evolutionary change appears in stars, organisms, and societies. A second difference is that the amount of detail that students are expected to learn is less than in traditional science, mathematics, and technology courses. Key concepts and thinking skills are emphasized instead of specialized vocabulary and memorized procedures. The ideas not only make sense at a simple level but also provide a lasting foundation for learning more science. Details are treated as a means of enhancing, not guaranteeing, students' understanding of a general idea.

Recommendations in *Science for All Americans* include topics that are not common in school curricula. Among those topics are the nature of the scientific enterprise and how science, mathematics, and technology relate to one another and to the social system in general. The report also calls for understanding something of the history of science and technology.

NATIONAL SCIENCE EDUCATION STANDARDS AND BENCHMARKS FOR SCIENCE LITERACY

In previous chapters we introduced the *National Science Education Standards* (NSES). In this section we direct attention to the *content standards,* in particular those for grades 5–8 and 9–12. (See Figures 7-1 and 7-2.) These standards describe the knowledge, understandings, and abilities that students should develop as a result of their educational experiences. They also represent one aspect of a comprehensive vision of science education, which also includes science teaching and assessment. We state this to make the point that as you consider the science curriculum, it is imperative to consider more than content. You also should review teaching and assessment in the consideration of any commercial program or the design of your local science curriculum.

Figures 7-1 and 7-2 present the conceptual organizers for the content standards. As you consider curriculum for middle school science, you should try to incorporate opportunities for students to develop the fundamental understandings and abilities associated with these conceptual organizers.

In 1993, Project 2061 also released *Benchmarks for Science Literacy,* based on *Science for All Americans.* The benchmarks consist of specific goals and objectives for science curriculum. Many local school districts and some national organizations began using the benchmarks for different models of science curriculum. Figure 7-3 presents the major conceptual organizers for benchmarks.

SOME CONSIDERATIONS IN THE DESIGN OF SCHOOL SCIENCE CURRICULA

The content standards presented in both the *National Standards* and *Benchmarks* elaborate what students should understand and be able to do in natural science, and the personal and social context that should be considered in the design of science curriculum. These standards emphasize inquiry-oriented activities, connections between science and technology, and the history and nature of science as students develop an understanding of fundamental ideas and abilities in science. The content standards of NSES represent one component of a comprehensive vision of the science curriculum, a vision that also includes science teaching, assessment, professional development, school programs, and the educational system. If you only review and use the content standards and ignore other standards, for example, on teaching and assessment, or only use a subset of content—such as subject matter for physical, life, and earth science—then the use of the *National Science Education Standards* in the science curriculum is incomplete.

Many different individuals and groups use the content standards for a variety of purposes. However, there are some groups who use them immediately and concretely—for example, curriculum developers, science supervisors at state and local levels, and classroom teachers of science. The concepts and understandings

Unifying Concepts and Processes	Science As Inquiry	Physical Science	Life Science	Earth and Space Science	Science and Technology	Science in Personal and Social Perspectives	History and Nature of Science
Systems, Order, and Organization	Abilities of Scientific Inquiry	Properties and Changes in Properties of Matter	Structure and Function in Living Systems	Structure of the Earth System	Abilities of Technological Design	Personal Health	Science As a Human Endeavor
Change, Constancy, and Measurement	Understandings of Scientific Inquiry	Motions and Forces	Reproduction and Heredity	Earth's History	Understandings About Science and Technology	Populations, Resources, and Environments	Nature of Science
Evolution and Equilibrium		Transfer of Energy	Regulation and Behavior	Earth in the Solar System		Natural Hazards	History of Science
Form and Function			Populations and Ecosystems			Risks and Benefits	
			Diversity and Adaptations of Organisms			Science and Technology in Society	

FIGURE 7–1   Conceptual Organizers from *National Science Education Standards* for Grades 5–8

Unifying Concepts and Processes	Science As Inquiry	Physical Science	Life Science	Earth and Space Science	Science and Technology	Science in Personal and Social Perspectives	History and Nature of Science
Systems, Order, and Organization	Abilities Necessary to Do Scientific Inquiry	Structure of Atoms	The Cell	Energy in the Earth System	Abilities of Technological Design	Personal and Community Health	Science As a Human Endeavor
Evidence, Models, and Explanation	Understandings About Scientific Inquiry	Structure and Properties of Matter	Molecular Basis of Heredity	Geochemical Cycles	Understandings About Science and Technology	Population Growth	Nature of Scientific Knowledge
Change, Constancy, and Measurement		Chemical Reactions	Biological Evolution	Origin and Evolution of the Earth System		Natural Resources	Historical Perspectives
Evolution and Equilibrium		Motions and Forces	Interdependence of Organisms	Origin and Evolution of the Universe		Environmental Quality	
Form and Function		Conservation of Energy and Increase in Disorder	Matter, Energy, and Organization in Living Systems			Natural and Human-Induced Hazards	
		Interactions of Energy and Matter	Behavior of Organisms			Science and Technology in Local, National, and Global Challenges	

FIGURE 7–2 Conceptual Organizers from *National Science Education Standards* for Grades 9–12

The Nature of Science	The Nature of Mathematics	The Nature of Technology	The Physical Setting

The Scientific Worldview
Scientific Inquiry
The Scientific Enterprise
	Patterns and Relationships
	Mathematics, Science,
	  and Technology
	Mathematical Inquiry
		Technology and Science
		Design and Systems
		Issues in Technology
			The Universe
			The Earth
			Processes That Shape the
			  Earth
			Energy Transformations
			Motion
			Forces of Nature

The Living Environment	The Human Organism	Human Society	The Designed World

Diversity of Life
Heredity
Cells
Interdependence of Life
Flow of Matter and
  Energy
Evolution of Life
	Human Identity
	Human Development
	Basic Functions
	Learning
	Physical Health
	Mental Health
	Group Interdependence
		Cultural Effects on Behavior
		Group Behavior
		Social Change
		Political and Economic
		  Systems
		Social Conflict
			Agriculture
			Materials and
			  Manufacturing
			Energy Sources and Use
			Communication
			Information Processing
			Health
			Technology

The Mathematical World	Historical Perspectives	Common Themes	Habits of Mind

Numbers
Symbolic Relationships
Shapes
Uncertainty
Reasoning
	Displacing Earth from
	  the Center of the Universe
	Uniting the Heavens
	  and Earth
	Relating Matter and Energy
	  and Time and Space
	Extending Time
	Moving the Continents
	Understanding Fire
	Splitting the Atom
	Explaining the Diversity
	  of Life
	Discovering Germs
	Harnessing Power
		Systems
		Models
		Constancy and Change
		Scale
			Values and Attitudes
			Computation and
			  Estimation
			Manipulation and
			  Observation
			Communication Skills
			Critical-Response Skills

FIGURE 7–3 Conceptual Organizers from *Benchmarks for Science Literacy*

described in the content standards do not represent a science curriculum. Content is what students should learn. Curriculum includes the way content is organized, what is emphasized, how it is taught, and how it is assessed. The science curriculum includes a structure, organization, balance, and presentation of the content in the classroom, and the curriculum can be organized in many different ways. The national standards indicate what should be learned, not how content should be organized in school science programs.

As you think about your science curricula, teaching, and assessment and begin incorporating the *National Science Education Standards,* consider the following criteria:

◆ Content standards must be used in coordination with the standards on teaching and assessment. Using the content standards with traditional teaching and assessment strategies misrepresents the in-

tentions of the *National Science Education Standards.*

◆ Science content, at the level of standards, cannot be eliminated. For instance, students should have opportunities to learn "Science in Personal and Social Perspectives" and "History and Nature of Science" in the school science program.

◆ Science content, at the level of conceptual organizers, cannot be eliminated. For instance, "Biological Evolution" cannot be eliminated from the life science standards.

◆ Science content can be added to elaborate conceptual organizers. In the translation of content to curriculum, the connections, depth, detail, and selection of topics can be varied as appropriate for students and school science programs.

The content standards, like the discipline of science itself, will continue to change. The national standards identify important and enduring ideas rather than current topics and contemporary research. The conceptual organizers, fundamental understandings, and abilities outlined in the national standards will provide students with basic concepts, a knowledge base, and skills that will continually improve their scientific literacy.

The *National Science Education Standards* and other reports on science education have identified important outcomes for all students. Although there are differences among the reports, they represent considerable agreement on the essential outcomes within the domains of science education. The *National Science Education Standards* incorporate many outcomes of the AAAS report. If you are actively involved in science curriculum, you should not view these as mutually exclusive reports. Having said this, it is also important to understand that the *National Science Education Standards* and the AAAS reports were developed over extended periods of time; had input from thousands of scientists, engineers, science educators, and science teachers; and used an overall conceptual framework for scientific literacy.

DESIGNING YOUR SCIENCE CURRICULUM

Discussion in this chapter has been directed toward national policies and the implications for development of instructional materials. In some cases, national groups will develop new programs. In these cases, large-scale projects will require a team of scientists, science educators, and classroom teachers of science. Often with the help of major funding, primarily from government agencies such as the NSF, materials are developed, field-tested, revised, field-tested again, revised, and then published. This is one approach to curriculum development. This model of curricular reform can be characterized as (1) occurring at a national or state level, (2) being heavily funded, and (3) approached from the top

down—that is, developed and published first and then implemented by classroom teachers.

Though there is a need for improvement, curriculum development in the near future will also be (1) at the local or district level; (2) funded within the usual budgets of schools and school districts, perhaps with some assistance from state, federal, or private agencies; and (3) approached from the bottom up—that is, initiated and developed by classroom teachers and then implemented within the school district.

The second approach to curriculum development is a smaller scale approach to change. Here an individual science teacher or team of science teachers is appointed to initiate, develop, and implement a science curriculum. This could encompass anything from a minor revision of an extant course to development of a new K–12 science program for the entire school district.

The new demands for educational improvement—combined with the level of funding at the national level for the "No Child Left Behind" legislation and the implementation of state standards and assessments—suggest that the burden for change will increasingly fall to the local school district and science-teaching personnel.

There is a third approach to curriculum development. The adoption of new science textbooks, software, and kit materials represents the selection and implementation of a science curriculum. The curriculum then can be *adapted* to align with the needs and requirements of local school districts and science teachers. In this approach, the emphasis is on adaptation through professional development.

With the preceding paragraphs as background and rationale, we direct your attention to a discussion that will be useful to science teachers confronting the task of designing a curriculum. We begin by noting several resources that form the basis of our discussion, starting with Ralph Tyler's 1949 classic, *Basic Principles of Curriculum and Instruction*.[15] More than 50 years of age, Tyler's model (see Figure 7–4) has not lost its vitality as

FIGURE 7–4 Ralph Tyler's Approach to Curriculum Development

I.   Examination of Traditional Factors Influencing the Curriculum to Determine an Initial Set of Instructional Goals
  • Examine student interests and characteristics
  • Analyze social trends and issues
  • Synthesize information from disciplines
II. Development of Preliminary Curriculum Program
  • Synthesize objectives from step I into a cohesive program
III. Reconsideration of Objectives in Terms of Philosophy and Psychology
  • Review program objectives for congruence with curriculum designer's philosophy
  • Review program objectives for congruence with current learning theories
IV. Development of Curriculum Program
  • Arrange curriculum objectives into an organized program
V.   Evaluation of Learning Experiences

an important process for identifying curricular objectives and learning experiences. This model is applicable today because it does not suggest a program; it outlines procedures for developing a curriculum. The utility and simplicity of Tyler's model is found in four basic questions:

- ◆ What educational purposes should the school seek to attain?
- ◆ How can learning experiences likely to attain these objectives be selected?
- ◆ How can learning experiences be effectively organized?
- ◆ How can we determine whether these purposes are being attained?[16]

There also are several helpful books that address various aspects of curriculum development: *Developing a Quality Curriculum* by Alan Glatthorn,[17] *Analyzing the Curriculum* by George Posner,[18] and *Understanding by Design* by Grant Wiggins and Jay McTighe.[19]

Although this discussion is about curriculum development by individual teachers and local teams of teachers, the national projects do have some important processes and advice. Joseph McInerney, director of the Biological Sciences Curriculum Study, outlined several criteria for the selection of content in curriculum development. These criteria are paraphrased:

1. How well does the information being considered illustrate the basic, enduring principles of the scientific discipline?
2. Do other teachers, administrators, and parents perceive the proposed materials as useful and important?
3. What is the relationship between the proposed curriculum materials and the prevailing context of general education?[20]

Asking and answering questions such as these will help with the difficult issue of deciding what content should be included and ensure that the program is understandable and acceptable to the scientific and educational communities.

The following discussion is our synthesis of approaches and recommended steps for redesigning and implementing a science curriculum.

 Visit http://www.prenhall.com/trowbridge and select Topic 1—Science Teaching Standards. Select "Web Links" and find the link on "Planning and Development of the School Science Program." Click on Science and Mathematics Advancement and Resources for Teachers (Smart), which gives a ten-point action plan for implementing change within a school district. Write a short synopsis of the suggested points and submit to your instructor using Electronic Bluebook.

Step 1—Review Influences on the Science Curriculum

In the first phase of curriculum improvement, you should spend some time reading, thinking, and discussing three traditional influences on the curriculum—science, society, and students. What are the recent advances in science and technology that are important for students to use in their personal lives and as citizens? Obviously, all scientific knowledge and technology advances cannot be incorporated into school science programs. Science teachers must decide what knowledge is of most worth.

What are the trends, issues, and problems in society that are related to science and technology? Reviewing some of these issues provides another goal component of the science program. An examination of student needs, interests, characteristics, and processes of learning is also essential. Here you can include the unique needs of students in your school or district. After reviewing current priorities regarding science, society, and students you can state a first set of general objectives. This first step is presented graphically in Figure 7–5, a flowchart for reviewing

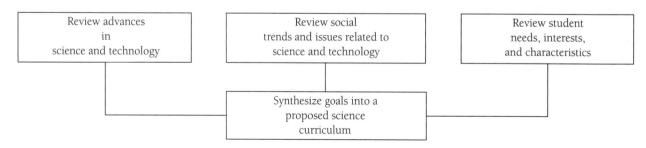

FIGURE 7–5   Curriculum Review and Synthesis Flowchart

major influences on the science curriculum. Figure 7–6 provides a flowchart of areas to review when considering the curriculum in the context of the school science programs.

Step 2—Synthesize Goals into a Proposed Science Curriculum

This phase consists of bringing the objectives identified in the first phase into a proposed curriculum framework. At this point, do not make an effort to evaluate or filter the objectives based on various constraints such as time, personnel, or budget. Synthesize your objectives into a program that has a scope and sequence, as well as classroom facilities, materials, equipment, instructional approach, and evaluation components. This can be an exciting exercise, so use your creativity.

Step 3—Describe the Present Science Curriculum

One mistake often made in local curriculum development is the omission of any consideration of the present curriculum. What are the present goals? What is the current textbook? What about the scope and sequence of the present program? What about the role and use of computers in the science program?

Reviewing the present program also includes reviewing any special topics, units, or lessons that you develop. This phase of development is a matter-of-fact approach, outlining what exists in terms of materials, equipment, time, space, budget, and your competencies. Use the categories of such as goals, instructional materials, teacher interests and competencies, classroom facilities and equipment, instructional methods, and assessment. This phase is represented in Figure 7–7, which is a chart for recording the proposed and present program characteristics.

Step 4—Analyze the Discrepancies Between the Proposed and Present Science Curriculum

Using the same categories—that is, material resources, instructional methods, classroom facilities, and teacher interests and competencies—provides a convenient way to identify the differences between where your science curriculum is and where you want it to be. As a result of this stage, you should have a good idea of what is needed in order to develop your science curriculum.

Step 5—Evaluate the Proposed Science Curriculum

This step is critical. This is the point at which you reevaluate what you propose doing in terms of what is possible. The phase is infused with reality. Things such as educational philosophy, learning theory, time, budget, and any other real-world items should be factored into the possible science curriculum. Screening everything at this point sets the stage for the review, purchase, development, or synthesis of materials; changes in goals; and suggestions for in-service programs appropriate to your proposed curriculum. At the end of this phase you should have a realistic picture of what can be done, who is required to do what, and how long it will take. The chart in Figure 7–8 provides one way to organize this information.

Step 6—Develop and Implement the Science Curriculum

There are two things to remember at this point. First, you do not have to develop the program *de novo*. You can select new materials and adapt materials in the current program. Second, the new science curriculum does not have to be developed in a week, a month, or even a year. As a result of your analysis and synthesis to this point, you should have a long-range plan for

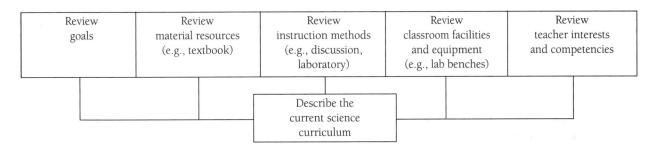

FIGURE 7–6 Curriculum Description Flowchart

	Proposed	Present
Goals (e.g., learn science knowledge and processes)		
Grade Levels (e.g., 5–8, 9–12)		
Time Requirements (e.g., 55 min./day at 9–12)		
Student Population (e.g., all students, at-risk)		
Type of Schools (e.g., urban, rural)		
Academic Subjects (e.g., life science, integrated)		
Description of Program (e.g., STS, standards-based)		
Relationship to Other Subjects (e.g., complements health, supports reading)		
Curriculum Materials (e.g., textbook, student modules)		
Instructional Emphasis (e.g., reading, active learning)		
Instructional Strategies (e.g., reading, active learning)		
Instructional Model (e.g., 5E model)		
Education Materials (e.g., kits, local equipment)		
Educational Courseware (e.g., MBI use of Internet)		
Evaluation (e.g., built into instruction, end-of-unit tests)		
Implementation (e.g., concerns-based adoption model, professional development)		
STS—Science–Technology–Society		
MBL—Microcomputer-Based Laboratory		

FIGURE 7–7   Characteristics of the Proposed and Present School Science Program

your professional development; material acquisition; development of lessons, units, or modules; adoption of new textbooks; and so on. Implementation can occur over an extended period of time.

Step 7—Evaluate the Science Curriculum

From time to time it will be necessary to reevaluate the science curriculum. Ideally, you will monitor and change the science curriculum continuously. Doing this will allow you to maintain those curricular components that are appropriate to the present state of science, society, and students, while changing those aspects of the program that have become outdated and outmoded.

The seven steps we have outlined are summarized in Figure 7–9.

Up to this point the process of designing or redesigning the science program has primarily focused on materials. The success of your curriculum development also depends on the awareness, interactions, and work of the people directly and indirectly involved in the process. The materials of the science curriculum are relatively easy to change, but while changing materials is necessary, it is not sufficient. Efforts to design a new science curriculum also must take into account the beliefs, attitudes, and perceptions that teachers, administrators, and the public have about science and technology education and the particular need to design a new program.

An Analysis of the Proposed and Current Curriculum and Instruction						
	What Is the Proposed Change?	*Who Has the Responsibility to Change?*	*Where Will Change Occur?*	*What Is the Actual Form of Change?*	*How Will the Change Be Implemented?*	*What Support Is Required?*
Goals						
Grade levels						
Time requirements						
Student population						
Type of schools						
Academic subjects						
Description of program						
Relationship to other subjects						
Curriculum materials						
Instructional emphasis						
Instructional strategies						
Instructional model						
Educational courseware						
Evaluation						
Implementation						

FIGURE 7–8 Changes in the School Programs

In regard to this assertion, we suggest the addition of other components for the successful development and implementation of a science curriculum:

- Establish the need to change the science education curriculum among the science faculty and with other teachers and administrators.
- Describe the nature, direction, and realities of change to those interested and concerned—especially administrators and the public.
- Obtain endorsement and support from the principal, school board, and community.
- Require and develop materials within the budget.
- Establish a realistic timeline for development and implementation.
- Provide for released time, in-service programs, and summertime pay for personnel directly involved in the project.
- Monitor and adjust the process of development and implementation.

SUMMARY

Adolescence is a unique period in life. Throughout our educational history we have seen changes in the science

curriculum for this age group. The junior high school was created in the late 1800s, and in the late 1900s, the middle school emerged. Junior high schools were junior versions of high school programs, but the middle school curriculum is uniquely designed for the early adolescent.

Although textbooks were significantly changed during the 1960s and 1970s, the 1980s and 1990s witnessed a return to models similar to those prior to the 1960s.

In the 1980s, a new wave of educational reform was initiated. Numerous national reports on education in general and on science education in particular have stimulated new interest in the science curriculum. Of particular importance are the *National Science Education Standards* and *Benchmarks for Science Literacy*. Aspects of the new emphasis can be summarized as follows:

- Standards (national, state, local) will be the basis for school science programs.
- Inquiry will be expanded to include cognitive abilities, knowledge about scientific inquiry, and teaching strategies.
- Laboratory activities will include both holistic and reductive analysis approaches.
- Decisions about science curricula will be largely determined by science teachers in local school districts.

FIGURE 7–9 A Proposed Process for Designing a Science Curriculum

I.   Review Influences on the Science Curriculum
 ■ Look at advances in science and technology that have personal and social utility for students
 ■ Evaluate social trends and issues related to science and technology
 ■ Consider student needs, interests, and characteristics, including national concerns and local issues
 ■ Outline goals relative to the three areas reviewed

II. Synthesize Goals into a Proposed Science Curriculum
 ■ Curriculum materials
 ■ Instructional strategies
 ■ Facilities, materials, equipment
 ■ Teacher competencies
 ■ Evaluation

III. Describe the Present Science Curriculum
 ■ Goals
 ■ Curriculum materials
 ■ Instructional strategies
 ■ Facilities, materials, equipment
 ■ Teacher interests and competencies
 ■ Evaluation

IV. Analyze Discrepancies Between Proposed and Present Program
 ■ Compare differences and identify priorities in terms of categories listed above

V.   Reevaluate the Proposed Science Curriculum
 ■ Reevaluate proposed program in terms of priorities and possibilities, e.g., budget
 ■ Review proposed program in terms of educational philosophy and policies of district, school, and/or science department
 ■ Revise proposed program incorporating contemporary educational psychology, e.g., development and learning theory

VI. Development and Implementation of the Science Curriculum
 ■ Review curriculum materials appropriate for the proposed program, e.g., textbooks, teaching modules
 ■ Consider adaptation of extant materials for proposed program
 ■ Develop curriculum materials, e.g., lessons, units, modules as necessary
 ■ Implement new materials in an organized fashion

VII. Evaluation of the Science Curriculum
 ■ Monitor and adjust curriculum periodically
 ■ Repeat process of redesign of science curriculum

◆ Interrelationships and interdependence of science, technology, and society will be contexts for study.

◆ Science and technology literacy for personal, social, and civic understanding will be the primary emphasis of the secondary science curriculum.

In the 1990s, the initial wave of reforms was sustained by development and implementation of national standards and benchmarks for science education. During the 2000s "No Child Left Behind" legislation (nochildleftbehind.gov), the emphasis on accountability, and the critical role of standards provide support and direction for the improvement of science education in general and the science curriculum in particular.

To design, develop, and implement your own science curriculum, we outlined seven steps:

1. Review influences on the science curriculum.
2. Synthesize goals into a proposed science curriculum.
3. Describe the present science curriculum.
4. Analyze the discrepancies between proposed and present programs.
5. Evaluate the proposed science curriculum.
6. Develop and implement the science curriculum.
7. Evaluate the science curriculum.

◆

REFERENCES

1. American Association for the Advancement of Science (AAAS), *Science for All Americans* (Washington, DC: Author, 1996).

2. American Association for the Advancement of Science, *Benchmarks for Science Literacy* (Washington, DC: Author, 1993).

3. National Research Council, *National Standards for Science Education* (Washington, DC: Author, 1996).

4. Commission on the Reorganization of Secondary Education, *Cardinal Principles of Secondary Education*, Bulletin 1918, no. 35 (Washington, DC: U.S. Bureau of Education, 1918), pp. 12–13.

5. W. T. Gruhn and N. R. Douglas, *The Modern Junior High School,* 3d ed. (New York: The Ronald Press, 1977), p. 133.

6. A. S. Brown and E. Obourn, Offerings and Enrollments (Washington, DC: U.S. Government Printing Office, 1961).

7. Paul DeHart Hurd, James T. Robinson, Mary McConnell, and Norris Ross, *The Status of Middle School and Junior High School Science* (Center for Educational Research and Evaluation. The Biological Sciences Curriculum Study (Colorado Springs, Colorado College, CO, 1981), p. 15.

8. Paul DeHart Hurd, *The Status of Middle School and Junior High School Science,* pp. 4–5.

9. Iris R. Weiss, Eric R. Banilower, Kelly C. McMahon, P. Sean Smith. *Report of the 2000 National Survey of Science and Mathematics Education* (Status Report) (December, 2001). Chapel Hill, NC: Horizon Research, Inc. [document can be downloaded at http://2000survey.-horizon-research.com/reports/status.php]

10. Ronald D. Anderson, Reforming Science Teaching: What Research Says about Inquiry, *Journal of Science Teacher Education* 13 (1) (2002): 1–12.

11. James A. Shymansky, William Kyle, and Jennifer Alport, "The Effects of New Science Curricula on Student Performance," *Journal of Research on Science Teaching,* 20 (5), (1983): 387–404.

12. Iris R. Weiss, Eric R. Banilower, Kelly C. McMahon, P. Sean Smith. Report of the 2000 National Survey of Science and Mathematics Education (Status Report) (December, 2001). Chapel Hill, NC: Horizon Research, Inc. [document can be downloaded at http://2000survey.-horizon-research.com/reports/status.php]

13. American Association for the Advancement of Science, *Benchmarks for Science Literacy* (Washington, DC: Author, 1993).

14. National Research Council, *National Standards for Science Education* (Washington, DC: Author, 1996).

15. Ralph W. Tyler, *Basic Principles of Curriculum and Instruction* (Chicago: University of Chicago Press, 1949).

16. Tyler, *Basic Principles of Curriculum and Instruction*, p. 1.

17. Alan Glatthorn, *Developing a Quality Curriculum* (Alexandria, Virginia: ASCD, 1994).

18. George Posner, *Analyzing the Curriculum* (New York: McGraw-Hill, 1994).

19. Grant Wiggens and Jay McTighe, *Understanding by Design* (Upper Saddle River, NJ: Prentice Hall, 2000).

20. Joseph McInerney, "Curriculum Development at the Biological Sciences Curriculum Study," *Educational Leadership* (December 1986/January 1987): 24–28.

◆ ———————————— INVESTIGATING SCIENCE TEACHING ———————————— ◆

ACTIVITY 7–1
GATHERING INFORMATION ABOUT CURRICULUM MATERIALS

The publishing industry has entered an electronic age, which allows for fairly rapid revisions of textbooks and curriculum materials. One of the greater challenges you will have as a teacher is trying to stay abreast of advances in science education outside of your own classroom, school, and district. The Internet is one of the places that you can quickly gather a lot of information without traveling, writing letters, or making phone calls. Use the information below to identify the usefulness in each web site. (Please note that the addresses listed were accurate late in 2002; if they do not work when you try them, do a search for the particular organization listed instead.)

Your Task

Visit each website below and respond to the following questions:

A. What are the strengths of this site?

B. What are the limitations or weaknesses of this site?

C. When would it be useful to access the information available at this website?

D. Based on when you think it would be useful to visit this site, what would be your next step after visiting this website?

Visit These Websites

The Textbook Letter
   http://www.textbookleague.org/
   This website publishes independent appraisals of textbooks that publishers are selling. Their emphasis is on textbooks. The Textbook League was established in 1989 to support the creation and acceptance of sound schoolbooks. They publish The Textbook Letter (or TTL), which is mailed to subscribers throughout the United States. The subscribers include classroom teachers, officers of local school districts, officers of state or county education agencies, and private citizens who take a serious interest in the quality of the instruction offered in the public schools.
   Each issue of TTL is built around reviews of schoolbooks, with emphasis on middle school and high school books in history, geography, social studies, health, and the various branches of natural science. These book reviews are augmented by evaluations of classroom videos and by articles about topics that are important to people who must choose instructional materials.

NSTA Science Suppliers list
   http://www.suppliers.nsta.org/
   The National Science Teachers Association has published a supplement to its journals each year called the Science Education Suppliers Guide. This useful tool includes the names and addresses of nonprofit organizations that work in science education as well as all the contact information for publishers, suppliers of materials and lab equipment, and companies that produce software. This supplement is now available on the Internet at the address listed above.

ACTIVITY 7–2
EVALUATING MIDDLE/JUNIOR HIGH SCHOOL SCIENCE PROGRAMS

At some time in your career, you will select a new science program. This activity introduces you to that process. The form you will complete is adapted from the American Association for the Advancement of Science publication Science Books & Films.

Select three programs from the discipline and grade level you intend to teach. Review the textbooks and complete the following chart. List the textbooks you compare by author(s), title, publisher, and copyright date.

Science Program

1. _____

2. _____

3. _____

General Evaluation	N/C	Poor	Fair	Adequate	Good	Excellent
Program aligned with standards						
Content accuracy						
Content currency						
Content scope						
Structure and methods as inquiry						
Organization and coherence of program						
Labs: in text/supplementals						
Comprehensibility of narrative						
Practicality of required materials and equipment						
Summary evaluation: text and supplementals						
Teach the nature of science						
Encourage students to develop the ability to inquire						
Stimulate awareness of science, technology, and society						

1. Were the programs for middle school, junior high school, or high school?
2. How were the programs similar? Different?
3. Describe an outstanding feature of each program.
4. Describe the weakest feature of each program.
5. Which program would you select to use? Why?

THE MIDDLE SCHOOL SCIENCE CURRICULUM

This chapter and the next one describe a number of curriculum programs that are consistent with reform efforts in science education. By now you probably recognize that curriculum is really more than content. Your curriculum includes science content, opportunities to conduct scientific inquiries, attitudes you wish students to develop, the context or environment of the classroom, various teaching strategies, and the means you use to assess student progress. There will be a difference between the science curriculum represented in your school district syllabus, the national standards, state and local frameworks, science textbooks, and what your students learn. Discussing the curriculum is more complex than it may seem. Rather than resolve all the issues surrounding curriculum, we direct attention in these chapters to the ideas of rigor, focus, and coherence—three features that are essential to meaningful learning in middle and high school science programs, and three features that should be reflected in the instructional materials you are using. The curriculum analysis conducted during the Third International Mathematics and Science Study (TIMSS) indicated that one possible explanation for U.S. students' low performance at eighth and twelfth grades was the lack of coherent, focused, rigorous curriculum materials that provide every student with an opportunity to learn science.[1] In this chapter we provide overviews of instructional materials for courses of study you may encounter at the middle level, which are more coherent, rigorous, and focused than the materials used in most schools.

SCIENCE CURRICULUM IN MIDDLE SCHOOLS

The 1980s initiated a period of transition and reform for middle/junior high school programs. In 1988, the NSF issued a request for proposals to develop programs for middle school science. The NSF solicitation contained descriptions of the orientation for middle school programs. "In middle school years, [the students] should begin to develop a more disciplined approach to inquiry and experimentation—improving their ability to organize and articulate knowledge, and to approach problems systematically."[2] Included in the solicitation were some characteristics of middle school materials. Those characteristics included the following:

- integration of science with other subjects,
- hands-on experiences,
- establishment of a coherent pattern of science topics,
- capitalization on the interests of students,
- use of recent research on teaching and learning, and
- identification of standards of student achievement.

In the early 1990s, the programs developed with these NSF grants became available. We describe a number of these programs in their latest editions later in the chapter. The challenge of finding appropriate curriculum for the middle level is captured by the very characteristics that describe early adolescents who are caught in the middle of growing up. These students are young and old, mature and immature, happy and angry, exuberant and despondent all at the same time! Hurd points out the need for a science curriculum to address the personal, social, developmental, and emotional needs of middle school students.[3] He recommends that the curriculum be based on solid science, be interdisciplinary in nature, and use everyday problems, such as human health issues, as the basis for learning key science concepts.

Hurd's recommendations build on some of the ideas from the "middle school movement" that was well documented by the mid-1980s. For example, in *A Middle School Curriculum*,[4] James Beane identified an insightful question about the middle school movement. Beane had the broad, underlying conception of the middle school in mind when he asked "the curriculum question." Beane was alluding to the fact that many aspects of middle level education had been addressed, but the curriculum continued with an "absent presence" as educators continued improving various aspects of middle schools. Based on the historical transition from junior high to middle schools, it comes as no surprise to learn that many educators have deep loyalties to, and identities with, subject-matter disciplines such as science, or even more specifically, life, earth, and physical science. With this view, Beane directly asked, "What should be the curriculum of the middle school?"

Beane argues that "academic disciplines," such as science, do not answer the curriculum question. He recommends a general education, as opposed to a specialized education approach. General education focuses on the common needs, concerns, and problems of individuals and society. Implementing this position would result in a curriculum that truly recognizes the intellectual, social, emotional, and physical perspectives of early adolescents. In addition, the curriculum would include social perspectives that center on themes such as interdependence, diversity, environment, and technology.

Unfortunately, the implementation of the middle school philosophy was interpreted as curriculum without substance, and critics feared that students were not making appropriate gains academically. Some of these criticisms were valid, but there are also successful examples of rigourous curricula that are child-centered.[5] In the successful implementation of the middle school philosophy, schools make sure that their curricula address these three components of academic excellence: (1) academic rigor; (2) equity; and (3) developmental appropriateness.[6]

Recent reforms in science education call for curricula designed to support students' construction of knowledge through inquiry. This approach to teaching is most effective when supported by instructional materials designed to address teacher as well as student learning. A study conducted at Michigan State University indicated that teachers used and learned from the materials and that the features that addressed content pedagogical knowledge were used more often and more effectively than those materials that addressed either pedagogical or content knowledge only.[7] In other words, if your curriculum materials support you and the student, it is easier to teach in a manner that encourages learning.

We recognize that the needs of science teachers and school districts use materials that fall along a continuum from traditional junior high school science to contemporary middle school curricula. In the program descriptions that follow, however, we have emphasized programs that are most closely aligned with standards, research, and the coherence, rigor, and focus identified in TIMSS.

 Visit http://www.prenhall.com/trowbridge and select Topic 2—Constructivism and Learning in Science. Select "Activities and Lesson Plans" and find the link "Ask Eric," which offers a set of edited lesson plans from teachers. Write a lesson plan of your own and submit it to your instructor using the Electronic Bluebook.

Multidisiplinary Programs

EVENT-BASED SCIENCE (EBS)

The *Event-Based Science (EBS)* series is a module-based program designed for students in grades 6–9, with a focus on current events. The series has 18 modules designed to last 4–6 weeks, each focusing on different themes and concepts across the domains of earth, life, and physical sciences. The modules can be sequenced over all middle school grade levels and combined with other instructional materials in order to build a comprehensive middle school science program. One or two modules typically are used in a year, with teachers selecting particular units based on the district's science standards, the local curriculum program, the interests of the student population, and their own background knowledge in specific topics. *EBS* is not a "standalone" curriculum. By design, teachers and students have to supplement each module with additional data about a specific event from various resources included as part of the materials, or suggested by the program.

Components: Teacher's guide, student edition, videotapes

Year Published: 1995–1999

Developer: Montgomery County Public Schools, Rockville, MD

Publisher: Dale Seymour Publications

Contact Information:

Dale Seymour Publications
P.O. Box 2500
Lebanon, IN 46052
(800)237-3142
(800)526-9907
Fax: (800)393-3156
www.pearsonlearning.com
www.eventbasedscience.com

FOUNDATIONS AND CHALLENGES TO ENCOURAGE TECHNOLOGY-BASED SCIENCE (FACETS)

Foundations and Challenges to Encourage Technology-Based Science (FACETS) is a set of 24 stand-alone, interdisciplinary investigation guides. Each guide presents science, mathematics, and other curricular topics on what is called a "need-to-know" basis. The nature of the modules suggests that teachers work with other content area teachers in the school to design cross-curricular experiences for the students. Units focus on a set of problem-solving and inquiry skills that reflect the processes and strategies used by scientists in investigative research: defining a problem, finding information, testing explanations, using models and simulations, designing investigations, collecting data, analyzing and checking data, drawing conclusions, communicating findings, and reflecting and connecting. Modules typically begin with an introduction to the topic followed by an average of six activities, taking two to four weeks to complete.

> **Components:** Student edition, teacher guide, laser discs
>
> **Developer/Distributor:** Education and International Activities Division of the American Chemical Society
>
> **Year Published:** 1996
>
> **Contact Information:**
>   www.chemistry.org
>   ACS Office of Society Services
>   (800)227-5558

Technology
Link

INTEGRATED SCIENCE

Integrated Science is a multi-year program designed around thematic integrating concepts that incorporates biology, chemistry, physics, and earth/space science. The curriculum is designed as a three-year program, grades 6–8 (also referred to as IS6, IS7, and IS8). Four thematic blocks cover six weeks of material in each grade level, and each block at each grade level has a single integrating concept organized around a central theme. All of the blocks offer multiple cross-curricular opportunities. The intention of the program is that through this integration across disciplines, students can understand the connections that every concept studied has between the different disciplines and to the real world. The Integrated Science curriculum approach to teaching and learning is a spiraling sequence of blocks of material, allowing students to obtain a base of knowledge upon which to build each year.

> **Components:** Classroom telecasts, hands-on activities, student books, and performance-based assessment strategies
>
> **Developer/Publisher:** Center for Communication and Educational Technology, University of Alabama
>
> **Year Published:** current, on the web
>
> **Contact Information:**
>   info@ccet.ua.edu
>   www.ccet.ua.edu/ishome.htm

THE *JASON* PROJECT

Technology
Link

Each year, the *JASON Project*—administered by the JASON Foundation for Education—embarks on a two-week scientific expedition to a remote location. The project develops a science and technology curriculum module to prepare students to participate in the expedition using interactive telecommunication. The *JASON Project* series currently consists of nine such modules. Two recent examples are described below.

The *JASON IV. Baja California Sur* contains 21 lessons and more than 70 activities that prepared students for live-satellite participation in a March 1993 expedition to Baja California Sur to study whales in the San Ignacio Lagoon and hydrothermal vent communities in the Guaymas Basin of the Sea of Cortez. During the module, students learn about past *JASON Projects* and about the goals of the *JASON IV* expedition. They also find out about the technological innovations that make such expeditions work—for example, robotics, sonar technology, and fiber optics. They learn about the science involved in the expedition—tectonic geological processes, photosynthesis, chemosynthesis, and the physiology, behavior, and migration pattern of gray whales—as well as about the social and cultural history of Baja California and the pros and cons of whaling.

JASON VI: Island Earth, Hawaii Expedition Curriculum contains 17 lessons, 31 activities, and more than 100 exercises that prepared students for live satellite participation in a 1995 research expedition to Hawaii to study volcanoes and what they reveal about the formation of the earth and the solar system. During the module, students learn about the organization of our solar system and about island ecology. They also learn about the technological innovations, such as planetary probes, robots, satellites, remote sensing, aerial photography, fiber optics, and computer communications that accompany many of today's expeditions. They study about geoscience concepts—plate tectonics, terrestrial volcanic activity, and planetary volcanism—as well as life science concepts relevant to the expedition—animal migration, island biogeography, and adaptation. They are introduced to the history, culture, and people of Hawaii both before and after the arrival of Captain James Cook.

> **Components:** Teacher's Guide includes objectives, step-by-step teaching procedures, and a materials list for each activity, as well as background materials for the teacher, reproducible student worksheets and readings, resource lists, and a glossary. Modules may also include posters, videotapes, maps of the ocean floor, several small maps, materials for several games and simulations.

Year Published: ongoing
Developer/Distributor: The Jason Foundation for Education
Contact Information: www.jason.org

Technology KIDS NETWORK PROGRAM

Link

The Kids Network Program, developed by TERC in collaboration with the National Geographic Society (NGS), offers middle grade students an interdisciplinary approach to science topics that are globally significant. Are We Getting Enough Oxygen? How Loud Is Too Loud? Is Our Water At Risk? What Is Our Soil Good For? What Stories Do the Data Tell? NGS Kids Network is a structured, telecommunications-based science curriculum.

Components: Website
Year Published: 1999/2000
Developer/Distributor: TERC
Publisher: National Geographic Society
Contact Information: www.projects.terc.edu/ LL Series

LIFE: HERE? THERE? ELSEWHERE? THE SEARCH FOR LIFE ON VENUS AND MARS

The *Life in the Universe Series* consists of six units, including the three volumes in the *SETI Academy Planet Project.* Each book in the *SETI Academy Planet Project* is designed to be a complete unit in itself as well as a subunit of a three-unit course. During the activities in the three units, each student plays the role of a "cadet" at the SETI [Search for Extraterrestrial Intelligence] Academy, a fictitious institution. (The SETI Institute is an actual scientific organization.) *Life: Here? There? Elsewhere?* engages students in 14 sequential "missions," or chapters, which can take four to six weeks to complete. The activities are designed to explore the possibility of life on Venus or Mars and to find out about methods used to detect life in the atmosphere and soil of earth. Comparative planetology and exobiology (the study of life outside or beyond the earth) are used to help students discover that life is not always intelligent, nor is it always easy to recognize. During the unit, students construct an orbital model of the earth, Mars, Venus, and the sun, and they learn about conditions on the three planets and why the search for life in the solar system is focused on these planets.

Components: Teacher's guide includes background information, directions for activities, discussion ideas, extensions, and reproducible blackline masters. Module also includes powers-of-10 cards, a poster, and a videotape—*Voyages to Earth, Mars, and Venus.*

Year Published: 1996
Developer: SETI
Multiple Distributors/Contact Information: www.seti.org/education/Welcome.html

Libraries Unlimited/Teacher Ideas Press
Dept. 9503
P.O. Box 6633
Englewood, CO 80155
Phone: (800)237-6124
Fax: (303)220-8843

Astronomical Society of the Pacific
390 Ashton Avenue
San Francisco, CA 94112-1787
Phone (800)962-3412
Fax: (415) 337-5205

Learning Technologies, Inc.
40 Cameron Avenue
Somerville, MA 02144
Phone: (800)537-8703

A copy of each guide will be available at NASA's Teacher Resource Centers and CORE (Central Operation of Resources for Educators) Centers.

FOUNDATIONAL APPROACHES IN SCIENCE TEACHING (FAST)

The *Foundational Approaches in Science Teaching (FAST)* series is an interdisciplinary science program consisting of three courses for middle, junior, and senior high school students. Each one-year course is organized in three strands—physical science (chemistry and physics), ecology (biological and earth sciences), and relational study. The ecology and physical science strands, which provide the formal science content, are intended to be presented concurrently by alternating short sequences of investigations from each strand.

Components: Student book, teacher's guide, several reference booklets for each course, and other optional teacher support materials. An instructional guide for teachers explains the philosophy and design of the FAST program and suggests schedules, sequences, and strategies for organizing and managing classes. An evaluation guide includes tests for assessing laboratory skills and understanding of concepts and an inventory of skills and concepts.
Year Published: 1994
Developer/Publisher: Curriculum Research and Development Group, University of Hawaii
Contact Information: Curriculum Research & Development Group

University of Hawaii
1776 University Avenue
Honolulu, HI 98622
Phone: (800)799–8111
www.hawaii.edu/crdg

MIDDLE SCHOOL SCIENCE AND TECHNOLOGY, THIRD EDITION

Biological Sciences Curriculum Study (BSCS), with support from the National Science Foundation, began developing this program in 1989. The first edition was published in 1991 and the second edition in late 1998, and now a third edition is available. This program is designed to help educators accomplish the following four goals:

1. Develop middle school students' understanding of basic concepts and skills related to science and technology.
2. Increase the participation and success of underrepresented populations in middle school science classes.
3. Improve middle school students' understanding of how science and technology relate to their lives.
4. Promote the development of critical thinking and problem-solving abilities in middle school students.

This three-year curriculum uses a thematic emphasis in each year that provides a unifying understanding of the sciences across disciplines. Within each year, one particular discipline is emphasized: earth/space science, physical science, or life science. The program uses a specific instructional model characterized by the BSCS 5E instructional Model: Engage, Explore, Explain, Elaborate, Evaluate. (This model is explained in detail in Chapter 15 of this book, Models for Effective Science Teaching.) BSCS sequenced and labeled all of the student activities in the program according to the 5E instructional model based on a constructivist model of learning. One tenet of the constructivist model is that all students have experiences from which they build (or construct) knowledge. Yet, in a classroom, attempting to help each student construct knowledge based on his or her previous experiences can be an overwhelming task. The task is further complicated by the fact that each student brings a different background to a lesson. The 5E instructional model in combination with other program features provides a solution to this dilemma for science teachers. The instructional model, cooperative learning theory, and the research on successful middle schools all support using a variety of strategies in the classroom. *Middle School Science & Technology* is more than 60 percent hands-on and minds-on investigations that keep students engaged in the study of science and technology. In addition to these investigations, the curriculum includes strategies, such as simulations, debates, plays, outdoor activities, research projects, and creative writing. Many of these strategies increase the participation

and success of underrepresented groups of students in the science classroom. Researchers have noted that certain strategies and topics help increase the success of minority students; these include cooperative learning, activities that help develop spatial skills, information that helps students prepare for careers, topics that are relevant to the students and that build on their prior experiences, and the reinforcement of basic skills.[8,9]

Components: Student book, Teacher's edition. Teacher's Guide and Resource book, videotapes, test bank, and Sci-Links.

Year Published: third edition will be released in 2003-2004

Developer: Biological Sciences Curriculum Study (BSCS)

Publisher: Kendall/Hunt Publishing

Contact Information:

BSCS
5415 Mark Dabling Boulevard
Colorado Springs, CO 80918
(719)531-5550
www.bscs.org

Kendall/Hunt Publishing Company
4050 Westmark Drive
P.O. Box 1840
Dubuque, IA 52004-1840
800-KH-BOOKS (800-542-6657)
www.kendallhunt.com

SCIENCE AND TECHNOLOGY CONCEPTS FOR MIDDLE SCHOOLS (STC/MS)

Science and Technology Concepts for Middle Schools (STC/MS) is an eight-module, inquiry-centered curriculum that provides opportunities for students to experience scientific phenomena firsthand. The modules can be sequenced for two one-year courses, each year consisting of a module from each of the four science/technology strands, or as four one-semester courses for earth science, life science, physical science, and technology. The *STC/MS* program materials include assessment components, suggestions for the use of educational technology, and reading selections to broaden student learning. Each *STC/MS* module is based on a four-stage learning cycle that is grounded in educational research and practice: focus, explore, reflect, and apply.

Components: Teacher's Guides, Student Guides, and kits

Developer: National Science Resources Center (NSRC)

Date Published: 2001

Publisher: Carolina Biological Supply Company

Contact Information:

NSRC
Outreach Office
(202)287-2065
www.si.edu/nsrc/stcms/overview.htm

Carolina
(800)227-1150
www.carolina.com/stcms/index.asp

Technology   **Link**

SEEKING SCIENCE

Seeking Science is a structured setting in which students investigate "driving questions" about science. These questions are the basis for students' research. Quality sites and online support guide students in their search for knowledge. During their investigations, students will use computers for the following tasks:

- to navigate through and take advantage of resources at the Seeking Science website
- to collect and critically evaluate information from the Internet
- to share questions and interesting sites with others
- to create products such as posters, reports, stories, and collages that represent their new understanding

Components: Seeking Science website and two Teacher's Guides
Year Published: current, online
Developer: University of Michigan
Publisher: Kendall/Hunt Publishing
Contact Information:

Kendall/Hunt Publishing Company
4050 Westmark Drive
P.O. Box 1840
Dubuque, IA 52004-1840
800-KH-BOOKS (800-542-6657)
www.kendallhunt.com

Earth/Space Science Programs

INVESTIGATING EARTH SYSTEMS

Investigating Earth Systems is a modular earth science curriculum component for middle school. It includes nine activity-based modules designed for grades 5-8. Modules are grouped into three grade levels: grades 5-6, 6-7, and 7-8. Modules introduce concepts through series of investigations (six to seven per unit), which are presented within a standard format that includes both the skills and the content students are expected to learn. Every investigation follows a learning cycle including: a problem or a question, a series of activities that lead students through finding possible answers to the challenge,

content notes for students' background information, and a review and reflect section that encourages students to reflect on what they have done and to summarize in their journals what they have learned. A section on thinking about scientific inquiry guides students on a process for thinking back on the use of the inquiry processes.

Components: Five student modules, teacher edition, materials kits, CD-ROMS, website
Year Published: 2000
Developer: American Geological Institute
Publisher: It's About Time
Contact Information:

American Geological Institute
4220 King Street
Alexandria, VA 22302-1502
www.agiweb.org

It's About Time, Inc.
84 Business Park Drive,
Armonk, NY 10504
(888)698-TIME (8463)
www.its-about-time.com

GLOBAL LAB

Technology   **Link**

Global Lab is a full-year, interdisciplinary, introductory science course. Using the latest Internet technology, *Global Lab* introduces students to science as inquiry, engaging them in collaborative scientific investigations. For their studies, students choose a local "study site" as the context for authentic, hands-on, integrated science explorations. Students study four essential scientific areas: the interaction of matter and energy, the biogeochemical cycles, biomes and biodiversity, and Earth as a system.

Components: Web tools online workspace
Year Published: 2001, online
Developer: TERC
Publisher: Kendall/Hunt Publishing
Contact Information:

TERC
www.terc.edu/TEMPLATE/products/
2067 Massachusetts Avenue
Cambridge, MA 02140
Phone: (617)547-0430
Fax: (617)349-3535
communications@terc.edu

Kendall/Hunt Publishing Company
4050 Westmark Drive
P.O. Box 1840
Dubuque, IA 52004-1840
800-KH-BOOKS (800-542-6657)
www.kendallhunt.com

Technology

Link

GLOBAL LEARNING AND OBSERVATIONS TO BENEFIT THE ENVIRONMENT PROGRAM (GLOBE)

The *Global Learning and Observations to Benefit the Environment (GLOBE)* Program is a hands-on international, environmental science and education program for grades K–12. *GLOBE* is a cooperative effort of schools, led in the United States by a Federal interagency program supported by NASA, NSF, EPA, and the U.S. State Department, in partnership with colleges and universities, state and local school systems, and non-government organizations. Internationally, *GLOBE* is a partnership between the United States and 100 other countries. *GLOBE* links students, teachers, and scientists in an effort to learn more about the environment through student data collection and observation. Students transmit their data to a central data processing facility via the Internet, receive vivid images composed of their data and data from other *GLOBE* schools around the world, acquire information from a variety of sources, and collaborate with scientists and other *GLOBE* students and communities worldwide in using these data for education and research.

> **Components:** Teacher's guides: How-to videos, website
> **Year Published:** online, ongoing
> **Developers:** TERC, NASA, NOAA
> **Contact Information:** www.GLOBE.gov

GEOKITS

National Geographic Society *GeoKits* provide teachers with a variety of resources and lesson plans designed to supplement an already-established earth science curriculum. The materials are also extensive enough that they could form the core of materials for the course. Each individual *GeoKit* addresses a broad topic traditionally taught in an earth science course: Earth's History, Dynamic Earth, Rocks and Minerals, Weather, Oceans, Pollution, and Astronomy. In addition to the earth science modules, there are 20 other modules that connect to other areas of the curriculum.

> **Components:** Teacher's Guide for consisting of 10 to 15 thematic lessons, each composed of one or more hands-on activities, reading and video assignments that include student response and discussion questions, map and chart activities, and many Internet-related research activities.
> **Developer:** National Geographic Society
> **Publisher:** National Geographic School Publishing
> **Years Published:** 1996–2000
> **Contact Information:**
>
> National Geographic
> Phone: (800)368.2728
> www.nationalgeographic.com/education/geokits/

Life Science Programs

BIODIVERSITY COUNTS

Biodiversity Counts is a middle school science program created by the American Museum of Natural History (AMNH). The program can be used in conjunction with a core life science curriculum or other biodiversity and environmental curricula. It brings students out of the classroom and into the field to study biodiversity. For example, students go into their backyards and schoolyards to inventory the plants and arthropods that live there. Students observe behavior, collect data, make identifications, and interpret and share their findings.

> **Components:** Teacher's Guide—the full supplementary curriculum unit, which may be downloaded in the Resources section; Biodiversity Resources—profiles and essays about the work of Museum staff and their colleagues, and materials about plants and arthropods, accessible in the Resources section
> **Developer:** National Center for Science Literacy, Education, and Technology at the American Museum of Natural History
> **Publisher:** American Museum of National History
> **Year Published:** online
> **Contact Information:**
> www.amnh.org/learn/biodiversity_counts/

MIDDLE SCHOOL LIFE SCIENCE, SECOND EDITION

Middle School Life Science is a full-year course organized around a series of learning cycles during which students work independently, with partners, and in small groups. They engage in hands-on laboratory activities to explore an idea or concept; develop the concept during class discussion and/or through readings or additional experiments; apply the concepts learned to other situations; and form connections between their new knowledge and other areas of inquiry. *Middle School Life Science* is a study of human biology, of people and the environment, and of choices people must make to stay healthy. The textbook is organized in 7 units: (1) "Ecosystems and Ecology," (2) "Body Structure," (3) "Foods and Digestion," (4) "Body Basics," (5) "Body Controls," (6) "Body Changes," and (7) "Cells and Genetics." When possible, the situations discussed relate to students' lives and involve general health topics such as fitness, nutrition, drug use, relationships with peers, and ecological topics such as recycling and environmental responsibilities.

> **Components:** Student book, teacher's guide, in three-ring-binder format, contains assessment options, strategies to use with reading assignments, unit overviews and materials lists,

and directions and guidelines for teaching all activities; teacher's resource book with worksheets, blackline masters for transparencies, optional lessons, additional print materials, and a test item bank

Developer: Judy Capra (principal author) and Jefferson County Public Schools

Publisher: Kendall/Hunt Publishing

Year Published: 2000

Contact Information: Kendall/Hunt Publishing Company
>   4050 Westmark Drive
>   P.O. Box 1840
>   Dubuque, IA 52004-1840
>   800-KH-BOOKS (800-542-6657)
>   www.kendallhunt.com

Physical Science Programs

CHEMICALS, HEALTH, ENVIRONMENT, AND ME (CHEM 2: ENHANCED PROGRAM)

Chemicals, Health, Environment, and Me is a series of 15 units on the nature of chemicals and how they interact with the environment. It is part of the Science Education for Public Understanding Program (SEPUP) series. Students learn to collect, process, and analyze information and to use scientific evidence as a basis for lifestyle-oriented decisions. The units can be used in any order. They focus on (1) the physical and chemical properties of common substances, (2) relationships and interactions between humans and their environment, (3) sound, (4) electricity and magnetism, (5) media techniques and how they are used for different purposes, (6) food additives, (7) sugar and sugar substitutes, (8) the threshold of toxicity, (9) smoking and health, (10) qualitative tests used to identify chemicals in highway spills, (11) the identification and disposal of potentially hazardous chemicals, (12) waste disposal and reduction, (13) the carbon cycle, (14) pharmacology, and (15) water quality.

Components: Teacher's guide, materials kit, reproducible blackline masters of student activity sheets

Year Published: 1997

Developer: Lawrence Hall of Science

Publisher/supplier: Lab-Aids, Inc.

Contact Information: www.lhs.berkeley.edu

>   Lab-Aids, Inc.
>   17 Colt Court
>   Ronkonkoma, NY 11779
>   Phone: (800) 381-8003
>   Fax: (631) 737-1286
>   www.sepup.com

INTRODUCTORY PHYSICAL SCIENCE

Introductory Physical Science is a sequential course that can be divided into three parts. Chapters 1–6 provide the progression from mixtures to compounds and elements. In the process, students learn about the characteristic properties by which substances are recognized and separated. Chapters 7–9 introduce the atomic model through radioactivity. Chapters 10–12 add the electric dimension to the atomic model, reinforcing material learned in previous chapters. The broad objectives of IPS include the development of laboratory skills, reasoning skills (for example, the application of knowledge to new situations), and communication skills in the context of science, while providing an understanding of the foundations of physical science. *IPS* relies on the fact that all students have some experience with matter in their daily life. Therefore, *IPS* has no prerequisites in the areas of science content. In this program, all new ideas are based on concrete student experiences in the laboratory, and all new terms are introduced only after the need for them has been established. *IPS* teaches science through experiments designed with clear goals. As students perform and analyze experiments, useful new terms are introduced to help students describe their experimental results. Through active participation in reaching their own conclusions, students are given opportunities to achieve a deeper level of understanding.

Components: Student textbook, teacher's guide and resource book, KaleidaGraph 3.09, and the assessment package.

Year Published: 1999

Developers: Uri Haber-Schaim and Harold Pratt

Publisher: Science Curriculum Inc.

Contact Information:

>   sci@shore.net
>   (800) 501.0957
>   (617) 489.2282
>   www.sci-ips.com

MODELS IN TECHNOLOGY AND SCIENCE (MITS)

Models in Technology and Science (MITS) is a module-based program designed for students in grades 5–8, with a focus on physical science and technology. The series has 11 modules designed to last six to eight weeks. The modules can be sequenced over grades 5–8 and combined with other instructional materials in order to build a comprehensive middle school program. Each module is a carefully sequenced, age-appropriate set of hands-on experiences that are student-centered and provide a context for constructing basic science concepts.

Publisher: Pitsco, Inc.

Year Published: 2001

Developer: EDC
Contact Information:

EDC
55 Chapel Street
Newton, Massachusetts 02158-1060
(617)969-7100
www.edc.org/CSE/

(880)835-0686
www.pitsco.com

The following sources were very helpful in developing the summaries of the instructional materials above: EDC K-12 Science Curriculum Dissemination Center [http://www2.edc.org/cse/work/k12dissem/materials] National Science Resources Center. *Resources For Teaching Middle School Science.* (Washington, DC: National Academy Press, 1998).

SCI Center at BSCS. *Profiles in Science: A Guide to NSF-Funded High School Instructional Materials* (2002) [http://www.scicenteratbscs.org].

◆
___

REFERENCES

1. William Schmidt, Curtis C. McKnight, Richard T. Houang, Hsing Chi Wang, David Wiley, Leland S. Cogan, and Richard G. Wolfe. *Why Schools Matter: A Cross-National Comparison of Curriculum and Learning.* (New York: Jossey-Bass, 2001).
2. National Science Foundation, *Program Solicitation: Programs for Middle School Science Instruction* (Washington, DC: National Science Foundation, 1988) p. 2.
3. Paul DeHart Hurd. *Transforming Middle School Science Education.* Ways of Knowing in Science Series (New York: Teachers College Press, 2000).
4. James Beane, *A Middle School Curriculum: From Rhetoric to Reality* (Columbus, OH: National Middle School Association, 1990).
5. Raymond J Bandlow. "The Misdirection of Middle School Reform: Is a Child-Centered Approach Incompatible with Achievement in Math and Science?" *Clearing House;* 75(2)(Nov–Dec 2001).
6. Rebecca M. Schneider and Joseph Krajcik. *The Role of Educative Curriculum Materials in Reforming Science Education.* ED445889, 1999.
7. Barbara Brauner Berns, Ilene Kantrov, Marian Pasquale, Doris Santamaria Makang, Bernie Zubrowski, and Lynn T. Goldsmith. *Guiding Curriculum Decisions for Middle-Grades Science.* (Portsmouth, NH: Heinemann, 2001).
8. D. W. Johnson and R. T. Johnson, *Learning Together and Alone: Cooperative, Competitive and Individualistic Learning,* 2nd ed. (Englewood Cliffs, NJ: Prentice-Hall, 1987).
9. J. B. Kahle, "SCORES: A Project for Change?" *International Journal of Science Education* 9 (3) (1987): 325–333.

◆ ───────────── **EVALUATING MIDDLE SCHOOL SCIENCE PROGRAMS** ───────── ◆

ACTIVITY 8–1
USING THE PROJECT 2061 CURRICULUM-ANALYSIS PROCEDURE

Project 2061 is the ongoing work of AAAS that included the development of *Benchmarks for Science Literacy*. With funding from the National Science Foundation and in collaboration with hundreds of K–12 teachers, curriculum specialists, teacher educators, scientists, and materials developers, Project 2061 has been developing a process for analyzing curriculum materials. Field tests suggest that Project 2061's curriculum-analysis procedure will not only serve the materials adoption needs of the schools but will also help teachers revise existing materials to increase their effectiveness, guide developers in the creation of new materials, and contribute to the professional development of those who use it. The Project 2061 curriculum-analysis procedure involves the following five steps:

1. *Identify specific learning goals to serve as the intellectual basis for the analysis.* This is done before beginning to examine any curriculum materials. The source for appropriate goals can be national standards or benchmark documents such as those mentioned above, state or local standards and curriculum frameworks, or sources like them. To be useful, the goals must be precise in describing the knowledge or skills they intend students to have. If the set of goals is large, a representative sample of them should be selected for purposes of analysis.

2. *Make a preliminary inspection of the curriculum materials to see whether they are likely to address the targeted learning goals.* If there appears to be little or no correspondence, the materials can be rejected without further analysis. If the outlook is more positive, go on to a content analysis.

3. *Analyze the curriculum materials for alignment between content and the selected learning goals.* The purpose here is to determine, citing evidence from the materials, whether the content in the material matches specific learning goals—not just whether the topic headings are similar. At the topic level, alignment is never difficult, since most topics—heredity, weather, magnetism, and so forth—lack specificity, making them easy to match. If the results of this analysis are positive, then reviewers can take the next step.

4. *Analyze the curriculum materials for alignment between instruction and the selected learning goals.* This involves estimating the degree to which the materials (including their accompanying teacher's guides) reflect what is known generally about student learning and effective teaching and, more important, the degree to which they support student learning of the specific knowledge and skills for which a content match has been found. Again, evidence from the materials must be shown.

5. *Summarize the relationship between the curriculum materials being evaluated and the selected learning goals.* The summary can take the form of a profile of the selected goals in terms of the content and instruction criteria, or a profile of the criteria in terms of the selected goals. In either case, a statement of strengths and weaknesses should be included. With this information in hand, reviewers can make more knowledgeable adoption decisions and suggest ways for improving the examined materials.

In addition to its careful focus on matching content and instruction to very specific learning goals, the Project 2061 procedure has other features that set it apart. For example, its emphasis on collecting explicit evidence (citing page numbers and other references) of a material's alignment with learning goals adds rigor and reliability to decisions about curriculum materials. Similarly, the Project 2061 procedure calls for a team approach to the analytical task, providing opportunities for reviewers to defend their own judgments about materials and to question those of other reviewers. These and other characteristics help make participation in the analytical process itself a powerful professional development experience.

Choose one middle school curriculum that interests you and try this adaptation of the Project 2061 procedure:

1. Identify specific learning goals to serve as the intellectual basis for the analysis.

2. Make a preliminary inspection of the curriculum materials to see whether they are likely to address the targeted learning goals.

3. Analyze the curriculum materials for alignment between content and the selected learning goals. Base this alignment on the degree of match between the relevant NSES or Benchmarks and the information in the curriculum you are examining. Use questions such as these:

◆ Does the content called for in the material address the substance of a specific benchmark/standard or only the benchmark/standard's general "topic"?

◆ Does the content reflect the level of sophistication of the specific standard/benchmark, or are the activities more appropriate for targeting standards/benchmarks at an earlier or later grade level?

◆ Does the content address all parts of a specific benchmark/standard or only some?

4. Analyze the curriculum materials for alignment between instruction and the selected learning goals. Seven criteria clusters have been identified to serve as a basis for the instructional analysis:

Cluster I. Providing a Sense of Purpose: Part of planning a coherent curriculum involves deciding on its purposes and on which learning experiences will likely contribute to those purposes. But while coherence from the curriculum designers' point of view is important, it may not give students an adequate sense of what they are doing and why. This cluster includes criteria to determine whether the material attempts to make its purposes explicit and meaningful to students, either by itself or by instructions to the teacher.

Cluster II. Taking Account of Student Ideas: Fostering better understanding in students requires taking time to attend to the ideas they already have, both ideas that are incorrect and ideas that can serve as a foundation for subsequent learning. Such attention requires that teachers be informed about prerequisite ideas/skills needed for understanding a benchmark or standard and what their students' initial ideas are—in particular, the ideas that may interfere with learning the scientific information. Moreover, teachers can help address students' ideas if they know what is likely to work. This cluster examines whether the material contains specific suggestions for identifying and relating to student ideas.

Cluster III. Engaging Students with Phenomena: Much of the point of science is explaining phenomena in terms of a small number of principles or ideas. For students to appreciate this explanatory power, they need to have a sense of the range of phenomena that science can explain.

Cluster IV. Developing and Using Scientific Ideas: Science literacy requires that students see the link between phenomena and ideas and see the ideas themselves as useful. This cluster includes criteria to determine whether the material attempts to provide links between phenomena and ideas and to demonstrate the usefulness of the ideas in varied contexts.

Cluster V. Promoting Student Reflection: No matter how clearly materials may present ideas, students (like all people) will assign their own meanings to them. Constructing meaning well is aided by having students (1) make their ideas and reasoning explicit, (2) hold their ideas and reasoning up to scrutiny, and (3) recast their ideas as needed.

Cluster VI. Assessing Progress: There are several important reasons for monitoring student progress toward specific learning goals. Having a collection of alternatives can ease the creative burden on teachers and increase the time available to analyze student responses and make adjustments in instruction based on those responses.

Cluster VII. Enhancing the Learning Environment: Many other important considerations are involved in the selection of curriculum materials: for example, the help they provide to teachers in encouraging student curiosity and creating a classroom community where all can succeed, or the material's scientific accuracy or attractiveness.

5. Summarize your assessment of what is being taught by the curriculum you selected and what instructional approach is being promoted. Are these materials you would use in the classroom? Why or why not?

CHAPTER 9

THE HIGH SCHOOL SCIENCE CURRICULUM

This chapter focuses on the science curriculum for grades 9–12. The programs described in this chapter emphasize the key ideas from the content, teaching, and assessment sections of the *National Science Education Standards,* as well as the essential ideas from other documents that have helped articulate a vision of reform in the later part of the 20th century. These programs are not necessarily the best-selling curriculum materials for high school science; however, they are the materials that are most consistent with current research about effective teaching and learning.

You can look forward to continuing improvements in the science curriculum that started in the 1990s. The formation of *National Science Education Standards*[1] and *Benchmarks for Science Literacy*[2] supports this statement because these documents provide a sense of vision that has specific suggestions for thinking about the content and instruction in school science settings.

SCIENCE CURRICULA FOR THE HIGH SCHOOL

In this section we present several examples of contemporary science curricula. These programs were supported by the NSF and published in the 1990s. Although some were developed prior to the publication of NRC standards and AAAS benchmarks, they represent a generation of high school science curricula closely aligned with the national standards and benchmarks. All of the developers have taken care to address standards and benchmarks in subsequent editions of their programs.

Earth/Space Science

EARTH SYSTEM SCIENCE IN THE COMMUNITY (EARTHCOMM)

EarthComm is the first high school earth science program developed by experts in earth science that addresses the *National Science Education Standards* (NSES). It is designed to work well with both block and traditional schedules and to be used in heterogeneous classes, providing access for all students to learn fundamental earth science concepts and to understand the nature of science and inquiry.

EarthComm emphasizes significant concepts, understandings, and abilities that all students can use to think critically, understand and appreciate the earth system, and make informed decisions.

EarthComm is an Earth Science curriculum developed by the American Geological Institute (AGI) and supported by the National Science Foundation and donors of the American Geological Institute Foundation. Through *EarthComm,* AGI focuses attention on the national deficiency in high school Earth Science education (grades 9–12) and on development of a complete high-school Earth Science curriculum. The EarthComm vision is the teaching, learning, and practice of Earth science by all students in all U.S. high schools. Their website contains resources for teachers, students, and parents as well as information on the development of the curricula.

EarthComm consists of five modules, each containing three stand-alone chapters connected to a common theme. Teachers can mix and match the chapters to create the program that best suits their needs. The modules are: Earth's Dynamic Geosphere (volcanoes, earthquakes, plate tectonics), Earth's Natural Resources (energy, mineral, water), Understanding Your Environment (bedrock geology, river systems, land use planning), Earth System Evolution (astronomy, climate change, changing life), and Earth's Fluid Spheres (oceans, severe weather, cryosphere).

Discipline: Earth Science
Grade Level: 9, 10, 11, or 12
Developer: American Geological Institute
Publisher: It's About Time
Copyright: 2001, varies with each module
Edition: First Edition

Components: The student text, teacher edition, *EarthComm* Kits, CD-ROMs, software

Contact Information:

American Geological Institute
4220 King Street
Alexandria, VA 22302-1502
www.agiweb.org

It's About Time, Inc.
84 Business Park Drive,
Armonk, NY 10504
(888)698-TIME (8463)
www.its-about-time.com

PROJECT STAR: THE UNIVERSE IN YOUR HANDS

Project STAR is a full-year course that uses astronomy as a vehicle for teaching students about real-world applications of mathematics and physics. The course stresses the importance of measurements, observations, and building models. The course focuses first on the solar system, then on stars and galaxies beyond the solar system, and finally on a model of the universe as a whole. Subjects covered in this textbook include the day and night sky; distances, sizes, and angles; the behavior of light; mirrors and lenses; the size and distance relationships of the earth, moon, and sun; paths of the planets; stars; the Milky Way galaxy; and galaxies and the universe.

Discipline: Astronomy
Grade Level: 11 or 12
Developer: Harvard-Smithsonian Center for Astrophysics
Publisher: Kendall/Hunt Publishing Company
Copyright: 1993
Edition: First

Each of the 15 chapters in *Project STAR* begins with several questions to test students' preconceptions about the subjects or concepts addressed in the chapter. In several hands-on activities, students then build and use simple but powerful tools to explore those concepts. For example, to answer questions about the position of the sun during the day, students learn how to measure the position of an object in the sky with their hands, plot the sun's apparent daily motion using a plastic hemisphere, and keep a journal of the sun's apparent motion. Other examples of the lab investigations that students conduct during the course include: determining the apparent size of an object as an angle measured in degrees; building scale models of the size and distance relations of the earth, moon, and sun to understand how the distances of these objects compare with their sizes; investigating what happens when different colors of the spectrum are projected onto the same place on a white screen; and estimating the size of the Milky Way galaxy and the distances to other galaxies using the apparent brightness-distance nomogram.

Components: Teacher's Guide, Student textbook, Individual *Project STAR* resource kits—for example, the Celestial Sphere Kit; the Refracting Telescope Kit, with Tubes; and the Solar System Scale Model Kit—contain most of the materials required to do an activity. A separate activity book—*Where We Are in Space and Time*—contains 21 additional hands-on activities.

Contact Information:

Kendall/Hunt Publishing Company
4050 Westmark Drive
P.O. Box 1840
Dubuque, IA 52004-1840
800-KH-BOOKS (800-542-6657)
www.kendallhunt.com

Chemistry

CHEMISTRY IN THE COMMUNITY (CHEMCOM)

Chemistry in the Community (*ChemCom*) is a yearlong high school chemistry program organized in seven units in a single textbook. Developed by the American Chemical Society (ACS), this program is designed to offer an engaging approach to the study of chemistry for a wide range of students. The course is organized around themes that use a societal issue with chemistry applications. Chemistry principles are presented on a need-to-know basis within each unit. The material emphasizes problem-solving techniques and critical-thinking skills to facilitate decision-making about scientific and technological issues.

Laboratory, decision-making, and problem-solving activities are an integral part of each unit and require student participation and cooperation for success.

ChemCom introduces considerably more content from organic, nuclear, industrial, and biochemistry than most conventional chemistry courses.

Discipline:	Chemistry
Grade Level:	9, 10, 11, or 12
Developer:	American Chemical Society
Publisher:	W.H. Freeman and Company
Copyright:	2002
Edition:	Fourth

The goals of *ChemCom* are to help students

♦ recognize and understand the importance of chemistry in their lives,

♦ develop problem-solving techniques and critical-thinking skills that enable the application of chemical principles in making informed decisions about scientific and technological issues, and

♦ acquire an awareness of the potential, as well as the limitations, of science and technology.

To accomplish these goals, *ChemCom*'s pedagogical approach introduces chemistry concepts as needed to help students understand complex, real-world social and technological issues. Each unit begins by providing a specific context designed to grab students' attention and ends with a task related to that context. The chemistry concepts and student activities within the unit build on and support the context. Concepts introduced in earlier units are often revisited and developed more fully in subsequent units. Student-centered instructional strategies emphasize social interactions, cooperative learning, and problem solving.

Components: Student text, teacher's edition, overhead transparency packet, blackline masters, workbook, skill-building handbook, test bank, CD-ROMs, *ChemCom* Connections Laserdisc

Contact Information:

www.whfreeman.com/chemcom
www.chemistry.org
ACS Office of Society Services
(800)227-5558

 Visit http://www.prenhall.com/trowbridge and select Topic 1—National Science Education Standards. Select "Science Teaching Standards" and find the link "The Creation of Communities of Science Learners" (ST5). The websites listed in this section include ones about "Planning Programs for High Ability Learners." Review the suggestions, choose several of interest, write a summary, and submit it to your instructor using the Electronic Bluebook.

Physics

ACTIVE PHYSICS

Active Physics is an introductory, activity-based physics course organized into six thematic units, each with a student book, supporting teacher's edition, and teaching videos. The thematic approach is designed to allow students to learn physics principles through the hands-on exploration of topics that interest them: sports, medicine, home, transportation predictions, and communication. Each of the thematic units contains three chapters which, although all related to the theme, are quite independent of each other and can be taught in any order. Each chapter focuses on a chapter challenge and contains eight to ten activities that provide students the opportunity to learn the physics principles they need in order to meet the challenge. Developed in conjunction with the American Association of Physics Teachers and the American Institute of Physics, this curriculum is designed to reach all high school students in grade 9, 10, 11, or 12. It can be used with both block and traditional schedules and is designed to be used with heterogeneous classes.

Discipline:	Physics
Grade Level:	9, 10, 11, or 12
Developer:	Arthur Eisenkraft, in association with the American Association of Physics Teachers and the American Institute of Physics
Publisher:	It's About Time
Copyright:	1998, 1999, 2000 (varies by module)
Edition:	First

Each chapter begins with a challenge that sets the stage for the learning activities and chapter assessments that follow. Chapter contents and activities are selectively aimed at the knowledge and skills needed to address the introductory challenge, providing a natural content filter (less is more). Each chapter's activities are designed around an inquiry learning cycle. The curriculum's constructivist approach elicits students' prior understanding, challenges students to investigate physics principles through activities, asks students to explain how the physics principles work, and develops logical explanations based on results. At the end of each chapter, students are given the opportunity to demonstrate what they have learned in a meaningful way by meeting the challenge offered at the beginning of the chapter. The activities and chapter challenges provide opportunities for students to use many different skills, including writing, drawing, graphing, computation, public speaking, graphic design, and use of computer technology.

Components: Teacher's Edition, student modules, material kits, videos, calculators, spreadsheets, computer-based and calculator-based labs, and other computer software programs

Contact Information:

It's About Time, Inc.
84 Business Park Drive
Armonk, NY 10504
(888)698-TIME (8463)
www.its-about-time.com

Technology **COMPREHENSIVE CONCEPTUAL CURRICULUM FOR PHYSICS (C^3P)**

Link

Comprehensive Conceptual Curriculum for Physics (C^3P) offers an integrated approach to physics content, instructional materials, and pedagogy. C^3P is a research-based curriculum developed at the Department of Physics at the University of Dallas. The project is available on a single CD-ROM that includes both the curriculum and resource materials. Other physics projects such as *PRISMS, CASTLE, Operation Physics, Tools for Scientific Thinking, Physics: Cinema Classics,* and *The Mechanical Universe High School Adaptation* have been used in the development of this curriculum.

Discipline:	Physics
Grade Level:	9 or 10
Developer:	Richard P. Olenick, Department of Physics, University of Dallas
Publisher:	Department of Physics, University of Dallas
Copyright:	2000
Edition:	Second

The goal of *Comprehensive Conceptual Curriculum for Physics* (C^3P) is to produce and disseminate a comprehensive, conceptually based physics curriculum suitable for all high schools, usable by all teachers, and effective for all students. To meet this goal, the program

♦ provides physics teachers with both materials and pedagogical approaches to enable them to teach a conceptual course in physics to all students,

♦ recognizes students' prior experiences and knowledge as expressed by their preconceptions,

♦ provides concrete experiences with phenomena, whenever possible, before introducing related terminology,

♦ employs a learning cycle that guides students from concrete experiences and descriptive expressions to quantitative reasoning,

♦ revisits concepts, principles, and theories in a spiral approach at successively higher levels of depth and abstraction,

♦ connects the physics learned to everyday applications, history, and other disciplines,

♦ reduces topical coverage with an increased emphasis on in-depth conceptual understanding,

♦ incorporates assessment procedures and instruments aligned to the curriculum to measure student skills, knowledge, understanding, and reasoning, and

♦ incorporates technologies, including calculator-based labs (CBL) and simulations when appropriate.

C^3P's integrated learning cycle approach is research-based and student-centered. It includes the following stages:

♦ Exploration—Students are involved in hands-on activities, model-building, computer simulations, and group activities. Students use materials to acquire information and learn through their own questions and actions.

♦ Concept Development—Teacher-led discussions, interactive presentations, videos, and simulations help answer students' questions. Student understanding is promoted through focus, and concept language is developed, and

♦ Application—Students are involved in real-life use of concepts, problem-solving, and decision-making connections to technologies. Students learn to accommodate new concepts into existing concepts.

Components: C^3P 2000 + CD-ROM, which is available only through workshop participation and contains both the curriculum and resource materials. A guided tour introduces the user to the navigation system and the various sections found on the CD-ROM.

Resources include a timeline; video; resource; physics cartoons and tunes; The CASTLE Project—provides an alternative approach to teaching electricity concepts; Interactive Physics Player—variety of simulations; and weblinks.

Contact Information: www.phys.udallas.edu/

www.phys.udallas.edu
Department of Physics
University of Dallas
1845 E. Northgate Drive
Irving, TX 75062-4799
(800)526-8472
Principal Investigator, Richard P. Olenick
olenick@acad.udallas.edu

MINDS-ON PHYSICS

Minds-On Physics (MOP) is an activity-based, full-year curriculum for high school physics. Although it was designed for level students, the materials may be adapted to other grades (including physical science for grades 8 or 9). Developed by Massachusetts Physics Education

Research Group, the design for *MOP* was guided by educational and cognitive research. The curriculum integrates physics topics traditionally taught at different times of the year. Students are expected to develop understanding of physics while improving problem-solving proficiency. Students work together, using simple equipment, fundamental physical concepts and principles, and how to apply them properly. The role of the teacher shifts from dispensing information to coach.

Discipline:	Physics
Grade Level:	11 or 12
Developer:	University of Massachusetts Physics Education Research Group (William Leonard, Robert Dufresne, William Gerace, Jose Mestre)
Publisher:	Kendall/Hunt Publishing Company
Copyright:	1999, 2000, 2001 (varies by volume)
Edition:	First

The goals of the *Minds-On Physics (MOP)* materials are to

- reveal and address students' misconceptions,
- help students develop analysis and reasoning skills,
- emphasize the role of concepts in problem solving,
- show students how to use concepts and principles to solve problems.
- discourage formulaic approaches to solving problems, and
- promote knowledge structuring and integration.

To accomplish these goals, the *MOP* program uses constructivist, activity-based, student-centered pedagogy to teach students to analyze physical situations conceptually, thereby improving both their understanding and problem-solving ability. MOP is based on a set of four basic principles:

- Knowledge is constructed by each learner, not simply transmitted by someone else,
- The construction of knowledge is an effort-driven process requiring significant time and engagement by the learner
- The construction of knowledge often takes place within the context of social interaction, and
- The construction of new knowledge is greatly influenced by the knowledge the learner already possesses.

In recognition of these principles, *MOP* uses an action-oriented approach to learning physics. This means that *MOP* decreases lecturing by the teacher, and requires minimal reading by the student prior to working on an activity. Instead, after introduction to the new topic, students are quickly engaged in activities that require them to interact with other students. Working in groups, students use concepts to analyze problem situations and answer open-ended questions, explore the concepts through inquiry and hands-on activities, and share personal reflections on prior experiences. The program approaches students as individuals possessing a unique way of looking at a situation or solving a problem. The *MOP* approach is on what students know, with an emphasis on processes such as analyzing, reasoning, explaining, and strategizing, over physics facts. Activities are organized to maximize students' attention, motivation, interest, involvement, and success.

Components: Student Activities and Reader, Teacher's Guide

Contact Information:

Kendall/Hunt Publishing Company
4050 Westmark Drive
P.O. Box 1840
Dubuque, IA 52004-1840
800-KH-BOOKS (800-542-6657)
www.kendallhunt.com

Biology

BIOLOGY: A COMMUNITY CONTEXT

Biology: A Community Context is a year-long introductory high school biology program organized in a single textbook containing eight units. This program is designed to offer an engaging approach for a wide range of students. The course is organized around themes that use a societal context requiring applications of major biological concepts. Each unit includes guided inquiries and posed problems, and culminates in a "Conference" providing students opportunities to develop inquiry and analytical skills while building understanding of how science works. The development of each unit reflects the view that an understanding of biology is a prerequisite for addressing environmental problems and that learning is best achieved by active, personal involvement with materials.

Discipline:	Biology
Grade Level:	9, 10, 11, or 12
Developer:	William Leonard (Clemson University) and John Penick (North Carolina State University)
Publisher:	Glencoe/McGraw-Hill
Copyright:	1998
Edition:	First

The emphasis throughout *Biology: A Community Context* is on active investigation. Students learn about the scientific process through hands-on inquiry into real-world problems. The seven-part instructional strategy of *Biology* is constructed to reflect the process of scientific inquiry and allow students to do science rather than just read about it. All *Biology: A Community Context* units are similar, beginning with active student involvement from the first day. This activity is designed so that most of a student's time during each unit is spent in active learning. Students make many decisions, initiate and design some investigations themselves, and as a group, take charge of the culminating activity in each unit. Because the design of each unit is similar, the instructional strategy follows a consistent pattern across all units. As a result, students come to anticipate the teacher's next instructional move. An understanding of the teacher's pattern is designed to facilitate classroom management and to empower the students, thereby providing effective learning. The instructional strategy is a significant component in developing the classroom climate.

Components: Student text, teacher's guide, resource book/implementation guide, student resource book, transparencies, test bank, videotapes, instructional resource

Contact Information:

Glencoe/McGraw-Hill
Customer Service Department
P.O. Box 543
Blacklick, OH 43004-0544
Phone: (800)334-7344
Fax: (614)755-5682
www.glencoe.com/sec/science/biology/bacc/index.html

BSCS BIOLOGY: A HUMAN APPROACH

BSCS Biology: A Human Approach is a standards-based, introductory biology program appropriate for students of all ages. The program is organized around six unifying themes in biology and teaches inquiry through collaborative, hands-on activities and the BSCS 5E model: Engage, Explore, Explain, Elaborate, and Evaluate. These unifying themes are designed for in-depth conceptual coverage, and the human perspective provides students with a relevant context for lifelong learning series of essays for each chapter and engaging videodisc sequences are designed to provide students with resources to construct an understanding of the concepts they are exploring.

Discipline:	Biology
Grade Level:	9 or 10
Developer:	Biological Sciences Curriculum Study (BSCS)
Publisher:	Kendall/Hunt Publishing Company
Copyright:	2003
Edition:	Second

BSCS Biology: A Human Approach uses a constructivist approach to instruction, which is designed to place the student in the center of their own learning and provide strategies for the teacher to guide this process. Students are first engaged in a new idea or concept. They then explore the concept through one or more activities. Next, in the explain phase, begin to construct an understanding of the concept based on their experiences during the explore phase. Students then elaborate on their understanding by applying it to a new situation. Finally, students and teachers have an opportunity to evaluate the students' understanding of a concept before moving on to a new concept. The program provides a variety of activities including hands-on labs, interactive simulations, role-playing scenarios and case studies, and readings with a storyline and addresses the needs of a diverse group of students.

Components: Student text, teacher's guide, teacher's resource CD-ROM (implementation guide, assessment guide, learning guide, correlation with standards, copy masters, optional activities), transparencies, software, and CD-ROMs,

Contact Information:

BSCS
5415 Mark Dabling Boulevard
Colorado Springs, CO 80918
(719)531-5550
www.bscs.org

Kendall/Hunt Publishing Company
4050 Westmark Drive
P.O. Box 1840
Dubuque, IA 52004-1840
800-KH-BOOKS (800-542-6657)
www.kendallhunt.com

RESOURCE AND ACKNOWLEDGEMENT

The program summaries in this chapter were adapted from the publication *Profiles in Science: A Guide to NSF-Funded High School Instructional Materials.* This document was developed by the staff of the Science Curriculum Implementation (SCI) Center at BSCS including Susan Rust, Jim Short, Sandy Smith, Aimeé Stephenson, Joe Taylor, and Ray Tschillard. The SCI Center is a national science education reform initiative focused on building leadership capacity for professional development that supports standards-based curriculum implementation. As a major program at BSCS in professional development, the SCI Center offers a variety of services and products to help teachers and administrators develop science programs for all students to learn science. *Profiles in Science* compiles information about 20 different comprehensive high school instructional materials (including life, earth, physical, and integrated science) that were developed with funding from the National Science Foundation and address the *National Science Education Standards*. The entire document can be downloaded from www.sci centeratbscs.org.

REFERENCES

1. National Research Council, *National Standards for Science Education* (Washington, DC: Author, 1996).

2. American Association for the Advancement of Science, *Benchmarks for Science Literacy* (Washington, DC: Author, 1993).

CHAPTER 10

SCIENCE AND OTHER DISCIPLINES: INTERDISCIPLINARY APPROACHES TO CURRICULUM

WHAT IS AN INTERDISCIPLINARY APPROACH?

As the world changes, more and more recognition is being given to the broad nature of education in science. No longer is it sufficient to think narrowly of Physics, Chemistry, or Biology, although these are the traditional main science subjects in our high schools. The advent of Earth sciences in the mid-20th century was a major step in recognizing the commonality of earth problems that demanded broad approaches to their solution. It has become more apparent that solutions to problems, as for example, environmental concerns, demand interdisciplinary viewpoints with their varied techniques and expertise. Similarly, integration of science with other disciplines such as mathematics, reading, social studies, history, technology, and other school subjects is an important step in bringing about a better understanding of how the world problems are tied together. At the same time, science teachers must realize the role science plays in one's overall education. At present there seems to be a lack of understanding of science principles among lay persons in society. Their "scientific literacy" appears to be at a low ebb right now. This makes your task even more important. Perhaps the solution is to develop greater recognition of the interdisciplinary nature of science in their education. Hopefully this chapter may bring forth some aspects of this recognition.

Many science teachers and school districts are integrating science with other disciplines. Justification for such approaches includes the fact that knowledge growth requires individuals to understand broader concepts that link several disciplines; the observation that

schools impose artificial boundaries and constraints on students; the common sense notion that real-world problems do not present themselves in discipline-bound packages; and the understanding that fragmentation of the curriculum reduces relevance and meaning for students. What do educators mean when they talk about interdisciplinary approaches to curriculum? We can begin with ideas of disciplines and curriculum. Disciplines such as physics, chemistry, and biology represent specific bodies of knowledge with their own history, procedure, and method. From these disciplines educators, curriculum developers, and science teachers select specific knowledge, methods, historical people, and advances to include in school science programs. As Bruner[1,2] points out, students must know the structure of science disciplines to further their development and acquire understandings of how things are related. From a teaching point of view, disciplinary approaches to the curriculum make sense because students can direct attention to specific content and closely related concepts and methods. Focusing on a subject for a period of time, for instance earth science for a year, allows students time and opportunity to progressively develop the fundamental concepts, methods, and history associated with the earth sciences. In science, the interdisciplinary approach begins with a theme, personal issue, social problem, school event, or science topic and applies the concepts and methods from more than one discipline to the realm of study or investigation. Where the disciplinary approach stresses thorough understanding of the conceptual schemes of a discipline such as biology or physics, interdisciplinary approaches emphasize connections and linkages among disciplines in the pursuit of understanding objects, organisms, and events in the natural and designed world. John Christensen,[3] a science teacher and curriculum developer, summarizes the interdisciplinary perspective:

> "In science, an integrated curriculum is a conceptual framework that weaves together the various concepts, skills and principles of the traditional subject-centered classrooms into a unified whole. This enables the curriculum to focus on the vital question: What from science is important for all students to know? The integrated curriculum is then built around the answer to that question. The relevant issues of our time can now be the primary focus. The concepts and skills of science can be built as these issues are addressed."

Heidi Hays-Jacobs[4] has pointed out some of the problems associated with content selection for interdisciplinary courses. One problem is what she terms the "potpourri" problem. That is, units are a sampling of knowledge from different disciplines without any central focus, scope, or sequence in the curriculum. A second issue emerges as a polarity problem where the differences between disciplinary and interdisciplinary approaches become polarized and result in conflicts with departments, schools, or states. To avoid these problems, Dr. Jacobs recommends two criteria for interdisciplinary programs. First, such programs must have carefully articulated designs that include a scope and sequence, a framework for thinking skills, indicators for attitudinal change, and thorough and consistent assessment. Second, the curriculum must include both disciplinary and interdisciplinary approaches. There are many good reasons to involve students in interdisciplinary studies as part of their science education. One way to encourage the development of understandings and abilities associated with science is to focus on epistemological issues through questions such as, "What do we know?" and "Why do we believe what we know?" Frequently, focusing on these questions brings forth interrelationships between disciplines not usually thought of. For example, what benefits accrued to industrial processes in the 19th century from the researches of chemists and physicists of that era in relation to thermodynamic processes, researches on the nature of electricity, and clarifications of the periodical table in chemistry? Students can gain a better understanding of the interdisciplinary nature of science by actively involving themselves in proposing new relationships. A technique sometimes used for this purpose is "morphological analysis," in which a two-axis chart is constructed with the horizontal axes listing forms of energy, such as light, heat, electrical, or nuclear, for example, and the vertical axes depicting various types of transportation systems such as automobiles, airplanes, submarines, rockets, human powered vehicles, animal powered vehicles, moving

sidewalks, and so forth. By imagining new vehicles that make use of some or all of the forms of energy available, creative designs can be invented that may have practical uses. The same technique may be used to broaden the vision of students in reference to other disciplines of art, music, social sciences, and others. Although many advocate interdisciplinary studies, there are some who urge caution. Kathleen Roth, who taught science at a middle school and at Michigan State University, has expressed some second thoughts about interdisciplinary studies. Her concerns grew out of work on a unit that combined science and history. After designing and teaching an interdisciplinary unit on "Seeds of Change," she realized the theme and teaching approach did not help students connect with the important concepts, especially science, that she had first thought they would. She also found that the interdisciplinary approach did not allow for adequate development of ideas and concepts related to science. It also seemed that the social studies connection constrained some science activities. In conclusion, Dr. Roth suggests, "Before we jump on the interdisciplinary bandwagon, let us engage in debate and study of the kinds of integration that are compelling, meaningful, and powerful for children."[5] Discussions about interdisciplinary curriculum often point to the use of themes as a central focus. Both the National Science Education Standards and Benchmarks for Science Literacy identified themes that you might use in the design of science curriculum (see Figures 10–1 and 10–2 for those concepts and processes). The national standards and benchmarks include conceptual and procedural schemes that cross traditional disciplinary boundaries and provide students with powerful ideas to help them understand the natural and designed world. The content of these unifying and common themes can be introduced at any

---

Order and Organization
Evidence, Models, and Explanation
Change and Measurement
Evolution and Equilibrium
Form and Function

FIGURE 10–1 *National Science Education Standards* Unifying Concepts and Processes

---

Systems
Models
Constancy and Change
Scale

FIGURE 10–2 AAAS *Benchmarks for Science Literacy* Common Themes

GUEST EDITORIAL ◆ MARIE DEL TORO

Earth Science Teacher
Fountain Valley School Colorado Springs, Colorado

THERE'S MORE TO SCIENCE TEACHING THAN FACTS, CONCEPTS, AND MEMORIZING

Whether one has been teaching science for ten years or ten months, in a public or private school, or to a classroom of 50 or five, there is the common belief that teaching is a demanding but very rewarding profession. As a new teacher, I have had my share of good and bad experiences, all of which proved very worthwhile. The purpose of this editorial is to relate some of my experiences and how they have helped me grow as a science teacher. Fountain Valley is a small college preparatory school located in Colorado Springs, Colorado. Its 220 students come from 28 states and eight foreign countries. As a result, there is a great diversity in student interests, values, and levels of academic performance. Although Fountain Valley encourages individualism, it also strives to further a community spirit. That spirit is exemplified in the following ways: students are assigned advisers to oversee their progress both academically and socially; students and faculty eat family-style dinners twice a week; and finally, faculty live on campus, providing personal interaction between students and faculty. Although the school is small, it offers many science courses. Obviously, every student in science will not choose science as a career. The school is sensitive to that fact. As a result, Fountain Valley has developed a broad curriculum ranging from traditional one-year courses in biology and chemistry to one-and two-term electives in oceanography, geology, and anthropology. The assumption is that through a diversity of offerings, something will appeal to every student.

Teaching in a boarding school requires a great deal of time and effort. It is not enough to teach a student the basics in math or science for, as teachers in a boarding school, we are obligated to a much larger commitment. In effect, we are serving as the student's parents, and so our teaching should encourage growth in all phases of a student's cognitive, affective, and psychomotor learning. If a student is to develop into a caring, sensitive, and intellectual person, the classroom atmosphere should be conducive to attaining those goals. Like any other subject, science could be five lectures a week. However, it seems that the essence of science, learning through discovery, is lost if this method is used. As a result, the best approach

to science I have found is an integration of methods such as experimentation, problem solving, reading and questions, student speeches, and field trips.

Two of my most interesting and rewarding experiences have been associated with field trips. One occurred very early in the fall during interim week. The purpose of this week is to provide students opportunities to expand their intellectual, cultural, social, and vocational horizons. I was fortunate enough to accompany another teacher and 13 students to the Oregon coast to study marine biology, rain-forest ecology, and coastal geology. Before the trip I knew few of the students, but after spending a week living, eating, and talking with them, I developed a very special relationship with some students which could not have been kindled in any other environment. They have seen me in a situation outside the classroom and they know how I can act. This additional contact with students helps them realize that a teacher is a person too and not just someone whose job it is to give A's and F's. The other very rewarding experience occurred during a field trip with my geology class. After spending the afternoon driving around Colorado Springs looking at various geologic oddities, two of my students told me that they had become highly motivated about geology due to my influence. They also expressed an interest in pursuing geology in college, which is ironic considering their lack of confidence at the start of the course. A few days later, one of these students asked me if I would help with her senior independent project which, surprisingly, dealt with geology.

Reflecting on the fall term, I must say that those students advanced in their understanding of geology and, more importantly, in their outlook toward science and in their newly-acquired confidence. Experiences such as these certainly make teaching worthwhile. However, it is not always that way. That is where the true challenge begins. The good student will learn regardless of the teacher and the poor student may or may not learn even with the most exciting, motivating teacher.

As a first-year teacher, my duties include teaching four courses, coaching two sports, supervising the girls' dorm one night a week and every sixth weekend, co-sponsoring the rock-climbing club, and chaperoning various trips to the school's mountain campus located in the Colorado mountains. With this spectrum of duties, I see many students other than those in my classes, and this contact is good. The hard part is in assuming so many roles: teacher, coach, disciplinarian, friend, and surrogate mother, father, brother, or sister. It must be exceedingly frustrating for a student not to know how I will react or, more importantly, how I will act in any given situation. A student rarely sees me perform all of these roles. Coaching allows me to see students in an environment outside the classroom. It is great to watch students enjoy a sport whether or not they are highly motivated in an academic situation. Sometimes students feel teachers judge them by their level of academic achievement, and so underachievers may tend to shy away from certain teachers. This

attitude is rather unfortunate, for there are certain traits, just as important in life as math or science formulas, which can be instilled only in competitive sports. A student who works hard at a sport is learning a great deal about patience, sportsmanship, teamwork, and modesty, all of which are valuable and are not limited to athletics but hopefully will carry over to the classroom.

Teaching is both demanding and rewarding. It is a profession which will take as much as you are willing to give. There are always days when nothing seems to be going right, but then there are days when your students excel. If I had to start again, I would make a concerted effort to listen more intently to various students' needs and excuses; keep my expectations high, for students need to strive for more than they think they can attain; and, finally, I would make it a point to be consistent in my treatment of various classroom activities.

level in the K–12 science program. In the following sections we provide examples and approaches to interdisciplinary approaches to science curricula.

HISTORY OF SCIENCE AND TECHNOLOGY IN SCIENCE CLASSES

There are several current trends that have relevance for integrating the teaching of the history and nature of science and technology in science classes.[6] There is a thrust for developing improved scientific literacy among students and the lay public. There is also renewed interest in instruction in history of science and technology as perceived by policy documents such as the NRC's National Science Education Standards,[7] the AAAS's Science for All Americans,[8] and Benchmarks for Science Literacy,[9] and (3) an additional trend toward inclusion of Science-Technology-Society themes in science classes in contemporary school programs as noted by the NSTA in its position statement titled "Science-Technology-Society: A New Effort for Providing Appropriate Science for All.[10] In the 1990s, an analysis of textbooks for science, U.S. History, World History, and U.S. Government courses reveals very limited attention to the history of science and technology—only about 2 percent of the total pages. An analysis of 27 state curriculum guides in science showed that less than half of them called for the study of history of science and technology. A similar situation was found with local and state social studies curriculum guides. One science guide (the Science Framework for California

Public Schools for 1990) includes some emphasis on the nature of science. The History-Social Science Framework for California Public Schools for 1988 stresses the importance of intellectual history. These efforts could presage increased attention to these important topics throughout the country.

SCIENCE AND MATHEMATICS

The alliance between science and mathematics has a long history, dating back many centuries. Science provides mathematics with interesting problems to investigate, and mathematics provides science with powerful tools to use in analyzing data. . . . Science and mathematics are both trying to discover general patterns and relationships, and in this sense, they are part of the same endeavor.[11]

No scientific discipline has become truly respectable until bolstered by data compiled and analyzed by mathematical methods. The evidence provided by natural phenomena, experimentally tested in the laboratory or in the field, and subjected to intensive scrutiny by mathematics forms the foundation on which science rests. For example, data collected by Tycho Brahe did not contribute substantially to the understanding of astronomy until the mathematical genius of Johannes Kepler put it into order and formulated several laws of planetary motion. A second example is more recent. The hypothesis, developed by Jonas Salk, of polio inoculation by weakened virus did not gain public acceptance until it was supported by statistical methods on a large scale.

Science teachers in middle and senior high school have an obligation to convey to students an understanding of the role of mathematics in science. Every opportunity should be used to show the integral nature of mathematics courses in grades 7–12, although little crossover between these disciplines is currently afforded. Students are led to believe that science and mathematics are unrelated entities. This attitude is often perpetuated by the teachers of both subjects, perhaps because they are unfamiliar with possible common objectives and applications. In practice, the difficulty of incorporating mathematics into science classes is compounded by extreme variations in mathematical ability among students. At any grade level, students in the science classes have mathematics competencies that range several grade levels above and below the average for the particular grade. Some students may have difficulties with simple addition and subtraction operations, while at the same time other students may have an understanding of ratio and proportion, percentage, and use of science notation. Science teachers confront this great variation and should plan science activities accordingly. The mathematical requirements for any given activity or experiment are also extremely varied. By suitably individualizing the instruction, students can be challenged at their level and in the process gain competence in the particular mathematical skill. See, for example, the Teaching Science Activities in Appendix A. Mathematics and science have many features in common. These include a belief in understandable order; an interplay of imagination and rigorous logic; ideals of honesty and openness; the critical importance of peer criticism; the value placed on being the first to make a key discovery; the international scope; and even, with the development of electronic computers, the ability to use technology to open up new fields of investigation.

The NCTM standards[12] emphasize problem solving, communication, reasoning, connections, estimation, measurement, patterns and relationships, and other areas that are equally important in science and mathematics education. Ronald Good also points out that we are likely to see more efforts to coordinate the curriculum and instruction of science and mathematics: The student who sits through math class from 9 a.m. to 10 a.m. is the same student who later sits (or moves around) in science class.[13] Occasional joint planning between the mathematics and science teachers can bring about improved conditions, in both areas, for relating mathematics and science. If mathematics teachers are aware of the uses of mathematics in the science classes at particular grade levels, they may point out the possible applications to their students. In assigning homework problems they may use currently significant examples from science.

Mathematics textbooks can be improved significantly on this point. The scientist is concerned with proper use of units and measurement. Attaching appropriate units to the figures given in word problems in mathematics can develop skills in usage, recognition, and manipulation of units by the students. The problems will take on increased meaning and show the applications of mathematics to science. Team-teaching arrangements between science and mathematics teachers can afford many opportunities for interrelating the two disciplines. Many teachers are trained equally well in both areas and have teaching responsibilities in both. In this case, maximum effectiveness should be achieved.

Visit http://www.prenhall.com/trowbridge and select Topic 1—National Science Education Standards. Select "Science Education Program Standards" and find the link entitled "The Coordination of the Science Program with Mathematics Education" (SEP3). This site describes the School Science and Mathematics Association, which is dedicated to providing leadership in the integration of science and mathematics. Obtain a copy of the journal published by SSMA, read a few articles, and submit a page of comments about the articles to your instructor using the Electronic Bluebook module.

MATHEMATICS AND ITS CONNECTIONS WITH SCIENCE DISCIPLINES

Too often the mathematics learned by secondary school science students seems to have little relevance to the mathematics used in their science courses. There needs to be increased cooperation and planning between mathematics and science teachers to bridge the gap that now exists to make the mathematics relevant to the science being studied. For example, developments in the teaching of biology at all levels reveal the need for students to have a mathematical background and an ability to bring mathematical experience and skills to bear on practical problems of measurement, classification, observation, and recording. It is equally clear that in studying biology meaningful, relevant situations can provide a springboard and motivation for learning and applying mathematics. The authors of biology textbooks assume that students understand the mathematics of measurement. The student may be asked to use a hand lens and to place the object being examined at the focal length of the lens, which is perhaps 6 centimeters (cm). Understanding of the metric system is required here. Reference may be made to the size of a human cell, which may be measured in micrometers and is frequently expressed using exponential notation. This also requires the student to be familiar with the metric system as well as the use of powers-of-ten notation. All sciences now work in the world of the very small. "Nanoscience" in biology, elementary particle physics, computer chip design and extremely short time intervals discussed in cosmology, and many other areas routinely use the prefix "nano" to refer to "billionths of" a meter, a second, or other measurement unit.

Ratio and proportion are other important mathematical concepts frequently used in biology. The ratio of length to width of plant leaves and the proportion of biomass to nutrition provided for plant growth are two concepts that require these mathematical understandings.

Statistical understanding is needed because frequently such things as the mean, median, and mode are expressed when talking about population and growth. When frequency tables are used, students must have the knowledge of collecting a sample in order to make a statistical count. It also is important for students to under-

stand the idea of using discrete and continuous data in graphing notations.

Calculating relationships between two sets of unit measurements such as Fahrenheit and Celsius temperature scales requires mathematical understanding. To be able to make conversions from one temperature scale to another is a skill required not only in biology but in many other sciences.

The concept of very small and very large numbers is another mathematical tool frequently used in biology. For example, giving students a problem involving bacteria growth where the number of bacteria doubles every 25 minutes provides a beautiful opportunity for them to calculate exponentially.

Another important concept is the idea of scaling and scaling factors. One exercise is to have students determine the food requirements of a small mammal, such as a mole, and of a very large animal, such as an elephant. Does the food requirement alter with respect to size, volume, mass, or other factors? This concept also can be applied to heat loss and the necessary rate of metabolism to maintain life. All of these are mathematical concepts that are needed in biology and whose application will

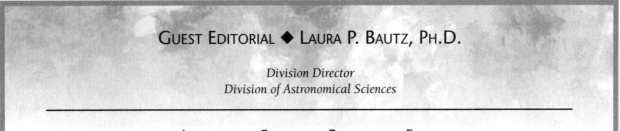

GUEST EDITORIAL ◆ LAURA P. BAUTZ, PH.D.

Division Director
Division of Astronomical Sciences

ASTRONOMY: EXPLORING BEYOND THE EARTH

In late February 1987, the explosion of a star 170,000 light years away became visible in the Southern Hemisphere. It immediately stimulated research all over the world as astronomers raced to observe and analyze this spectacular event. Press coverage of this occurrence attested to the public's interest in the phenomenon by which a star, many times more massive than our own sun, blew itself apart in the last stages of its life. Events such as the 1987 supernova are not the only ones in astronomy to capture the imagination. Astronomy is the science that leads to understanding conditions found on other planets, how stars form and evolve, what happened to shape the present universe, and other questions. On an immediate level, astronomy assists in measuring time, in explaining tides and seasons, and in enhancing pleasure at viewing the night sky. Professional astronomers gather and analyze information

that comes from distant celestial objects. Most of this information comes to earth as light, which we view through telescopes, or radio waves, which we collect through enormous antennae. We then process our data using computers. One does not need sophisticated equipment to view the skies, however. A pair of binoculars is sufficient to reveal craters on the moon, and if there are no city lights to interfere, one can see clouds of stars, bright gas among some stars, and the rich diversity of astronomical objects. These can all be seen in more depth at planetariums, observatories, and science museums.

Astronomy is a physical science and one that requires an initial effort to master the basic principles. Students who want to become astronomers should keep their options open and study mathematics and basic science courses.

Mathematics, science, and environmental sciences find common ground in technological advances.

help students to better understand the use of mathematics in science.

Mathematics concepts used in chemistry at a more sophisticated level are those of ratio and proportion. Concepts of pressure, volume, and temperature change and the use of the general gas laws provide opportunities for students to apply these mathematical operations. Manipulations of equations and formulas also require mathematics. Calculations need to be made in balancing equations. A chemical equation is similar to a mathematical formula in its application. It is evident that mathematics has much to offer chemistry, biology, and other science subjects. Conversely, mathematics also can gain greatly from these subjects if the teachers of mathematics and the sciences make an effort to plan and to standardize the notation systems they use. If the mathematics teachers in their applications will use science examples and if the science teachers will apply the mathematics at every opportunity in working science problems, students will understand that mathematics and science are inseparable entities and highly important to scientific endeavor.

Simple Statistics

An aspect of mathematics in science that needs greater attention is the use of simple statistical techniques. Students should have opportunities to assemble data, con-struct frequency distributions, and calculate certain measures of central tendency (such as the mode, median, and mean) and certain measures of dispersion (such as the range, average deviation, and standard deviation). Exercises requiring these operations will emphasize the intimate relationships between science and mathematics. Certain experiments lend themselves well to statistical computations, particularly those dealing with biological populations or probability problems.

SCIENCE AND READING

A frequently neglected connection is that of reading and science. Because students obtain information from science textbooks, their reading skills play an important role, yet too often the level of the reading matter is inappropriate for their grade level. Often students are unaware that reading and understanding science material is quite different from reading novels or short stories. As a result, they lose effectiveness in their reading.

Larry Yore has noted several points bearing on the beliefs and attitudes school teachers have regarding reading in science.[14] He believes that science teachers place high value on reading as an important strategy to promote learning in science and generally accept responsibility for teaching content reading skills to science students. Many accept the importance of science reading as a component of scientific literacy and as a means of

GUEST EDITORIAL ◆ WILLIAM A. ANDERSON, PH.D.

Program Director Earthquake Hazard Mitigation Program
Division of Critical Engineering Systems

EARTHQUAKES: REDUCING DEATH AND DAMAGE

On September 19, 1985, a large earthquake rocked Mexico City, left thousands of people dead, and caused millions of dollars in property damage. Some years before, on March 27, 1964, an earthquake in Alaska killed over a hundred people and caused millions of dollars in property damage. I studied the social and economic impact of the Alaskan earthquake as a graduate student in sociology. As a result of my work, I realized that many parts of the world are threatened by earthquakes such as these in the United States alone, 39 states are subject to earthquakes. Because earthquake hazards touch many countries, a global community of researchers study the phenomena. When appropriate, the United States has joined in establishing cooperative international programs for joint research and the sharing of vital information. I have worked with researchers from Japan, China, and Mexico. In particular I have been active in a program that was established with Mexico following the Great 1985 Mexico City-Earthquake, which has taught us many lessons on how to reduce earthquake hazards. Many people in different scientific and technical disciplines are required to extend our understanding of earthquakes. Some of the researchers I work with include seismologists, geologists, engineers, and sociol-ogists like me. Through their investigations, seismologists and geologists are developing a basic understanding of what causes earthquakes. Their goal is to understand seismic events well enough to predict earthquakes, thereby giving the public time to prepare. Engineers are completing equally-important work in the design and development of buildings that can withstand the enormous structural strains and stresses caused by earthquakes. More earthquake casualties result from collapsed and damaged buildings than from any other cause, so improved buildings would save many lives. Sociologists are also contributing to our growing knowledge about the effects of earthquakes. As a sociologist, I study the actions that people and organizations must take to prepare for and respond to earthquakes; some of these actions include finding effective ways to educate the public about the earthquake hazard; reducing the exposure of populations to earthquakes through land-use planning; and organizing such emergency actions as medical response, and search and rescue. The common goal of the researchers who study earthquakes is to reduce the property damage and loss of life that result from these disasters. I find it very satisfying to work with those who are exploring this frontier of science.

improving science achievement. Jeffrey Mallow has concluded that students have a great range of misconceptions regarding science reading. Among these misconceptions, students believe: (1) science vocabulary is the same as ordinary vocabulary, (2) science textbook materials are to be memorized, (3) one can read science as rapidly as literature, and (4) all science reading is of the same sort and at the same level. Students commonly think, "If I can't understand a popular account of science, then I must be incapable of grasping science altogether." Some suggestions Mallow makes regarding improving students' ability to read science materials are: (1) use objectives and reviews for orientation toward the material, (2) read slowly and reread, going back and forth between sections, and read any margin notes provided, (3) use questions and exercises interactively with specific chapter sections, and (4) use problems interactively with the whole chapter.[15] An Integrated Approach to Middle School Science and Technology Professional associations, reports, and national standards and benchmarks call for changes in middle level science education that affect the science curriculum.[16,17,18,19,20,21] Some of the key recommendations include: emphasizing science as inquiry, especially higher-order thinking skills; focusing on personal and social issues and the connections among science, technology, and society; integrating science disciplines with one another and other disciplines; and organizing the curriculum around unifying themes.

Mathematics and science teachers must work together and with students to make better connections between mathematics and science curriculums.

An Integrated Approach to High School Science and Technology

Global Science: Energy, Resources, Environment is an environmental science program designed for high school students. This program integrates chemistry, biology, physics, and earth science into a laboratory-oriented curriculum. Labs or classes allow students to analyze social problems and understand how science is relevant to their personal lives. By viewing the world as a dynamic, self-supporting ecosystem, students gain a new appreciation of our planet and the knowledge to manage its resources intelligently. Figure 10–3 provides an annotated table of contents for Global Science, which gives an indication of the program's integrated approach. We also include the science disciplines in Global Science (see Figure 10–4). This is an example of the second criteria outlined by Hayes-Jacobs; namely, curriculum must include both disciplinary and interdisciplinary approaches.

Summary

Justification for interdisciplinary approaches to curriculum vary. Some authors think that fewer students are interested in science courses because of economic reasons; they do not see job possibilities in science, so they pursue other studies. Another proposed explanation for a lack of interest in science is that students often think science is dull, particularly when the only science they encounter is presented in a form that lacks

connections to personal and social contexts. Many individuals and reports have proposed that the scientific and technologic understanding and skills that students need should be developed in personally meaningful and socially relevant contexts. These recommendations support an interdisciplinary approach to the science curriculum; that is, curriculum connections should exist not only between science disciplines but also among other areas of educational and intellectual growth. Increasingly, science teachers recognize the need to integrate science with other disciplines. The ability to synthesize information, to view world problems holistically, and to look at the interrelated dimensions of problems that affect human life are becoming more important.

Interdisciplinary programs and unified approaches to studying science appear to be growing. There is a need for greater emphasis on relating mathematics and secondary school sciences. Students of mathematics should have opportunities to apply their mathematical skills to the solution of scientific problems; applications should be called to their attention. The use of inquiry methods in science teaching provides many opportunities for incorporating mathematics. In this way mathematics is seen as a tool of science for quantifying and testing hypotheses. Students practice, on a realistic and meaningful level, the skills learned in their mathematics classes. In addition to practice in the usual skills of addition, subtraction, scientific notation, logrithms, use of calculators, and so forth, students in modern science learn to evaluate measurements, express precision of data and results, work with significant figures, and apply statistical tests to their data. These skills are practiced at

1. *The Grand Oasis in Space*
   Students build an understanding of ecosystems.
2. *Basic Energy/Resource Concepts*
   Students develop an understanding of the laws governing energy and mineral resource use.
3. *Mineral Resources*
   Students learn how mineral deposits are formed, where they are located, and how they are mined.
4. *Growth and Population*
   Students learn about exponential growth and population issues.
5. *Food, Agriculture, and Population Interactions*
   Students examine nutrition and the fundamentals of food production, modern agricultural practices, and the world food situation.
6. *Energy Today*
   Students build understandings of the energy sources for modern societies.
7. *Nonrenewable Resource Depletion*
   Students examine the depletion pattern for nonrenewable resources and examine resource lifetimes.
8. *Nuclear Energy*
   Students understand the basic principles of nuclear energy and consider its potential as an energy option.
9. *Energy Alternatives*
   This chapter focuses on the energy source alternatives to oil, gas, coal, and nuclear power.
10. *Strategies for Using Energy*
    Students examine energy options and consider options for future planning.
11. *Water: Quantity and Quality*
    This chapter builds an understanding of the importance of having adequate quantities of high-quality water for modern societies.
12. *Resource Management: Air and Land*
    Students examine ways of improving our ability to use air and land.
13. *The Economics of Resources and Environment*
    Students combine scientific information and economic principles related to resource and environmental challenges.
14. *Options for the Future*
    Students develop models of the future.

FIGURE 10–3 *Global Science: Energy-Resources-Environment* Annotated Table of Contents

Chapter	Life Science	Earth Science	Chemistry	Physical Science	Physics
1. The Grand Oasis in Space	•	•	•	•	
2. Basic Energy/Resource Concepts	•		•	•	•
3. Mineral Resources		•	•	•	•
4. Growth and Population	•				•
5. Food, Agriculture, and Population Interactions	•	•	•		
6. Energy Today		•	•	•	•
7. Nonrenewable Resource Depletion		•		•	•
8. Nuclear Energy	•	•	•	•	•
9. Energy Alternatives	•	•	•	•	•
10. Strategies for Using Energy		•	•	•	•
11. Water: Quantity and Quality	•	•	•	•	
12. Resource Management: Air and Land	•	•	•	•	•
13. The Economics of Resources and Environment					•
14. Options for the Future	•	•	•	•	•

FIGURE 10–4 Disciplinary Representation in *Global Science*

all levels of junior and senior high school. The National Science Education Standards and Benchmarks for Science Literacy encourage the inclusion of other areas such as technology, history and nature of science, and personal and social issues in the curriculum. There are examples of interdisciplinary approaches to curriculum that emphasize science concepts and skills as well as other disciplines.

◆
_____

REFERENCES

1. Jerome Bruner, *The Process of Education* (Cambridge, MA: Harvard University Press, 1960).

2. Jerome Bruner, *Toward a Theory of Instruction* (New York: W.W. Norton & Company, 1968).

3. John Christensen, "Integrated Secondary Science: The Time is Now," in New Directions in Education (Dubuque, IA: Kendall/Hunt Publishing Company, 1994).

4. Heidi Hayes-Jacobs, *Interdisciplinary Curriculum: Design and Implementation* (Alexandria, VA: Association for Supervisors and Curriculum Development, 1989).

5. Kathleen Roth, "Second Thoughts About Interdisciplinary Studies," *American Educator,* 18 (1) (1994): 48.

6. Rodger W. Bybee, et al., "Teaching History and Nature of Science: A Rationale," *Science Education,* 75 (1) (1991).

7. National Research Council (NRC), *National Science Education Standards* (Washington, DC: Author, 1996).

8. American Association for the Advancement of Science (AAAS), *Science for All Americans* (Washington, DC: Author, 1989).

9. American Association for the Advancement of Science (AAAS), *Benchmarks for Science Literacy* (Washington, DC: Author, 1993).

10. National Science Teachers Association, "Science Education for Middle and Junior High Students," *Science and Children,* 24 (3) (1986): 62–63.

11. AAAS, *Science for All Americans:* 34.

12. National Council of Teachers of Mathematics, *Curriculum and Evaluation Standards for School Mathematics* (Reston, VA: Author, 1989).

13. Ronald Good, "Editorial: Research on Science-Mathematics Connections," *Journal of Research in Science Teaching* (February 1991): 109.

14. Larry D. Yore, "Secondary Science Teachers Attitudes Toward and Beliefs About Science Reading and Science Textbooks," *Journal of Research in Science Teaching,* 28 (1) (1991): 55–72.

15. Jeffrey V. Mallow, "Reading Science," *Journal of Reading,* 34 (1991): 324–328.

16. AAAS, *Science for All Americans.*

17. J. A. Beane, *A Middle School Curriculum: From Rhetoric to Reality* (Columbus, OH: National Middle School Association, 1990).

18. R. W. Bybee, C. E. Buchwald, S. Crissman, D. R. Heil, P. J. Kuerbis, C. Matsumoto, and J. D. McInerney, *Science and Technology Education for the Middle Years: Frameworks for Curriculum and Instruction* (Washington, DC: The National Center for Improving Science Education, 1990).

19. California State Department of Education, *Caught in the Middle* (Sacramento: Author, 1988).

20. Carnegie Council on Adolescent Development, *Turning Points* (New York: Carnegie Corporation of New York, 1989).

21. AAAS, *Benchmarks for Science Literacy.*

PLANNING FOR INSTRUCTION AND ASSESSMENT

The fun of teaching science involves figuring out the most interesting strategies and techniques to enhance learning. The most dismal thing that can happen is to get in a rut and keep teaching in the same ways day after day. Students soon get bored, and soon you will become jaded, too.

The solution to this is to create new, effective, and innovative ways to present material, use games to stimulate interest, and get students personally involved in their learning. For too long science teachers have looked at students as receptacles for knowledge—the fount for which is the teachers themselves, or the science textbook. But things are changing as we employ new ways of teaching and learning. If we look at science classes as a place where students can use their fertile minds to solve problems, gather data, explore new avenues, or create different solutions, we will find that they respond favorably and learn science. There will be some excitement in every class as students look for changes in things they are growing, see the results of an experiment, or learn of some exciting information that relates to the natural or designed world. Students are curious and responsive to new challenges. Our job is to direct these traits so that learning occurs. This is what makes our jobs interesting.

In the process of becoming involved in their own learning, students develop certain desirable knowledge, skills, and attitudes that stay with them throughout their lives. Whether they go into science as a career or not, certain understandings, habits of careful observation, deliberation before drawing conclusions, and healthy skepticism all will be useful characteristics in any field of endeavor. The development of scientific literacy is not merely being able to read science materials with understanding, but also to develop a full appreciation of where scientific information comes from, the differences between science and technology, and how each of these impinges on society.

Our goal as science teachers should be to produce scientifical-literate citizens who can make valid and considered judgments about decisions relating to science and technology. It certainly is true that we live in an increasingly scientific and technologic world that is likely to become even more complex in the future. Citizens of the 21st century are in middle and high schools today. What a responsibility we have as science teachers to ensure that these children will be well equipped to cope with the challenges ahead! You have chosen an exciting career in science instruction for secondary school students. With thoughtful preparation, you are destined for success.

INQUIRY AND CONCEPTUAL CHANGE

Inquiry is the process by which scientists pose questions about the natural world and seek answers and deeper understanding, rather than knowing by authority or other processes.[1]

This quote, taken from the draft edition of the *National Science Education Standards* document of 1992, suggests that teaching school science might be more in tune with the practice of science if it were taught in a questioning mode rather than in the traditional expository mode used in most science classes. This chapter proposes that teaching in an inquiry manner may result in students learning science in a way that expresses more accurately the true nature of science; this method may also bring about conceptual changes in students' minds more effectively and more permanently.

To emphasize the importance of inquiry teaching methods in science, the *National Science Education Standards,* published in 1996, stated in their *Teaching Standard A* that "Teachers of science plan an inquiry-based science program for their students." They continue by stating that "Inquiry into authentic questions generated from student experiences is the central strategy for teaching science. Teachers focus inquiry predominantly on real phenomena, in classrooms, outdoors, or in laboratory settings, where students are given investigations or guided toward fashioning investigations that are demanding but within their capabilities."[2]

INQUIRY

It is important to begin by saying that inquiry is not solely within the domain of science. Other areas of intellectual endeavor, such as social problems, mathematics, analysis of literature, and history also use inquiry effectively. For example, suppose that one wishes to study the potential effects of increasing populations (including human, animal species, and plant life) on the environment in a given part of the world. To study this topic, certain questions would need to be asked, certain hypotheses formulated, experiments designed, data gathered and analyzed, and conclusions drawn. These activities represent inquiry and investigation. The information could not be obtained simply by referring to books or authorities because the information may not be available. Inquiry becomes a necessary method of attacking the problem.

When students study science using investigation and inquiry, they employ many different skills. Some of these skills are psychomotor that involve doing something physical, such as gathering and setting up apparatus, making observations and measurements, recording data, and drawing graphs. Other skills students employ are intellectual or academic, such as analyzing data, making comparisons, evaluating results, preparing reports, and communicating results to other students or teachers. Students engage in a full range of performances to fully explore a problem, an experience that prepares them for the future when other problems confront them. They are not limited to rote memorization and recitation as is often the case in traditional methods of learning. Instead, students have developed certain lifelong learning skills that will serve them well in the future.

The *National Science Education Standards* suggest several inquiry skills twelfth graders should have mastered.[3] They are as follows.

Developing the abilities of scientific inquiry is an important goal of science teaching.

Students should be able to:

1. Formulate usable questions by:
   a. generating a number of possible questions;
   b. recognizing which questions are in the domain of scientific inquiry;
   c. being aware of the complexity of questions being generated.
2. Plan experiments by:
   a. selecting a question that can be explored through experimental procedures;
   b. designing a procedure for the systematic collection of data; and
   c. choosing appropriate measuring tools.
3. Conduct systematic observations by:
   a. choosing and/or designing and building tools and apparatus;
   b. using tools and apparatus;
   c. collecting and recording data (judging their precision and accuracy);
   d. organizing data; and
   e. representing data.
4. Interpret and analyze data by:
   a. graphing data; and
   b. retrieving, using, and comparing data from other investigations.
5. Draw conclusions by:
   a. relating conclusions to data and their analysis;
   b. relating their experiment to other experiments;
   c. relating their experiment to models and theories; and
   d. suggesting further investigations (formulating new questions).

6. Communicate by:
   a. using words, graphs, pictures, charts, and diagrams to describe the results of their experiments;
   b. producing summaries or abstracts of their work;
   c. using technology to improve communications; and
   d. analyzing critically other people's experimental work.
7. Coordinate and implement a full investigation by:
   a. formulating questions;
   b. planning experiments;
   c. conducting systematic observations;
   d. interpreting and analyzing data; and
   e. drawing conclusions and communicating the entire process.

Students should be able to demonstrate each skill in a new experiment. Evidence of individual skills and the ability to conduct a full investigation will be documented in the reports that students write during the communication component.

In addition to skill development, certain attitudes are fostered that give a realistic picture of how science proceeds in real life. It becomes obvious to students experiencing inquiry and investigation that ready-made answers to problems do not automatically appear. Much hard work and thinking are necessary to solve most problems. Rarely can answers to problems be found by simple reference to authority. Becoming aware of this fact and developing the necessary skills to proceed on one's own gives students a feeling of self-sufficiency that pays dividends in the future.

As one prepares to teach an inquiry lesson, certain fundamental qualities of the teaching process stand out. The following list represents a variety of recognizable behaviors found in inquiry-based or investigative lessons. Not all behaviors will be found in each lesson, but a majority of them will be present if the lesson is to qualify as an inquiry experience.

1. There should be a recognizable question. The question may be student-initiated or teacher-initiated. It may be identified in reading material, life experiences (daydreaming or other wakeful encounters) or from other sources.
2. There should be a plan of attack to answer the question. The plan may include data-gathering through the use of library resources, reference to authorities, experimentation, or alert attention to serendipitous events. Systematic records should be established for all information gathered in the process.
3. There should be a period of analysis in which relationships between entities are explored and examined. This may be a period when hypotheses are formulated and tentatively evaluated.

4. There should be a period of testing and checking to look for inconsistencies or verification of hypotheses. Careful records should be kept for future reference and examination.

5. Tentative conclusions should be drawn and stated in written form, with the expectation that further data collection may force reevaluation of the conclusions. With this caveat in mind, the conclusions may be circulated among classmates and other interested parties for comments and suggestions.

6. An effort should be made to review the problem, the procedures used in attacking the problem, data-gathering processes, and analysis of results. Conclusions should be based objectively on the data gathered. Avoid unsupported opinions and subjective statements in the conclusions.

Visit http://www.prenhall.com/trowbridge and select Topic 1—Science Teaching Standards. Select "Web Links" and find the link for "Planning inquiry-based programs" (ST1). Find the link that suggests an annotated list of inquiry based classroom activities for science teachers. Pick one activity and submit a response to your instructor using the Electronic Bluebook module.

Following are several examples of short inquiry-based lessons that examplify the above points:

◆

Finding Out About Light Switches

Problem: How can you design a switch that can turn a circuit on or off from two locations. (For example, you might want a switch at the bottom and at the top of a staircase.)

Plan of attack: Gather information (have students decide what information they might need (i.e., flowing electricity needs conducting wires, a complete circuit, a source of current, etc.). Draw a wiring diagram (straight lines for wires, proper symbols for battery or current source, switches, light bulbs, etc.). Check the workability of the circuit. Discuss this plan with classmates.

Construction and testing: Gather materials and construct the circuit using the wiring diagram as a guide. Make proper connections with correct materials and tools. Test the completed circuit. If it fails to work, recheck all connections and wiring. Continue until successful.

Report results: Communicate what you have learned to a classmate who was not involved with this investigation.

(Note: Do not study the solution on the next page until you have made a sincere effort to solve the problem yourself.)

Three-way light switch (Solution) It is convenient to have a light that can be turned on and off from two locations, such as at the bottom and at the top of a stairs. How can a circuit be arranged to accomplish this?(See Figure 11–4).

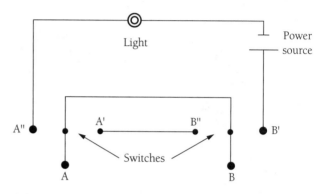

FIGURE 11–A Schematic Diagram of a Three-way Light Switch

Step 1 Bottom of stairs	B is to the right
	Move A to the left
	Light goes on
Step 2 Top of stairs	A is to the left
	Move B to the left
	Light goes off
Step 3 Bottom of stairs	A is to the left
Visitor wishes to come up	B is to the left
	Move B to the right
	Light goes on
Step 4 Top of stairs	A is to the left
	B is to the right
	Move B to the left
	Light goes off
Step 5 Top of stairs	A is to the left
Both wish to descend	B is to the left
	Move B to the right
	Light goes on
Step 6 Bottom of stairs	A is to the left
	B is to the right
	Move A to the right
	Light goes off

◆

Teaching Half-Life Concepts

The concept of half-life is often misunderstood by secondary school science students. A simple inquiry experiment may be set up using water flowing from a large graduated cylinder through a small rubber tube. See Figure 11–B.

Problem: How can you determine the "age"? (i.e., the time when the large graduated cylinder was full of water)

Plan of attack: Fill a 1000 ml graduated cylinder with water and attach a small rubber tube over the top lip of the cylinder. Start water flowing by siphon action into another empty 1000 ml cylinder. Use a stopwatch to determine elapsed times. Control the water flow by using a small screw clamp on the discharge tube.

Data-gathering: What elapsed times should you observe? What volume markings on the graduated cylinders should you observe? What do you observe regarding the rate of emptying of the first cylinder and the rate of filling of the second cylinder? What was the "half-life" of the draining water? (i.e., the time it took for half of the water to drain) What was the "half-life" in the second stage? (time it took for half of the water to drain) What was the "half-life" of the third stage? The fourth stage? How do these half-lives compare?

Analysis: Set six 100 ml graduated cylinders over a light box as shown in Figure 11–C. Fill each with colored water to the level shown in the figure. On a piece of stiff cardboard placed behind the cylinders, draw a curved line through the midpoints of each of the respective levels of water shown. Predict where the curved line would continue if there were seventh and eighth cylinders with water in them. In which cylinder

FIGURE 11–B Set-up for Half-Life Inquiry

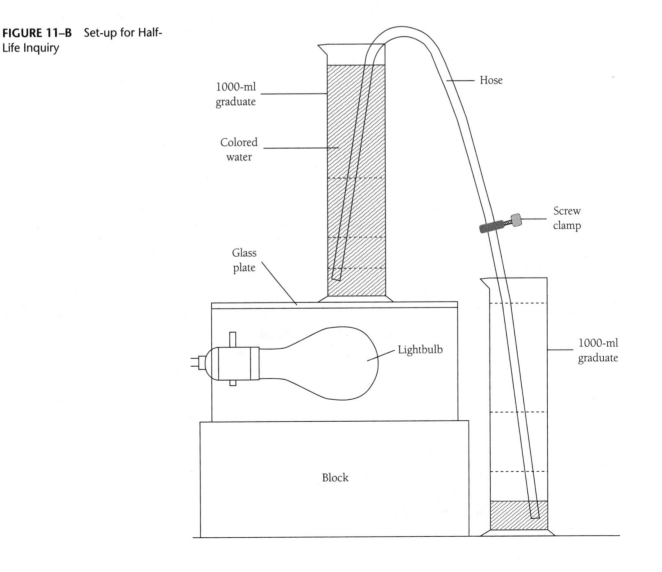

FIGURE 11–C   Graph Showing
Half-Life Determination

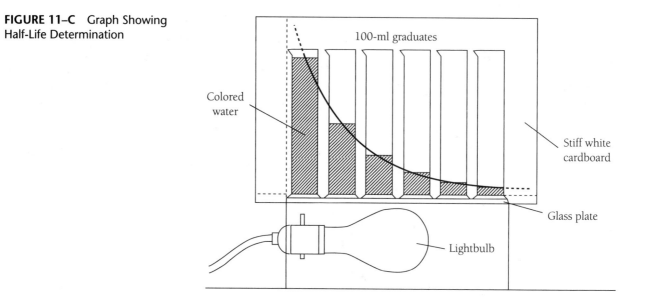

would there be NO water? What conclusion can you draw from this experiment? From your experiment, how long ago was the large cylinder completely full? This is the "age" of the water in the beginning large cylinder. These concepts can be applied to the decay of radioactive substances to determine their age.

◆

CONCEPTUAL CHANGE

Children entering our science classes at the middle school or high school level already have a vast store of knowledge of science from previous classes and personal experiences. One mistake new teachers make is to assume that their students are somewhat like blank slates and that what one needs to do is start from scratch and build new science concepts in their minds. This would be fine if it were not for the fact that the new concepts have to compete with old information already present. Sometimes these two entities are quite different, and they may even be incompatible. In addition, the old information may be preferred. It is often uncomfortable to be told that one's knowledge is incomplete or wrong.

As children construct their world from observations, trial-and-error experiences, instruction from classroom teachers, words of wisdom from their parents, and numerous other sources, they form concepts of how the world works and behaves. Being pragmatists, children use the knowledge they have gained to explain the unfamiliar things they encounter. If the information seems to offer satisfactory explanations and it appears to work for them, it becomes ingrained in their

behavior. "What works is true" is a familiar quotation from the famous psychologist, William James. As children process information, many apparent explanations they formulate may not agree with scientists' understandings of the phenomena.

Thus, when these children reach school age and are given formal instruction, the previous concepts retained in their minds may be naive, incomplete, tentative, or incorrect, and it may interfere strongly with what the teacher is trying to convey. It has been found that such misconceptions are amazingly tenacious and difficult to change.

Consider how humans approach their understanding of the world around them. All knowledge comes through our senses. All normal human beings have five sensory organs that continually bring information that is somehow accepted and assimilated into our prior knowledge. This accumulation of knowledge forms the basis on which we respond to the world and to new events. Much of what we learn is based upon common sense. This forms an interpretation of events in which the information provided by our senses forms a strong and convincing argument for what we believe.

Unfortunately, common sense is often uncommonly unreliable. For example, a simple illustration of the unreliability of our sense of touch might be shown by placing each hand in water of different temperatures, one cool and one warm. After a minute or two, put both hands in a third container of water in which the temperature is midway between those of the other two. The sensation we get is that one hand tells us that the water is cool and the other tells us the water is warm. In other words, the hands are very unreliable indicators of the temperature of water.

Another sensory organ that sometimes fools us is the ears. For example, perhaps a helicopter is approaching from a distance. Perhaps we are on a street in which there are several houses on both sides of the thoroughfare. We may, for example, hear the helicopter approach from the south, and then suddenly, just as clearly, it may seem to be approaching from the north. What the ear has given us is response to sound waves that were echoing from one or more of the buildings on the street, so we have a temporary misconception of the location of the helicopter.

There are hundreds of incidents that occur in the life of a growing child that could be illustrated in simple examples like these. As long as they are temporary misunderstandings and are soon corrected by further experiences or a word from a parent or friend, they do no harm. But a more complex situation, for example the observation of a bright crescent moon, might pose a tougher problem. If children think about why the moon is in a crescent shape, perhaps they might think that the earth's shadow is somehow falling on the portion of the moon that they cannot see. After all, an object produces a shadow when it cuts off the light from the source. Perhaps the earth gets in the way of the light from the sun and casts a shadow on the moon. From this it is easy to extend the ideas that sometimes the moon is covered by an even larger shadow, even to the point when it is entirely covered and becomes completely invisible, and that maybe this is why we cannot see the moon during certain times of the month.

This misconception is further reinforced by the very idea that sometimes, as during a lunar eclipse, the shadow of the earth really does block the light from the sun, thus producing the eclipse. Children in elementary and middle schools are fascinated by eclipses; perhaps this concept assumes an inordinate level of importance in their minds, which they naturally extend to the explanation of the moon's monthly phases. Unfortunately, some teachers themselves may be confused on this matter, and they may even reinforce the incorrect concept.

This leads us to the ultimate problem, which concerns teachers at all levels. How can we structure our science classes and other experiences that will help children acquire understandings more in line with those held by scientists or other informed individuals who consider the manner in which the world works?

Most of the time, information in science classes is presented in an expository manner by the teacher. Additional information comes from textbooks, films, videotapes, and other sources. A small fraction of class time is devoted to laboratory work. Some of that time is oriented toward student inquiry or investigations but probably not more than 2 to 3 percent of the class day. There is little investigative kinds of teaching in most of our science classes.

Is the kind of traditional science teaching described above conducive to overcoming misconceptions that are held rather persistently and stubbornly by most learners? The results seem to show that it is not. We do not appear to be making much progress in increasing science literacy among our students or among members of the lay public. Reports keep pointing to the lack of science knowledge in school children in the United States. During the heyday of science curriculum development projects of the 1960s, we seemed to be making gains as reported by the NAEP. Since then, however, science scores have been declining, and our standings as a nation when compared with other industrialized nations usually show children near the bottom in terms of science knowledge.

To overcome these deficiencies, we are faced with the problem of devising different and better teaching strategies in science. Some of the research on generative learning and constructivism may give some clues as to how these problems might be attacked. For example, we might consider:

1. First the action then the words.   Use of this concept might help teachers structure their science lessons so that students encounter firsthand the phenomena under study, rather than simply be told about it as a bit of information they must remember and recall for a test. Strictly verbal learning, which tends to foster a false sense of security about one's knowledge, might thereby be minimized. Students would be able to demonstrate the concepts under study, or state principles in their own words, or suggest ways to apply principles in other contexts. Today, students concentrate so intensely on memorizing a concept's exact words or wording that they fail to grasp the meaning. The types of factual tests we frequently give students reinforces this limited manner of study.

2. Talk through the new concept.   On an individual basis, if possible, have students explain their interpretation of the phenomenon. Try to elicit the reasons why students hold a particular point of view. Ask questions tactfully to identify the points where clarification is needed. Use the basic premise of science, which is that every cause has an effect and every effect is produced by a cause. During this time, use simple demonstrations where possible and examine each phase of the demonstration in detail. Present new information or new points of logical reasoning that are nonthreatening and nonjudgmental. Avoid casting aspersions on previous poor teaching or previous experiences, as such comments might elicit resistance from students. Finalize the session by having students explain in their own words their revised understanding of the phenomenon.

3. Teach the concept to someone else.   We have all experienced the truth of the maxim that "One really learns a subject when one teaches it." Use this truism to help reinforce the new understanding in the students' minds.

Active involvement in science investigations helps students learn.

On a one-to-one basis to start with, have students explain the phenomenon to each other. Have students ask questions of their pupils to see whether the explanation has been clear and logical. Later, you might have students explain or demonstrate the phenomenon in a classroom environment.

4. Don't let the concept die.   Every teacher has probably experienced the situation of memory lapse when explaining a science phenomenon before a class. It is frustrating to suddenly realize that you have forgotten some small point and you get yourself in trouble when explaining the concept. The more frequently you can refresh your memory through repetitions, the more likely you can avoid this embarrassment. It is like regular practice on a musical instrument. Without such practice, things begin to fall apart. This principle applies also in the case of restructuring science concepts. One successful performance does not guarantee success for all time. It has been found that when under pressure, such as during tests, students have a tendency to revert to former knowledge. Frequent repetitions of the newly learned information is necessary, and use of the information in contexts helps to reinforce it in students' minds.

FOSTERING CONCEPTUAL CHANGE THROUGH INQUIRY

Cognitive psychologists have examined our traditional approaches to teaching and have concluded that American pedagogy has been dominated by a behaviorist

Visit http://www.prenhall.com/trowbridge and select Topic 2—Constructivism and Learning in Science. Select "Activities and Lesson Plans" and find the link on Newton's Apple. This popular science program on the Public Broadcasting Service features many science activities and teacher information for science classrooms. Order the teachers' guides available from this website and share with your instructor using the Electronic Bluebook module.

model: In the behaviorist approach, the teacher's task consists of providing a set of stimuli and reinforcements that are likely to get students to emit an appropriate response. If the goal is to get students to replicate a certain behavior, this model works well; but if understanding, synthesis, eventual application, and the ability to use information is our goal in education, a behaviorist approach is not successful. Because there is no place in the model for understanding, it is not surprising that behaviorist training rarely produces it.[4]

The constructivist model of learning, discussed elsewhere in this book, provides greater emphasis on understanding, forming relationships between concepts, relating new learnings to schema already present in the brain, and developing applications of new knowledge to events and problems that the student encounters. It is within this context that inquiry and investigative approaches to problem-solving may be the most beneficial method. To see how this may come about, consider the following examples.

To begin, identify some of the procedures that characterize learning through a constructivist approach. Among these are encouraging student input of creative ideas, using alternative sources of information, using open-ended questions (questions that may have several possible answers), encouraging students to suggest causes for events, making predictions, testing out one's ideas before acceptance, challenging the ideas of others, collecting evidence to support one's ideas, and restructuring one's concepts on the basis of new evidence.

All of these procedures also characterize investigative activities. Students who engage in inquiry perform all of the procedures repeatedly as they study problems. In doing so they develop habits of inquiry in much the same way as do scientists or other investigators. To illustrate, look at the following example.

Suppose an eighth grade science class is faced with the task of measuring the diameter of the sun, a problem found in many earth science textbooks. The class is divided into groups of four people per group. The first task each group must address is, "What kind of measurements would give this information?" Discussion among the group members might lead to the realization that only inexpensive equipment is available, that measurements could only be made during the daytime when the sun is visible, and certain precautions against direct observation of the sun must be observed. A group prediction of the sun's diameter might be made.

Further discussion, perhaps with teacher assistance, might stimulate the idea that one could use proportions between similar triangles to get the answer. Perhaps the group decides that drawing a diagram of the setup would help. The task of selecting equipment becomes easier now because it only needs to fit within a classroom or a convenient outdoor area.

Procurement and construction of the equipment comes next. A metric ruler, some three-by-five index cards, a marking pen, and a paper punch are all that is needed. One bit of necessary information is the distance from the earth to the sun in metric units. This information usually can be obtained from an astronomy textbook. A circle exactly one centimeter in diameter can be drawn on a three-by-five index card. This circle should be drawn carefully to increase accuracy of the measurement. The card should be affixed to the end of the metric ruler in a position perpendicular to the ruler. Another card can have a small diameter hole punched in the center of it. For best results, the hole should only be about two millimeters in diameter.

To obtain the measurements, point the metric ruler at the sun while holding the punched card at some small distance (perhaps 50 centimeters) from the affixed card at the other end of the ruler. An image of the sun will fall on the affixed card. Move the punched card back and forth until the sun's image exactly covers the dot on the affixed card. Now measure the distance from the punched card to the affixed card.

A proportion may now be written as follows:

Distance between the two cards is to the distance of the earth from the sun as the diameter of the sun's image is to the diameter of the sun. From this proportion the diameter of the sun can be obtained.

What skills and procedures were used by students in this investigation? We can identify discussion, sharing of ideas, seeking information from an authority, construction of an apparatus, making a prediction, gathering data, and solving a mathematical relationship, among others. Solution of problems in this manner invariably allows the students to employ and practice many useable skills. Such procedures should be used frequently enough in science classrooms to give students repeated practice. This way it will become second nature to the students and will provide them with a realistic picture of how science advances.

SUMMARY

The strategies of inquiry teaching are emphasized in the *National Science Education Standards* as primary methods of conducting science classes to acquaint students with investigative procedures used by scientists and other problem-solvers. Among the inquiry skills needed to conduct investigations are formulating questions, planning experiments, conducting systematic observations, interpreting and analyzing data, drawing conclusions, communicating results, and coordinating an investigation.

In addition to the skill competencies needed, attitudes such as persistence, willingness to do hard work, and developing abilities to proceed on one's own are essential.

Much discussion is now held among science teachers about how children conceptualize subject material. Ideas of constructivism are proposed, in which it is theorized that learners "construct" their own world of ideas from the sensory input they receive. In the process of doing this, many misconceptions arise, which must be dealt with by their teachers. The chapter discusses methods for dealing with misconceptions. Also several examples of investigative activities are provided as models.

REFERENCES

1. National Committee on Science Education Standards and Assessment, *National Science Education Standards: A Sampler* (Washington, DC: National Research Council, 1992.)

2. *National Science Education Standards,* National Academy Press (Washington, DC: National Research Council, 1996).

3. *National Science Education Standards.*

4. Robert E. Yager, "The Constructivist Learning Model," *The Science Teacher* (September 1991): 54.

CHAPTER 12

QUESTIONING AND DISCUSSION

STUDYING SCIENCE IN DEPTH

Many students fall into a pattern of superficial study of science with their objective being to learn just enough to recognize some vocabulary and to memorize a few facts that may appear on an approaching test. Other students may become sufficiently interested to study the subject more deeply and to explore the concepts and interrelationships. These are sometimes called a *surface approach* as opposed to a *deep approach*. A comparison of these two approaches has been reported by Chin and Brown.[1] They found that "when students used a deep approach, they ventured their ideas more spontaneously, gave more elaborate explanations which described mechanisms and cause and effect relationships, or referred to personal experiences, asked questions which focused on explanations and causes, predictions, or on resolving discrepancies in knowledge, and engaged in 'on-line theorizing'. Students using a surface approach gave explanations that were reformulations of the question, a 'black box' variety which did not refer to a mechanism, or macroscopic descriptions which referred only to what was visible."

An Inquiry Discussion	
1. What have you found out about the pendulum?	This is a good question because it is divergent. It allows for a number of responses. Students will have found out something, and being able to tell it to the instructor will help clarify any problems.
2. What seems to affect the frequency, i.e., the number of times it swings a second?	This is a more convergent question. It helps students center on frequency. They may not have thought of this before. Students replied that they didn't know.
3. Try some things to find out.	The teacher then leaves and moves on to other students requiring some assistance. Later, the teacher returns.
4. What have you done to find out about the frequency?	Here again the instructor is asking a relatively divergent question since the students may have done many things. The students reply that they have used different weights.
5. How did the use of different weights affect the frequency?	The instructor is asking students to interpret data. Students, however, still have not discovered that the length of the string affects the frequency.
6. What do you think the length of the string would have to do with the frequency?	This question is fairly directive-convergent. The instructor is helping students to center on a particular variable.
7. How would you determine this?	This question asks students to devise an experimental procedure.

Obviously, science teachers want to encourage deep approaches instead of surface approaches. How can this be done? One way is to embrace an investigative or inquiry-based approach to teaching science as recommended by the *National Science Education Standards*. Central to this method is liberal and effective use of questioning and discussion.

THE NATURE OF INQUIRY-BASED TEACHING

Inquiry-based teaching has two main elements: arrange the learning environment to facilitate student-centered instruction, and give sufficient guidance to ensure direction and success in discovering scientific concepts and principles. One way that a teacher helps students obtain a sense of direction and use their minds is through questioning. The art of being a good conversationalist requires listening and posing insightful questions. Good inquiry-oriented teachers are excellent conversationalists. They listen well and ask appropriate questions, assisting individuals in organizing their thoughts and gaining insights. Inquiry-oriented teachers seldom tell but often question. A properly given question is a hint. If students are studying a pendulum but have not discovered that its frequency is related to its length, the instructor may notice that the students seem to be having difficulty. The instructor can guide the students by asking a series of questions. Listed on the previous page on the left are the questions asked. On the right is an analysis of what the instructor is doing.

Notice that the instructor aided students, through artful questions, to make their own discoveries and to use their minds. The teacher did not steal the thrill of discovery from the students but instead facilitated it. Proper questioning is a sophisticated teaching art. To practice it, teachers must know where the students' thoughts are and must switch from the classical concept of teaching-telling to listening and questioning and being open to the students' ideas. Consequently, the emphasis changes from teaching to student learning. After perceiving students' difficulties, an instructor must formulate a question that will be a challenge yet that will give guidance. To do so, instructors must know what they are trying to teach in a conceptual way and adapt the question so it is appropriate to the students. Moving about the class, teachers must constantly adapt this procedure from student to student. This process requires unusual awareness and ability. It is no wonder so many teachers fall back into the classical mode of teaching. To move about a classroom in this manner is to truly individualize instruction, teach for the person and, if done constantly in a positive setting, to humanize instruction. Good questioning practices are critical in all areas of science instruction, including discussion, demonstrations, informal lectures, field trips, and others. For interesting activities to engage in to practice your questioning skills in a variety of situations, try those suggested at the end of this chapter.

TYPES OF QUESTIONS

Questions may be planned before class or may arise spontaneously because of student interaction. It is always wise to prepare a series of questions before entering

By moving about the laboratory, the teacher can question and listen to students individually.

an inquiry-oriented class, preparing questions positively to your questioning ability. Having thought about the questions gives you direction and a sense of security, thus enhancing your ability to carry on a discussion.

Inquiry-oriented teachers must remain constantly flexible. Even though they have planned a series of questions, they must be willing to deviate from them and formulate new ones as they interact with students. These unplanned, spontaneous questions may be difficult to create at first, but through developing good questioning techniques, instructors become more sophisticated and more likely to interact appropriately with students.

Before you devise your questions you should decide:

1. What talents are you going to try to develop?
2. What critical thinking processes will you try to nurture?
3. What subject matter objectives do you want to develop?
4. What types of answers will you accept?
5. What skills do you wish to develop?
6. What attitudes and values do you wish to emphasize?

Educational Objectives and Questions

Just as objectives can be classified by this taxonomy, so can questions. Refer to the questions in the previous section and classify them, on the left, according to the taxonomy. Then list five of the best questions and decide why you believe they are good. Bloom's abbreviated taxonomy is repeated to help you (see Chapter 6). An example of how you might use it is shown as a guide.

BLOOM'S TAXONOMY

Cognitive Domain	Affective Domain
Evaluation	Receiving
Synthesis	Responding
Analysis	Valuing
Application	Organizing
Comprehension	Characterizing
Knowledge	

Questions requiring responses from the higher levels of the hierarchy are more desirable because answering them involves more critical and creative thinking and indicates a better understanding of concepts.

USING BLOOM'S AND KRATHWOHL'S TAXONOMIES TO CLASSIFY QUESTIONS

Classification	Sample Question
Knowledge	1. How many legs has an insect?
Synthesis	2. What hypotheses would you make about this problem?
Application	3. Knowing what you do about heat, how would you get a tightly fitted lid off a jar?
Analysis	4. What things do birds and lizards have in common?
Comprehension	5. Operationally define a magnet.
Evaluation	6. If you were going to repeat the experiment, how would you do it better?
Receiving	7. Do you watch science shows on television?
Responding	8. Do you talk to your friends about science?
Valuing	9. What is your interest in earth science now compared to when you began the course?
Valuing	10. What do you value about this film?
Organizing	11. Can you argue using scientific facts, evidence, and data?
Characterizing	12. Do you use problem solving techniques for solving problems at school or at work?

PROCESSES OF SCIENCE AND QUESTIONS

Another way to classify questions is to use science processes. This approach ensures that the basic structure of science and critical thinking is taught. Shown below is a guide of how you might classify questions using science processes such as hypothesizing, designing, observing, graphing, and others.

CLASSIFYING USING SCIENCE PROCESSES

Classification	Sample Question
Observing	1. What do you observe about the landscape?
Hypothesizing	2. What do you think will happen to the solution when I heat it?
Designing an Experiment	3. How would you determine the absorption of the different wavelengths of light in water?
Graphing	4. How would you graph these data?

Setting up Equipment	5. Obtain the following equipment and set it up as directed.
Reducing Experimental Error	6. How many measurements should be made to report accurate data?
Inferring	7. What inferences can you make from the data?

Convergent and Divergent Questions

Another way to classify questions is to determine whether they encourage many answers or just a few. Questions allowing for a limited number of responses and moving toward a conclusion are called *convergent*. Questions allowing for a number of answers are called *divergent*; they provide for wider responses plus more creative, critically considered answers. In an inquiry discussion it is generally desirable to start with divergent questions and move toward more convergent ones if students appear to be having difficulties.

Generally speaking, convergent questions, particularly those requiring only a "yes" or "no" answer, should be avoided because they allow for fewer responses, thereby giving students little opportunity to think critically. The fundamental purpose in using the inquiry approach is to stimulate and develop critical thinking, creative behavior, and multiple talents. Convergent questions generally do little to achieve this end. Remember that, in an inquiry investigation, it is important that students have a chance to use their minds. Learning to think rationally and creatively does much to increase a person's self-concept. Unfortunately, some teachers are so concerned with getting the right answer that they prevent students from going through a thought process. Even though students may come up with wrong conclusions, the students still have had a mental experience in thinking about the problem. Having this experience is probably more important than a right answer. We as teachers would, of course, like for students to think and obtain the correct answer as well. However, recall for a moment a mathematics teacher who only accepts the correct answer to a problem, ignoring the procedures used in obtaining it. Students may have used very good thinking processes to obtain the answer yet misplaced the decimal point. Is the teacher justified in saying that students have not learned because they don't have the right answer? Students probably will never have that problem again but they undoubtedly will have many situations requiring them to use similar logical strategies. It is the thinking that is most important! Teachers who do not reward thinking may stifle students.

Teleological and Anthropomorphic Questions

Teleological (Greek—*teleos*—an end) questions are those that imply that natural phenomena have an end or purpose. The word *anthropomorphic* comes from two Greek words: *anthropos*, meaning *man*, and *morphos*, meaning *form*. An anthropomorphic question implies that some natural phenomenon has the characteristics of humanity. For example, such a question might state that some natural phenomenon has a want or wish: rocks fall because they want to.

Why do you think teleological questions should be avoided? What do they do as far as developing critical thinking and leading to further investigation? How do they contribute to misconceptions?

Talent-Oriented Questions

Although the procedures thus far have mainly emphasized the importance of cognitive questions, other types of questions are also important. Teachers should spend a considerable amount of time formulating talent-oriented questions to help them know their students.

We believe that you should not only determine talent but help to manifest it by rewarding students for all types of talent. Some teachers and administrators may argue that the only function of a science teacher is to develop scientific awareness. It is our view that this awareness will occur to a higher degree if students have opportunities to develop and demonstrate their best talents, thereby building their self-esteem and developing more positive feelings about science. Some examples of talent-oriented questions are listed below.

Questioning to Discover Talent

Talent	*Question*
Artistic	1. What important ideas should be put on a mural to be hung in our laboratory?
Organizing	2. How should we organize the field trip?
Communicating	3. What should be included in a short article about the science fair for the school paper?
Creative	4. In what ways can we convey to the rest of the school how exciting biology, earth

	science, chemistry, and physics are?
Social	5. What shall be the social activities for the science picnic?
Planning	6. How shall we plan our investigations of the pond community throughout the year?

Teachers also should ask questions to find out students' interests. What gets them involved? Determining these interests helps teachers plan increasingly relevant lessons. Asking students individually about their concerns also lets the students know you are interested in them as people and not as sponges to soak up scientific information.

Piaget pointed out that proper questioning gives insights into a student's thought patterns. To do so, the instructor must hypothesize how the student is thinking, then pose questions to see if the hypothesis was correct. The student's response either confirms the hypothesis or indicates a need for further investigation. The instructor may have to formulate a new hypothesis and construct questions to determine its validity. This type of questioning is particularly helpful when the student seems to be having difficulty in discovering or conceptualizing. Excellent teachers in mathematics, physics, chemistry, and other courses often use this approach to diagnose students' thinking-process difficulties and to help them resolve problems.

QUESTIONING PROCEDURES

Wait-Time Affects Quality of Responses

Mary Budd Rowe and her coworkers have done an extensive study of the questioning behavior of teachers.[2] In their analysis of taped classroom discussions, they discovered that teachers, on an average, wait less than a second for students to reply to their questions. Further

Visit http://www.prenhall.com/trowbridge and select Topic 2—Constructivism and Learning in Science. Select "Activities and Lesson Plans." Find the link "Ask Jeeves," which provides a medium for students to ask questions, and Jeeves will search for websites where answers can be found. This practice teaches students to formulate better questions and get quicker results. Summarize the main points brought out in this website and present them to your instructor for discussion using the Electronic Bluebook module.

investigations revealed that some instructors waited an average of three seconds for students to answer questions. An analysis of student responses revealed that teachers with longer wait-times (three seconds or more) obtained greater speculation, conversation, and argument than those with shorter wait-times.

Dr. Rowe found further that when teachers were trained to wait five seconds, on the average, before responding, the following occurred:

1. Students gave longer and more complete answers instead of short phrases.
2. There was an increase in speculative, creative thinking.
3. The number of suggested questions and experiments increased.
4. Slower students increased their participation.
5. Teachers became more flexible in their responses to students.
6. Teachers asked fewer questions, but the ones they asked required more reflection.
7. Students gave a greater number of qualified inferences.
8. Teacher expectations for student performance changed; teachers were less likely to expect only the brighter students to reply.

Dr. Rowe believed that the expectancy levels of students are more likely to change positively if students are given a longer time to respond. She also found that the typical pattern of discussion: teacher-student-teacher can be altered by training instructors to get student-student-teacher responses. This pattern will occur when students are involved in some controversy, for example, determining the best design for an experiment or deciding what conclusions can be drawn from data.

For inquiry-based teaching to occur, most instructors should increase their wait-time tolerance so that students have more opportunities to think and create.

In addition, sociocultural factors may play a part in the effectiveness of the questioning and wait-time procedures. In school systems where high-authoritarian classroom environments prevail, low levels of student questioning may exist, which would tend to negate teachers' efforts to apply suitable wait-time and inquiry techniques, especially in discussion situations in the science classroom.[3]

Good Discussions Are Student-Centered

Most teachers, when they are involved in a class discussion, dominate it to a considerable extent; an inquiry-based class should be student-centered, which means the proportion of time that the teacher talks should be kept to a minimum. Note the two diagrams of discussion interaction in a class in Figure 12–1.

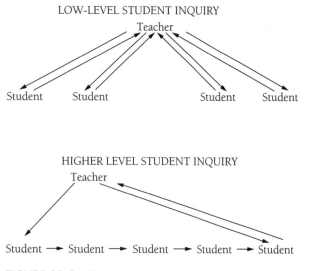

FIGURE 12–1   Discussion Interaction Diagrams

It is not easy to develop techniques so that the second type of interaction operates. How would you as a teacher get the second pattern to operate in your classes?

SOME PRECAUTIONS IN QUESTIONING

It has long been thought that the practice of questioning promotes student thinking and participation, and in most cases it does. However, sometimes certain questioning techniques have the reverse effect and actually shut off student thinking. Frequently what the teacher actually does is initiate a question-and-answer practice that does not evolve into true classroom discussion and does not promote expressiveness, active participation, or independent thinking. Instead, the process may encourage student passivity and dependency. A few precautions are outlined in the following paragraphs to alert teachers to practices that may hinder discussion.

First, sometimes using questions simply results in a back-and-forth interchange between teacher and students in which the teacher is the questioner and the student is the respondent. Instead, try holding back from asking questions at the start, thus encouraging students to take some responsibility for carrying on the discussion, rather than simply being targets of teacher questions.

Second, questions are sometimes used to make a point in which a particular piece of information or idea is underscored. This practice can be counterproductive, because the same information would be more effective as a declarative statement.

Third, questions are often asked to help students who pause or falter in their responses. We sometimes condition students to speak in short bursts in answer to our direct questions, and students don't expect to have to do anything beyond this. True discussion, however, requires thoughtful, sustained reasoning on the part of the students. It requires more time to express complex thoughts or interpretations. If the teacher pushes in too quickly with a question, the effect halts student thought processes and substitutes the teacher's thoughts.

Fourth, questions are sometimes used to elicit predetermined answers. In this case, the teacher has a particular answer in mind and phrases questions so that the student produces the expected answer. This again shuts off speculative responses from students.

Fifth, teachers occasionally ask questions in reply to a student's question. While sometimes recommended as a way of promoting inquiry, the danger is that it may convey the idea that only the teacher gets to ask the questions and that whenever students ask questions, all they get is a redirected question.

Sixth, questions are sometimes used to draw out the nonparticipating students. This assumes that every student is in the frame of mind to respond equally when compared to every other student. The practice may instead intimidate some students and cause others to become wary of future questions. Students may thus prepare answers in advance and fail to listen to the argument or the discussion. Such practices may cause students to withdraw even more rather than to draw them out.

Seventh, using questions to probe the students' personal feelings and experiences in the classroom is risky. This may make the student feel fear and resentment. Such questions should be saved for more "low-pressure"? or "one-on-one" private contacts in which the teacher and the student can talk together comfortably.

Alternative practices can help you avoid these pitfalls. For example, instead of asking a question, make a declarative statement. This can still present the problem or issue to the students and open up avenues for further discussion.

Another alternative to questioning would be to restate the speaker's words. Try to make a statement that interprets what the student has said, thus giving the class an opportunity to reconsider the information. Declare your perplexity when you do not understand something a student has said. Simply state, "I am confused about what you are saying." Invite elaboration. Use a statement such as, "I'd like to hear more of your views on that." Encourage class questions. In a discussion it should be possible for students to ask other students questions or to direct their questions to the person who is speaking, whether the speaker is a teacher or a student. Let the speaker pause and ask a question. This promotes discussion, indicates the speculative nature of the statements that are being made, and gives the student an opportunity to obtain feedback.

Finally, simply maintain silence. Use a longer wait-time to indicate to the student that you are conducting a leisurely practice and you want to provide opportunities for reflection, introspection, and thoughtful answers.[4]

USING QUESTIONING IN A COMPETITIVE LEARNING STRATEGY

A useful technique that employs classroom questioning by the teacher has been described by a group of high school teachers in a Colorado school.[5] This approach takes the form of oral quizzing, which normally happens once a week, usually during a Wednesday class period.

The rules for the oral quizzing are given in Figure 12–2. The numbers on the seating chart represent the average numerical grade the student currently holds. Each student has an equal opportunity to move upward from the C section to the B section to the A section by successfully answering teacher questions on the day of the oral quiz. The strategy has superior motivating potential as well as serves as an excellent mechanism for classroom control.

Advance planning is necessary to ensure that the questions asked give proper attention to higher levels of cognition. Teachers who have used this questioning strategy have reported excellent results and recommend its use to others. It is important to recognize that the competitive spirit is emphasized in this strategy, a fact that may cause some teachers to seek alternatives to this method.

RESEARCH ON QUESTIONING IN THE CLASSROOM

Because of its potential in stimulating thinking and learning, questioning remains one of the most influential teaching behaviors in the classroom. The first major systematic research on questioning was conducted by Stevens at Columbia University in 1912. Almost all the research conducted from that time until the 1950s focused primarily on describing teacher questioning behavior. Results uniformly supported the finding that questions stimulating memory and recall were the type being emphasized in classrooms.

Around 1970, a new increase of activity on teacher questioning began. The emphasis in this research was on identifying specific questioning levels and skills that had an impact on pupil growth.

Full-functioning teachers almost certainly have educational objectives not only at the fact level but also at

WHEN: Any Day

SEATING:

```
76  83  88  94  100
75  82  87  93  99
74  81  86  92  98
73  80  85  91  97
72  79  84  90  96
71  78  83  89  95
```

RULES:

1. Students in A or B seats cannot use notes or text during quizzing.
2. Students in C seats can use notes and text.
3. The student to whom the question is being directed must answer quickly. When the instructor calls for the next person this student's turn is over.
4. By design the questioning must start at the top A with the first question.
5. For missed questions, the first student with the correct answer moves to where the question started. All the students in between move back one seat.
6. Tardy students or those who have been absent *for any reason* must move to the last seat in the last row.
7. Inappropriate behavior will also send a student to the last seat.
8. All students must keep track of where their earned seats are. If there is a dispute or someone forgets where to sit, he or she must move to the last seat in the last row.
9. Questions will *only be asked once.* Some questions may be clarified with the student asking, "What do you mean by _____?"

GRADING:

1. Grades for earned seats will be recorded on Wednesday at the end of the period.
2. Oral quizzing grade will be used to replace the lowest test grade each quarter.

FIGURE 12–2   Oral Quizzing

the concept level and even at the personal meaning and values levels. This necessitates asking high-order questions of students. Teachers then need not determine whether to ask high-level questions but rather need to determine how to find an appropriate balance of lower- and higher-order questions to achieve instructional goals.

There has been much research on the use of questions as a learning strategy. Questions in textual material have been defended on the basis that they provide "advance organizers" for the material to be learned. The use of questions at the higher levels of cognition (such as application, analysis, synthesis, and evaluation) has been shown to have a significant positive effect on student learning. Questions placed within the text material appear to produce better understanding and retention than text material without questions. And in a study on presentation style, groups of students reading material with questions at the beginnings of paragraphs scored higher on an immediate post-test than did groups reading without questions.

As a result of the research over the past 75 years, we can draw several tentative conclusions concerning questioning in the classroom. Teachers appear to persist in asking questions that require students primarily to recall knowledge and information. It is important to consider stressing high-level questions and devising a variety of instructional objectives that balance low-level memory questions with preplanned high-convergent and divergent questions. Teachers can be effectively trained to raise the cognitive emphasis of their questions. There is a tendency for the cognitive levels of questions asked by teachers and responses from pupils to be positively related.

The extent of wait-time teachers use after asking questions dramatically influences the quantity and quality of pupil responses. Teacher educators need to provide training opportunities for teachers to practice increasing their wait-time to a minimum of three seconds.

At the primary level, there is a tendency for the use of lower cognitive level questions to be related to pupil achievement. Teachers need to stress the importance of balancing low and high cognitive level questions to stimulate productive thinking at all grade levels.[6]

Questioning in the Content Areas

Students in science classes experience general questioning techniques but also encounter questioning in the content of their science classes. The skills of formulating good questions in science and of seeking solutions to questions posed by their teachers, their textbooks, and their laboratory experiments are practiced and developed in the context of the science discipline being studied.

Research on reading and questioning in content areas is reported by Bonnie Armbruster and others.[7] Results showed that most questions were directly related to textbook material that was to have been read by the students in their assignments and were largely questions on factual information. Only about 15 percent of the questions required students to analyze, predict, or apply information from the text. These questions came from only a small number of the teachers involved in the study, indicating that the use of high-level questions was somehow related to individual teaching styles. There was also a high percentage of rhetorical questions whose purpose was not clear other than perhaps to form a bridge to foster continuity in class discussions.

Visit http://www.prenhall.com/trowbridge and select Topic 2—Constructivism and Learning in Science. Select "Activities and Lesson Plans" and find the link for "Amusement Park Physics". This site will help students formulate meaningful questions on science principles related to the content of physics. Study the suggestions here and discuss in class what scientific principles are at work in the amusement park.

Gender Differences

Science educators are becoming increasingly concerned about gender differences with respect to expectations, types of experiences, and participation in science classrooms. Roberta Barba and Loretta Cardinale have investigated student questioning interactions in secondary school science classrooms.[8] Results of the study suggest that female students have fewer interactions with science teachers and receive less attention than males. Questions asked of female students were predominantly low-level questions. Males received more teacher interaction, including more questions of higher levels. This trend in questioning female students seems to give females a signal that they have low ability in the sciences. It is also apparent that such behavior occurs before the secondary school level is reached, causing many females to believe that they are incapable of success in science.

Levels of Questions

Studies of teachers' classroom interactions indicate that 60 to 80 percent of teachers' questions require the lowest level of thinking for satisfactory answers.[9]

A practical questioning technique divides teacher questions into soliciting moves and reacting moves. Soliciting moves are categorized as:

◆ recall questions that draw upon past experience or knowledge;
◆ data-collecting questions where students react to direct observations;
◆ data-processing questions, where students hypothesize, analyze, compare, or suggest solutions; and
◆ verification questions, where students evaluate or judge responses.

Reacting moves by the teacher involve the following:

◆ accepting or informing the student that the response is correct;
◆ rejecting or informing the student of the incorrectness of the response;

◆ requesting clarification or further evidence; or

◆ asking another person.

Employment of the above strategies can raise the level of questions, provide opportunities to practice thinking skills beyond mere factual recall, and foster skills that support inquiry and investigative methods.

Development of effective questioning skills among students is as important as developing better questioning techniques among teachers. As science classes adopt more investigative learning and teaching methods, the ability to ask higher-order questions becomes imperative. As with all learning, frequent opportunities to practice the desired skills results in greater improvement.

DISCUSSION AS A MEANS OF INQUIRY

An excellent model for leading a discussion is that of a clever talk show host. What is it that such a person does to stimulate the interesting, even exciting discussions that frequently are held on radio and television programs?

A number of clues can be found in the manner in which the host conducts the show—both in preparation and during the show itself. While each host is different, there are certain common elements. A good talk show host:

1. studies the topic before the show,
2. presents an interesting background analysis before eliciting comments from the participants,
3. relaxes the guests,
4. avoids embarrassing anyone,
5. keeps the discussion moving at a good pace,
6. rewords any comments that might be misunderstood,
7. prevents anyone from monopolizing the discussion or going off on a tangent,
8. encourages the participants to speak about their feelings,
9. uses humor to reduce tension,
10. asks good questions of a divergent variety.[10]

With these guidelines, a teacher can conduct a similarly interesting discussion that will stimulate students to open up and participate. There is no shortage of interesting topics in science to bring up for discussion, particularly now that the interrelationships of science to technology and society are fair game in science classes.

Advantages of Discussion

Students become more interested when they are involved, thus discussion is a desirable approach for class procedures. Since an objective of modern science instruction is to teach science as a process, with an emphasis on the individual's cognitive development, students must have time and opportunities to think. A student can't think unless given opportunities to do so. The presentation of problems in a discussion requires students to think before they can formulate answers. A teacher who tells students all about a subject offers only boredom. In addition, the students have been robbed of an opportunity to use their minds. All they have to do is soak up information and memorize it.

Discussion is more likely to develop inquiry behavior. A discussion leader interested in developing inquiring behavior seldom gives answers but asks questions instead. In answering, students learn to evaluate, analyze, and synthesize knowledge. They are often thrilled to discover fundamental ideas for themselves. Another benefit of discussion is that the teacher receives feedback. An astute discussion leader learns quickly from student comments about how much students understand. The leader then guides the discussion, moving it rapidly when students understand the information and slowing it down when they have difficulty. A lecture-oriented teacher seldom knows what students are comprehending. This teacher may concentrate on a point that the class understands or may speed through information that confuses students. One of the greatest mistakes a beginning teacher can make is to assume that the lecture method will work well in a secondary school.

How to Lead a Discussion

Leading a discussion is an art that is not easily learned. There is nothing more exciting than to see a master teacher conducting an interesting and exciting discussion. How can you bring students to this point? Excellent class discussions do not just happen. Inexperienced instructors may think they will walk into a class and talk about a subject off the top of their head. After all, don't they know more about the subject than the students? While it's true they may know about the material, they are faced with the problem of helping students discover information and develop their talents. This process requires as much preparation as any other class procedure. The first step in preparing for a discussion is to determine what it is you wish to accomplish—ask yourself, "What are your objectives"? Next, outline questions you think may help students to reach these objectives. Good discussion leaders use the "What do you think?" approach to learning. They ask questions such as were suggested in the section on questioning. For example:

1. Why did you do this experiment?
2. What did the data show?
3. Why did you use this approach?
4. How would you go about finding answers to this problem?

5. How else could you find the answer?
6. How does this answer relate to your daily life?
7. What mental steps did you take in solving the problem?
8. How many variables were involved in the experiment?
9. How do you feel about science?

Spend Time Analyzing Thought Processes

Every discussion should stimulate critical and creative thinking. You should spend time analyzing the types of questions you will ask in a discussion to ensure that they require the exercise of these abilities. This way you indicate to your students a belief in their becoming more well-rounded people. You will also contribute positively to their expectancy level of their critical thinking. Showing students that they are performing relatively sophisticated mental operations—inferring, hypothesizing, evaluating data, and so forth—will encourage them to accept that they can use their minds to derive answers to relatively complex problems. We come to believe that we are good thinkers only by being successful in thinking and by receiving feedback about our thinking abilities from others. Furthermore, teachers build positive student self-concepts when they involve students in tasks requiring thinking and show them how they are developing their minds. An actual inquiry discussion might follow these steps.

Present a problem such as, "What is the lifetime of a burning candle?" Encourage students to formulate hypotheses or give evidence. For example, say an apparatus is set up as follows: a burning candle is placed upright in a pan in which there is some water, and the candle is then covered with a glass container. Show how the experiment is set up by projecting a transparency of it on a screen. Some types of questions to ask are: "What will happen to the candle when it is covered?" "What else will happen to the apparatus as this is done?" "What would happen if the candle were lengthened, the size of the jar above it were increased, or the amount of water in the container holding the candle were decreased?" "How would you find out?"

After the students have progressed this far, have some students reflect back on what has been said and summarize the high points of the discussion. As a discussion leader, at times you might have to assist a student in doing this by repeating, "What was the problem?" Review the cognitive processes students used in solving the problem. Ask: "What hypotheses were made?" "What was the best hypothesis and why?" "How were the conclusions reached?" "On what are they based?" and "What is required to make better conclusions?"

Questions Must Be Directed at the Students' Level

A less-experienced discussion leader often starts a discussion with a question that is too difficult. If there is no response to a question, the teacher should rephrase it to make it simpler. This procedure may have to be followed several times before there is a response. A question implies an answer. Similarly, if the question is too vague, the students may not respond, and rephrasing it may give them some insight. Leading a discussion by questioning without giving answers is a skill that brings great satisfaction, but to be an astute questioner requires practice and a keen awareness of students' comprehension. By questioning correctly, the experienced discussion leader can guide students toward understanding the concepts and principles involved in the lesson or experiment. The questions must be deep enough to require critical thinking rather than a simple "yes" or "no" answer.

Eye contact is also an important aspect in leading a discussion. A teacher's eyes should sweep a class, constantly looking for boredom, a student with an answer or a question, or one with a puzzled look. Eye contact gives the instructor feedback and motivates students to think and participate in the discussion. It also shows that you are more interested in the students than in the information being covered.

A Discussion Started in a Novel Way Gains Attention

A motivational technique useful in beginning a discussion is to start it with an interesting demonstration. A vial of blood placed on a demonstration desk can stimulate questions, leading to a discussion of blood or the circulatory system. Burning a candle can lead to a discussion of several scientific concepts and principles. A good rule to follow is to start a discussion with a precept or observation whenever possible. Not all discussions will lend themselves to this procedure, but those that involve the discovery of a concept almost always do (see, for example, the Teaching Science Activity-Discovery Demonstration: Inquiring into Falling Bodies in the Appendix).

Use Overhead Projectors When Appropriate

The use of overhead projection with transparencies sometimes helps concentrate the class's attention on clarifying a problem. For example, focusing students' attention on some of the approaches to devising a classification scheme can be done easily with an overhead projection. Use different-colored acetate cut to various sizes and shapes and ask students how they would group the materials. A discussion can arise from the demonstration of such cognitive processes as analysis, discrimination, and ordering. Another demonstration using the overhead projector might include a discussion of magnetism and magnetic lines of force; using a magnet and iron fillings sprinkled on top of transparent plastic sets the stage for a discussion of the properties of magnetism.

GENERAL RULES FOR LEADING A LARGE GROUP DISCUSSION

Some general rules to follow in using discussions are:

1. Create an atmosphere in the class in which questions are not only welcomed but are expected. Be warm, open, and receptive.

2. As much as possible, include students' interests.

3. When you give reinforcement, do it positively and as often as you can. Use very little negative feedback. Say: "That's a good answer. "That's right, you have the idea." "Osgood, you're thinking; keep it up." "You have something there. Who would like to react to this answer?" Do not ignore the students; always give some recognition to their answers. No response should be a form of negative feedback. If students have the wrong answer, do not say, "That's wrong" or "No, that answer is no good." Rather, say: "Well, that is not quite right." "You may have something there, but I am not sure I understand the point," or "Good, you are thinking; but that is not quite what I was leading up to."

4. When you encourage a student to think, evaluate the product on the basis of the student's level of comprehension. Even when you, with a more extensive background, are aware that the student's idea is either incomplete or incorrect, accept it or even praise it if it indicates that the student has made effective use of the information required by this stage of the course.

5. Praise a student for being a good listener when the student calls attention to a mistake you have made.

6. When leading a discussion, try to remember previous comments and interrelate them. If at all possible, give recognition by referring to the name of the student who made the comment. For example, a teacher in responding to the idea of a student might say, "Joan believes that there are other factors besides temperature determining the rate of expansion of a metal. George has just suggested that possibly humidity and air pressure may have a minor effect." The teacher has acted as a summarizer for two students' views and has given them recognition by using their names.

7. Maintain a positive and accepting attitude. Your attitude in leading a discussion does much to determine the quality of that discussion. If you walk into a class feeling and looking very glum and with the weight of the discussion on your shoulders, the students' response will be lukewarm. However, if you start a discussion with the attitude that you and the students are going to have fun wrestling with ideas, their response is more likely to be impressive. In leading a discussion with adolescents, you must be able to laugh at yourself; discreet use of humor captures interest and gains participation.

8. When questions arise for which science does not yet provide an adequate explanation, state that, as yet, there is no answer. This gives students insight into avenues of research which we still need to explore.

9. When necessary, restate a student's answer before going on to your next remarks. Doing so often gives other students time to think about their answers.

10. Call on both students who are willing to answer and those who are not.

11. Do not rush discussions. Remember that the major reason for having discussions is to give students time to think. When there is silence during a discussion, this may be the period where most of the thinking is going on. Remember that a desirable wait-time averages five seconds.

Breaking the class into smaller groups can also provide variety. A sample design for this type of discussion is found in the Small Group Problem Solving in Appendix B.

Special Precautions in Leading a Discussion

At times, the following suggestions are proper, but the teacher should give serious consideration to their potential disadvantages as well:

1. Repeat a question back to a class when it is asked of you. Or have another student repeat the question in its entirety. Ask a student to speak up so that the entire class can hear. Ask a student to research an answer to the question.
2. Encourage the entire class to take notes.
3. Avoid the appearance of carrying on a private conversation with the person who asked the question.
4. Deliberately let your eyes roam over the entire class while giving the answer.
5. Use questions requiring hypothesis formation.
6. Avoid sarcasm.
7. Encourage students to seek recognition before answering or have them be courteous of another and wait until that person finishes before they respond.

8. Do not let students make derogatory remarks about another student's question or answer, since this is demeaning to the person.

9. Suggest an individual conference with the student when:

   ◆ The degree of difficulty in answering is greater than that expected of the class as a whole.

   ◆ The subject matter involved bears little relation to the key ideas being stressed.

   ◆ The answer is both detailed and lengthy.

   ◆ The time spent in answering the question may destroy the sequence of thought being developed.

SPECIAL DISCUSSION TECHNIQUES

Invitations to Inquiry

In its Biology Teacher's Handbook, the BSCS gives 44 class-discussion outlines under the title "Invitations to Inquiry." The main purpose of these outlines is to involve students in the strategies of solving scientific problems—not to teach science subject matter. The invitations engage students in the process of solving problems in the way that scientists are engaged. A typical outline for an invitation is given below.

FORMAT FOR AN INVITATION

Present a problem to the students and ask how they would go about solving it. Describe the actual experimental design used by the scientist. Ask the students what they would hypothesize about the experimental results.

Then give the students the data the scientists collected and ask: "What conclusions can you make about these data?" Finally, ask: "If you were the scientist, what

would be your next problem and why?" BSCS authors state that the primary aim [of invitations] is an understanding of enquiry. It is mainly for the sake of this aim that the active participation of the student is invoked. Both practical experience and experimental study indicate that concepts are understood best and retained longest when the student contributes to his own understanding.[11] You can easily make your own invitations. The steps are as follows:

1. Decide what your science processes and subject-matter objectives are.

2. State a problem related to your objectives. The idea for problems can come from actual scientific research reported in journals.

3. Devise questions that give students opportunities to set up experiments, make hypotheses, analyze and synthesize, and record data. Stress the understanding of science as a process and the cognitive skills involved.

4. Write the invitation as a series of steps. In different sections insert additional information to help students progress in depth in the topic or methods of research.

5. Evaluate your invitation, comparing it with the science-process list on page 161 and rewrite it to include more of these processes.

Invitations to inquiry can be written for various levels of learning. As much as possible, they should stress the development of students' cognitive abilities. In addition to the science processes, students should also learn the necessity for having a control, understand cause-and-effect relationships, learn when to use quantitative data and how to interpret it, learn the role of argument and inference in the design of experiments, and so forth.

Dividing the class into small groups permits more individual attention and opportunities to answer in laboratory activities.

Write an invitation! Your first invitation probably won't be very sophisticated, but in the process of writing it you will gain insight into how to construct invitations and gain a better understanding of how to involve students in understanding science as a process.

Pictorial Riddles

Another technique for developing motivation and interest in a discussion is to use pictorial riddles: that is, pictures or drawings made by the teacher to elicit student response. A riddle is drawn on the chalkboard or on poster board or is projected on a transparency, and the teacher asks a question about the picture.

Pictorial riddles are relatively easy to devise. They can be as simple or as complex as a teacher desires. In devising a riddle follow these steps:

1. Select some concept or principle he wishes to teach or emphasize.
2. Draw a picture or show an illustration that demonstrates the concept.
3. An alternate procedure is to change something in a picture and ask students to find out what is wrong in the picture. An example might be a picture of a large child being held up on a seesaw by a small child. Ask, "How is this possible?" Or show a farming community in which all of the ecological principles are misapplied and ask what is wrong with what has been done in the community.
4. Finally, devise a series of questions related to the picture which will help students gain insights into the principles involved.

There are two general types of pictorial riddles. The first type shows an actual situation. The instructor asks why the situation occurred. Figure 12–3 is of this type.

1. What questions can you ask about this riddle?
2. What is wrong with this diagram?
3. Where do pine trees grow?
4. Why do they grow where they do?
5. If you were going to change the riddle to make it more accurate, what would you do and why?
6. What does the wind have to do with the ecology of the area?
7. Where would you expect to find the most and the least amount of vegetation on the mountain? Why?
8. How could you change this riddle to teach some additional science concepts?

In the second type of pictorial riddles, the teacher manipulates something in a drawing or a series of drawings and then asks what is wrong with the diagram. Figure 12–4 is an example of this type. Some questions that might be asked about each riddle follow each picture:

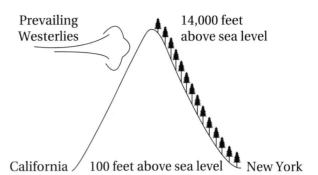

FIGURE 12–3 Pictorial Riddle (biology)

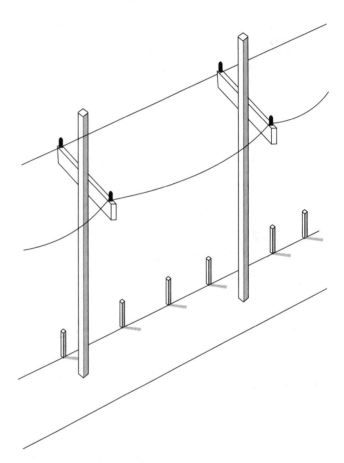

FIGURE 12–4 Pictorial Riddle (physical science)

1. What do you notice about the things in this picture?
2. What is similar in the picture?
3. Why do the fence and the telephone line appear to be similar?
4. Why would you expect the two telephone lines to be the same?
5. What do you think is the season of the year for each line and why?
6. What does temperature have to do with the appearance of the telephone lines and why?

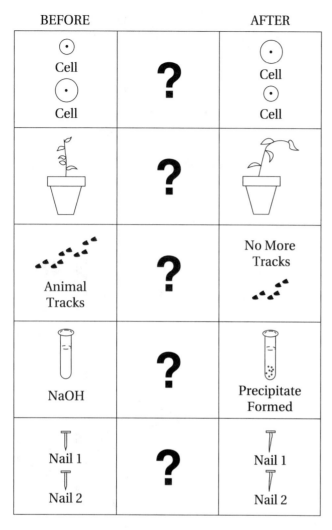

FIGURE 12–5 Sequential Pictorial Riddles. Can You Supply the Missing Form?

OTHER TECHNIQUES TO MOTIVATE DISCUSSION

Case Histories

Another technique to motivate discussion is to use case histories in science. These histories tell stories about the development of some science concepts. The instructor may tell the students part of what was done and then ask what they think the next step was. Case histories can be constructed from a classic experiment in the history of science.

Covers of Science Magazines

An activity to supplement a science lesson can be constructed around magazine covers depicting various aspects of science. Science, the journal of the AAAS, has some very interesting covers that lend themselves well to this approach. The instructor holds up the cover picture and asks questions to give students hints about the topic represented.

The Magic Circle As a Facilitator of Discussion

The magic circle is another means of stimulating discussion in the science classroom. This is simply a teaching technique designed to develop listening and

7. At what time of year would you expect to see the sagging telephone line and why?

The format for a riddle which lends itself particularly well to overhead projection is the before-and-after type of riddle. Students are shown a diagram or picture, some factor is then altered, and the students are shown another picture of the same situation after modification. Students are to hypothesize what happened in the before situation to reach the modification shown in the after diagram. Figure 12–5 shows some examples of before-and-after riddles.

The riddle in Figure 12–6 is constructed like the face of a clock. The arms are turned to different organisms and the class is asked what the ecological relationships are between them.

Riddles may be prepared from many types of materials, such as photographs and Polaroid 35-mm slides, magazine pictures, diagrams, cartoons, greeting cards, and objects.

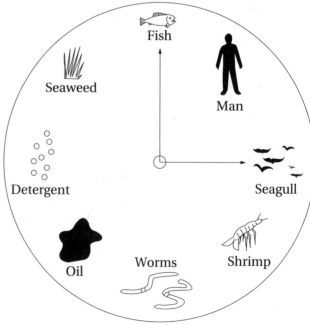

FIGURE 12–6 Riddles to Show Relationships

communication skills, an awareness of self-worth, and an interest in and respect for other people's ideas.

To promote these objectives, it is necessary to ask questions that students will react to with personal feelings. For example, ask humanistic questions ("How do you feel about. . .?"). Also, ask divergent questions to encourage a variety of responses.

You, the teacher, must positively reinforce statements made by the students so that they will feel that their contribution is worthwhile and that they, as people, are valuable and able to achieve success. Be sure to encourage the other students to listen to the speaker. Students also should reinforce what the speaker has said with their own ideas and experiences so that the entire discussion is a sharing session.

Creativity

Teaching creatively is another means of stimulating discussion. Defining *teaching creatively* is difficult. To get at the meaning and value of creative teaching, consider the following questions:

1. What is creativity?
2. Do you perceive of yourself as a creative individual? Why do you feel this way? How can you use creativity in the classroom?
3. When you have used creative teaching methods, what has been the response of your students?
4. How did they feel about their experience?
5. How did you feel about using creative teaching techniques in the classroom?
6. How might creative teaching be used in the science classroom?
7. How can we help students to be more creative in their thinking?
8. What, if any, are the limitations of creative teaching?
9. What are the advantages and disadvantages of creative teaching?
10. If you had the choice of studying in a creative versus a noncreative classroom, which would you choose? Explain your answer.
11. Select any topic which you traditionally teach in your classroom. How could you make the teaching of that topic more creative?
12. What are some ideas for creative teaching techniques you have used in your classroom?
13. If a student teacher were to ask you about teaching creatively, what would your response be? Would you recommend trying some creative ideas?
14. If you believe creativity is important in education, how might you encourage a traditionalist to give this method a try?

DISCUSSION AS A TECHNIQUE OF REVIEW

All of the preceding discussion techniques can be used to good advantage for class review. Discussion also may be used as an excellent review for laboratory work. After you have had a class conduct several experiments in a unit, take time to discuss the conclusions that can be drawn from the laboratory work. Also consider how the information was obtained, what types of problem-solving and cognitive behaviors were involved in determining the answers, and what assurance the students have that their information is correct. A discussion of this type can do much to reinforce learning and divide the trivia from the really important aspects of learning.

The One-Word Type of Review

The one-word approach may be used to involve all students in the review process. After students have read, seen a film, performed a laboratory exercise, or been involved in other types of investigative work, ask them to write their impressions in one word on a piece of paper. These papers should then be passed to the front of the class, and several of them should be written on the board. The students should then be asked to explain why they wrote their words. After they give their explanations, they should be asked to take any three words and construct a sentence. This technique provides an excellent review of the material and involves all the students.

Persuasion and Discussion

Discussion and formal lecturing are somewhat alike because both activities involve elements of persuasion. A useful definition of persuasion is that "persuasion is the conscious attempt to bring about a jointly developed mental state common to both source and receiver through the use of symbolic cues."[12]

Persuasion and instruction appear to have a great deal in common. Both involve communication that includes giving arguments and evidence for the purpose of getting someone to believe something or to do something. Both are influenced by constructivism. People respond to formal instruction and persuasion in terms of their preexisting perspectives. Both require conscious cognitive activity on the part of the recipient while also seeking understanding.

Discussion plays an important role in persuasion, because a common objective of discussion in science classes is to develop a new behavior or to modify an existing behavior with respect to learning science. In investigative modes, these behaviors frequently are unfamiliar to the students because of previous repeated exposure to traditional expository methods of teaching. Discussions among students or between students and their teacher provide opportunities for persuasive evidence to be examined and analyzed. These opportunities are particularly necessary when dealing with overcoming misconceptions or with faulty premises in science.

Learning to Lead a Good Discussion Never Ends

Teachers never quite perfect their ability as discussion leaders, but they should never stop trying to improve. Excellence in discussion comes only with wisdom, not only in subject matter but in learning how to develop talents and self-concepts. For dedicated teachers, there is probably no greater satisfaction than to walk out of class knowing that they have developed the students' mental abilities to the point where their presence is practically unneeded except as an organizer. To acquire this facility requires preparation and constant self-analysis, but it is one of the intellectual satisfactions that comes only with good teaching.

SUMMARY

The ability of the teacher to ask questions to stimulate creative and critical thinking and to manifest multiple talents is basic to inquiry teaching. Inquiry types of questions may be involved in all areas of science teaching, such as discussion, laboratory demonstrations, student worksheets, visual aids, and evaluations. Instructors should plan their questions before class but remain flexible and adapt their instruction as dictated by student interaction. Before outlining the question, teachers should decide what talents, critical thinking processes, and subject matter objectives they hope to develop and the answers they will accept.

Questions may be classified as convergent or divergent according to Bloom's Taxonomy, by the science processes, and/or by the multiple talents they are trying to develop. Divergent types of questions and those requiring more cognitive sophistication should be stressed. Teleological questions, anthropomorphic questions, and those that could be answered by "yes" or "no" responses should be avoided.

The time a teacher waits for a response, called "wait-time," is very important. Most teachers wait, on an average, less than one second. A five-second average wait-time results in more responses by slow learners, more creative answers, more complete-sentence answers, more questions, and more suggestions for experiments.

This chapter suggests questioning techniques to involve students in investigations and to stimulate creativity. Research indicates that teachers trained in questioning techniques do change their questioning behavior in the classroom, asking questions requiring greater cognitive ability. Teachers who emphasize higher-level types of questions are more likely to see their students do better on national tests, which tend to test for all cognitive levels.

The lecture method should play a relatively minor role in instruction in the secondary schools. Inquiry-based discussions motivate students and involve them more in cognitive processes than do lectures. There are definite techniques to be used in leading inquiry-oriented discussions. Primarily, the instructor should question and give minimal information; the type of question asked by the teacher helps students discover concepts and principles.

To lead a good discussion requires extensive preparation. Discussion leaders should know their objectives, outline a series of relevant questions, and spend time at the end of the discussion analyzing how conclusions were reached. Part of the discussion should be devoted to reflecting on the thought processes used in arriving at these conclusions. This ensures better understanding and development of the cognitive processes.

Discussion leaders should give as much positive reinforcement as possible. They should compliment students on good ideas and suggestions and never deride or make sarcastic remarks about poor suggestions. Regardless of the answers given in a discussion, teachers should try to react positively to the participants; ignoring a response is a poor procedure. Eye contact is important as a motivator and a means of receiving feedback. A good method for starting a discussion is to use a demonstration or overhead projection pertaining to a subject or topic of interest to students. In leading the discussion, attempt to recall previous comments and interrelate the suggestions with the names of the individuals who made them. Remember that students occasionally will test your judgment to determine your competence as a teacher.

Some special techniques used in stimulating discussion are invitations to inquiry, pictorial riddles, case histories in science, questions organized around covers of science magazines, and the magic circle technique. All of these methods can be used to suggest open-ended experiments if students are aware of the factors involved in experimentation. Discussion is also an excellent vehicle for review, both in class and laboratory work. The one-word approach may be used to involve all the students in the review process.

◆
_____

REFERENCES

1. Christine Chin and David E. Brown, "Learning in Science: A Comparison of Deep and Surface Approaches," *Journal of Research in Science Teaching,* 37 (2) (2000): 100–138.

2. Mary Budd Rowe, "Wait-Time and Rewards as Instructional Variables: Influence on Inquiry and Sense of Fate Control," *New Science in the Inner City* (New York: Teachers College, Columbia University, September 1970). Unpublished paper.

3. Olugbemiro J. Jegede and Janet O. Olajide, "Wait-time, Classroom Discourse, and the Influence of Sociocultural Factors in Science Teaching," *Science Education,* 79 (3) (1995): 233–249.

4. J. T. Diller, "Do Your Questions Promote or Prevent Thinking?" *Learning,* 11 (October 1982): 56–57.

5. Boyce Baker and others, "Oral Quizzes," Conversations with Baker and other teachers at Grand Junction High School, Grand Junction, Colorado (conducted by the author, 1988).

6. William Wilen, "Implications of Research on Questioning for the Teacher Educator," *Journal of Research and Development in Education,* 2 (1984).

7. Bonnie B. Armbruster and others, "Reading and Questioning in Content Area Lessons," *Journal of Reading Behavior,* 23 (1) (1991): 35–39.

8. Roberta Barba and Loretta Cardinale, "Are Females Invisible Students?" An Investigation of Teacher-Student Questioning Interactions," *School Science and Mathematics,* 91 (7) (November 1991): 306–310.

9. Paul B. Otto, "What Research Says: Finding an Answer in Questioning Strategies," *Science and Children,* 28 (April 1991): 44–47.

10. Jeff Passe, "Phil Donahue: An Excellent Model for Leading a Discussion," *Journal of Teacher Education,* 35 (43) (January/February, 1984).

11. William V. Mayer, Editor, "The Golden Age of Biological Education 1960–1975," in *Biology Teachers Handbook, 3rd ed.* (New York: John Wiley & Sons), p. 47.

12. T. R. Kobala, "Persuasion and Attitude Change in Science Education," *Journal of Research in Science Teaching,* 29 (January 1992): 63–80.

◆ ————————— **Investigating Science Teaching** ————————— ◆

Activity 12–1
Recognizing Good Questions, Part 1

Read the following questions and mark them according to whether they are poor (P), fair (F), good (G), or excellent (E).

_____ 1. Why do roots thirst for water?

_____ 2. Why does water seek its own level?

_____ 3. Are all big trees the same size, shape, and age?

_____ 4. How does a siphon work?

_____ 5. How do seeds sprout?

_____ 6. How does soap clean?

_____ 7. What will happen if clothes are soaked with a bleach before instead of after washing?

_____ 8. How can the bleaching action be accelerated?

_____ 9. If ethylene glycol prevents avalanches, what other chemicals do you suspect might also prevent them?

_____ 10. If you were going to repeat the experiment with yeast, how would you improve it?

_____ 11. How would you design an experiment to _____?

_____ 12. If you have a straight-line graph indicating a relationship between population growth and time but the period ends at two days, what could you say about the population at four days?

_____ 13. How would you define a magnet operationally?

_____ 14. How could you be more certain about the conclusions you made from the data?

_____ 15. What do you think will happen to a potted geranium plant if it is placed near a window?

_____ 16. What evidence does the process of diffusion contribute to the molecular theory?

_____ 17. Look at the culture plates and describe what you see.

_____ 18. Place the organisms into any two groups you wish.

_____ 19. If the distance is doubled between two masses in Newton's gravitational formula, what will happen to the force?

Now provide an explanation for your responses. Why do you think some questions are poor, fair, good, or excellent?

Activity 12–2
Recognizing Good Questions, Part 2

Below are several questions related to the preceding activity. Read each question and attempt to answer it. Record your answers in the space provided and refer to them again after completing this chapter to see how well you did.

_____ 1. Of the preceding questions, which three are the best?

_____ 2. Which are teleological or anthropomorphic questions?

_____ 3. Which questions require the student to analyze?

_____ 4. Which questions require the student to synthesize?

_____ 5. Which questions require the student to evaluate?

_____ 6. Which questions are convergent?

_____ 7. Which questions are divergent?

_____ 8. Which questions require students to demonstrate in their responses the processes of science?

_____ 9. Which questions require students to reason quantitatively and what are they required to do?

_____ 10. Which questions require creative responses?

_____ 11. Which questions require students to formulate an operational definition?

_____ 12. Which questions require students mainly to observe?

_____ 13. Which questions require students mainly to classify?

_____ 14. Which questions require students to demonstrate experimental procedure?

_____ 15. Which questions require students to formulate a model?

_____ 16. Which questions require students to hypothesize?

_____ 17. Which question would an authoritarian personality most likely guess at if he or she didn't know the answer?

_____ 18. Which of the following two types of questions suggest a test?

   a. How do seeds sprout?

   b. What is needed for seeds to sprout?

_____ 19. It has been said that "how" questions do not lead to experimentation. Comment on this statement.

After you have answered these questions, compare and discuss your answers with other students in the class.

ACTIVITY 12–3
CLASSIFYING QUESTIONS IN NORMAL CONVERSATION

Observe normal conversation and classify the questions asked according to one of the classification systems suggested in this chapter.

ACTIVITY 12–4
CLASSIFYING QUESTIONS USING BLOOM'S TAXONOMY

Write some discussion questions to be used in a class discussion and classify them according to Bloom's Taxonomy and science processes.

ACTIVITY 12–5
CLASSIFYING QUESTIONS: DIVERGENT OR CONVERGENT?

In the blank before each question, place a "D" if you think the question is divergent, a "C" if you think it is convergent.

_____ 1. What do you think I am going to do with this apparatus?

_____ 2. What conclusions can you make from the data?

_____ 3. Can anything else be done to improve the growth of the plants?

_____ 4. Is heat an important factor in the experiment?

_____ 5. Do you think the salt precipitated because the solution was cooled?

_____ 6. Which of these three rocks is hardest?

_____ 7. What can you tell me about the geology of this area from the picture?

_____ 8. Would you say you have sufficient data?

_____ 9. In what ways can you make the lights burn with the wire, switch, and power supply?

_____ 10. What things can you tell me about the biological make-up of this earthworm from your observations?

Which questions are the most convergent? What answers are possible for these questions? What words start these sentences? How would you change the sentences to make them more divergent?

ACTIVITY 12–6
CLASSIFYING QUESTIONS: TELEOLOGICAL OR ANTHROPOMORPHIC?

In the blank before each question, indicate whether the question is teleological (T) or anthropomorphic (A).

_____ 1. How do you think bacteria feel when ultraviolet light is shined on them?

_____ 2. Why does water seek its own level?

_____ 3. Why do plants seek the light?

_____ 4. Why will a body in motion want to stay in motion?

_____ 5. Why is the end of evolution to become increasingly more complex?

ACTIVITY 12–7
LEADING A DISCUSSION

Lead a small discussion and have someone check your wait-time and how well you get students to talk to students instead of students to teacher to student.

ACTIVITY 12–8
SELF-EVALUATION INSTRUMENT FOR RATING YOUR QUESTIONING ABILITY

Lead a discussion and use a cassette tape recorder to record it. Read through the following questions. Then listen to the tape. Put a check mark in the blank before the statement for each time the action described in the statement occurred.

_____ 1. You asked what students knew about the topic before starting the discussion.

_____ 2. You asked a convergent question.

_____ 3. You developed student-student rather than teacher-student interaction.

_____ 4. You asked an effective question.

_____ 5. You reinforced an answer without saying that the response was correct.

_____ 6. You did not stop discussing a point when the right answer was given but asked students if there were other answers or further discussion.

_____ 7. You asked a question requiring science-process thinking (e.g., hypothesizing, designing an experiment, inferring).

_____ 8. You interrupted a student without giving him or her time to complete his or her thought.

_____ 9. You paraphrased a student's statement to clarify or focus for others on the topics.

Conclude this activity by noting the following information for future reference.

_____ 1. Measure how many seconds on the average you waited for a response.

_____ 2. Measure how much class time (in seconds) you devoted to routine (e.g., roll taking, announcements), student activity, and teacher talk.

     _____ Routine:

     _____ Student activity:

     _____ Teacher talk:

_____ 3. Rate yourself as a listener:

     1   2   3   4   5   6   7   8   9   10

     Poor listener   Average   Good listener

_____ 4. Rate yourself as a questioner:

     1   2   3   4   5   6   7   8   9   10

     Poor questioner   Average   Good questioner

Evaluate your responses and list those things you most want to change in your teaching. Record and rate yourself again at a later date or have a student or aide do it and note your improvement.

CHAPTER 13

INVESTIGATION AND PROBLEM SOLVING

INTRODUCTION TO INQUIRY TEACHING

With the publication of the *National Science Education Standards* by the National Research Council in 1996, the notion of teaching science by inquiry and investigation received a tremendous boost in recognition and familiarization by science teachers in the United States. This teaching strategy was listed as a top priority for science teaching. Since then much activity has taken place in school systems and in state departments of education throughout the nation to develop goals and strategies to bring about appropriate changes to achieve the desired results. For the past three decades, science teachers have read, talked about, and experimented with methods of teaching using investigative, inquiry approaches to learning the content and processes of science. These efforts have met with varying success for many reasons that will be discussed in this chapter. The challenges of inquiry teaching are still very evident, and the shift from traditional, expository methods has been very slow.

Pinchas Tamir states, "The notion of inquiry has been central to science education for the last twenty years."[1] In studying science education literature, Tamir recognized that inquiry has been central to the learning process in secondary school science.

In 1966, Dr. Richard Suchman, of the University of Illinois, did research on inquiry teaching. He said, "Inquiry is the fundamental means of human learning."[2] This is a very important statement when we consider how much of our science teaching is not done by inquiry.

In 1980–81, a large research project was done in the United States that examined science teaching methods being used at that time. The authors of this project stated,

"Because the development of inquiry skills is one of the goals for science education, it is a natural focal topic for the study of science education carried out by a group of scholars under the auspices of Project Synthesis."[3]

The position statement of NSTA, the largest science teachers' organization in the world, states:

> The major goal of science teaching is the development of scientific literacy for all people. Incorporated within the concept of scientific literacy is both the understanding of key principles in science and the understanding of how scientific ideas are developed.[4]

In a different study Leopold Klopfer stated, "A major emphasis for education for scientific literacy must be placed on the processes of scientific inquiry."[5] These are several authors who have declared inquiry to be an important and fundamental method of learning and particularly useful in science.

DEVELOPMENT OF INQUIRY TEACHING IN THE SCHOOLS

Scientific inquiry and investigation as we presently understand it (much less the practice of science in any important way) did not enter our schools until the mid 19th century. Instead, faith was at least as important as empirical data and in many instances it dominated the practice of science. This faith was often a complex mixture of Christian theology, idealism, and entrenched traditions. It also was a condition that had its roots in many centuries of disagreements between the Church and the practices of science.[6]

Changes in the way science was studied—and taught—may be observed more clearly by looking at the innovations of individual scientists and teachers, rather than through any organized curricular movements. Examples include the methods of Louis Agassiz at Harvard's Lawrence Scientific School, in which he invited students to visit his lab, study specimens firsthand, and thereby gain direct knowledge. He directed field trips to the countryside and seashore, encouraged students to make their own collections, and conducted instruction by correspondence with specimen collectors around the country.[7]

During the late 1800s and early 1900s, inquiry teaching was generally a rarity in science classrooms. Pestalozzi's object method of the early 1900s may have had the germs of inquiry embedded in it, but it was many decades before firsthand study of objects and phenomena became an accepted practice in science classrooms. Even today, many teachers avoid inquiry teaching because of several perceived problems with this method of instruction. These include the necessity for a slower pace, more time consumption, the need for large quantities of materials, a more active and perhaps chaotic classroom, the urgency to cover material to prepare for the next grade level, and high emphasis of most tests on factual memorization instead of focusing on skill development, processes of science, and investigative strategies. These perceived problems are accompanied by the normal inertia and resistance to changes in methods of instruction. The burdensome problems facing teachers today leave little time for probing new methods of teaching.

Students learn about acceleration by gravity in a hands-on experiment.

DEFINING INQUIRY

Welch and others define inquiry as, "a general process by which human beings seek information or understanding. Broadly conceived, inquiry is a way of thought. Scientific inquiry, a subset of general inquiry, is concerned with the natural world and is guided by certain beliefs and assumptions."[8] J. T. Wilson defines inquiry in the following terms:

> Inquiry is a process model of instruction based upon learning theory and behavior. Too often it is confused with open-ended, undirected activity which is assumed to simulate scientific activity. This is not the case. Inquiry results wherever and whenever stimuli challenge the existing expectations of the participant. The situation may occur in a well-equipped laboratory, but it may also occur in a well-planned and produced lecture, a stimulating reading assignment, or a simple novel situation. The emphasis of inquiry is not the mere acquisition of science knowledge or the production of scientists. It is rather an emphasis upon how humans process information in order to make intellectual decisions of all sorts.[9]

Some authors writing on the subject of inquiry make a distinction between general and scientific inquiry. Specifically:

> Scientific inquiry is defined as a systematic and investigative activity with the purpose of uncovering and describing relationships among objects and events. It is characterized by the use of orderly, repeatable processes, reduction of the object of investigation to its most simple scale and form, and the use of logical frameworks for explanation and prediction. The operations of inquiry include observing, questioning, experimenting, comparing, inferring, generalizing, communicating, applying and others.[10]

Scientific inquiry has also been defined as "a systematic investigative performance ability which incorporates unrestrained inductive thinking capabilities after a person has acquired a broad and critical knowledge of particular subject matter through formal learning processes."[11]

Some authors believe that, particularly in secondary schools, inquiry teaching is a way of developing the mental processes of curiosity and investigation so that students learn how information is obtained. Other authors believe teachers should not use scientific inquiry in the classrooms of the secondary school. They believe that it is a mistake to lead students to think that they are acting like scientists when, in fact, they may only be exhibiting general inquiry characteristics. They also believe that true scientific inquiry cannot be done until one has a strong grasp on the subject far in advance, which would limit inquiry to graduate students and laboratory researchers. We believe that it is necessary to introduce the ideas of inquiry and investigation to children in the secondary schools, and perhaps even earlier, even though they may not know much science before they have this instruction. See "Additional Teaching Science Activities" in Appendix A p. 373, for examples of classroom exercises designed for students with minimal science backgrounds.

DISCOVERY AND INQUIRY STRATEGIES DISTINGUISHED

Over the last 50 years, most of the programs funded by the United States government for developing modern instruction in elementary and secondary schools have stressed student involvement in discovery- or inquiry-oriented activities. Millions of dollars have gone into constructing science and mathematics studies and curricula for this purpose.

What is *discovery* or *inquiry?* Many educators use these terms interchangeably, whereas others prefer to differentiate their meanings. In our terminology, *discovery occurs when an individual is mainly involved in using his or her mental processes to mediate (or discover) some concept or principle.*

For students to make discoveries, they must perform certain mental processes, such as observing, classifying, measuring, predicting, describing, and inferring. Many elementary school curriculum-project materials of the past 40 years mainly were designed to involve children in discovery activities.

Discovery

Discovery is the mental process of assimilating concepts and principles. Discovery processes include observing, classifying, measuring, predicting, inferring, and others.

Starting in the middle school and becoming increasingly more sophisticated as students progress through high school, materials are designed to stress inquiry. Inquiry teaching, however, is built on and includes discovery, because students must use their discovery capabilities in addition to other capabilities. In

true inquiry, the individual tends to act more like a maturing adult. Adults behave in a number of ways to unravel the hidden relationships relative to a problem. They define problems, formulate hypotheses, design experiments, and so forth. They perform certain relatively sophisticated mental processes, such as originating problems, formulating hypotheses, designing investigative approaches, testing out ideas with experiments, synthesizing knowledge, and developing attitudes of open-mindedness, suspension of judgment, checking results, and others. These are all inquiry practices.

Secondary students may be asked to choose and investigate an organism and report their research. If they define their own problems, design experiments, collect data, and so forth, they are behaving in an inquiry manner. Refer to the paragraphs on discovery and inquiry. How do these processes differ? How would you design a discovery-oriented lesson in your subject field? How would you design an inquiry-oriented lesson?

Inquiry

Inquiry is the process of defining and investigating problems, formulating hypotheses, designing experiments, gathering data, and drawing conclusions about problems.

Because secondary teachers often do not clearly distinguish between discovery and inquiry, they tend to overemphasize discovery activities. Piaget indicated that adolescents are in the process of developing formal thought and should, therefore, have opportunities to use a higher level of thinking. Hypothetical-deductive and reflexive thinking are two characteristics of this stage of development. Formulating hypotheses, designing investigations, evaluating data, and looking over an investigation to determine how it can be improved all require these mental operations. Middle and secondary instruction should, therefore, not only include discovery but an increasing number of inquiry activities.

Clearly, one develops discovery and inquiry thinking abilities only by being involved in activities requiring these mental tasks. Since an individual never really masters any of them completely, there is only a degree to which one becomes proficient in learning how to discover and inquire. Even the most sophisticated Nobel Prize scientist, author, painter, mathematician, or sociologist is still moving forward in developing these skills. The task of the school system is to construct its curriculum so students develop and demonstrate these human investigative abilities.

The *National Science Education Standards* have placed inquiry teaching at the forefront of current science-teaching methods. As teachers struggle with the shifting emphases, certain teachers have come forth with helpful suggestions about new approaches. Huber and Moore have developed a model for taking advantage of the current interest in hands-on experiences.[12] They make the observations that "Hands-on does not guarantee inquiry. However, many seemingly limited hands-on activities can be extended into the realm of inquiry using a model that involves (a) discrepant events to engage students and direct inquiry, (b) teacher supported brainstorming activities to guide students in planning investigations, (c) suitable written job performance aids to provide structure and support, and (d) the requirement that students provide a product of their research which typically includes a class presentation and a graph." An example of this approach can be found in Appendix A.

ADVANTAGES OF DISCOVERY AND INQUIRY TEACHING

You are probably beginning to see some of the reasons that discovery and inquiry teaching are used in the schools. Jerome Bruner has been instrumental in leading the movement toward discovery teaching. He outlined four reasons for using this approach:

1. Intellectual potency
2. Intrinsic rather than extrinsic motives
3. Learning the heuristics of discovery
4. Conservation of memory

By intellectual potency, Bruner means that an individual learns and develops her or his mind only by using it to think. His second point means that, as a consequence of succeeding at discovery, the student receives a satisfying intellectual thrill—an intrinsic reward. Teachers often give extrinsic rewards (A's, for example), but if they want students to learn for the fun of it, they must devise instructional systems that enable students to obtain intrinsic satisfaction in performing their tasks. In Bruner's third point, he emphasizes that the only way a person learns the techniques of discovery is to have opportunities to discover. Through discovering, a student slowly learns how to organize and conduct investigations. Bruner argues in his fourth point that one of the greatest benefits of the discovery approach is that it aids in better memory retention. Think for a moment of some scientific idea you have thought out yourself and compare it with information you were given in a class. The material you reasoned out and came to some conclusion about is probably still in your mind, even though you may have learned it years ago. On the other hand, concepts you were told often escape recall.

Although these four justifications have been outlined for discovery teaching, they also have relevance for inquiry. The teaching strategies for the two approaches are similar because they stress the importance of students using their cognitive mental processes to work out the meaning of things they encounter in their environment.

Although Bruner has suggested the salient justifications for modern teaching, there are at least six additional reasons for using student investigative approaches. They are as in the following sections.

Instruction Becomes Student Centered

One of the basic psychological principles of learning implies that the greater the student involvement, the greater the learning. Usually when teachers think about learning, they picture the student assimilating information. This view of learning is very limited, for learning involves those aspects that contribute to the individual becoming a fully-functioning person. For example, in inquiry situations, students learn not only concepts and principles, but self-direction, responsibility, and social communication. In teacher-centered instruction, however, many of the opportunities for developing these talents are denied to the student. The instructor provides the self-direction and retains the responsibility. If you look at instruction as enabling a person to improve in all the facets that make up a human being, it is difficult to justify a teacher-centered learning environment.

Inquiry Learning Builds the "Self-Concept" of the Student

Each of us has a self-concept. If it is good, we feel psychologically secure, are open to new experiences, are willing to take chances and explore, tolerate minor failures relatively well, are more creative, generally have good mental health, and eventually become fully functioning individuals. Part of the task of becoming a better person is to build one's self-concept. We can do this only by being involved in learning because through involvement we manifest our potential and gain insights into self. Inquiry teaching allows for greater involvement, thereby giving students more chances to gain insights and better develop their self-concepts.

Expectancy Level Increases

Part of a person's self-concept is his or her expectancy level, which means that the student believes or expects that he or she can accomplish a task on his or her own. He or she has learned from previous discovery and inquiry experiences that he or she can think autonomously. In other words, from having had many successful experiences in using investigative talents, this individual has learned, "I can solve a problem on my own without the help of a teacher, parent, or anyone else." As a consequence, there is an "I-can-ness."

Inquiry Learning Develops Talent

Humans possess more than 120 talents. Academic talent is related to only a few of them. The more freedom we have to use these academic talents, the more opportunities we have to develop others, such as creative, social, organizing, and planning talents.

Inquiry Methods Avoid Learning Only at the Verbal Level

When you learned the definitions for words such as osmosis, photosynthesis, logarithm, and others, did you play memorization games, or did you work out the meaning in your mind and really understand what you were learning? Could you define these terms operationally, or could you give memorized definitions only? Inquiry teaching, since it involves students working out the meaning of their work, tends to avoid learning only at the verbal level.

Inquiry Learning Permits Time for Students to Mentally Assimilate and Accommodate Information

Teachers often rush learning, which results in students playing recall games. Students need time to think and use their minds to reason through and gain insights into the concepts, principles, and investigative techniques they are involved in. It takes time for such information to become a meaningful part of the mind. Piaget believed that there is no true learning unless the students mentally act on information, and, in the process, assimilate or accommodate what they encounter in their environment. Unless this assimilation occurs, teacher and students are involved only in pseudo-learning, which is knowledge retained only for a short time.

GUIDED VERSUS FREE INQUIRY

How much structure should be provided in inquiry situations? There should be enough to ensure that students are successful in understanding the important implications of their studies. If students have not had experience in learning through inquiry, initially they should be given considerable structure in their lessons. After they have gained some experience on how to conduct an investigation, the structure then should be lessened. In this text, a general term *investigative* is used to include both discovery and inquiry teaching approaches. The term *guided discovery and inquiry* is used where there is considerable structure given, and *free discovery and inquiry* indicates that there is little guidance provided by the instructor. Following is an example of

a portion of a guided-inquiry lesson. Note that much of the planning is outlined by the teacher. The students, for example, do not originate the problem, and considerable guidance is provided on how to set up and record the data. In a free-type lesson, the students may originate the problem and determine how to resolve it.

Guided Inquiry

In a guided inquiry approach, the instructor provides the problem and encourages students to work out the procedures to resolve it. Examples of problems teachers might give to involve students in this type of process are:

1. How is algebra used in our community?
2. Given the story up to this point, how would you end it?
3. How would you write a poem to indicate your feeling about seeing the ocean?
4. What do you think about intermarriage?
5. How could you make a better salad dressing?
6. Here are some snails. Find out as much as possible about them.
7. Here is a pond and some apparatus. Find out as much as possible about how this pond changes over a year.
8. How could we make poetry more popular in our school?
9. A new highway is built through the jungles of Brazil and passes by an Indian village that has had little contact with modern civilization. What will happen?
10. Here is some apparatus for studying motion. Set it up in any way you choose to study the movement of an object.
11. How does using a different language change a person's perceptions of other cultures?
12. Here is some apparatus for studying circuits. Use it to find out as much as possible about circuits.
13. Do whatever you wish with this salt to determine its physical and chemical properties.
14. What should be done to improve the environment of our school?
15. Here is some water that is supposed to be polluted. How will you prove that it is?
16. If you were going to produce a piece of art to show contentment, what would you do and why?

In a guided inquiry plan, students are encouraged to resolve problems either on their own or in groups. The teacher is available as a resource person, giving only enough aid to ensure that the students do not become too frustrated or experience failure. The assistance the teacher gives, however, should be in the form of questions to help students think about possible investigative procedures. Ask students questions, giving them direction rather than telling them what to do. Good questions, at the right time, may provide just the needed stimulus for students to become more involved in creative investigation. Contrast this method with that of a teacher who says, "Study groups and tell how they are different." In the second instance, the teacher has robbed the students of many opportunities for thought and creativity.

◆

Example of a Guided Inquiry Lesson (Middle School Level)

Learning About Bulbs, Batteries, and Circuits

Here are some materials for studying electrical circuits. Use them to find out as much as you can about circuits. Work in groups of two.

Materials: Six or eight small flashlight bulbs and sockets, 8–10 inch lengths of insulated copper wire, similar lengths of uninsulated copper wire, a dozen flashlight dry cells with holders, switches, small screwdriver, pliers, scout knife

Procedure: Examine the dry cells. (1) What are the advantages of dry cells? (2) Why not just use the electricity from a wall socket? (3) What are some differences between the electricity from a dry cell and that from a wall socket? (4) Which is the positive end of a dry cell? (5) Describe the negative end. (6) How could you connect two or more dry cells together to make the output stronger?

Examine the bulbs carefully. (7) What actually produces the light when connected in a circuit? (8) Why does it produce light? (9) How does the current go into and out of the light bulb? Examine the copper wires. (10) Which kind should you use, insulated or uninsulated? (11) Why? (12) What do you need to do to an insulated wire in order to connect it in a circuit?

Try connecting bulbs, dry cells, wires, and switches together to make a bulb light. (13) Write down some simple rules to follow so your classmates could also succeed.

Try to light several bulbs at once. Draw a simple wiring diagram for your successful setup. Use standard symbols for bulb, switch, dry cell. Consider at least two different ways to connect the bulbs for successful results.

Try connecting dry cells together to give a brighter or longer-lasting light. Draw a simple wiring diagram for your successful setup. Consider at least two different ways to connect the dry cells.

(14) What is a short circuit? Connect a dry cell, a light bulb, and a switch to illustrate a short circuit. When we say "short circuit," what we really mean is "short of resistance." (15) What often happens when you have a short circuit? (16) Why?

Summarize what you have learned about light bulbs, dry cells, switches, and circuits in this exercise.

◆

Free Inquiry

After students have studied and learned how to attack a problem, gained sufficient knowledge about the subject, and performed modified inquiry, the instructor might invite them to become involved in free inquiry. This method differs from the modified approach because the students identify what it is they would like to study. The following questions are suggested as a basis for this type of class activity:

1. If you were the teacher of this class and you were going to select the most exciting things to investigate this term, what would they be?

2. What are some problems related to our community that you would like to study?

3. Now that you have studied, for example, salts, algae, light, heat, radiation, animal behaviors, and so forth, what problems can you come up with that you would like to investigate individually or in teams?

4. Now that you have finished this experiment, for example in population, what other experiments can you think of and which of them would you like to do?

5. When you see problems in the community, such as pollution, or some problem related to science that you would like to discuss, bring it to the class's attention.

6. What types of mathematical investigations would you like to conduct (e.g., determining the acceleration of a skier or a race-car driver)?

7. What authors would you like to read?

8. What biographies would you like to write or read?

9. What kind of play would you like to write, read, or produce?

CONDITIONS FOR INQUIRY TEACHING

Suchman lists four conditions for good inquiry teaching.[13] The first one he calls *the condition of freedom,* meaning the freedom of learners to seek out desired information. They must be allowed to try out ideas and invent ways of accounting for what they see. This is the essence of the inquiry approach.

The second condition is *the condition of the responsive environment*. A responsive environment is a classroom, a laboratory, or the outdoors on a field trip—anywhere that provides many opportunities for inquiry. It cannot be a sterile classroom or lecture hall. Teachers must have books, apparatus, experiments, aquaria, and many other things for students to work with. Inquiry can take place only in a responsive environment. The teacher must provide the information the students seek or the sources for that information. The teacher must make available a wide range of materials and facts from which the students can choose to meet their needs of the moment. This is the second important condition for inquiry teaching.

The third condition listed by Suchman is *the condition of focus*. Inquiry is a purposeful activity, a search for greater meaning in some event, object, or condition that raises questions in the inquirer's mind. It is directed toward one goal, toward the solution of a problem. It is not scattered; the energies are not dissipated. This is what is meant by the condition of focus.

Suchman's fourth condition is *the condition of low pressure*. Students will gain their reinforcement directly from the success of their own ideas in adding meaning to the environment or to their understanding of it. The teacher must respond positively to the student but neutrally to the product of the student's thinking. The teacher must recognize that not all students learn at the same rate. The condition of low pressure provides for students with different rates of learning to progress in the same classroom. Contemporary education sometimes defeats that purpose by putting too much emphasis on the class being 50 minutes long. The bell rings and the students must move to another class, which emphasizes educational uniformity. There is very little flexibility for teachers to provide for different rates of learning.

When you teach by inquiry, there are several important elements of an inquiry lesson that must be followed. The basic elements of such a plan are described below:

- *The problem*. This is the basic requirement and meets the condition of focus described by Suchman. If at all possible, the problem should be real, meaningful, and capable of study. If the problem can be elicited from the class, so much the better. A practical substitute, however, is one identified by the teacher and elaborated for the class.
- *The background information*. Some means must be found to provide the necessary information to put the class on a fairly common level of understanding. This may be in the form of a brief class discussion, some common reading matter, a textbook, or a preliminary experiment to give general understanding to all members of the class.
- *The materials*. This refers to Suchman's condition of a responsive environment. Provisions must be made to have adequate quantities of materials at hand, opportunities for individual work with the materials, and a chance for students to choose the materials they will need to solve the problem.
- *The guiding questions*. This consists of an anticipated list of questions to be asked by the teacher to direct students' thought processes. Prepare a skeleton outline of these but allow for ample deviation from the basic list in order to provide for student input.
- *The hypotheses*. These should be formulated as a result of discussions and guiding questions. Permit a condition of freedom so as not to inhibit discussion.
- *The data gathering and analysis*. This is the hands-on, experimental part of the inquiry lesson. Permit a condition of low pressure here to allow for mistakes and repeats. Emphasize record-keeping and a systematic approach to the problem.
- *The conclusion*. This refers to the lesson's closure and should culminate in some final result based on experimentation and discussion. Group conclusions are acceptable.

RESEARCH FINDINGS ABOUT USING INVESTIGATIVE TEACHING APPROACHES

Although the research findings still need further investigation, particularly concerning how students vary in feelings about the different approaches (affectivity) and the development of more than just subject-matter achievement differences (i.e., multitalents, self-concept, and so forth), they do indicate that investigative approaches have been successful. Shulman, as a result of a Conference on Learning by Discovery, summarizes the research in discovery as follows: "In the published studies, guided discovery treatments generally have done well both at the level of immediate learning and later transfer."[14]

An early examination of inquiry teaching set up a three-year longitudinal study to determine the differences this type of teaching made on students' learning behavior. Investigators at Carnegie-Mellon University found that an inquiry-oriented social studies curriculum significantly increased students' abilities to inquire about human affairs, compared to those studying non-inquiry materials.[15] This study is important because it shows that inquiry teaching over a prolonged period can help individuals become better investigators. When teachers first begin to use this approach, they often become frustrated and think they are not making sufficient progress. These instructors suffer from a covering compulsion; they feel better as teachers if they cover something because they have a mistaken idea of the function of teaching. They are surprised to learn that often students do not assimilate material covered by lecture (see Figure 13–1).

FIGURE 13–1   Differences
Between Inquiry and Noninquiry
Teaching

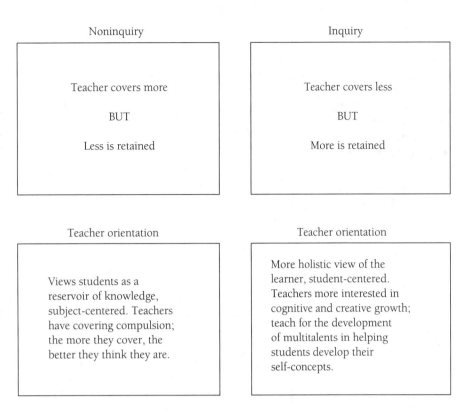

Noninquiry

Teacher covers more

BUT

Less is retained

Teacher orientation

Views students as a
reservoir of knowledge,
subject-centered. Teachers
have covering compulsion;
the more they cover, the
better they think they are.

Inquiry

Teacher covers less

BUT

More is retained

Teacher orientation

More holistic view of the
learner, student-centered.
Teachers more interested in
cognitive and creative growth;
teach for the development
of multitalents in helping
students develop their
self-concepts.

Six key characteristics of an inquiry-based classroom were identified by Crawford after researching new roles for science teachers in today's schools.[16] These consist of situating instruction in authentic problems, grappling with data, collaborating with other students and the teacher, making connections with society, teacher modeling behaviors of a scientist, and development of student ownership in the problem. It is important that students feel connected with the problem under study and practice the behaviors usually ascribed to scientists when they tackle tough questions that interest them.

Highly significant research concerning inquiry teaching has been completed using meta-analysis (the analysis of previous analytical studies using a common statistical framework).[17] This meta-research involved a careful study of 25 years of research comparing student performance in newer science curricula (i.e., post-Sputnik) to student performance in traditional courses.

Five measures were used in the comparison-achievement, attitudes, process, analytic abilities, and related skills. On a composite basis across all junior high and senior high school curricula in science, the average student in the new science curricula exceeded the performance of 64 percent of the students in traditional courses. This consistent pattern of positive effects clearly established the superiority of the new

curricula over traditional courses. Students' achievement scores were effectively raised 9–14 percentile points when the students were placed in a classroom using a new program.

Teacher enthusiasm is a prime characteristic for those who instruct children in inquiry methods and attempt to infuse the spirit of investigation among students in science classes. A study by MacKenzie[18] described how a "teacher's stance of wonder, curiosity, and exploration during the use of hypothetical inquiry situations served as a way for the teacher to address her goals for students to be more vocal members of the learning community; to encourage critical and creative thinking in the students; to provide them with meaningful, context-rich opportunities for synthesizing personal past experiences with ongoing classroom instruction; to enhance socialization skills in the middle school environment; and to provide an improvisational environment for both learning and teaching."

As teachers engage in efforts to modernize their science teaching styles, certain areas of research are needed in reference to teacher beliefs, teachers' knowledge base for implementing inquiry, teacher practices, and student learning from inquiry-based instruction. In addition, Keys and Bryan[19] have pointed out that "particular attention be paid to research on inquiry in diverse classrooms, and to modes of inquiry-based instruction that are designed by teachers."

Problem Solving

The history of science clearly demonstrates the reliance upon observation and identification of problems." Charles Darwin clearly expressed a view when he stated, "How odd it is that anyone should not see that all observation must be for or against some view if it is to be of any service." And it appears that Albert Einstein agreed when he told his audience during a Herbert Spencer Lecture at Oxford, "Do not believe those scientists who say that their methods are inductive." Most recently, Sir Karl Popper felt obliged to again challenge what he called an "integral part of the Baconian religion" by stating that, "Science begins with theories, with prejudices, superstitions, and myths. . . . Science begins with problems, practical problems or theoretical problems. . . . "

We possess extensive knowledge of both the physical and theoretical world. Admittedly, this knowledge is subject to change, but it is the best knowledge we can achieve and is, therefore, used to guide our current and future actions. However, it is just as true that every addition of new knowledge brings with it the recognition of how little we really know. This is quite a paradox, but it is the tension (as Popper would put it) between what we think we know and our awareness of how little we know that inexorably results in problems."[20]

Investigations in the science classroom begin with a problem. Problem solving as a teaching strategy embodies most of the techniques and learning skills science educators consider important when learning science by investigative methods.

Several approaches to problem solving were researched and discussed by Donald Wood.[21] The first approach involves the following:

1. Begin with a task embedded in a familiar setting.
2. Introduce problem-solving techniques that might be applicable.
3. Allow students to create their own paths to a solution.
4. Emphasize collaborative learning and problem solving.
5. Help develop collaborative working skills.
6. Provide different roles for individuals in a group setting.
7. Identify, confront, and discuss misconceptions.

In a study by Taconis, et al, dealing with determination of the variables that characterize effective strategies for teaching science problem-solving, it was learned that "providing the learners with guidelines and criteria they can use in judging their own problem-solving process and products, and providing immediate feedback to them were found to be important prerequisites for the acquisition of problem-solving skills. Group work did not lead to positive effects unless combined with other variables, such as guidelines and feedback."[22] It was also pointed out that "the complexity of a problem depends on the number of variables involved, the number of sub-problems that have to be solved to reach the final answer, and the number of formulas, laws and principles from which the solver has to make a choice when planning the solution. A problem can be closed or open: that is to say, have one unique answer or be open to a variety of possible solutions." It is apparent from the above that many cognitive activities such as analysis, planning, hypothesis formulation and testing are needed for successful problem-solving.

The teacher's role in the problem-solving methods discussed above involve thinking about and presenting everyday situations and experiences that relate to each concept or fundamental law discussed. The teacher should be a facilitator and suppress the urge to tell students what they should try or what they should discover. Encourage sharing of ideas in class and devise a wide range of options for solving the problem.

Teachers using problem-solving approaches to learning science will inevitably find some elements of resistance. There will be a reluctance on the part of students to change their learning styles from what they have been used to in traditional learning. Similarly, teachers may express concern about assessment and testing methods because emphasis on factual memorization will be minimized.

Teachers themselves may have serious reservations about using problem-solving methods because of the additional time required and a de-emphasis on coverage of textbook materials. There may also be increased expense because of the wide range of resources needed to fully explore solutions to the problems selected.

The NSTA Search for Excellence in Science Education begun in 1981 sought exemplary programs in secondary school science teaching throughout the United States. Many programs were found and reported on in the *Focus on Excellence* published by the NSTA in 1987. At the college level a similar search was conducted by the Society for College Science Teachers (SCST). Results were published in Innovations in College Science Teaching by John Dunkhase and John Penick in 1988.[23]

In both of these efforts, criteria for exemplary programs in science teaching focused heavily on the use of inquiry and investigative teaching methods. Three main components were deemed necessary to qualify as an exemplary problem-solving type of teaching strategy: identification of a problem, investigation and analysis of the problem, and presentation of the results.

Programs did not qualify as exemplary if the main attention was on presentation of facts and concepts, manipulations of numbers and equations to get a so-called "right answer," or verification of scientific phenomena to get a prescribed result in laboratory work.

Students in exemplary programs were introduced to the process of identifying problems, gathering information, organizing and analyzing information, and presenting the best analysis. Active participation in identification and investigation of science-related problems and human endeavors was considered important. Attention was paid to acquisition of new knowledge and the processes by which scientific information is generated and applied to the solution of real problems.

The types of activities in which students engage in classrooms reflect the degree of inquiry practiced in these classes. An analysis of the inquiry level of science activities in junior high school science textbooks was done by Pizzini, and others.[24] They found a significant variation in the frequency of inquiry level activities among science textbooks and activity guides. Four levels of inquiry were identified, ranging from confirmation or verification activities through structured inquiry and guided inquiry to open inquiry in which students formulate hypotheses and design procedures for investigating problems.

The researchers concluded that the first three levels do not produce the mindset nor the skills needed to practice inquiry and investigative problem solving. Only open inquiry provides these experiences. They also concluded that science activities in junior high school science textbooks and commercially published supplementary activity guides are essentially noninquiry approaches to science teaching.

The researchers produced a helpful list of suggestions needed to achieve the goal of science instruction based on open inquiry. To accomplish this, students should:

1. Identify problems and potential solutions, and design plans to test the solutions.
2. Formulate and test hypotheses and test their predictions.
3. Design their own procedures and analyze the processes used.
4. Formulate new questions.
5. Analyze and discuss the underlying assumptions.
6. Share and discuss predictions, procedures, products, and solutions.
7. Consider and develop alternative predictions, procedures, products, and solutions.
8. Develop a questioning base for prior knowledge.
9. Link their own experiences to activities, concepts, and principles.

Although inquiry teaching should receive a major emphasis in science teaching, not everything can or should be taught by inquiry. For example, for students to learn the names of chemical compounds, they must memorize them. If you want students to learn how to handle and use a microscope, you will probably have to show them. If there are safety precautions to be aware of, the instructor must tell the students about them.

You, as a teacher, will have to establish a value system and use it as a guide in determining when you will or will not teach something by inquiry.

SUMMARY

Many of the modern curriculum materials for the middle and secondary school are discovery- and inquiry-oriented. In discovery teaching, students use their minds to gain insights into some concept or principle. In the process of discovering, an individual performs such mental operations as measuring, predicting, observing, inferring, and classifying. In inquiry, an individual may use all of the discovery mental processes plus those characterizing a mature adult, such as formulating problems, hypothesizing, designing experiments, synthesizing knowledge, and demonstrating such attitudes as objectivity, curiosity, open-mindedness, and respect for theoretical models, values, and attitudes. Discovery and inquiry teaching may vary from a relatively structured approach (where considerable guidance is provided by the instructor) to free investigation (where the students originate problems).

Why use these investigative approaches? The philosophical and psychological advantages appear to be many. These methods increase intellectual potency; cause a shift from extrinsic to intrinsic rewards; help students learn how to investigate; increase memory retention; make instruction student-centered, thereby contributing to a person's self-concept; increase expectancy levels; develop multiple, not just academic talents; avoid learning only on the verbal level; and allow more time for students to assimilate and accommodate information.

Although there is a need to further assess the value of these approaches (particularly relative to attitudes, values, and self-concept attainment), there is much evidence that students taught by these methods perform significantly better on cognitive tasks involving critical thinking than those taught by traditional instruction.

Teachers often suffer from a "covering syndrome." If they cover the material, they feel that their responsibility as teachers has been met. But because a teacher covers something is little assurance that students have learned it. Student-centered instruction, because it often requires more time, results in less covering than does traditional teaching. The retention and critical-thinking ability of students in investigative-oriented classes, however, has been found to be greater.

◆
─────

REFERENCES

1. Pinchas Tamir, "Inquiry and the Science Teacher," *Science Education,* 67 (5) (1983): 657–672.

2. Richard Suchman, *Developing Inquiry* (Chicago: Science Research Associates, 1966).

3. Norris Harms and Robert Yager, "Project Synthesis," *What Research Says to the Science Teacher,* 3 (1981): 53–72.

4. *Science Education for the 80s* (1) (Washington, DC: NSTA, 1979).

5. Leopold Klopfer, "The Teaching of Science and the History of Science," *Journal of Research in Science Teaching,* 6 (1) (1969): 87–95.

6. Carlton H. Stedman, "Fortuitous Strategies on Inquiry in the Good Ole Days," *Science Education,* 71 (5) (1987): 657–665.

7. *Ibid.*

8. Wayne Welch, Leopold Klopfer, Glen Aikenhead, and J. T. Robinson, "The Role of Inquiry in Science Education: Analysis and Recommendations," *Science Education,* 65 (1) (1981): 33–50.

9. J. T. Wilson, "Processes of Scientific Inquiry: A Model for Teaching and Learning Science," *Science Education,* 58 (1) (1974): 127–133.

10. K. D. Peterson, "Scientific Inquiry for High School Students," *Journal of Research in Science Teaching,* 15 (2) (1978): 153–159.

11. William Kyle, Jr., "The Distinction Between Inquiry and Scientific Inquiry and Why High School Students Should Be Cognizant of the Distinction," *Journal of Research in Science Teaching,* 17 (2) (1980): 123–130.

12. Richard A. Huber and Christopher J. Moore, "A Model for Extending Hands-on Science to Be Inquiry Based," *School Science and Mathematics,* 101 (1) (January, 2001): 32–41.

13. J. Richard Suchman, *Developing Inquiry* (Chicago: Science Research Associates), pp. 14–18.

14. Lee S. Shulman, "Psychological Controversies in the Teaching of Science and Mathematics," *Science Teacher* (September 1968) 90.

15. John M. Good, John U. Forley, and Edwin Featon, "Developing Inquiry Skills With an Experimental Social Studies Curriculum," *Journal of Educational Research,* 63 (1) (1969): 35.

16. Barbara Crawford, "Embracing the Essence of Inquiry: New Roles for Science Teachers," *Journal of Research in Science Teaching,* 37 (9) (November, 2000).

17. James A. Shymansky, William C. Kyle, Jr., and Jennifer M. Alport, "The Effects of New Science Curricula on Student Performance," Journal of Research in Science Teaching, 20 (5) (1983): 387–404

18. Ann Haley MacKenzie, "The Role of Teacher Stance When Infusing Inquiry Questioning Into Middle School Science Classrooms," *School Science and Mathematics,* 101 (3) (March, 2000): 143–153.

19. Carolyn W. Keys, Lynn A. Bryan, "Co-Constructing Inquiry-Based Science With Teachers: Essential Research for Lasting Reform," *Journal of Research in Science Teaching,* 38 (6) (2001): 631–645.

20. Norman G. Lederman and Margaret L Niess, "Problem 'less' Research: 'Less' Is Not More!" Editorial: *Science Education,* 96 (8) (December, 1996): 393–394.

21. Donald R. Woods, "Three More Approaches to Problem-Solving," *Journal of College Science Teaching* (September/October, 1991).

22. R. Taconis, M.G.M. Ferguson-Hessler, H. Broekkamp, "Teaching Science Problem-Solving: An Overview of Experimental Work," Journal of Research in Science Teaching, 38 (4) (2001): 442–468.

23. John A. Dunkhase and John E. Penick, "Problem-Solving for the Real World", *Journal of College Science Teaching,* 21 (November 1991): 100–105.

24. Edward L. Pizzini and others, "Inquiry Level of Junior High Activity," *Journal of Research in Science Teaching* (February 1991): 111.

DEMONSTRATION AND LABORATORY WORK

THE ROLE OF DEMONSTRATIONS AND LABORATORY WORK

The two aspects of science teaching that have long characterized the nature of this endeavor are demonstrations and laboratory experiences. Some would say that science teaching without these two components is really not science. Regardless of one's position on this topic, the two strategies remain at a high level in most science classrooms. With increased emphasis on inquiry teaching, it is likely that demonstrations and experiments will remain important, though probably with shifts toward open-ended styles and investigative approaches being used more frequently.

In the first-period general-science class, Mr. O'Brien took a candle out of a box and placed it on the demonstration desk. He told the class he would show them the difference between a physical and chemical change. He struck a match and placed the candle over the flame until the wick burned. Soon some of the wax was melting, dripping, and then solidifying. He said, "This is an example of a physical change. When the candle partially burns, the wax changes to carbon dioxide and water— and then there is a chemical change." The students watched the demonstration and some took notes.

Across the hall, Mr. Jackson was teaching the same unit. He also wanted to have students learn about physical and chemical changes. Uncertain of how he was going to do this, Mr. Jackson asked Mr. O'Brien if he knew a good demonstration to show these changes. Mr. O'Brien suggested he burn a candle. Mr. Jackson, however, taught these concepts differently. After the bell rang and the students were seated, he took a candle and a match box out of his demonstration desk, placed them on top of the desk, and asked, "What am I going to do with the candle and match?" Art answered, "You are going to light it." Mr. Jackson replied, "That's right, but what will happen to the match and candle when I light them? How will they change? What will happen to the candle when it burns? Will it drip?"

Several students raised their hands and suggested answers to his questions. He lit the candle, and it started to drip. He asked, "Why does the candle drip? What will happen if we try to burn the dripped material? Where did the dripped material come from, and how did it change while the candle was burning?"

George explained that the material merely melted and then solidified. Mr. Jackson asked the rest of the class what they thought of George's explanation, "What evidence was there for his suggestion?" Several members of the class discussed the matter and agreed that this material had only changed form in the process of melting and resolidifying. Mr. Jackson asked, "What is this type of change called?"

Two students raised their hands and suggested that it might be a physical change. Mr. Jackson then asked what was happening to the candle as it burned. What caused it to get shorter, and why would it eventually have to be replaced? The class considered this and eventually realized that the candle was also changing chemically.

INQUIRY THROUGH DEMONSTRATION

Which of these teaching methods do you think would be the more effective way to demonstrate physical and chemical changes and why? What did students learn from Mr. Jackson's approach that they might not have learned from Mr. O'Brien's? Which of the methods stressed the inquiry approach and why? Which method do you think took instructors more time to prepare? Which would be more inductive in its approach? Why do you think teachers have traditionally emphasized the deductive method in giving demonstrations? If you were going to teach this lesson, how would you do it?

A demonstration has been defined as the process of showing something to another person or group. Clearly, there are several ways in which things can be shown. You can hold up an object such as a piece of sulfur and say, "This is sulfur," or you can state, "Sulfur burns; light some sulfur, and show that it burns." Showing things in this way mainly involves observation or verification. Mr. O'Brien's use of demonstration was of this type.

A demonstration can also be given inductively by the instructor asking several questions but seldom giving answers. An inductive demonstration has the advantage of stressing inquiry, which encourages students to analyze and make hypotheses based on their knowledge. Their motivation is high because they like riddles, and in an inductive demonstration they are constantly confronted with riddles. The strength of this motivation becomes apparent if you consider the popularity of puzzles. Inviting students to inquire why something occurs taxes their minds and requires them to think. Thinking is an active mental process. The only way in which students learn to think is by having opportunities to do so. An inductive demonstration provides this opportunity because students' answers to the instructor's questions act as feedback. The teacher has a better understanding of students' comprehension of the demonstration. The feedback acts as a guide for further questioning until the students discover the concepts and principles involved in the demonstration, and the teacher is sure that they know its meaning and purpose.

Demonstrations, in addition to serving as simple observations of material and verification of a process, may also be experimental in nature. A demonstration can become an experiment if it involves a problem for which the solution is not immediately apparent to the class. Students particularly like experimental demonstrations because they usually have more action. Students enjoy action more than words! They love to watch something happening before their eyes.

 Visit http://www.prenhall.com/trowbridge and select Topic 2—Constructivism and Learning in Science. Select "Activities and Lesson Plans" and find the link for "Cool Science for Curious Kids." Obtain ideas on these activities and try out several in your methods class for response and discussion. Submit these to your instructor by using the Electronic Bluebook module.

Demonstration Versus Individual Experimentation

Educators have stressed the importance of self-instruction and less reliance on large-group or class instruction. Education should be preparation for life, and part of that preparation must be to ensure that the individual continues to learn long after formal education ends. It is important that the school reinforce habits and patterns of learning that will prepare students to continue their education many years after they leave organized instruction. Laboratory work, because it involves the individual directly in the learning process, as well as imparting working skills, is thought to be superior to teaching by demonstration. Students working on a laboratory problem have learned far more than just the answer to the problem. They may learn to be efficient, self-reliant, and analytical; to observe, manipulate, measure, and reason; to use apparatus; and, most importantly, to learn on their own. Individual laboratory experimentation helps to attain these goals better than do demonstrations. For this reason, demonstrations should play a lesser role in science instruction, with individual student investigation receiving top priority.

Demonstrations, however, are not entirely without value. Demonstrations can be justified for the following reasons:

1. *Lower cost.* Less equipment and fewer materials are needed by an instructor doing a demonstration. It is, therefore, cheaper than having an entire class conduct experiments. Note however, that cheaper education is not always necessarily better education.

2. *Availability of equipment.* Certain demonstrations require equipment not available in sufficient numbers for all students to use. For example, not every student in a physics class needs to have an oscilloscope to study sound waves.

3. *Economy of time.* Often the time required to set up equipment for a laboratory exercise cannot be justified for the educational value received. A teacher can set up the demonstration and use the rest of the time for other instruction.

4. *Less hazard from dangerous materials.* A teacher may more safely handle dangerous chemicals or apparatus requiring sophisticated skills.

5. *Direction of the thinking process.* In a demonstration, a teacher has a better indication of the students' thinking processes and can do much to stimulate the students to be more analytical and synthetic in their reasoning.

6. *Show the use of equipment.* An instructor may want to show the students how to use and prevent damage to a microscope, balance, oscilloscope, and so forth.

Planning a Demonstration

To plan an efficient and effective demonstration requires extensive organization and consideration of the following points:

1. Identify the concept and principles you wish to teach. Direct the design of the entire demonstration to their attainment.

2. If the principle you wish to teach is complex, break it down into concepts and give several examples for each concept. For example, photosynthesis involves understanding concepts of radiant energy, chlorophyll, carbon dioxide, glucose, water, temperature, a chemical change, and gases. Students memorizing that green plants can make sugar in light with water results in little understanding if they do not know the meaning of these concepts.

3. Choose an activity that will show the concepts you wish to teach. Consult the sources at the end of this chapter for possible suggestions for activities.

4. Design the activity so that each student becomes as involved as possible. Personal participation will strengthen students' understanding of the concepts involved.

5. Gather and assemble the necessary equipment.

6. Practice the demonstration at least once before class begins.

7. Outline the questions you will ask during the demonstration. This procedure is especially important in doing an inquiry-oriented demonstration.

8. Consider how you may use visual aids, such as the overhead projector, to supplement the demonstration.

9. Decide on the evaluation technique to use.

   Written Techniques

   a. Essay: Have students take notes and record data during the demonstration, and then have them write a summary of the demonstration.

   b. Quiz: Have students write answers to questions or prepare diagrams to see if they really understood the demonstration. Stress application of scientific principles.

   Verbal Techniques

   a. Ask students to summarize the purpose of the demonstration.

   b. Give them problems in which they must apply the principles they have learned.

10. Consider the time a demonstration will take. Try to move it rapidly enough to keep students attentive. Prolonged or complicated demonstrations are generally undesirable because they don't hold the students' attention.

11. When you plan a demonstration, do it well, with the intention that you will probably use it for several years. It will then take less time to prepare in the future. Evaluate a demonstration immediately after giving it to determine its weaknesses and strengths. Add any questions that will contribute to the inquiry presentation when you use the demonstration again.

Giving a Demonstration

When giving a demonstration, keep the following guidelines in mind:

1. Make it easily visible. If you are working with small things, can you use an overhead projector to make them more visible?

2. Speak loudly enough to be heard in the back of the room. Do you speak loudly enough and modulate the tone and volume of your voice to avoid monotonous delivery? When a student responds, do you ask him or her to speak up so other students can hear? Do you repeat students' questions and answers for emphasis and audibility?

3. Do you display excitement in giving the demonstration? Do you make it "come alive"? A good demonstrator is somewhat of a ham. This kind of instructor uses dramatic techniques to excite and involve students. The way in which a teacher makes a demonstration come alive is as much an art as is reading Shakespeare well to an enraptured audience.

4. How do you stage the demonstration? How do you start it to involve everyone immediately? One suggestion is to place unique objects on a demonstration desk. For example, a transfusion container or a Van de Graff generator placed on a desk immediately motivates students' inquisitive minds. Before you even begin, you have the students with you, wondering what you are going to do.

   a. Teach inductively. Start your demonstration with a question. If you have interesting equipment, ask your students what they think you are going to do with it. Spend some time just asking questions about the apparatus. In the construction of a transfusion container, for example, there are several scientific principles involved, such as partial vacuum, air pressure, sterile conditions, nutrient for the cells placed in the bottle, and anticoagulants to prevent clotting of the blood.

   b. Ask questions constantly about what you are going to do, what's happening, why they think it is happening, and what the demonstration is proving or illustrating.

   c. Know the purpose of what you are demonstrating. Use your questions as a guide only. The questions you have anticipated may be excellent, but also be ready to pick up suggestions from the questions students ask while they are observing the demonstration.

   d. Give positive reinforcement. Always recognize an answer: "Say, I think you have something there." "Good, you're thinking." "What do the rest of you think of John's remarks?" When a student gives a good explanation, be complimentary. Seldom react negatively to a student's answer. Don't say, "That's wrong." Rather say, "It's good you're thinking, but your answer is not quite right."

5. Allow at least three seconds for students to reply to your questions. This wait-time is important so that the students may think about and reason out the demonstration.

6. Use the blackboard to describe the purpose of the demonstration. Verbal explanations are seldom enough. Any picture or diagram you make on the board immediately attracts the students' attention. Remember that your students have lived in a TV-centered environment; as soon as they see a visual representation on the board, they are drawn to it. A beginning teacher often fails to realize or ever consider how the blackboard can complement the learning activity.

7. At the conclusion of the demonstration, have a student summarize what has occurred and its purpose. This summation helps to fix the purpose of the demonstration in the minds of the students.

8. Evaluate your lesson, orally or in a written summary.

Ways to Present a Demonstration

Of the several ways in which a demonstration can be given, a teacher-centered demonstration is seldom the best method, because it does not provide enough student involvement. When students participate actively in giving a demonstration, they are more interested and, consequently, learn more. Several types of student-participative demonstrations are shown in Appendix A for example, "Discovery Demonstration: Bottle and Key," p. 392; "How Long Can You Boil Water in a Paper Cup?" p. 395; "Discovery Demonstration: Inquiring into Falling Bodies," p. 395; "Small Group Problem Solving," p. 397; and "Evaluation of Student Understanding of a Basic Physical Principle," p. 393. Here are five ways in which a demonstration can be presented.

1. Teacher demonstration.   The teacher prepares and gives the demonstration to the class. This approach has the advantage usually of better organization and more sophisticated presentation.

2. Teacher-student demonstration.   This is a team approach in which the student assists the teacher. This type of demonstration recognizes the student. The class may be more attentive because they like to watch one of their peers perform.

3. Student-group demonstration.   This method can be used on occasion; it has the advantage of more actively involving students. The group approach can be used to advantage if students are allowed to select their group members. The teacher should evaluate the group as a whole and assign the same grade to each group. The groups will form at first among friends. However, if some of the members are not productive, they will be rejected the next time groups are selected. The peer pressure to produce and become actively involved replaces the necessity for a teacher to encourage students to work. This group arrangement may also be effective in organizing laboratory work. The only problem is that the teacher must be patient until group pressure is brought to bear on the nonproductive students in the class.

4. Individual student demonstration.   This method can produce very effective demonstrations, especially if the student has peer status. An effective way to have individual student demonstrations is to have upperclassmen, from advanced science classes, demonstrate to the lowerclassmen. A freshman general-science class may become enthralled when a physics or chemistry senior comes into the class to give a demonstration. An upperclassman, excited about giving a demonstration, helps to convey that excitement to the students.

5. Guest demonstration.   Guest demonstrators can do much to relieve a boring pattern of routine class activities. Other science teachers in the school may be called in to present a demonstration or activity in which they have some special competence. Professional scientists are also often willing to give special demonstrations.

Silent Demonstration

Some authors have stressed the importance and desirability of the silent demonstration. In the passage below a verbal demonstration is compared with a silent one.

> The usual kind of demonstration by which science teachers give their students visual or auditory experiences is the teacher-talking demonstration. In this performance the teacher is actor and commentator. The pupils, who are supposed to be learning from the new experience how to attack a difficulty or develop a concept, are spectators. But they do not necessarily learn scientific facts or

When giving a demonstration, ask questions constantly about what you're going to do, what's happening, and why.

principles from a demonstration in which everything is done for them. Pupils really learn when they observe and react to what is presented.

There is a kind of demonstration that is likely to ensure, on the part of the student, careful observation, accurate recording of data, and practical application, later, of the ideas gained from the experience. This procedure is the silent demonstration. The following comparison of the silent demonstration and the teacher-talking demonstration shows how they differ.[1]

The silent demonstration, since it cannot be supplemented or strengthened by explanation, requires more careful planning than does the teacher-talking demonstration (see Table 14-1). In preparing the silent demonstration, the teacher may find this general procedure a good one. First, fix clearly in mind the object of the demonstration, and select the apparatus and materials best suited for the demonstration. Then determine the beginning point of the demonstration. The beginning is based on what the teacher assumes that pupils know.

Consider difficulties as learning steps. Perform the techniques so that they can be observed from all areas of the room. The steps should follow some order in relation to the learning steps. Give pupils an outline of the steps to be used. Outlines may be photocopied, mimeographed, or put on the chalkboard.

Silent demonstrations should not be used frequently because there is no way for the teacher to determine if the students are achieving the objectives while the demonstration is being given. Silent demonstrations can, however, provide a welcome change in the routine activity of the class. They can be used effectively if an instructor's movements are accentuated so that the students can see and have some hints about what is relevant. In a silent

demonstration, visibility is extremely important and must be ensured; otherwise, the students will quickly become frustrated and discipline problems will ensue.

Storage of Demonstration Equipment

Equipment made by you or your students can lend an added fascination to a science demonstration, because students are often more impressed by homemade equipment. Parents, industrial companies, and students will often construct or provide apparatus for the school without cost. Having students build equipment also involves them in improving the science instruction of the school. This personal investment helps to build student morale and to show the community that the science department is an active and dynamic part of their school.

Store equipment after use so that it may be found easily in the future and set up again with little effort. One way to do so is to establish a list of headings under which to store materials. For example, in physics, storage areas might be labeled: "electricity," "magnetism," "heat," "light," "sound," "atomic structure," and so on. In biology, storage categories might be: glassware, chemicals, slides, preserved plant and animal specimens, etc. The next time you wish to find the equipment, it is readily available under the proper storage title. Such a system also makes it easy for students to assist you in storing or obtaining equipment for use in demonstrations.

An efficient way to store small demonstration materials is to use several shoe boxes. Place all the materials you need for a demonstration in the box and label the end. For example, a box might be labeled "electrostatic demonstration materials." You might also include in the box a sheet of paper describing the demonstration.

TABLE 14–1 Comparison of Teacher-Talking and Silent Demonstration

Teacher-Talking Demonstration	Silent Demonstration
Teacher states purposes of the demonstration.	Pupil must discover purpose as the demonstration progresses.
Teacher names pieces of apparatus and describes arrangement.	Teacher uses apparatus. Pupils observe equipment and arrangement.
Teacher is manipulator and technician, tells what is being done, points out and usually explains results.	Teacher performs experiment. Pupils observe what is being done and then describe results.
Teacher often points out the things that should have happened and accounts for unexpected results.	Pupils record results as observed. Teacher checks for accuracy and honesty in reporting. Teacher repeats the experiment if necessary.
Teacher summarizes the results and states the conclusion to be drawn. Pupils usually copy the conclusions as stated.	Pupils summarize data and draw their own conclusions based on what they observed. Teacher checks conclusions and repeats experiment if necessary.
Teacher explains the importance of the experiment and tells how it is applied in everyday life.	Pupils attempt to answer application questions related to the demonstration.

This helps lessen future preparation time for the same demonstration. A student laboratory assistant can get the box down, read the included sheet, check to see if all of the equipment needed is present, and replenish needed supplies. The box then will be ready for use, and you will require practically no preparation time. This storage procedure works particularly well with general science and simple physical materials. A drawback is that when many materials and articles of equipment are stored in the boxes, they are not then easily available for other demonstration work during the year.

Special Equipment

FREE SOURCES OF EQUIPMENT

Science courses often require special science equipment. Some of this specialized equipment may be available to teachers without cost if they go through the proper channels. In some areas of the country, there are companies willing to donate materials to the schools when they receive a written request from the teacher. Consult with experienced teachers or professional scientists in your community to determine what is available.

The journals and periodic reports of the National Science Teachers Association frequently have sections devoted to sources of free and inexpensive materials for science teaching. They are usually available in your school library, or you may choose to join the Association and receive the journal of your choice. A career-oriented science teacher will find this a valuable source of materials and teaching topics.

OVERHEAD PROJECTOR

Every science class should have an overhead projector with suitable transparency supplies. Such a projector can become a valuable teaching aid during a demonstration or discussion. For example, in biology a teacher may want to show how to make a wet-mount slide. This procedure cannot be demonstrated easily except by using an overhead projector. Many of the properties of magnetism can also be demonstrated by the use of such a projector.

OTHER PROJECTION AND DEMONSTRATION EQUIPMENT

Advances in technology in recent years have produced many kinds of projection equipment which are reliable and serviceable. One example is the Macintosh "PowerPoint" system, which enables projection of high-quality images using a laptop computer and integrated projector for total flexibility and convenience. Attendance at regional or national conventions of science teaching associations provides an opportunity to observe a wide variety of demonstration apparatus for use in science classes.

Stressing the Higher Levels of Learning

A demonstration should contribute to the objectives of the course and school. It should be used to stimulate critical thinking and offer opportunities for creativity. A demonstration may further be used to develop understanding of the philosophical basis of science. For example, the instructor may ask questions that elicit responses relating to the degrees of certainty or uncertainty in the data, the social implications of new findings in science, and the responsibilities of scientists in the release of new findings to the public. What questions need to be asked and what decisions need to be made?

Questions of this type can be used discriminately throughout a series of demonstrations to build a philosophical awareness of the foundations of modern science. The responsibility to impart knowledge of this sort offers great challenge to the teacher in formulating lessons. An activity that embodies higher understanding, more students' individuality, and creative reactions is illustrated in "Evaluating Food Choices" in Appendix A, p. 374.

INQUIRY THROUGH LABORATORY WORK

It has often been said that science is not really science unless it is accompanied by experimentation and laboratory work. In the secondary schools, there continues to be interest in the laboratory as the focal point for the study of science. It is worth noting that this is not the first time in the history of science education in the United States that the laboratory has come into prominence. The late 1800s saw the construction of laboratories in secondary schools and colleges with a corresponding change in emphasis in the methods of science instruction. The recitation method and the catechetical approach for learning science principles were gradually replaced by experiments in laboratories with the expressed purpose of verifying the laws of physics and chemistry. It was believed that students would learn science best by repeating, in an abbreviated fashion, the classical experiments of Newton, Galileo, Hooke, Priestley, Boyle, and many others. Students would see principles of natural science at work, enabling them to understand the underlying science concepts. Laboratories and apparatus were designed to duplicate as nearly as possible the materials and equipment used in the original experiments, with modern refinements to ensure reasonable accuracy in the hands of science students.

Christina Hart[2] has commented on the role of laboratory work in science classes. "Laboratory work is almost ubiquitously seen as being of great importance to science education, by some as almost the defining characteristic of this component of the school curriculum. However, research on aspects of laboratory work and its consequences does not provide strong support for this view. Gunstone and Champagne (1990) argued that laboratory work could successfully be used to promote conceptual change if small qualitative laboratory tasks are used. Such tasks aid in students reconstructing their thinking as less time is spent on interacting with apparatus, instructions, and recipes, and more time spent on discussion and reflection."

The Inquiry Approach

Beginning in the late 1950s, there was a definite shift in emphasis in high school science. The laboratory became the center of attention at all levels of secondary science, including the junior high school. The particular goals and methods used in the various new curriculum projects of the Physical Science Study Committee, the Biological Sciences Curriculum Study, the Chemical Education Materials Study, the Chemical Bond Approach Project, the Earth Science Curriculum Project, and others are discussed in detail in Chapter 3. Without exception, these projects emphasized and provided for inquiry methods in which students themselves were the investigators, and which gave many opportunities for creativity.

The inquiry method in the science laboratory can be promoted by several fairly simple but important changes. Paul Brandwein and Joseph Schwab, in describing the inquiry curriculum, had this to say about inquiry methods:

> In general, conversion of the laboratory from the dogmatic to the inquiring mode is achieved by making two changes. First, a substantial part of the laboratory work is made to lead rather than lag the classroom phase of science teaching. . . . Second, the merely demonstrative function of the laboratory (which serves the purpose of the dogmatic curriculum) is subordinated to two other functions.
>
> One of these functions consists in a new service to the classroom phase of instruction. With classroom materials converted from a rhetoric of conclusions to an exhibition of the course of inquiry, conclusions alone will no longer be the major component. Instead, we will deal with units which consist of the statement of a scientific problem, a view of the data needed for its solution, an account of the interpretation of these data, and a statement of the conclusions forged by the interpretation. Such units as these will convey the wanted meta-lesson about the nature of inquiry. But they will appear exceedingly easy and simple, conveying little of the real flavor of scientific inquiries, unless the verbal statement of the problem situation and of the difficulties involved in the acquisition of data is given meaning by an exhibition of their real physical referents. . . .
>
> The second function of the inquiring laboratory is to provide occasions for an invitation to the conduct of miniature but exemplary programs of inquiry. The manual for such a laboratory ceases to be a volume that tells students what to do and what to expect.[3]

The inquiry mode of teaching, in addition to requiring a different philosophical approach by the teacher and students, also demands higher levels of proficiency in the use of the tools of inquiry. These tools consist of the skills needed to inquire into natural events and conditions. For example, one could not learn very much about how forces cause masses to accelerate unless one could make careful measurements of distance, time, force, and mass. To learn the interrelationships between all of these factors requires that students refine their measurement skills. It is necessary to know how to use a meter stick or measuring tape, to read the units correctly, to read a stop watch, to operate a beam balance correctly, and to measure force with a spring scale or some other method. In the classroom, students must have opportunities to practice the skills required for a particular inquiry situation; otherwise, the experience will probably be frustrating and the learning minimal.

Traditional laboratory experiments do not provide enough opportunities for students to use their minds to solve problems posed in the laboratory. Frequently, all that is required is to make sure all the detailed instructions found in the laboratory manual are carried out, and that all the blanks are filled in after the experiment is completed. Laboratory manuals have often been compared to a cookbook, which fails to excite students very much and often leaves them unsure about what they were studying, or what they found out in the activity. Paul German and others analyzed several biology textbooks and found little evidence of scientific inquiry.[4] They reported that "Results indicated that while some manuals have made efforts to include a few science process skills, they seldom call upon students to use their knowledge and experience to pose questions, solve problems, investigate natural phenomena or construct answers or generalizations."

Some suggestions for "uncookbooking" laboratory experiments have been offered by William Leonard.[5] These suggestions are included here for consideration by science teachers in secondary schools because of their relevance to investigative methods of teaching.

1. Give the student a simple task or goal to accomplish. This task can be explained verbally by the teacher or by brief explanations in written form. The purpose is to focus students' attention on a problem and to encourage creative thinking in solving it.

2. Give the student only essential procedures. Some general suggestions may be made to get the student started but only to spark some creative thinking. Let students tussle with these matters for awhile. If frustration becomes apparent, give some help in the form of possible exploration.

3. Have students work in small, cooperative groups. Ideas for possible procedures can be shared and discussed. Try to see that ideas are not monopolized by one person in the group and that real sharing is taking place.

4. Provide students with ideas and lists of potential resources to use in investigating the problem. When technical procedures are needed, let students recognize the need and call for assistance.

5. Resist telling students how to carry out the investigation. Although this will undoubtedly require more time, it will provide opportunities for reflection and deliberation by the students themselves and help to develop necessary investigative skills.

6. Add some meaningful questions at the end of the investigation. Do not stress obtaining the "right" answer, but do emphasize analyzing why certain procedures were used, why certain hypotheses were tested, and why certain conclusions were drawn. The purpose of these questions is to cause students to think about their work, the decisions they made, and even the possible faulty pathways they took in arriving at a result.

The American Association for the Advancement of Science (AAAS) has argued for an open-ended approach in laboratory work rather than the use of the confirmatory approach that leaves students with an inaccurate view of the practice of science. Instead, it contributes to the notion that the purpose of experimentation is the verification of hypotheses rather than their refutation.

The Advent of Computerized Science Laboratories

Careful thought should be given to replacement of traditional laboratory experiments with computer simulations of the experiments. Certain skills used in traditional laboratory experiments are not capable of being developed or experienced in computer simulations. Such skill development as organizing and recording data, for example, may be taken over by the microcomputer, thereby eliminating that experience for students in the laboratory. When microcomputers are used in the laboratory, their usage should be carefully integrated into the curriculum, thus providing exposure to important aspects of computer technology while preserving concrete experiences provided by hands-on experiences.

Five skill categories are identified on page 199 of this chapter. Of the five, acquisitive, organizational, creative, manipulative, and communicative, it would seem very difficult to develop the skills of manipulation and communication through computer simulations. An additional skill, use of safe laboratory procedures, also would be nearly impossible to achieve. A. Winders and B. Yates have commented on the replacement of hands-on laboratory experiments with computer simulations:

> In summary, the time honored hands-on science laboratories have, and will continue to provide essential academic and practical skills for our students. The use of computer technology, chosen carefully and used wisely, will be of great benefit in augmenting traditional laboratories. The challenge before us is to successfully balance the old and the new to gain the best both have to offer[6]

Research on the Laboratory's Role in Science Teaching

Over the years, science educators have examined the influence of the laboratory on achievement and other variables such as reasoning, critical thinking, understanding science, process skills, manipulative skills, interests, retention, and ability to do independent work, among others. Much of this research gave inconclusive results, but science teachers in general feel that the laboratory is a vital part of science teaching.

Joseph Novak described the problems graphically:

The science laboratory has always been regarded as the place where students should learn the process of doing science. But summaries of research on the value of laboratory for learning science did not favor laboratory over lecture-demonstrations . . . and more recent studies also show an appalling lack of effectiveness of laboratory instruction. . . . Our studies showed that most students in laboratories gained little insight regarding the key science concepts involved or toward the process of knowledge construction.[7]

Some positive findings can be cited. Three studies done between 1969 and 1979 found that laboratory instruction increased student problem-solving abilities. Other researchers reported positive results encouraging cognitive development, introducing scientific ideas, giving concrete examples, and learning how to manipulate materials when working with disadvantaged students in the laboratory.[8]

Data from a national survey in 1978 show that laboratory work and hands-on science activities are not used optimally in science teaching. Many teachers say students are apathetic about laboratory work and that labs are difficult to stock, maintain, and control. However, it is not likely students will experience much of the nature, methods, and spirit of science without this important component of science teaching.

In Texas, the legislature in 1984 mandated that all secondary school science classes must have at least 40 percent of their time devoted to laboratory work. Prior to that date, science classroom teachers had not allocated that much time to laboratory instruction. The first reaction by the teachers was shock and anger. A study by Robert James confirmed that even two years later teachers had difficulty seeing the potential benefits of the mandate, were concerned about the impact of the rule on them, and felt that they have better ideas as to how they should use class time.[9]

Thus, while much lip service is commonly given to the value of laboratory work in science classes, many science teachers appear to discount its value when faced with the realities of organization, materials procurement, time constraints, and lack of familiarity with investigative approaches to laboratory instruction.

Skill Development in the Laboratory

The complaint has frequently been lodged against science teaching that students and teachers alike have difficulty in expressing exactly what the goals of science teaching should be. In taking up this challenge, we will identify the types of skills that science students ought to be able to do better after having taken junior and senior high school science. We have listed five categories of skills: acquisitive, organizational, creative, manipula-

tive, and communicative. No attempt is made to rank these categories in order of importance, or even to imply that any one category may be more important than any other. Within each of the categories, however, specific skills are listed in order of increasing difficulty. In general, those skills that require only the use of one's own unaided senses are simpler than those that require use of instruments or higher orders of manual and mental dexterity.

CATEGORIES OF SKILLS

A. Acquisitive skills—Skills of gathering information
   1. Listening—being attentive, alert, questioning
   2. Observing—being accurate, alert, systematic
   3. Searching—locating sources, using several sources, being self-reliant, acquiring library skills
   4. Inquiring—asking, interviewing, corresponding
   5. Investigating—reading background information, formulating problems
   6. Gathering data—tabulating, organizing, classifying, recording
   7. Research—locating a problem, learning background, setting up experiments, analyzing data, drawing conclusions
B. Organizational skills—Skills of putting information in systematic order
   1. Recording—tabulating, charting, working systematically, working regularly, recording completely
   2. Comparing—noticing how things are alike, looking for similarities, noticing identical features
   3. Contrasting—noticing how things differ, looking for dissimilarities, noticing unlike features
   4. Classifying—putting things into groups and subgroups, identifying categories, deciding between alternatives
   5. Organizing—putting items in order, establishing a system, filing, labeling, arranging
   6. Outlining—employing major headings and subheadings, using sequential, logical organization
   7. Reviewing—picking out important items, memorizing, associating
   8. Evaluating—recognizing good and poor features, knowing how to improve grades
   9. Analyzing—seeing implications and relationships, picking out causes and effects, locating new problems
C. Creative skills—Skills of developing new approaches and new ways of thinking
   1. Planning ahead—seeing possible results and probable modes of attack, setting up hypotheses
   2. Designing—creating a new problem, a new approach, a new device or system
   3. Inventing—creating a method, device, or technique

4. Synthesizing—putting familiar things together in a new arrangement, hybridizing, drawing together

D. Manipulative skills—Skills of handling materials and instruments

1. Using an instrument—knowing the instrument's parts, how it works, how to adjust it, its proper use for a given task, its limitations

2. Caring for an instrument—knowing how to store it, using proper settings, keeping it clean, handling it properly, knowing its rate capacity, transporting it safely

3. Demonstrating—setting up apparatus, making it work, describing parts and functions, illustrating scientific principles

4. Experimentation—recognizing a problem, planning a procedure, collecting data, recording data, analyzing data, drawing conclusions

5. Repair—repairing and maintaining equipment, instruments, etc.

6. Construction—making simple equipment for demonstrations and experimentation

7. Calibration—learning the basic information about calibration, calibrating a thermometer, balance, timer, or other instrument

E. Communication skills—Skills of transferring information correctly from one experimenter to another

1. Asking questions—learning to formulate good questions, to be selective in asking, to resort to own devices for finding answers whenever possible

2. Discussion—learning to contribute own ideas, listening to ideas of others, keeping on the topic, sharing available time equitably, arriving at conclusions

3. Explanation—describing to someone else clearly, clarifying major points, exhibiting patience, being willing to repeat

4. Reporting—orally reporting to a class or teacher in capsule form the significant material on a science topic

5. Writing—writing a report of an experiment or demonstration, not just filling in a blank but starting with a blank sheet of paper, describing the problem, the method of attack, the data collected, the methods of analysis, the conclusions drawn, and the implications for further work

6. Criticism—constructively criticizing or evaluating a piece of work, a scientific procedure or conclusion

7. Graphing—putting in graphical form the results of a study or experiment, being able to interpret the graph for someone else

8. Teaching—after becoming familiar with a topic or semi-expert in it, teaching the material to one's classmates in such a manner that it will not have to be retaught by the teacher

Is There a Need for Science Skill Development?

Courses in elementary and secondary schools should emphasize the processes of science as much as the concepts and generalizations. Understanding a process improves skill competencies, while learning how to learn requires adequate learning tools. In addition, students need confidence in their ability to perform the tasks needed in self-learning. Skill competency strengthens self-reliance.

Can Skill Development Be Guided Through a Graded Sequence of Difficulty—From Simple to Complex?

This progression is possible because of certain characteristics of skills themselves, such as level of difficulty and complexity. For example, skills requiring the use of unaided senses are usually simpler than those requiring the use of instruments. It is easier for students to use their unaided eyes to compare the colors of minerals than to operate a petrographic microscope to do the same thing at a higher level of sophistication. Also, groups of simple skills may be included in more difficult complex skills. Graphing, for example, requires competency in the simpler skills of counting, measuring, and using a ruler (instrument). In the same way, higher levels of learning—such as analysis, synthesis, and evaluation—require higher levels of skill proficiency.

Does Skill Development Enhance or Preclude Concept Development?

Growth in conceptual understanding is enhanced by expertise in skill usage. In teaching skills, concepts form the vehicle by which the skills are learned. One cannot learn a skill in a void—there must be substantive information on which to operate. The skill of comparing, for example, is useless unless there are things to compare. In the same context, a hierarchy of skills forms a framework to which concepts can be attached. As one learns increasingly sophisticated skills, the subject matter (concepts) can be adapted and changed as required.

Can Achievement of Skill Competencies Be Tested?

There is ample evidence that skill achievements can be structured in behavioral terms. Performance can be observed and evaluated. Various performance levels of individual skills can be graded on a continuum from minimum to maximum success. Not only is it possible for teachers to create testing situations using performance objectives, but it is equally possible to provide self-evaluation opportunities for students to gain knowledge of their own progress and levels of performance.

What Are the Implications of the Skill-Development Approach in the Science Classroom?

Conditions necessary for success when emphasizing the skill or process goals are:

1. Time must be provided for practice and experience in the skills being developed. One does not become proficient without practice and drill.
2. Teachers must clearly understand the skill objectives. Planning must revolve around these objectives rather than traditional content goals alone.
3. Ample materials must be available. There must be a responsive environment permitting students to operate with the materials of science.
4. A variety of conceptual materials may be selected to facilitate skill development. Most conceptual themes or topics provide ample opportunities for teaching varied skills. In planning for teaching, however, it is important to concentrate on a few skills in any particular lesson.
5. Evaluation emphasis must be placed on performance or behavioral terms, not mere factual memorization or recitation. The superficial coverage of content must be de-emphasized and performance and depth of understanding brought to the foreground.

Mere identification of skills to be taught is only a first step in the realization of a science objective. To aid in skill development and ultimate mastery of the desired skills, the teacher must devise suitable teaching plans and student activities. In this type of learning, learning by doing is an important maxim. Pupils must be involved in activities that give repeated practice in the desired skills. The laboratory becomes an important facility at this point because most of the skills involve procedures that, to a greater or lesser extent, require materials and apparatus.

A sample lesson, oriented toward skill development, is given in the "Teaching Inquiry Skills" section in Appendix A, p. 396.

Organizing Laboratory Work

Effectiveness of the laboratory experience is directly related to the amount of students' individual participation. Such participation means active involvement in the experiment with definite responsibilities for its progress and success. In theory the ideal arrangement would be to have each student wholly responsible for conducting the experiment from start to finish. In this way, the preliminary planning, gathering materials, preparation of apparatus, designing the method, collecting data, analyzing results, and drawing conclusions are unmistakably the work of the individual student, with a maximum level of learning.

In reality, for certain students, maximum learning may be achieved by working in pairs or very small groups. With good cooperation and shared duties, the stimulation of pair or small-group activity may be beneficial. In group work, a shy student may be stimulated into action and thought processes not possible when working alone. An extroverted student may assume directive and leadership qualities not developed in individual work. The science teacher must be aware of these possibilities and plan the methodology of laboratory work accordingly. There should be opportunities in the laboratory to provide experiences using both arrangements. Avoiding stereotyped and inflexible arrangements should be of concern to the teacher of laboratory sciences.

Experiments will vary greatly in complexity. Even in a typical laboratory science, such as chemistry, experiments may be no more than carrying out a pre-planned exercise of observation and data-gathering, or they may be as extensive and demanding as research on a problem whose solution is totally unknown. Arrangements for laboratory work must accommodate these extremes. Students of general science in the junior high school may need more of the exercise type of experiment to gain the skills needed for complex experiments. However, they should also be given opportunities to work on true experiments so that they might sense the joy of discovery in the same way as a practicing scientist.

The Use of Laboratory Assistants

Preparations for laboratory work require exorbitant amounts of time on the part of the conscientious science teacher. Ordering materials, providing for their storage, inventorying, repairing equipment, and preparing for laboratory experiments daily are a tremendous drain on the science teacher's time and energy. Some teachers have developed systems where student laboratory assistants are used to perform many of the tasks needed to carry on successful laboratory programs. One teacher has prepared a handbook for laboratory assistants included here to illustrate the organization of such a program.[10] Students are given credit for participation.

Handbook for Laboratory Assistants

PHILOSOPHY

Each laboratory assistant should constantly be working to make the Science Department more successful. There are definite responsibilities, duties, and dangers involved in the program for assistants. The department of science depends on you to a great extent. It is expected that each assistant is to be trusted and relied upon to perform his/her duties properly without the necessity of close supervision.

RESPONSIBILITIES AND DUTIES

It is the purpose of the Laboratory Assistant Program to aid science teachers, help maintain and organize the equipment and supplies of the department, and to improve the science program. Specifically, this includes:

1. the care and organization of the stockroom,
2. the preparation of laboratory exercises and demonstrations for teachers,
3. the preparation of papers, information sheets, class lists and other clerical work for the teachers,
4. the inventorying of supplies,
5. the correction of papers for teachers, and
6. the preparation of charts, posters, signs and labeling of shelves, etc.

REQUIRED INDIVIDUAL PROJECT

In all classes you will have tests and homework, but in the Laboratory Assistants Program, an individual project is required instead. One project is required each semester, or a partially completed project will be accepted the first semester if the project is extremely complex and permission has been given in advance.

PROJECT PROPOSAL (PLAN)

At the end of the first quarter, a proposal should be submitted. If accepted by the science department, the student will then take data in the experiment.

The Project: The project should include a substantial report discussing the nature of the project, theories, procedure, data, etc. The report is due the last day of the semester.

SPECIAL SHORT COURSES

Classes on special skills will be conducted at the weekly meetings to improve your abilities.

1. Handling glassware I (cleaning)
2. Handling glassware II (cutting, bending, and assembling)
3. Preparation of solutions (molarity, normality)
4. Safety in the laboratory
5. Analytical weighing
6. Setting up a biology lab
7. Setting up a chemistry lab

GRADING

Grades will be determined and recorded objectively. A conscientious student should receive an "A" or "B" in science. However, it is possible to receive a lower grade for unsatisfactory performance. Grades will be based on the following items:

Required Projects: Each laboratory assistant will be required to complete one project each semester. This project may be in any area of science.

Special Projects: Each laboratory assistant should be constantly working to make the science department better. Any ideas you may have for improving the department will be considered a special project when organized and completed by the student. Projects of a student's own initiative must be cleared through a faculty member before starting.

Demonstrations: Teachers will assign demonstrations to the laboratory assistants whose responsibility it will be to find the equipment, set up the demonstration, and run it at least twice to make certain it works properly.

Laboratory Experiments: Teachers will assign experiments to be set up and tried by the laboratory assistants. This will include Physics, Biology, Chemistry, Advanced Biology, Biological Science Laboratory Practicals, and Freshman Science. Students are required to clean up the laboratory after the experiments.

Sections: Each laboratory assistant will have an assigned section in the preparation room and will be responsible for organizing, inventorying, and seeing to the cleanliness of the section. The section assignments will be rotated on a regular basis.

Attendance at Meetings: Failure to come to a meeting may drop your grade.

Daily Grades: Teachers will be evaluating the laboratory assistants at all times for cooperation, fulfillment of responsibilities, and adherence to rules and regulations.

Log Book: Keep a notebook to include daily accomplishments, notes of meetings and special classes, to be turned in at the end of each quarter.

Point System	Maximum Points
Section grade	= 100 points/week
Preparation of laboratory experiments	= 100 points/experiment prepared
Special projects	= 200 points/special project
Demonstrations	= 100 points/demonstration (if performed for a class)

Semester Grade: Determined from the average of the two quarter grades and the semester special science project.

MEETINGS

All laboratory assistants are required to attend all meetings since this is a credit course.

Meeting Schedule: Noon meetings every other week on Monday. All students must be present promptly at noon. Bring your lunch.

Seventh period meetings on the week when there are no noon meetings (Tuesday, 7th period at 2:10 to 3:05 p.m.). These meetings are for organizing sections, working on special projects, classes, and individual projects.

PROCEDURE FOR PREPARING A CHEMISTRY EXPERIMENT

I. Obtain experiment number and approximate date it is to be ready
II. Preparation
   a. Read experiment in laboratory manual
   b. Read directions in teacher's manual
     (1) Equipment needed
     (2) Precautions
     (3) Laboratory hints
III. Setup
   a. Check all chemicals, etc. (Report anything not available in proper quantities)
   b. Check to see if solutions are old
   c. Make all necessary solutions in proper quantities
   d. Make one set of chemicals per table. Label solutions with formula and concentration. Use correct size bottles.
   e. If experiment has an unknown, prepare a key to unknowns to be turned in
IV. Perform experiment
   a. Make certain experiment is completely set up
   b. Check to see if proper results were obtained
   c. Record data
V. Experiment report ready
VI. Clean up all glassware and put away all materials after experiment is completed.

PROCEDURE FOR PREPARATION OF DEMONSTRATIONS

I. Find a demonstration to prepare
   a. Use any source you can find
   b. Consult with a science teacher
   c. Use special demonstration books in science department
II. Read demonstration carefully
III. Organize, collect all material necessary
IV. Try demonstration, perfect it, be certain that it works

V. Find out when teachers could utilize demonstration
VI. Store chemicals in proper place for safekeeping, and clean up work area
VII. Perform demonstration
   a. Give demonstration for proper class, or
   b. Bring in all material for the demonstration (on a cart) for the teacher at the proper time
   c. Don't leave demonstration or experiment equipment lying around if you don't complete it in one period—always put material in proper place even if overnight.

Orienting Students for Laboratory Work

In general, students of the sciences look forward to a laboratory class with pleasant anticipation. Being pragmatic by nature, they sense that this is truly science and that an exciting experience awaits them. This attitude, most prevalent in the junior high school, must be carefully nurtured and guided as the student progresses to more rigorous disciplines. If laboratory work becomes a bore because of excessively rigid formality, unexciting exercises, cookbook techniques, or for other reasons, the student will probably be lost as a potential science participant. An atmosphere of excitement, curiosity, interest, and enthusiasm for science should be encouraged in the laboratory, tempered by care and restraint in use of apparatus and diligence in the tasks assigned. Obviously, a hands-off policy regarding equipment cannot be adopted, nor can a complete *laissez-faire* attitude be condoned. Respect for the problem, the materials, and the probable results of experimentation must be developed. The laboratory experience is but one vehicle by which the objectives of science teaching are developed. Suitably carried out, it can be one of the most effective methods of teaching and learning.

Orientation for laboratory work may involve creating a suitable frame of mind for investigating a problem. The problem must appear real to students and worthy of study. Students must have some knowledge of possible methods of attack, and they should know what equipment or apparatus is needed and be familiar with its use.

Students also must have time to work on the problem. In a given situation, the science teacher may need to give attention to one or more of these factors to begin students on their laboratory investigations.

The Place of Discussion in Laboratory Work

In recent years, there has been a trend toward placing laboratory work at the beginning of a new unit of study. The laboratory guidebook or manual is designed to identify problems requiring observation and solution. Students perform the assigned tasks or devise procedures to arrive at a solution to the problem. While doing so, they discover the need for further information to explain their observations. They are motivated to read a textbook, search for information in a sourcebook or handbook, read supplementary material, or consult their teacher.

Laboratory work is followed by class discussion or question periods. During these activities, student questions are answered, observed phenomena are clarified, and certain misconceptions may be discussed. Other activities—such as problem assignments, projects, extra reading, reports, tests, and demonstrations—may follow in their proper context as part of the teaching and learning process.

In this method it is likely that more than half of the total class time is spent in laboratory activities. Follow-up sessions become extremely important. The teacher usually must ascertain the accuracy of the learned concepts, correct misconceptions, and promote maximum learning more than in a conventional course. At the same time, students are more directly involved in the task and may be more highly motivated than they would be otherwise.

Laboratory Work in the Middle School and Junior High School

Extension of laboratory practices to middle and junior high schools is occurring with greater frequency. Facilities for effective laboratory work are being built into modern junior high schools and students of this age level are beginning to experience laboratory work on a regular, planned basis.

Middle and junior high school students are enthusiastic participants in the laboratory method of teaching. Curiosity and a buoyant approach to learning make this group responsive to the laboratory method, and proper teacher guidance can make this method a fruitful one. Because junior high school science leads to more rigorous and laboratory-oriented sciences in the senior high school, it is worthwhile to consider its contributions to more effective learning when the student reaches biology, chemistry, or physics. It is reasonable to assume that certain attitudes, knowledge, and skills learned in the junior high school contribute to better and perhaps more rapid learning in the senior high school.

Following is a suggested list of basic knowledge and skills that might be developed in fifth-through ninth-grade science and that are considered desirable prerequisites for senior high science:

1. to understand the purposes of the laboratory in the study of science
2. to understand and be familiar with the simple tools of the laboratory
3. to understand and use the metric system in simple measurement and computation
4. to attain the understanding necessary to properly report observations of an experiment
5. to keep neat and accurate records of laboratory experiments
6. to understand the operation of simple ratios and proportions
7. to understand the construction and reading of simple graphs
8. to understand and use the simpler forms of exponential notation
9. to understand the proper use and operation of the Bunsen burner
10. to use the calculator for simple operations
11. to understand and demonstrate the use of a trip balance
12. to work with glass tubing in performing laboratory experiments
13. to keep glassware and equipment clean
14. to put together simple equipment in performing laboratory experiments
15. to measure accurately in linear, cubic, and weight units, and
16. to use the microcomputer for data gathering, record keeping, word processing, and data storage.

A difficult problem in any effort to emphasize inquiry strategies in laboratory experiences is to get students to create or design experiments that will hold promise of producing answers or solutions to problems selected for study. Care must be taken to design experiments that are not too simple nor too ambitious, that have controls, that can be replicated, and that make clear to the students the need to have a structured and organized approach. Paul German, et al., have researched the problems of experiment design among seventh grade students.[11] They have concluded that "development of the science process skills of formulating hypotheses and identifying variables, together with model examples, may be a means to facilitate student success in designing science experiments."

Laboratory work in the middle and junior high school can be broadened to include such features as out-of-doors observations, excursions, and certain types of project activities, as well as conventional experimentation in laboratory surroundings. Systematic nighttime observations of planets, constellations, meteors, the moon, and other astronomical objects may properly be considered laboratory work. Similarly, meteorological observations and experiments involving record keeping and correlations of data are included under this heading. Excursions for collecting purposes, observations of topographical features, studies of pond life, and ecological investigations are true laboratory work. The narrow connotation of laboratory work as something that takes place only in a specially designed room called a laboratory must be avoided in the junior high and middle school sciences.

The range and variety of activities performed by students in laboratory work make it necessary to use many evaluation methods. A teacher of science must be aware of these prerequisites and alert to new possibilities as well. Increasing emphasis on laboratory methods is almost certain to broaden, rather than narrow, the range of individual differences among students. Suitable means must be devised for evaluating the progress and achievement of these students in their laboratory experiences.

SAFETY PRECAUTIONS IN THE LABORATORY

An inevitable result of greater student participation in laboratory work is increased exposure to potentially dangerous apparatus and materials. Instead of viewing this fact as a deterrent to the laboratory method of teaching, the alert and dedicated science teacher will approach the problem realistically and will take the proper precautions to avoid accidents among students in the laboratory.

Accidents and injuries often occur because students lack knowledge of the proper techniques and procedures. If the teacher plans properly, these techniques can be taught in advance. Certain minimum standards of acceptable procedures may be demanded of students before they are allowed to work in the laboratory. The

motivation to engage in laboratory work is usually strong enough to overcome students' reluctance to develop the requisite skills, particularly if they are convinced of the inherent dangers and the need for proper safety precautions.

According to the National Safety Council, about 32,000 school-related accidents occur each school year, about 5,000 of which are science-related. Junior high grades 7–9 experience the highest frequency of accidents, while elementary grades report the lowest accident frequency. Another source estimates one major accident per 40 students per year in laboratory settings throughout the country.[12]

A 1970 study on high school science safety revealed the following:

♦ Advanced placement groups have the most accidents.
♦ Class enrollment and laboratory space have a significant relationship to laboratory accidents; the higher the classroom enrollment and the smaller the laboratory space, the higher the frequency of accidents.
♦ Fewer accidents occur when individual laboratory stations exist.
♦ The chemistry class is more prone than other classes to laboratory accidents.[13]

The prevention of accidents can be accomplished through a positive science safety educational program that emphasizes teacher and student awareness of the potential dangers in science-related activities. "Safety First"

Students learn about behavior of liquids and solids by personal involvement under safe conditions.

should be the basic motto for the school science program. However, safety considerations should seldom rule out a science lesson. Effective planning sometimes can be used to capitalize on safety problems. Developing and maintaining positive attitudes toward safety require continual efforts in safety education. It is hoped that safety training in the science program will instill in the student the importance of safety in all areas of work and play.[14]

Some general laboratory skills that will prepare the student to work safely are these abilities:

1. to handle glass tubing—cutting, bending, fire-polishing, drawing tubing into capillaries, inserting tubing into rubber stoppers, and removing tubing from rubber stoppers
2. to heat test tubes of chemicals—knowledge of proper rate of heating, direction, use of test tube racks, etc.
3. to handle acids—pouring, proper use of stoppers to avoid contamination, dilution in water, return of acid bottles to designated shelves, etc.
4. to test for presence of noxious gases safely
5. to treat acid spillage or burns from caustic solutions
6. to operate fire extinguishers
7. to set up gas generators properly
8. to use standard carpenter's tools
9. to use dissecting equipment, scalpels, etc.

An excellent publication dealing with safety in the secondary school science classroom is published by the NSTA.[15] In a section entitled "Suggestions for a Safe Science Program," the publication provides many excellent guidelines for teachers and students in science classes. A survey of accidents in high school chemistry laboratories in California, reported by Robert McComber, showed that accidents were usually caused by poor laboratory techniques. There were more serious accidents in large classes, and accidents were more frequent when horseplay was involved. Forty percent of the accidents occurred among students who were above average in scientific inquisitiveness. The types of accidents that most frequently had serious results were explosions and burns from phosphorus; the easy availability of dangerous chemicals used occasionally in the normal chemistry course seemed to contribute to accidents as well.[16] The following safety precautions to be observed in the chemistry laboratory may be put into effect in a school by discussing them with the students, supplying copies for students' notebooks, and posting them in a prominent place in the laboratory.

A LIST OF SAFETY PRECAUTIONS IN THE CHEMISTRY LABORATORY

The work you do in the chemistry laboratory is a very important part of your chemistry course. Here you will learn to observe experiments and draw your own conclusions about your observations. The following is a list of safety rules to follow in making your laboratory work as safe and efficient as possible:

1. Observe all instructions given by the teacher. Ask for help when you need it.
2. In case of an accident, report to your teacher immediately.
3. Be careful in using flames. Keep clothing away from the flame, and do not use flames near inflammable liquids.
4. Follow the directions carefully when handling all chemicals.
5. If acids or bases are spilled, wash immediately with plenty of water. Be sure you know where the neutralizing solution is located in the laboratory. Ask your teacher how to use it.
6. Read the labels on all reagents very carefully. Make a habit of reading each label twice on any reagent used in an experiment.
7. Dispose of waste materials in the proper receptacles. Solid materials should be placed in special crocks provided for the purpose.
8. Be sure you know the location and proper usage of the fire extinguishers and fire blankets provided in the laboratory.
9. Consider the laboratory a place for serious work. There is no excuse for horseplay or practical jokes in a science laboratory.

SAFETY AND THE LAW

The principal is responsible for the overall supervision of the entire school's safety program. The science teacher is similarly responsible for the supervision of safety in the science class.

Individual teachers can be held liable for negligent acts resulting in personal injury to students. Some school boards have liability coverage that might support teachers if legal action is brought against them. Teachers should inquire about the nature of local board coverage

Visit http://www.prenhall.com/trowbridge and select Topic 4—Science Safety. Select "Web Links" and find the website of the "Maryland School Performance Program Safety Manual," which gives a comprehensive collection of the major safety issues to consider when teaching science. Initiate a class discussion about safety and explore the best ways of making children aware of certain dangers in doing demonstrations or laboratory work. Engage your instructor by using the Electronic Bluebook module.

and/or their own personal liability coverage. The extent of a teacher's liability is discussed in the NSTA publication, *Safety in the Secondary Science Classroom.*[17]

SUMMARY

A demonstration has been defined as showing something to a person or group. The techniques of planning a demonstration involve determining the concepts and principles to be taught, deciding on activities, gathering the materials, practicing the demonstration, outlining the questions to be asked, and deciding on the evaluation methods to be used.

Plan a demonstration with the intention of using it again. A teacher, in giving a demonstration, should be aware of visibility, audibility, and all of the aspects that go with good staging. The teacher should have zest, present the demonstration inductively, ask inquiry-oriented questions, give positive techniques, and summarize and evaluate the demonstration. A demonstration may be conducted by the teacher, by the teacher and students together, by a group of students, by an individual student, or by a guest. More attention should be given to demonstrations other than those presented by the teacher, with accompanying comments. Silent demonstrations offer a different approach and emphasize observational techniques.

Technology Link Equipment should be stored so that it is easily located for future demonstrations. Special equipment can often be secured from local industries without cost. The overhead projector, LCD projector, and TV screen are excellent teaching aids for demonstrations.

Individual experimentation is usually a more desirable teaching technique than are demonstrations, but demonstrations have the advantage of economy of time and money, allow for greater direction by the teacher, and provide certain safety precautions. Demonstrations should contribute to the higher levels of learning—those requiring critical thinking and creativity.

Laboratory work in the junior and senior high school is constantly changing. From the emphasis on verification experiments in the traditional mode, the student is now invited to inquire into or investigate a problem. Laboratory experience becomes the initial introduction to a new topic of subject matter, followed by discussion, reading, and further experimentation. The experiment may lead to new problems that warrant investigation.

The junior high school is becoming increasingly oriented toward a laboratory approach. Not only does this approach give students an early start in learning science methods, but it introduces and allows practice of certain skills that will have value in senior high school sciences.

With more of the responsibility for learning in the laboratory being allocated to the student, the matter of safety becomes even more important. The science teacher must carefully train students in the use of laboratory apparatus and materials. This training may precede actual work in the laboratory or be an intrinsic part of the laboratory work early in the students' experience. The promise of science for the future continues. A breakthrough has been achieved in which students at last have become participants in the search for knowledge, not mere recipients of facts and generalizations dispensed by authoritative teachers and textbooks. The laboratory is the key instrument in science teaching.

◆

REFERENCES

1. E. S. Obourn, Aids for Teaching Science Observation—Basis for Effective Science Learning, Office of Education Publication No. 29024 (Washington, DC: U.S. Government Printing Office, 1961).

2. Christina Hart, et al., *Journal of Research in Science Teaching,* 37 (7) (2000): 655–675.

3. Paul F. Brandwein and Joseph J. Schwab, *The Teaching of Science as Enquiry* (Cambridge: Harvard University Press, 1962), pp. 52–53.

4. Paul G, German, Sandra Haskins, and Stephanie Avis, "Analysis of Nine High School Biology Laboratory Manuals Promoting Scientific Inquiry," *Journal of Research in Science Teaching,* 33 (5) (May 1996): 475–500.

5. William H. Leonard, "A Recipe for Uncookbooking Laboratory Investigations," *Journal of College Science Teaching,* 21 (November 1991): 84–87.

6. A. Winders and B. Yates, "The Traditional Science Laboratory Versus a Computerized Science Laboratory: Think Carefully Before Supplanting the Old with the New," *Journal of Computers in Science and Mathematics Teaching,* 9 (Spring 1990): 11–15.

7. Joseph D. Novak, "Learning Science and the Science of Learning," *Studies in Science Education,* 15: 77–101.

8. Patricia Blosser, "The Role of the Laboratory in Science Teaching," *School Science and Mathematics,* 83 (2) (February 1983).

9. Robert K. James, "The Concerns of Secondary Science Teachers About Required Amounts of Laboratory Instruc-tion," *School Science and Mathematics,* 91 (February 1991): 73–76.

10. Clifford Hofwolt, Laboratory Science Course Handbook for Laboratory Assistants (University of Northern Colorado, Greeley: Department of Science Education mimeograph, 1968).

11. Paul German, Roberta Aram, and Gerald Burke, "Identifying Patterns and Relationships Among the Responses of Seventh-Grade Students to the Science Process Skill of Designing Experiments," *Journal Of Research in Science Teaching,* 33 (1) (January 1996): 78–99.

12. George J. O'Neill, Television Series Program #1, *Safety in the Science Laboratory* (Sponsored by the NE Tennessee Section of the American Chemical Society in cooperation with WSJK, Knoxville, TN, 1975).

13. John Wesley Brennan, "An Investigation of Factors Related to Safety in the High School Science Program," Ed.D dissertation (University of Denver, Colorado, 1970), ED 085 179.

14. *Safety First in Science Teaching,* Division of Science, North Carolina Dept. of Public Instruction, Raleigh, NC (1977).

15. NSTA, *Safety in the Secondary Science Classroom* (Washington, DC: NSTA Subcommittee on Safety, 1978).

16. Robert McComber, "Chemistry Accidents in High School," *Journal of Chemical Education* (July 1961): 367–368.

17. NSTA, *Safety in the Secondary Science Classroom.*

CHAPTER
15

MODELS FOR EFFECTIVE SCIENCE TEACHING

Publication of the *National Science Education Standards* places *Science As Inquiry* very high on science teachers' instructional agenda. The standards on inquiry focus science teachers' attention on developing students' abilities to use observations and knowledge as they construct scientific explanations. The *Standards* incorporate the traditional processes of science with instructional strategies that require students to use scientific knowledge and evidence from their investigations to formulate scientific explanations. The *Standards* shift instructional emphasis toward empirical criteria, critical thinking about evidence, and scientific reasoning in the construction of explanations.

Figures 15–1 and 15–2 summarize the inquiry abilities in the national standards. These standards do not represent an instructional model. They do present learn-

ing outcomes that should be based in student investigations. Because inquiry is a central theme in the *Standards*, we emphasize that "Science As Inquiry" as represented in Figures 15–1 and 15–2, present learning outcomes for students. *An assumption underlying these outcomes is that students will engage in laboratory-oriented investigations.*

We begin this chapter with a section on the use of textbooks. Most science teachers use textbooks, so we provide some background and suggestions that will help you use textbooks to optimize learning.

The next section outlines models that will help you organize for effective instruction. These constitute the planned sequence of instruction. The flexible component is something you will develop with experience in science teaching. The chapter concludes with a general instructional model that incorporates many elements of other models. This model is presented in detail and is recommended as a model that is both usable and effective for science teaching.

Identify questions that can be answered through scientific investigations.

Design and conduct a scientific investigation.

Use appropriate tools and technologies to gather, analyze, and interpret data.

Develop descriptions, explanations, predictions, and models using evidence.

Think critically and logically to make the relationships between evidence and explanation.

Recognize and analyze alternative explanations and predictions.

Communicate scientific procedures and explanations.

Use mathematics in all aspects of scientific inquiry.

FIGURE 15–1 Science As Inquiry: Grades 5–8

Identify questions and concepts that guide scientific investigations.

Design and conduct scientific investigations.

Use technology and mathematics to improve investigations and communications.

Formulate and revise scientific explanations and models using logic and evidence.

Recognize and analyze alternative explanations and models.

Communicate and defend a scientific argument.

FIGURE 15–2 Science As Inquiry: Grades 9–12

USING TEXTBOOKS EFFECTIVELY

You may think it unusual to have a section on using textbooks, but textbooks are central to science teaching. In spite of some common myths, textbooks in and of themselves are not bad; most good teachers use textbooks, and textbooks can enhance student learning.

The majority of teachers use textbooks. In a 1985 survey, Iris Weiss found that 93 percent of science teachers in grades 7–12 used a published textbook.[1] Interestingly, the majority of science teachers did not consider textbook quality to be a significant problem in their schools. The most high-rated aspects of science textbooks were their organization, clarity, and reading level. However, a number of individuals and groups do see problems with the quality and usability of textbooks.[2-5]

Since the 1960s, the prevailing view in science education has been that programs should be activity-based and not textbook dominated. Research reported in 2001 shows that the opposite is the case—teachers are using fewer activities and relying more on the textbook.[6] Use of textbooks is prevalent in science teaching due to several factors: the need for science teachers to plan for several subjects, the reduction of budgets, and the scheduling of science classes in nonlaboratory rooms.

In this section we assist you in becoming an intelligent user of the textbook—that is, to help you recognize the potentials and limitations of textbooks, and to use them to enhance learning. The section relies on the research of Kathleen Roth and Charles Anderson.[7]

Science teachers use textbooks in several ways. Textbooks help teachers make decisions about the curriculum. Questions about topics, activities of coverage, depth, sequence, and emphasis are answered by reference to the textbook. Keep in mind that although the textbook helps teachers make efficient decisions, they do not necessarily help them make the best decisions for student experiences and learnings.

Textbooks help teachers select teaching strategies. Again, this use of textbooks has both advantages and disadvantages. The clear advantage is efficiency. It takes considerable effort to manage an activity-based program. It is much easier to have students read the textbook. The disadvantage is that reading the textbook may not facilitate student learning. We discuss this in detail later.

Textbooks provide scientific explanations. Descriptions of key concepts and information are usually straightforward and succinct in textbooks. Providing students with good descriptions of scientific ideas is difficult; it is especially difficult when teachers are teaching out of their discipline. So textbooks can be a useful resource for scientific explanations.

Given the function of textbooks, it is easy to see why the majority of teachers rely on them. What do science teachers need to understand in order to use textbooks more effectively? First in importance is to understand how students use textbooks.

We have pointed out that students have prior knowledge about science. Often this knowledge is inadequate or incomplete when compared to accepted scientific knowledge. Students' prior knowledge is important to understand when considering students' reading strategies. What happens when students are asked to read a text that has explanations about phenomena that are incompatible with their current explanations? Students seem to use several strategies to accommodate the difference between their conceptions and those presented in textbooks.[8] Here are the different strategies students use.

 Visit http://www.prenhall.com/trowbridge and select Topic 6—Professional Development. Select "Web Links" and find the website for the National Science Teachers Association (NSTA). Exhibits of a plethora of textbooks for all levels can be found in the convention venues at regional and national locations. Plan to visit one of these conventions to familiarize yourself with the vast amount of material available for your choosing.

Reading for Conceptual Change

A few students use the text to change current conceptions to more appropriately scientific conceptions. As students confront concepts that conflict with their own ideas, they give up their concepts and assimilate those presented as formal scientific explanations in the textbook.

Overrelying on Prior Knowledge and Distorting Text to Make It Compatible with Prior Knowledge

Here students use elaborate strategies to link prior knowledge with text knowledge. These students genuinely try to make sense of the text and integrate text ideas with their own knowledge. Still, they just cannot give up their own strongly held ideas. Theirs is the strategy of linking scientific knowledge with their own ideas.

Overrelying on Facts in the Text with an Additional Notion of Learning—Separating Prior Knowledge and Text Knowledge

These students focus on the memorization of vocabulary and facts. They do not relate the facts and vocabulary to each other or to their prior knowledge. Reading for conceptual change is not possible.

◆ **STEPS FOR DESIGNING LESSONS** ◆

Using Textbooks Effectively

1. Direct students' attention to important concepts.
2. Challenge students' thinking and misconceptions.
3. Ask students to construct explanations of everyday phenomena.
4. Probe student responses.
5. Provide accurate feedback to students.
6. Construct alternative representations of textbook explanations.
7. Make explicit the connections between textbook explanations and student misconceptions.
8. Select activities that create conceptual conflict and encourage conceptual understanding.

Overrelying on Details in the Text—Separating Prior Knowledge and Text Knowledge

These students pay great attention to the text. They attend to the details, as opposed to concepts, and fail to attach any meaning to details. The details, most often specialized vocabulary of science, are isolated words that have no relationship to anything. These students think they understand science if they are able to decode the words and identify details in the textbook.

Overrelying on Prior Knowledge and Ignoring Text Knowledge

Some students rely on their own experiential knowledge to interpret the textbook. If asked about text knowledge, they equate textbook explanations with their own explanations, ones that have nothing to do with scientific explanations. To them the text makes sense in terms of their prior knowledge.

What can teachers do? There are a few recommendations for effective use of science textbooks. The principles are based on studies of text-based science teaching[9] and understandings gained from studies of students' reading strategies.[10]

Directing Students' Attention to Important Concepts

Textbooks typically contain numerous ideas and vocabulary words. This situation causes students to memorize facts and lists of words rather than focus on strategies that will result in conceptual change. Focusing students on central issues that are problematic, keeping lessons related to the concepts, and keeping vocabulary to a minimum will contribute to conceptual change.

Challenging Students' Thinking and Misconceptions

Most textbooks are written from a scientist's perspective. Seldom do textbook authors consider students' perspectives as they organize textbooks. Still, students will interpret text material in terms of their prior knowledge. Effective teachers identify the differences between students' concepts and those in the textbook. By asking questions and challenging students' thinking, teachers can initiate the process of conceptual change. The questions should be stated in relation to ideas in the textbooks, or students may not make the connections.

Asking Students to Construct Explanations of Everyday Phenomena

Questions in textbooks seldom have students apply knowledge to everyday experiences. Encouraging students to compare, challenge, and debate each other's explanations are all methods that result in conceptual change.

Probing Student Responses

Listen for students' thinking rather than for right answers. Ask questions that will have students justify and clarify their responses.

Providing Accurate Feedback to Students

Teachers typically respond to student answers by praising correct answers and ignoring incorrect answers. The greatest concern is the latter. Although teachers think this approach helps students, in actuality it does not. Giving positive feedback for any answer encourages students to maintain their current conceptions and to use ineffective strategies to find correct answers. You should give clear and accurate feedback about the strengths and limitations of student responses.

Constructing Alternative Representations of Textbook Explanations That Make Explicit the Relationships Between Scientific Explanations and Student Misconceptions

Give the students time to struggle with explanations in the textbook. Most textbooks are packed with explanations that are presented in one way only, and then the text moves to the next explanation. There is little time and variation to help students consider alternative explanations and construct new concepts. After students have time to grapple with concepts, you should provide different representations of the ideas. The representations will be most effective if they clearly contrast the students' and the text's explanations.

Selecting Activities That Create Conceptual Conflict and Encourage Conceptual Understanding

Selection of activities is based on criteria such as student interest, a sense of important science concepts, and the need to do inquiry-oriented activities. Discrepant events are good examples of the types of activities that create conceptual change. In the end, doing activities is not as important as helping students make sense of their experiences.

Designing Your Instructional Sequence

Using the textbook, facilitating learning, grouping students, and sequencing instruction are examples of factors you must consider in designing an instructional sequence. Many talented individuals have considered instructional strategies and sequences that you can use. This section reviews some of the prominent models for science teaching.

The Learning Cycle

The learning cycle originated in the 1960s with the work of Robert Karplus and his colleagues during the development of the Science Curriculum Improvement Study (SCIS). Originally, the learning cycle was based on the theoretical insights of Piaget, but it is also consistent with other theories of learning, such as those developed by Ausubel.[11]

Originally there were three phases to the learning cycle: *Exploration, Invention,* and *Discovery.* Later, these terms were modified to *Exploration, Concept Introduction,* and *Concept Application.* Although other terms have been used for the three original phases, the goals and pedagogy of the phases have remained similar.

In the exploration stage of the learning cycle, students are actively involved in exploring new materials and ideas.

During the first, or *Exploration,* phase of the learning cycle, students learn through their involvement and actions. New materials, ideas, and relationships are introduced with minimal teacher guidance. The goal is to allow students to apply previous knowledge, develop interests, and initiate and maintain a curiosity toward the materials. The materials should be carefully structured so involvement with them cannot help but engage concepts and ideas fundamental to the lesson's objectives. During the exploration, teachers can also assess students' understanding and background relative to the lesson's objectives.

Concept Introduction is the next phase. Various teaching strategies can be used to introduce the concept. For example, a demonstration, video, CD-ROM, textbook, or lecture can be used. This phase should relate directly to the initial exploration and clarify concepts central to the lesson. Although the exploration was minimally teacher-directed, this phase tends to be more teacher-guided.

In the next phase, *Concept Application,* students apply the newly learned concepts to other examples. The teaching goal is to have students generalize or transfer ideas to other examples used as illustrations of the central concept. For some students, the period of psychological self-regulation, equilibration, and mental reorganization of concepts may take time. Having several activities where a concept is applied can provide the valuable time needed for learning. An excellent introduction to and science teaching examples of the learning cycle have been developed by Howard Birnie[12] and Karplus and colleagues.[13]

John Renner and his colleagues examined the effectiveness of altering the sequence of the learning cycle. They found that the normal sequence (described above) is the optimum sequence for achievement of content knowledge.[14]

Anton Lawson has made important connections between research on student misconceptions and use of the learning cycle.[15] Lawson suggests that use of the learning cycle provides opportunities for students to reveal prior knowledge (particularly, their misconceptions) and opportunities to argue and debate their ideas. This process can result in cognitive disequilibrium and the possibility of developing higher levels of reasoning.

Lawson proposes three types of learning cycles: *descriptive, empirical-inductive,* and *hypothetical-deductive.* Although the sequence is similar to that described above, the difference among the types of learning cycles is the degree to which students gather data in a descriptive manner, or in a manner that empirically tests alternative explanations. In descriptive learning cycles, students observe natural phenomena, identify patterns, and seek similar patterns elsewhere. According to Lawson, little or no disequilibrium occurs in descriptive learning cycles.

Empirical-inductive learning cycles require students to explain phenomena, thus expressing any misconceptions and providing opportunities for dialogue and debate. Hypothetical-deductive learning cycles require students to make explicit statements of alternative explanations of phenomena. Higher order reasoning patterns are required to test alternative explanations.

COOPERATIVE LEARNING

As a science teacher, you will be in a position to structure lessons in several different ways. Most commonly, lessons are structured so students compete with one another for recognition and grades. You also might design your lessons so students can follow an individual approach, or learn on their own. There is a third option that lends itself to science teaching, especially when the laboratory is a central part of instruction. This is a cooperative approach where students are arranged in pairs or small groups to help each other learn the assigned material. David Johnson, Roger Johnson, and their colleagues have developed a substantial research base for the use of a cooperative learning model.[16] Over the years, the Johnsons also have developed the practical instructional approach based on their model. We base

---

◆ STEPS FOR DESIGNING LESSONS ◆

Applying the Learning Cycle

Concept Exploration

1. Identify interesting objects, events, or situations that students can observe. Student experiences can occur in the classroom, laboratory, or field. Many instructional methods can be used to explore a concept.

2. Allow students time to explore the objects, events, or situations. During this experience, students may establish relationships, observe patterns, identify variables, and question events. In this phase, the unexpected can be used to your advantage. Students may have questions or experiences that motivate them to study what they have observed.

3. The primary aim of the exploration is to have students think about concepts associated with the lesson.

Concept Introduction

4. The teacher directs student attention to specific aspects of the exploration experience. Initially, the lesson should be clearly based on student explorations. In this phase, the key is to present the concepts in a simple, clear, and direct manner.

Concept Application

5. Identify different activities in which students extend the concepts in new and different situations. Several different activities will facilitate generalization of the concept by the students. Encourage students to identify patterns, discover relationships among variables, and reason through new problems.

In the Exploration phase of the learning cycle, students are actively involved in exploring new materials and ideas.

---

this discussion on their book *Circles of Learning: Cooperation in the Classroom.*[17] (We recommend that you read the guest editorial by David and Roger Johnson, "A Message to Teachers on Structuring Student Interactions in the Classroom.")

There are four basic elements in cooperative learning models. To be truly cooperative, small groups must be structured for *positive interdependence, face-to-face interactions, individual accountability,* and *use of interpersonal and small-group skills.*

Positive interdependence is established when students perceive that they are in affirming and cooperative relationships with other members of their group. There are several ways of achieving positive interdependence. You can establish mutual goals for the group; establish a division of labor for a mutual task; divide materials, resources, or information to ensure cooperation among group members; assign students different roles, such as recorder, researcher, organizer; or create joint rewards for the group.

Face-to-face interactions among students is a central aspect of cooperative learning. Cooperative work and verbal exchanges among students form the learning experience. Though they work in groups, students must still be individually accountable for learning the assigned materials. Cooperative learning is not having one person do a report for two or three others. The aim is for all students to learn the material. To accomplish this, it is necessary to determine the level of mastery among students and then assign groups to maximize achievement.

Finally, students have to learn to use interpersonal and small-group skills. Students are not naturally skilled at cooperative learning. They must learn the social skills of collaboration, they must be given time and experience in collaboration, and they must be taught to analyze the group process to see if effective working relationships have been maintained.

Science teachers will have to teach students the skills of cooperation. This statement leads to the obvious questions, "What skills need to be taught?" and "How does one teach these skills?" In answer to the first question, there are four levels of cooperative skills. First, there are *forming skills*—that is, the basic skills needed to organize a group and establish norms of behavior for cooperative interaction. Here are some suggestions to help the initial formation of cooperative groups:

- Students should move into groups without undue noise and unnecessary interaction with other students.
- Students should stay in their group.
- Students should speak softly.
- Students should encourage each other to participate.
- Students should use names and look at each other during discussions.
- Students should avoid sarcastic remarks toward other people.

Group functioning is the second skill level that you will need to develop. Here the lessons involve those skills that will maintain the group and facilitate effective working relationships. Important skills of group maintenance include:

- Students should understand the purpose, time allotment, and most effective procedures to complete their work.

- Students should support each other's ideas and work.
- Students should feel free to ask for help, information, or clarification from other group members or the science teacher.
- Students might learn how to paraphrase and summarize another student's ideas.
- As appropriate, students should learn how to express their feelings about the assignment and group process.

The next phase is *formulating understanding* of the concepts, processes, and skills of the assigned lesson. The skills are designed to maximize each student's learning. Here are some suggestions:

- Each student should summarize—aloud—important ideas contained in the material.
- Other students should correct and clarify summaries.
- Students should elaborate on each other's summary.
- Students can give hints about ways to remember ideas.
- All group members should participate in the discussion.

The last stage is *fermenting ideas and understandings*. Students should develop skills that will help reconceptualize and extend ideas. At this level, there is already a firmly developed group structure, so it is possible to introduce challenges, conflicts, and controversies. Because of already developed skills, challenging situations can bring about deeper thinking, further synthesis of ideas, gathering of more information, and constructive arguments about conclusions, decisions, and solutions. In this case, the science teacher may be the person who encourages the extension of ideas. It is possible, even desirable, for students to function at this level. The teacher will have to decide about the degree of group development and level of interaction as this level is reached. Skills that facilitate this stage include:

- Criticize ideas, not other students.
- Clarify disagreements within the group.
- Synthesize different ideas into a single statement.
- Ask other students to justify their conclusions.
- Ask probing, clarifying questions.
- Generate several answers or conclusions, and select the best for the given situation.

We now turn to the second question, "How does one teach these skills?" As a science teacher interested in cooperative learning, it will be critical to identify students who have not developed the group skills discussed earlier. There are several ways that you can teach the skills required for cooperative learning:

- Be sure that students understand the need for group skills.

GUEST EDITORIAL ◆

ROGER JOHNSON
Professor of Science Education
University of Minnesota, Minneapolis

DAVID JOHNSON
Professor of Social Psychology
University of Minnesota, Minneapolis

A MESSAGE TO TEACHERS ON STRUCTURING STUDENT INTERACTIONS IN THE CLASSROOM

There are instances where traditional practice in schools has gone one way, while empirical research indicated that another course was more productive and desirable. Such is the case with the use of cooperative, competitive, and individualistic student-student interaction patterns for instruction. In the past forty years, competition among students has been emphasized in most American schools. In the past fifteen years, individualistic efforts toward achieving learning goals have been increasingly emphasized. The research indicates, however, that cooperative interaction among students would be more productive on a wide range of cognitive and affective instructional outcomes than either competitive or individualistic interaction patterns.

Perhaps the major reason for this discrepancy between educational practice and research is the fact that how students interact with one another has not been emphasized in the development of curriculum and in teacher preparation. The spotlight has been on the ways that students interact with materials and the role of the teacher; however, how students interact with each other during instruction has powerful and important effects on their learning and socialization.

There are three basic choices for student-student interaction patterns: competitive, individualistic, or cooperative. A competitive interaction pattern exists when students see that they can obtain their goals if and only if the other students with whom they are linked fail to obtain their goals. An example would be a spelling bee where students spell against each other to find the best speller in the class. Norm-referenced evaluation systems, such as rank-ordering students from best to worst or grading on a curve, set up competitive interaction between students. An individualistic interaction pattern exists when the achievement of students' learning goals are unrelated to the goal achievement of other students. An exam-

ple of this we're-all-in-this-alone situation would be a spelling class where each student has his or her own set of words to learn and a criterion for measuring individual success, so that the achievement of one student has no effect on the achievement of another.

A cooperative interaction pattern exists when the students perceive that they can obtain their goal if and only if the other students with whom they are linked obtain their goals. An example of this sink-or-swim-together situation is a group of students working together as a spelling group, preparing each other to take the spelling test individually on Friday. Each student's score is the number of words his or her group spells correctly. In competition there is a negative interdependence in terms of goal attainment, in the individualistic situation there is independence between goal attainment, and in cooperation there is a positive interdependence in terms of goal attainment.

There are many research studies which have compared cognitive and affective results for students working cooperatively, competitively, and individualistically. The results indicate that, in comparison to competition and working individually, cooperation produces:

1. Higher achievement and longer retention of the material learned;
2. More positive attitudes about the subject matter and the teacher;
3. Higher self-esteem;
4. More effective use of social skills; and
5. More positive feelings about each other. (This *positive cathexis* works regardless of differences between students and has implications for the integration of different ethnic groups, mainstreaming of handicapped students into regular

classroom settings, and managing the heterogeneity present in every classroom.)

These results represent only a few of the many which have been researched, but they emphasize the powerful nature of cooperative learning. Furthermore, the importance of cooperative learning experiences goes beyond improving instruction and making teaching more satisfying and productive for teachers, although these are worthwhile goals. The ability of all students to cooperate with others is the keystone to building and maintaining friendships, stable families, career success, neighborhood and community membership, and contributions to a society. Knowledge and skills are of no use if the students cannot apply them in cooperative interaction with other people.

With strong empirical support for cooperative learning and the fact that it makes sense for students growing up in society, we must be careful not to overgeneralize. The research into cooperative learning does not say that having students work together cooperatively is a magic wand that will solve all classroom problems. It does say that those problems probably have a better chance of being solved in a cooperative than in a competitive or an individualistic setting, but it is not reasonable to expect hyperactive students to suddenly become calm or low mathematics students to suddenly master all the material. It does give the teacher a powerful edge to go to work on the problems of orchestrating effective instruction for students.

We recommend that all three interaction patterns be used in a classroom setting. Students must learn how to compete appropriately and enjoy the competition, win or lose; they must learn how to work independently and take responsibility for following through on a task; and they must learn how to work with one another effectively in cooperative relationships. Each of these interaction patterns must be used appropriately and integrated effectively within instruction, realizing that cooperation is the most powerful of the three.

There is little doubt that teachers who master the strategies needed to set up appropriate interaction patterns, maximizing the use of cooperation, will have a powerful and positive effect on their classroom learning environment. This addition to the teacher's repertoire does not mean a new curriculum. It takes only a few minutes to make clear to students the kind of student-student interaction that is expected, with some additional time needed at first to teach the appropriate interaction skills to the students.

The initial effort on the teacher's part and the time needed to carefully structure student-student interaction are effort and time well spent. It would be exciting to see the gap between the research findings and traditional classroom practice disappear so the students would say, "School is a place where we work together to learn and share our ideas, argue our point of view, and help each other find the most appropriate answers and understand the materials. Sometimes we have a fun competition and sometimes we work individually, but most of the time we learn together."

◆ Be sure that students understand the skill and when to use it.
◆ Be sure that students have time and situations where they can practice the skills.
◆ Be sure that students have the opportunity and procedures for discussing their use of group skills.
◆ Be sure that students continue using the skills until they are a natural part of group work.

Since work in science classes, and later life, is dependent on group work, we think your time and effort required to implement cooperative skills will be well spent. There is still a time and place for individual and competitive learning. The cooperative learning model provides an excellent complement to other models used in science teaching.

THE MADELINE HUNTER MODEL

The late Dr. Madeline Hunter endeavored to develop materials and a teaching model designed to increase instructional effectiveness. Her model is based on psychological theory, primarily behaviorism, and educational research. The model is quite practical. It seems a simple and complete way to integrate many essential aspects of instruction into a teachable plan. This discussion is based on two of Dr. Hunter's books.[18]

The first step is a prelesson evaluation. The aim of the evaluation is to place your objectives at the correct level and best sequence for your students. Although this seems simple enough, it is often not done. As a part of this process, you also may consider analyzing the task of achieving your objectives and designing an activity to

---

◆   **STEPS FOR DESIGNING LESSONS**   ◆

Applying the Cooperative Learning Model

Objectives

1. *Clearly specify the objectives for the lesson.* You should make clear the two types of objectives: academic and collaborative skills. The former objective is used in most science lessons. The latter provides students with the specific skills used for cooperative learning.

Decisions

2. *Decide on group size.* This decision may be influenced by time, materials, equipment, and facilities. A general recommendation is to use pairs or groups of three.

3. *Decide on who is in the group.* Generally, it is best to have heterogeneous groups randomly assigned. Other alternatives include homogeneous grouping and having students select their own group.

4. *Decide on the room arrangement.* Again, this decision may be influenced by facilities and equipment. For optimum cooperative learning, group members should sit in a circle and be close enough for effective communication.

5. *Decide on the instructional materials to promote interdependence.* In early stages of developing cooperative learning groups, pay attention to the ways materials are used to facilitate interdependence. Three ways are suggested: materials interdependence (e.g., one set of materials for the group); information interdependence (e.g., each group member has a resource needed by the group); and interdependence with other groups (e.g., intergroup competition).

6. *Decide on roles to ensure interdependence.* You can assign roles—such as summarizer, researcher, recorder, and observer—that will encourage cooperation among group members.

Explanations

7. *Explain the assignment.* Be sure students are clear about the academic task. Make connections to past experience, concepts, and lessons. Define any relevant concepts, and explain procedures and safety precautions. Check on students' understanding of the assignment.

8. *Explain the collaborative goal.* Students must understand that they are responsible for doing the assignment and learning the material, and that all group members are to learn the material and successfully complete the assignment.

9. *Explain individual accountability.* All individuals should understand that they are responsible for learning, and that you will assess learning at the individual level.

10. *Explain intergroup cooperation.* Sometimes you may want to extend the cooperative group idea to include the entire class. If so, the method and criteria of success should be clear.

11. *Explain the criteria for success.* In the cooperative learning model, evaluation is based on successful completion of the assignment. It is therefore important to explain the criteria by which work will be evaluated.

12. *Explain the specific cooperative behaviors.* Since students may not understand what is meant by cooperative work, you should give specific examples of your expectations of their behaviors. For instance: "stay as a group," "talk quietly," "each person should explain how he got the answer," "listen to other group members," and "criticize ideas, not people."

Monitoring and Intervention

13. *Monitor student work.* Once the students begin work, your task is to observe the various groups and help solve any problems that emerge.

14. *Provide task assistance.* As needed, you may wish to clarify the assignment, introduce concepts, review material, model a skill, answer questions, and redirect discussions.

15. *Teach collaborative skills.* Because collaboration is new, it may be important to intervene in groups and help them learn the skills of collaboration.

16. *Provide closure for the lesson.* At the end of the lesson, it may be important for you to intervene and bring closure. Summarize what has been presented, review concepts and skills, and reinforce their work.

Evaluation

17. *Evaluate the quality and quantity of student learning.* Evaluate the previously decided-upon product (e.g., a report).

Processing

18. *Assess how well the groups functioned.* If group collaboration is truly a goal, then some time should be spent on assessment. Point out how the groups could improve next time.

diagnose student understanding before and *en route* to your final objective.

Next, design the beginning of your lesson. Three components should be considered. A readiness activity, in which the present lesson relates to the learner's past, involves the learner and establishes relevance of the instructional objectives. Another aspect of the readiness activity is to inform the students of your objective—that is, what they will learn and how you will know if they have learned it.

After the readiness section of the lesson, consider the actual input of information, processes, or skills. For instance, you might review the catalogues of instructional strategies outlined in Chapter 2 and consider which methods will best deliver the material. Teaching efficiency, learning effectiveness, and availability of facilities, materials, and equipment should be the criteria of evaluation and choice.

Next comes a consideration of assessment. How can you check for student understanding and comprehension? You may wish to sample the class, give a quiz, have a discussion, or ask questions of individual students. This assessment need not be formal, but there should be some type of feedback, for you and the students, concerning the lesson's effectiveness.

Finally, there should be closure: the lesson should not just stop. There should be an ending in which you and/or the students summarize what has been learned.

This discussion has been on planning the lesson; the obvious next step is teaching it. What is it that will make the lesson effective? Once you have formulated instructional objectives, be sure you teach to the objective. Include actions and strategies that relate to the objective. Are your questions, concepts, processes, skills, and activities clearly related?

As you teach the lesson, you will want to monitor student progress and adjust instruction accordingly. Monitoring student progress can be done overtly by asking students to do something indicating the degree to which they have learned the material. Or, monitoring can be done covertly by observing student work and listening to student discussions of the assignment. Based on this feedback, you will have to make one of several decisions: continue the lesson as planned, alter the lesson, reteach the lesson, or end the lesson and prepare a new one.

THE 5E INSTRUCTIONAL MODEL: AN INTRODUCTION

In the early 1960s, J. Myron Atkin and Robert Karplus first proposed a learning cycle.[19] Karplus, Herb Thier, and their colleagues based the original learning cycle on the psychological theories of Piaget and used the cycle as the basis for organizing lessons in Science Cur-

◆ STEPS FOR DESIGNING LESSONS ◆

Applying the Hunter Model

Before designing a daily lesson, you should complete the following evaluation:

Prelesson Assessment

- Determine the continuing strand or theme of science concepts and processes.
- Identify a major objective based on science concepts and processes. Then locate the students' understanding relative to the major objective.
- Select specific objectives for daily lessons.

Lesson Planning and Lesson Sequencing

For each teaching sequence, you should use the following steps to determine whether and how they are appropriate for your objectives and to the students' mastery of past and present concepts and processes.

Anticipatory Set

Early in the lesson, you should include an activity that will elicit students' attention to the content and processes. The anticipatory set will

- focus the students' attention during the period of transition,
- elicit attending behavior and mental readiness for the day's lesson,
- provide a connection between past lessons and the lesson to be taught, and
- last long enough to orient students to the immediate objectives and lesson.

Objective and Purpose

This step is one of communicating to the students the day's objectives. The objective and purpose statement will

- inform the students of the day's objectives and outline what they will be able to do at the end of the lesson, and
- clarify how and why the lesson is important and useful.

Instructional Input

Here, the teacher actually teachers. Instructional input will

- require the teacher to determine the content and processes that relate directly to the objectives, and

♦ select the best means available to facilitate students' learning of the desired objectives.

Modeling

Where appropriate, you should try to provide examples of the science content and processes included in your objectives. Modeling will

♦ provide examples of expected learning outcomes, and

♦ give the students visual and auditory input.

Monitoring Student Understanding

Monitoring is assessment that occurs during the lesson. You should check for students' understanding of essential information and concepts by sampling, signaling, and explaining. Monitoring will

♦ identify students' understanding, and

♦ provide ways and means to adjust the instructional sequence.

Practice

Lessons should include opportunities for students to practice the content and processes they have learned. Initial attempts should be teacher-guided; later practice can be done on an individual basis. Practice will

♦ provide opportunities to apply concepts and processes with your supervision, and

♦ extend student understanding to new situations.

Postlesson Assessment

Sometime after the lesson, you will assess students' understanding of the concepts and processes. Base the assessment on the major objectives identified in the prelesson assessment and the specific objectives of the lessons.

riculum Improvement Study (SCIS) materials. A variation on this teaching model was also proposed by David Hawkins and used in the Elementary Science Study.[20] We have extended and elaborated the original

design for a learning cycle by Atkin and Karplus and have based the 5E model proposed in this chapter on that work.

Over the years, many curriculum designers have elaborated, modified, and applied teaching models in different educational programs.[21] The approach in this chapter is the first to describe the form and function of a teaching model, then to discuss the psychological basis for the proposed model, and finally to describe the model.

Form and Function

The 5E instructional model has five phases: engagement, exploration, explanation, elaboration, and evaluation. Each phase has a specific function and is intended to contribute to the learning process. We have described the phases in terms of (1) assumptions about the mental activity of students, (2) activities that students would be involved in, and (3) strategies used by the teacher. Later in this section we shall discuss the five phases in detail.

An instructional model has two functions. A model provides guidance for curriculum developers as they design a program. Depending on the instructional model, curriculum developers can use the model at different levels of organization. One level is equivalent to a year-long sequence; another is equivalent to a unit; and another is equivalent to an activity or series of daily lessons. The second function of an instructional model is to help the classroom teacher improve instructional effectiveness through a systematic approach to and use of strategies closely aligned with models of learning and educational outcomes.

A Constructivist Orientation

Historically, educators have explained learning by classifying it into one of three broad categories. In simple terms, these are transmission, maturation, and construction (see Figure 15–3). In recent years, cognitive scientists and science educators have focused on a constructivist model in their work on the misconceptions

Perspective	View of Students	View of Knowledge	Approach to Teaching
Transmission	They must be filled with information and concepts.	Core concepts are a copy of reality.	External to Internal
Maturation	They must be allowed to mature and develop.	Emergence of core concepts.	Internal to External
Construction	They are actively involved in learning.	Construction of core concepts.	Interaction between Internal and External

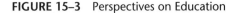

FIGURE 15–3 Perspectives on Education

of students, that is, differences between novice and expert explanations of phenomena, and naive versus canonical theories individuals hold.[22,23,24]

In the constructivist model of learning, students reconstruct core concepts, or intellectual structures, through continuous interactions between themselves and their environment (which includes other people). Applying the constructivist approach to teaching requires the teacher to understand that students have some conceptions or prior knowledge of the world. Such conceptions may be inadequate (i.e., misconceptions) and need further development (i.e., conceptual change).[25] In teaching for conceptual change, teachers should be sure that students are focusing on objects or events that engage concepts of interest to the science teacher—that is, objects or events that are related to science or technology. Then, students can encounter problematic situations that are slightly beyond the current level of understanding. In so doing, the student will experience a form of cognitive disequilibrium. Teachers then structure learning experiences that assist the reconstruction of core concepts. New constructions can then be applied to different situations and tested against other conceptions of the world.

Science teachers are beginning to implement the constructivist view.[26,27] Doing so requires (1) teaching in a manner that recognizes the students' level of conceptual understanding and (2) an understanding that the students' construction of knowledge occurs through the confrontation and resolution of problem situations. The key here is that confrontation should be intellectually challenging but within students' parameters of intellectual accommodation. Intellectual challenges that are actually included as instructional strategies are described by terms such as moderate novelty, appropriate dissonance, optimal discord, tolerable mismatch, and reasonable disequilibrium.

Research by Peter Hewson and his colleagues suggests that conceptual change may occur in several different ways.[28,29,30,31] There may be the addition of new conceptions, a reorganization of current conceptions, and a rejection of conceptions. An important instructional aspect of the model proposed by Hewson and others is that students must be *dissatisfied* with the current conception, the new conception must be *intelligible*, the new conception must be *plausible*, and the new conception must be *fruitful*. You can imagine this from a teacher-students interaction point of view. A science teacher introduces a new concept, and students are unable to reconcile the new concept with current knowledge and experience. The teacher then provides experiences and information that helps students make sense of the new conception. As students consider and try to incorporate the new conception, they must see that a world in which the conception is true is generally reconcilable with their worldview. Fi-

nally, students must see that there are instances where there is good reason to supply the new conception—namely, it works and it helps explain things. Regardless of the specific instructional model, helping students to develop more adequate scientific concepts is an important goal of science teaching. It is also a difficult task.

An assumption of the 5E model is that using sequences of lessons designed to facilitate the process described above will assist in students' construction of knowledge. Another is that concrete experiences and computer-assisted activities will assist in the process of constructing knowledge. The following are general strategies based on the constructivist view of learning:

◆ Recognize students' current concepts of objects, events, or phenomena.

◆ Present situations slightly beyond the students' current conceptual understanding. One could also present the student with problems, situation conflicts, paradoxes, and puzzles.

◆ Choose problems and situations that are challenging but achievable.

◆ Have students present their explanations (concepts) to other students.

◆ When students are struggling with inadequate explanations (misconceptions), first help them by accepting their explanations; second, by suggesting other explanations of the same phenomena or activities designed to provide insights; and third, by allowing them time to reconstruct their explanations.

The 5E instructional model is based on a constructivist view. Because this model of learning is important, we summarize it before introducing the different phases of the 5E model. Constructivism is a dynamic and interactive conception of human learning. Students redefine, reorganize, elaborate, and change their initial concepts through interactions among the environment, classroom activities and experiences, and other individuals. Individual learners interpret objects and phenomena and internalize the interpretation in terms of their current concepts similar to the experiences being presented or encountered. In other words, changing and improving conceptions often require challenging the current conceptions and showing them to be inadequate. From a science teacher's point of view, the instructional and psychological problem is to avoid leaving students with an overall sense of inadequacy. If a current conception is challenged, there must be opportunity, in the form of time and experiences, to reconstruct a more adequate conception than the original. In short, the students' construction of knowledge can be assisted by using sequences of lessons designed to challenge current concepts and provide opportunities for reconstruction to occur.

Visit http://www.prenhall/trowbridge and select Topic 2—Constructivism and Learning in Science. Select "Web Links" and find the link for "The Constructivist Zone," which will describe the notion of constructivism from an historical perspective. Outline the main steps in the development and prepare a discussion period for students in your class by using the Chat function to engage in a class discussion of constructivism.

The 5E Instructional Model: The Phases

Again, the model's five phases are engagement, exploration, explanation, elaboration, and evaluation.

Visit http://www.prenhall.com/trowbridge and select Topic 2—Constructivism and Learning in Science. Select "Web Links" and find the link for the "Southwest Educational Developmental Laboratory" (SEDL). Review the topics featured at the site. Choose a topic of interest and write a synopsis. Submit it for inspection by your instructor by using the Electronic Bluebook module located on the navigation bar of the website.

ENGAGEMENT

In the first phase, you engage the student in the learning task. The student mentally focuses on a problem, situation, or event. The activities of this phase make connections to past and future activities. The connections depend on the learning task and the different dimensions of scientific literacy (see Chapter 4); they may be conceptual or procedural.

Asking a question, defining a problem, and showing a discrepant event are all ways to engage students and focus them on the instructional task. The teacher's role is to present the situation and identify the instructional task. The teacher also sets the rules and procedures for establishing the task.

Successful engagement results in students being puzzled and actively motivated in the learning activity. Here we are using *activity* in both the constructivist and behavioral sense—that is, students are mentally and physically active; in other words, they have a "mindson, hands-on" experience. If we combine the external events with the basic needs and interests of the students, instruction contributes to successful learning. Figure 15–4 summarizes the engagement phase.

EXPLORATION

Once you have engaged the students' interest in ideas, students need to have time to explore these ideas. You can specifically design exploration activities so that stu-

Orientation

This phase of the teaching model initiates the instructional task. The activity should (1) make connections between past and present learning experiences and (2) anticipate activities and organize students' thinking toward the learning outcomes of current activities.

Students

Establish an interest in, and develop an approach to, the instructional task.

Teachers

Identify the instructional task.

Activities

May vary, but should be interesting, motivational, and meaningful to students.

Learning

Initiated by, exposure to, and experience with concepts, processes, and skills.

FIGURE 15–4 Engagement

dents in the class have common, concrete experiences that begin building concepts, processes, and skills. Engagement brings about disequilibrium, while exploration initiates the process of equilibration. Some of the key words used to describe the type of activities used in this phase are *concrete* and *hands-on*. Courseware can be used in the phase, but it should be carefully designed to assist the initial process of conceptual reconstruction.

Visit http://www.prenhall.com/trowbridge and select Topic 2—Constructivism and Learning in Science. Select "Web Links" and find the website for the "School of Education at the University of Colorado at Denver." To expand your understanding of constructivism, this website will provide unlimited information for you.

The aim of exploration activities is to establish experiences that a teacher can use later to formally introduce a concept, process, or skill. During the activity, the students have time in which they explore objects, events, or situations.

As a result of their mental and physical involvement in the exploration activity, students establish relationships, observe patterns, identify variables, and question events.

The teacher's role in the exploration phase is that of facilitator or coach. The teacher initiates the activity and allows students the time and opportunity to investigate objects, materials, and situations based on each student's own concepts about phenomena. If called upon, the

Orientation

This phase of the teaching model provides the students with a common base of experiences within which current concepts, processes, and skills may be identified and developed.

Students

Complete activities directed toward learning outcomes.

Teachers

Facilitate and monitor interaction between students and instructional situations, materials, and/or courseware.

Activities

Provide mental and physical experiences relative to the learning outcomes. These activities provide an initial context for students' explanations as they have unanswered questions based on the exploration.

Learning

Directed by objects, events or situations.

FIGURE 15–5   Exploration

teacher may coach or guide students through questions, suggesting avenues of activity or thought, and hints that may avoid frustration and begin the process of mental reconstruction. Use of concrete materials and experiences is essential. However, it is important to remember that the teacher's role is subordinate to the students' activity. The exploration phase is an excellent time to use cooperative learning. Figure 15–5 summarizes the exploration phase.

EXPLANATION

The word *explanation* means the act or process in which concepts, processes, or skills are made plain, comprehensible, and clear. The process of explanation provides the students and teacher with a common use of terms relative to the learning task. In this phase, the teacher directs student attention to specific aspects of the engagement and exploration experiences. First, students are asked to give their explanations. Second, the teacher introduces scientific or technological explanations in a direct and formal manner. Explanations are ways of ordering the exploratory experiences. The teacher should base the initial part of this phase on students' explanations and clearly connect the explanations to experiences in the engagement and exploration phases of the instructional model. The key to this phase is to present scientific concepts, processes, or skills in a simple, clear, and direct manner, and move on to the next phase. You should not equate telling with learning. The explanation phase can be relatively short because the next phase allows time for restructuring and extends this formal introduction to concepts, processes, and skills.

The explanation phase can be teacher-, textbook-, or technology-directed. Teachers have a variety of techniques and strategies at their disposal. Educators com-

**Technology
Link**

Orientation

This phase of the teaching model focuses students' attention on a particular aspect of their engagement and exploration experiences and provides opportunities to demonstrate their conceptual understanding, process skills, or behaviors. This phase also provides specific opportunities for teachers to introduce concepts or skills.

Students

Describe their understanding, use of their skills, and express their attitudes.

Teachers

Direct student learning by clarifying misconceptions, providing vocabulary for concepts, giving examples of skills, modifying behaviors, and suggesting further learning experiences.

Activities

Provide opportunities to identify student knowledge, skills and values, and to introduce language and/or behaviors related to learning outcomes.

Learning

Directed by teacher and instructional courseware.

FIGURE 15–6   Explanation

monly use oral explanations, but there are other strategies such as reading, video, film, and educational courseware. This phase continues the process of cognitive construction and provides scientific words for explanations. In the end, students should be able to explain exploratory experiences using common scientific terms. Students will not immediately express and apply the explanations—learning takes time. Students need time and experience to establish and expand concepts, processes, and skills. For a summary of the explanation phase, see Figure 15–6.

ELABORATION

Once students begin developing an explanation of their learning tasks, it is important to involve students in further experiences that extend or clarify the concepts, processes, or skills. In some cases, students may still have misconceptions, or they may only understand a concept in terms of the exploratory experience.

Elaboration activities provide further time and experiences that contribute to learning. According to Audrey Champagne:

> During the elaboration phase, students engage in discussions and information-seeking activities. The group's goal is to identify and execute a small number of promising approaches to the task. During the group discussion, students present and defend their approaches to the instructional task. This discussion results in better definition and gathering of information that is necessary for successful completion of the task. The teaching cycle is not closed to information from the outside. Students get infor-

Orientation

This phase of the teaching model challenges and extends students' conceptual understanding and skills. Through new experiences students develop deeper and broader understanding, more information, and adequate skills.

Students

Present and defend their explanations and identify and complete several experiences related to the learning task.

Teachers

Provide an occasion for students to cooperate on activities, discuss their current understanding, and demonstrate their skills.

Activities

Provide experiences through challenges, repetition, new activities, practice, and time.

Learning

Encouraged through challenges, repetition, new experiences, practices, and time.

FIGURE 15–7   Elaboration

mation from each other, the teacher, printed materials, experts, electronic databases, and experiments they conduct. This is called the information base. As a result of participation in the group's discussion, individual students are able to elaborate upon the conception of the tasks, information bases, and possible strategies for its completion.[32]

Interactions within student groups is an application of Vygotsky's psychology to the teaching model. Group discussions and cooperative learning situations provide opportunities for students to express their understanding of the subject and receive feedback from others who are close to their own level of understanding.

The phase is also an opportunity to involve students in new situations and problems that require the application of identical or similar explanations. Figure 15–7 is a summary of the elaboration phase of the teaching model.

EVALUATION

At some point, students should receive feedback on their achievements. Informal assessment can occur from the beginning of the teaching sequence. The teacher can complete a formal assessment after the elaboration phase. As a practical educational matter, teachers must assess student learning. This is the phase in which teachers administer tests or performance activities to determine each student's understanding. This is also the important opportunity for students to use the skills they have acquired and evaluate their own understanding. In addition, one justification for such a model lies in providing adequate opportunities for all students to learn science.

The 5E instructional model is aligned with many processes involved in scientific inquiry. In science, the methods of scientific inquiry are an excellent means for

Orientation

This phase of the teaching model encourages students to assess their understandings and abilities and provides opportunities for teachers to evaluate student progress toward achieving the educational objectives.

Students

Examine the adequacy of their explanations, behaviors, and attitudes in new situations.

Teachers

Use a variety of formal and informal procedures for assessing student understanding.

Activities

Evaluate concepts, attitudes, and skills of the students.

Learning

Repeat different phases of the teaching model to improve conceptual understanding and/or skills.

FIGURE 15–8   Evaluation

students to evaluate their explanations. These methods are, after all, congruent with science. How well do student explanations stand up to review by peers and teachers? Is there a need to reform ideas based on experience?

Figure 15–8 summarizes the evaluation phase.

Figure 15–9 provides additional details about what the teacher does and what the student does at different stages in the instructional model. We have provided descriptions of methods and activities that are both consistent and inconsistent with this model.

In addition, one author (Rodger Bybee) has provided a detailed discussion of the 5E model in *Achieving Scientific Literacy: From Purposes to Practices.*[33]

SUMMARY

This chapter describes several instructional models. Although textbooks are used by the majority of science teachers, there has been little effort to use them effectively. Science teachers should recognize that students' use of textbooks is influenced by their prior knowledge (i.e., misconceptions) and that this prior knowledge can dominate or distort text material. Some recommendations for using a textbook include the following:

- Direct students' attention to important concepts.
- Challenge students' misconceptions.
- Ask students to construct explanations of everyday phenomena.
- Probe student responses.
- Provide accurate feedback to students.
- Construct alternative representations of textbook explanations.
- Select activities that create conceptual conflict.

Stage of the Instructional Model	What the Student Does	
	That Is Consistent with This Model	*That Is Inconsistent with This Model*
Engage	Creates interest	Explains concepts
	Generates curiosity	Provides definitions and answers
	Raises questions	States conclusions
	Identifies what the students know about the topic	Provides closure
		Lectures
Explore	Encourages students to work together without direct instruction from the teacher	Provides answers
	Observes and listens to students as they interact	Explains how to solve the problem
	Asks probing questions to redirect students' investigations when necessary	Provides closure
	Provides time for students to puzzle through problems	Tells students that they are wrong
	Acts as a consultant for students	Gives information that answers the question
		Leads students step-by-step to a solution
Explain	Encourages students to explain concepts and definitions in their own words	Accepts explanations that have no justification
	Asks for justification (evidence) and clarification from students	Neglects to solicit students' explanations
	Formally provides definitions, explanations, and new labels	Introduces unrelated concepts or skills
	Uses students' previous experiences as the basis for explaining concepts	
Elaborate	Expects students to use formal definitions and explanations	Provides definite answers
	Encourages students to apply the concepts and skills in new situations	Tells students that they are wrong
	Reminds students of alternative explanations	Lectures
	Refers students to data and evidence and asks: What do you already know? Why do you think . . . ?	Leads students step-by-step to an answer
		Explains how to work through the problem
Evaluate	Observes students as they apply new concepts and skills	Tests vocabulary words, terms, and isolated facts
	Assesses students' knowledge and/or skills	Introduces new ideas or concepts
	Looks for evidence that students have changed their thinking or behaviors	Creates ambiguity
	Allows students to assess their own learning and group-process skills	Promotes open-minded discussion unrelated to the concept or skill
	Asks open-ended questions, such as: Why do you think . . . ? What evidence do you have? What do you know about? How would you explain . . . ?	

FIGURE 15–9   Applying the 5E Instructional Model

Another instructional model is the learning cycle. This cycle is a three-step instructional sequence that includes

◆ concept exploration,
◆ concept introduction, and
◆ concept application.

Cooperative learning is an effective strategy in the science classroom. Students learn a number of strategies that help them develop and function as a group. Formation of a group, group functioning, formulating understanding of the task, and time to discuss and reform concepts are all important aspects of cooperative groups.

Hunter's model is described in this chapter. The teaching sequence in this model includes

◆ anticipating set,
◆ objectives and purpose,
◆ instructional input,
◆ modeling,
◆ monitoring student understanding, and
◆ practice.

The 5E instructional model includes the phases of engagement, exploration, explanation, elaboration, and evaluation. The basis of the 5E instructional model is

Stage of the Instructional Model	What the Student Does	
	That Is Consistent with This Model	*That Is Inconsistent with This Model*
Engage	Asks questions, such as: Why did this happen? What do I already know about this? What can I find out about his? Shows interest in the topic	Asks for the "right" answer Offers the "right" answer Insists on answers or explanations Seeks one solution
Explore	Thinks freely, but within the limits of the activity Tests predictions and hypotheses Forms new predictions and hypotheses Tries alternatives and discusses them with others Records observations and ideas Suspends judgment	Lets others do the thinking and exploring (passive involvement) Works quietly with little or no interaction with others (only appropriate when exploring ideas or feelings) Plays around indiscriminately with no goal in mind Stops with one solution
Explain	Explains possible solutions or answers to others Listens critically to another student's explanations Questions other explanations Listens to and tries to comprehend explanations offered by the teacher Refers to previous activities Uses recorded observations in scientific explanations	Proposes explanations from thin air with no relationship to previous experiences Brings up irrelevant experiences and examples Accepts explanations without justification Does not attend to other plausible explanations
Elaborate	Applies new labels, definitions, explanations, and skills in new, but similar, situations Uses previous information to ask questions, propose answers, make decisions, design experiments Draws reasonable conclusions from evidence Records observations and explanations Checks for understanding among peers	Plays around with no goal in mind Ignores previous information or evidence Draws conclusions from thin air Uses in discussions only those labels that the teacher provided
Evaluate	Answers open-ended questions by using observations, evidence, and previously accepted explanations Demonstrates an understanding or knowledge of the concept or skill Evaluates his or her own progress and knowledge Asks related questions that would encourage future investigations	Draws conclusions, not using evidence or previously accepted explanations Offers only yes-or-no answers, memorized definitions or explanations as answers Fails to express satisfactory explanations in his or her own words Introduces new, irrelevant topics

FIGURE 15–9   (Continued)

the original learning cycle used in the SCIS program. We have modified and extended this learning cycle and drawn on research in the cognitive sciences—research that deals primarily with student misconception and conceptual change. Three factors support the use of this instructional model: (1) research from the cognitive sciences, (2) concordance of the model with the scientific process, and (3) utility to curriculum developers and classroom teachers.

◆

REFERENCES

1. Iris Weiss, *Report of the 1985–86 National Survey of Science and Mathematics Education* (Research Triangle Park, NC: Research Triangle Institute, November 1987).
2. Jean Osbourn, Beau Jones, and Marcy Stein, "The Case for Improving Textbooks," *Educational Leadership* (April 1985).
3. Stephen Jay Gould, "The Case of the Creeping Fox Terrier Clone," *Natural History* (January 1988).
4. Joseph D. McInerney, "Biology Textbooks—Whose Business?" *American Biology Teacher,* 48 (7) (October 1986).

5. Audrey Champagne et al., "Middle School Science Texts: What's Wrong That Could Be Made Right?" *American Association for the Advancement of Science Books & Films* (May/June 1987).

6. Iris Weiss, *Report of the 2000 National Survey of Science and Mathematics Education* (Chapel Hill, NC: Horizon Research, Inc., 2000).

7. Kathleen Roth and Charles Anderson, "Promoting Conceptual Change Learning from Science Textbooks," in *Improving Learning: New Perspectives*, P. Ramsden, ed. (New York: Kogan Page Publishers, 1988).

8. Kathleen Roth, *Conceptual Learning and Student Processing of Science Texts* (Research Series No. 167) (East Lansing, MI: Institute for Research on Teaching, Michigan State University, 1985).

9. Charles Anderson and Edward Smith, *Teacher Behavior Associated with Conceptual Learning in Science*, paper presented at the annual meeting of the American Educational Research Association, Montreal, Canada, 1983.

10. Roth, *Conceptual Learning and Student Processing of Science Texts*.

11. Robert Karplus, "Teaching for the Development of Reasoning," in 1980 Association for the Education of Teachers of Science Yearbook, *The Psychology of Teaching for Thinking and Creativity*, Anton E. Lawson, ed. (Columbus, OH: ERIC Clearinghouse for Science, Mathematics, and Environmental Education, 1979).

12. Howard Birnie, *An Introduction to the Learning Cycle* (Saskatoon, Canada: University of Kastachewan Press, 1982).

13. Robert Karplus et al., *Teaching and the Development of Reasoning* (Berkeley: University of California Press, 1977).

14. John Renner, Michael Abraham, and Howard Birnie, "The Importance of the FORM of Student Acquisition of Data in Physics Learning Cycles," *Journal of Research in Science Teaching*, 22 (4) (1985): 303–326.

15. Anton Lawson, "A Better Way to Teach Biology," *American Biology Teacher*, 50 (5) (May 1988): 266–278.

16. See for example, David Johnson et al., "Effects of Cooperative, Competitive and Individualistic Goal Structures on Achievement: A Meta-Analysis," *Psychological Bulletin*, 89 (1981): 47–62; and Roger Johnson and David Johnson, "What Research Says about Student Interaction in Science Classrooms," in *Education in the 80s: Science*, Mary Budd Rowe, ed. (Washington, DC: National Education Association, 1984), pp. 25–37.

17. David Johnson, Roger Johnson, Edith Johnson Holubec, and Patricia Roy, *Circles of Learning: Cooperation in the Classroom* (Alexandria, VA: Association for Supervision and Curriculum Development, 1986).

18. Madeline Hunter, *Mastery Teaching* (El Segundo, CA: TIP Publications, 1982); and *Improved Instruction* (El Segundo, CA: TIP Publications, 1976).

19. J. Myron Atkin and Robert Karplus, "Discovery or Invention?" *Science Teacher*, 29 (1986): 45–51.

20. David Hawkins, "Messing About in Science," *Science and Children*, 2 (6) (1965): 5–9.

21. John W. Renner and Michael Abraham, "The Sequence of Learning Cycle Activities in High School Chemistry," *Journal of Research in Science Teaching*, 23 (2) (1986): 121–143.

22. Charles W. Anderson, "Incorporating Recent Research on Learning into the Process of Science Curriculum Development," commissioned paper for IBM-supported design project (Colorado Springs, CO: Biological Sciences Curriculum Study, 1987).

23. Audrey Champagne, "The Psychological Basis for a Model of Science Instruction," commissioned paper for IBM-supported design project (Colorado Springs, CO: Biological Sciences Curriculum Study, 1987).

24. John Bransford, Ann Brown, and Rodney Cocking, eds., *How People Learn: Brain, Mind, Experience, and School* (Washington, DC: National Academy Press, 2000).

25. James Wandersee, Joel Mintzes, and Joseph Novak, "Research on Alternative Conceptions in Science," in *Handbook of Research on Science Teaching and Learning*, D. Gabel, ed. (New York: Macmillan Publishing Company, 1994).

26. W. Kyle and J. Shymansky, "Enhancing Learning through Conceptual Change in Teaching," in *Research Matters to the Science Teacher*, 21 (1989), National Association for Research in Science Teaching.

27. C. W. Anderson, "Strategic Teaching in Science," in *Strategic Teaching and Learning: Cognitive Instruction in the Content Areas*, Joens, ed. (Alexandria, VA: Association for Supervision and Curriculum Development, 1987).

28. Peter Hewson, "A Conceptual Change Approach to Learning Science," *European Journal of Science Education*, 3 (4) (1981): 383–396.

29. Peter Hewson and N. Richard Thorley, "The Conditions of Conceptual Change in the Classroom," *International Journal of Science Education*, 11 (Special Issue) (1989): 541–653.

30. Peter Hewson and Mariana Hewson, "An Appropriate Conception of Teaching Science: A View from Studies of Science Learning," *Science Education*, 72 (5) (1988): 597–614.

31. G. J. Posner, K. A. Strike, P. W. Hewson, and W. A. Gerzog, "Accommodation of a Scientific Conception: Toward a Theory of Conceptual Change," *Science Education*, 66 (2) (1982): 211–227.

32. Audrey Champagne, "The Psychological Basis for a Model of Science Instruction," p. 82.

33. Rodger Bybee, *Achieving Scientific Literacy: From Purposes to Practices* (Portmouth, NH: Heinemann, 1997).

◆ ————————— **ENGAGING IN ACTION RESEARCH** ————————— ◆

ACTIVITY 15-1
WHAT DOES IT MEAN TO CONSTRUCT AN UNDERSTANDING OF A SCIENTIFIC CONCEPT?

In this chapter we have discussed various models for organizing your approach to how you present ideas and opportunities in the classroom to maximize learning. A constructivist approach is one of the key ideas emerging in many areas of educational reform, including science education. Despite the support in the research for the value of this approach, it is probably the least common approach of instruction. Use this activity to think about what the value of a constructivist approach might be and why it is seldom used.

1. Draw a concept map that demonstrates your understanding of the concept "photosynthesis." Your map should answer this question: What are the key ideas related to the concept and how are they related?

2. Circle the areas on the map that you think should be taught in middle school in one color and the areas that should be taught in high school in another color.

3. Watch the video *Lessons from Thin Air*, and then prepare to discuss these questions:

   ◆ What does the teacher do to help students build an understanding of photosynthesis?
   ◆ What else could the teacher do?
   ◆ What do you think of the student's reaction to his own videotape?
   ◆ Do you think photosynthesis is a valuable concept to teach? Why?
   ◆ What is your explanation about why so few people could accurately explain how an acorn grows into a large oak tree?

4. Look at your concept map in light of what you learned watching the video. How does your map represent both accuracies and inaccuracies in understanding the big ideas behind the concept of photosynthesis?

5. Review the areas on your map that you indicated as being appropriate to teach in middle and high school. What changes would you make based on the video and the discussion?

6. What do you see as the role of an instructional model in helping students develop accurate understandings of key scientific concepts?

   If you would like to learn more about videos like *Lessons from Thin Air*, check the Annenberg website at www.learner.org.

PLANNING FOR EFFECTIVE SCIENCE TEACHING

Science teachers are especially fortunate because of the many interesting and motivational things connected with science that they can use in their teaching. Examples of natural and scientific phenomena abound. The daily cycle of news events, the endless variety of clouds and weather, the growth of plants and animals, the passage of the seasons—all contribute to an endless store of materials for scientific and technologic discussions. There are rocks and minerals to be collected, flora and fauna to be investigated, and many examples of scientific ideas and technological devices to be used as teaching aids in science classes.

Alert and enthusiastic science teachers do not miss the opportunity to incorporate these in their teaching plans. Clever use of appropriate items and examples will inject a degree of interest and spontaneity into science classes that is unmatched in other disciplines. How does the science teacher put the things of science to use? Are there meaningful ways to plan for effective teaching? Can the teacher maintain sequence and organization and at the same time stimulate interest? Can the objectives of science teaching be realized while permitting the objects of science to dominate the scene? These are questions teachers must face when planning their yearly and daily work.

At this point, we recommend that you complete at least one of the following activities—Planning a Simple Lesson and Evaluating a Lesson—located at the end of this chapter.

In the next sections, we introduce some elements and strategies of effective teaching. These are the "pieces" that science teachers use in designing individual lessons or teaching units. The chapter is structured so that you develop an idea of different types of planning for effective science teaching. This chapter pre-

sents the practical, how-to of science teaching—the actual planning of a science program, a teaching unit, and daily lesson plans.

PLANNING A UNIT OR COURSE OF STUDY

The prospects of designing a course, unit, or even a daily lesson plan may be quite daunting for a new teacher. Fortunately, the instructional materials you will use will have done much of the preplanning of the organization and content of your prospective unit. Your particular goals and objectives, however, will certainly dictate the specific manner in which the accomplishment of these goals and objectives will be met.

In your planning there are several components to consider. First, you should have a clear idea of the rationale for the course or unit. Why is this material being included? How does the new information fit into the overall course or unit? You will need to think about the intended learning outcomes. What specific student objectives are to be accomplished? Which of these are conceptual, which are skill objectives, and which are expected values outcomes?

It is helpful to construct some type of conceptual framework showing the relationships among the ideas of the unit or course. Which are major ideas? Which are minor or subordinate ideas? In what order should they be presented?

A very important component is the instructional plan, which will consume much of your planning time. How can you best accomplish your objectives? What materials lend themselves best to the task? How can you make it interesting? How will students become actively involved? How can you avoid a traditional didactic

Good advance planning for a lesson or unit is essential for effective teaching. Sharing of ideas with other teachers is important.

approach and employ inquiry methods? These are all important questions you will need to answer.

Finally, you need to think about your evaluation plan. There are many forms of evaluation, each of which can serve a specific purpose in your teaching. Think about evaluation as you plan your unit or course, not as you approach the end of it. One very helpful approach is called "backward design." In this process you begin by identifying the desired results and next determine acceptable evidence that would indicate the students attained your goals. Then, and only then, you plan the learning experiences for your program. This process is based on the work of Grant Wiggins and Jay McTighe and elaborated in their book, *Understanding by Design.*[1]

Visit http://www.prenhall.com/trowbridge and select Topic 1—Science Teaching Standard. Select "Web Links" and find the website on Benchmarks for Science Literacy prepared by the American Association for the Advancement of Science (AAAS). This link offers guides and policies for developing science curricula. Identify three such guides and arrange to discuss them in your class by using the Electronic Bluebook module.

SOME ELEMENTS AND STRATEGIES OF EFFECTIVE SCIENCE TEACHING

Effective teaching requires a great deal of thought, preparation, and design. In the following sections we introduce some ideas that you might keep in mind while designing a lesson, teaching unit, or entire science curriculum.

Before a Lesson

Several times in this book we have indicated the importance of goals and objectives. They emerge here as the fundamental consideration of the planning process.

Goals and objectives are like maps. They indicate the journey and the destination, respectively. Goals and objectives indicate where you are going and tell you when you have arrived. In teaching, it is often important to remember that, like travel, the destination defines the trip, and the means of travel accommodates other aspects of the trip (e.g., budget, time, and access). We recommend careful thought and identification of the desired results and the evidence that you have attained those results. Once you actually have designed the lesson and begun teaching, it is important to continually direct and redirect teaching to your goals and objectives. To use the trip analogy again, one can have educational side trips, but it is essential to continue in the general direction of your objectives and your goals.

Beginning a Lesson

How you begin sets the stage for the lesson. The beginning of a lesson should achieve several things. First, it should connect what has been learned in the past with what is going to be learned in the present lesson. While the connections may seem obvious to you as the teacher, it is not always as clear to the students. Second, a good beginning can provide a focus or context for the present lesson. Effective beginnings answer the why and what questions that students may have. Third, the beginning should be exciting and engaging. Students should be enthusiastic about what they are going to study.

There are many effective ways to begin a lesson. Current events, confrontation with problems, pictorial riddles, discrepant events, counterintuitive situations, and challenging questions are but some of the ways to begin a teaching sequence.

The Middle of a Lesson

Once the lesson or unit is under way, you can incorporate more elements and strategies into science teaching. Here are a few initial ideas to consider as you design lessons. Active participation with materials, equipment, and media is a good way to engage the learner's attention and develop the concepts, skills, and values of your objectives. You want to optimize the amount of time students are engaged in learning tasks.

There are different means of capturing, maintaining, and enhancing students' attention. These motivational strategies include showing the personal meaning of the lesson in the students' lives. Personal meaning can be provided through a rationale, or by connecting an idea or concept to the students' lives or answering a personal question. Success is another motivator. New objects and experiences can improve student interest and attention as much as success.

Once you are into the lesson, remember to apply the principles of learning and development. At a minimum, use reinforcement to discourage nonproductive behaviors. When introducing skills it is often essential to model what you want the students to do. For example, demonstrate how you want them to set up and dismantle laboratory equipment or use the probes of a computer-based laboratory.

Practice is another element of learning. Some ideas, skills, and values are learned because they have great personal meaning. In others, proficiency is achieved through repetition of a task. Don't hesitate to schedule time to practice the skills that you perceive to be important. Sometimes practice can be done with the entire class, usually at the initial stages of learning; other times practice can be individualized and either distributed throughout or clustered at the end of the learning sequence.

As you teach the lesson, it is valuable to monitor student progress. How are they doing? Do they understand what has been taught? If students are not progressing as you had anticipated, it is well worth adapting the sequence or method to better enhance student learning. The assessment can be as simple as spot-checking papers, asking questions, or giving a quiz. The crucial point is to change instruction based on the assessment.

There is another, sometimes elusive, set of factors that is important for planning and teaching. These factors can be thought of as the classroom climate. What plans should be made to establish a classroom environment that enhances student learning? Planning your lesson or unit should include communicating expectations of achievement—your goals, procedures for a safe and orderly work environment, anticipation and sensible management of disruptive behavior, and establishment of cooperative learning.[2]

There is a lot that goes into teaching. Some of the factors described above can actually be a part of your planning, while others are part of your instructional theory.

Ending a Lesson or Unit

Too often lessons and units just stop. Plan an ending to your lesson. There should be closure, an opportunity for you or your students to summarize what has been taught. At the lesson's end, you should be able to indicate how well the objectives were met. Students ought to leave the room with a feeling of accomplishment and closure for the day's lesson or the unit.

After a Lesson or Unit

When a lesson or unit is over, you should have some measure of the lesson and student achievement. The measure can be an informal assessment of how things went and what they learned, or a formal evaluation of the lesson through a quiz or test of student achievement. These procedures are feedback for you and the students. They indicate what might be changed in the instructional sequence and the problems students may be having with the material. The next section is a more complete description of planning for effective science teaching.

DESIGNING PROGRAMS, UNITS, AND LESSONS

This section is designed to have you take steps toward the practical, everyday matter of science teaching. You have just read about some general strategies of effective teaching. Here many of the elements and methods are combined into a sequence of instruction. Although there are many models and methods for teaching science, the purpose of this section is for you to begin thinking generally about your science program and specifically about planning science lessons. We take the approach of beginning with the science program, the year-long plan. Although this is probably not your most immediate concern, having the "big picture" of your science program provides the framework for consistent and coherent units and lessons. The sequence is the science program, unit plans, and lesson plans.

THE LONG-RANGE PLAN: A SCIENCE PROGRAM

Our goal for this section is to have you begin thinking about a full year's science program. The essential elements for this section are discussed in length in the chapters on curriculum. To accomplish our goal of conceptualizing a total science program—seeing the forest before looking at trees—you should complete Activity 16–4, Designing a Full-Year Program, at the end of this chapter. Designing your science program will be a major challenge. You will have to synthesize many diverse ideas and recommendations into your program. Remember to begin with the desired outcomes and acceptable evidence that you have achieved those outcomes. Topics and activities come from a variety of sources. These sources may include the following:

- ◆ science department requirements,
- ◆ district syllabi,
- ◆ state guidelines,
- ◆ textbook organization, and
- ◆ national organizations.

Sorting all of these recommendations is not easy. Fortunately, many of the recommendations are more consistent than not. In the end, you will decide on your science program. That is why we encourage you to begin thinking about how to organize your program. There are several ways to organize programs. We briefly describe some of those ways in the next sections.

Structure of the Discipline

Science disciplines are organized by major conceptual structure. Themes such as thermodynamics in physics, bonding in chemistry, and diversity in biology are examples of conceptual schemes that organize disciplines. Many contemporary curriculum projects are organized by the structure of disciplines.

Nature of Scientific Inquiry

Inquiry refers to the ways scientists within disciplines determine the truth or falsehood, validity or invalidity, of knowledge claims. The inquiry includes the processes scientists use—observation, classification, controlling variables, forming hypotheses, and designing experiments. But organizing on the basis of inquiry includes more—the study of how and why scientific propositions are accepted or rejected. If scientists have competing theories, how does one know which is acceptable?

Topics of Science Disciplines

Topics can be used to organize science courses. Electricity, magnets, rocks and minerals, cell division, and photosynthesis are examples of topics.

Issues Related to Science

In recent years, there has been a trend toward using issues to organize courses. If carefully and properly done, organizing a program by issues can be exciting for students and will include many important science concepts and processes. Issues include the following: air quality and atmosphere, water resources, land use, population growth, food resources, mineral resources, and environmental quality.

Organizing a science program can take the form of a yearly calendar. The calendar indicates the order of units and time allotted to them. Table 16–1 is a calendar for a course organized by both integrating concepts and social issues. Examination of textbooks and state syllabi will provide other examples of yearly calendars.

In preparing this calendar, the order of issues and concepts generally moves from simple to complex. The more complex problems come later in the year, and more time is allotted for study of these issues. The calendar includes 180 days, the average number of classes a science teacher has in a school year.

THE MIDDLE-RANGE PLAN: A SCIENCE UNIT

A beginning teacher is assisted by a teaching-unit plan designed in moderate detail for a period of a month or six weeks. The unit topic is usually a cohesive area of study that fits into long-range plans and objectives. The teaching unit frequently contains the following sections and characteristics:

1. Title
2. Purpose statement
3. Objectives
4. Content
5. Methods
6. Materials
7. Evaluation
8. Teaching sequence

The *title* is simply an identifying name for the unit. It need not be anything complicated; for example, "An Introduction to Physics," "Human Ecology," or "Earth Processes: Folds and Faults."

Table 16–1 Yearly Calendar for a Course Organized by Concepts and Issues

Unit	Issue	Concepts	Days Allotted
I	Science and technology in society	The nature of science and technology	10
II	Air quality	Cycles	20
III	Land use	Scale	20
IV	Water quality	Equilibrium	20
V	Hazardous substances	Gradient	25
VI	Space exploration	Systems	40
VII	Population, resources, environment	Interactions	45
			(Total 180 days)

A *purpose statement* is a synopsis of why this unit is important and generally what will be accomplished by the teaching unit.

The *objectives* should be specific, brief statements of purpose for the unit. They should serve as constant reminders to the teacher of the things to be accomplished in the time allotted. They should be practical, timely, and carefully suited to the capabilities of the class. Objectives should be clearly written and testable.

Content refers to the actual material to be taught in the unit. Because this material may be extensive, the teaching-unit plan cannot list all of it in minute detail; however, the plan may list major principles, pertinent facts of major importance, examples and illustrations, and references to specific knowledge in text material deemed important for the unit. An outline form may be used in this part of the unit plan. Because of the chronological nature of the teaching unit, specific content and references to subject matter can be distributed sequentially throughout the unit.

Methods to be used in teaching should be planned as carefully as possible. This is where the use of one (or a combination) of the instructional models is highly recommended. Plan through the sequence of lessons using a model. Based on the model and your objectives, certain parts of the teaching sequence may be taught more suitably by one method than by another. For example, a film may be the most effective teaching agent for an introduction (e.g. engagement, anticipatory set), and a simulation game may be most appropriate as an elaboration of the lesson's concepts. At another time you may deem a discussion or individual project to be the best teaching method.

Materials must be planned with care to ensure their availability when they are needed. In some cases, ordering a few weeks in advance is necessary. Apparatus should be checked to see whether it is in working order. Development of the teaching unit will undoubtedly involve hours of library work, getting ideas for reading materials and activities. Consideration should be given to the needs of slow and gifted learners, and suitable materials should be arranged for them.

Evaluation should be thought of as a continuing process throughout the unit. One of the major functions of evaluation is to keep students informed of their progress and to give them realistic assessments of their own abilities. Assigned work, short quizzes, conferences, and unit tests must be planned in the teaching unit. Not all of the evaluative devices and techniques can be planned in detail in advance, but provision for them can be made. Evaluation should be based on the objectives of the unit.

The *teaching sequence* may be outlined for the period of time involved, but flexibility for change must be provided. This can be done by arranging for alternative procedures, omitting or adding certain subject matter, and providing for unplanned periods that can occasionally be interspersed to take up slack or give needed time for completing a topic. The teaching unit should be thought of as a guide for action rather than a calendar of events. Reasonable attention to the sequence, objectives, and procedures of the teaching unit can promote better learning, satisfaction, and accomplishment. A general outline for a unit is presented here.

Outline for a Science Teaching Unit

- Title
- Purpose Statement
- Outline for a Year Program (Use Activity 16–4, Designing a Full-Year Program, and indicate where your unit is located in the total program.)
- Objectives for the Unit
- Weekly Schedule for the Unit (See Table 16–2 for an example.)
- Pretest
- Daily Lesson Plans (Use a specific model or combination of models.)
- Unit Test

TABLE 16–2 Example of a Weekly Schedule for a Middle School Science Class Studying Environmental Change

Content Outline	Class Period	Phase of Teaching Model	Class Activity
Environmental problems in paper	Homework	Engagement	Students collect examples of newspaper articles dealing with environmental problems, e.g., hazardous substances or pollution.
Evidence of environmental change • Change is common • There are good, bad, and neutral changes	1	Exploration	Class goes outside and gathers evidence of changes in local environment. They should find good, bad, and neutral changes.
Factors related to environmental change • Immediate • Delayed • Cycles • Growth	2	Explanation	Show film *The Saga of DDT.* Use film to focus discussion on key concepts. End class with short lecture, defining and giving examples of immediate change, delayed change, cyclical change, and change through growth.
Changing environmental systems	3	Elaboration	Do silent demonstrations of changes in aquatic and terrestrial ecosystems. Have students identify potential immediate, delayed, cyclical, and growth changes.
Limits to change in environmental systems	4	Elaboration	Do invitation to inquiry on "Tragedy of the Commons." Use cooperative groups.
End of section	5	Evaluation	Quiz on concepts. Students will define concept and give one local and one global example.

CHECKLIST OF REQUIREMENTS FOR THE SCIENCE UNIT

Your instructor may indicate requirements for a science unit. You can use this checklist to organize your science unit.

1. *Title Page.* Give the title of the unit, grade level, and whether it is based on a new curriculum. If it uses a modern curriculum, state its name. List your name, the title and number of the course, and leave a space for the unit evaluation.
2. *Purpose Statement.* Give the reason for the scope and sequence of the unit. Indicate the broad goals to be achieved through the unit.
3. *Objectives.* These should be clearly stated.
4. *Weekly Schedule of the Unit.* A brief, one-page survey of what will take place each day as shown in Table 16–2.
   a. Include reading assignments.
   b. Include homework activities.
5. *Laboratory Exercises.* These should be some of your own laboratory activities, including the following:
   a. The subject-matter objectives (concepts) the laboratory will teach.
   b. Critical-thinking and problem-solving processes the lesson will develop, indicated in the margin of the activity.
   c. A discussion section preceding the lesson and open-ended possibilities following the lesson.

   d. Other (assigned by your instructor).
6. *Invitations to Inquiry.* (You are to prepare these invitations.)
7. *Discussion Questions during or at the End of the Unit.*
   a. List the questions you will ask to determine whether the students understood the material studied and whether they can apply what they have learned.
   b. When possible, the questions should develop critical-thinking and problem-solving processes. The type of mental process the student must use—for example, predicting or inferring—should be placed in the margin to indicate what is required.
8. *Demonstrations.* Include only if they are required because of a shortage of equipment or for safety reasons.
9. *Bulletin Board Display.* Prepare a diagram for at least one bulletin board display, indicating how it will appear.
10. *Supplemental Materials.*
    a. Laboratories or investigations
    b. Reading materials
11. *Multimedia Materials.*
    a. CD-ROMs
    b. Use of the Internet
    c. Videos
    d. PowerPoint Presentations
    e. Models, charts

Stimulating interest in science and technology is an important goal in resource or teaching units.

12. *Consideration of Safety Precautions.* What special considerations should be made about safety?
13. *Consideration of Special Students.* You might wish to include the variations on the lesson you would implement if you have special students.

Technology

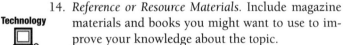

Link

14. *Reference or Resource Materials.* Include magazine materials and books you might want to use to improve your knowledge about the topic.
15. *Assessments.* Assessments should evaluate your objectives.
    a. Quizzes
    b. Performance
    c. Assessments
16. *Self-Evaluation of the Unit.*
    a. After compiling this unit outline, go back over it and write what problems you think you might have in teaching.
    b. After teaching this unit, evaluate how you think it could be improved.

THE RESOURCE UNIT

Many science teachers prepare a resource unit for the different topics they teach. A resource unit is, as the title indicates, a collection of resource materials that can be used for a specified topic (e.g., acids and bases, the laws of thermodynamics, the rock cycle, or photosynthesis) or various issues (e.g., population growth, air quality, world hunger, or health and disease). Rather than assemble the resources in a teaching sequence such

as we have discussed previously, a resource unit is usually arranged by teaching strategies or methods. If you begin organizing resource units now, in only a few years you will have an extensive collection of ideas and methods. Although you will have to determine the topics or issues for your science program, we can provide some general organizational categories for resource units. You would probably want to develop resource units for each of the major topics in your curriculum.

Possible Organizational Categories for Resource Units

◆ Goals
◆ Objectives
◆ Bulletin Boards
◆ Computer Software
◆ Demonstrations
◆ Discussion Topics
◆ Field Trips
◆ Homework
◆ Invitations to Inquiry
◆ Lecture Notes
◆ Multimedia
◆ PowerPoint
◆ Projects
◆ Supplementary Readings
◆ Assessments
◆ Videos
◆ Websites
◆ Miscellaneous

Technology

Link

You will probably not use all of these categories, and will perhaps add some of your own, but this list should

TABLE 16–3   Resource Unit: Examples of Categories and Contents

Categories	Contents
Aims and Goals	Lists of aims and goals from your local district, state education agency, national organizations, and textbooks.
Objectives	Lists of objectives from your local district, state education agency, national organizations, and textbooks.
Bulletin Boards	Sketches and designs, newspaper and magazine articles, pictures, and maps.
Computer Software	CAI programs, microcomputer-based laboratory, tutorial, simulation, HyperCard, models.
Demonstrations	Collections of good demonstrations from journals such as *Science Scope,* the *Science Teacher,* the *American Biology Teacher,* the *Physics Teacher;* ideas from workshops and college courses.
Discussion Topics	Questions and issues that are successful with students.
Field Trips	Description of where to go, what to do, and who to contact.
Games	List of games in science department, local media center.
Homework	Unique and interesting homework assignments for the topic.
Invitations to Inquiry	Lists of appropriate invitations from *Biology Teachers Handbook,* invitations you have developed, ideas for invitations.
PowerPoints	List (by title or content) of PowerPoints on file.
Lecture Notes	Revised notes from past courses.
Projects	Problems and ideas for projects.
Supplementary Readings	List of books and articles in media center, your file, or public library.
Assessments	Quizzes, tests, and questions for the unit.
Videos	List of videos from *NOVA, DISCOVERY,* etc., for VCR replay.
Websites	List of sites that relate to the concepts and topics of the unit.

Technology Link

help you begin organizing your resource units. Use of a personal computer and a database or HyperCard program will greatly enhance your organization, filing, and search capacity. Table 16–3 is a more complete description of the categories and examples of materials for a resource unit.

THE SHORT-RANGE PLAN: THE SCIENCE LESSON

The sequence of topics in this chapter may have seemed unusual to the science teacher facing a first lesson. We think there is added advantage for all teachers who have thought through their year's program and a unit before writing a daily lesson plan. Planning gives direction. A yearly plan guards against disconnected units, and unit plans protect against disconnected lessons. For all teachers, planning is an essential component of effective instruction. Approaching a science class with a well-organized plan gives the teacher personal assurance and leaves the students with confidence in the teacher's abilities. Thought planning should precede any written plans. Ask yourself questions such as

◆ What are my goals?
◆ How can I best achieve my goals?
◆ How will I know that students have achieved the goals?

◆ How can the concepts, processes, or skills be presented most effectively?
◆ How can I evaluate the lesson's effectiveness?

Since students vary in abilities and interests, plans must provide for these variations. Only by knowing something of the background of each student can the teacher be effective. This fact argues strongly for taking a personal interest in the students in one's classes. The small human contacts in a friendly classroom, an interested question here and there, can motivate students better than any other method.

Planning for effective science teaching is more than just making sure that there is something to do for the entire class period. For example, unless it is the very first lesson of the year, it is probable that assignments have been made and that the nature of the subject matter is understood. Thus, the basis for planning has already been established.

To conduct an interesting class period, the teacher must vary the methods from day to day and even within the class period itself. It is eventually ineffective to use the same pattern of teaching every day. Even an excellent method can suffer from overuse. With the great variety of methods from which to choose and with the potential excitement of inventing a new technique or of modifying an existing one, the science teacher is in an excellent position to plan a highly effective lesson.

The written plan should be concise and functional. The format may vary with the situation and individual teacher, but most important, it should be a practical, usable plan. In general, provision should be made for listing objectives and the related concepts. The learning activities and required procedures should be listed. The procedures ought to be given in adequate detail—for example, written questions and directions ensure a smooth class. All materials needed for the class period should be listed and checked. Two last essentials are assignments and evaluation. A skeletal form for a daily lesson would include the topics listed below:

1. Objectives
2. Concepts
3. Activities/Procedures
4. Materials
5. Assignments
6. Assessments

During the class hour, a teaching plan should be as unobtrusive as possible, yet referred to when needed. Main ideas, questions, and procedures may be memorized. Be sure the plan is handy if you need it for reference. As we mentioned above, a plan gives direction. You should also plan for flexibility: Realize that you will have to make some decisions about the direction of a particular lesson based on circumstances that arise in class.

After each lesson, we recommend evaluating the lesson plan. The experience gained in teaching a lesson should be recorded with brief notations on the written plan, either during the class period or immediately after class. Suggestions for timing, organization, student involvement, or modification of a technique can be noted for future use. (See Evaluation of Instructional Skills, at the end of this chapter.)

We will conclude this section with some helpful hints for contemporary lesson planning that includes goals such as inquiry. To help organize your planning in advance, the following are some features of lessons for inquiry-oriented science teaching.

- Students are involved in broad, open-ended questions related to science, technology, and/or social issues related to science and technology. Generally, students do not know the answer to the question.
- Students are required to understand the question before designing an investigation.
- Students design investigations and make observations and conclusions.
- Students write their results using the standard protocol of science papers.

Planning for such experiences should be done with the following points in mind:

TABLE 16–4 An Instructional Sequence for Planning Lessons

Engagement

This phase of the instructional sequence initiates the learning task. The activity should (1) make connections between past and present learning experiences, and (2) anticipate activities and focus students' thinking on the learning outcomes of current activities. The student should become mentally engaged in the concept, process, or skill to be explored.

Exploration

This phase of the teaching sequence provides students with a common base of experiences within which they identify and develop current concepts, processes, and skills. During this phase, students actively explore their environment or manipulate materials.

Explanation

This phase of the instructional sequence focuses students' attention on a particular aspect of their engagement and exploration experiences and provides opportunities for them to verbalize their conceptual understanding, or demonstrate their skills or behaviors. This phase also provides opportunities for teachers to introduce a formal label or definition for a concept, process, skill, or behavior.

Elaboration

This phase of the teaching sequence challenges and extends students' conceptual understanding and allows further opportunity for students to practice desired skills and behaviors. Through new experiences, the students develop deeper and broader understanding, more information, and adequate skills.

Evaluation

This phase of the teaching sequence encourages students to assess their understanding and abilities and provides opportunities for teachers to evaluate student progress toward achieving the educational objectives.

- Students probably have not had many previous opportunities of this type. Some may feel the need for explicit directions. The initial progress made by these students may be disappointing and frustrating, both to student and teacher.
- Accepting responsibility for one's own learning is a challenge that some students may tend to resist. Passive learning in which the teacher has been the key person for initiating a course of action has probably been the students' experience.
- First attempts should be on a small scale, with opportunities for greater choice and greater responsibility increasing as the student gains experience.
- The teacher should provide situations in which questions are asked. Students should be encouraged

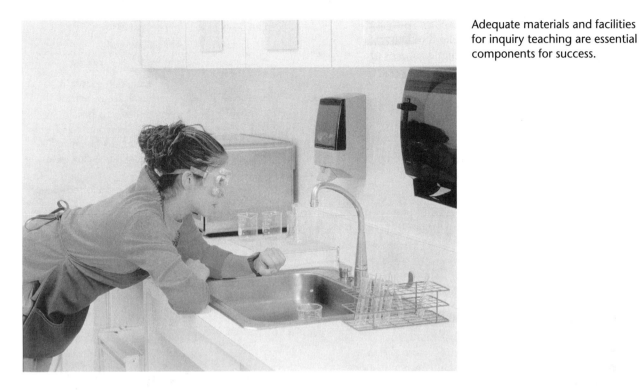

Adequate materials and facilities for inquiry teaching are essential components for success.

to formulate and ask questions that can be answered through inquiry.

♦ Means must be provided for students to gain experience in analyzing the results of an inquiry. The ability to see relationships, to organize data so that meaningful patterns emerge, to draw inferences, and to visualize ways of improving the investigation is a necessary skill that must be developed for effective learning.

♦

Sample Inquiry Lesson Plan—Grades 8–10

Overall Plan of the Lesson

The Problem
Objectives
Materials
Class Groupings
Background and Discussion (entire class)
Pupil Investigation (in groups)
Post-experiment Discussion (entire class)
    a. Hypotheses
    b. Concepts
    c. Comparison of group results
    d. Conclusions
Teacher's Notes

Problem: How can we measure the speed of sound by resonance?

Objectives: Pupils should be able to

a. Explain what causes resonance
b. Perform the experiment to measure the speed of sound by resonance
c. Hypothesize what effect temperature may have on the speed of sound

Materials:

Tuning fork—Middle C (256 vps or G-384 vps)
Rubber mallet for striking the tuning fork
Glass tube at least 1 inch in diameter and 16-inches long
Deep container for water, such as a tall cylinder

Class groupings: Suggest 5–7 persons per group

Background and Discussion: (This can be established by discussion and questioning of the pupils, with some information provided by the teacher.)

1. Have you ever pushed a playmate on a swing? How did you decide when to push? Was it decided for you by when the swing came back to you?
2. If you pushed each time the swing came back to you, what happened to the height of the swing? If you stopped pushing, what happened to the height of the swing?

3. This was an example of resonance because you added energy periodically to make the swing go higher. Can you think of any other examples of resonance?

4. What is a tuning fork used for?

5. In music, what might be the vibration rate (frequency) of a common tuning fork used for getting the proper pitch?

6. How fast does sound travel through air? Does this change sometimes? What might cause it to change?

7. How might we find the speed of sound in air? (The method we will use will involve a tuning fork and resonance.)

Pupil Investigation:

1. Obtain a tuning fork with the number of vibrations per second marked on it.

2. Obtain a glass tube about 16-inches long and 1 inch in diameter, open at both ends. Hold the tube upright with the lower end in a tall container of water (see Figure 16A).

3. Strike the tuning fork a sharp blow with a rubber mallet and hold it above the open end of the glass tube.

4. Slowly move the glass tube up and down, keeping the vibrating tuning fork close to the open end of the tube, until a place is found where the sound of the tuning fork is greatly magnified.

5. When you have found the best resonance, measure the length of the tube from the top to the surface of the water in the bottom of the tube.

6. Multiply the length you have measured (in feet) by 4 and then by the number of vibrations per second marked on the tuning fork. This gives you the speed of sound in feet per second.

Post-investigation Discussion:

1. Why do you multiply the length of the tube by 4? Why do you multiply by the frequency of the

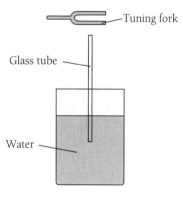

Figure 16A

Explanation of Resonance in a Closed Tube
While tuning fork goes from:

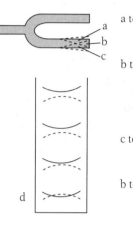

a to b – Downward-produced condensation goes from c to d and starts to reflect.

b to c – Reflected condensation goes from d to c and reinforces new condensation being formed above tuning fork.

c to b – Rarefaction formed under tuning fork goes from c to d and starts to reflect.

b to a – Reflected rarefaction goes from d to c and reinforces a new rarefaction being formed above tuning fork, thus giving louder sound.

Figure 16B

tuning fork? Why do you use water in the large container? Could you use another liquid? Try it.

2. The glass tube closed at the bottom by water is called a "closed tube." Could you obtain resonance with an "open tube"? How could you perform this experiment with an open tube?

Conclusion:

What do you conclude from this investigation? State your conclusion in one sentence.

Teachers' notes:

The relationship among wavelength, frequency, and speed of sound is wavelength times frequency equals speed of sound. To get the wavelength in this investigation, the length of the glass tube is multiplied by 4 because the sound wave travels the length of the tube four times for each wave before resonance is produced (see Figure 16B).

5E Model Lesson Plan—Lung Capacity

A useful strategy for teaching science to middle school pupils is that of the 5E Model. There are five parts to this format as follows:

Engagement
Exploration

Explanation
Elaboration
Evaluation

Problem: To find the lung capacity of each pupil

Materials:

Large glass container of at least 2 liters capacity. A cider jug may serve the purpose for this
Large open plastic or metal container for water. The container should hold at least five liters of water. Rubber tubing, about 5 millimeters inside diameter, and about 30 centimeters in length (see Figure 16C for the proper setup of the apparatus).
Small container of water in which a few milliliters of chlorine bleach has been mixed for disinfectant.

Engagement:

What is lung capacity? Why is a large lung capacity desirable for humans? Who would be best served by a larger lung capacity on average—people who live at sea level or those who live at high altitudes? Suggest why this might be true. How might we determine a person's lung capacity?

Exploration:

A. Have pupils, in sequence, exhaust the air completely from their lungs and then take a very deep breath from the rubber tube. Note the height the water reaches in the cider jug.
B. Carefully measure the difference in height between the initial height and the final height with a metric ruler. Record this measurement for each person. (Note: Be sure to dip the end of the rubber tube into the bleach water after each use.)
C. After students have measured their "intake lung capacity," have them perform the experiment again—this time by filling their lungs to capacity and then expelling the air into the cider jug that has been filled with water. Measure the difference in height of the water in the jug after all lung air has been expelled. Record this measurement next to the measurement of "intake lung capacity."
D. To obtain the lung capacity of each pupil in liters, multiply the height difference you measured by p times r squared. The formula for volume of a cylinder is height times p times r squared. For example if the height measurement was 10 centimeters and the radius of the cider jug was 8 centimeters, the volume would be 10 centimeters times 64 square centimeters times p, which equals 2011.6 cubic centimeters, or 2.012 liters.

Explanation:

What caused the water to go into the cider jug on the intake phase of the experiment? (Remember a vacuum cannot "pull" on anything. There must have been "pushing" to get the water to go into the jug. What might it have been?)

What caused the water to leave the jug on the "expelling" phase of the experiment?

Generally, how did the two measurements obtained in the two phases compare for each pupil? What might account for any differences noticed?

Elaboration:

In some countries, divers take a deep breath and dive for oysters or other shellfish. They can stay under water for several minutes. What kind of lung capacity must they have? How could you increase your lung capacity?

Whales are mammals that breathe air. They dive and remain below the surface for many minutes. What might happen to your lung capacity if you breathed pure oxygen instead of ordinary air? (Be careful how you answer this.)

Evaluation:

What factors should be evaluated in this experiment?

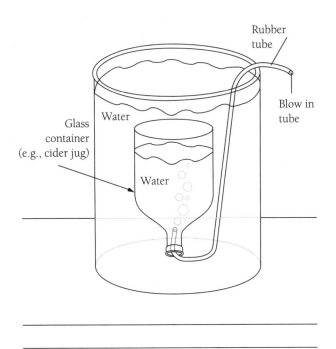

Rubber tube

Blow in tube

Glass container (e.g., cider jug)

Water

Water

Figure 16C

Was the apparatus functional? How could you improve it?

How many trials should one take to obtain a representative lung capacity measurement for each pupil?

What conclusions might you draw after completing this experiment?

◆

SUMMARY

Planning is one of the critical aspects of effective science teaching. When designing a lesson, teaching unit, or total course, keep in mind some ideas that are fundamental to effective instruction: use objectives, focus teaching on the objective, be sure students actively participate, apply principles of learning and motivation, and develop lessons with a beginning, middle, and end that are educationally productive.

A variety of methods are used in contemporary science teaching. Some of the key methods are questioning, discussing, demonstrating, reading, role-playing, presenting reports, doing projects, working in the laboratory, solving problems, taking field trips, preparing multimedia presentations, conducting simulations, and debating.

Science teachers can use models of teaching that combine strategies and methods into an instructional sequence. Using teaching models contributes to more efficient design of science lessons, and the synthesis of many elements of instruction into a workable and effective form.

The long-range plan of science teaching is the full-year program. This idea has been introduced briefly. There are at least two kinds of middle-range unit lesson plans. The teaching unit is planned with a time sequence in mind and usually provides for statements of objectives, outlines of content, methods, materials, and assessment techniques. The resource unit is not usually concerned with chronology but a reservoir that the teacher uses for daily lesson planning. It may contain lists of aims, important knowledge objectives, lists of activities and projects, computer software, suitable demonstrations and experiments, references, bibliographies, sample tests, assignments, and other teaching aids.

The lesson plan is a guide for action, not a rigid blueprint to be followed unswervingly. It should be flexible and should be modified when necessary. Much thought precedes the writing of a lesson plan. Consider such questions as, "What is the purpose of the lesson?" "What major generalizations are to be taught?" "How is the material best presented?" and "What kinds of individuals are in the class?" before planning the sequence on paper.

The format of the lesson plan should be functional and comfortable to the teacher. Individual teachers select the format most useful to them. Lesson plans should be as concise as possible within the limitations of effective teaching. While teaching, the lesson plan should be unobtrusive but available for reference.

Planning for contemporary science teaching usually requires a somewhat different approach than more traditional methods. The role of the teacher becomes one of guidance and direction, with students accepting greater responsibility for learning. Plans must provide more time, more questioning, greater variety of materials, and willingness on the part of the teacher to allow individual variations in progress by students.

Thorough lesson planning is a necessary facet of effective science teaching. Good teaching does not happen by accident. It is particularly important that a prospective teacher of science recognizes the value and benefit to be derived from careful, inspired planning in the art of science teaching.

◆

REFERENCES

1. Grant Wiggins and Jay McTighe, *Understanding by Design* (Alexandria, VA: Association for Supervision and Curriculum Development, 1998).

2. David Berliner, "The Half-Full Glass: A Review of Research in Teaching," in *Using What We Know about Teaching*, Philip Hosford, ed. (Alexandria, VA: Association for Supervision and Curriculum Development, 1984), pp. 51–77.

◆ ———————————— **INVESTIGATING SCIENCE TEACHING** ———————————— ◆

ACTIVITY 16–1
PLANNING A SIMPLE LESSON

1. Select a simple and specific short-range objective for a science class, such as "to develop skill in correct use of the microscope," or "to learn how to use a balance," or "to operate a microcomputer." Plan a lesson to achieve this objective, incorporating the features of a good lesson plan.

2. Using the lesson plan prepared above, or a similar one, teach your classmates the lesson. Invite them to play the role of secondary science class, with appropriate questions and activities. Solicit their constructive criticisms and comments on your lesson and the effectiveness of your teaching.

ACTIVITY 16–2
EVALUATING A LESSON

A lesson plan for an eighth grade science class is described below. Read through the description of the teacher's preparation and topic, and study the teacher's written lesson plan. Then respond to the questions at the end of the section.

Mr. Foster looked forward to planning the eighth grade science class on Monday morning. The topic for consideration was the simple Mendelian ratio of 1:2:1 for the offspring in the first generation produced by crossing of two pure strains. As he thought of the students in his class, it seemed that he might involve them in class participation and generate enthusiasm by doing a demonstration experiment. He would use the crossing of pure white and pure black guinea pigs as a simple case to illustrate this phenomenon.

In pure strains the genes for coat color in the parents could be represented by BB and ww. The only possible combinations in the first generation offspring would be Bw. These animals would be black, but each would carry the gene for white. If animals of this genetic makeup were crossed, the possible combinations in their offspring (second generation) would be BB, Bw, wB, and ww.

To demonstrate the purely statistical nature of the results obtained in this cross and of the effect of dominant over recessive genes, Mr. Foster decided to make a simple arrow spinner that would be attached to the blackboard with a suction cup. Then a circle could be drawn on the blackboard, around the spinner, and labeled as shown in the figure. With this device, he could engage the class in a "game of chance," give them practice in keeping a record of the data shown as follows, and put across the point of the lesson in an interesting manner.

After constructing the spinner, Mr. Foster decided to give it a trial run to see whether it would perform satisfactorily and whether the demonstration could be accommodated in the 50-minute class period. Out of 40 trials, the results he obtained in his trial run were

	BB	BW	WB	WW
Trials:	11	8	11	10

The activity took ten minutes and the results appeared to be close enough to the expected values to illustrate the point. He decided to plan his class period around this demonstration experiment.

On paper, Mr. Foster's lesson plan looked like this:

Life Science 8

Topic: Simple Mendelian ratio
Purpose: To show the statistical nature of the Mendelian ratio
Objective: At the completion of this lesson the student should be able to predict the approximate proportions of each gene combination obtained with 100 trials of the spinner.

Introductory remarks and questions (10 min.):

1. What is meant by dominant gene? By recessive gene?
2. Suppose a pure-bred black and a pure-bred white guinea pig (BB, ww) were mated. What genes have they for color? What would be the color of their offspring?
3. What are the possible combinations of dominant and recessive genes for color of coat? (BB, Bw, wB, ww)
4. What might be the proportions of each of these combinations in the offspring? (1:1:1:1—since Bw and wB are the same, the ratios appear as 1:2:1)
5. How would we show that this is the result of statistical probability?

Activity: Set up the blackboard spinner. Select a volunteer to spin it. Select another volunteer to keep a record on the blackboard under the headings BB, Bw, wB, and ww. Continue for 10–15 minutes.

Discussion (20 min.):

1. What are the actual colors of offspring that have each of the possible gene combinations? (three black and one white)
2. Why aren't the results in an exact ratio of 1:2:1? (change variations when few trials are used)
3. Could we improve the results? (more trials)
4. Student questions (anticipated)

Assignment (a volunteer assignment): Two boys or girls might run this experiment for more trials to see what the results would be.

Evaluation:

Time OK?_____ Interest?_____ Understanding?_____ Student Learning?_____

1. How would you improve Mr. Foster's lesson?
2. What pitfalls and precautions would you advise Mr. Foster about?
3. What features would you identify as a well-planned lesson?

ACTIVITY 16–3
PLANNING A UNIT: PRELIMINARY QUESTIONS

Suppose you are faced with the task of planning and carrying out a unit of work (e.g., four to five weeks) in your teaching area. What questions might you ask yourself? How will you organize your thoughts and plans? Consider each of the following questions:

1. What will be some important factors to take into consideration?

2. How might you involve students in the planning? How much student involvement is desirable?

3. What different levels of planning will probably be necessary?

4. What parts of your plans will you, of necessity, put down in written form?

5. What parts of your plans might you prefer to note mentally but not necessarily write down?

6. How much importance will you grant to a time budget?

7. How will you provide for the anticipated procedure questions and activities of the class? For the unanticipated questions and activities?

8. How will you provide for flexibility so that unexpected events can be handled adequately?

9. What purpose will evaluation serve in subsequent planning?
   a. From the standpoint of knowledge acquired by the students?

   b. From the standpoint of modification of the plans for the next teaching session?

ACTIVITY 16–4
DESIGNING A FULL-YEAR PROGRAM

As best you can, design a year's science program. We have found it best to complete the preliminary items as a way of thinking through your ideas. Then, complete the weekly schedule. You may wish to indicate major units within the weekly outline. Finally, complete the question at the end of the investigation.

Title of Program: Preliminary Textbook:
Discipline: Supplemental Textbook(s):
Grade Level:
Purpose Statement:

Weekly Schedule for an Academic Year: *Unit Topics for an Academic Year:*

1.
2.
3.

Question:

What was your rationale for the sequence, or order, of topics outlined?

ACTIVITY 16–5
A COMPLETE LESSON PLAN

Think through all aspects of a lesson plan. The experience will contribute to your doing this on a less formal basis for future lessons.

Topic
Goals
Objectives
Materials
Instructional Plan
Assessment

ACTIVITY 16–6
EVALUATION OF INSTRUCTIONAL SKILLS

This form is provided for a self-evaluation of a lesson you teach. The evaluation is directed toward the use of strategies, methods, and models discussed in this chapter.

	Highly skilled, superior application and integration	Very skilled, instruction is integrated, evenly consistent, and smooth	Good use of skill but does not apply consistently	Poor application of skill	Unable to observe
Selects appropriate objectives	1	2	3	4	5
Makes objectives and purposes of lesson clear to students	1	2	3	4	5
Teaches to the objective	1	2	3	4	5
1. Asks questions relevant to objective	1	2	3	4	5
2. Provides information relative to objective	1	2	3	4	5
3. Responds to learned questions/ problems related to objectives	1	2	3	4	5
Demonstrates continuity in lesson	1	2	3	4	5
1. Beginning	1	2	3	4	5
2. Middle	1	2	3	4	5
3. End	1	2	3	4	5
Uses different methods	1	2	3	4	5

	Highly skilled, superior application and integration	Very skilled, instruction is integrated, evenly consistent, and smooth	Good use of skill but does not apply consistently	Poor application of skill	Unable to observe
Applies a model of teaching	1	2	3	4	5
1. Concept Mapping	1	2	3	4	5
2. The Learning Cycle	1	2	3	4	5
3. Cooperative Learning	1	2	3	4	5
4. Madeline Hunter	1	2	3	4	5
5. Textbook	1	2	3	4	5
6. 4MAT	1	2	3	4	
Shows continuity of plans	1	2	3	4	5
1. Long Range (year)	1	2	3	4	5
2. Middle Range (unit)	1	2	3	4	5
3. Short Range (daily)	1	2	3	4	5

ACTIVITY 16–7
STUDENT ATTENTION

The following technique can be used to analyze student attention in class. Enlist the aid of another teacher or friend to observe your teaching for a full class period. Provide her with a form similar to the following:

OBSERVATION SHEET

Name _____ Class _____

Date _____ Time _____

Instructions: (a) At intervals of three minutes, count the class members and determine the number of students who are actively paying attention to the lesson or activity. Use your best judgment as to whether a student is paying attention. (b) Keep a record of the types of activities engaged in by the teacher and/or class (e.g., lecture, discussion, demonstration, experiment, film, student report). Note the time of transition from one type of activity to another. Note any major occurrences, such as disciplinary action, public address system coming on, entrance of a visitor, or any unusually distracting event. Plot a graph of percent attention versus time for each class observed.

Total attendance _____

Time	Class Count	Percent	Comments
0	_____	_____	_____
3	_____	_____	_____
6	_____	_____	_____
•			
•			
•			
•			
•			

ACTIVITY 16–8
EFFECTIVENESS OF METHODS

The effectiveness of different teaching methods can often be judged by student attention. In this investigation you are provided with a class attention record for a middle school physical science class. The record is for a week, and the different activities are noted. You are to review the high and low points of the week and draw conclusions about the different methods used and pupil attentiveness.

- How many methods did the teacher use?
- Which methods seemed most effective?

- What can you tell about transitions between activities?
- If you were to redesign the lessons for this, what would you change?

Good advance planning for a lesson or unit is essential for effective teaching. Sharing of ideas with other teachers is important.

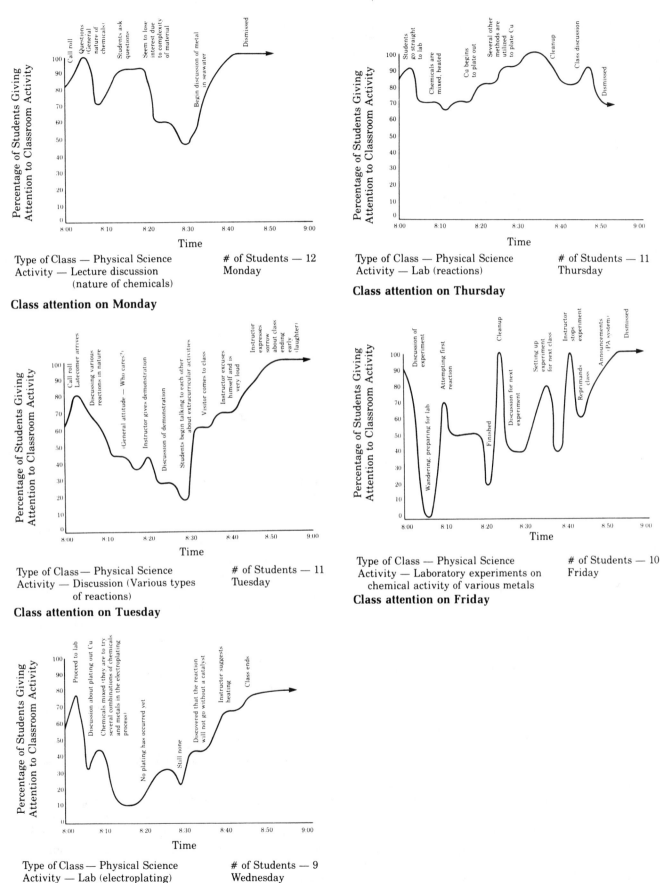

Type of Class — Physical Science   # of Students — 12
Activity — Lecture discussion   Monday
           (nature of chemicals)

Class attention on Monday

Type of Class — Physical Science   # of Students — 11
Activity — Lab (reactions)   Thursday

Class attention on Thursday

Type of Class — Physical Science   # of Students — 11
Activity — Discussion (Various types   Tuesday
           of reactions)

Class attention on Tuesday

Type of Class — Physical Science   # of Students — 10
Activity — Laboratory experiments on   Friday
           chemical activity of various metals

Class attention on Friday

Type of Class — Physical Science   # of Students — 9
Activity — Lab (electroplating)   Wednesday

Class attention on Wednesday

ASSESSING STUDENT LEARNING

As a teacher of science, you have incredible power. The power to help others learn. The power to improve your teaching. Where do you get this power? From assessment! Do you know that you can influence the motivation of students to learn science? That you can modify the study habits of students in your classes? That you have the power to change attitudes and develop new interests and directions for learning?

Most science teachers look at assessment as an unpleasant task—one that unfortunately has to be done and the quicker the better! Because of this, assessment is frequently left until the end of a unit or lesson. Then some kind of test is hastily developed and given to the student: sometimes the test fits what was taught, sometimes it is far removed. However absurd, this happens frequently. These test results are then often put into the form of grades and given to the students, mainly for ranking students and providing reports to parents. The teacher relaxes in the knowledge that the students have been tested, at least for another month or so.

Happily, there is much more to assessment than this. With careful planning and sufficient time to prepare the form of assessment, evaluation can be an integral part of the teaching and learning process. This is what it should be. There is diagnostic evaluation that helps you understand your students' background, knowledge, and skills as you begin teaching. There is formative evaluation in which the assessment helps you learn about student difficulties as you go through class instruction. The kind of assessment you do at the end of your instruction is called summative evaluation and is generally used for giving grades, ranking students, or placing them in groups.

Throughout this book we have been talking about innovative and effective teaching and learning strategies, such as investigative learning and inquiry. These methods require different kinds of assessment than is found in traditional, expository teaching. Especially with the greater emphasis on developing lifelong learning skills, new tests have to be devised that assess those skills.

A common perception among teachers is that evaluation is limited to giving tests. The broader aspects of evaluation—including self-evaluation by students, evaluation of laboratory work, diagnostic, formative, and summative evaluation, and other aspects of the total evaluation process—are sometimes misunderstood by teachers. Most teachers have received little formal training in evaluation, and so their evaluation methods have traditionally tended to be formal, concentrating on quizzes and end-of-term tests.

As a result, instruction and evaluation are thought of as separate entities. In addition, an adversarial relationship seems to exist between the evaluator and those being evaluated, thus minimizing the evaluation's effectiveness and destroying one of the very reasons for doing it—the valid assessment of achievement, attitudes, skill development, and progress. Evaluation should be considered a vital part of instruction and inseparable from it. In this chapter, many illustrations will show the connections between instruction and evaluation.

ASSESSMENT STANDARDS

Science Assessment Standards prepared by the National Committee on Science Education Standards and Assessment (NCSESA) serve as criteria against which to judge the quality of assessment practices used to determine student attainment in science and to determine the opportunity provided students to learn science. These standards serve as guides and statements of principles identifying essential characteristics of exemplary assessment practices. Following is a short list of the standards prepared by the National Research Council.[1,2]

Visit http://www.prenhall.com/trowbridge and select Topic 1—Science Teaching Standards. Select "National Science Teaching Standards," check the hot link for Professional Development Standards and find the website by "EduTel Communications," whose goal is to assist teachers to incorporate existing and emerging technologies into interdisciplinary curricula. This website is particularly useful in handling controversial issues and ethical questions of today, such as human cloning. Use the Chat function to engage in a class discussion about human cloning.

Assessment Standard A provides for Coordination with Intended Purposes in which assessments are deliberately designed, and have explicitly stated purposes.

Under Assessment Standard B—Measuring Student Achievement and Opportunity to Learn—the data collected should focus on science content that is most important for students, and equal attention should be given both to opportunities to learn and to assessment of student achievement.

Under Assessment Standard C—Matching Technical Quality of Data with Consequences—it should be clear that features that are claimed to be measured are actually measured and that assessment tasks are authentic, that is, that they represent similar tasks or performance that is being assessed. Students should have adequate opportunities to demonstrate their achievements.

In Assessment Standard D—Avoiding Bias—assessment practices must be fair. Avoid the use of stereotypes or language that may be offensive to a particular group. Do not assume that experiences or perspectives of a particular group will apply equally to other groups with different backgrounds.

Visit http://www.prenhall.com/trowbridge and select Topic 2—Constructivism and Learning in Science. Select "Activities and Lesson Plans" and find the link for Bad Science. The information found here alerts you to the fact that not all you see, read, or hear is true from a scientific point of view. Think of several examples that may have occurred in your own experience that illustrate this fact and prepare to lead a discussion in your class topic.

An important goal of assessment is to develop self-directed learners. Thus, the students must understand the purpose of the assessment and have opportunities for conversations and input into the assessment practices.

In summary, the standards include focusing on what is most important for students to learn in science and providing data that may lead to valid inferences about students' science attainment. The data collected should be consistent with the particular aspect of science attainment being assessed and should be equally fair for all students. Science teachers should be involved in the design and implementation of the assessment materials and procedures and should consider the intended use of the resulting information. Finally, equal attention should be given to the assessment of the opportunities to learn as well as to student attainment.

Visit http://www.prenhall.com/trowbridge and select Topic 1—Science Teaching Standards. Select "National Science Teaching Standards," click on the assessment standards hot link, and find the link to "Assessing the Nature of Learners' Science Content" using on-line resources. Try this resource and share with other students by using the Electronic Bluebook module.

THE CASE FOR STRENGTHENING ASSESSMENT IN THE SCIENCE CLASSROOM

Evaluation involves the total assessment of students' learning. It includes evaluating their understanding of the process of science, subject-matter competence and achievement, multiple talents, scientific attitudes, laboratory skills, and willingness to work. The progress of the students toward the objectives of the course and goals of the school, as well as the effectiveness of instruction, are considered. Good evaluation indicates the strengths and weaknesses of instruction. Once a teacher has made a thorough assessment, she has an indication of how to improve her teaching. Evaluation acts as feedback in the experimental process of teaching. A teacher must experiment in order to progress and become more skilled. She must be willing to try new methods and new techniques, and, by so doing, evolve toward teaching mastery.

Visit http://www.prenhall.com/trowbridge and select Topic 2—Constructivism and Learning in Science. Select "National Science Teaching Standards," click on the hot link for the assessment standards, and find the website on "Incorporating Assessment into the Learning Process." This site points out the importance of making assessment and instruction two parts of one entity. Devise some ways of doing this in your classroom and share your thoughts with other students in your methods class.

Multiple Purposes of Assessment

Science teaching is an inquiry, not only in the laboratory but in the daily classroom methods and activities. An inquiry approach assumes collection of data to verify the success of the methods used. Assessment techniques are a great source of data. The better the evaluation instruments, the greater the information available to the teacher for improving teaching. Classroom assessment usually falls into one of three categories: diagnostic, formative, or summative.

Diagnostic evaluation normally precedes instruction but may be used during instruction to discover student learning problems. Diagnostic evaluation can provide information to teachers about the knowledge, attitudes, and skills of the students entering a course and can be used as a basis for individual remediation or special instruction.

Formative evaluation is carried on during the instructional period to provide feedback to students and teachers on how well the material is being taught and learned. Since teaching is a dynamic process, formative evaluation can provide useful information that teachers can use to modify instruction and can improve teaching effectiveness so that greater learning and understanding occurs. Black and William define formative assessment as "all those activities undertaken by teachers and by their students [that] provide information to be used as feedback to modify the teaching and learning activities in which they are engaged."[3]

The third kind of evaluation, *summative,* is the kind that is used most often by teachers and is primarily aimed toward providing student grades and reports of achievement. It is most frequently based upon cognitive gains and rarely takes into consideration other areas of the intellect. Summative assessment is generally used at the end of an instructional unit to assess the final outcome of that unit in terms of student learning.

The authors of *Classroom Assessment* and the *National Science Education Standards* recommend that you consider three questions when designing and integrating assessment into your classroom practice:

- Where are you now?
- Where are you trying to go?
- How can you get there?

Visit http://www.prenhall.com/trowbridge and select Topic 2—Constructivism and Learning in Science. Select "National Science Teaching Standards," find the hot link for assessment standards, and find the "How Can Assessment Serve Our Students?" link. This website reflects the voice of experience in attempts at assessing student learning in an authentic manner.

If you keep these questions in mind when you are planning your assessments, you will be able to keep a focus, communicate expectations clearly to your students, and achieve more in your classroom.

The Case for Formative Assessment

There is research that supports the importance of formative assessment in ensuring student understanding of science. For example in Black and William's review of more than 250 articles and books they were able to conclude that formative assessment is an essential component of classroom instruction and, in fact, a necessary component when attempting to raise standards. The significance of formative assessment can only be realized, however, when teachers and students *use* the information gained from the assessment to inform teaching and influence learning. The learning gains possible from systematic attention to the data from formative assessment has been documented to be larger than for any other type of educational intervention.[4] To make sure that formative assessment is an effective tool for increased learning, teachers must focus on the *quality* of their feedback. Research indicates that the use of descriptive, criterion-based feedback is much more useful and effective for the student than numerical scoring or letter grades that do not relate back to clear criteria.[5,6,7,8,9]

The Case for Summative Assessment

Effective summative assessment has a clear and valued target, attends to many facets of learning, including content understanding, application, processes, and reasoning, and includes a role for student reflection.[10,11,12,13] You can accomplish all this in your summative assessment if you plan ahead, use assessment resources, and vary the types of assessments you use. Table 17–1 offers a way to think about approaches for classroom assessment.

The Impact of High-Stakes Assessment

The United States is in an era of high-stakes, large-scale testing that has not been seen since standardized tests were introduced in the early 1900s. At that time, standards tests were used by the Army to determine which specialty to assign to each recruit in preparation for World War I. In the 1920s, IQ tests were used by schools to sort students into different programs, such as college preparation, general education, or vocational program. Then in the 30s and 40s colleges began using national examination as part of the admission process. These uses of national testing pale in comparison to the use of state and national level assessments today.[14]

TABLE 17-1 Assessment Approaches in the Classroom[13]

Selected Response Format	Constructed Response Format			
Multiple choice True-false	Brief Constructed Response	Performance Assessment		
Matching	Fill in the blank	Product	Performance	Process-Focused
Enhanced multiple	Words	Research paper	Oral presentation	Debate
choice	Phrases	Poem	Lab demonstration	Teach-a-lesson
	Short answer	Portfolio	Enactment	Oral question
	Sentences	Project		Observation
	Paragraphs	Model		Interview
	Label a diagram	Video/audio tape		Conference
	Visual	Spreadsheet		Think aloud
	representation	Lab report		Journal
	essay			

These assessments are now administered to every student in districts at multiple grade levels. Public officials then use the scores to rank schools, make financial decisions, determine continued certification, and set teachers' salaries. When you are visiting schools during your teacher education, ask about the role and influence of standardized tests in each school. Use what you learn to formulate questions to ask when you are interviewing for teaching positions.

EVERYONE HAS A ROLE IN ASSESSMENT

The Teacher's Role

Because good assessment is varied, the role of the teacher is varied, also. Above all, the teacher must be prepared. Know what you want your students to learn and what sort of information will count as evidence that the learning has occurred. You will need to have clear criteria that you communicate to students and you will have to allow time to teach your expectations and criteria to the students. Good assessment is not an afterthought; it takes instructional time and should be part of your planning. If you plan for multiple and varied assessments, you will find that you play many roles—coach, facilitator, negotiator, responder, provider of feedback. At the end of this chapter you will see a variety of assessment examples. Review these examples and consider what role you would have for each type of assessment.

The Student's Role

One of the key activities that students must engage in is self-assessment. Most middle and high school students are not inclined to be reflective about their school work. In your role as coach, you will want to encourage self-

reflection and assessment. The goal of this is to help students bridge the gap between what they know and understand and what they *can* know and understand. Brown points out that learning is most effective when the learner has insights into his or her own strengths and weaknesses as a learner.[15] To encourage this type of reflection you can try providing students with journaling tasks, conduct class discussions about learning, or use a peer assessment strategy, helping students set goals and develop plans, or teaching time management skills.

The School's Role

To be able to use a variety of assessment tools comfortably and effectively, it is critical that the school and the district support the use of varied assessments. If teachers do not have this type of support, it will limit their effectiveness in the classroom. As indicated in the assessment standards listed earlier in the chapter, as well as by the data supporting the roles of formative and summative assessment, learning is more effective if instruction and assessment are seamless. To learn more about support for varied assessment, find out the district and school's policies on these issues. Also ask an administrator if s/he would be willing to talk to you about the role of the school in supporting varied assessment in addition to high-stakes assessments.

AN OVERVIEW OF ASSESSMENT TECHNIQUES

Forms of Assessment That Are Not Tests

With the realization that teaching methods in science are expanding to include more inquiry and investigative techniques, there has come an equally important realization that assessment methods must be adjusted to match the newer teaching methods. No longer can teachers rely on traditional paper-and-pencil tests as the sole means of assessing student progress and achievement. Students are aware that for fairness in evaluation of their work in science classes, efforts must be made to develop authentic assessment techniques that get to the heart of the tasks they are expected to perform. Teachers sensitive to this need are developing a host of alternative assessment techniques to deal with the enlarged variety of activities students engage in during their studies in science. Among these techniques are concept mapping, creative assessments, journals, oral interviews, essay, portfolios, observations, projects, extended tasks, open-ended labs, and others. These techniques should be planned to fit the type of activity or instruction in which students are engaged.

Concept Mapping

Concept mapping is a means of organizing ideas. It is used in instruction and can be used in assessment as well. Students begin by identifying the major and minor concepts of a topic under study, then organizing these concepts in hierarchical relationships. When used as assessment tools, concept maps provide the teacher with information on how students relate the concepts they have learned. In this way, a better picture of the students' understanding of the topic can be ascertained.

When analyzing the concept maps produced by students, the teacher should look for concepts that are definitely related to the topic at hand, show a hierarchical relationship from simple to more complex, are informative as to scientific accuracy, and are replete with examples showing how the concepts are or can be applied in real situations. Assessments of this type are of necessity quite subjective and should be used to glean clues as to the students' misunderstandings or misconceptions.

Creative Assessment

In creative assessment, students are given the opportunity to show what they have learned in a nontraditional manner. Some students might use scrap books, home videos, or cartoons to show information and relationships that illustrate what they have learned in the unit. Instead of simply recalling facts, they can use higher level thinking skills, such as application, analysis, synthesis, or evaluation. To implement creative assessment in the classroom, the teacher might spend a short time suggesting the kinds of things students could do to show their knowledge. This should not in any way limit their creativity, but many students need guidance to avoid frustration, especially if this is the first time they have been exposed to nontraditional ways of assessing

their progress. By its very nature, this form of assessment is quite subjective and should be used as motivation or formative evaluation during instruction in a unit.

Visit http://www.prenhall.com/trowbridge and select Topic 3—Alternative Assessments. Select "Web Links" and find the website for "Alternative Assessment in K–12 Science Education." This paper discusses the changing face of assessment in science education and is an important source of ideas. Take a position on "accountability" actions in many states and on the national scene. Submit your thoughts to your instructor by using the Electronic Bluebook module.

Journals and Oral Interviews

The first of these provides a teacher with information of a sequential nature showing how students have progressed in their study of the science material. Some teacher guidance is needed to help students focus on the topics at hand and avoid irrelevancies. Some questions of the type "How might this information help you plan a traveling vacation?" or "What new facts did you learn that could make your life more interesting?" might help guide the students' responses. Journal entries should be regular and need not be voluminous. They should promote reflective thinking and may generate further questions for study.

Some students are more adept at speaking than writing. Oral interviews in a relaxed atmosphere may supply information to the teacher and student alike that will benefit future work. They give the teacher an opportunity to provide verbal support to students as well as to obtain clues about their study habits, difficulties of understanding certain topics, misconceptions, and gaps in knowledge. Students, at the same time, may gain a better understanding of what is expected, the location of resources, and a realistic measure of their own strengths and weaknesses. This type of assessment is most useful when coordinated with instruction in the formative stages of development of the unit or chapter.

Portfolios

A portfolio is put together by a teacher for individual students, using materials produced by the student. These materials can include a large variety of products, such as worksheets, pictures, assignments completed, data sheets, written conclusions, experiment reports, maps, stories, plans, and any other written materials related to the work completed for a unit or course. It is usually long range—perhaps up to a year, or longer—and can form the basis for other types of assessments, such as interviews and conferences. An advantage of a portfolio is that it is highly individualized and avoids to some extent the syndrome all teachers have—that of comparing students with other students in a competitive atmosphere. Another advantage is that the students can use the enclosed materials to evaluate themselves and gain a more realistic picture of their own accomplishments.

 Visit http://www.prenhall.com/trowbridge and select Topic 3—Alternative Assessments. Select "Web Links" and find the website on "Assessment Resources," which has been prepared by the Columbia Education Center. This website can help you design alternative assessments in an effective manner. Prepare a presentation on alternative assessment for your instructor by using the Electronic Bluebook module.

Practical Assessment

This method of assessment provides information on students' skill and problem-solving abilities through the use of apparatus setups, experiments, and open-ended situations that can reveal certain thinking processes. Students who have become familiar with investigative learning will be able to display their abilities to best advantage. Students who have been taught in highly traditional, expository classes will find this method of assessment distasteful and possibly unfair. One should not expect students to perform satisfactorily in an assessment procedure that is strange or different from the instructional methods they have experienced.

GENERAL GUIDELINES FOR USING TESTS

When you are confronted with the prospect of preparing a test, there are several methods that will contribute to appropriate, effective evaluation. Some guidelines for testing are listed here:

1. Use tests humanely as learning and diagnostic devices. Give students opportunities to demonstrate that they have learned what they missed on a test; adjust the grade.
2. Never use a test as a punishment.
3. Minimize the use of completion and matching questions.
4. Use tests or self-evaluation inventories to evaluate all of your behavioral objectives, including science processes and attitudes.
5. Spend time with each student going over missed questions. This may be done while the class is involved in laboratory work.

6. Remember that tests are only a sample of what has been learned, and probably not a very good one. Therefore, they should not be used as the only means of evaluation.
7. Ask questions to determine how students feel about the material being used.
8. Place the easier questions at the beginning of the test so students gain confidence and minimize their frustration and nervousness.
9. Consider the time factor. How long will it take students to complete the test? Some students will finish much sooner than others. What will you do with them? If you do not have some work outlined, they are likely to present discipline problems.
10. Design the test to be easily scored. Leave a space for all the answers on one margin.
11. Rather than having the students write on the test, have them place their responses on an answer sheet. This procedure ensures ease of recording and saves paper since the test may be used for more than one class.
12. Encourage honesty. Remove the temptation to copy by spreading students out or by making two versions of the same test and alternating them when you pass out the tests. You may wish to try the honor system; some instructors in high school have used this with success. Set a pattern of honesty immediately in your classes.

Accounting for Student Individuality When Using Science Tests

Problems in interpreting and using tests may occur for students who are not native English speakers, have a learning disability or read below grade level, have low motivation, or have test anxiety. The results of such tests are usually suspect when there are wide differences in home environments, which may not provide opportunities to learn the types of tasks included on the tests. Some of the techniques a science teacher can use to minimize the differences in test results include the following:

1. Nonverbal tests can be prepared, using diagrams and pictures familiar to the various culture groups being tested. In the case of language difficulties, use of translations might be considered.
2. Attempts can be made to use items that are intrinsically interesting to the students to encourage motivation. Selection of items that have relevance to the experiences of the test takers will increase their likelihood of success.
3. Make time less of a factor—write tests so they are not dependent on speed as an important condition for success on the test.

4. Keep the test procedures simple and the instructions clear.
5. Base the content of the test on intellectual skills and knowledge that are familiar to the group being tested.

Problem Tests

This kind of test presents a problem and asks the students to work on it. A problem test is similar to an invitation to inquiry except that it is done by an individual student. The test usually contains a series of questions that the students must answer to solve the problem. A problem test can be constructed with relative ease if it is based on a problem that has actually confronted a scientist—problems that can be easily obtained from a scientific journal. The teacher gives the students information about the problem and has them devise their own hypotheses, research designs, or methods of collecting and recording data. A problem test can best be used to acquaint students with scientific processes. The test may have an answer sheet similar to that for a self-test, or it may be used to stimulate discussion.

Open-ended scientific problems are preferable for this kind of test. Some examples of problems that might be used in constructing a test of this nature are:

1. How would you reduce the amount of pollution from a smoke stack?
2. A citizen thought the local river was polluted. How could he find out? What experiments could he do?
3. A scientist thought fungus might produce a chemical that inhibits the growth of bacteria. What kind of experiments must she conduct to verify her hypothesis?
4. What are some general considerations to be kept in mind when making a true-false, a multiple-choice, and a completion test?
5. Prepare a picture or problem test.

True-False Tests

If the examination is limited to true or false questions, statistics show that 75 or more items are necessary to overcome the guessing factor. On a 100-question true-or-false test, students should be able to answer about 50 questions correctly merely by guessing. According to some, this problem can be eliminated by subtracting the number of wrong answers from the number of right ones to determine the score; they penalize for guessing. This procedure is not recommended, however, because students usually think the instructor is using the technique maliciously. It is also undesirable because the student is penalized for guessing; in science, we wish to have students make hypotheses—that is, good guesses.

Avoid overbalancing the test with too many true or too many false questions. Try to make them fairly even in number so that a student who knows a little about the material cannot get a high score simply by assuming that more questions are true (or false). Here are some other suggestions:

- Avoid using statements that might trick students.
- Do not use the same language as in the text, or students will tend to memorize.
- Do not use double negatives in a statement.
- Avoid ambiguous statements. For example, do not write, "Erosion is prevented by seeding."
- Avoid using complex sentences in your statements.
- Do not use qualitative language if you can possibly avoid it. Do not write, for example, "Good corn grows at a slower rate than hybrid corn," or "The better metals conduct electricity faster."
- Arrange your statements in groups of 10 to 20. This procedure relieves excessive tension for students.
- Put answer blocks on one margin so that they can be easily checked using a key.

Multiple-Choice Tests

A multiple-choice test is composed of items having more than three responses. If there are not at least four possible responses to each question, a correction formula should be used. A multiple-choice test differs from a multiple-response test in that only one answer is correct for each question in the first type of test. We suggest the following approaches:

- In a multiple-choice test, make all responses plausible.
- All answers should be grammatically consistent.
- Try to keep all responses about the same length.
- Randomize the correct answers so that there is no pattern in the examination. Students often look for a pattern.
- Remember that the correct response often can be determined by a process of elimination as well as by knowing the correct answer. Try to prevent this in phrasing the answers.
- Present first the term or concept you wish to test for.
- Test for the higher levels of understanding as much as possible.
- Require a simple method for the response. Provide short lines for the answers along one margin of a page so they can be easily keyed.
- Group your items in sections. This system makes it easy to refer to various sections of the test and helps break the monotony in taking the test.
- Group together all questions with the same number of choices.

Completion and Matching Tests

Since completion and matching tests usually emphasize recall and are often verbally tricky, they should be minimized. If matching questions are used, they should be grouped. When there are more than 15 matching items in a group, the test becomes cumbersome. Number your questions and use letters for your answers, or the reverse, but be consistent. Have more matching choices than questions to minimize obtaining answers by elimination. Although matching tests have traditionally stressed simple recall, they can be used to test for recognition or application principles. Three sample matching questions follow:

1. A machine that would require the least amount of friction to move it 20 feet.
2. A machine that could best be used to pry open a box.
3. Which of the listed devices is made up of the greatest number of simple machines?
   a. Pliers
   b. Wheelbarrow
   c. Ice tongs
   d. Seesaw
   e. Doorknob

f. Pencil sharpener
g. Saw

SUMMARY

Classroom assessment can be characterized as diagnostic, formative, or summative. In addition, students and teachers may have to participate in district or state mandated assessments. In designing classroom assessments it is important to remember the significance of high-quality formative assessments as a powerful, positive effect on student learning and achievement. Teachers should think of assessment as a means for improving their own classroom practice, planning curricula, developing self-reflecting learners, and reporting student progress. Student participation in the assessment process is essential. You will need to vary your assessment tools and techniques to provide ample opportunities for students to demonstrate their growing competencies and understandings. By making assessment seamless with instruction, you will not lose instructional time when you stop to assess—you will gain it!

◆

REFERENCES

1. National Research Council, *National Science Education Standards* (Washington, DC: National Academy Press, 1996), pp. IV–6 to IV–18. [also available online at www.nap.edu]
2. National Research Council, *Classroom Assessment and the National Science Education Standards* (Washington, DC: National Academy Press, 2001). [also available online at www.nap.edu]
3. P. Williams and D. William. "Assessment and Classroom Learning," *Assessment in Education,* 5 (1), (1998): 7–74. [Quotation is from page 7.]
4. P. Williams and D. William. "Inside the Black Box: Raising Standards through Classroom Assessment," *Phi Delta Kappan* 80 (2) (1998): 139–148.
5. R. L. Bangert-Downs, C. C-L. Kulik, J. A. Kulik, and M.T. Morgan, "The Instructional Effect of Feedback in Test-Like Events," *Review of Education Research* 61 (2) (1991): 213–238.
6. R. Sadler, "Formative Assessment and the Design of Instructional Systems," *Instructional Science* 18 (1989): 119–144.
7. R. Butler and O. Neuman, "Effects of Task and Ego-Achievement Goals on Help-seeking Behaviours and Attitudes," *Journal of Educational Psychology* 87 (2) (1995): 261–271.
8. J. Cameron and D. P. Pierce, "Reinforcement, Reward, and Intrinsic Motivation: A Meta-analysis," *Review of Educational Research* 64 (3) (1994): 363–423.
9. A. N. Kluger and A. deNisi, "The Effects of Feedback Interventions on Performance: A Historical Review, A Meta-analysis, and a Preliminary Feedback Intervention Theory," *Psychological Bulletin* 119 (2) (1996): 254–284.
10. National Research Council, *Classroom Assessment and the National Science Education Standards* (Washington, DC: National Academy Press, 2001). [also available online at www.nap.edu]
11. R. J. Stiggins, *Student-involved Classroom Assessment* (3rd ed. Columbus, OH: Merrill Prentice Hall 2001).
12. R. Sadler, "Formative Assessment and the Design of Instructional Systems," *Instructional Science,* 18 (1989): 119–144.
13. J. McTighe and S. Ferrara, *Assessing Learning in the Classroom* (Washington, DC: National Education Association, 1998).
14. National Research Council, *Classroom Assessment and the National Science Education Standards* (Washington, DC: National Academy Press, 2001). [also available online at www.nap.edu]
15. A. L. Brown, "The Advancement of Learning," *Educational Researcher* 23 (8) (1994): 4–12.

THE PSYCHOLOGICAL BASIS
FOR EFFECTIVE SCIENCE TEACHING

In this chapter we review the general areas of *motivation, learning, development,* and *group behavior.* We place this review in the context of science teaching, which will provide you with a meaningful perspective on psychology. This chapter uses a set of *Learner-Centered Psychological Principles* adapted from a report from the American Psychological Association (APA)[1] and the Mid-continent Regional Educational Laboratory (McREL), the National Science Teachers Association's *Handbook of Research on Science Teaching and Learning,*[2] and two National Research Council publications, *The Science of Learning,*[3] and *How People Learn: Brain, Mind, Experience, and School*[4] as foundations. As a science teacher you also will be interested in the publication, *Learning Science and the Science of Learning,*[5] which translates many of the ideas from these publications, especially *How People Learn,* into practical strategies for science teaching. This chapter also includes several activities that you can use to investigate various aspects of psychology and science teaching.

LEARNER-CENTERED
PSYCHOLOGICAL PRINCIPLES

In 1990, Charles D. Spielberger initiated a Presidential Task Force on Psychology in Education with the goal of synthesizing the knowledge base from psychology and education and applying it to learners and learning. That project resulted in a publication titled *Learner-Centered Psychological Principles.* In this section, we present the principles as they were reproduced in a 1993 report from the APA and McREL. The first ten principles refer

to metacognitive and cognitive, affective, developmental, and social factors. The remaining two principles address individual differences. In the discussion following these principles, we have adapted the original discussions for science teaching. The *Learner-Centered Psychological Principles* provides you with a holistic perspective of students. The following discussion includes many ideas and theories that have direct application to your work as a science teacher. You will recognize the ideas of theorists such as David Ausubel, Albert Bandura, and Abraham Maslow,[6,7,8] Jean Piaget,[9,10] and Carl Rogers,[11] as well as contemporary ideas such as constructivism,[12] conceptual change,[13,14,15] and cooperative learning.[16,17,18]

Metacognitive and Cognitive Factors

PRINCIPLE 1: THE NATURE OF THE LEARNING PROCESS

Learning occurs naturally, through pursuit of personally meaningful goals. It is an active, volitional, and internally mediated process of discovering and constructing meaning from information and experience. Experiences, including those with the natural and designed world, are filtered through the learner's unique perceptions, thoughts, and feelings.

You should assume that science students want to pursue personally relevant learning goals. They are capable of assuming personal responsibility for learning; for example, monitoring their progress, checking for understanding, and engaging in self-directed learning. Science teachers should establish an environment that recognizes past learning, ties new learning to personal goals, and engages students in the learning process. During this process, students develop meanings and in-

Careful attention must be paid to details of measurement, observation, and data-gathering in order for learning in laboratory work to be successful.

terpretations based on current knowledge, understandings, and beliefs. Support for this principle comes from a constructivist/cognitive learning perspective.[19–32]

PRINCIPLE 2: GOALS OF THE LEARNING PROCESS

Learners create meaningful, coherent representations of knowledge regardless of the quantity and quality of data available.

As students learn science, they generate integrated mental representations and subsequent verbal explanations for their experiences. Sometimes those explanations may demonstrate poorly understood or inadequately developed facts, concepts, principles, or theories of science. Learning processes operate holistically in the sense that science students develop internally consistent understandings that may be inconsistent with an objective, externally oriented perspective of scientific knowledge. As learners internalize values and meanings within science, however, they can refine their conceptions by incorporating missing ideas, resolving inconsistencies, and changing current conceptions so they are consistent with accepted scientific explanations. The second principle is supported by research on human learning, memory, and cognition.[33,34]

PRINCIPLE 3: THE CONSTRUCTION OF KNOWLEDGE

Learners link new information with extant and future-oriented knowledge in uniquely meaningful ways.

Science teachers understand that learners organize information in ways that are important and understandable to the individual. The unique knowledge construction of students is the result of their backgrounds and experiences. Their understanding of science is based on constructions of knowledge through linkages of experience with mental concepts.

Given that backgrounds and experiences of individual students can differ dramatically, and that the mind works to link information, science education aims to have all learners create shared understandings and conceptions regarding fundamental knowledge and skills that define and lead to valued outcomes relative to the sciences—for example, the *National Science Education Standards*[35] and *Benchmarks for Science Literacy*.[36]

Science teachers can assist learners in acquiring and integrating knowledge by helping them with strategies for constructing meaning, organizing content, accessing prior knowledge, relating new knowledge to science concepts and principles, storing or practicing what they have learned, and visualizing future uses for the science knowledge. Research supporting principle number three is from developmental and cognitive psychology.[37–41]

PRINCIPLE 4: HIGHER-ORDER THINKING

Higher-order strategies for *thinking about thinking* (i.e., for reflecting on and monitoring one's own mental operations) can facilitate creative and critical thinking and the development of expertise.

By the time science students enter middle school, they are generally capable of thinking about their own thinking. Such metacognitive strategies include self-awareness; self-inquiry or dialogue; self-monitoring; and self-regulation of the processes and contents of thoughts, knowledge structures, and memories. As science students become aware of and use metacognitive strategies, they also develop higher levels of commitment, persistence, and involvement in learning. From a science teacher's perspective, you should understand that learners require settings where their personal interests, values, and goals are respected and accommodated. Research in the areas of metacognition, cognitive learning strategies, and novice/expert development form the research base for this principle.[42]

Affective Factors

PRINCIPLE 5: MOTIVATIONAL INFLUENCES ON LEARNING

The depth and breadth of information processed, and what and how much is learned and remembered, are influenced by (1) self-awareness and beliefs about personal control, competence, and ability; (2) clarity and saliency of personal values, interests, and goals; (3) personal expectations for success or failure; (4) affect, emotion, and general states of mind; and (5) the resulting motivation to learn.

Students' constellation of beliefs, goals, expectations, and feelings can enhance or interfere with their quality of thinking and processing of scientific information. The relationship among thoughts, mood, and behavior underlies individuals' mental health and ability to learn. As a science teacher, you should recognize that learners' cognitive constructions of reality affect motivation, learning, and performance. Positive learning experiences in science can change any negative thoughts and feelings and enhance student motivation to learn science. Research on intrinsic motivation, attribution theory, emotion, and self-esteem (as it relates to motivation) support this principle.[43-46]

PRINCIPLE 6: INTRINSIC MOTIVATION TO LEARN

Individuals are naturally curious and enjoy learning, but intense negative cognitions and emotions (e.g., feeling insecure; worrying about failure; being self-conscious or shy; and fearing corporal punishment, ridicule, or stigmatizing labels) thwart this enthusiasm.

Science teachers who support and develop students' natural curiosity and intrinsic motivation to learn, rather than using fear of corporal punishment, will experience greater interest and learning in the classroom. Both positive interpersonal support and instruction in self-control strategies can enhance learning by offsetting factors that interfere with optimal learning—factors such as low self-awareness, negative beliefs, lack of learning goals, negative expectations for success, anxiety, insecurity, or pressure. Research supporting this principle was synthesized from the areas of intrinsic motivation, anxiety, and curiosity.[47,48,49]

PRINCIPLE 7: CHARACTERISTICS OF MOTIVATION-ENHANCING LEARNING TASKS

Curiosity, creativity, and higher-order thinking are stimulated by relevant, authentic learning tasks of optimal difficulty and novelty.

As science teachers create classrooms that learners perceive as personally relevant and meaningful, they also will witness positive effect, creativity, and insight. For example, science students need opportunities to make choices based on their interests and to have the freedom to change the course of learning in light of self-awareness, discovery, or insights. Science investigations similar to real-world situations in complexity and duration will develop students' higher-order thinking skills and creativity. In addition, curiosity is enhanced when students work on personally significant tasks of optimal difficulty and novelty. Motivation, learning goals, and higher-order thinking provide the research foundation for this principle.[50-53]

Developmental Factors

PRINCIPLE 8: DEVELOPMENTAL CONSTRAINTS AND OPPORTUNITIES

Individuals progress through stages of physical, intellectual, emotional, and social development. Developmental stages are a function of unique genetic and environmental factors.

Science students learn best when instructional material is both appropriate to their developmental level and is presented in an enjoyable and interesting way. Investigations and activities in the science classroom should appropriately challenge students' intellectual, emotional, physical, and social development. Unique environmental factors—such as the quality of language interactions between teachers and students, and parental involvement in students' schooling—can significantly influence development. An overemphasis on developmental readiness, however, may preclude learners from demonstrating that they are more capable intellectually than schools, teachers, or parents understand. Awareness and understanding of developmental differences of students with special emotional, physical, or intellectual disabilities, as well as special abilities, can greatly affect efforts to create optimal contexts for learning. This principle is based on research from developmental psychology.[54]

Personal and Social Factors

PRINCIPLE 9: SOCIAL AND CULTURAL DIVERSITY

Learning is facilitated by social interactions and communication with others in flexible (i.e., small groups, personal discussions), diverse (i.e., different ages, cultures, family backgrounds), and adaptive (i.e., laboratory settings, field trips, computers) instructional settings.

Technology Link

Learning science is facilitated when students have an opportunity to interact with students of different cultural and family backgrounds, interests, and values. Classroom situations and student groups that allow for and respect diversity encourage flexible thinking as well as social competence and moral development. Individual students should have opportunities to hear and respond to different perspectives, express one's own perspective, and reflect on the thoughts and views of others, thereby developing insights and formulating new levels of science comprehension. Research in social constructivism, adaptive instruction, and cultural diversity supports this principle.[55,56,57]

PRINCIPLE 10: SOCIAL ACCEPTANCE, SELF-ESTEEM, AND LEARNING

Learning and self-esteem are heightened when individuals are in respectful and caring relationships with others who see their potential, genuinely appreciate their unique talents, and accept them as individuals.

Students need personal relationships that give them access to higher-order, healthier levels of thinking, feeling, and behaving. Teachers' states of mind, stability, trust, and caring are preconditions to help students establish a sense of belonging, self-respect, and self-acceptance. Self-esteem and learning can be mutually reinforcing in the science classroom. Research from social psychology, personality theory, and self-esteem support this principle.[58,59,60]

Individual Differences

PRINCIPLE 11: INDIVIDUAL DIFFERENCES IN LEARNING

Although basic principles of learning, motivation, and effective instruction apply to all students regardless of ethnicity, race, gender, physical ability, religion, or socioeconomic status, learners have different capabilities, strategies, and preferences for learning. These differences are a function of environment (i.e., what is learned and communicated in different cultures or other social groups) and heredity (i.e., what occurs naturally as a function of genes).

Curricular and environmental conditions are important factors that also affect learning outcomes. As a science teacher you should try to understand and value cultural differences and the cultural contexts in which learners develop. Such an understanding enhances the possibilities for designing and implementing a learning environment of a science classroom that encourages science literacy for all students. This principle is based on research from social and developmental psychology, and individual differences.[61]

PRINCIPLE 12: COGNITIVE FILTERS

Personal beliefs, knowledge, and perceptions resulting from prior learning and current interpretations form an individual's basis for constructing reality and interpreting life experiences.

Science students have unique cognitive constructions that form a basis for beliefs and attitudes about others. Individuals use these *separate realities* as if they were true for everyone. Such behaviors can lead to misconceptions and cognitive conflict. Awareness of these

phenomena allows greater choice in what students believe. It also offers more control over the degree to which students' beliefs influence their actions and enable them to see and take into account other points of view. The cognitive, emotional, and social development of a student and the way that student interprets life experiences result from prior schooling, home, culture, and community factors. Research on belief systems, thinking, and self-system variables support this principle.[62–65]

IMPLICATIONS FOR SCIENCE TEACHING

As a science teacher you recognize the importance of research and its role in the formulation of knowledge about the natural world. Research from psychology in areas such as cognition, motivation, development, and social interactions provides the science teacher with valuable insights about students—their classroom behavior and their ability to learn. The only trouble is, you have to apply this knowledge in the instructional strategies you use, the curriculum you design, and the criteria you use for assessment. In this section, we outline some implications of the discussion on learner-centered psychological principles. Our theme is applying psychology for effective science teaching, science curriculum, and science assessment.

Effective Science Teaching

The learner-centered principles have implications for science teachers and teaching. We have limited the discussion to those implications that are based on the APA and McREL report, those described in the *Handbook of Research on Science Teaching and Learning,* and those that are consistent with recommendations of the *National Science Education Standards:*

- Effective science teaching involves students in inquiry-oriented activities that engage their curiosity.
- Effective science teaching provides opportunities for students to explore ideas and make connections among extant scientific knowledge, new information, and their current conceptions.
- Effective science teaching provides opportunities for student-teacher and student-student interactions that center on science-related experiences.
- Effective science teaching includes a concern for extant scientific knowledge and the incorporation of that knowledge into students' formulation of meaning and understanding.
- Effective science teaching encourages students to elaborate and generalize their understandings through new inquiries, investigations, debates, group

projects, and personal actions that require higher-order thinking.

- Effective science teaching employs policies and strategies that ensure fairness, a regard for students, and a safe learning atmosphere.

Effective Science Curriculum

Although you will probably inherit a school district's curriculum framework, instructional materials, and textbooks, you will have opportunities to improve the science curriculum through your modifications and additions and through the adoptions of new instructional materials and development of new school science programs. An important consideration of curriculum improvement would certainly include the following principles:

- Effective science curricula include inquiry-oriented activities and investigations that engage students in the development of scientific knowledge and their cognitive abilities.
- Effective science curricula provide a variety of opportunities for students to actively engage in the construction of scientific explanations, the testing of those explanations against scientific knowledge, and the opportunity to communicate scientific explanations.
- Effective science curricula are developmentally appropriate for the unique aspects of students—intellectual, emotional, social, and physical.
- Effective science curricula include authentic tasks and performance assessments.
- Effective science curricula incorporate activities and strategies that encourage all students to interact and develop positive perceptions of other students regardless of race, gender, culture, physical abilities, or other individual differences.
- Effective science curricula recognize the importance of psychological factors, such as affective and emotional development, higher-order thinking, metacognitive strategies, reflective self-awareness, and personal goal setting.

Effective Science Assessments

Science teachers continually assess student progress. Some assessments are informal and rely on qualitative judgment about student work. Other assessments are formal in the sense that they are included in the curriculum and instruction and provide explicit feedback about student learning. We provide some ideas about effective science assessments:

- Effective science assessments are embedded in the instructional activities and are consistent with the goals of the science program.
- Effective science assessments focus on personal achievement more than group comparisons.
- Effective science assessments provide teachers, students, and parents with information about (1) the opportunities students have had to learn science concepts and processes as described in standards, and (2) student growth and performance relative to developmentally appropriate standards.
- Effective science assessments provide opportunities for students to identify examples of successful work and progress.
- Effective science assessments strive to avoid bias and provide a fair evaluation of student learning.
- Effective science assessments incorporate opportunities for students' reflection on their progress and on feedback from others.

SUMMARY

This chapter used *Learner-Centered Psychological Principles* based on a synthesis of research from psychology and the *Handbook of Research in Science Teaching and Learning, How People Learn,* and *Learning Science and the Science of Learning* as the basis for discussion. Those 12 principles included

1. the nature of the learning process;
2. goals of the learning process;
3. the construction of knowledge;
4. higher-order thinking;
5. motivational influences on learning;
6. intrinsic motivation to learn;
7. characteristics of motivation-enhancing learning tasks;
8. developmental constraints and opportunities;
9. social and cultural diversity;
10. social acceptance, self-esteem, and learning;
11. individual difference in learning; and
12. cognitive filters.

Science teachers should consider these principles as they are consistent with decades of psychological research from a variety of areas, such as clinical, developmental, social, cognitive, and personality. Very important, these principles offer science teachers a holistic view of students and the various factors that affect learning.

The chapter also included implications of these psychological principles for teaching, curriculum, and assessment.

◆
_____

REFERENCES

1. American Psychological Association and the Mid-continent Regional Educational Laboratory (McCrel), *Learner-Centered Psychological Principles: Guidelines for School Redesign and Reform* (Washington, DC: American Psychological Association, January 1993).

2. National Science Teachers Association, *Handbook of Research on Science Teaching and Learning,* D. Gabel, ed. (New York: Macmillan Publishing Company, 1994).

3. National Research Council, *The Science of Learning* (Washington, DC: National Academy Press, 1998).

4. John Bransford, Ann Brown, and Rodney Cocking, eds., *How People Learn: Brain, Mind, Experience, and School* (Washington, DC: National Academy Press, 2000).

5. Rodger W. Bybee, ed., *Learning Science and the Science of Learning* (Arlington, VA: NSTA Press, 2002).

6. Abraham Maslow, *Motivation and Personality* (New York: Harper & Row, 1970).

7. Abraham Maslow, *The Farther Reaches of Human Nature* (New York: Viking Press, 1971).

8. Abraham Maslow, *Toward a Psychology of Being* (New York: Van Nostrand Reinhold, 1968).

9. Jean Piaget, *The Development of Thought: Equilibration of Cognitive Structures* (New York: Viking Press, 1977).

10. Jean Piaget and Barbel Inhelder, *The Psychology of the Child* (New York: Basic Books, 1969).

11. Carl R. Rogers, *Freedom to Learn* (Columbus, OH: Charles E. Merrill, 1969). See also Rogers, *Freedom to Learn for the '80s* (Columbus, OH: Charles E. Merrill, 1983).

12. Ken Tobin, W. Capie, and A. Bettencourt, "Active Teaching for Higher Cognitive Learning in Science," *International Journal of Science Education,* 10 (1) (1988): 17–27.

13. B. Watson and R. Konicek, "Teaching for Conceptual Change: Confronting Children's Experience," *Phi Delta Kappan,* 71 (9) (1990): 680–685.

14. Peter Hewson, "A Conceptual Change Approach to Learning Science," *European Journal of Science Education,* 3 (4) (1981): 383–396.

15. P. Hewson and M. Hewson, "An Appropriate Conception of Teaching Science: A View from Studies in Learning," *Science Education,* 72 (5) (1988): 597–614.

16. David Johnson and Roger Johnson, "The Socialization and Achievement Crisis: Are Cooperative Learning Experiences the Solution?" *Applied Social Psychology Annual 4,* L. Bickman, ed. (Beverly Hills, CA: Sage Publications, 1983).

17. David Johnson et al., "Effects of Cooperative, Competitive, and Individualistic Goal Structures on Achievement: A Meta-Analysis," *Psychological Bulletin,* 89 (1) (1981): 47–62.

18. R. E. Slavin, "Cooperative Learning and Student Achievement," *Educational Leadership,* 45 (2) (1988): 31–33.

19. A. Bandura, "Human Agency in Social Cognitive Theory," *American Psychologist,* 44 (9) (1989): 1,175–1,184.

20. J. G. Brooks and M. G. Brooks, *The Case for Constructivist Classrooms* (Alexandria, VA: Association for Supervision and Curriculum Development, 1993).

21. H. Gardner and W. Boix-Mansilla, "Teaching for Understanding—Within and Across the Disciplines," *Educational Leadership,* 51 (1994): 14–18.

22. R. Glaser, "Education and Thinking: The Role of Knowledge." *American Psychologist,* 39 (1984): 93–104.

23. J. W. Getzels and P. W. Jackson, *Creativity and Intelligence* (New York: John Wiley and Sons, Inc., 1962).

24. Abraham Maslow, *The Farther Reaches of Human Nature* (London: Penguin, 1983). (Original work published 1971.)

25. B. L. McCombs, "Learner-Centered Psychological Principles for Enhancing Education: Applications in School Settings," in *The Challenge in Mathematics and Science Education: Psychology's Response,* L. A. Penner, G. M. Batsche, H. M. Knoff, and D. L. Nelson, eds. (Washington, DC: American Psychological Association, 1993.)

26. B. L. McCombs and R. J. Marzano, "Putting the Self in Self-Regulated Learning," *Educational Psychologist,* 25 (1) (1990): 51–69.

27. Jean Piaget, "Development and Learning, Part I of Cognitive Development in Children," *Journal of Research in Science Teaching,* 2 (3) (1964): 1–10.

28. Jean Piaget, *The Construction of Reality in the Child,* trans. M. Cook (New York: Basic Books, 1954).

29. D. Kuhn, "Thinking As Argument," *Harvard Educational Review,* 62 (2) (1992): 155–178.

30. N. Burbules and M. Linn, "Response to Contradiction: Scientific Reasoning during Adolescence," *Journal of Educational Psychology,* 80 (1) (1988): 67–75.

31. B. Eylon and M. Linn, "Learning and Instruction: An Examination of Four Research Perspectives in Science Education," *Review of Educational Research,* 58 (3) (1988): 251–301.

32. Anton E. Lawson, "Research on the Acquisition of Science Knowledge: Epistemological Foundation of Recognition," in *Handbook of Research on Science Teaching and Learning,* D. Gabel, ed. (New York: Macmillan Publishing Company, 1994).

33. David P. Ausubel, *Educational Psychology: A Cognitive View* (New York: Academic Press, 1968).

34. James Wondersee, Joel Mintzes, and Joseph Novak, "Research on Alternative Conceptions in Science," in the *Handbook of Research on Science Teaching and Learning,* D. Gabel, ed. (New York: Macmillan Publishing Company, 1994).

35. National Research Council, *National Science Education Standards* (Washington, DC: Author, 1996).

36. American Association for the Advancement of Science, *Benchmarks for Science Literacy* (Washington, DC: Author, 1993).

37. J. Anderson, *The Architecture of Cognition* (Cambridge, MA: Harvard University Press, 1983).

38. S. Carey, "Cognitive Science and Science Education," *American Psychologist,* 41 (10) (1986): 1,123–1,130.

39. M. Linn, C. Clement, S. Pulos, and S. Sullivan, "Scientific Reasoning during Adolescence: The Influence of Instruction in Science Knowledge and Reasoning Strategies," *Journal of Research in Science Teaching,* 26 (2) (1989): 171–187.

40. Lawson, "Research on the Acquisition of Science Knowledge."

41. Wondersee et al., "Research on Alternative Conceptions in Science."

42. F. Barron, "The Needs for Order and for Disorder As Motives in Creative Activity," in *Scientific Creativity: Its Recognition and Development,* C. W. Taylor and F. Barron, eds. (New York: John Wiley and Sons, Inc., 1963), pp. 153–162.

43. C. Ames, "Achievement Goals and the Classroom Climate," in *Student Perceptions in the Classroom,* D. H. Schunk and J. L. Meece, eds. (Hillsdale, NJ: Lawrence Erlbaum Associates, Inc., 1992), pp. 327–348.

44. R. Ames and C. Ames, "Motivation and Effective Teaching," in *Advances in Motivation and Achievement: Motivation Enhancing Environments,* vol. 6, M. L. Maehr and C. Ames, eds. (1989), pp. 247–271.

45. A. Bandura, "Self-Efficacy Mechanism in Human Agency," *American Psychologist,* 37 (1982): 122–147.

46. Ronald Simpson, Thomas Koballa, Jr., J. Steve Oliver, and Frank Crawley, "Research on the Affective Dimension of Science Learning," in the *Handbook of Research on Science Teaching and Learning,* D. Gabel, ed. (New York: Macmillan Publishing Company, 1994).

47. E. L. Deci and R. M. Ryan, "A Motivational Approach to Self: Integration in Personality," in *Nebraska Symposium on Motivation,* R. Dienstbier, ed., vol. 38, *Perspectives on Motivation* (Lincoln, NE: University of Nebraska Press, 1991).

48. J. P. Connell and R. M. Ryan, "A Developmental Theory of Motivation in the Classroom," *Teacher Education Quality,* 11 (1984): 64–77.

49. Simpson et al., "Research on the Affective Dimension of Science Learning."

50. Maslow, *Motivation and Personality.*

51. Maslow, *The Farther Reaches of Human Nature.*

52. Barron, "The Needs for Order and for Disorder As Motives in Creative Activity."

53. Connell and Ryan, "A Developmental Theory of Motivation in the Classroom."

54. S. Harter, "Affective and Motivational Correlates of Self-Esteem," in *Nebraska Symposium on Motivation,* R. Dienstbier, ed., vol. 40, *Developmental Perspectives on Motivation* (Lincoln, NE: University of Nebraska Press, 1992).

55. D. W. Johnson and R. T. Johnson, *Cooperation and Competition: Theory and Research* (Edina, MN: Interaction Book Company, 1989).

56. Mary Atwater "Research on Cultural Diversity in the Classroom," in *Handbook of Research on Science Teaching and Learning,* D. Gabel, ed. (New York: Macmillan Publishing Company, 1994).

57. Jane Butler Kahle and Judith Meese, "Research on Gender Issues in the Classroom," in *Handbook of Research on Science Teaching and Learning,* D. Gabel, ed. (New York: Macmillan Publishing Company, 1994).

58. Bandura, "Human Agency in Social Cognitive Theory."

59. Brooks and Brooks, *The Case for Constructivist Classrooms.*

60. Harter, "Affective and Motivational Correlates of Self-Esteem."

61. M. Almy, *Young Children's Thinking* (New York: Teachers College Press, 1966).

62. Ames, "Achievement Goals and the Classroom Climate."

63. Brooks and Brooks, *The Case for Constructivist Classrooms.*

64. McCombs and Marzano, "Putting the Self in Self-Regulated Learning."

65. Rogers, *Freedom to Learn.*

◆ ──────────── **ENGAGING IN ACTION RESEARCH** ──────────── ◆

ACTIVITY 18–1
STUDENT MOTIVATION

Compete this activity during an observation period in a science classroom. First, identify three students of differing motivation levels—one highly motivated, the second about average, and the third unmotivated. You may have to ask the science teacher for recommendations. Second, observe these students for fifteen minutes each. During this time note the behaviors that you think reveal their level of motivation. Finally, indicate what you would recommend to increase their motivation.

1. How would you modify the science class to increase student motivation?
2. What role do the curriculum materials play in student motivation?
3. What role do instructional methods play in student motivation?

ACTIVITY 18–2
HOW CAN I MOTIVATE STUDENTS TO LEARN?

This activity is based on an analysis of external motivation. You are to spend a period of time (at least one class period and preferably two or three) observing a science teacher. During this observation period try to note examples of the factors that you think will increase student motivation.

Motivational Factors	Observations	Effect on Students
Level of students' concern		
Students' perception of climate in classroom		
Students' success		
Students' interest in subject		
Students' knowledge of results of their activity		

HOW DO THESE FACTORS INTERACT?

Provide your own examples of the way you would implement these (or other) factors to increase student motivation.

1.

2.

3.

ACTIVITY 18–3
MOTIVATIONAL NEEDS

Imagine that you observed these behaviors in a tenth-grade biology class.

Mary was restless and fidgeting during the lesson; something seemed to be competing for her attention. The science teacher ignored her. Two desks away Robert sat quietly, head on his desk, sleeping. The teacher awakened Robert and firmly suggested that he pay attention. Karen paid close attention to the teacher. She was careful to record the important points of the lesson and then started her assignment. After completing her work and handing it to the teacher, she was given recognition that was earned and deserved. Martin came into the class and immediately started clowning around, climbing on desks and causing a commotion. He was also given recognition—it was also earned and deserved; however, the teacher had to make a great effort to get him to behave in an appropriate manner.

1. What do you think might be motivating these students' behaviors?

2. How could you find out more about the motivations of these students?

3. How would you respond to the students in a different ways?

ACTIVITY 18–4
REWARDS AND PUNISHMENTS

In connection with learning about psychology as it is applied in education, you should plan to spend several hours in observation of a science class. Your task is to determine the reinforcements and punishments that are given. Use the following guide to help systematize your observations. Review the definitions involved and then make a check each time you observe a reinforcement or punishment.

	Present Stimulus	Remove Stimulus
Pleasant Stimulus		
Aversive Stimulus		

1. Which did the teacher use most—reinforcement or punishment?

2. What types of reinforcers and punishments were used?

3. Did any particular method seem effective? Ineffective?

4. What did you learn about the use of reinforcement and punishment in the science classroom?

ACTIVITY 18–5
ASSESSING COGNITIVE DEVELOPMENT: CONCRETE OPERATIONS

The administration of tasks outlined in this section should provide you with insights into the cognitive abilities of students. Administering the tasks will require making arrangements for the interview session and preparing the required materials. Interpreting the results may present problems. For this reason, some discussion is provided on how tasks can be interpreted. The experiences of questioning students about their reasoning will provide valuable insights into students' cognitive development.

Here are some specific suggestions for administering the tasks. Also, we provide a suggested interview form.

Each of the tasks to be administered outlines a basic structure for the interview. Certain specific suggestions for giving the tasks should be followed:

1. Establish rapport. It is important that the person giving the interview establish good rapport with the student before administering the tasks (i.e., ask the student's name, age, etc., as suggested on the interview form that follows). Tell the student you have some games to play, and that all answers are acceptable. Try to make the tasks fun to do, smile while the student does them, and do what you can to lessen the student's feeling that the interview is a threatening experience.

2. Do not give answers. Do not tell the student that she is wrong or right; just accept her answers and either you or another student record them on the interview form.

3. Always ask for the justification of an answer. In the interview we are interested in determining how the student thinks (i.e., is she really conserving or is she just giving a correct answer?)

4. Hypothesize about the student's thinking. Formulate in your mind certain hypotheses about how the student is thinking. Ask the student questions to test your hypotheses to determine whether they are correct.

5. Use the "another student told me" approach. In asking the student to justify an answer, you may ask her why she thinks it is correct. Experience shows that some students will not respond to "why" questions. Generally, however, if you restructure your questions giving an episode like the following, they will respond: "The other day a boy told me that the rolled out clay in the form of a hot dog weighed just as much as the clay before it was changed. What would you say to him?"

6. Allow for wait-time. Remember that most tasks require some form of logical-mathematical reasoning. Thinking takes time. Therefore, do not rush the student in your interview. Allow time for thinking: five or more seconds of time allowance is not too much.

7. Have fun. Most of all, have fun giving the tasks and try to see that students have similar experiences.

Outlined below is an interview form to be used to note the task achievement of the student. It will probably be best for you to record the responses while you interview. The interview form needs some clarification. In each session you should plan on giving six or seven tasks. The time for administering these will vary from twenty to forty minutes, depending on the age and cognitive level of the student. Place a description of each task in the left-hand column. Check in the appropriate column whether the student achieved or did not achieve the task. In the column provided for the level of cognition, write the period the student demonstrated. With many students you will not get a clear demarcation of stage. They might perform preoperationally on three tasks and concrete operationally on four. You probably would indicate the transitional stage on the basis of your limited interviewing measures.

Piagetian Interview Form: Concrete Operational Period

Name of Student _____   Interviewer's Name _____   Location _____

Age _____   Grade _____   Gender _____

Activity description (e.g., conservation of substance, class inclusion)	Achievement: Task achieved Not achieved	Indication of cognitive level (e.g., operational). Note: If student doesn't achieve level of task, it is assumed she is at a lower level.	Other comments about the student's behavior or statements	Justification (student's reason for responding as she did)

1. _____

2. _____

3. _____

4. _____

5. _____

6. _____

7. _____

8. _____

9. _____

10. _____

How many tasks were achieved?

How would you classify this student's level of development? Transitional? Concrete operational?

How would you justify this classification?

How could you confirm this level?

What are the educational implications of your interview?

Piagetian Interview Activities

Time and distance. Tell the student two persons are walking the same speed and distance, except one is walking on a straight path and one is walking on a crooked path. Ask, "Which one reaches his house first?" "Why?" Use two strings of equal length to represent the paths.

Discussion: Up to age nine, children usually have difficulty comparing the time taken and distance covered by two moving persons or objects. They believe going farther (in direction) takes more time. They do not compensate by increasing or decreasing the speed. For this reason, preoperational and early concrete operational children believe Person A will take more time.

Seriation. Prepare ten cards of stickpeople, dolls, flowers, or some animal so that they progressively increase in size. Place the first and last of the series on a table and tell the child to place the rest of them in order.

Discussion: During the concrete operational period, a child develops the ordering ability. This ability usually occurs during ages 7 and 8. Many children, however, even in the third grade, cannot do the task. If they cannot do it, they probably also have difficulty with number because ordering is basic to understanding mathematics.

Ordering. Show children, ages 6 through 8, stages of a developing moth, including the egg, larva, pupa, and adult. Discuss how the moth develops through these stages. Let the children look at the various stages of the organism and have them draw the stages in order of development. Next, show them a picture of one of the stages and ask, "What would be the next stage?" "What was the stage before this?" "Why do you think so?"

Discussion: If the children can do this and give reasons for their placement of the stages, they probably are able to order. Many young children will not be able to do this. The activity is still valuable because it helps children grasp some concepts of development, although they may not be able yet to interrelate them. If they do not order correctly, they probably do not see the stages as a continuum of an organism slowly progressing to maturity. Children unable to do this probably reason by transduction.

Speed. Obtain two toy cars of different colors. Draw on a piece of paper a line to indicate the end of a race. Place one of the cars behind the other at the start. Move both of these cars with each of your hands so that they come to the finish line at the same time. Ask, "Which of the cars was going faster, or did they both move the same?" "How do you know?" "How about the distance traveled?" "Did one cover a greater distance?" "When was one car ahead of the other?" "Why?" "Which one moved faster?"

Discussion: Young children believe that if the cars finish the race together, they must be moving at the same speed. This is because they believe order, being in front or together, indicates speed. Usually at age 9 or 10 children take into consideration where an object started and stopped, distance traveled, and the time it took. If the child does not grasp this realization, he will have difficulty doing mathematical speed problems. This difficulty may occur even into the fifth and sixth grades. If a child cannot do such problems, use toy cars and other objects to help him discover the relationship of speed to time and distance, so that he eventually will understand that speed = distance/time.

Conservation of substance. Show a student a diagram of a kernel of popcorn, and then draw a picture of it after it has popped. Ask, "Is there more corn after it is popped than before it is popped?" "Why has the volume changed?"

Discussion: Preoperational children, being perception-bound, believe there is more corn to eat after it is popped. Concrete children know that altering the corn's state does not change its amount.

Reversibility. Have students grow bean seeds or show them plants in various stages of development. After they have raised some plants, have them draw how the plants grew. Give the students a diagram of a young plant and ask them to draw how it would look in stages before and after this picture. Next, have the students draw several pictures showing the stages of development of plants in reverse order. Ask, "Why do you think your pictures are true?"

Discussion: If the students can reverse properly and give you reasons why they are drawing the plants in this order, they have probably achieved reversibility in their thinking. Checking for reversibility can be easily done whenever the children have prepared and learned something in one order and are then asked to reverse the order.

Reverse seriation. Obtain twenty straws. The straws should be cut so that you have two series of ten straws, each that progress in length. Set up one series from short to long, and then ask the children to take the other set and place them in reverse order.

Discussion: This task identifies whether children can reverse the order of a series of objects. Children around age 7 can usually seriate, but many children ages 8 through 9 still have difficulty in reversing the order.

Classification—Ascending and descending hierarchy. Prepare a number of cards, some labeled birds with pictures of birds on them, some labeled ducks with pictures of ducks on them, and some labeled animals with pictures of various animals on them. Show these to a group of eight- to ten-year-old children. Ask them to arrange the cards in groups according to each of the three labels. Next, place the bird pile on the duck pile and ask, "Is the bird label, now on top, still appropriate?" "Why?" Now place the animal pile on the others. Ask, "Is this appropriate?" "Why?" "Do all the cards belong in this pile?" "Are birds animals?" "Are ducks animals?" "If all the animals in the world died, would there be any ducks?" "Why or why not?"

Discussion: This activity determines whether a child understands class inclusion; that is, ducks are not only ducks but also birds (an ascending hierarchy). Ducks are a subgroup belonging to birds, a higher major group. Asking if ducks would remain if all the animals are killed determines whether the child can also descend a hierarchy (go from animals, a major group, to ducks, a subgroup).

Conservation. Rip a newspaper in half. Ask, "Do I have more, less, or the same amount of newspaper as I had before?" (conservation of substance). Ask, "Do the combined pieces of newspaper weigh more, less, or the same as the paper did before it was torn?" "Why?" (conservation of weight). Ask, "If I put these torn pieces of newspaper in a large tank of water, would they occupy more, less, or the same amount of space as when the paper was whole?" "Why?" (conservation of volume).

Discussion: Children usually do not develop conservation until after age 6. In other words, they do not realize that physically altering one property of matter does not necessarily change its amount, weight, or the volume it will occupy. Conservation of substance and weight usually develop by age 8, while conservation of volume occurs later.

Number. Obtain ten straws. If the child can count, have him count them one through ten. Point to a middle straw and ask, "If the last straw is ten, what is the number of this straw?" Place the straws together and have the child count them. Move the straws apart. Ask, "Do I have more, fewer, or the same number of straws now as before?"

Discussion: Preoperational children often can count but do not know number. To fully comprehend number children must understand the following:

1. *Classification* —realize that the straws, although they may not look alike, are still straws.
2. *Cardination* —realize that no matter how you arrange objects in a set, you still have the same number.
3. *Ordination* —place the straws in order and realize that where the object is in the order determines its number.

Class Inclusion. Show the students some fruit (e.g., ten raisins and two pears). Ask, "In what ways are these alike?" "What do you call them?" "Are there more raisins than fruit?" "If I took the fruit and you took the raisins, would I have more, or would you have more?" "How would you be able to prove who had more?"

Discussion: This activity tests again for class inclusion. Does the child realize that the subclass *raisins* is included in the major class *fruit?* Is the child overcome by the perception of a large number of raisins?

ACTIVITY 18–6
ASSESSING COGNITIVE DEVELOPMENT: FORMAL OPERATIONS

Valuable insights concerning patterns of reasoning can be gained from interviewing students and asking them to respond to simple tasks. The tasks in this activity are designed for assessment of formal operations. You may wish to include some tasks from Activity 18-5, Assessing Cognitive Development: Concrete Operations. You should also review the suggestions for interviewing in that activity.

Piagetian Interview Tasks: Formal Operational Period

Name _____   School _____

Class or Subject _____   Teacher _____

Gender_____   Level _____

Age _____   (years) _____   (months) _____   Gender Demeanor _____

Date _____   Other _____

Proportional Reasoning

This task assesses the student's ability to apply the concept of ratio and proportion. The student is given an 8 1/2 × 11-inch card. Stickpeople are drawn on each side of the card, one being two-thirds the height of the other. The small and large stickpeople should be constructed to measure four and six jumbo paper clips respectively. Ask the student to measure the height of each of the stickpeople with a set of eight connected jumbo paper clips. After the student has measured and recorded the heights of the two stickpeople, the jumbo clips are replaced with a set of small paper clips. Ask the student to measure only the short stickperson with the new set of clips. Remove the stickperson. Then ask, "How tall is the large stickperson in terms of the small paper clips?"

Task 1—Proportional Reasoning Responses

1. Predicted height of tall stickperson: _____
2. Justification for prediction: _____
3. Key statements indicating cognitive level: _____
4. Classification of cognitive level: _____
5. Suggestions for teaching: _____

Discussion: The measurement of the tall stickperson should be six jumbo clips and nine small clips in length, and the small stickperson should measure four jumbo clips and six small clips. The criterion for success on this task is the ability of the student to accurately predict the height of the tall stickperson in terms of small clips (i.e., nine clips). The student's justification must include a reference to direct ratio or proportion. The student may just guess and give you a number. If the child does, she is not demonstrating the use of formal thought. If, however, the child tries to solve the problem on paper or reasons in a rational way, indicating that the situation is a simple proportion, she is demonstrating formal thought:

Small Stickperson		*Large Stickperson*
4 clips	5	6 clips
6 clips	5	*x* clips

Separation and Control of Variables

This task utilizes a simple pendulum consisting of a length of string about 80 centimeters long and a set of varying weights. Ask the student to determine which variable or variables affect the frequency of oscillation of the pendulum (the number of swings per unit of time, e.g., second). (Note: Since the length of the string is the only relevant variable, the problem is to isolate it from the others. Only in this way can the student solve the problem and explain the frequency of oscillations.)

Task 2—Separation and Control of Variables Responses

1. Question: Which variable or variables affect the frequency of oscillation of this pendulum?

Response: _____

_____

2. Question: Can you design an experiment to prove that your choice is correct?

Response: _____

_____

3. Key statements indicating cognitive level: _____

_____

4. Classification of cognitive level: _____

_____

5. Suggestions for teaching: _____

_____

Discussion: The criterion for success on this task is the student's ability to identify the one variable (length of string) that affects the oscillation of the pendulum. The student's justification must indicate that he held all variables constant while manipulating only one variable in reaching a conclusion. The student should initially indicate that variables involved in the problem could be weight, length of string, or height at which the pendulum is dropped. The student may initially think a combination of these may affect the frequency. He may then describe a set of hypotheses to test these variables. However, before finishing, the student should design an experiment controlling one variable at a time, such as length of string, to find out whether his hypothesis is correct. In this way he should systematically eliminate the irrelevant variables. The ability to plan experiments to separate and control—or manipulate—one variable at a time, observe it accurately, and make proper conclusions characterizes formal thought.

Proportional Reasoning

The student is presented with a balance scale consisting of a wooden rod with equally spaced numbered positions. Weights are attached as indicated in the diagram. Begin by using equal weights (10 grams) equidistant from the fulcrum (pivoting point). Remove one. Maintain equilibrium of the balance by holding the force arm. Ask, "Using any of the weights in front of you, how could you get the scale to balance?" After the student responds, ask, "What other ways are there to balance the scale besides the one you chose?" Remove the weight from the scale. Place another weight nearer the fulcrum and maintain equilibrium by holding the force arm. Ask, "How may the scale be balanced by using the weights?" "How do you justify your responses?"

Task 3—Proportional Reasoning Responses

1. Question: Using any of the weights presented here, how could you get the scale to balance?

Response: _____

_____

2. Question (justification): How did you arrive at this answer?

Response: _____

_____

3. Key statements indicating cognitive level: _____
_____

4. Classification of cognitive level: _____
_____

5. Suggestions for teaching: _____
_____

Discussion: The criterion for success on this task is the student's ability to equate length times weight on one arm of the fulcrum with length times weight on the other arm, or to figure out the problem by using proportions. To balance the scale, the student must apply the principle of levers.

Task 4—Hypothetical Reasoning Response

1. Student's description of rule: _____
_____

2. Justification for the rule: _____
_____

3. Key statements indicating cognitive level: _____
_____

4. Classification of cognitive level: _____
_____

5. Suggestions for teaching: _____
_____

Discussion: The student should, in his own words, state that the angle of incidence equals the angle of reflection. If the student does state this rule, ask the student to explain the meaning of the rule to ensure that he has not simply memorized it. The student need not use the above words, as long as he can explain the rule.

Group Structure You will need to spend at least one class period observing a secondary school science class. During the class, try to direct your attention to the students as a group.

To gain insights into group structure in a science class, you should answer the following questions. Use the one-to-seven continuum to indicate the degree to which the group characteristic is present. These questions are based on the earlier discussion of the defining characteristics of groups.

	Low			*Medium*		*High*	
1. To what degree do the students have a *solidarity* of opinion, purpose, and interests when they work in this class?	1	2	3	4	5	6	7
2. To what degree are the students *satisfied* with the class?	1	2	3	4	5	6	7
3. To what degree are members of other classes *attracted* to this class?	1	2	3	4	5	6	7
4. To what degree do students in the class group feel they are *wanted* and *belong* in the class?	1	2	3	4	5	6	7
5. To what degree (both quality and quantity) do students *interact* through various types of communication?	1	2	3	4	5	6	7
6. To what degree is the group *structure* beneficial to achieving goals?	1	2	3	4	5	6	7
7. To what degree are the *norms* of behavior adhered to by group members?	1	2	3	4	5	6	7

What behaviors did you observe that allowed you to make these decisions? How can you identify these properties of groups? After each of the words listed below place two or three behaviors that you think support your judgment.

Solidarity of group:

Satisfaction with group:

Attraction of group:

Interaction of group:

Structure of group:

Norms of group:

UNIT 6

UNDERSTANDING AND WORKING WITH STUDENTS

For several decades, the issue of equity in science classes has received attention but little action. Beginning in the 1990s, science educators rallied to the slogan "science for all students," as this was a prominent theme in *Science for All Americans*,[1] *Benchmarks for Science Literacy*,[2] and the *National Science Education Standards*.[3] Embracing science for all students means that science teachers will have to translate general ideas such as "all students can learn" and "all students can participate in science activities" into actual classroom practices.

Whether the discussion centers on helping girls succeed in science,[4] multicultural education,[5,6,7] or disabilities,[8] the unifying value that science teachers should recognize is equity. Equity in this case means that all students, regardless of gender, race, ethnicity, or disability, will have access to high-quality science education programs and fair opportunities and treatment in science classrooms. Equity in science classrooms also means that students develop an understanding of views and perspectives of groups and cultures other than their own. It is certainly the case that science teachers must maintain a balance among the unique perspectives of individuals, common values and ideals of society, and the defining characteristics of science. Science, mathematics, and engineering have been predominately spheres dominated by white males. The issue now is not recitation of past sins but a remedy of future practices. As a beginning teacher, what do you need to know and do to implement the goal of science for all students in your classroom? Chapter 19 focuses on issues related to various special needs that individual learners may have. While Chapter 20 looks at a bigger picture by examining the research about female students and nonwhite

learners. The implications of this research are easiest to apply when you think of your class as a multicultural environment. Chapters 21 and 22 turn to the practical matters of attending to controversial issues, classroom management, and conflict resolution. To work with *all* the students in your classroom, you will need to synthesize the information in all four chapters, consider each child as an individual, and then try different combinations of ideas and strategies with each child to help bring out his or her best every day.

Banks says that multicultural education "tries to create equal educational opportunities for all students by ensuring that the total school environment reflects the diversity of groups in classrooms, schools, and the society as a whole.[9] He goes on to point out that in this environment students learn to form knowledge for themselves. Another way to think about a multicultural environment is to consider what type of environment facilitates the internalization of a value system that helps those who feel disempowered to do or learn science become aware, knowledgeable, and empowered for change.[10]

Therefore, a multicultural environment is one in which the diversity of the people in the environment is celebrated and used to improve the quality and quantity of learning that takes place. This environment can be an informal setting such as a neighborhood, community center, or a local park, or it can be a more formal setting such as a church, school, or city government. In this chapter, we will limit the discussion to multicultural environments in the school setting. We will discuss general strategies for developing multicultural environments and look at some of the learning characteristics of different cultures.

CHAPTER
19

INDIVIDUAL DIFFERENCES IN SCIENCE CLASSROOMS

A great diversity of students come to science classes. They come from urban, suburban, and rural environments; they come from poor, middle-class, and affluent homes. Some can read, others cannot; some are interested in science, others are not. Some are gifted, some are slow, and most are average. The list could go on and on. In fact, if we started a classification system, it could continue until we described each individual in each school. Saying that each student is a unique individual is to state the obvious. And few teachers disagree, in principle, with the logical educational implication of such a statement—namely, all students require individual attention and opportunities to learn.

EXCEPTIONAL STUDENTS IN EDUCATION: A RATIONALE

Of the many issues that educators face in the future, perhaps one of the most encompassing is that of a right to education for *all* students. In the late 1970s, attention was focused on the educational rights of students who were traditionally placed in restricted, special-education programs. One result of this movement is the recognition of individual differences and the conclusion that has been clear to many teachers for a long time—all students are exceptional.

All educators stand to gain from having exceptional students in science classrooms. Although it is only natural to expect some initial hesitation, frustration, or fear on the part of students and teachers alike, once these feelings pass, the gains are clear: Exceptional students encounter a whole new range of educational opportuni-

ties; regular students learn that in terms of basic human needs and wants, exceptional students are not very different from themselves; and teachers become more sensitive to the realities of different learning styles, subtleties of instruction, and modifying curricula to meet students' personal needs. In the end, we all learn more about what it means to be human.

Aside from the points made in the preceding paragraph, there is another reason for having exceptional students in science classrooms: it is the just thing for science teachers to do. We have a responsibility to provide the best science program for all our students. Science teachers know that students have unique needs that are not fulfilled by curriculum materials alone. An essential task for science teachers is accommodating our programs and teaching to the needs of students, not to making students adapt to our science programs and teaching strategies.

EXCEPTIONAL STUDENTS IN SCIENCE PROGRAMS: THE LAW

Appeals to personal and professional benefit and to justice do not completely convince teachers of the need to include exceptional students in the science classroom. The most immediate and forceful argument seems to be the law. We have a legal responsibility to include exceptional students in the mainstream of school programs.

One of the first laws that included protection of the rights of exceptional students was the Rehabilitation Act of 1973, Public Law 93-112, Section 504, which states:

No otherwise qualified handicapped individual in the United States . . . shall, solely by reason of his handicap, be excluded from participation in, be denied the benefits of, or be subjected to discrimination under any program or activity receiving federal financial assistance.

Since most, if not all, school systems receive federal financial assistance under this law, exceptional students must be allowed to participate in, receive the benefits of, and have open access to educational programs.

Other federal legislation that included safeguards concerning the rights of exceptional students was Public Law 93-380, the Education Amendments of 1974. This law mandated due process procedures at the state and local levels for the placement of exceptional students, ensured placement of exceptional students in the least restrictive environment, and set a goal of providing full educational opportunities for all handicapped students within each state. Public Law 94-142, the Education for All Handicapped Children Act of 1975—the regulation with which most United States school personnel are probably familiar—requires that exceptional students be integrated into regular classrooms whenever possible:

It is the purpose of this Act to assure that all handicapped children have available to them . . . a free appropriate public education which emphasizes special attention and related services designed to meet their unique needs, to assure that the rights of handicapped children and their parents or guardians are protected, to assist states and localities to provide for the education of all handicapped children, and to assess and assure the effectiveness of efforts to educate handicapped children.

Specifically, Public Law 94-142 requires the following of school personnel:

1. Zero rejection. No student may be rejected from a free public education and related services. Court cases, such as *Pennsylvania Association for Retarded Children v. Commonwealth of Pennsylvania*, 334 F. Supp. 1257 (E. D. PA 1971) and *Mills v. Board of Education of the District of Columbia*, 348 F. Supp. 886 (D. D. C., 1972) have resulted in a legal commitment to the public schools for the education of all school-age students. That all students have a "right to education, regardless of their present level of functioning" results in a principle of zero rejection. You also should note that education is defined as the development of students from their present level to the next appropriate level. In brief, the assumption is that all students are educable.

2. Classification and placement. Evaluation of students shall be nondiscriminatory. Diagnostic and assessment procedures are to be established by each state to ensure that cultural and racial bias are not evident in the system used for identifying exceptional students.

Tests shall be a fair evaluation of the student's strengths and weaknesses.

3. Appropriate education. This stipulation is a requirement for an Individualized Education Program (IEP). An IEP should have statements concerning the student's present level of performance, how he or she will participate in the regular educational program, the type of special services needed, the date special services were initiated, and the expected length of services. In addition, the IEP should set short- and long-term minimum standards, measures of achievement, and an evaluation of educational progress that includes a conference among school personnel, parents, and the exceptional student.

4. Least restrictive placement. To the maximum extent possible, exceptional students will be educated with all other students. "Least Restrictive Placement" means that exceptional students should be educated in the "mainstream," the regular educational environment. They can be educated in special programs when the nature or severity of their handicap requires such treatment.

5. Due process. The exceptional student (usually through parents or a guardian) has a right to question testing and placement; that is, exceptional students are guaranteed procedural safeguards in the placement and provision of special services.

6. Parental participation. Parents of the handicapped student have the right to be present for their child's evaluation, placement, and development of the IEP.

Visit http://www.prenhall.com/trowbridge and select Topic 5—Science Education and Special Needs. Select "Strategies and Techniques for Teaching Students with Learning Disabilities." Find out how to adapt your science instruction for children with learning disabilities. Write a response and submit it to your instructor using the Electronic Bluebook module.

Public Law 101-476 was passed in 1990 to reauthorize P.L. 94-142. This reauthorization accomplished several things, including changing the name of the law to the "Individuals with Disabilities Education Act" (IDEA) with the purpose of reflecting a more contemporary philosophy. Rather than focusing on handicapped people, the language was changed to emphasize the *individuals* with disabilities and send a "person-first" message. The reauthorization upheld the major provisions of the original law, but added provisions for very young children with disabilities, added students with traumatic brain injuries and those with autism, and for students preparing to leave secondary school. The transition services are designed to make sure disabled students who are leaving high school receive assistance when finding a job or attending vocational school or a university or college. P.L. 101-476 emphasized inclusion of *all* students, even those with severe disabilities.[1]

Public Laws 93-112, 93-380, 94-142, and 101-476 stand on fundamental principles guaranteed in the Constitution. Exceptional students have been systematically excluded from many educational programs, which, in essence, has been a violation of the constitutional rights of approximately 35 million Americans. The Fourteenth Amendment guarantees equal protection under the law for all Americans. Recall that the *Brown v. Board of Education of Topeka,* 347 U. S. 483 (1954) overturned the earlier "separate but equal" ruling of *Plessy v. Ferguson,* 163, U. S. 537 (1896). It is instructive to read the *Brown v. Board* decision and make appropriate changes in the wording, such as *disabled* or *challenged* for *Negro* or *race,* and *classroom* for *school.* Separate educational facilities for some students are, by definition, unequal; thus, exceptional students have been deprived of the equal protection of the laws guaranteed by the Fourteenth Amendment of our Constitution.

Of these laws, Public Law 94-142 was probably the most significant piece of educational legislation of the 1970s, and its effect will continue to be felt into the 21st century. There are several reasons for this fact. First, Public Law 94-142 incorporates parts of the other laws and clarifies the fundamental right of all students to an education. Second, because it is a federal law, it establishes the right to education as a national priority. Third, Public Law 94-142 commits us to recognize individual differences and to appropriate educational programs for all students because it is permanent legislation with no expiration date. This fact demonstrates the importance Congress placed on this legislation.

RACIAL INEQUITIES IN SPECIAL EDUCATION

Minority students are overrepresented in public school special education programs and underrepresented in gifted education programs. African American students are one and one half to four times more likely to be identified as mentally retarded or emotionally disturbed. Native American students tend to be overrepresented in categories related to cognitive disabilities. Asian American students are typically underrepresented in special education and well represented in gifted education. Even more disturbing is that students of color are more often placed in a restrictive, substantially separate setting. As elaborated

in Chapter 20, the low expectations that teachers have for students of color is part of the problem in special education placements as well as in regular classroom settings.[2]

EXCEPTIONAL STUDENTS IN SCIENCE CLASS: SOME GUIDELINES

Teachers' concerns are not in understanding why exceptional students should be in science classrooms but rather in dealing with the fact that they are in our classrooms. And so the problems may be stated: What can be done to provide the best science education program possible? What are the first steps? What should I do now? The following sections address these questions. The ideas about teaching exceptional students have been synthesized from many sources and should give you some information, some confidence, and some direction in working with exceptional students.

> Visit http://www.prenhall.com/trowbridge and select Topic 5—Science Education and Special Needs. Select "Web Links" and find the website on "Inclusion in Science Education for Students with Disabilities." Arrange with your instructor to have the class discuss special features in science teaching to accommodate students with disabilities. Use the Electronic Bluebook module to submit your ideas.

There are some simple, straightforward things that you can do that will help most students. Certainly, there are unique problems in integrating any exceptional student into the science classroom. You can anticipate some personal tension and educational problems during the period of adjustment. And, understandably, we cannot provide suggestions that will cover all situations. Nevertheless, there are some approaches that have proved helpful with most exceptional students.

General Guidelines for Helping Exceptional Students

1. Obtain and read all the background information available on the student.
2. Spend time educating yourself on the physical and/or psychological nature of the student's exceptionality and how it affects the student's potential for learning.
3. Determine whether special help is available to you through the resources of experts within and outside the school system.

4. Determine any special equipment needed by the student.

5. Talk with the student about limitations and about particular needs in the science class.

6. Use resource teachers and aides to assist you.

7. Establish a team of fellow teachers (including resource teachers and aides) to share information and ideas about the school's exceptional students. A team approach is helpful in overcoming initial fears and the sense of isolation in dealing with the student. You may need to take responsibility for contacting appropriate school personnel and establishing the team; if so, have courage and do it.

8. Other students are often willing to help exceptional students. Encourage them to do so.

9. Be aware of barriers, both physical and psychological, to the fullest possible functioning of each student.

10. Consider how to modify or adapt curriculum materials and teaching strategies for exceptional students without sacrificing content, processes, or activities.

11. Do not underestimate the capabilities of exceptional students. Teachers' perceptions of students' abilities have a way of becoming self-fulfilling prophecies. If these perceptions are negative, they may detrimentally affect students and your ability to create new options for them.

12. Use the same standards of grading and discipline for exceptional students as you do for the rest of the class.

13. Develop a trusting relationship with all students.

14. Educate the other students about exceptionality in general, as well as about specific handicaps of students in their class.

Visit http://www.prenhall.com/trowbridge and select Topic 5—Science Education and Special Needs. Select "Web Links" and find the link to the "Curriculum and Instruction Program at Pennsylvania State University" that flags papers from the Association of Educators of Teachers of Science. A treat awaits you with dozens of suggestions for handling issues concerning diverse populations of students in science education. Select one or two to read and reflect on. Make plans to incorporate some of the ideas in your lesson planning for teaching special needs children.

Auditorially Challenged Students

From an early age, most children learn through listening—and there is every indication that most teaching is through telling. So, it becomes quite difficult for students with hearing problems; science teachers have to adjust. Hearing impairment is defined as an auditory problem that may adversely affect the student's educational performance. Students with hearing impairments often have developmental delays in speech and language. These delays have obvious effects on the ability to communicate. Students with hearing impairments will not necessarily have problems acquiring science concepts, although they may have difficulty learning the written or oral language to communicate their understanding.

Helping Auditorially Challenged Students Learn Science

1. Individuals with hearing impairments depend heavily on visual perception. Therefore, seat the student for optimal viewing.

2. Determine whether an interpreter will be needed and the nature of the student's speech/language problems.

3. Learn the student's most effective way of communicating.

4. Find the student a listening helper.

Visually Challenged Students

Like students with hearing impairments, students with visual impairments are those whose vision is limited enough to require adaptations in materials and strategies. Students who can read material with the use of magnifying devices and/or enlarged print are classified as partially seeing. Students who require Braille or taped materials are classified as educationally blind.

Helping Visually Challenged Students Learn Science

1. Students with visual impairments learn through sensory channels other than vision, primarily hearing. Therefore, seat students for optimal listening.

2. Determine from the student what constitutes the best lighting.

3. Change the room arrangement whenever necessary, but always make a special effort to reorient the student.

4. Allow the student to manipulate tangible materials, models, and, when possible, real objects. Do not unduly protect students from materials.

5. Speak aloud what you have written on the board and charts.

6. Use the student's name; otherwise, the student may not know when he or she is being addressed.

7. Since smiles and facial gestures might not be seen, touching is the most effective means of reinforcing the student's work.

8. Be aware of eye fatigue. This fatigue can be overcome by varying activities, using good lighting, and providing close visual work.
9. Have the student use his visual capacity when possible (unless otherwise directed).

Physically Challenged Students

Students with physical and health impairments represent a diverse group of special needs, for this category includes students with allergies, asthma, arthritis, amputations, diabetes, epilepsy, cerebral palsy, spina bifida, and muscular dystrophy. Some are mobile and others are confined to wheelchairs; some have good use of their limbs and others do not. Some have a single condition and some have multiple disabilities. The range of needs is such that some can work in the regular science classroom with little or no problem, whereas others require full-time care.

Helping Physically Challenged Students Learn Science

1. Eliminate architectural barriers.
2. Become familiar with the basic mechanics and maintenance of braces, prostheses, and wheelchairs.
3. Understand the effects of medication on students and know the prescribed dosage.
4. Obtain special devices, such as pencil holders or reading aids, for students who need them.
5. Learn about the symptoms of special health problems and appropriate responses.

Speech- and Language-Challenged Students

Until recently, classroom teachers had more contact with students with speech and language impairments than with any others with disabling conditions. This situation may still be true in most schools, but learning disabilities programs are growing rapidly. Speech and language disabilities that you might encounter are articulation (the most common problem), dyslexia, delayed speech, voice problems, and stuttering. In addition, students with other disabilities, such as cleft palate, cerebral palsy, and hearing loss, may have speech and language problems.

Helping Speech- and Language-Challenged Students Learn Science

1. Help the student become aware of the problem; students must be able to hear their own errors.
2. Incorporate and draw attention to newly learned sounds in familiar words.
3. Know what to listen for and match appropriate remedial exercises with the student's problem.

4. Be sure your speech is articulated; students often develop speech and language patterns through modeling.

Students with Learning Disabilities and Mild Mental Disabilities

Because the difference is far too technical to summarize here, suffice to say there is a distinction between learning disabilities and mild mental disabilities. Students with mild mental disabilities should be identified only through the use of multiple criteria. Classroom teachers may observe indications of mental disabilities in a student's social interaction, general intelligence, emotional maturity, and academic achievement. In contrast, students with learning disabilities show a significant discrepancy between their achievements and the apparent ability to achieve. The problem is manifest as a disorder of learning and not mental ability. Science teachers may observe learning disabilities in the areas of arithmetic, listening, reading, spelling, logical thinking, speaking, and writing.

Helping Learning Disabled and Mentally Challenged Students Learn Science

1. Listen closely so you can understand the student's perception and understanding of concepts and procedures.
2. Use an individualized approach based on the student's learning style, level of understanding, and readiness.
3. Use multisensory approaches to learning: visual, auditory, kinesthetic, and tactile.
4. Find and use the student's most refined sensory mode to aid in development of mental capacities.
5. Make use of the students' strengths and work on diminishing their deficiencies.
6. Since many exceptional students have short attention spans, reduce or control interruptions.
7. Stay within the students' limits of frustration. Rely on your judgment, not the level of curriculum materials.
8. Begin conceptual development at a sensory-motor or concrete level, and work toward more abstract levels.
9. Work on speech and language development.
10. Help students to develop self-esteem; a good, firmly grounded self-concept is essential to their continued development.

Emotionally Challenged Students

These students probably cause the greatest concern and frustration for science teachers. As it turns out, they also are the ones who have been in science classrooms all along.

GUEST EDITORIAL ◆ ELIZABETH KARPLUS

Special Education
Campolindo High School
Moraga, California

SCIENCE FOR EXCEPTIONAL STUDENTS

Every science teacher is familiar with the case of Albert Einstein who failed mathematics as a young student because he could not memorize and had a nonverbal style of thinking. Or, they have heard of Thomas Edison, who was declared mentally retarded and whose mother taught him at home because she did not believe he was stupid.

Einstein and Edison are not just special isolated cases. I remember Alan, a very tall, skinny, slightly stooped, dark-haired student. In high school, he carried all of his books and papers in total disarray in a large backpack. As a child, he had been diagnosed as dyslexic, dysgraphia, and dyscalculic at the California State Diagnostic School for the Neurologically Handicapped. This diagnosis was based on his profound problems with orientation in time and space and mild cerebral palsy evidenced in shaking hands, poor coordination, and poor throat-muscle control (and, therefore, poor speech). He was very distracted by the sensory stimuli around him and unable to attend selectively because he could not decide which signal of many was the important one for the current task.

After diagnosis, he was placed in a self-contained class for the learning disabled, where remedial mathematics and reading were begun by a large, loving woman. He ran away from school. The drill on symbols and phonics frustrated him because he was unable to get meaning from them in isolation. What he needed was an awareness that the events in the world, including symbols, were consistent and made sense and that the symbols were only useful in helping to describe that sense. He needed hands-on experiences where he could observe what happened. He needed contact with ideas and with other bright students who could discuss those ideas, since reading about them was so difficult. Alan needed to learn to sequence his symbols (writing 73, not 37, when he meant seven tens and three units) and sequence directions according to the meaning or the expected result rather than trying to remember them in detail step-by-step since his memory was so poor. He needed taped textbooks so that he could listen to

them to get information. He needed to ask "why" and "what." He needed the encouragement of accepting teachers who weren't dismayed by his poor writing or his unusual approaches to problems. Those teachers, in turn, often needed to reword their explanations as class work became increasingly abstract, because words never carried quite the same meaning for him that they did for most of the class.

It was in the science classes that he had the greatest triumphs, and it was the activities in these classes that provided the best environment for him to learn from his mistakes and to monitor his own learning, developing a style of learning he could apply to other subject areas. He went on to major in physics at a California State University—a modern success story.

Learning-disabled students, such as Alan, need science or other activity courses (shop, home economics, arts, crafts) as much or more than nondisabled students. In science classes, the students themselves can control variables, change conditions, observe results, and learn to discriminate between variables that affect the outcome of the experiment and those that do not.

The science classes can provide exposure to new equipment and ideas in a hands-on setting. New learning can be firmly embedded in a situational context so that it is easier to remember and reapply. Old learning can be applied in new situations so that concepts are refined. Language usage itself can be refined and vocabulary increased. Science activities are filled with opportunities to measure along, around, through, diagonally, up, and down. The student can easily distinguish among thin, narrow, short, light, and weak, and learn when each is an appropriate replacement for "little." Position and direction are encoded in the prepositions in, out, among, under, over, between, by, and up, as well as in adjectives such as contiguous or nouns such as circuit, test tube, or beaker.

In science classes, instructions make sense and are usually monitored by the progress of the experiment, not by remembering an *a priori* order. You cannot filter a precipitate before the two interacting solutions have been mixed. If you haven't connected the battery, the bulb will not light. Most importantly, the student learns that failures do not represent disaster but are useful as sources of new information. The creative teacher can use each failure of an experiment, each mismeasurement, to help the student to a new understanding of the phenomenon.

However, there are two cautions the science teacher of the learning-disabled student must observe. You must take special pains to recognize the learning-disabled student's preferred sensory channels (visual-reading; auditory-listening; kinesthetic-demonstration) for information input and his or her preferred channels for output or reporting his or her understandings to you (visual-writing or diagrams; auditory-oral speech; kinesthetic-demonstration). You also may need to change your preferred methods of presentation to match the student's methods; otherwise, he or she may not be able to understand the lesson or you may not be able to discover how much he or she has actually learned. In my classes, we often read test questions or put laboratory instructions and text on cassette tapes so that the student may listen and understand rather than read and misunderstand.

Sometimes, it is necessary to change laboratory setups to make them more usable for students, particularly the physically handicapped, whose movements may be jerky or ill-defined. Equipment can be clamped tightly to the desk or otherwise anchored. Special laboratory measuring devices are available for the blind or deaf, and they are often useful to the learning-disabled student, who can then use more than one sense and thus monitor his or her own collecting of accurate information.

Science classes are for everyone, including the learning-handicapped student. Learning science involves attention, reasoning, and questioning skills that are of constant value throughout life. Learning science can bring great satisfaction to the learning-disabled high school student because it is an important academic discipline and because he or she can develop skills so necessary for self-esteem in these classes. We owe these students their chance to learn how to learn—a skill most easily taught through well-designed science experiments.

Emotionally challenged and disruptive students show behavior that ranges from mild, attention-getting pranks to violent assault. They also may demonstrate withdrawn behavior ranging from mildly withdrawn to clinically depressed and suicidal. Other examples of behavior that teachers might identify as disturbed or disruptive include regression, fears and phobias, chronic complaints of pains and illness, aggressiveness, overdependence, social isolation, perfectionism, excessive dieting, obesity, chemical dependency, defiance, and vandalism.

The student's behavior may be a result of forces within or from the environment. The first may be either physiological or psychological in origin. Environmental factors might include violence in the home, school pressures, and/or social problems. In some cases, schools and teachers may contribute to the development of disruptive behaviors, in the form of extreme emphasis on grades, teacher comments, harsh and punitive treatment, unwarranted social comparison, unrealistic physical and academic requirements, and teacher conversations about student behavior that in turn become fulfilled prophecies when other teachers have the same student.

Helping Emotionally Challenged Students Learn Science

1. Spend time with students when they are not being disruptive.
2. Make rules reasonable and clear.
3. Provide realistic, reasonable, and appropriate consequences if rules are broken.
4. Disruptive behavior ranges from low levels at which a student may merely be looking for attention or recognition through a spectrum that ends in rages, tantrums, or complete withdrawal. Always try to be alert to behaviors that, though minimally disruptive, could become more serious problems.
5. Avoid personal confrontations or situations that provoke troubled students.
6. Make directions for assignments, class work, and laboratory procedures direct, clear, and complete.
7. Be aware of and prepare for transitional times in the classroom.
8. Provide troubled students with success experiences.
9. Resolve conflicts by talking about specific behaviors, reasoning, and involving the student in the problem-solving process. Once a course toward aggressive or uncontrolled behavior begins, it is hard to stop.
10. Convey your intention to help resolve the problem mutually: "We have a problem here, and we are going to resolve it."
11. If behavior problems escalate, try to talk about the process while providing solutions to the problem. For example, "We are both getting angry; can't we settle this calmly?" or "I see you are upset; let's try to solve the problem."
12. Avoid using comparison, embarrassment, ridicule, and unwarranted threats to change behavior.

Academically Unsuccessful Students

These students have normal abilities and do not have any significant physical or psychological disabilities, yet they are below their expected level of achievement. Their challenges may be caused by such things as extreme poverty, a home environment that does not encourage learning, poor reading abilities, diminished self-concept, negative attitudes toward school, and language problems due to a first language other than English. In the past, these students were labeled culturally deprived, slow learners, economically disadvantaged, and underachievers. We have used the words academically unsuccessful to suggest that the science teacher's attention should be directed toward the educational problems and their remediation or resolution, not to the student's culture, home, or economic condition. The role of the science teacher is to help these students overcome their educational problems and continue their development. It is neither to identify a cause for the problem nor to excuse one's self from important educational goals, such as developing scientific literacy.

Helping Academically Unsuccessful Students Learn Science

1. Identify the educational problem—for example, reading—and concentrate on resolving this problem.
2. Convey your expectations for achievement within a realm of reasonable possibilities for the student.
3. See that physiological, physical, and psychological needs are fulfilled.
4. Use concrete learning experiences, such as the laboratory.
5. Provide experiences where the student will succeed.
6. Eliminate educational approaches that have not worked and try something new.
7. Give recognition to talents the student does have.
8. Approach the educational impairment with an attitude of, "When you are in science, we are going to work on this."
9. Provide time, materials, and experiences within the learning capabilities of the student.
10. Adapt instruction and the curriculum to the student, not the reverse.

GIFTED AND TALENTED STUDENTS IN SCIENCE CLASS: PERSPECTIVE AND RESOURCES

If you had a serious illness, you would want the best physician. If you had economic problems, you would want the best financial adviser. Everybody recognizes the need for unusual gifts and talents, yet this is a much-reglected area in education.

Definitions of giftedness vary. Most, however, are paraphrased from the congressional report submitted by past Commissioner of Education Sidney Marland in *Education of the Gifted and Talented*.[3] Gifted and talented students are those identified by professionals who, by virtue of their abilities, are capable of high achievement. These students require educational programs beyond those normally provided to fulfill their personal potentials and to encourage their contribution to society. In a less-cumbersome definition: gifted students have superior academic abilities. Talented students have special aptitudes in specific areas. The difference between giftedness and talents is not distinct, since most gifted students have talents and most talented students are gifted in some areas. Gifted and talented students may have demonstrated abilities in any of the following areas: academics (general or specific), leadership, visual and performing arts, music, creativity, mechanics, and athletics.

As a science teacher you should be interested in the characteristics of giftedness that you may encounter in the classroom.

Characteristics of the Gifted and Talented Student in Science Class

1. Enjoys asking scientific questions.
2. Solves problems easily and logically.
3. Demonstrates advanced ethical, cognitive, and aesthetic development.
4. Learns science faster than other students.
5. Understands scientific concepts quickly.
6. Asks many questions about science.
7. Shows an awareness of science far beyond that of other students.
8. Is motivated to read and study science independently.
9. Demonstrates unique abilities in designing laboratory equipment to solve problems.
10. Is highly creative.

In addition, there are a few negative behaviors—such as boredom, frustration, acting out, and complaints—that you may observe. This list gives a subjective and preliminary means of identifying gifted and talented students. If you think you have such a student, it is best to consult the school counselor so that appropriate tests can be administered to confirm your initial impressions.

Adapting school programs for gifted and talented students can be achieved in many ways. Businesses, industries, colleges, and universities often have programs for students showing special abilities. There are special honors classes, programs, and schools. Gifted students can work on advanced placement courses and accelerated schedules, take extra classes, enter college early, and work part-time and/or summers in projects where they can develop their talents. You can easily find many options for the gifted students in your school.

Although resources are available, probably the crucial question is, "What can I do to help the gifted and talented student in science class?"

Helping Gifted and Talented Students Learn Science

1. Use questions, problems, and projects that will facilitate higher levels of cognitive, affective, and psychomotor development.
2. Develop independent study programs.
3. Have special honors seminars.
4. Initiate extracurricular science activities, such as having science fairs or having gifted students help teach an elementary science club.
5. Assign special projects in lieu of routine work that is boring the students.
6. Emphasize scientific inquiry and problem-solving in your teaching.
7. Individualize a program based on the student's interests.

TEACHING SCIENCE FOR INDIVIDUAL DIFFERENCES

After reading the previous sections, it should be clear that, as a science teacher, you will encounter a broad range of students. All students have individual differences that should be recognized in the science classroom. With increased recognition of the science-for-all orientation and because of the laws cited earlier, more and more school systems are modifying their instructional programs to give greater attention to individual differences. Psychological research indicates that there are human differences that have implications for teaching. This research indicates that:

1. Individuals come to the classroom with different conceptions of natural phenomena.
2. Individuals vary in the rate at which they learn concepts.
3. Individuals have different levels of motivation toward learning.
4. Individuals have different levels of psychomotor skills.
5. Individuals have different attitudes, values, and concepts in regard to science.

 Visit http://www.prenhall.com/trowbridge and select Topic 5—Science Education and Special Needs. Select "Web Links" and find the website on "Modifying Science Lessons for Students with Special Needs." Select a lesson and modify it to accommodate students with disabilities. Using the Electronic Bluebook, submit these lesson plans to your instructor for discussion and action.

There are many more such statements that could be made concerning individual differences among students in the science classroom. Common sense and observation confirm the statements as much as research evidence. Yet, there has been reluctance on the part of teachers to modify instruction. In this section, we describe several ways you can individualize instruction in your science classroom.

Individualized instruction is a process of adapting curriculum materials and instructional procedures to the student's needs. The aim of individualization is to maximize student learning. Many schools have used grouping as a way of reducing instructional differences in a classroom or grade level. However, grouping alone cannot meet the needs of all students. Other approaches are important.

There are some variations on individualized instruction in science. The entire science program may be individualized for all students, or only for students with exceptional needs. Individualized instruction may be based on any or all of the following: rate of learning (e.g., accelerated, extra time), direction of learning (e.g., independent study, student-selected projects), different methods (e.g., alone, small-group, teacher-directed), different materials (e.g., reading, laboratory activities), and levels of achievement (e.g., assessments, projects completed). Clearly there are many variations available to science teachers. These approaches only describe things you can do in the classroom and do not include approaches requiring administrative or school-wide reorganization. The following sections are brief descriptions of different approaches to teaching science for individual differences.

Grouping

In one plan, the students are grouped according to ability. They are assigned units of work to complete, and when they finish these units, they may be moved at the end of the semester to another group of higher ability and achievement. Sometimes teachers group within a classroom so that there might be high, middle, and low groups in a class of 30. This system allows the teacher to adjust instruction to the different levels. It is usually not a good idea to maintain these groups on a permanent basis, because such grouping defines a class structure, the disadvantages of which outweigh the advantages.

Continuous Progress

A second approach is the continuous-progress plan. It allows students to progress from subject to subject with no time restriction. A student who finishes biology in six weeks and passes an examination is then eligible to move into chemistry. This approach is linear—that is, it progresses through the regular sequence of science courses.

Enrichment Programs

Enrichment programs provide extra opportunities for students who complete the regular program and the extra time needed for others to complete the chapter or unit. Here, the faster students have the opportunity to work in depth and breadth within the science course. Using an enrichment program may require extra materials and a resource center.

Team Teaching

Another attempt to give greater attention to individual differences is to use some large-group instruction in a team-teaching situation on certain days, with small-group and individualized instruction on other days. This method is a compromise between having traditional group instruction and completely individualized instruction. This approach has the advantage of releasing teachers during the large-group instruction so that they may prepare and organize materials. When this method is used, there is no reason why the students cannot be taught on an individualized basis when the group is divided into smaller sections.

TEACHING SCIENCE FOR INDIVIDUAL DIFFERENCES: ADVANTAGES AND DISADVANTAGES

Now that you have some information about what is possible, it is appropriate to review some of the advantages and disadvantages in teaching science for individual differences. The aforementioned approaches endeavor to respond to the overwhelming evidence on individual variation. They are efforts to respect the person. Science teachers who have gone from group-centered to more individualized instruction often state that they didn't realize how futile it was in the traditional approach to try

to have all students learn particularly difficult material at the same rate. The fact that the slower academic students are not demeaned and frustrated because they don't learn rapidly or gifted students are not held back until their classmates catch up is perhaps the major advantage of recognizing individual differences.

Furthermore, there is a shift in emphasis from extrinsic to intrinsic rewards. Students doing an assignment at their own rate gain self-confidence and a sense of competence that may not manifest themselves so easily in group instruction. The real joy of learning in this manner comes in students completing the task on their own initiative, not simply because of grades given by the teacher.

Although an individualized approach ideally has many practical advantages, there also are several disadvantages. A science teacher considering taking a position in a school or seriously thinking about the implementation of such a system should be aware of these disadvantages before making the pertinent decisions.

 Visit http://www.prenhall.com/trowbridge and select Topic 2—Constructivism and Learning in Science. Select "Activities and Lesson Plans" and find the link for "Science Is Fun in the lab of Shakhashiri." Using this resource, design a plan for alternative assessment that emphasizes development and use of creative ideas or projects that give clues to the teacher about their students' understanding of concepts in science. Submit your plan to your instructor by using the Electronic Bluebook module.

Staff

Individualizing a science program means that the faculty must operate as teams. Instructors must be well prepared in several subjects, because they may be supervising a large laboratory containing students working on units spread over several areas in different subjects. Because students are often working on different units within each of these subjects, a teacher cannot read a chapter ahead of the students the night before and be prepared. Teachers of individualized instruction must know the subjects and curriculum well to interact appropriately with each student's needs.

Acting as a member of a fully functioning team is often difficult because of the differences in how members view their functions as teachers and because of what they think are appropriate requirements for the learners. For example, if some teachers believe that students should be directed to cover a lot of material, and other teachers think students should be given considerable freedom to become autonomous investigators, there are bound to be conflicts among the faculty team members.

Materials

Individualized science instruction demands more reading matter and audiovisual aids than does conventional teaching since multilevel learning aids must be available to adjust materials to students academic abilities. For example, some students may read college-level books or use computers and videodiscs while others work on laboratory investigations.

SUMMARY

Because of the call to educate *all* students in science and because of clear legal mandates, science teaching requires that teachers recognize the unique disabilities, gifts, and talents of their students. Exceptional students will be mainstreamed in regular classrooms, and the gifted also will receive special attention. Although each exceptional student, whether disabled or gifted, presents a distinctive case, there are some guides and suggestions that can help the science teacher meet the specific needs of students.

Science teachers have recognized the needs of students at either end of a continuum, from disabled to gifted. The process has clarified individual differences in general, and it emphasizes the theme of this chapter—*all students can learn science.*

Students vary in their perceptions of school and science and in their cognitive, affective, and psychomotor development. Schools ordinarily have not taught for individual differences because of traditional philosophy and practices, problems of scheduling, poor teacher preparation, instructional costs, poor facilities, and poor equipment. In spite of these problems, many schools are now endeavoring to change the traditional pattern of instruction. This change also has been encouraged by laws requiring individualized programs for exceptional students who are being taught in the regular classroom. Individualized grouping, continuous progress, enrichment programs, team teaching, honors classes, seminars, second-level science courses, and special science classes have been successful.

Although there are advantages and disadvantages to teaching science for individual differences, on balance, the advantages outweigh the disadvantages. To achieve the goals of teaching science for individual differences, all students must develop their understanding of science and abilities of inquiry. You can embody these aspirations in a vision that includes expectations that all students will achieve national standards in science, provision for rich and varied experiences with science content, instruction that accommodates different needs and learning styles, direct action on equity issues, and appropriate assessment strategies.

◆
___
RESOURCES

Technology National Center for Learning Disabilities: www.ld.org
Link Council for Exceptional Children: www.cec.sped.org

LD Resources: www.ldresources.com
Gifted Students: www.kidsource.com

◆
___
REFERENCES

1. Marilyn Friend and William Bursuck, *Including Students with Special Needs: A Practical Guide for Classroom Teachers* (Boston, MA: Allyn and Bacon, 1996).
2. The Civil Rights Project, Daniel Losen and Gary Orfield, editors, *Racial Inequity in Special Education* (Cambridge, MA: Harvard Education Press, 2002).
3. Sidney Marland, *Education of the Gifted and Talented* (Washington, DC: U.S. Government Printing Office, 1972).

CHAPTER
20

TEACHING SCIENCE FOR GENDER AND CULTURAL DIFFERENCES

Research on classroom interactions among teachers and students and between students sheds light on the ways boys, girls, and students of color can have quite different experiences in school. Most of the differences are subtle, some are blatant, yet both can be powerful in molding students' identities. In this chapter, we present an overview of gender issues, which have been studied extensively, and issues related to cultural differences, which have not been studied as extensively, and then conclude with ideas that you can implement in your classroom to make sure that *all* students learn science.

Myra and David Sadker have spent several decades studying gender differences in schools. Their 1994 book, *Failing at Fairness: How Our Schools Cheat Girls,* documents the variable treatment that boys and girls receive in the classroom. They note that the differences are often so subtle and engrained in our culture that when others watch a classroom video full of gender bias, they don't see any of it until it is pointed out. Then participants in their workshops have an "aha!" experience about what subtle gender bias is all about. The Sadkers also illustrate the gender bias pervasive in course materials and how significantly the images presented in these materials can influence students' perceptions of male and female ability. Additionally, parents play an important role in classroom culture through the expectations they maintain for their children and the ways they reinforce or challenge the gendered expectations students encounter at school. In sum, these various forces help create the particular culture of a classroom that, when biased against girls' full participation, can be detrimental to girls' academic and social development.

TEACHER BIAS

In my A.P. physics class in high school there were only three girls and 27 boys. The three girls, myself included, consistently scored at the top end of the scale. On one test I earned a 98. The next closest boy earned an 88. The teacher handed the tests back saying, "Boys, you are failing. These three pretty cookies are outscoring you guys on every test." He told the boys it was embarrassing for them to be beaten by a girl.[1]

Teachers play a central role in determining the climate of their classrooms. While most teachers are unaware that they treat boys and girls differently and some make a conscious effort to avoid gender bias, an examination of many classrooms reveals a subtle and pervasive gender bias that undermines girls' confidence. For example, Sadker and Sadker report that boys call out responses more than girls and demand more of the teacher's attention. While teachers get frustrated with the calling out and set rules that students must raise their hands and wait to be called on, the girls are more often reprimanded for breaking the rule. They write that this "system of silencing operates covertly and repeatedly"[2] throughout years of schooling and socializes girls not to be disruptive, aggressive, or demanding.

Boys' disruptive behavior is reprimanded, but expected, so it gets framed and tolerated differently by teachers than girls' disruptive behavior. Peggy Orenstein's qualitative study of adolescent girls provides many rich examples of some of the phenomena discussed more broadly in Sadker and Sadker's book.

In mid-November, Mrs. Richter is giving out grades. . . The teacher sits at her desk in the back corner of the room, and the students come up one by one. . . When Dawn's turn comes, Mrs. Richter speaks sharply to her. "You're getting a B," the teacher says, "but for citizenship, you're getting 'disruptive.' You've been talking a lot and there have been some outbursts." Dawn scrunches her mouth over to one side of her face, lowers her eyes, and returns to her seat.

"Disruptive?" yells Nate from across the room where the teacher's voice has carried. She's not disruptive, I'm disruptive." Mrs. Richter laughs. "You've got that right," she says. When his turn comes, Nate gets a B plus. "It would've been an A minus if you turned in your last homework assignment," Mrs. Richter says. As predicted, his citizenship comment is also 'disruptive,' but the bad news isn't delivered with the same sting as it was to Dawn—it's conferred with an indulgent smile. There is a tacit acceptance of a disruptive boy, because boys are disruptive. Girls are too, sometimes, as Dawn illustrates, but with different consequences. . . .

Over the course of the semester, Dawn slowly stops disrupting; she stops participating too. At the semester break, when I check with Mrs. Richter on the classes' progress, she tells me, "Dawn hardly talks at all now because she's overpowered by the boys. She can't get the attention in class, so she's calmed down."

Nate, however, hasn't changed a bit, but whereas Dawn's behavior is viewed as containable, the teacher sees Nate's as inevitable. "I'll go through two weeks of torture before I'll give him detention," Mrs. Richter says. "But you have to tolerate that behavior to a certain extent or he won't want to be there at all, he'll get himself kicked out."[3]

As a result of different expectations, girls and boys learn what they can and can't get away with in class. Many girls learn too well the lesson that they are to be cooperative, and their education suffers because of it. Girls are often model students. They get better grades and receive fewer punishments than boys. Their good behavior allows the teacher more time to work with the more difficult to manage boys. As a result, girls receive "less time, less help and fewer challenges. Reinforced for passivity, their independence and self-esteem suffer. As victims of benign neglect, girls are penalized for doing what they should and lose ground as they go through school."[4]

Visit http://www.prenhall.com/trowbridge and select Topic 5—Science Education and Special Needs. Select "Web Links" and find the link for the "National Association for Research in Science Teaching (NARST)." This website addresses matters of gender in artricles on "Teaching for Gender Difference" and others. Open discussion of this matter serves to better inform students in classes on "Methods of Teaching Science" to take appropriate measure in their planning. Use the Chat function to engage in a class discussion on this topic.

Girls are cognizant of these behavior differences and often consider themselves superior to boys, especially at the elementary level. They complain that boys are more off-task, raise their hands even when they don't know an answer, and dominate the class in inappropriate ways. This early confidence fades as girls progress through school. By middle school, many girls place so much importance on being correct and not looking foolish in class that they are afraid to be wrong. A female student in the gifted program at her suburban middle school explained, "Boys never care if they're wrong. They can say totally off-the-wall things, things that have nothing to do with class sometimes. They're not afraid to get in trouble or anything. I'm not shy. But it's like, when I get into class, I just. . . . " She shrugs her shoulders helplessly. "I just can't talk. I don't know why."[5]

Because girls are often afraid of being wrong, they may take longer to respond to a question posed in class. This also works to their detriment, as wait-time analyses have shown that teachers usually give students less than a second to begin to respond to a question. As a result, girls are often bypassed as boys are more willing to offer an answer. Studies have also shown that boys are given slightly longer wait-times but the reasons for this preference are unclear. However, the message sent to students who are given more time to respond is that the teacher has confidence that they will get the answer right.[6,7]

Girls are also sometimes the victims of blatant teacher bias. Blatant bias against girls is often most pronounced in science, math, and technology classrooms in which some teachers believe that boys are more suited to excel in these fields than girls. One student teacher told Sadker and Sadker, "A lot of my female students complained about a science teacher who persisted in referring to them as 'dizzy' or 'ditzy' or 'airhead.' He often told the class, 'You can't expect these girls to know anything.'" A teacher from Louisiana told them about a science teacher who called the boys "Mr." or "Professor" but called the girls by their first names, if they were lucky, or "Blondie." In one extreme case, there is a story of a girl in a high school chemistry class whose repeated question to the male teacher was ignored until he threw a beaker at her and yelled, "What do you want?" Afterward, he told the researcher that girls aren't suited to do science.

The American Association of University Women's (AAUW) Educational Foundation has spearheaded several landmark publications synthesizing the literature regarding girls' experiences in schools. Their 1998 publication, Gender Gaps: Where schools still fail our children, sought to examine the progress that had been made in the 1990s to reduce gender differences in educational outcomes. While there were some signs of improvement, they noted that studies of teacher-student interactions continued to document male domination in the classroom in both large and small groups. The most notable inequities occurred in math, science, and technology classrooms.[8]

What Is the Root of Teacher Bias?

These inequities are not surprising when one considers the cultural bias at work in which girls are expected to excel in the humanities and boys in the sciences.[9,10,11] Many teachers and students believe these generalities exist, and middle and high school level standardized test scores support it. But the root of how these generalizations come about is a topic of intense debate. Are girls biologically predisposed to excel at language and relationships and boys to excel at math and spatial relations? Most educational researchers and scientists maintain that it is impossible to separate "nature" from "nurture" in determining the relative impact of the many forces that shape people's lives.[12,13] Cultural expectations and constructions of gender are extremely powerful in shaping individuals' behavior and are so engrained that it is difficult to examine one's own culture. In the equity literature, it is assumed that differences in educational outcomes among large groups of people are primarily the result of cultural expectations and classroom experiences, not biology.

For example, Sadker and Sadker note that teachers' beliefs that boys are smarter in mathematics and science begin in the earliest school years, at the very time when girls are getting better grades and equal scores on standardized tests. Many adults (teachers included) think that boys possess innate (i.e. biologically based) mathematical and scientific abilities. They believe girls can achieve too, but they must work much harder. As a result of these gendered expectations, teachers send messages to students in line with their beliefs that can shape educational outcomes. Also, a marked reduction in the gender gap in secondary mathematics achievement over the past decade and longstanding equal performance in elementary school strongly supports the notion that if biological differences do exist, they need not determine educational achievement.[14,15,16,17] The literature that documents subtle and blatant teacher bias against girls is one piece of a puzzle that has negative implications for girls' confident participation in school. Decreased confidence is especially probable in subject areas such as science, math, and technology, areas in which many teachers assume that girls' have less natural talent than boys.

STUDENT BIAS

Beliefs about what boys and girls are supposed to do are also transmitted through peer relationships. The messages boys send to girls are both subtle and blatant, and, as with teachers, powerful in defining girls' "place" in areas such as science and math. As stated in the teacher bias section, student bias against girls is most pronounced in areas such as science, math, and technology because of a cultural belief that boys should outperform girls in these areas. The following examples also illustrate this point. McLaren and Gaskell interviewed high school girls in physics class about their experiences and found that girls identified more biased treatment by boys than by teachers.

> In our class there is one guy and he is really, really smart; he has a 90% average and over and he kind of looks at me as if I'm not supposed to be in that class. And he kind of thinks that he's smarter than me and that I'm wasting my time in that class. And then when I get a good mark on my test, I feel really good because I proved to him that I'm not stupid, that I can do it too.[18]

McLaren and Gaskell suggest that boys may feel freer to harass girls in science than in other classes because of larger cultural messages that science is a male domain. They argue that gender should be an official part of the science curriculum to affect change in these attitudes, instead of leaving students to deal with it informally.

Girls may also act as if they don't want to or can't do science because "acting girly" brings attention from boys. For example, Peggy Orenstein observed middle school girls shrieking when a boy dangled a spider in front of them that he had captured for extra credit in science class. They made a big deal about it, and the boys did, too. After the hoopla, a girl told Orenstein, "I'm not *really* afraid of that stuff, except snakes and blood. But guys like it if you act all helpless and girly, so you do."[19] Orenstein reflected on these scenes she witnessed again and again and wrote,

> With each flight toward traditional femininity, I thought about who has permission, who has the right in our culture, to explore the natural world, to get dirty and muddy, to think spiders and worms and frogs are neat, to bring them in for extra credit in science. In fact, to be engaged in science at all.[20]

She also observed several other incidents that reflect how peer interactions shape expected gender roles in science class. In one lab group comprised of two girls and one boy, the girls watch the boy complete a Cartesian diver experiment, offering encouragement but no criticism. The girls squeal with delight when he gets it right and then he lets them each take one turn with the diver before recovering it and continuing to play by himself.

In one final example, several girls are having trouble getting their Cartesian diver to work and ask a boy for help. A girl tells Orenstein, "I told him he could do it for us because he has man's hands." Another boy watching the scene exclaims, "Yes! A *man* had to do it!" when his friend completes the experiment. When a girl in the group asks the boy how he did it, he laughs and answers, "I have magic hands. *Man* hands." Orenstein writes that the girls laugh too—acting appropriately "helpless and girly"—but they never learn how to do the experiment.[21]

These examples illustrate that boys and girls are very aware of the cultural expectations for males and females in science. Both boys and girls reinforce these stereotypes through the comments they make to each other, the types of activities they feel free to engage in, and the types of activities they view as gender-specific. As a result, girls learn that their full participation is not expected in science, in fact it is sometimes actively discouraged, so they are more likely to lose confidence and interest in the subject than boys.

A loss in academic confidence is one piece of a larger picture of diminishing confidence experienced by adolescent girls in our society. Research on developmental issues unique to the adolescent years has shed light on how challenging these years are for all children.[22] It is generally the middle school years, ages 11–14, in which students must grapple with changes in their bodies, increased social pressure to conform to peer culture, hormonal ups and downs, increased awareness of sexuality and desire, and greater awareness of gender roles that apply to themselves. Both boys and girls struggle with these issues, but in general, girls emerge from the storm with their self-esteem less intact than boys. This plunge in self-confidence unique to adolescence is one of the major forces that has implications for middle school girls' participation, interest, and learning in school, especially in science.

COURSE MATERIAL BIAS

Students continue to encounter a male-dominated world in their textbooks, classroom posters, and course presentations. The historical contributions of men make up the majority of history (in all subject areas) that students learn in school. They study male inventors, writers, poets, artists, leaders, and warriors much more than they study women who also filled these roles and other roles that are not as valued in our culture. Not only do textbooks and other materials ignore all but the most "notable" women (e.g. Joan of Arc, Marie Curie, Amelia Earhart, Harriet Tubman), they also do not discuss *why* women are omitted. Just as there is evidence of white men taking credit for the accomplishments of black men in U.S. history, the same is true for women. Historical education ideally would examine how having the legal power to vote, own property, publish, attend college, etc. have framed the contributions of men and women to society, but they often do not.[23]

The researchers have students examine the posters in the room and count the number of men and women represented in them. They find more than 300 men but only 11 women. The students are surprised by the disparity. A girl asks, "But did women really do anything worthwhile? I mean, like Mark says, maybe we were irrelevant." They then display books about the lives of girls and women and mount posters of women in the room. A girl comes up to them and says, "I'm very glad to know this. I hardly know any famous women, and it makes me feel bad, as though I can't do anything. I like science, but this is the first time I've seen books about women scientists. Can I please borrow the book about Barbara McClintock? I want to learn more."[24]

As this illustrates, students want to learn about interesting people, and learning about more women may help girls (and boys) expand their vision of life's possibilities. In fact, there are many women from history and today that merit inclusion in curricula who are omitted due to precedence, oversight, or discrimination.

Course material bias in male-dominated areas such as science is especially problematic for students' developing identities because it reinforces larger cultural stereotypes and girls' self-doubt that they can excel in "male" domains. The same girl in McLaren and Gaskell's study who admitted self-doubt because of putdowns by boys in science class also attributed her lack of confidence to curricular materials. She continued:

> You start thinking, in all the textbooks and stuff all you see is guys. . . . In the textbook you see, this guy invented this sort of thing, a lot in the math and sciences. That's all you really see. You start thinking, "Oh, maybe it's because females can't really do that," and I think, that sort of affects [girls], maybe not because they really particularly think about it, but I think that it may have something to do with it unconsciously or whatever. I just sort of get that impression.[25]

The 1998 literature review by the AAUW indicates that textbooks are somewhat more balanced than they were in 1992, but critics argue that the inclusion of more women into the materials is more about quantity than quality. Women have a greater visual presence in texts, but they are often pictured in stereotypical roles, and the overall historical narrative presented to students has not changed significantly since the research done by Sadker and Sadker.

Boys continue to outperform girls on standard measures of achievement in secondary science (except biology), and girls opt out of advanced science coursework in greater numbers than boys. Science, like math, is often presented as factual, linear, numeric, and objective. "Cookbook" science "experiments" are designed to lead students to one right answer and have dominated the curriculum. Scientists would point out that these exercises, commonly referred to as "experiments," are not experiments at all, but only demonstrations or exercises in following a particular procedure. True experiments are far more creative, engaging, and open-ended. Additionally, units or courses in science can vary so much that previous work may not seem relevant to new material (e.g., chemistry versus physics). Thus, like in math, the probability for difficulty in understanding new concepts and doubting one's ability is greater than in language courses where concepts have more of a spiraling nature.

PARENTAL BIAS

Parents' attitudes about their children's abilities also can have a powerful impact on the development of self-concept. While some parents actively resist gender-stereotyped expectations for their children, less-critical parents may inadvertently contribute to larger cultural stereotypes. For example, many parents foster their sons' interest in traditionally masculine fields such as math, science, and computers by buying mechanical toys for them and putting a computer in their room while assuming these items wouldn't interest their daughters. Early exposure to science-related toys and hobbies has been shown to positively correlate with later science achievement.[28] Some parents maintain different expectations for the types of courses their sons and daughters should pursue and achievement in those courses based on gender stereotypes.

Orenstein recounts a story about Lindsay, a girl in the advanced math track at a suburban middle school. Lindsay was experiencing anxiety attacks at school and home, and doctors could find nothing wrong with her. It turned out that she was failing math and she was terrified of her parents' reaction. Interestingly, her parents were so relieved to find out what was wrong with her that they weren't angry at all. In a discussion with Lindsay's mother, Orenstein asked if the panic attacks could be seen as a warning that Lindsay was placing too much pressure on herself. Her mother instead thought that they were a result of her being placed in a class beyond her capabilities.

> We were surprised that Lindsay was placed in algebra at all. She has always gotten B's in math, so that's not her strong subject. . . . I think the panic was just from not knowing what was going to happen if she brought home an F. We didn't kill her, and I think she was surprised. But I said, "Now if there's any other class where you *should* be doing well and you get and F—*then* you'll be killed for sure."[27]

Perhaps Lindsay's mother really was basing this attitude on her daughter's academic record and not gender stereotypes, but given a larger culture in which women are

viewed as less capable in math (and science) than men, her parents did nothing to counteract gender stereotypes and gave Lindsay permission to opt out of advanced math coursework. It is in this way that parents may reinforce the culture of the classroom and contribute to girls' lack of confidence in areas considered male domains.

ADDING ETHNICITY AND CULTURE TO THE MIX

Much research has been done on girls' passage through adolescence in the 1990s which offers meaningful perspectives on ways in which our cultural expectations demean girls. Individual girls and those from different ethnic groups have many varied experiences and responses to the challenges of these years. For example, far more African-American girls retain their overall self-esteem during adolescence than white or Latina girls. They are almost twice as likely to say they are "happy with the way I am" (despite the messages from school) than girls from other groups and say "they are pretty good at a lot of things" at nearly the rate of white boys (AAUW, 1991). Latina girls, on the other hand, suffer the worst self-esteem drop. The number of Latina girls who are "happy with the way I am" plunges between the ages of nine and fifteen by 38 percentage points, compared to a 33 percent drop for white girls and a 7 percent drop for black girls.[28] Numerous studies illuminate the complexities in girls' lives and indicate that some girls maintain a sense of self and direction better than others. These authors share the conclusion that many girls experience a loss of confidence through their interactions with others and in response to American culture; a loss that takes years to recover from, and, in some cases, only if one is aware of what has happened.[29,30]

Despite the number of studies about girls' passages, there has been little research on boys or the cognitive, metacognitive, and motivational characteristics of students in relationship to their ethnic or cultural background.[31,32] This dearth of work also means that the few studies that exist may not be parallel, so it is difficult to compare studies or begin to make generalizations for the multicultural populations found in many school settings. In this section, we will describe the characteristics that influence learning of a variety of ethnic groups.

There is not clear agreement that various cultural/ethnic groups learn significantly differently from each other. Wang did work that suggests that the differences among ethnic groups are not significant enough to be considered when thinking about how students learn. Rather he suggests that socioeconomic status is a more significant factor than either race or culture.[33] This study suggests that theories emphasizing racial differences in cognitive and metacognitive skills should be rethought in terms of the influences of a combination of cultural-familial factors.

> Visit http://www.prenhall.com/trowbridge and go to Topic 5—National Science Teaching Standards, then select "Science Education System Standards." Find the websites under "equity embodied in science education policies." Among the better ones is the National Science Teachers Association's "Position Statement on Multicultural Education," which clarifies the commitment of NSTA toward all children in science. Write a brief paper summarizing the main points of this position statement and submit to your instructor using the Electronic Bluebook module.

When considering the characteristics of any large group, consider this caution: "One reason that the linkage between culture and learning styles is controversial is that generalizations about a group of people have often led to naive inferences about individuals within that group."[34] Below are some of the characteristics that help describe the strengths different groups of learners bring to the classroom based on the funds of knowledge taught within their culture. The purpose of these lists is to provide a sense of the range of strengths for each population in general. In reality, the lists oversimplify the whole issue. The hope is that this information will help you as a teacher recognize the great chasm between traditional Anglo ways and the strengths that non-Anglo children may bring to the classroom that are now being ignored or "assimilated." The learning characteristics emphasized by Anglo culture are listed first for comparison purposes. These are the characteristics that most curricula and instruction are focused on enhancing. Keeping this perspective in mind makes the differences on other lists even more noticeable. The learning characteristics of Anglo culture[35,36,37] include the following characteristics:

- Value individuality highly
- Believe that reality is material
- Encourage positive self-talk
- Relate to adults in a formal and task-oriented manner
- Reward makes for achievement in academics and athletics, females for friendliness and physical appearance
- Value objectivity, analytical thinking, and accuracy

The learning characteristics of Mexican American culture include the following characteristics:

- Seek friendly, personal adult relationships
- Do not sanction physical contact among adolescent boys and girls
- Become bicultural/bicognitive to succeed
- Are more highly motivated in a cooperative learning environment than in a competitive environment (friends and family form a safety net and support system in daily life)
- Have greater verbal productivity than whites
- Tend to need affiliation
- Family rituals form the basis of social networks and solidarity (families are large and extended)
- Social interactions developed from infancy and maintained through adult life
- Wide latitude given for error; lots of encouragement to try again
- Children learn by modeling adults at home
- Develop a "zone of comfort" at home due to the previous three characteristics; not reinforced at school

The learning characteristics of the African American culture[38-41] include the following:

- Value oral experience; use expressive language
- Emphasize social well-being, solidarity, interdependence and cooperation to benefit society
- Stress loyalty in interpersonal relationships
- Believe that human beings are spiritual
- Treat human behavior as subjective
- Use an effective approach to knowledge
- Believe that the sense of self is collective
- Have a sense of mutual responsibility for other African people
- Get involved physically, cognitively, and emotionally in learning

The learning characteristics of the Native American culture[42,43] include the following:

- Need to understand the whole picture (global learners)
- Make many observations before performing a task
- Find true/false and multiple-choice tests more difficult than essay tests
- Are stronger at synthesis and interrelating ideas
- Like to have "discussions with self"
- Come from a strong oral tradition
- Believe in balance in the universe
- Believe that humans are a part of nature, not superior to it
- Treat every individual with dignity
- Believe that reality is spiritual
- Value cooperation and harmony highly
- Believe that making eye contact with adults is disrespectful
- Include learning by doing, symbols, dreams, and humor in traditional education

♦ Show respect to adults by disagreeing with the elders
♦ Discourage the demonstration of achievement and individual competition unless it benefits the group in some way (Jim Thorpe at the Olympics)

Many of the dominant characteristics of nonwhite learners align well with ideas about how to improve students' success in learning science such as making observations, being able to consider the whole picture rather than the parts, and having strong social skills. What does not align well are the Western definitions of some of the attributes. For example, consider the terms *academic time management, practice, goal-directedness,* and *sense of self-efficacy* in light of the characteristics of white learners and dominant white culture: We mean learners who can stick to a task, use their time wisely, and believe in their ability to do the task. This perspective favors a learner who works quickly, quietly, and efficiently and is willing to tell the teacher what a good job she has done.

If we reframe those characteristics from a nonwhite perspective, we need to focus on characteristics like putting the task into perspective, that is, fitting it into the big picture, doing the task cooperatively, creatively, and so that it honors the learner's culture. The more holistic approach of most nonwhite learners allows for greater reflection, if the instructor and the curriculum recognize this asset.

Technology 🖥️ **Link**

SCIENCE, COMPUTING, AND EQUITY

The computing culture shares many similarities with the culture of science. Research indicates that computer technology is also viewed as a heavily masculine domain and that girls experience biased treatment by teachers, peers, parents, and course materials that contributes to their lack of interest in the field when compared with boys. When computer technology is used in the science classroom, as is becoming more commonplace, the combination of the science and computing cultures may compound these notions of masculinity and further alienate girls and others already disengaged from science. Much research has been conducted on students' responses to the use of computer technology in the classroom and evidence suggests that most students, both boys and girls, have positive attitudes toward computers.[44,45]

In particular, research has shown that students enjoy the change from typical classroom instruction that using computers brings, and that so far there has not been a novelty effect in which interest has dissipated over time. Computer lab environments are typically more social and offer students more opportunities for personal control than the regular classroom environment, contributing to increased motivation. Collaborative Internet projects, in particular, offer unique opportunities that have been shown to positively affect student interest. Gender differences in computer use at school are remarkably similar to gender differences noted in science classes. Boys tend to do the work while girls watch when in mixed-sex groups, or girls perform the secretarial tasks while the boys make project decisions. Girls in advanced high school computer science classes are few and far between and are often subject to more sexual harassment and isolation in these classes than in others. The higher ratio of boys to girls in these courses has been offered as an explanation for this occurrence. In one case study, the only girl who managed to interact respectfully with the boys in an advanced computer science class publicly denigrated her own abilities and fit accepted feminine images (she was attractive, nice, and a cheerleader).[46,47,48]

The gender equity literatures in science and computer technology share some common goals. The works examine how the cultures of scientific and computer technology communities create climates that are open and closed to different groups of people. They contend that cultural barriers, not innate or biological differences are responsible for disparities in achievement and participation. Today, both pieces of literature suggest that it is not the girls who need to catch up with science or computers, but that science and computers need to catch up with them. In other words, girls' legitimate concerns should focus attention on changing the software and curricula, pedagogy, and goals for science and computer technology education. A successful transformation would enable more women and other reticent groups to be able to visualize themselves as legitimate participants and those fields as interesting and meaningful. The pieces of literature share the belief that increasing the participation of women in scientific and computer professions will benefit the fields by bringing in more diverse perspectives. Both argue that changing educational practices, curricula, and culture will ultimately benefit both the "haves" and "have-nots" by creating more opportunities for engagement, and will not eliminate what has worked for those already engaged.[49]

WHAT ARE THE IMPLICATIONS FOR CURRICULUM AND INSTRUCTION?

To help all learners have the opportunity to develop as successful science learners, change is necessary in three major areas of school: curriculum, instruction, and assessment. Banks[50] and Ladson-Billings[51] both endorse a transformation approach to curriculum. The essence of the transformation approach, according to Banks, is that it "changes the structure, assumptions, and perspectives of the curriculum so that subject matter is viewed from the perspectives and experiences of a range of groups."

An advantage of this approach is that it brings awareness of marginalized groups to all learners and therefore legitimates their experiences. In addition, it helps learners construct their own understanding of their culture and the cultures of others. Increased understanding decreases the stereotype images often reinforced by the "festival" approach to multicultural education. Think about the instructional materials described in Chapters 8 and 9—how do they fit with a transformation view of curriculum?

 Visit http://www.prenhall.com/trowbridge and select Topic 2—Constructivism and Science Learning. Select "Activities and Lesson Plans" and find the website on "Amateur Science." This site will open up possibilities for projects that may emphasize equity matters such as diverse groups working together. Capture some ideas for future use by referencing this website in your notes for application when you begin teaching.

In terms of instruction, the single biggest change that teachers in multicultural environments can make is to include cooperative learning strategies in their teaching.[52-55] This does not necessarily mean doing more group work. These opportunities for cooperative learning must allow for students to construct their knowledge in a safe, social environment that allows all students to articulate their understanding.

In addition to this major change in instruction, there are a variety of strategies teachers can employ to help all students succeed in science.[56-64] For example, try the following in your classroom:

- set expectations as high for nonwhite students as for white students,
- accept all students' experiences as legitimate,
- use the language and understandings of the children, and
- provide access to higher-order thinking skills for all students, and use other students as language and cultural brokers.

Consider the following actions to help you develop a multicultural classroom.

Show Respect for Cultural Differences

Develop a perspective of cultural differences rather than cultural deficits. The former will help you see that cultural groups have different views and learning styles, the accommodation of which will greatly enhance learning science. The latter perspective perpetuates the myth that differences equal deficits and that girls, minorities, and exceptional students have problems learning science.

Respect for cultural differences means that you understand that there is not one best way to learn science and that every student has a unique perspective and approach to learning. Value what each student brings to the classroom, whether it is another language, travel to other countries, or just a different way of completing routine activities.

Consider the Cultural Resources of Your Students

Although diverse groups may be in your science class, it is difficult to know exactly which groups (and how many individuals) will predominate. The point here is your openness to understanding the groups represented in your classes. You might consider home visits, involvement in community activities, talking with parents, observing students in nonclassroom and nonschool settings, and reading about different cultures.

Use Understanding to Enhance Learning

In numerous sections of this book we have discussed the model of learning that begins with students' current conceptions of science and constructs more adequate conceptions aligned with science. So it is that some students will have prior knowledge influenced by their culture-bound experiences. You should not avoid using this as a foundation for teaching and learning.

Make Decisions That Enhance Learning

From the moment you begin teaching a lesson, you will receive feedback from students about their interest, attention, and understanding. You will have to decide what to do—how to adjust your plans—in order to enhance learning. In classrooms with culturally different groups, you will have to be more sensitive to student signals because some may vary from what you have previously experienced. Although the subtleties of culturally influenced responses may take some time to understand, it is not too early to be aware of their influences and to carefully evaluate each lesson, asking where students had difficulty, if all students were involved, which students seemed interested, and what evidence you have that learning occurred.

Provide Time

Students need time to activate their prior knowledge. If activated, they will have more to share in class. Writing in journals, working in small groups on focus questions, or participating in paired brainstorming sessions are examples of strategies that will provide opportunities for you and the students to identify what is known and what is not.

Provide Positive Role Models

Students should learn from individuals who represent different cultural groups. Students have to recognize that women, minorities, and individuals with handicaps can all do science and make contributions to society.

As part of fulfilling the national standards on the History and Nature of Science, you should introduce students to the diversity of individuals who have contributed to advances in science, engineering, medicine, and other related professions.

Use Cooperative Groups

Research shows that cooperative groups, when adequately implemented, help all students become involved and learn science. Cooperative groups shift responsibilities among members and thus subtly confront stereotypes and prejudices while allowing for individual and cultural differences.

Use Hands-On Investigations

In general, all students are motivated through active involvement. The physical manipulation of materials, the intellectual encounter, and cooperation with peers that occurs while doing investigations contribute to all students learning more science.

Provide Equal Opportunities and Expectations

All students should have experiences with science equipment, computers, field trips, and materials. Again, we point out the advantage of cooperative group work in achieving the goal of equal opportunity for student involvement. You should also make it clear that you expect all students to become involved and develop the abilities associated with inquiry and the use of facilities, materials, and equipment.

Use Appropriate Language

When teaching science, you will often use analogies and metaphors. Try to balance male and female metaphors and use examples that incorporate other cultures.

Be Sensitive in Questioning

Science teachers ask a lot of questions. When you ask a question—WAIT—so all students have time to ponder and reflect on the answer. You should also be aware of who responds and who you ask to respond. Teachers often have different reactions to different students, and the differences too often reveal the teacher's perceptions of student abilities.

Communicate with Parents

Parents are your allies. Assume they care about what is happening in school as well as with their own children. But remember that caring does not translate into specific knowledge about how to support their children in school. Let parents know about achievement gaps from national and international data that show the inequities by gender, race, culture, and geographic region. Often this awareness helps parents support higher standards at school and at home. Emphasize the importance of reading for improving all academic performance, and provide parents with book lists of reading that appeal to your students.

Keep parents informed by sending advance notice about major assignments and assessments. Prepare a copy of the syllabus to send home with students, in the mail, or by email. Send updates regularly. When talking to parents about their own children, point out what the student has done well and what is not going well and the reasons for each. Conduct workshops for parents that model what you are doing in class or that help connect science to real life.

Maintain High Expectations

Regardless of the diversity in your science class, you should make it clear that you expect all students to achieve higher levels of achievement. You should expect all students to participate, use complete sentences, and use correct grammar when speaking or writing, and make clear that you will do everything you can to help all students succeed in science class.

SUMMARY

Science teachers need to recognize the unique influences of culture on students' perceptions and learning styles. Two large ideas that are developed in other chapters in this book and in the *National Science Education Standards* will help you attend to each child in your classroom as a unique learner. The first is to use a constructivist approach to organize your teaching (see Chapter 16), and the second is to use authentic assessment strategies (see Chapter 17).

Constructivism blends well with cooperative learning strategies and provides a methodology for accepting and legitimating all learners' explanations. Adherence to a constructivist philosophy also changes the pace in the classroom so that each learner has time to construct an understanding of a concept. Constructivist strategies in the classroom encourage learners to make use of what they already know and build new knowledge connections from there.

Authentic assessment tasks will build on the strengths many female and non-Anglo learners bring to the classroom, because they place the assessment in a context that is meaningful for the learner. Traditional forms of assessment remove this context, thereby handicapping most nonwhite learners. By authentic, we mean the use of assessment tasks that reflect the teaching and learning environment. For instance, in a science classroom that is rich in hands-on, inquiry-oriented laboratory activities, it is not authentic to use paper-and-pencil tests as the only form of assessment. Authentic assessment for this classroom would include hands-on, inquiry-oriented tasks.

Regardless of which specific changes you or your school chooses to implement to improve the learning opportunities for all students, we all must move away from deficit models that emphasize what non-Anglo learners *can't* do (or don't do) when compared to white learners. Schools should celebrate the diversity and range of approaches and experiences that each learner brings to the classroom. This celebration allows all learners to develop to the best of their ability and increases their chances of becoming lifelong, self-regulating learners.

◆
_____

REFERENCES

1. Myra Sadker and David Sadker, *Failing at Fairness: How Our Schools Cheat Girls* (New York, NY: Macmillan Publishing Company, 1994).
2. *Ibid.*, p. 43.
3. Peggy Orenstein, *SchoolGirls. Young Women, Self-Esteem, and the Confidence Gap* (New York, NY: Bantam Doubleday Dell Publishing Group 1994), pp. 16–17.
4. Sadker & Sadker, 1994, p. 44.
5. Orenstein, 1994.
6. American Association of University Women Educational Foundation (AAUW), *Gender Gaps: Where Schools Still Fail Our Children* (Washington, DC: Author, 1998).
7. Sadker & Sadker, 1994.
8. AAUW, 1998.
9. Jane Butler Kahle, *Measuring Progress toward Equity in Science and Mathematics Education* (Madison, WI: National Institute for Science Education, 1998).
10. Orenstein, 1994.
11. Sadker & Sadker, 1994.
12. T. Berry Brazelton and Stanley I. Greenspan, *The Irreducible Needs of Children: What Every Child Must Have To Grow, Learn, and Flourish* (Boulder, CO: Perseus Book Group, 2000).
13. Bryant, A. & Clark, E. (Fall/Winter, 2000). How parents raise boys and girls. Newsweek, pp. 64–65.
14. American Association of University Women Educational Foundation, *How Schools Shortchange Girls* (Washington, DC: Author, 1992).
15. AAUW, 1998.
16. National Center for Education Statistics, *Digest of Education Statistics* (Washington, DC: U.S. Department of Education, May, 2001).
17. A. McLaren and P.J. Gaskell, "Now you see it, now you don't: Gender as an issue in school science." In J. Gaskell & J. Willinsky, Eds., *Gender in/forms curriculum: from enrichment to transformation* (New York, NY: Teachers College Press, 1995), pp. 136–156.
18. Orenstein, 1994, p.22.
19. *Ibid.*
20. *Ibid.*, p. 26.
21. Paul deHart Hurd, *Transforming Middle School Science Education. Ways of Knowing in Science Series* (New York, NY: Teachers College Press, 2000).
22. AAUW, 1998.
23. Sadker & Sadker, 1994.
24. *Ibid.*, pp. 129–130.
25. *Ibid.*, p. 148.
26. Kahle, 1998.
27. Orenstein, 1994, p. 49.
28. *Ibid.*
29. Mary Pipher, *Reviving Ophelia: Saving the Selves of Adolescent Girls* (New York, NY: Ballantine Books, 1994).
30. Lyn M. Brown and Carol Gilligan, *Meeting at the Crossroads: Women's Psychology and Girls' Development* (Cambridge, MA: Harvard University Press, 1992).
31. Deborah Taylor and Maureen Lorimer, "Helping Boys Succeed," *Educational Leadership* 60 (4) (2002): 68–71.
32. P. Guild, "The Culture/Learning Style Connection," *Educational Leadership*, 51 (8) (1994): 16–21.
33. A. Y. Wang, "Cultural Familial Predicators Predictors of Children's Metacognitive and Academic Performance," *Journal of Research in Childhood Education*, 7 (2) (1993): 83–90.
34. P. Guild, 1994.
35. C. R. G. Bert and M. Bert, *The Native American: An Exceptionality in Education and Counseling* (1992). (ERIC Document Reproduction Service No. ED351 168).
36. B. C. Howard, *Learning to Persist—Persisting to Learn* (1989). (ERIC Document Reproduction Service No. ED325 592).
37. Taylor and Lorimar, 2002.
38. P. Guild, 1994.
39. B. C. Howard, 1989.
40. K. Murtadha, "An African-Centered Pedagogy in Dialog with Liberatory Multiculturalism," in *Multicultural Education, Critical Pedagogy, and the Politics of Difference,*

C. E. Sleeter and P. L. McLaren, eds. (Albany, NY: SUNY, 1995), pp. 349–370.

41. Kay Lovelace Taylor, "Through the Eyes of Students," *Educational Leadership* 60 (4) (2002): 72–75.

42. C. R. G. Bert and M. Bert, *The Native American: An Exceptionality in Education and Counseling* (1992). (ERIC Document Reproduction Service No. ED351 168).

43. Howard, 1989.

44. Megan Mistler-Jackson and Nancy Butler Songer, "Student Motivation and Internet Technology: Are Students Empowered to Learn Science?" *Journal of Research in Science Teaching* 37 (5) (May, 2000): 459–79.

45. Janet Ward Schofield, *Computers and Classroom Culture* (New York, NY: Cambridge University Press, 1995).

46. AAUW, 2000.

47. Freeman A. Hrabowski, "Raising Minority Achievement in Science and Math," *Educational Leadership,* 60 (4) (2002): 44–48.

48. Schofield, 1995.

49. AAUW, 2000.

50. James A. Banks, "Transforming the Mainstream Curriculum." Educational Leadership 51 (8) (1994): 4–8.

51. G. Ladson-Billings, "What We Can Learn from Multicultural Education Research," *Educational Leadership* 51 (8) (1994): 22–27.

52. A. Darder, "Buscando America: The Contributions of Critical Latino Educators to the Academic Development and Empowerment of Latino Students in the U.S.," in *Multicultural Education, Critical Pedagogy, and the Politics of Difference,* C. E. Sleeter and P. L. McLaren, eds. (Albany, NY: SUNY, 1995), pp. 319–348.

53. R. Donato and D. Hernández, "Metacognitive Equity for Mexican American Language-Minority Students," in *Compendium of Readings in Bilingual Education: Issues and Practices,* R. Rodriquez, ed. (San Antonio, TX: Texas Association for Bilingual Education, 1994), pp. 22–30.

54. Ladson-Billings, 1994.

55. Murtadha, 1995.

56. C. K. Howe, "Improving the Achievement of Hispanic Students," *Educational Leadership,* 51 (8) (1994): 42–44.

57. Ladson-Billings, 1994.

58. R. Donato and D. Hernandez, 1994.

59. S. Pogrow, "Teaching Thinking to At-Risk Elementary Students," *Educational Leadership* (1988): 79–85.

60. Ana Maria Villegas, "Culturally Responsive Teaching," in *Foundations for Tomorrow's Teachers #1* (Princeton, NJ: Educational Testing Service, 1991).

61. Hrabowski, 2002.

62. Carmen A. Rolón, "Educating Latino Students," *Educational Leadership* 60 (4) (2002): 40–43.

63. Larry I. Bell, "Strategies that Close the Gap," *Educational Leadership* 60 (4) (2002): 32–34.

64. Taylor, 2002.

Author's Note: Megan Mistler-Jackson was a primary author on this chapter

CONTROVERSY IN THE CLASSROOM

Every science teacher encounters controversial issues in discussions in the science classroom. These may emerge unexpectedly, or they may be an integral part of lessons. If they are anticipated, you will have the advantage of preplanning, thinking through strategies, and arranging for necessary materials and information. If they occur unexpectedly, our advice is to have an understanding of the science, the ethics, and a general plan of action that has been considered and prepared in advance. It is wise to take the point of view that students have mind-sets, opinions, or even biases (which may reflect opinions learned at home), that they have a right to those opinions, and that the teacher's role is not one of promoting a particular point of view, but rather one of fostering orderly discussion of the issues.

Controversial issues may include a wide range of topics and will often reflect national, state, or local conflicts of ideas or values. The latter may occur frequently on the occasion of state or local elections, at which time the electorate will consider a variety of referendums. For example, issues that have gained notoriety in the media are doctor-assisted suicide, environmental concerns regarding protection of endangered species, research on human embryos, use of human fetuses in medical research, teaching of creationism versus evolution, controlling population growth, controlling growth of cities, use of water resources, and restrictions on smoking in public places. There is no foreseeable end to these issues, nor to the inevitable controversies that develop among the public.

Part of science education for students in our schools is learning how to deal with opinions of persons whose views differ from their own. Avoiding discussion of the issues will not bring about necessary learning,

changes in attitudes, understanding of others' opinions, or interaction skills with people with differing ideas. Incorporating activities that address controversial issues will enhance student learning and present opportunities to develop abilities to think critically and resolve conflicts. In addition, students will build a foundation of civic responsibility.

Controversy in the classroom confronts the teacher with issues of ethics and conflict resolution. In this chapter we present a brief introduction to these areas.

ETHICS IN THE SCIENCE CLASSROOM

Ethics is the study of the general nature of morals and of the moral choices made by individuals and groups. In everyday terms, ethics is concerned with right or wrong actions and judgments about whether individuals are good or bad persons. For most of the controversial issues in science classrooms, ethics relates to the moral quality of a course of action. For example, decisions about the use or nonuse of medicines, cutting or not cutting forests, or using or not using human growth hormones.

As a science teacher you will encounter ethical positions, and it is best to understand the many origins of these positions. The various sources for ethical positions include the law, family traditions, community expectations, religious traditions, and the influence of friends. These are some of the most frequently involved sources. Because of this variety, addressing ethical issues in the science classroom can be frustrating and confusing. With care and attention you can use controversy to help students develop their ability to think critically. However, you will have to focus on *ethics as a process of critical thinking* and not on picking a solution or deciding on an answer.

It is safe to assume that the future will require citizens to make personal and social decisions that involve aspects of science and technology. For the most part, such decisions will center on issues such as population growth, resource use, agriculture, environmental quality, and health. This is where ethics enters, and where these citizens will be presented with competing points of view. How can you best help students decide between (or among) competing points of view? You can help them develop the language and skills to

- clearly communicate their moral concerns;
- understand others' points of view;
- rigorously analyze our own points of view and those of others; and
- respectfully argue about and criticize differing points of view.

In short, approach ethics in the science classroom as a process of thinking critically about morally difficult matters. This process of critical thinking should be approached in a way that promotes respect for and serious consideration of the views of others. When implemented in careful, consistent, and patient ways, ethics in the science classroom contributes directly to one of the primary aims of education—citizenship.

ETHICAL ANALYSIS IN THE SCIENCE CLASSROOM

Ethical analysis and scientific inquiry share the commitment to rational discourse. Scientific inquiry is a form of rational analysis of facts and empirical matters. Scientists ask, What is the case, and how can we best explain it? Ethics is a form of rational analysis into right and wrong action and good and bad character. Ethicists ask, What ought we to do or be, and what justifies our answers to such questions? Scientific inquiry insists on rigor and on following rules of rational analysis for developing an explanation for natural phenomena. Ethics insists on the following as its rules for rational analysis and discourse:

Assumptions about rules and character must be examined and supported. Opinions have no weight. This requirement is similar to the requirement in science that proposed explanations be supported by empirical data. Unsupported explanations command no respect. In the absence of justification, the process of ethics breaks down.

Arguments justifying a point of view must appeal to reasons that any reasonable person can accept, regardless of his or her particular beliefs. Justifications must be as universal and objective as possible. Here, "objective" means they should be as free of idiosyncrasy as possible. "Universal" means that they should be widely shareable.

Arguments justifying a point of view must always be open to criticism, including and especially self-criticism. "How could I be mistaken, confused, or inconsistent?" is a question that is essential for ethical analysis.

The results of ethical analysis are arguments that establish a point of view as reasonable, a point of view that reasonable people should be willing to accept. The persuasive power of ethics, like that of science, relies on the mutual commitment to rational, disciplined inquiry.

Results of ethical analysis are, therefore, tentative; they are never final or certain, any more than the results of a scientific inquiry. One must, as a result, always be open to the possibility of ending with poor results, or "getting it wrong," thus, the possibility of beginning another round of ethical analysis.

There are four elements to the process of ethical analysis that you can develop in the classroom.

1. Interpretation. This task involves helping students communicate clearly and carefully what each has to say. The task of interpretation requires students to define and clarify terms. Thus, the first element of ethical analysis is to establish clearly the meaning of key terms and to use those terms with *consistent meaning* throughout the process of justification.

2. Analysis. The task here is to identify the nature of the reasons that someone is proposing as the justification for a point of view. The conceptual tools of ethics are brought to bear at this stage of ethical analysis in an attempt to answer the question, "What is the focus of a justification?" The nature of the reasons that students use include negative consequences, for example, results are detrimental to health or safety; or positive consequences, for example, eliminating hunger or disease. Other reasons include respect for individual rights and beliefs. Finally, fairness or justice is often one of the reasons students argue in analysis.

3. Argument. This task involves giving and testing reasons that together support or justify a point of view. The task here has several steps. First, we need to identify the premises that are asserted in support of a conclusion. Arguments, to be complete, must have both premises and conclusions. Second, we need to examine the warrants for premises—why their proponent thinks them to be true. Third, we need to determine whether the conclusion does indeed follow the premises.

4. Critique of the justification.   Critique proceeds by asking these questions about each of the first three elements of doing ethics:

   a. Has the proponent been clear and consistent in the use of key terms?

   b. Has the proponent focused on all of the relevant moral considerations? Has the proponent identified the full range of ethical implications of the science or technology issue being considered? That is, has the proponent appreciated the fact that ethical analysis requires a solid, complete, and rational foundation?

   c. How good is the proponent's argument?

     (1) Is it complete? Are there missing premises?

     (2) Are the warrants for its premises established on rational grounds? How could one disagree with the warrants that are offered?

     (3) Does the conclusion follow from the premises? Do other conclusions follow from the premises?

This is an excellent place to stop and turn to Activity 21-1 at the conclusion of the chapter. This activity centers on the distribution of resources and provides an introduction to the process of ethical analysis.

ETHICAL DEVELOPMENT OF STUDENTS

Many of the issues that pose controversial problems for discussion in science classrooms are of an ethical nature. This situation creates the need to consider the development and maturity of students with respect to their innate abilities to deal with complex ethical problems. In the 1970s, Lawrence Kohlberg[1] studied matters of moral development of children. Kohlberg used Piaget's research on moral development as the foundation for his studies. He carried out numerous studies in the United States and in other countries striving to better define moral development.

One of his main works, started in 1958, involved a longitudinal study of boys at ages 10 and 16, and followed their development past the ages of 24 and 30. Kohlberg also made several cross-cultural investigations. His research generally substantiated Piaget's proposition that moral development is hierarchical in character. Kohlberg proposed that moral development consists of three levels, each containing stages identified as *preconventional, conventional,* and *postconventional.* The following paragraphs describe these levels.

At the preconventional level, children are responsive to such rules and labels as good and bad, right and wrong. They interpret these labels in purely physical or hedonistic terms—if they are bad, they are punished; if

they are good, they are rewarded. They also interpret labels in terms of the physical power of those who enumerate them. Two stages in this level consist of punishment avoidance and reward seeking.

At the conventional level, expectations of the individual's family, group, or nation are perceived as valuable in their own right, regardless of immediate and obvious consequences. The attitude is one not only of conformity to the social order but also of loyalty to it—of actively maintaining, supporting, and justifying the order, and of identifying with the persons or group involved in it. Two stages are recognized in this level: socially approved orientation and law-and-order orientation.

At the postconventional level, there is a clear effort to teach to others a personal definition of moral values—to define principles that have validity and application apart from the authority of groups or persons and apart from the individual's own identification with these groups. Two stages in this level consist of a social-contract legalistic orientation and an orientation toward universal ethical principles. In the first of these stages, there is a clear awareness of the importance of personal values and opinions, and a corresponding emphasis on procedural rules for resolving conflicts. In the latter stage, rights are defined by the conscience in accordance with self-chosen principles, which are based on logical comprehensiveness, universality, and consistency. These principles are abstract and ethical (e.g., the golden rule).

Because Kohlberg's study population was all male, more recent studies have been conducted to find out whether his ideas could be universally applied to all students.[2,3,4] This scholarship shows that females are relational, connected learners. In other words, girls and women tend to view the world holistically and see how things are connected together. This means that females are more likely to follow an ethic of care and responsibility while males are more likely to view things separate and independent of each other. You may see this difference in approaches when you ask students to support a specific side of an issue. Students who view things as connected will have difficulty choosing one idea over another because they may see the strengths and weakness in both choices.

CONFLICT RESOLUTION IN THE SCIENCE CLASSROOM

By their very nature, incorporation of science-related social issues within science classes brings forth many situations subject to differing interpretations, differing values, and differing points of view. Frequently, environmental concerns come to the foreground. Matters of resource allocation and conservation generate intense interest and strong opinions among students. Pitting the economic benefits of cutting forests against the endangerment of flora and fauna living in these areas is often personalized by students, who take strong positions. Such situations present opportunities for students to learn how to resolve science and technology-related social conflicts. The Key Issues Program of Keystone Science School has developed a mediation process for resolving conflicts. It is especially important to understand that individuals have preferred ways of resolving conflicts and that any one way of resolving a conflict is appropriate in some cases and inappropriate in others. Table 21-1 displays five different ways of resolving controversial issues.

In addition to the problems of providing opportunities for fair and objective discussions of the conflicting points of view found in one's classes, the teacher must also be concerned about student achievement and anxiety while sensitive topics are being discussed. Such concerns take one beyond the realms of simple evaluation and grading into areas of concern for feelings, attitude development, and values formation.

Jon Pedersen studied the effects of controversy relating to a science-technology-society issue on achievement and anxiety among secondary school science students. He found that "A controversy can exist when one student's ideas, information, conclusions, theories, or opinions are incompatible with those of another student or when incompatible activities occur and the students involved try to reach an agreement."[5]

A group of students studying the CHEM-COM chemistry program was divided into two subgroups. One group used a method called cooperative controversy, and the other group used individualistic study. In the cooperative controversy model, student groups of four each were formed and divided into pairs—one pair to present a pro position, and the other pair to present a con position of the issue being studied. Each pair, after sufficient preparation, presented its position, and the positions were debated by the group which then reached a consensus and wrote a collaborative report.

In the individualistic model, students worked on their own and were told to read, study, and research the assigned issue using any resources available.

The period of time involved was 20 days (four weeks). At the end of the period, two measures were used for evaluation. Anxiety levels were measured using a State-Trait Anxiety Inventory. Class achievement was measured by a teacher-made achievement test.

The researchers concluded that the cooperative controversy treatment had a positive effect on the dependent variable, anxiety, but no effect on the depend-

TABLE 21–1

Methods	What Happens When Used	Appropriate to Use When. . .	Inappropriate to Use When. . .
Denial or Withdrawal	Person withdraws to solve the problem.	The issue is relatively unimportant, timing is wrong, cooling off period is needed, withdrawal offers a short-term solution.	The issue is important, will not disappear, and builds.
Suppression or Smoothing Over	Differences are played down; *surface* harmony exists. May result in resentment, defensiveness, and possible sabotage if primary issues remain unresolved.	Preservation of the relationship between parties is more important than resolving the controversy.	Reluctance to deal with the conflict leads to evasion of an important issue or when players are ready and willing to deal with the issue.
Power or Dominance	One's authority, position, majority rule, or a persuasive minority settles the conflict.	Power comes with the position of authority and when this method has been agreed upon.	Losers have no way to express their needs. Could result in future disruptions.
Compromise or Negotiation	Each party gives up something in order to meet halfway.	Both parties have enough leeway to give, resources are limited, or when win/lose stance is undesirable.	The original position is inflated and unrealistic, the solution is too diluted to be effective, and the commitment is doubted by the parties involved.
Collaboration or Mediation	Each player's position is clear and the abilities, values, interests, and expertise of all are recognized.	Time is available to complete the process, parties are committed and trained in use of the process.	The conditions of time, abilities, commitment are not present.

Adapted from Key Issues Mediation Techniques, a program of the Keystone Science School, Keystone, Colorado. Used with permission.

ent variable, achievement. Anxiety was reduced, possibly because of the opportunities for sharing information and tasks, which may have minimized difficulties of understanding among individuals. Working independently on an issue did not provide this kind of help and reinforcement.

DESIGNING CONTROVERSIES FOR THE SCIENCE CLASSROOM

Before continuing, you may wish to complete Activity 21-2 on issues in the science classroom.

For the teacher, consideration of the moral development and maturity of students provides clues for structuring discussions of controversial issues. Damon argues that it is not enough for children to distinguish right from wrong, they must develop a commitment to acting on their ideals.[6] Here is a suggested flow of steps to guide your students through in their study of science-based social issues:

1. Identify the conflict and theme for the controversy (e.g., life, liberty, justice, truth, etc.).
2. Introduce the scientific or technological problem.
3. Clarify the conflict.
4. Be sure there is a controversy (i.e., a choice between two or more alternatives).
5. Describe the situation and controversy to the student in understandable terms.
6. Delineate the possible decision in the dilemma.
7. Review the ethical positions and describe what you perceive to be the pro/con positions for each stage.
8. Ask for a definitive decision with reference to the controversy.
9. Remember that a good controversy is simple, straightforward, and relevant to students.
10. Ask for a justification for the response.

After introducing the controversy, the science teacher should guide the discussion, making sure the students stay on the topic. The teacher can point out inconsistencies in reasoning and more adequate resolutions to the controversy. Be sure to let the students answer and justify their positions.

OTHER STRATEGIES FOR TEACHING ABOUT CONTROVERSIAL ISSUES

Areas of biology teaching are fraught with issues that are controversial in today's world. One is the issue of genetic engineering. This is a topic that deals with genetic screening/eugenics, cloning, gene therapy (modification of human genes that cause disease), and gene al-

teration (of plants and animals including humans). A teaching strategy for dealing with this and similar issues in the classroom is debate. An experimental procedure carried out by two teachers in Rosemont, Minnesota, has taught us much about what makes debate an effective strategy for teaching.[7]

Objectives for the unit included understanding of topics of genetic engineering and biotechnology; identification of different issues within the field, such as cloning; gene therapy and gene alteration; and production of a final essay summarizing the students' learning in genetic engineering.

After thorough planning and adherence to the rules of debate, the *debate format* worked well. A selected judge monitored the debate procedures, and a jury of peers rendered a decision at the end of the debate. The total time required to carry out the sequence of preparation, debate time, and final discussions was seven days of class time, which was considered reasonable considering the benefits achieved.

Some of the obvious benefits were that many students indicated they had formed their own opinions on the issues, rather than just following the crowd. Pre- and posttest results showed a decrease in the number of unsure responses concerning resolution of the issues. Each student was accountable for some part of the exercise, and students maintained a high interest level throughout the period.

For teachers faced with the perplexing problem of how to approach discussion of controversial issues in class, the debate format described above offers a positive strategy. The benefit of using this approach is the opportunity for creative modifications and diversions of the method.

Other effective methods to use in science classrooms when exploring and discussing current issues of concern are role-playing, morphological analysis, creativity-synectics, and others. *Role-playing* is a particularly useful technique because it allows students to place themselves in someone else's shoes. One example deals with the problem of the proposed construction of a superhighway through valuable agricultural land. The issue centers on the selection of an appropriate route that would minimize the agricultural damage. Obviously, there are more than two positions or views to such an issue.

To set up the situation, the instructor described the following: There is the head of the federal transportation department, a cabinet-level appointee, who has jurisdiction over interstate highways. There is the truckers' union, which is concerned with economy of delivering goods. The agricultural community, represented by several state and federal agencies, is intimately concerned and affected by any decisions. In addition, a number of organizations are concerned with environmental issues; business groups from small cities and towns that might be bypassed by such a superhighway express their concerns; and other groups interested in aesthetics and general quality of life are also vocal in their expressions of concern.

To get the teaching activities started, the instructor suggested a number of roles that might properly be included in the exercise. Such roles might include the representative of the highway department, chair of one or more agricultural agencies, president of a local environmental club, a number of farmers along the proposed route who would be directly affected by the construction, a lawyer for the highway department, as well as a lawyer for the agricultural agencies, and others. Students were encouraged to suggest other roles that might enhance the discussion of the issues.

A short prospectus was written by the instructor for each of the proposed roles. The prospectus in each case was general and suggested points of view that the player might take. Ample opportunity was provided for role-players to create, amplify, or embellish their points of view. This generated superb interest on the part of class members and led to much humor and good feeling. Roles were chosen or assigned, and the portion of the class not involved in the role-playing function were assigned the task of evaluating the effectiveness of each presentation and deciding on the outcome.

After one or two days of preparation to gather facts and figures, prepare statements, discuss pros and cons, and research data, a day was chosen for the meeting of the various representatives. This hearing was open to the public, that is, other members of the class. The meeting was chaired by an impartial moderator and was carried on during a normal 50-minute class period.

An obvious benefit of this teaching strategy was the high interest generated by the discussion. No students were apathetic or bored, even those with a peripheral role to play. Preparation for the event was excellent as students sought out supporting data for their arguments. An extension of the role-playing strategy could be made by inviting other classes to sit in as observers. The author's experience led him to believe the method

could be used frequently, with variations on other issues and topics covered in the science class.

Morphological analysis has potential as a method for exploring and explicating solutions for problems arising in controversial situations. This is a creative problem-solving strategy that helps to identify and relate various independent variables or factors. The approach involves several steps:

1. A problem is stated in terms as general as possible.
2. Students are invited to identify as many independent variables as possible.
3. Students state these variables or factors in as many ways as possible.
4. Each of the factors becomes an axis on a grid of a two-dimensional or three-dimensional model.
5. Students then combine the axes or locate intersections within the grid that provide multiple ways of viewing and resolving the problem. To illustrate: suppose the issue was how to rationalize the problem of replacing all of the vehicles dependent on burning fossil fuels in the United States with vehicles that use some other nonpolluting source of energy, such as electricity, solar power, or wind power.

The first step would be to have the class identify independent variables associated with each form of energy (presently in use or proposed). Two axes of a grid might be type of energy versus efficacy of use in a national transportation system. In the first category might be listed fossil fuels, solar energy, nuclear energy, wind energy, water power, or others. The second axis might contain cost per mile, average highway speed, maintenance of vehicles, convenience of use, conversion costs, and other factors.

A grid might be set up as shown in Table 21-2.

Studying the grid by placing intersecting points at desired places and by inserting estimated but realistic values for each factor would enable students to decide what traits of the new transportation system to consider as viable alternatives to the present system. The exercise could be done in a group or individual format as desired. A general discussion could be held after the exercise to consider the advantages or flaws of each system

TABLE 21–2 Model Grid

		Type of Energy				
		Fossil	Solar	Nuclear	Water Power	Wind Power
Efficacy	Cost	___ /	___ /	___ /	___ /	___
of	Speed	___ /	___ /	___ /	___ /	___
Use	Upkeep	___ /	___ /	___ /	___ /	___
	Convenience	___ /	___ /	___ /	___ /	___
	Conversion	___ /	___ /	___ /	___ /	___
	Other	___ /	___ /	___ /	___ /	___

suggested. The level of interest in this exercise would likely be higher than traditional methods of lecture, recitation, or discussion.

Another technique, *creativity-synectics* developed by William J. J. Gordon and colleagues in the 1960s, offers a teaching strategy for stimulating creative talents.[8]

Synectics requires students to form three types of metaphors to gain different perceptions of a problem. These are used to break mental *structures* or *psychological set* in looking at a problem, thereby contributing to the stimulation of creative thought. The three metaphors are *direct analogy, personal analogy,* and *compressed conflict.*

In *direct analogy,* students compare and contrast two objects or concepts and state how they are similar or different. For example, in a controversy about cutting down the rain forest, they might be asked to compare and contrast birds with airplanes, or tropical woods with corn, or pharmacists with medicine men.

In *personal analogies,* students state how they would feel if they were an endangered species of animal. They might be encouraged to identify with an object or concept such as a river or an evaporating water molecule. They might express their feelings about their potential future or fate in the rain forest.

The two steps above may then lead to a situation of *compressed conflict.* Students are asked to identify contradictions in the analogies and work to resolve them by making certain concessions or accommodations.

The above strategy helps students perceive problems in a more diverse and creative manner. They will have motivation to explore something unfamiliar and create something new or different. One desirable outcome also may be the ability to see a problem from another person's point of view and to avoid responding to problems in stereotypical ways.

Small-group discussions on an identified topic, followed by an all-class discussion, with small-group leaders presenting the consensus of their groups, will become an effective method of dealing with controversial issues in the classroom. The creativity-synectics strategy will set the stage for more fruitful class discussion.

SUMMARY

Facing the prospect of dealing with controversial issues in science classes is almost a certainty for science teachers. Well-prepared teachers will not wait until a serious issue suddenly makes its appearance in the classroom. Instead, the teacher will think through many possibilities and potential strategies for dealing with the issues and plan to teach their students the basics of ethical analysis.

Current issues may develop out of various referendums that appear on the ballot during elections or that have a global nature, frequently have an environmental context, and are invariably extremely complex, affecting many segments of society in diverse ways. In addition, highly vocal groups often express their points of view through the media, committees, and political agendas. Rather than to be feared, these should be looked upon as opportunities for students to think critically and develop ethically.

Teachers should understand some of the basic ideas of ethics and ethical analysis, as these are the bases for a rational inquiry into controversial topics. Strategies for teaching about controversies suggested in this chapter include class debates, role-playing, morphological analysis, creativity-synectics, and small-group discussions, and other techniques.

An important principle when dealing with controversial issues is that the teacher's job is to provide suitable opportunities for discussion and explication of the issues and maintain a culture of respect in the classroom for all views, while at the same time avoiding injecting personal views.[9] To do otherwise is to invite repercussions from parents, school authorities, and community groups.

◆

REFERENCES

1. Lawrence Kohlberg, "The Cognitive-Developmental Approach to Moral Education," *Phi Delta Kappan* (June 1977): 670–677.
2. Carol Gilligan, *In a Different Voice* (Boston: Harvard University Press, 1985).
3. M. Belenky, B. Clinchy, N. Goldberger, and J. Tarule, *Women's Ways of Knowing: The Development of Self, Voice, and Mind* (New York: Basic Books, 1986).
4. Nel Noddings, "The Gender Issue," *Educational Leadership,* 49 (4) (1992): 65–70.
5. Jon E. Pedersen, "The Effects of a Cooperative Controversy, Presented as an STS Issue, on Achievement and Anxiety in Secondary Science," *School Science and Mathematics,* 92 (7) (November 1992): 374–380.
6. William Damon, "The Moral Development of Children," *Scientific American* 281 (2) (Aug 1999): 72–78.
7. Kerri Armstrong and Kurt Weber, "Genetic Engineering—A Lesson on Bioethics for the Classroom," *American Biology Teacher,* 53 (May 1991): 294–297.
8. William J. J. Gordon, *Creativity-Synectics,* Synectics Educational Systems, 121 Brattle Street, Cambridge, MA 02138.
9. Wiel Veugelers, "Different Ways of Teaching Values," *Educational Review* 52 (1) (Feb 2000): 37–46.

◆ ———————————— **EXPERIENCING ETHICAL ANALYSIS** ———————————— ◆

ACTIVITY 21–1
AN EXPLORATION OF ETHICAL ANALYSIS IN THE SCIENCE CLASSROOM

DISTRIBUTING RESOURCES

This activity is designed as an introduction to ethical analysis. The openness and ambiguity of the task is intentional. It provides ample opportunity for discussion about an issue that is not laden with prior information or understanding. Thus, you can concentrate on the elements of ethical analysis, which are

1. **Interpretation.**   Clarifying and defining terms and using them consistently.
2. **Analysis.**   Identifying the reasons that various individuals propose as justification for their point of view. Do they want to

   ◆ avoid negative consequences,
   ◆ nurture positive consequences,
   ◆ honor individual values and beliefs,
   ◆ pursue fair and equitable solutions?

3. **Argument.**   Developing a rationale for the position. Do the individuals provide

   ◆ premises and conclusions,
   ◆ support for premises,
   ◆ premises and conclusions that are consistent?

4. **Critique.**   Analyzing the arguments and information presented. You should pursue answers to the interpretation, analysis, and argument as part of the ethical analysis.

Your problem is to decide how to distribute resources among three groups who have requested your help. For this activity we are using the term *resources* to include many different things, such as food, minerals, fuels, and other items needed by people. Here is the only information you have to make your decisions:

You have 300 units of resources.

You presently use 200 units of resources.

You can survive on 100 units of resources.

Three groups want some of your resources. Here are their situations:

Group 1—needs 250 units of resources to survive; wants 250 units of resources

Group 2—needs 100 units of resources to survive; wants 200 units for survival *and* improvement

Group 3—needs 50 units for survival; wants 100 units for improvement

Group 4—needs no units for survival; wants 200 units for improvement

First, decide how you would distribute the resources. Complete the chart below.

Individual Decisions

Distribution of Resources	Group 1	Group 2	Group 3	Group 4

Reasons for Decision

Now join a group of three or four individuals and use the process of ethical analysis on the discussion of a group decision about the allocation of resources.

Distribution of Resources	Group 1	Group 2	Group 3	Group 4
Reasons for Decision				

Activity 21–2
Which Issues Would You Introduce in School Programs?

Take a few minutes and complete the following survey. Your responses will be the basis for discussing the inclusion of controversial issues in science programs. There are many public policy problems confronting citizens. The policy concerns below are related to one another. This makes selection of one problem over another somewhat difficult. With this understanding, we ask that you do your best to rank the most significant policy issues with a number 1, the second with a number 2, and so on to number 12.

The easiest way to rank the twelve issues is to first rank those items you think are most important (i.e., 1, 2, 3, 4). Then rank the least important items (i.e., 12, 11, 10, 9). Finally, rank the middle options from most to least important (i.e., 5, 6, 7, 8).

_____ Air Quality and Atmosphere (acid rain, CO_2, depletion of ozone, global warming)

_____ Energy Shortages (synthetic fuels, solar power, fossil fuels, conservation, oil production)

_____ Extinction of Plants and Animals (reducing genetic diversity)

_____ Hazardous Substances (waste dumps, toxic chemicals, lead paints)

_____ Human Health and Disease (infectious and noninfectious disease, stress, diet and nutrition, exercise, mental health)

_____ Land Use (soil erosion, reclamation, urban development, wildlife habitat loss, deforestation, desertification)

_____ Mineral Resources (nonfuel minerals, metallic and nonmetallic minerals, mining, technology, low-grade deposits, recycling, reuse)

_____ Nuclear Reactors (nuclear waste management, breeder reactors, cost of construction, safety)

_____ Population Growth (world population, immigration, carrying capacity, foresight capability)

_____ War Technology (bioterrorism, nerve gas, nuclear development, nuclear arms threat)

_____ Water Resources (waste disposal, estuaries, supply, distribution, groundwater contamination, fertilizer contamination)

_____ World Hunger and Food Resources (genetically modified organisms, food production and distribution, agriculture, cropland conservation)

_____ Other (please specify)

CLASSROOM MANAGEMENT AND CONFLICT RESOLUTION

Two major concerns for beginning science teachers are student discipline and classroom management. You have probably asked yourself, "How will the students behave?" "Will they do what I tell them to do?" "What can I do if a student is disruptive in science class?" In this chapter we provide some answers to such questions.

Many individuals share your concern about discipline. The American public consistently indicates that lack of discipline is one of the most important problems facing public schools. What about science teachers? Do they perceive discipline as an important problem? Actually, the majority of science teachers do not believe that discipline is a serious problem. In a 2000 survey, Weiss found that only 6 percent of teachers in grades 7–9 and 5 percent of teachers in grades 10–12 reported "maintaining discipline" as a serious problem in their school. If you include "lack of student interest in science," those percentages are increased by an additional 4 percent and 8 percent respectively.[1]

What do science teachers consider "lack of interest," and what is meant by "maintaining discipline"? There are many answers to these questions. Our discussion is primarily directed to conflicts between teachers and students and to the constructive resolution of conflicts.

Before proceeding, you should complete the first two activities on Engaging in Action Research at the end of this chapter, Conflicts: What Would You Have Done? and Resolving Conflicts. Doing these will give you some information about the ways you resolve conflicts and so will serve as a useful preparation for this chapter.

CLASSROOM CONFLICTS

Classroom conflicts occur when the activities of one or more individuals are incompatible; such conflicts can be interpersonal or intergroup. An action that is incompatible with another action interferes, obstructs, or reduces the effectiveness of the action.[2] For the most part, we can discuss conflicts between teachers and students, since a teacher must often take some action, even when two students are in conflict. In most classrooms, the difference between compatible and incompatible activities is defined by rules, policies, or expectations of behavior. A classroom conflict usually results in disruption of normal activities and educational objectives.

Note the neutrality of the preceding definition. We have not defined rules or passed judgment on whether certain rules or expectations of behavior are good or bad. Science teachers have a wide range of rules and expectations for students. Similarly, students have a remarkable ability to adapt to different teachers and classroom situations. Rather than trying to define rules, it is better to focus on classroom conflicts and suggest ways that science teachers can either prevent conflicts or resolve them constructively.

We begin by presenting two views of the same conflict. First is the report of a student teacher who had eight weeks of experience; the second is the report of the student teacher's supervisor, a science teacher with ten years of experience.

The Student Teacher's Perceptions

A new seating chart was set up for the class. In the shuffle, a student (the most openly aggressive and hostile student I've seen) started to swing at a student sitting behind him. I'm not sure of the reason, but I suspect that the boy behind him had his feet sticking out under the desk and the student either kicked him or tripped over him or slid his chair into his feet, and words were exchanged. I was close enough to verbally stop him and then collar him and send him up to the front of the class. My words were something like, "All right, you're moved, right now, up to the front; turn forward and don't turn back around or away from the chalkboard or you'll be out of here immediately. If you can't get along with the people around you, then you can sit by yourself with no privileges until you're ready to be part of the class." I thought for a minute he was going to explode (both mentally and physically), but he moved, sat and did nothing, very belligerently withdrawn, incredibly strong, and negative.

The Teacher's Perceptions

A new seating chart was established in the class. As one student took his newly assigned seat he appeared to be belligerent but not verbally so. Another student immediately behind made a comment, and he responded by turning around and pushing the table, and made a comment which I did not hear. The action was bad enough to get the attention of the majority of the class.

The instructor (student teacher) responded by giving the student a seat at a lone table in the front corner of the room. He took the seat but refused to do any work in class for the next three days. Whenever he attempted to turn or communicate with others, he was told to turn around. The student remained belligerent during this entire three-day period. After the teacher made corrections or comments he, usually, unknown to the instructor, had some obscene comment or verbal reaction to the correction.

Teachers' perceptions of the same situation can vary. Teachers' perceptions of students can also influence the way they interact with the student to resolve the conflict. This conflict was not unique as classroom conflicts go—it was short, resolved by the teacher, and ended with little difficulty.

We can continue by looking at another typical classroom conflict. What is unique about this conflict is that it has been described by *both* the student and the teacher.

The Student's View

I was sitting at a table in the science laboratory with a few friends. We had finished our work and were engaged in normal conversation. The teacher approached our table and told us to get some work out, "You can't just sit there and talk."

I ignored her, and after she left our presence, we resumed our conversation. She came back soon after that, a bit more perturbed, and repeated her previous order. This time I spoke and told her I must be responsible enough to know when and how to do my schoolwork since I had an A average in school. "So," I said, "I don't need you to supervise my study habits." I reminded her we weren't being noisy, just talking among ourselves; that we weren't bothering anyone.

She became angry. She told us we were bothering others and stated that there was a rule of no talking in the science laboratory. In general, she tried to control the situation with power and authority instead of tact and reason. I, in turn, got a little indignant, lost my temper, and smarted off. She then kicked me out of science for the remainder of that day.

The Teacher's View

It was about halfway through the period when I noticed three boys sitting at a table talking. I went over to the table and told them that this is a science class and they should finish their science laboratory. I said they should do something besides talk.

I went about my business until, a few minutes later, I noticed that the boys were still talking. So I went to the table again and explained that they should be working. I hadn't even finished what I was saying when one of the boys said he was "smart enough to take care of himself so you can just leave me alone."

At this, I told the boy that a few students do not have the right to talk and disturb other students who wanted to work. The boy got angry and said, "The hell with you and the other students." At this, I asked the boy to leave the room and he did.

This situation is a typical classroom conflict in several respects. The context was related to undefined time in class, apparently the conflict lasted only four to five minutes, and there apparently was a rule governing conduct.

The reports described above reveal several other factors common to school conflicts. The perceptions of the individuals in conflict were very different, as is clear in the descriptions of the confrontation. Communication was somewhat accurate at the beginning but deteriorated as the situation continued to the point of threats, name-calling, and assertions of power. Characteristics of a trusting attitude were lacking. Finally, each party to the conflict thought he or she was correct; thus, the problem belonged to the other person. Note also that the conflict ended but was not resolved. Left the way it was, there is every reason to suspect that future problems would occur between the student and the teacher, and, in fact, they did.

All conflicts are different. Figure 22–1 outlines different levels of student behavior that may result in classroom conflicts. Understanding different student (and teacher) behaviors that lead to conflict situations can help prevent some conflicts and give direction and guidelines on the intervention and resolution of others. Also, such understanding clarifies how conflicts escalate; that is, each party moves to a higher level, hoping the other party will withdraw. In some unfortunate cases, simple conflicts can escalate to violent and destructive episodes within the school.

Level I: Normal conflicts for individuals of this age and stage. Although the behavior may have violated general rules or norms of peers or society, the conduct is not a typical pattern for the individual.

FIGURE 22–1 Levels of School Conflicts

Active	*Passive*
Mischievous	Aloof
Temperamental	Sulky
Overeager	Slow to Warm Up

Level II: Occasional conflicts for the individual. The conflicts are violations of minor school policies, classroom rules, and age-appropriate societal norms. There may be an emerging pattern that is subtle but should not be overlooked.

Active	*Passive*
Clowning	Dawdler
Impulsive	Shy
Acting Out	Dreamer
Seeks Affirmation	Alienated

Level III: A pattern of behaviors that consistently conflict with minor school policies, classroom rules, and age-appropriate societal norms. The pattern is clear, but the major rules and basic rights of others are seldom violated.

Active	*Passive*
Disobedient	Avoidant
Oppositional	Shut Down
Negativistic	Withdrawn
Provocative	Alienated

Level IV: A pattern of behaviors that persistently violated major school policies, classroom rules, and the basic rights of others. The pattern is clear to school personnel and peers.

Active	*Passive*
Aggressive	Depressive
Destructive	Self-destructive
Angry	Substance Abuse

Level V: Episodes of behaviors directed toward the physical harm of self, others, or property.

Active	*Passive*
Violent	Substance Addiction
Vandalism	Suicidal

CAUSES OF CONFLICTS

Understanding the origins and causes of disruptive behavior can provide you with responses that prevent many conflicts. The causes discussed below are arranged from origins common to almost all adolescents to the beginnings of unique disorders of only a few adolescents.

The Middle School Student

The fifth through ninth grade student is going through the period of early adolescence. Students at this period are sometimes mature and reflective; they are also sometimes immature and impulsive. They sometimes want to separate themselves from adult authorities, such as science teachers, and they sometimes want to be directed by adults. They sometimes want to be treated as individuals who can make decisions and act responsibly, and they sometimes want to be told what to do

and when to do it. You can probably see from this discussion that it is difficult to know the appropriate way to respond to early adolescents.

The classroom can be a place where there is a certain amount of testing of adult roles and learning to be responsible. The result can be real bursts of energy for learning science and, also, great energy lulls. Frustrating? Yes. What can you do? First and foremost, try to understand that these behaviors are part of the developmental process and more often than not you should not internalize them as something directed at you, your teaching, or science. Second, establish the limits of tolerable activity for your class. The limits vary from teacher to teacher, and so we cannot define your limits. But you must have limits, and it is in your interest to identify them early, be sure they are clear, and make them known to your students.

Classroom management for this age level is largely a matter of instilling controlled self-discipline. Thus, limited freedom must be permitted so that self-discipline can be exercised. Students will not develop self-discipline and reliability if they are never given the opportunity to practice them. Overly rigid, authoritarian control, in which the primary motivation for good behavior is fear of the teacher's reprisal, will not develop the kind of student who is capable of self-discipline. At the same time, you cannot permit chaos by allowing uncontrolled behavior. A productive environment allows students to show initiative and be responsible for their actions within a framework of supervisory control by the teacher.

Early adolescents are usually quite responsive and sensitive to their peers. You can provide a positive approach to discipline by showing them that their actions influence the actions of other class members. Where students misbehave and take up valuable class time, they are infringing on the study time of classmates. As a result, they are likely to lose the favor of peers and be seen as troublemakers; their status will correspondingly change.

The middle school science teacher can use peer pressure to bring about improved classroom behavior. You should constantly refer to the need for cooperation, the value of class time, the real purposes of the study of science, and mutual obligations to one's classmates.

The Senior High School Student

Sharp character differences between middle school students and senior high students do not exist. You can easily find younger students who are as mature as those in the senior high school. The reverse also is true. In general, however, as students mature, one finds more inhibition and less boisterous behavior in the classroom. This change is a natural result of the student's nearing adulthood. More thought is given to future plans, career choices, or decisions about advanced education.

From the standpoint of discipline, this increased maturity is salutary. The frequency of classroom incidents requiring disciplinary measures usually decreases. The student is more likely to respond to treatment normally accorded adults. Because of the student's sensitivity in this regard, the most effective measures you can use in disciplinary matters are those that treat the student as an adult, with responsibilities for adult behavior.

Some students cause discipline problems because they are bored with the activities. Although you may think that science is interesting and exciting, many students do not. Many students may not understand the concept being discussed or demonstrated, but some may. These difficulties can cause boredom and subsequent behaviors that lead to conflicts. Gearing class activities to the needs and interests of a wide range of students is certainly desirable. We also recommend having interesting and relevant lessons.

For some students, "negative attention is better than no attention at all." Often students who are not successful academically, athletically, musically, and

so on, become the class clowns or enact other behaviors that result in minor conflicts with the science teacher's activities. Attention-seeking behavior is often hard for teachers to change because the responses that teachers think reduce or eliminate the disruptive behavior are the very responses that reinforce the students' behavior.

The best way to reduce this behavior is to give the student attention in educationally constructive ways. Give recognition for the types of behavior you desire and try to ignore the attention-seeking behaviors you do not wish to have reoccur.

Maslow's hierarchy of basic needs—food, water, sleep, safety and security, love and belongingness, and self-esteem—describes another source of discipline problems. Sometimes students' basic needs have not been fulfilled, and the result is inappropriate behavior as they attempt to fulfill their needs. The teacher's response is to try and fulfill those needs in the best way possible and in a way that is also educationally productive.

In other cases, students can be frustrated with the amount of effort required in science versus the amount of learning and the rewards they receive. Other problems can be students' resistance to required subjects; that is, they feel forced to do activities they are not interested in or do not like, and they occasionally must comply with rules that conflict with personal preferences (for example, wearing safety goggles).

We are not suggesting that you can provide a frustration-free environment. If frustrations are mounting, you can change the pace, switch activities, take a break, let the students have a discussion day, and so on. Forcing a tense situation can result in a conflict that could have been avoided.

We turn to the origin of one of the more persistent and difficult discipline problems, alienation. Simply defined, alienation is a feeling of being separated or removed from one's group or from society. There is also a weakening of the social bond between the individual and society or the school system as a subsystem of society. The latter situation results in the student's rejection of school and the appropriate behaviors for those in school. Melvin Seeman, a sociologist, suggests five components that influence alienation.[3] We present this discussion as background for many school-related problems, such as assaults, gangs, guns, and general alienation of youth in schools.

First, there is *powerlessness*. This is the individual's belief that he is unable to influence his life under the present rules. This feeling was described by Rowe as fate control.[4] Control over one's life is directed by something besides the individual. Here, science teachers can show individuals that they can achieve and that there are positive results for appropriate behavior.

Second, there is *meaninglessness*. This is the absence of a clear set of values and connections between the individual and society. We have heard this problem discussed as relevance of instruction and the curriculum. Trying to present the concepts and processes of science in a context that is meaningful to the student helps reduce this problem.

Third, *normlessness* is a reduction in the regulatory power of social rules and laws over individual behavior. To overcome this problem, the science teacher should make classroom rules clear and enforce them consistently and fairly. Let the students know that there are rules, that you intend that rules be obeyed, and that all students are subject to the same rules and consequences for rule violation.

Fourth is the feeling of *isolation*. Here the individual feels left out of the group, class, or school. This problem occurs most frequently in large and impersonal schools and science classes. Be sure students know that you care for them and want them in your classroom, and that you show some personal attention to their work.

Finally, there is *self-estrangement*. The individual comes to rely on external rewards and is easily frustrated when they are not received. The individual lacks self-confidence. This problem suggests a need for experiences where the student's confidence in completing a task is supported, and he learns that there are some internal rewards for learning science.

Our discussion of the origin of students' discipline has been general. There are more specific descriptions and recommendations concerning behavior problems of adolescents. Too often science teachers construct their own explanations for adolescent behavior, and they do not consult individuals or resources who are knowledgeable. Science teachers provide explanations of adolescent behavior such as, "He only wanted attention," "She comes from a broken home," or "He associates with the wrong group." Although these are explanations, they are also incomplete and hold every possibility of having misconceptions about the causes of adolescent behavior. If you do not think you have an adequate understanding of a particular student, or if you think something is seriously wrong, consult a counselor, school psychologist, or a book on behavior problems of adolescents. If you are wondering about a student's behavior, ask yourself these questions:

- Is there a *pattern* of behaviors? Does the student behave the same way in other classes?
- Does the student continually demonstrate inappropriate behaviors for his or her age?
- Are the basic rights of others (including you) consistently violated?
- Is there the possibility of personal harm, either to the student in question or to others?

If you find yourself answering "yes" to these and similar questions, you should consult other resources because the behaviors are probably not in the acceptable range for your classroom and school. There is no need to try and solve the problem yourself. Many of your colleagues in the school system—special educators and school psychologists—are immediate and valuable resources.

DISCIPLINE PROBLEMS AND THE SCIENCE CLASSROOM

Science has numerous applications to the daily lives of students. This relevance gives you many opportunities to engage students in the study of science and avoid discipline problems. Science classes also have the advantage of demonstration devices and other laboratory equipment that stimulate interest. Students may find themselves drawn away from unruly influences and toward scientific interests. Furthermore, for students whose poor behavior may stem from lack of recognition, science classes may offer opportunities to gain prestige in the eyes of their peers.

On the negative side, certain unique problems exist in science classes. The laboratory, by its very nature, offers freedom of movement that may lead to discipline problems. Students without self-discipline will find many opportunities to cause trouble. The teacher's control must be completely effective, although not rigid, or the learning opportunities of the laboratory will be sacrificed. Learning requires considerable self-direction and attention to the task, and the laboratory, under skillful guidance of the teacher, can be a place where students develop self-discipline. We recommend completing the activity Classroom Discipline, at the end of this chapter.

CONFLICT RESOLUTION AND REGULATION

Social psychologists have studied the resolution and regulation of conflicts. *The Resolution of Conflict* by Morton Deutsch is probably the single most important synthesis of these research findings.[5] For this reason, we rely on Deutsch's ideas in this discussion.

We assume that conflicts will occur in the science classroom. We also assume that you are interested in their *constructive resolution*. Further, we assume that in those rare situations of intense conflict, you are interested in regulating the conflict so that the results are not destructive to you or others.

David and Roger Johnson and their colleagues have used the *cooperative learning model* to help students learn how to mediate conflicts in the classroom. Science teachers will find such strategies helpful.[6]

Avoiding Destructive Conflicts

Destructive conflicts tend to escalate from minor encounters to major events in the classroom. Involved persons increasingly rely on power and authority to resolve, regulate, and finally control the situation. As the conflict takes a destructive course, threats, coercion, and demonstrations of power steadily displace open discussion and the processes of peaceful resolution. The destructive course is set once (1) the conflict becomes a win-lose situation, (2) communication decreases and, thus, misperceptions increase, and (3) commitments for personal and social consistency decrease. We can look to the opposite of these three ideas for some means to avoid destructive classroom conflicts. We suggest that you consider the following to avoid destructive conflicts:

+ Encourage cooperation.
+ Communicate clearly.
+ Commit yourself personally and socially to resolve the conflicts peacefully.

Visit http://www.prenhall.com/trowbridge and select Topic 3—Alternative Assessments. Select "National Science Teaching Standards" and find the link for "Science Education Program Standards." Then locate the website that discusses learning styles. Accommodating individual learning styles often solves problems of discipline and engenders self-discipline. Write a brief comment on students' learning styles and submit to your instructor using the Electronic Bluebook module.

Encouraging Constructive Resolutions

Conflicts will take a constructive course when science teachers use a creative problem-solving model for intervention. This model includes (1) motivation to resolve the problem, (2) finding conditions to redefine the problem, and (3) suggesting ideas that might solve the problem. Following are suggestions that contribute to constructive resolutions of conflicts:

+ Define the conflict as small.
+ Resolve the conflict as soon as possible.
+ Focus on the problem, not the person.
+ Reduce the conflict to several smaller problems and resolve them.
+ Emphasize similarities and common goals.
+ Be sure all parties agree on the problem.
+ Acknowledge that a conflict exists.
+ Use a third party to resolve the conflict.

On some occasions, problems persist and for many reasons cannot be easily resolved. What should one do when conflicts cannot be constructively resolved? When a situation such as this exists, try to *regulate* the conflict so it does not take a destructive course.

Regulating Classroom Conflicts

In regulating conflicts, you attempt to set limits or boundaries on the interaction between conflicting parties. Regulating conflicts is obviously harder than re-

solving them. Both parties are often on a thin edge leading to destructive conflict. In such situations, teachers fear both for their safety and of having intense emotional responses. Likewise, students who find themselves in these situations have similar reactions. Although we must accept the legitimacy of these human responses, we must also guard against the detrimental consequences of a destructive conflict. What can a science teacher do? The following recommendations will help you regulate conflicts:

+ Wait until parties are calm, rational, and organized, and then begin talking about the conflict.
+ Demonstrate the legitimacy of all parties in conflict.
+ Reach agreement on the limits of interaction.
+ Use new and different approaches when other ones have failed.
+ Develop a sense of community for all parties.
+ Make sure rules are known, clear, and unbiased.
+ Remedy rule violations as soon as possible.
+ Use counselors for third-party regulation when necessary.

This is an excellent time to complete the activity Resolution and Regulation of Conflicts at the end of this chapter.

SOME RECOMMENDATIONS FOR SCIENCE TEACHERS

Developing Self-Discipline

The goal of all discipline training should be the development of responsible self-discipline. Students should reach a point of inner motivation to complete learning tasks. Discipline of this type is positive and self-rewarding.

To reach this goal, students should have numerous opportunities to practice self-discipline or peer-group discipline. As with the development of any skill, there must be time to practice.

Teaching science by inquiry methods provides a setting for developing self-discipline. Individual work in the laboratory or on projects carried out in the classroom or at home gives many opportunities to develop good work habits and qualities of self-reliance, persistence, and reliability.

The following suggestions may assist the science teacher in providing an environment in which student self-discipline can be developed:

+ Capture interest through activities, experiments, projects, and other student-oriented learning methods.
+ Allow a degree of unstructured work commensurate with the maturity and experience level of the students.

- Give suitable guidance to students who require direction and external control, until it is no longer needed.
- Treat students as adults from whom you expect mature behavior and evidence of self-discipline.

Developing Techniques to Influence Behavior

Science teachers have techniques they use to influence student behavior. In light of earlier discussions of conflicts, many of these techniques are early-warning signals for the student. In this respect, the actual conflict is prevented, usually because the student responds to the signal.

Here are some suggestions you may consider:

- Use nonverbal signals, such as staring, clearing your throat, shaking your head, or stopping discussion and waiting.
- Use physical closeness or proximity control. While continuing the discussion, move near the disruptive student.
- Use humor to let the student know that enough is enough. Humor should not be sarcastic or personally demeaning.
- Ask the disruptive student a simple, direct, and easy question that will bring him or her into the discussion.
- Provide individualized help for particularly difficult problems, laboratories, or assignments.
- Help the students through transitional periods in class, such as shifting from a laboratory to seat work. Provide the time and be sure not to expect immediate responses during transitional periods.
- Establish patterns for laboratory work, cleanup, and other routine or common activities in the classroom.
- Modify routines such as attendance and distributing papers.
- Remove particularly tempting laboratory equipment.
- Have well-prepared lessons, use a variety of instructional methods, and show a personal interest in students.

 Visit http://www.prenhall.com/trowbridge and select Topic 6—Professional Development. Select "National Science Teaching Standards" and find the link for the "Discovery Channel School." The main page allows the visitor to choose from teachers, students, and parents as well as recommends suitable activities working with pupils to solve discipline problems. Collect a few of these recommendations for discussion in your science methods class.

Developing Means to Resolve Classroom Conflicts

The following recommendations may help avoid serious conflicts and bring about constructive, as opposed to destructive, consequences:

- Try to recognize the consistent patterns of behavior that can result in conflicts (see Figure 22–1).
- Clarify classroom rules. This may require mentioning particular rules relating to daily activities.
- Clarify each person's perceptions of the conflict situation. "How does this situation seem to you?"
- Maintain communication between the parties in conflict. You should be able to keep the lines of communication open for several minutes by avoiding personal insults, threats, or the use of power.
- Define the conflict as a mutual problem. "Look, you would like to visit, and I would like it quiet so students can work. How can we resolve this?"
- Avoid using power to resolve the conflict. Use of power can escalate the conflict and/or end it without resolution.

Developing a Discipline Policy

One of the strongest recommendations we can make to science teachers is to develop a discipline policy. Having a policy will result in consistency and clear expectations for both you and your students. Once you have developed a set of rules (and we suggest you do this with the students), the following suggestions should be considered when there are rule violations or conflicts:

- Request that the student stop the behavior and remind the student of the rule being violated.
- If the behavior continues, inform the student that the behavior must stop and that "we will have to resolve the problem."
- Establish what the problem is and what can be done to resolve it.
- Help establish the new rules and procedures of the student's behavior, and make clear the consequences for any further rule violations.
- Avoid using personally or physically harsh or abusive measures.
- Be consistent with the rules and consequences you have both agreed to. Be kind and firm. Being kind shows respect for the student; being firm shows respect for yourself as a person and as a science teacher.

Meeting Parents to Solve a Discipline Problem

Occasionally, you will find it necessary to meet with parents concerning their child's behavior in school. As a

FIGURE 22–2 Steps in Assessment of a Discipline Problem

Understand the Problem
- What happened in the last forty-eight hours of the student's life?
- What were the circumstances of the problem?
- What patterns of behavior are identifiable?

Clarification of Current Difficulties
- What is the nature of present school-related problems?
- What is the duration of all problems, i.e., academic, behavioral, with peers?
- Have there been any recent changes in behavior? Achievement? Friendships?

Review of Background
- What is the relevant family background?
- What is the student's relation to peers?
- How has the student related to other teachers? Administrators? Counselors?

Identification of Coping Style
- How does the student handle stress?
- What triggers a discipline event?
- How does the student think problems could be avoided.
- What resources are available to help the student avoid difficult situations?

Assessment of Psychological and Developmental Status
- What is the student's mood?
- What are the student's cognitive, moral, social, and emotional levels of development?

List All Current Problems
- What are the present problems as perceived by (1) the student, (2) school personnel, and, if appropriate, (3) parents?
- Which problems have highest/lowest priority?

Establish Help That Is Required
- What does the student want (or agree) to do?
- What do school personnel recommend?
- What will all parties agree to?
- Should anyone else be involved?

Develop a Contract
- What terms are acceptable to student, school personnel, and parents?
- Who is responsible for doing what? When? How?

first step, we recommend you do a thorough assessment of the student's discipline problems; the steps are outlined in Figure 22–2. Scheduling a meeting with parents indicates a high level of concern about the student, which suggests the need for information, documentation, and understanding of the problems and their potential resolution.

As you approach the meeting, keep several things in mind. First, have with you the information (and examples) concerning the student's problems. Second, realize that you have two goals: to gain further understanding of the student's background and role in the family, and to join with the family in a cooperative approach to intervene and improve the student's behavior.

Outside of the natural nervousness about meeting with parents, you have other challenges to bear in mind. The family usually will be very concerned and often quite defensive about being called to school. To work effectively, you must have the cooperation of other school personnel. Finally, to develop a plan of action to be im-

plemented, you will have to identify and work with the central decision makers in the family. The following are some suggestions for a meeting with parents to solve a discipline problem. Note that some of the ideas in this section are applicable to any meeting with parents concerning school-related problems, whether academic, social, or behavioral.

- Be sure the meeting is scheduled. Do not plan to just see the parents after school or stop by their home unannounced.
- Have data, documentation, and examples. The more specific you can be, the more the parents will realize the seriousness of the problem.
- Try to recognize and overcome the parents' anxiety and defensiveness. Some simple statements such as "I'm sure you are concerned about your child's problems" will help. Also acknowledge that the parents know about their child and can contribute to the problem's resolution.

- Define and clarify the current problem. Present the problem in a clear and concise manner. Direct the discussion toward actual behaviors, and avoid derogatory comments relative to the student.
- Allow the parents time to respond. If the parents do not respond, then review the problems to impress on them the serious nature of the issues. If the parents seem confrontational, then direct their attention to the problem and not other issues, such as the personalities of school personnel. If the parents are cooperative, then develop a list of means that might be used to help resolve the problems.
- Develop a Plan of Action

1. Identify the behaviors to be increased/decreased.
2. Are there other educational problems that should be attended to—for example, reading difficulties or learning disabilities?
3. Identify the consequences of inappropriate behaviors. A logical-consequence approach often works very well.
4. Decide on who, what, when, where, and how the plan will be implemented.
5. Clarify the responsibilities of school personnel, parents, and others.
6. Determine what all parties would see as improvement.
7. Schedule other meetings to review progress.

SUMMARY

The matter of class control and management is of primary concern to science teachers. The multiple problems of preparing for class, devising suitable teaching methods, and keeping the class orderly are frequently overwhelming.

The actual statistics indicate that most science teachers do not perceive maintaining discipline as a problem. Nor do they think that they need assistance with discipline and class management. Although statistics indicate that discipline problems are not a major concern, it is nonetheless true that inevitably there will be conflicts in the science classroom. Conflicts occur when the activities of one individual or group are incompatible with the activities of another individual or group.

The causes of conflicts vary, but some of the more prevalent origins of conflict are adolescent need for separation and individuation, the need for attention, boredom, frustration, tension, and alienation. It is also true that the very nature of the science classroom—laboratory work, small-group discussions, transitions from one activity to another—can cause some problems.

Conflicts can be resolved using a few simple procedures: define the conflict when it is small, work to resolve the conflict immediately, focus on the problem, reduce the problem to smaller parts, be sure there is agreement on the problem, and use a third party if necessary. If conflicts are headed in a destructive direction, you should wait until all parties are calm; recognize legitimacy; reach limits on interactions; use new approaches if old ones do not work; make rules clear, known, and unbiased; and, again, use a third party if necessary.

There are many possible ways to resolve conflicts in the classroom. For students, an important first step is to develop self-discipline. A second step is developing a set of techniques that can prevent or resolve a conflict before it develops. Next, it is recommended that the teacher use the various means of resolving conflicts. Finally, each teacher must develop a discipline policy. Such a policy will result in a fair and consistent pattern of conflict resolution in the science classroom. All of these methods converge in the recommendation to be firm, friendly, fair, and consistent in your interactions with disruptive students.

◆

REFERENCES

1. Iris Weiss, *Report of the 2000 National Survey of Science and Mathematics Education* (Chapel Hill, NC: Horizon Research, Inc., 2001).
2. Morton Deutsch, *The Resolution of Conflict* (New Haven: Yale University Press, 1973).
3. Melvin Seeman, "The Meaning of Alienation," *American Sociological Review,* 24 (December 1959): 783–791.
4. Mary Budd Rowe, *Teaching Science by Continuous Inquiry* (New York: McGraw Hill, 1979).
5. Morton Deutsch, *The Resolution of Conflict.* (New Haven, CT: Yale University Press, 1973).
6. David Johnson, Roger Johnson, B. Dudley, and R. Burnett, "Teaching Students to Be Peer Mediators," *Educational Leadership* (1992): 10–13.

◆ ─────── ──── **ENGAGING IN ACTION RESEARCH** ──── ─────── ◆

ACTIVITY 22–1
CONFLICTS: WHAT WOULD YOU HAVE DONE?

The following three incidents were recorded by student teachers. The incidents occurred in science classrooms and represent discipline situations you might encounter. Read each incident and decide what you would have done had you been in the situation. After this you might share your response with other students in class to see what they would have done.

Incident 1

I was tutoring seven students who had fallen behind in their ninth grade general-chemistry class. As I proceeded, two male students made sly remarks that related to my subject material. I laughed at first, but then said, "OK, fun is fun, but let's get down to business." Since they did not take this as a warning, I told them that if they did not keep quiet and listen, they would have to return to the classroom. At this point I realized that I had "threatened" them in the form of a warning—the old "do-or-die" situation.

The two students continued this behavior, so I asked them to leave and just stand and wait. It was tough for me since I really did not want them to leave. They needed the help I was there to provide, but they infringed on the learning opportunity of the five other students. Class went well after the two boys left.

What would you have done in this situation?

Incident 2

This was a conflict between two students during a laboratory period. I stepped in to try to resolve it before it grew out of control.

The laboratory required a perch made of books. One student borrowed a book from a laboratory partner that was large enough to meet his needs. However, the partner decided he wanted to have the book available for reading during the period and asked for his book back. The first student didn't want to move his setup since it was all prepared and checked, so he refused the other's demands. The partner was slowly losing patience when I stepped in. Since the problem wasn't very grave to me, I told the two that we could easily solve the conflict and asked for the student's help in exchanging the book and rechecking the setup while the partner cooled off. The tension subsided, and they were able to work together during the period.

What would you have done in this situation?

Incident 3

I passed out a test. An A$^+$ student forgot to do one section of the test. I graded all the tests. This student received a B$^+$. She is a talkative student, always making some jokes or puns in class to gain attention. After I returned the test, she said nothing in class for two days.

On the second day, I approached the student to help her on some problems in balancing equations. She had some trouble, so I was able to help her. After class she came up to me and insisted that I change her grade. I listened to her explain her mistake. Then I asked her what she thought should be done. She said I should change her grade. She decided that it would be fair to give her a better grade.

What would you have done in this situation?

ACTIVITY 22–2
RESOLVING CONFLICTS

There are many factors that influence the direction and resolution of a conflict. In this activity you are going to examine your preferred methods for resolving problems. In other words, how do you typically try to resolve conflicts with other people? The insights you gain from the exercise will be beneficial when you have to resolve conflicts with students in your science class.*

The following sayings can be thought of as descriptions of different ways individuals resolve conflicts. Read each of the statements carefully. Using a scale of 1 through 5, indicate how typical each saying is of your actions in a conflict situation.

5—Very typical of the way I act in a conflict

4—Frequently typical of the way I act in a conflict

3—Sometimes typical of the way I act in a conflict

2—Seldom typical of the way I act in a conflict

1—Never typical of the way I act in a conflict

_____ 1. Soft words win hard hearts.

_____ 2. Come now and let us reason together.

_____ 3. Arguments of the strongest have the most weight.

_____ 4. You scratch my back, I'll scratch yours.

_____ 5. The best way of handling conflicts is to avoid them.

_____ 6. If someone hits you with a stone, hit the person with a piece of cotton.

_____ 7. A question must be decided by knowledge and not by numbers if it is to have a right decision.

_____ 8. If you cannot make a person think as you do, make the person do as you think.

_____ 9. Better half a loaf than no bread at all.

_____ 10. If someone is ready to quarrel with you, the person isn't worth knowing.

_____ 11. Smooth words make smooth ways.

_____ 12. By digging and digging, the truth is discovered.

_____ 13. One who fights and runs away lives to fight another day.

_____ 14. A fair exchange brings no quarrel.

_____ 15. There is nothing so important that you have to fight for it.

_____ 16. Kill your enemies with kindness.

_____ 17. Seek till you find, and you'll not lose your labor.

_____ 18. Might overcomes right.

_____ 19. Tit for tat is fair play.

_____ 20. Avoid quarrelsome people—they will only make you unhappy.

Some insights about your typical style of resolving conflicts can be gained by adding the responses to different sayings. Add your typical responses to the sayings as indicated.

Sayings	Total	Response Style
1, 6, 11, 16	___	Smoothing
2, 7, 12, 17	___	Negotiating
3, 8, 13, 18	___	Forcing
4, 9, 14, 19	___	Compromising
5, 10, 15, 20	___	Withdrawing

* This activity is based on ideas from P. Lawrence and J. Torsch, *Organization and Environment: Managing Differentiation and Integration* (Cambridge, MA: Division of Research, Graduate School of Business Administration, Harvard University, 1967), and from David Johnson, *Human Relations and Your Career: A Guide to Interpersonal Skills* (Upper Saddle River, NJ: Prentice Hall, 1978).

Science teachers are concerned with two goals as they resolve conflicts. One goal is personal and involves achieving, gaining, or maintaining something; for example, achieving an educational goal, gaining personal recognition, or maintaining one's sense of security in the science classroom. The second goal has to do with preserving or changing the relationship with the conflicting party. In the science classroom, this usually means preserving the relationship with a student, while changing the patterns of behavior.

The five different response styles to conflicts have direct bearing on the personal and relational goals of science teachers. We describe briefly the results of typical conflict responses relative to personal and relational goals of teachers.

Withdrawing

Withdrawing from a conflict fulfills neither the personal nor the relational goals. Essentially it is a lose/lose approach to conflict resolution since the educator gives up whatever educational goals she had and does not try to maintain the relationship with the student. In brief it is

PERSONAL—LOSE
RELATIONAL—LOSE

Smoothing

Smoothing over the conflict gives highest priority to maintaining the relationship, often at all costs, including giving up personal goals. This is a resolution that usually results in

PERSONAL—LOSE
RELATIONAL—WIN

Forcing

Here, personal goals are achieved at any cost. The cost is often to give up a personal relationship with the students. We have a situation of

PERSONAL—WIN
RELATIONAL—LOSE

Compromising

The educator gives up some personal goals, and some relational goals are modified in order to resolve the conflict. All parties to the conflict give up something and are often dissatisfied with the results. The grounds for resentment by both educator and students have been established. The amount of resentment will depend on the perceived amount of compromise by each party to the conflict. In essence, this is a resolution of

PERSONAL—TIE
RELATIONAL—TIE

Negotiating

Educators and students resolve conflicts through cooperative problem solving. Though some changes occur, essentially the goals of both educators and students are achieved and relationships are maintained. This approach is one of

PERSONAL—WIN
RELATIONAL—WIN

There are times when each of the different means of resolving conflicts is an appropriate course of action. Science teachers should understand this and make judgments concerning the situation, the student, and their personal and relational goals.

Think of a classroom situation where each of the response styles would be appropriate.

Withdrawing:

Smoothing:

Forcing:

Compromising:

Negotiating:

INDUCTION AND PROFESSIONAL DEVELOPMENT

You are rapidly reaching the culmination of many years of study in preparation for the career you have chosen. Soon you will be in charge of real live classes in science for which you have been prepared. This is an exciting prospect full of promise for your future.

Now you will face students and see their enthusiasm or disinterested natures, their understandings or perplexities. You will have a chance to interact with them, give help when they need it, praise them when warranted. At the same time, you will be gaining confidence as a teacher yourself.

Many new teachers become discouraged after a few months on the job. It may not be what they expected, or perhaps the particular teaching situation is too daunting. Try not to become disheartened. Make friends with dedicated, experienced teachers with whom you can converse. All have faced many of the same problems you are facing. Do not be influenced by certain cynical teachers who may try to dissuade you. They may decry what they think is your idealism for the task. But schools need idealistic teachers who can think creatively and who are willing to try new methods. An understanding principal will look favorably upon people with ideas. Within the rules and norms of the school, use every opportunity to bring out the best in students. Above all, be enthusiastic yourself. Show that you know your subject and that you want to share your knowledge with others. Students will respond favorably.

The chapters which follow provide many ideas and suggestions for finding materials for teaching and for making a successful transition to practicing teacher of science. We have called this section "Induction and Professional Development" because we realize the importance of making a good transfer to the job you have prepared yourself for. And of course, we are hopeful you will be happy in your new employment and will make it a lifelong career. Speaking from experience, the authors believe your choice is an excellent one and that you will discover untold joys in being a participant and contributor to a most noble profession, the education of young people in science.

CHAPTER 23

MATERIALS FOR SCIENCE TEACHING

AVAILABILITY OF SCIENCE TEACHING MATERIALS

Technology

Link

Recent years have seen the proliferation of new teaching materials for science classes. Teachers are now faced with making choices which they may not have experienced before. Technology has provided new kinds of equipment and apparatus, as well as new audio and video materials Publishers of science textbooks have produced creative and colorful new approaches that excite teachers and students alike. Using the Internet to expand and update the offerings of traditional textbooks is now a reality through SciLinks, an innovative connection between the National Science Teachers Association and several publishing houses.

Judiciously used, these new materials may serve well to accomplish the goals of producing scientifically literate students, and by extension, similarly educated adults in the near future.

Science teachers are fortunate in having an abundance of teaching materials to draw on. Their problem is selecting the proper materials and techniques to accomplish this task. Recent years have seen a proliferation of teaching materials of every description; the display areas of any large convention of science teachers present an overwhelming variety of these materials.

With so many teaching aids available, it helps to consider their purposes in the process of educating science students:

1. More of the students' senses are stimulated by teaching aids. They frequently activate the avenues of learning involving sight, sound, touch, smell, and taste. Combinations of senses are appealed to more often.
2. Teaching aids maintain interest. Students are likely to be in a receptive frame of mind for maximum learning.
3. Teaching becomes less fatiguing when a variety of methods and materials is used and the teacher's enthusiasm is maintained.
4. Individual differences are most adequately served by a variety of teaching aids. Students frequently learn better by one method than by another.
5. Teaching aids provide opportunities for frequent changes of pace, which is particularly useful in middle school teaching.
6. Specific materials designed for specific teaching tasks are more effective because of their refined nature. For example, a well-designed model of certain geological features may illustrate a point better than a photograph—or in some cases better than an actual field trip.

USING SCIENCE-LEARNING MATERIALS

Printed materials will continue to be important in science teaching. Textbooks are still a basic source of information in science classes, and when they are used judiciously and with recognition of their limitations, textbooks contribute substantially to the teaching-learning situation.

A publication by the NSTA provides some guidelines concerning science-learning materials.[1] Their recommendations are intended to offer guidance in determining kind and quantity.

1. When needed for learning, individual textbooks and laboratory manuals should be available without cost to every student.
2. The science textbooks used by students at any time should be no more than four years past the date of the last major revision.
3. For each science course, there should be an ample supply of diverse printed materials to supplement the textbook and laboratory manual.
4. The school science library should contain an adequate selection of books, periodicals, and pamphlets on the sciences, the applications of science, and the history, philosophy, and sociology of science.
5. An adequate supply of modern science equipment should be available for individual and small-group activities and experiments.
6. A diverse supply of audiovisual learning materials must be readily available for each science course.
7. Certain items of audiovisual equipment should be provided as permanent equipment for individual courses.

USE OF TEXTBOOKS

The teaching of science in general and of physics in particular has been textbook-centered in the English-speaking world since the 1820s. Countless teachers of science have learned their basic information from textbooks. They have transferred this information to their students and may have considered that doing this successfully has satisfied their objectives of teaching science to the best of their ability.

Arthur Stinner maintains that rigid adherence to the textbook formulations of scientific information, with their inherent mathematical emphasis, frequently leaves a large vacuum in students' understanding of science concepts. Because of the apparent efficiency of this method, learning science really becomes a matter of memorizing facts, principles, and mathematical formulas, and using these to solve textbook problems that may or may not have relevance to the real world.[2] The physicist and science writer Hans Christian von Baeyer (quoted in Stinner) has said:

> Having students memorize formulas and problems on paper is easier and cheaper than staging experiments and demonstrations. But it avoids the confrontation between the real and the abstract, so it misses the essence of physics. A student learns a mechanical sequence of mathematical manipulations—an algorithm—and executes it adeptly, with wide variety of input data. Instead of a set of ideas to be matched against the real world, physics becomes a sequence to be carried out swiftly and accurately.[3]

Recent research on the applicability of a learning cycle strategy when teaching from textbooks has been reported by Macheno and Lawson in the *Journal of Research in Science Teaching*.[4] They report that "Science textbooks are traditionally written in a manner contrary to the learning cycle approach, with term introduction preceding the exploration of examples." Continuing, they say that "Students who read the learning cycle passages earned higher scores on concept comprehension questions than those who read the traditional passages, at all reasoning levels." Also, they found that "The present science textbooks and methods of instruction, far from helping, often actually impede progress toward scientific literacy. They emphasize the learning of answers more than exploration of questions, memory at the expense of critical thought, bits and pieces of information instead of understandings in context, recitation over argument, and reading instead of doing."

What does this tell the new teacher about the use of textbooks in science teaching? While much of the information of science in the classroom will continue to come from textbooks, the teacher is advised to be duly forewarned of their possible deleterious effects; the teacher also must constantly guard against their misuse as the sole source of information, their highly abbreviated nature, and their emphasis on results rather than on the ways in which the information has been obtained. Frequent use of investigative methods to ferret out the solutions to real problems may help to minimize the inherent dangers of overuse of textbooks alone.

There is much evidence that the single textbook is still the source of most science information taught in science classes at the secondary level. Research by R. E. Stake and J. A. Easley produced the following conclusion:

> The source of knowledge authority was not so much the teacher—it was the textbook. Teachers were prepared to intercede, to explain, but the direct confrontation with knowledge for most students was with printed information statements. Teachers did it differently from classroom to classroom, but regularly there was deference to the textbook, or lab manual, or encyclopedia, map, or chart. Knowing was not so much a matter of experiencing, even vicariously (self-knowledge perhaps was not to be trusted), but of being familiar with certain information or knowing how to produce the answers to questions that would be asked.[5]

Because of the wide range of reading abilities, problems arise with respect to providing suitable reading materials for all students. David Memory and Kenneth Uhlhorn suggest one response to the dilemma by the use of multiple textbooks at different readability levels.[6] Several benefits of the use of multilevel textbooks are suggested:

1. The approach enables teachers to hold each student responsible for assigned reading because suitable reading levels are available to all.

2. Using more advanced reading materials can better challenge the able readers and challenge them to higher achievement.

3. The approach allows students to practice the comprehension, vocabulary, and study skills taught to them in English and reading classes.

4. It increases the likelihood of success for mainstreamed handicapped students.

5. The approach provides exposure to different viewpoints of authors and instills appropriate scientific skepticism.

6. It reinforces the idea of fluid inquiry—the idea that the overall concept of an area of science can change over time (for example, plate tectonics, genetics, particle physics, etc.).

7. It reduces the need to simply repeat the content of single texts in class discussions and fosters better individual comprehension by students.

8. The approach results in improved student attitudes because of generally higher levels of achieved success.

Selecting Textbooks

The selection of science textbooks frequently reflects concerns for readability, topical content, recency or currency of information, and other factors that emphasize the practical and pragmatic matters associated with textbook choice. Decisions based on what is best for particular students sometimes lack perspective. An ex-

ample of an attempt to use a sociological perspective in selecting science textbooks was reported by Lynn M. Mulkey at Hunter College in New York City.[7] The main research question was, "Does selection of science textbooks deprive younger children in working-class school districts the benefits of perspectives that will help make them 'participants' in science while simultaneously enriching the scientific preparation of older children in middle-class school districts?"

The findings indicated that the availability of (textbook) knowledge important for the development of a scientific role (career) was, on the average, the same for both middle- and working-class districts. However, social class had a distinctive effect on orientation to cognitive flexibility. The middle-class child is more likely to receive encouragement in developing cognitive flexibility (the privilege to be nonconforming). Textbooks appear to be written and selected for children who are perceived as prepared for cognitive flexibility and may have "an accumulated advantage which may or may not be attributable to differences in capacity."[8] Science teachers must place the textbook in its proper perspective in their classes. Students generally feel more comfortable with a textbook than without one. It serves to organize information, stress important concepts, direct activity, and set goals for the study of a particular science. All of these contributions are important. It must be remembered, however, that a textbook alone cannot achieve even a majority of the objectives of science teaching. It cannot provide labo-

A wealth of instructional materials is a necessary component in inquiry teaching for consistent success.

ratory experiences, develop true inquiry skills, or teach self-reliance in solving problems. These are objectives that are achieved best by other methods and materials. In collaboration with a variety of other materials, the textbook is an important contributor to these objectives.

Selecting a textbook for a given science class is frequently a haphazard affair. Textbooks are often chosen after superficial inspection. Color may influence one's choice more than content; photographs may carry more weight than organization of subject matter; advertising appeal may be more of a deciding factor than usefulness.

In selecting a textbook in science, establish criteria against which competing books can be rated. These criteria include:

A. Factors that deal with the subject-matter content and organization.
   1. Logical organization, sequence of difficulty, grouping of topics.
   2. Emphasis on principles and concepts.
   3. Accuracy of information.
   4. Usefulness of information, applications, and functional nature of the material.
   5. Recent information, modern concepts, theories, and applications.
B. Factors that deal with development of noncontent objectives.
   1. Attention given to development of interests, appreciations, and attitudes.
   2. Attention given to problem-solving approach.
   3. Attention given to skills of science learning.
   4. Attention given to the role of science in society and to scientific literacy.
C. Factors that deal with experiments, demonstrations, and activities.
   1. Inquiry or verification approach.
   2. Student participation, activity, and investigation.
   3. Use of simple materials, degree of structure in laboratories.
   4. Emphasis on drawing conclusions on the basis of observation and experimentation.
D. Factors that deal with mechanical features of the textbook.
   1. Binding, size, durability, attractiveness.
   2. Size of type, level of reading difficulty, summaries, glossaries, index.
   3. Illustrations, maps, charts, graphs, captions.
   4. General ease in using the book.
E. Factors that deal with authors of the textbook.
   1. Qualifications (experience, level of preparation).
   2. Quality of writing, interest, and readability.
   3. References to purposes of the book and intended use.
F. Factors that deal with prospective useful life of the textbook.
   1. Copyright date, revisions, and reprintings.
   2. Nature of material, rate of obsolescence, years of usability.

It is suggested that these criteria be used with a rating scale for comparison with competing textbooks. A scale like the one that follows might be used:

0_____ Book totally lacking in the characteristic
1_____ Occasional evidence of the characteristic
2_____ Greater evidence of the characteristic but below average
3_____ Reasonably frequent evidence of the characteristic
4_____ Excellent evidence of the characteristic
5_____ Superior in all aspects of the characteristic

Readability Analysis

Perhaps the most important consideration when analyzing textbooks for a science class is their readability. The reading level of students in any given class varies by several grade levels. To meet individual differences, to avoid discouraging students with low reading levels, and to avoid frustration, it is necessary to select a book that will meet the needs of a variety of students. Usually, these criteria result in the selection of books with reading levels at or slightly below the grade level for the class.

What is readability? Readability refers to reading difficulty of a book, paragraph, or prose passage. Many factors enter into readability, such as types of sentence construction, length of sentences, vocabulary, number of syllables in words, type of print, and concept density. At present, there are several readability formulas that are frequently used in analyzing textbooks. Unfortunately, the results obtained by the various formulas do not agree. (See Activity 23–1)

AUDIOVISUAL MATERIALS

Recent years have seen the development of many audiovisual aids for the science teacher. These materials have not always enjoyed the best possible usage because of certain limiting conditions. It is important for the science teacher to have a good working knowledge of several audiovisual devices and to be aware of their teaching possibilities.

In using an audiovisual aid, the teacher's most important consideration is, "Is this the most effective method at my disposal for teaching these concepts?" If the answer is yes, every effort should be made to incorporate the aid into classroom planning. Mental inertia or unwillingness to try a new device should not remain a deterrent to good teaching in science.

Some of the older, reliable audio-visual techniques used in science classrooms are still in use today. The key question for a science teacher is embodied in the previous paragraph—"Is this the most effective method for teaching 'these' concepts?" Considerations of time, energy, convenience, and potential effectiveness should determine the teacher's decision. If overhead projection, films, filmstrips, television, videotapes, or other audiovisual materials appear to be the most suitable for the particular circumstances, these are the ones that should be used.

On the other hand, if you as science teacher are familiar with the use and operation of newer technologies, these should be seriously considered. Examples that might serve your needs effectively are PowerPoint, a projection system that has excellent clarity, great flexibility, ease of use, reliability, and currency. Computer literacy, not only for word processing but for opening the enormous potential of the Internet, is an essential skill required by all science teachers. Increasingly, more science textbook publishers are incorporating a feature called SciLinks into their publications. This permits readers of content in the textbooks to explore further and to update their knowledge about certain topics by using certain icons identified in the narrative to turn to the Internet for more recent information. Students can then be wholly current on scientific information—perhaps as recent as "today's news." By using the SciLinks feature, students can be directed to current films broadcast on television on Public Service stations or National Geographic Specials to obtain up-to-date information in an interesting form.

Materials for the Laboratory

Science deals with the phenomena of nature. These phenomena cannot be studied effectively through abstract or theoretical discussion alone, although this may be necessary at times. Most science students find that actual objects, models, or living specimens make a phenomenon concrete enough to be understood. Science materials and apparatus—demonstration equipment, as well as materials for experimentation—are designed to fulfill this function.

One of the major problems for the junior and senior high school science teacher is the procurement and maintenance of laboratory equipment. Questions of what and how much to order, how to use the apparatus most effectively, and how to store it conveniently for future use are difficult ones, especially for a beginning science teacher. Frequently, it is the teacher moving into a new position who faces these problems in their most acute form. If the preceding teacher has not kept careful records of apparatus and equipment and maintained them in good working order, the job of inventorying can be overwhelming.

If possible, it is wise for a teacher beginning a new science position to plan on spending several days in advance of the regular opening of school to work on inventorying equipment, checking its condition, and preparing orders for needed supplies for the year. This preparation will contribute to more effective teaching. Teaching plans may be built around certain materials that are available in sufficient quantities for classroom demonstrations and experiments. It is highly recommended that schools and science departments use their microcomputers to inventory their materials and equipment.

Ordering and Inventorying

Factors to be considered in purchasing equipment and laboratory materials are:

1. Is this the best available item for the teaching purpose intended? Because of the importance of the teaching

Students develop observational skills in conjunction with cognitive knowledge in investigative science classes.

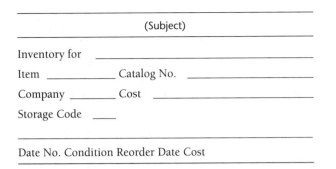

FIGURE 23–1   Inventory Card

| Inventory of Expendables, Chemistry | | | | | |
Date	Item	Condition	On Hand	Needed	Cost
4 81	Tubing glass (4 mm)	Ex.	10 lbs.	0	
4 81	Tubing glass (5 mm)	Ex.	10 lbs.	0	
4 81	Tubing glass (16 mm)	Ex.	0	5 lbs.	$6.85/lb.
4 81	Tubing rubber (4 mm)	Good	50 ft.	0	
4 81	Tubing rubber (5 mm)	Good	10 ft.	40 ft.	$175.00/ 100 ft.

FIGURE 23–2   Inventory Checklist

task and the limitations of time, it is essential to have the best possible tools at hand. The equipment must be basically simple, be capable of illustrating the intended principles, and be engineered to work well.

2. Will the materials serve their intended purpose for a reasonable length of time? Classroom equipment and other materials receive hard use as successive classes work with them. They must be designed to withstand rough handling for several years. A poorly engineered and poorly constructed apparatus, though possibly less expensive to purchase, is rarely economical in the long run.

3. Are the materials functional? Can they be stored easily without excessive disassembly? Do they lend themselves to student use? It is generally a mistake to purchase overly-delicate apparatus or equipment with unnecessary precision capabilities for the secondary science class.

4. Is the cost reasonable for the quality of equipment purchased? Comparing catalog prices from several companies can result in savings. It is essential to check the specifications carefully on all apparatus ordered, to ensure that they meet the requirements of the situation.

New equipment and materials of the nonexpendable variety should be inventoried on receipt. A three-by-five card file system is a useful method to keep a record of new purchases and current stock of materials and apparatus. A suggested form for an inventory card is shown in Figure 23–1.

Each nonexpendable item in stock should be inventoried on a card of this type. Expendable items should be inventoried on a longer form of the checklist variety. With a well-kept inventory checklist it should be possible to ascertain the amount and condition of expendable items at a glance. Since the preparation of such a list and the effort required to keep it current is quite time-consuming, this task should be assigned to student laboratory assistants if possible.

An inventory checklist might look like the one shown in Figure 23–2.

SUPPLEMENTARY TEACHING AIDS

The sources of supplementary teaching materials are multiplying year by year. For the science teacher, a major problem in using them is proper selection. Educational departments of industrial companies have created or made available to teachers innumerable aids for science teaching. Many of these materials are free or can be obtained at minimal expense. Many kits and project materials for the use of junior and senior high school students are now available. Some of them are free if ordered in small quantities.

A very useful type of supplementary teaching aid is student science periodicals, such as *Science News, Current Science, Science World,* and *Science and Math Weekly.* Subscription rates for students are nominal. In addition to highly informative articles on current science topics, these publications frequently contain suggested student activities and experiments. A teacher's edition is sometimes provided, containing suggestions on how to use the activities and other materials. The science teacher of today would be remiss in failing to use these teaching aids.

Some activities require minimal materials, often very simple items the students can make themselves. For an example, see the "Teaching Science Activity: The Evolution Simulation Game," in the Appendix, pp. 375-379.

As with the standard equipment and materials discussed earlier, storage and availability for effective use are problems in the classroom. A storage file for printed materials, indexed by subject, is a necessary item, and periodic updating is required.

THE ROLE OF THE SCIENCE STAFF IN PLANNING FACILITIES

Assisting in the planning of modern science complexes and the remodeling of old facilities to meet the demands of new instructional methods is the responsibility of the science teacher. It is a rare teacher who will not be involved in this type of activity during a professional career.

Planning a facility that will be educationally effective and efficient for 30 to 40 years requires the best minds available. Several well-qualified persons should be involved in the planning, including science teachers with vast experience, science educators, and local, state, and national science supervisors. Building a structure that may cost millions of dollars certainly warrants expenditures for planning. It is desirable that some science teachers be hired during the summer so that they can devote their full time to this task.

A teacher's philosophy of education defines activities that suggest facilities. It is important that teachers consider what they wish to accomplish educationally and then what type of facilities will enable them to reach these objectives. Teachers must remember, however, that they will not be the only instructors to use the plan: It will undoubtedly be in use long after they have retired. It is paramount that teachers think to the future, to science teaching in the 21st century, and ask, "What can I help design today that will not hinder other teachers two or three decades from now?"

It is the responsibility of science teachers to outline the educational specifications for the architect, but the science teacher does not design the room. Designing the area for optimum fulfillment of the educational specifications is the responsibility of the architect. The design of the science area obviously must fit into the total scheme for the school.

The science staff has a role to play in site selection. Before the site is selected, they should urge the administration to consider how the site can add to the school's instructional program. Such a consideration is of particular importance in biology, where field work complements class instruction. The final decision in this matter is the responsibility of the Board of Education and must be based on cost and other factors. For example, a site desirable because it offers a good natural area for science work may present a problem in transporting students to and from school.

INFLUENCES ON SCIENCE FACILITIES

Trends in Science Instruction

To ensure that facilities will not be outdated, the science staff must be aware of instruction trends. Science education has undergone a dynamic revolution in curricu-

A well stocked library provides materials for students to develop research skills in inquiry classes.

lum and in teaching methods and techniques. Modern technology and research in learning theory alter the present methods of instruction. To guard against facilities restricting new methods of instruction, they should be designed to be flexible, easily modifiable, and able to take into account the trends in science education.

Teaching Methods

Two instructional approaches that are receiving attention are team teaching and individualized instruction. Team teaching involves some large-group instruction for 80 to 100 students, with smaller laboratory sections. Instruction for large lecture-demonstration classes is afforded by lecture complexes or by rooms divided by operable walls that open for large groups. Individualized instruction is designed to allow each student to progress at his or her own rate. This approach requires many individual work areas. Both group and individualized instruction require diverse facilities far removed from those of the traditional classroom.

A variation on this concept is that of differentiated staffing. In this concept, various groups of teachers serve different functions. There may be one or more master teachers in each subject matter discipline. Other teachers serve in supporting roles, along with noncertified teacher aides, specialists, and other individuals. The differentiated concept is considered more efficient in the use of the school's time and allows more teacher-student interaction. It also provides a basis for differentiation of pay scales and the application of merit-pay concepts.

In recent years, a different concept of education has been tried, namely, that of the open school (sometimes called free school). There are several examples of this type in the United States and in Europe. The open school may be completely ungraded, yet it may extend from ages four or five up through ages 17 and 18, corresponding to the twelfth grade. Some of the innovations in the open school are the use of noncompulsory attendance, freedom of choice by the students for the classes they wish, and the use of teacher aides, parents, specialists, and individuals who can work through a broad spectrum of problems. To be effective, the open school must have a responsive and rich environment with ample materials available for students to work with. At the present time, most open schools are at the elementary level, but there are several exceptions that continue to ages 17 and 18.

It appears that a developing trend throughout science education is the application of more humane methods of teaching. There is more concern about student attitudes and interests and other aspects of the affective domain. Teachers are beginning to make an effort to develop feelings of mutual trust between the students and themselves. They consider that each student has individual worth. Increasingly, teachers attempt to develop and maintain positive attitudes for education and schooling. There is an increased use of audiovisual aids by small groups and individuals engaged in special work. Tape recorders are being used more often to enrich class instruction. Some of the new schools have multiple tape-recording outlets and a series of tapes so that individual students can listen to various tapes at the same time. This arrangement is similar, on a limited basis, to the type of activity that goes on in language laboratories. Provision must be made to ensure widened use of audiovisual material on both individual and group bases.

♦   **REFLECTING ON SCIENCE TEACHING**   ♦

Designing Facilities

1. Discuss what Winston Churchill meant by the statement, "We shape our facilities; thereafter they shape us."
2. What relevance does the statement "form follows function" have for science teachers?
3. Who should be involved in the planning of science facilities and why?
4. Many schools are built with little or no consultation with school personnel. Why is this an undesirable practice?
5. What does a teacher's philosophy of education have to do with facilities?

Another development is emphasis on more varied instruction. Not all students necessarily perform the same experiment in the same class period. In one class, students may be engaged in several different activities.

More space for both equipment and storage is being provided in many schools. This change includes the provision of more preparation areas.

♦   **REFLECTING ON SCIENCE TEACHING**   ♦

Trends and Facilities

1. What trends of science education have implications for facilities?
2. Can you think of other trends that have implications for science facilities?

Curriculum

In the past 20 years, certain curriculum changes have become more and more evident. Among them are the use of new curricula at the middle school, junior high, and senior high levels. Frequently the sequence in the junior high is living sciences in the seventh grade, physical science in the eighth grade, and earth science in the ninth grade. Some schools have developed minicourses, which are one-semester courses on rather specialized topics offered on an elective basis, so that students may choose them to satisfy individual needs. In recent years, various courses in environmental sciences have been developed as part of the minicourse offerings.

A discernible change in the interpretation of the word laboratory seems to be evident in recent years. Rather than thinking of the laboratory as merely a room equipped with gas, water, and electricity, it now is thought of as a place where experiments can be conducted. This conception might include the outdoors as well as the indoors, and it might include observational experiments, particularly with respect to the life and earth sciences. Modern curricula emphasize laboratory approaches, which require more laboratory space and supporting facilities, such as preparation rooms, live rooms, greenhouses, and student research and project areas.

Most of the modern curriculum developments emphasize inquiry. Facilities must be provided to allow for inquiring in several ways, such as reading, observation, experimentation, study of models, charts, preserved specimens, field work, slides, overhead projection, and videos. Information from a variety of sources is becoming more available to students, requiring greater flexibility in space utilization.

GUEST EDITORIAL ◆ SUSAN STEWART

Physical Science Teacher
Kenny C. Guinn Junior High, Las Vegas, Nevada

PREPARING FOR THE FIRST YEAR

Are there really slot machines in the classrooms? Do cacti grow on the playground? Do most of the teachers lose their paychecks in the local casino once a week? These and similar questions were asked by the folks back home when I left my conservative midwestern hometown to start an adventure as an eighth-grade science teacher in Las Vegas. Regardless of the different images people have of this city, I am certain that my experiences as a first-year teacher here are very much like those of my fellow graduates in other parts of the country. Adolescents are adolescents no matter where they live. The first year of teaching junior high is frustrating and exhausting. But as my colleagues assure me, it gets easier with experience, and I believe them.

Las Vegas is growing by leaps and bounds and consequently is one of the few places in this country crying for teachers. Kenny C. Guinn Junior High just opened this fall with 1,150 students drawn mainly from a rapidly-expanding part of town. Most of the parents in this area are employed by the hotels on the Strip. Because of the growth of this town and the fact that in most cases both parents work, Clark County is a fairly wealthy district. Comprehensive special education programs, vocational-technical education, and career exploration are emphasized at all levels. Strong emphasis is placed on basics, and comprehensive programs are offered in all schools for youngsters who need special help in reading and mathematics. The Clark County School District reflects all ethnic backgrounds in its student population, staff, and approach to learning. The ethnic distribution of students is 78 percent Caucasian, 15 percent Black, 5 percent Spanish-American, 0.4 percent American Indian, and 1.6 percent others.

With three new schools opening the district had 110 schools. It is a privilege to be a member of the staff that opened one of these new schools. It is exciting and challenging to participate in setting precedents and in creating new curricula for over 1,100 students. Other "thrills of opening a new school" (as my principal loves to say) include dealing with unfinished rooms and laboratory facilities, as well as undelivered supplies and equipment; waiting for defective doors and pencil sharpeners to be repaired; and running a program that has never been tried before. These are times that call for the highest virtues a teacher can possess: flexibility, creativity, and patience.

This first year as a junior high science teacher is an eye-opening experience. There are so many things I am facing now for which no college course or textbook ever prepared me. Who could have taught me how to handle the politics within an administration or of a district school board? What course trained me to deal with the parents of different students? Was there a textbook recipe on how to deal with the normal day-to-day stress that confronts anyone who works with teenagers up to eight hours a day?

I am very thankful for the preparation I did have in my undergraduate years. There I developed very important organization skills. I learned how to express my creativity and my love for science through writing curricula. I was challenged to develop an educational philosophy and to learn how to apply it to practical and realistic objectives for the classroom.

My strength as a teacher lies in my enthusiasm for my subject and in my wholehearted conviction that it is valuable for every youngster. I also have a certain empathy for junior high students and a genuine concern for guiding them through "those difficult years." Supposedly, those qualities are enough to start the young teacher off with a smooth-running classroom. Well, if you do not discover it in student teaching, you soon find out on your first job how fragile all those idealistic goals and perceptions of education are; they shatter before your eyes within the first three months. It takes persistence and faith to piece together again a modified educational philosophy consistent with the classroom realities.

One of the major areas for which college courses have failed to prepare teachers in the past is discipline. As a first-year teacher, I did not anticipate spending 70 percent of the class time in teaching students that there are logical consequences to their actions. Genuine concern, conscientious hard work, and creative lesson plans are not enough. The prospective teacher needs to be trained in effective classroom control. I, like many other teachers, have learned classroom management by trial-and-error and have ended up using methods that just seem to work. For certain periods of time, my actions became mechanical and/or inconsistent; they were designed to eliminate my stress and they did not always consider the best interests of the child. To create a workable and consistent philosophy of discipline, the young teacher needs more background in adolescent psychology and more practical experience in the classroom with time to apply, evaluate, and revise this philosophy.

Teaching is not an eight-hour-a-day job; you are a teacher around the clock. The demands by the public for what a good teacher should be are increasing. The trend to make teachers accountable for cranking out reading, writing, and calculating students is on the uprise. More and more guidelines and restrictions are being established as to what you can teach. College is the place to learn some self-preservation and sanity-saver techniques. Gather ideas for your future curricula. Learn how to express your creativity in concrete objectives. Spend as much time as you can in the classroom—observing, experimenting, and evaluating. Solidify what you believe about children, the role of the teacher, and the role of the school, and start to observe how it works in practice.

There are still several things for which no text or course can prepare you. At times, as a first-year teacher, there will appear to be few rewards, and even those few will not be immediately visible. You need to be aware of the potential morale problems you will face among your faculty. Although you confront disillusionment, you must resist being drawn into a negative attitude. Keep hold of those ideals; you may have to reconstruct them, but do not ever abandon them. Budget cuts, crowded classrooms, and apathetic parents are other challenges which await you. It is part of the occupation, however, and your decision to stick with it boils down to your own conviction that you possess a potential power to make a dent in it all.

My personal conviction is strong enough that I know I want to make teaching my career. I plan to finish coursework for a Master's degree in geology or biology. With that, I would like to try teaching overseas for a few years. Environmental education also appeals to me, and I may want to move into the position of consultant. This first year is just the beginning, of course, and there are many possibilities ahead.

Some curriculum developers discern a recent trend in science classrooms toward a return to teacher demonstrations and seatwork.[9] This trend may reflect higher costs of laboratory equipment.

Some schools use the block approach to learning science. This method is most advanced in the BSCS biology course, in which students concentrate on laboratory work in depth for four to six weeks. This arrangement requires greater storage space, as do some other modern developments in science instruction. Advanced science courses, such as science seminars or advanced placement, are frequently used and require more work areas.

Trends in Science Facilities

Flexibility of design is an important feature of science facilities. This means that the facilities must be designed so that they can be changed or defined by the people who use them. In other words: (1) the equipment used should have optimal functionality and mobility, and (2) the degree of flexibility is determined by the number of usable changes; that is, the more usable changes, the greater the degree of flexibility. There should be the capacity for immediate change (changes that require only minutes to make) and long-range changeability (something that might take place over a weekend or during a vacation period).

The adaptation gaining popularity is the "service sandwich," a 36-inch space between floors in which are contained wiring, lighting fixtures, TV conduits, air ducts, plumbing, and other utilities. Access to these utilities may be through the ceiling at designated points, spaced so that rooms may be changed at will but utilities will be easily accessible. There is not much point in being able to change partitions around if one cannot also change the lighting arrangements, plumbing, air conditioning controls, and other services. Grid troughs containing electrical conduits, ducts for hot and cold air and return ducts, fluorescent light tubes, telephone lines, electrical wiring conduits, switches, outlets, radio and TV circuitry, and intercom systems are designed into the service sandwich.

Between 1970 and 1972, exemplary science facilities were studied by the NSTA.[10] Six task force members visited more than 140 schools in the United States. These schools had been nominated by individuals, state science groups, and the National Science Supervisors Association (NSSA). The purpose of the study was to assess the status of science teaching facilities in the middle, junior high, senior high, and junior college levels.

Two characteristics of science facilities were considered necessary to earn the judgment of exemplary. They were flexibility and provision for individualization. Early in the study it was found that facilities themselves could not be studied separately or isolated from

FIGURE 23–3   Contrasting Modes of Science Instruction

other characteristics of science teaching, including programs, curriculum materials, and instructional staff. Two modes of science instruction, showing the trend toward greater emphasis on student-centered learning through the use of materials and facilities, are shown in Figure 23–3. In the first mode, the traditional teaching situation involves a teacher, resource materials, books, and other sources of information impinging on the student from many directions. The student has little control over what he or she receives. In the second emerging pattern of school instruction, the student finds him or herself at the center of learning, with freedom and opportunities to select from a variety of teaching modes—including resource rooms, carrels, laboratories, resource persons, lectures, textbooks, and other materials. The difference between these two modes is based on the place at which the student is put in the learning pattern.

The evolving patterns in facilities and programs are shown in Figure 23–4. The arrows indicate the transition from rigid, traditional patterns near the bottom to flexible and optional modes at the top of each ladder.

Trends in School Buildings

One of these trends is that of the open-concept school. Schools designed along this line frequently do not have interior walls—or if they do, walls are minimal and frequently not load-bearing. Movable partitions are often used, and bookcases and room dividers replace cinderblock walls. The environment in such schools is usually pleasant, particularly if the interior of the building has been acoustically treated. This treatment includes carpeting of the floors and walls, if possible, and the use of acoustical tile or varied ceilings to break up sound patterns.

The open-concept schools give considerable freedom of movement and, when combined with flexible scheduling patterns, provide a casual and aesthetically pleasing atmosphere. Students move from area to area in small groups or individually, and the typical clatter of the traditional classroom (with its bell at the end of a class period) is usually absent. Freedom of movement requires flexible furniture and ample work areas for small groups. Laboratories are often placed along the perimeter or are designed in some kind of movable fashion, leading to innovation in laboratory furniture. One trend is the use of power islands, which include electricity, gas, and water, as well as waste disposal units. For maximum flexibility there is access through the floor for connections to all the necessary utilities. Using such connections enables one to cover the floor access port completely, move the power island out of the way, and redesign the room as much as one wishes. Movable laboratory tables, which can be used to form work areas, are usually associated with the power island; these extend from the power center.

A new innovation in laboratory furniture is a portable carrel. Such a carrel stands about six feet high and is about three feet wide and folds into a compact unit that may be locked. When a student wishes to use his or her carrel, he or she unlocks the combination, pulls out a door, and a seat appears with bookshelves and writing surfaces immediately available.

Another innovation, which is appearing in new schools and is conducive to better science teaching, is computer terminals for using computer-assisted instruction facilities. A second innovation is the provision of a combined teacher-office work area to facilitate team planning. This area is particularly useful when curriculum planning is done by the individual teachers in the district or in team-teaching situations. The use of ramps

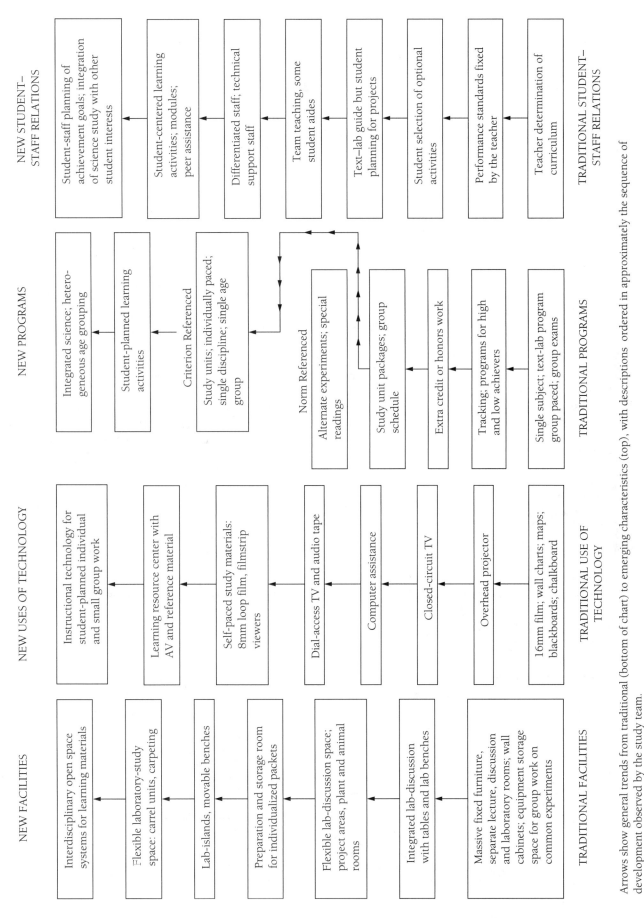

FIGURE 23–4 Evolving Patterns in Facilities, Technology, Programs, and Student-Staff Relations in Science Teaching

Arrows show general trends from traditional (bottom of chart) to emerging characteristics (top), with descriptions ordered in approximately the sequence of development observed by the study team.

to accommodate wheelchairs is another important change. The use of color and of aesthetically pleasing work areas is also a welcome change. Another innovation is the use of adjoining outdoor-environment centers to which students in the earth science and biology classes may have immediate access.

As teachers remove themselves more and more from the position of being the primary information source, their role changes to that of director of learning or diagnostician. Consequently, students have more control over the rate at which they proceed and the sequence of information with which they interact. Information from a wide variety of sources is becoming more available to the students, thus there is a demand for greater flexibility in space utilization.

Large, open laboratories are becoming more common, as is the growth of technologically assisted study. Calculators and computer terminals are sometimes installed for individualized instruction. The open laboratories must be large enough for sufficient separation between groups. This space acts as a sound barrier and works adequately as long as the total number of students is not excessive. Other methods of breaking up the large, open areas while retaining flexibility include using bookshelves as room dividers, varied furniture arrangements to give visual and aesthetic satisfaction, or movable self-supporting partitions.

GUIDELINES FOR PLANNING A SCIENCE COMPLEX

It is clear that the science complex must contain more of everything and must be designed with an emphasis on flexibility. In planning science facilities, attention should be given to the following principles.[11]

Planning Facilities

1. Those who select the school site should consider the potential contributions of the surroundings to the teaching of science. The location of science rooms within the science complex in relation to supply, outdoor areas, and sunlight exposure needs consideration. For example, a biology classroom is best located on a ground floor with access to growing areas.
2. Planning of science rooms should incorporate the ideas of many qualified individuals who have had experience in planning science facilities, not just the architect's ideas.
3. The needs of science should be considered in floor planning, illumination, ventilation, plumbing, and placement of sinks and water taps. Electric plugs for each student should be provided if necessary.

4. Consideration should be given to windowless classrooms, since they do have some advantages for storage, thermal control, and audiovisual programs.

Area and Space Resources

1. The amount of floor space provided should be 35 to 45 square feet or more per student (50 square feet if storage area is included).
2. The number of rooms and how much they will be used throughout the day should be carefully determined. If a room will not be filled with science students all day, what other classes will be in it?
3. There should be enough space for projects to remain assembled for varying periods of time.
4. Enough space should be provided for proper storage of all materials.
5. Space should be provided for displaying student-constructed projects and other products and devices.
6. Space should be provided for the science teacher to work.
7. More aisle space must be provided in multipurpose laboratories because of greater student movement.

 Visit http://www.prenhall.com/trowbridge and select Topic 6—Professional Development. Select "Web Links" and find the website of the "National Science Teachers Association." They have publications on construction and renovation of school science labs, which have many ideas and recommendations about space requirements. Use this information to draw sketches and room plans for a science area of your choice. Submit these plans to your instructor using the Electronic Bluebook module.

Different Learning Activities

1. The science rooms should provide for a wide range of learning activities for individuals, small groups, and the entire class.
2. Facilities should permit students to experiment with many materials.
3. Areas should be provided where experiments and projects may be conducted for others to observe.

 Visit http://www.prenhall.com/trowbridge and select Topic 2—Constructivism and Learning in Science. Select "Activities and Lesson Plans" and find the link for "TOPS." This will have many ideas for constructible projects that require work space to function. From this survey, write a brief paper on what it takes to facilitate project building in a science area. Submit this paper to your instructor for discussion using the Electronic Bluebook module.

♦ **REFLECTING ON SCIENCE TEACHING** ♦

Instructional Facilities

1. What five considerations do you think are most important in facility design for science teaching?
2. Design a modern floor plan for a science complex. Justify your design.
3. How do the facility requirements for individualized instruction vary from those of group instruction?
4. Facilities should be available for individual experimental work.
5. There should be provision for small-group or individual conferences with the science teacher.

Furniture and Decor

1. Rooms should be pleasant and attractive. Using several colors in cabinets and display cabinets helps to give the room a pleasant appearance.
2. Rooms should be flexible, to accommodate a variety of uses. Furniture that is not permanently installed ensures greater flexibility, since it can be easily moved as conditions warrant.
3. Adaptable furniture should be provided.

Auxiliary Facilities

1. Planning science facilities should include consideration of the community resources that can be used to supplement the program (i.e., libraries, museums, parks, etc.).
2. There should be a facility for construction and repair of equipment.
3. Provisions should be made for published materials to be available.
4. Facilities should be provided for effective use of audiovisual aids.

In planning a science complex, careful consideration must be given to the study of space relationships. Where should the biology rooms be located in relation to the physics, chemistry, and other science rooms? What relationship should they have to the storage areas? Should there be a central storage area with access to all classrooms, or should each classroom have a storage facility? The advantage of the former arrangement is that it requires less space and makes equipment available for multiple use. For example, a vacuum pump may be eas-

ily available to physics, chemistry, physical science, and general science classes. A central storage area, however, requires greater organization and agreement among the faculty involved on how the equipment will be used and returned to the storage area.

The NSTA, through its Commission on Professional Standards and Practices, has prepared a document entitled "Conditions for Good Science Teaching."[12] In its recommendations, it has dealt with resources for learning, among which are science rooms and laboratories. A list of its recommendations follows:

Conditions for Good Science Teaching

1. There should be at least one separate laboratory for each kind of science course offered.
2. There must be enough laboratory rooms provided for each science course to accommodate all students who can profit from the course and who wish to take it.
3. Each laboratory must be large enough to accommodate real experimentation.
4. Each laboratory should have ceilings that are at least 10 feet (3 meters) high.
5. Each laboratory should be appropriately furnished for each science.
6. Each laboratory should have conveniently located electric, gas, and water outlets.
7. Waste-disposal facilities must be provided in all laboratories.
8. For work efficiency and safety, laboratories should have lighting that takes into account the variations in working conditions common to science laboratories.
9. Reasonable considerations of comfort and health require that each laboratory have the capability of renewing the room air at a rate compatible with normal student occupancy and the potential uses of science laboratories, such as maintenance of animals, noxious gases, etc.
10. Fire blankets and fully operable fire extinguishers must be located where they are quickly accessible. Every laboratory should be protected by automatic overhead sprinklers.
11. Chemistry laboratories must contain an emergency shower, an eye-wash fountain, and safety goggles for all students.
12. Every science laboratory must have two unobstructed exits.
13. There should be an annual, verified safety check of each laboratory.
14. No more than 24 students should be assigned to a space intended for group discussion and activity (as distinct from large-group lecture).

15. A science classroom should have full audiovisual capability and facilities for conducting scientific demonstrations.
16. Specialized facilities are needed (plant growth facilities, animal room, darkroom, and science shop).
17. Individual project areas are needed for students working on special experiments.
18. Ample science-library space must be available.
19. Conference rooms are needed for teacher-student conferences.
20. Ample space is needed for the storage of supplies and equipment.
21. Every science teacher requires access to a preparation area free from students.
22. Every science teacher should have private office space.
23. The science department budget should appear as a separate account within the whole school budget, and it should be subdivided functionally.
24. Supplies should be budgeted on a per capita basis with the amount varying according to the nature of the course and the consumables involved.
25. Budgets should provide leeway for items to be ordered during the school year for new projects, perishable materials, and unforeseen contingencies.

SCIENCE FACILITIES AND STUDENTS WITH DISABILITIES

In 1977, Joseph A. Califano, then Secretary of Health, Education, and Welfare, signed the regulations implementing Section 504 of the Rehabilitation Act of 1973. Section 504 provides that "No otherwise qualified handicapped individual . . . shall solely by reason of his handicap be excluded from the participation in, be denied the benefits of, or be subjected to discrimination under any program or activity receiving federal financial assistance."

In many cases, there have been dramatic changes in the actions and attitudes of institutions and individuals receiving federal funds. Some of the implications of the regulation are as follows:

1. All new facilities must be barrier-free.
2. Programs or activities must be made accessible to persons with disabilities, and/or structural changes must be made within a given time period.
3. Qualified persons with disabilities may not, on the basis of a disability, be denied admission or employment even if facilities have not been made barrier-free.
4. Colleges and universities must make reasonable modifications in academic requirements, where

necessary, to ensure full educational opportunity for students with disabilities.
5. Educational institutions must provide auxiliary aids, such as readers for the blind or interpreters for the deaf.

It is evident that the educational systems and the design professions, as well as material and product manufacturers, must determine the needs of persons with disabilities. In turn, this understanding must be translated into practical, economical ways of providing opportunities for these individuals so that they may achieve educational accomplishment.

In the past, architects and educators have been content to function with respect to the so-called average person. They have often been unaware of the many individuals with physical disabilities who are striving to function as productive citizens. This has been true not only in the design of buildings but also in the design of the science curricula.

Since, as much as possible, persons with disabilities should participate equally in campus activities with those who are nondisabled, it is imperative that the entire educational facility be considered. This consideration not only benefits the participant who has a disability, but it also aids staff members and visitors who may have disabilities.

Various institutions have been modified so that they are accessible to persons with disabilities. Stairways are being supplemented with ramps and elevators. Braille letters and symbols are used for signs. The problem is not easily solved in laboratories, however. In many cases, spacing work areas in the laboratories requires complete remodeling. Since the standard laboratory table does not accommodate a person using a wheelchair, many facilities are totally inadequate for compliance with the new laws.

Furthermore, a laboratory that has been modified to accommodate a person using a wheelchair does not necessarily meet the needs of every individual with a disability. Problems involving manual dexterity require additional modifications that have an impact on not only the station but also on the specific items of equipment associated with that station.

Physical barriers present just one phase of the problem of accessibility for persons with disabilities. Another aspect relates to the affective approach to the problem. For this reason, the overall environment for the student must be considered.

The new regulations may encourage more students with disabilities to study science. One of the reasons that individuals with disabilities may have avoided the science field, or any other program requiring science courses, could be their inability to find appropriate means of completing laboratory requirements. For the first time, these students may have the opportunity to satisfy the requirements for a particular major.

 Visit http://www.prenhall.com/trowbridge and select Topic 5—Science Education and Special Needs. Select "National Science Teaching Standards," then click on the link for the "Science Teaching Standards," and find the website entitled www.tsbvi.edu. Study this website for a comprehensive list of accessibility guidelines.

SUMMARY

Science teachers in today's schools have almost unlimited choices of materials with which to enhance their teaching. Wise selection of appropriate materials is a major problem. In making these choices, it is important to recognize the basic reasons for using a variety of materials in science teaching. Individual differences among students demand variations in methods and materials. The psychology of learning supports the thesis that variety of materials promotes better learning. More of the senses are stimulated, and more avenues of learning are activated. Availability of many materials gives opportunity for individual work and experimentation.

Published materials form a large segment of today's science-teaching arsenal. Textbooks continue to be essential tools, although their limitations are better recognized. It is still important to select textbooks in science carefully and with an understanding of their contribution to learning. Many supplementary monographs and pamphlets are now available. These materials usually are written at a level suitable for junior and senior high school students. Authors of these publications have done an excellent job of communicating difficult concepts from the research frontiers as understandable science for the nontechnical reader. At the same time, they have demonstrated the processes of science admirably and conveyed realistic ideas of the role of science in society. Audiovisual equipment and materials continue to gain in sophistication. Although radio and television have not yet realized their potential as teaching aids in the average classroom, increasing strides are being made in their use. New techniques with overhead projectors, film-loop projectors, and single-concept films are finding increased popularity. Individual differences are being better served by these materials, and individualized instruction is enhanced by more flexible audiovisual aids.

Science teaching depends greatly on laboratory work. Materials for the laboratory are increasing, both in variety and in abundance in science classrooms. The science teacher must become familiar with sources of laboratory apparatus and supplies. In choosing equipment, educational value is paramount. In addition, durability and usefulness are important considerations. Once purchased, equipment must be maintained in usable condition. An up-to-date inventory is necessary, and an adequate budget for purchase of new materials must be available.

In this chapter we have not attempted to give an exhaustive treatment of the problems of facilities design. Instead, we have tried to show teachers' responsibilities in ensuring that new facilities are an improvement over the old ones; we have also pointed out some considerations in providing modern facilities. Science teachers are the most competent at knowing what facilities are needed for efficient and effective teaching. It is their responsibility to work toward getting these facilities.

In writing educational specifications, teachers must take care that the facilities will not be outdated in 20 or 30 years. This problem can be avoided if facilities are made flexible and if teachers understand trends in teaching that have implications for science instruction.

New federal requirements mandate that students with disabilities be provided with suitable facilities, materials, and services to ensure full educational opportunities for this group. Substantial modification of laboratory space and facilities is required.

◆

REFERENCES

1. National Science Teachers Association, *Conditions for Good Science Teaching in Secondary Schools* (Washington, DC: Author, 1970), p. 6.
2. Arthur Stinner, "Science Textbooks and Science Teaching: From Logic to Evidence," *Science Education,* 76 (1) (1992): 1–16.
3. Hans Christian von Baeyer, quoted in Stinner, pp. 13–15.
4. Musheno and Lawson, "Effects of Learning Cycle and Traditional Text on Comprehension of Science Concepts by Students at Different Reasoning Levels," *Journal of Research in Science Teaching,* 36 (1) (1999): 23–27.
5. R. E. Stake and J. A. Easley, Case Studies in Science Education (Urbana, IL: Center for Instructional Research and Curriculum Evaluation, University of Illinois, 1978).
6. David M. Memory and Kenneth W. Uhlhorn, "Multiple Textbooks at Different Readability Levels in the Science

Classroom," *School Science and Mathematics,* 91 (February 1991): 64–72.

7. Lynn M. Mulkey, "The Use of a Sociological Perspective in the Development of a Science Textbook Evaluation Instrument," *Science Education,* 71 (4) (1987): 511–522.

8. Mulkey, pp. 511–522.

9. Marjorie Gardner, "Ten Trends in Science Education," The Science Teacher (January 1979): 30–32.

10. J. D. Novak, *Facilities for Secondary School Science Teaching: Evolving Patterns in Facilities and Programs*

(Washington, DC: National Science Teachers Association, 1972).

11. This list has been modified from *Science Facilities for our Schools,* Publication K-12 (Washington, DC: National Science Teachers Association, 1963).

12. *Conditions for Good Science Teaching in Secondary Schools* (Washington, DC: National Science Teachers Association, 1984).

◆ ──────────── **INVESTIGATING SCIENCE TEACHING** ──────────── ◆

ACTIVITY 23–1

Readability Analysis

For the busy teacher or review committee selecting textbooks, a primary consideration is ease of use. Fortunately, one of the readability formulas, the Fry Readability Graph, is a simple tool which can be used by the average classroom teacher in selecting textbooks. It is a good exercise to try your hand at determining the readability of a textbook that you might use for your particular subject, to familiarize yourself with the difficulty and usefulness of such a formula. Remember, however, that the results are only approximate and largely dependent on the technical nature of the material being analyzed. Many of the readability formulas do not take into adequate consideration the technical nature of many science subjects.

Fry's Readability Graph

The Fry graph is used for narrative and expository writing only; do not use it for poetry, dialogue, drama, or unusual styles of writing. The Fry graph assesses technical difficulty, not interest, style, or content.

Directions for Using the Readability Graph

1. Select three 100-word passages from near the beginning, middle, and end of the book. For anthologies, average nine samples (three samples from each of three stories or essays).

2. Avoid samples from the beginnings and ends of chapters.

3. Include proper nouns (except for common names like Dick or Sue) in your word count.

4. Count the total number of sentences in each 100-word passage (estimating to the nearest tenth of a sentence). Average these three numbers.

5. Count the total number of syllables in each 100-word sample. There is a syllable for each vowel sound; for example: cat (1), blackbird (2), continental (4). Don't be fooled by word size; for example: polio (3), through (1). Endings such as -y, -ed, -el, or -le usually make a syllable; for example: ready (2), bottle (2). Average the total number of syllables for the three samples.

6. Count numbers in figures (1973) as one syllable. If the number is written out, count it in full syllables.

7. Plot on the graph the average number of sentences per hundred words and the average number of syllables per hundred words. The point where these plots coincide designates the grade level. If your computation places the estimated reading level in the shaded area on the graph, start over again with different samples. (Plot these two points on the Fry Graph shown as follows. What is the approximate grade difficulty level of this material?) Most plot points fall near the heavy curved line. Perpendicular lines mark off approximately grade level areas.

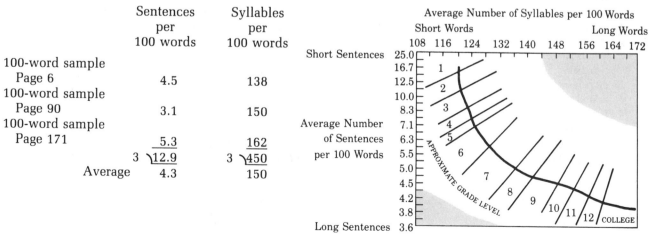

	Sentences per 100 words	Syllables per 100 words
100-word sample Page 6	4.5	138
100-word sample Page 90	3.1	150
100-word sample Page 171	5.3	162
	3 ⟍12.9	3 ⟍450
Average	4.3	150

8. If the material has been translated from another language, add one year to the estimated reading level.

9. If the material was written before 1900, add one year to the estimated reading level.

10. If great variability is encountered either in sentence length or in the syllable count for the three selections, randomly select several more passages and compute their average before plotting.

Textbook

	A	B	C

I. Content (sample all units/chapters)
   A. Most of the necessary topics/units for this level
   B. Historical development of science/scientists
   C. Present-day environment/energy/social/scientific issues
   D. Balance of life/physical/earth topics/units
   E. Appropriate level of mathematics/science content (i.e., Piaget)

II. Presentation (sample all units/chapters)
   A. Balance of content vs. inductive laboratory skills/methods/inquiry
   B. Development of ideas prior to use of scientific vocabulary
   C. Interesting informal writing style
   D. Unfamiliar/important terms/principles in italics/boldface
   E. Problem solving and scientific methods are integrated

III. Accuracy (sample 5–10 of each item)
   A. Indexed topics were scientifically correct
   B. Measures are only SI metric and technically correct
   C. Glossary is scientifically correct and understandable
   D. Directions for structured activities are precise and they work
   E. Appropriate safety is stressed at all times

IV. Organization (sample 2–3 units)
   A. Unit introduction/abstract sets the stage for student involvement
   B. Sequential development of ideas/concepts/skills
   C. Investigations are integral, not just add-on
   D. End of unit questions require thinking/application
   E. Well-indexed cross references

V. Readability
   A. Words per sentence = _____ (for grades 5–6, below 21 = outstanding)
   B. 60 percent of sentences are simple or compound (not complex)
   C. Reading level is .5 to 1.5 grade levels below text level
   D. 3–4 personal references per 100 words
   E. 1–2 examples/applications of abstract principles (low concept density)

Textbook

	A	B	C

VI. Adaptability
   A. Provisions for wide range of student skills/interests/learning styles
   B. Useable as a reference book
   C. Provides for a wide range of learning activities (not just verbal)
   D. Chapters/units can be omitted
   E. Includes appropriate controversial topics (e.g., evolution)

VII. Teaching Aids
   A. Annotated references for teachers
   B. Annotated references for students (books, periodicals, films, etc.)
   C. Publisher provides appropriate in-service
   D. Teacher's Guide includes wide variety of activities, methods, etc., besides answers
   E. Complete lists of permanent/consumable kit materials and sources

VIII. Illustrations
   A. Boy/girl and white/minority balance sex/minority stereotype
   B. Photos/art: large, clear, and appropriate (not too "arty")
   C. Illustrations integrated as direct references
   D. Adequate labels for all art/photos
   E. Modern art/photos, except for historical settings

IX. Activities
   A. At least 1/3 of activities are laboratory-oriented
   B. Balance of large/small muscle, in/out of seat activities
   C. Wide range of difficulty = success for all levels
   D. Balance of structured/inquiry activities
   E. Activities stress understanding/application, not just memorization

X. Appearance
   A. Size/style/layout of print makes for easy reading
   B. Appropriate pleasing page balance/placement of art/copy
   C. Size/shape of book is appropriate for grade level
   D. Durable, nonglare, opaque paper
   E. Attractive/durable binding and cover

Total

ACTIVITY 23–2
LEARNING MATERIALS

1. Begin a file of free and inexpensive materials related to your teaching area. Arrange an indexing system for easy access and location of items when needed.
2. Survey the current research in science education for information on the effectiveness of teaching by television. On the basis of your findings, what conclusions can you draw concerning the future of educational television in the field of science?

ACTIVITY 23–3
DESIGNING THE SCIENCE FACILITIES FOR A SMALL MIDDLE-SENIOR HIGH SCHOOL

At some point in your teaching career, you may be called upon to participate on a committee to design or contribute plans for a science room, or science wing of an existing building, or perhaps to help plan an entirely new structure, including science classrooms and laboratories. For practice in this, use the following information to design a science wing for a school of 600 pupils, grades 7–12. Assume there are 350 students in the sciences in a given year. The classes include two 7th grade life science, two 8th grade physical science, two 9th grade earth science, three 10th grade biology classes (required), two classes of 11th grade chemistry (optional) and one 12th grade physics class, also optional.

After discussing this with your classmates and considering all the possibilities, draw the plans for the science wing giving attention to the following points:

1. Number and size of science classrooms required
2. Number of laboratories—either combined with classrooms or separate
3. Required storage space for equipment, chemicals, and projects
4. Plant growing room and animal facilities
5. Safety factors, traffic flow for students, gas, water, and electrical services
6. Site selection, facilities for science outdoors
7. Any other factors of importance

Remember as you plan, you are building for at least 25 years into the future. Consider possible changes in enrollment patterns of growth or decline. Be able to justify your choices in class discussions. Remember, a science facility should be built to accommodate a variety of teaching methods and should be planned with flexibility in mind.

CHAPTER 24

STUDENT TEACHING AND PROFESSIONAL GROWTH

Students nearing the end of their teacher training grow increasingly anxious to get on the job. They may look forward with anticipation to trying their wings as full-fledged teachers in charge of a class. At the same time, they are apt to feel apprehensive at the prospect of facing a roomful of students. Will they be able to hide their nervousness? Will their knowledge of the subject be adequate for the task? Will they be able to handle discipline problems? These questions and many others may cause concern as they face the future—a future that will see them transformed from science students to teachers of science.

WHY STUDENT TEACH?

The student-teaching experience is designed to smooth the transition from the role of student to that of teacher. It is the students' opportunity to test their liking for the teaching task. They will discover whether they really enjoy teaching the subject for which they have prepared themselves. They will learn through their close contacts with children whether they are really interested in teaching children of the particular age level for which they are assigned. Most important of all, they will, it is hoped, find a genuine enthusiasm in the teaching task, an enthusiasm sufficient to convince them that this should be their chosen vocation. At the same time, the student-teaching assignment will give the training institution an opportunity to evaluate students' teaching capabilities. Successful student-teaching experiences, under the supervision of qualified classroom teachers, will enable the training institution to place its "stamp of

approval" on the student teacher's work, with reasonable assurance of their future success.

The prospective science teacher can confidently expect to gain the following values from the student-teaching experience. These values will not accrue automatically. Much of the responsibility rests with the student teachers as they attempt to profit from this culminating experience in their teacher training.

1. Improvement in Confidence. Actual experience with a science class will take away the fear of the unknown that everyone experiences when faced with a new situation. Many of these fears may turn out to be groundless. The experience actually will prove to be fun and exhilarating once the initial uneasiness is overcome. Psychologists have learned that the way to overcome the butterflies of fear of the unexpected is to become deeply involved in the experience. The immediacy of the routine problems then supersedes the anticipated difficulties.

2. Putting Theories into Practice. Here new teachers will be able to test what they have learned in methods classes (and in other classes) about ways of handling various problems. Handling individual differences among students, discipline cases, techniques of presenting science material, laboratory methods, working with small groups, and so forth, will provide situations in which student teachers can apply educational theories to classroom reality.

3. Learning About Student Behavior. Firsthand, responsible relationships with students will give student teachers the chance to study them, observe their behavior under a variety of conditions, and learn about motivation, competition, enthusiasm, boredom, and many other factors that make up the climate of a typical classroom.

4. Testing Knowledge of Subject Matter.   Regardless of the student teachers' self-assurance and confidence in their own knowledge of the subject they are planning to teach, they are likely to have a certain amount of apprehension about their ability to transmit this knowledge to others. The responsibility of teaching enthusiastic and sometimes critical students can be unnerving and is certain to convince student teachers of the necessity of knowing their subject thoroughly and of preparing for their contacts with the class. One frequently hears the comment, even among experienced teachers, "I really learned my subject when I had to teach it."

5. Receiving Constructive Criticism.   At no other time in their long-term teaching experiences will student teachers have the benefit of prolonged, intensive observation of their teaching by an experienced teacher who can be constructive in criticism and advice. This valuable benefit is not to be taken lightly. If the criticism and suggestions are taken receptively, with the intention of putting them into practice, this experience can be the most valuable part of the student teacher's assignment. It is important, therefore, to select one's supervising teacher wisely. The chance to observe and be observed by a master teacher in an atmosphere of mutual respect and helpfulness is immeasurably worthwhile.

6. Discovering Teaching Strengths and Weaknesses.   Student teachers will have the opportunity to discover their own strong and weak points in the handling of science classes. They may find that performing demonstrations results in the most successful teaching and gives them the most pleasure. It may be that organizing classes into effective discussion groups brings about maximum learning under their direction. The questioning technique and the Socratic method of conducting teacher-pupil discussions may be most successful under their guidance. Conversely, these same activities may be the least effective for them. Knowing these facts early in their career will enable teachers to improve their weaknesses and capitalize on their strengths. It is certainly to the advantage of a science teacher to be highly competent in many methods of teaching, but it is equally important to recognize that individual teachers have certain innate teaching strengths and should use techniques that capitalize on these strengths.

7. Gaining Poise and Finesse.   Because teaching is as much an art as a technique, experience should improve ways of handling classes (such as anticipating student questions and problems, timing, exploiting enthusiastic and dramatic classroom events, sensing the proper time for introducing a new activity, and commending good work). These factors will contribute to smoother functioning of class activities and to generally more effective learning. It is important to recognize, of course, that this kind of improvement will continue as long as a teacher teaches and that rarely, if ever, does a teacher reach complete perfection in the art.

Selecting Your Supervising Teacher

Frequently, a certain amount of latitude is allowed the prospective student teachers in their choice of school, subject, and teacher under whom they wish to work. The extent of this freedom will vary with the institution and circumstances in which the student-teaching program is operated, and it is entirely possible that assignments may be made quite arbitrarily. However, it is more likely that, within certain limitations, the wishes of the student will be taken into consideration.

Therefore, it is to the advantage of the student teacher to make a careful selection of school, subject, and supervising teacher. Often, new teachers feel that their student-teaching assignment was the most valuable experience in their training program. This can be true if the selection is well made and the experience fulfills its potential.

Prospective student teachers should obtain the maximum advantage by teaching in their major field. It is this area for which they are best prepared and in which they probably will feel the greatest confidence. If the situation permits, teaching in their minor field also, under a different supervising teacher, may be advantageous; they will benefit from constructive help from two experienced teachers. This experience may be analogous to an actual situation as a full-time teacher in a small or medium-sized school system.

It would be wise to visit several classes in a number of schools in the quarter or semester before your student-teaching assignment. Arrangements can be made through the principal of the school, and advance notice can be given to the teachers involved. If the purpose of the visits is explained, the prospective student teacher will probably be favorably received, particularly if it is a school in which student teachers customarily have been supervised.

The advantages of the visit can be manifold. Prospective student teachers will be able to refresh their memory of the atmosphere and activities of a high school classroom. They will be able to observe an experienced teacher in action. They will mentally attempt to project themselves into an equivalent situation as a teacher in charge of a class, a desirable step in preparation for their actual student-teaching assignment. They may be able to talk briefly with the teacher at the close of class to gain further insights. After several such visits to a variety of classes (including several outside the field of science), prospective student teachers will be able to

Keen interest and rapt attention are key hallmarks of science students in inquiry classes.

choose more intelligently the kind of teaching situation they wish to select for their student-teaching experience.

Some suggestions of criteria to look for in the teaching situation are:

1. Is the teacher well prepared, and is she teaching in his/her major field?
2. Does the teacher have good control of the class?
3. Do the students appear to be alert and interested in the activities?
4. Is there a genuine atmosphere of learning?
5. Do the facilities and materials appear to be adequate for the kind of science being taught?
6. Does it appear that the teacher is a person from whom one can learn valuable teaching techniques?
7. Is there opportunity for a certain degree of flexibility in carrying out one's teaching plans?
8. Does the teacher have a moderate workload, thus affording time for constructive help for a student teacher?
9. Does the teacher appear to be interested in serving as a supervisor for a student teacher in his/her charge?

Meeting Your Supervising Teacher

Once the assignment is made for a particular school, class, and teacher, it is imperative that the student teacher arrange for a short interview before attendance at the first class. This interview can be brief but should be a day or two in advance and by appointment. You will then avoid incurring the displeasure of the supervising teacher by intruding on his last-minute preparation for class and will provide for an interchange of questions and answers.

At the interview, the student teacher should be punctual, interested, enthusiastic, and suitably dressed. The purpose of the interview is to become acquainted and to exchange ideas and information. The supervising teacher is interested in knowing the background and preparation of the student teacher. He/She is also interested in any special qualifications the student teacher may have, such as the ability to handle audio-visual equipment, take charge of a science club, or talk about travel experiences. The student teacher is interested in learning what his/her role is to be in the classroom, what meetings to attend, what text materials are in use, and so forth.

The supervising teacher will probably suggest a period of class observation, perhaps a week or two at the outset. There may be certain room duties to perform, such as roll-taking, reading announcements, and distributing materials. Each of these tasks will enable the student teacher to quickly learn the names of pupils, a necessary step in establishing rapport with members of the class. The student teacher probably will be encouraged to prepare a seating chart immediately. Text materials may be discussed and the teacher's long-range objectives clarified. The student teacher will probably be asked to read certain assignments so that he/she will be acquainted with the students' present studies. He/she will find it imperative to do this regularly in order to best assist students who need help.

Facilities and apparatus available for teaching the science class may be shown to the student teacher during the interview. Location of the library and special preparation rooms may be pointed out. The place in the classroom where the student teacher may observe the activities of the class may be designated. (In one school, it was customary for the student teacher to sit next to the

A new student teacher tries out her skills while the supervising teacher looks on.

demonstration desk, facing the class. In this way, she learned to recognize pupils more quickly; but, more important, this arrangement enabled the student teacher to see the expressions on the pupils' faces as they responded to questions or watched a demonstration, as they showed perplexity, or as they registered insight into problems under discussion.)

Students who intend to teach in urban-area schools are advised to seek out student-teaching experiences that will give them the best possible preparation for such an assignment. Such an experience might involve student teaching in a school similar to the type in which they wish to be teaching ultimately.

BEING A STUDENT TEACHER

Your First Days in the Class

Observing pupils in the science class can be a profitable experience the first few days or weeks. Student teachers have an advantage in this situation because they are not preoccupied with teaching plans and conducting the class, as is the regular teacher. The alert observing student teacher can, in fact, be of assistance to the regular teacher in recognizing incipient discipline problems, lack of interest, or special conditions that might lead to better teaching if recognized early. Student teachers may wish to follow a systematic observation program to become familiar with all class members. For this purpose, a checklist of individual differences is suggested. Place a check mark in the column opposite the observed characteristic. The numbers represent individual pupils observed.

RECOGNIZING INDIVIDUAL DIFFERENCES IN A NEW CLASS DURING THE FIRST FEW WEEKS[1]

Things to observe and consider:

Pupils 1 2 3 4

1. Health
2. Physical defects and differences
3. Personality
4. Basic skills
5. Relationships with fellow pupils
6. Relationship with teacher
7. Class participation
8. Class attitude and cooperation
9. Dependability
10. Probable ability combined with effort

The first days in the student-teaching class should afford opportunities to give individual help to pupils who need it. Do not answer questions directly, but use inquiry methods—that is, ask guiding questions. It is wise to confer with the supervising teacher about the extent of such help. There may be some reason to withhold assistance on certain assignments. At the same time, contact with students on an individual basis is an excellent way to gain confidence in your ability to explain, teach, or convey information. The student teacher should capitalize on every possible opportunity to develop this skill.

If the science class is one in which laboratory work plays a large part (i.e., chemistry, physics, biology, or earth science), there will be many opportunities to give individual help. The student teacher can also be of significant help to the regular teacher in preparing laboratory apparatus and supplies. In this situation, the student teacher will realize that teaching a laboratory science requires extensive planning and attention to detail.

Because the initial period of observation may be rather brief, perhaps only a few days or a week, student teachers will do well to begin thinking about the choice of a teaching area or unit. Such a choice may have already been made in conference with the supervising teacher. It will certainly depend on the subject-matter goals of the course during the semester or quarter of the assignment. In anticipation of their student teaching, students will wish to gather appropriate materials and to prepare general plans. Some of the details of the preliminary planning are considered in the next section.

Preparing to Teach a Lesson

Some of the problems involved in lesson planning are detailed in Chapter 16. However, a brief review of the salient factors may be worthwhile.

A teacher facing a class for the first time may expect to accomplish far too much in a given amount of time. Although it is not necessarily wasteful to overplan a lesson, it is a mistake to try to teach everything on the lesson plan just because it is there. Sometimes the learning pace of the pupils does not allow the entire lesson plan to be completed. You must be in tune with your class constantly, sensing the proper pace and modifying your presentation as the situation demands.

A second common fault of the beginning teacher is the tendency to teach beyond the students' comprehension. This fault may be a result of recent contact with college courses, in which the level is very high, or the inability to place abstract ideas into concrete terms for comprehension by secondary school students. The problem is important enough that beginning teachers should make certain that their presentation is at the appropriate level for the class involved. Perhaps they could try a few test trials with individual students to acquire a realistic sense of the proper difficulty level before they teach the entire class.

Construction of unit and daily lesson plans is an important task at this stage (see Chapter 16 for suggested formats). It is important to have a clear idea of what you wish to accomplish in the allotted time and what specific objectives are to be met. Student teachers should attempt to place themselves in the position of a science pupil who is learning about the material for the first time. They should consider factors of interest, motivation, individual differences, time limitations, facilities, and equipment; they should try to anticipate the kinds of problems that may occur and prepare possible solutions. When student teachers have considered these elements, they will feel more secure and will have fewer discipline problems.

Beginning teachers should also anticipate questions from the class. First attempts at planning tend to neglect preparation for handling these questions and fail to provide enough time for dealing with them in the class period. Yet the frank interchange of ideas between teacher and students, which is provoked by questions, can be an effective teaching technique and should not be ignored. In planning, try to anticipate the kinds of questions students may ask. If you remember that the students may be encountering the subject matter for the first time, it is not too difficult to foretell what questions may come to their minds. Jot down these probable questions on your lesson plan, along with suitable answers or with suggested procedures for finding the answers. Time spent in this manner is not wasted, even if the specific anticipated questions do not arise. Beginning teachers will gain confidence in their own understanding of the subject matter and in their ability to provide suitable answers.

A final point to consider is that of proper pacing and timing of the class period. The written lesson plans may have suggested time allotments for various activities, but the actual class is certain to deviate to some extent. The important idea to remember is to be flexible enough to accommodate minor variations within the class period. However, to avoid gross miscalculations of time requirements for certain activities, rehearse them in advance. A short lecture, for example, can be tried out on one's roommate, who will be able to give critical comments on clarity and organization, as well as timing. In the case of student activities or laboratory work, it is usually advisable to allot about 50 percent more time than appears adequate for the teacher to do the work. This leeway is also recommended in giving written tests.

At all stages of planning for the first day of teaching, it is imperative that student teachers keep the supervising teacher informed of their plans, solicit advice and assistance, and, in general, plan in such a way as to make the transition from regular teacher to student teacher as smooth as possible.

The First Day of Teaching

If student teachers have had frequent opportunities to work with individuals and small groups before their first day of actual teaching, they will find the new experience a natural extension of these tasks and a challenging opportunity for growth in the art of teaching. A good introduction will get the class off to an interesting start. A brief explanation of the purpose of the lesson and the work at hand, followed immediately by plunging into the class activities, will convey to the students an appreciation of the tasks to be accomplished. A forthright and businesslike manner by the student teacher will elicit class cooperation and leave no doubt about who is in charge.

Attention should be given to proper speech and voice modulation. A good pace should be maintained, and, above all, genuine enthusiasm must be displayed. This enthusiasm will normally be infectious and will secure an enthusiastic response from the class. If possible, students should be encouraged to participate. Questions from students should be encouraged and a relaxed atmosphere maintained for free interchange of ideas.

It is usually advisable, especially with junior high school classes, to vary the activity once or twice during the class period. Perhaps a short lecture can be followed by a brief film and the period concluded with a summarizing discussion. Or a demonstration by the teacher might be followed by a period of individual experimentation. It is true that planning and execution of a varied class period requires more work on the part of the teacher, but the dividends appear in the form of enthusiasm, alert attention, and better learning.

The last five or ten minutes of a class period are often used to summarize the major points of the lesson and to make appropriate assignments. It is important to recognize that students need to have a feeling of accomplishment and progress to keep their motivation high. A final clarification of what is expected of them in preparation for succeeding lessons is worth a few minutes at the close of a class period.

Completion of the student teacher's first day of teaching should be followed as soon as possible by reflection on the successes and failures of the class period and an effort to diagnose any problems that may have arisen. This evaluation can usually be done profitably in conference with the supervising teacher and can be a useful follow-up to the day. Any required adjustments in future plans can be made at this time, necessary additional materials can be gathered, and the stage can be set for a new day of teaching to follow.

Your Responsibilities

The opportunity to student teach in a given school system under a competent supervising teacher should be considered a privilege. Contrary to an apprentice in a typical trade situation, the apprentice teacher is not working with inanimate materials, such as wood and metal, but with live human beings of infinite worth. Student teachers must never forget their responsibility to provide the best possible education for the students and to avoid possible harmful measures.

It is, therefore, extremely important to make lesson plans with care, to consider individual differences in interest and ability, and to conduct the class in an atmosphere of friendly helpfulness. Each student should be considered a potential "learning being" with capabilities for infinite growth. The teacher's responsibility is to develop this potential to the maximum extent.

The student teacher's responsibility to the supervising teacher rests in the area of recognition of authority and respect for experience. Certainly, there may be disagreements about teaching methods, but the final authority is the supervising teacher, who is officially responsible for the class. At the same time, an alert student teacher can be of great help by anticipating the needs of the class, suggesting materials, preparing materials, and in general earning the title of assistant teacher, which is used in some school systems. The varied backgrounds of student teachers and their willingness to share experiences and special talents can make the science classroom more interesting and educationally effective.

Also important is the responsibility of student teachers toward themselves and their potential as science teachers. It would be relatively easy to sit casually by, waiting for things to happen in the student-teaching assignment. The student teachers who gain the most, however, from the standpoint of personal growth, will be those who enter the experience with a dynamic approach, intent on learning everything they can in the time allotted. They will participate, when permitted, in meetings of the school faculty, in attendance and assistance at school athletic events, in dramatic and musical productions of the school, and in other functions relating to school life. In this way, they will see their pupils in many roles outside of the science classroom and will gain insight into the total school program. They will be able to achieve a balanced perspective of their own role as teachers of science among the other academic disciplines and curricular activities. Such experience will enable them to become mature teachers of science and will complete the metamorphosis from the role of college science student.

Concerns of the Student Teacher

A questionnaire listing nine areas of preparation was distributed to 40 student teachers of secondary science at the University of Northern Colorado. They were asked to indicate those areas in which they felt the need for greater preparation.

Four areas receiving the greatest number of responses were evaluating students and grading, handling discipline problems, answering students' questions, and stronger preparation in subject matter, in that order. Other areas of consideration were lesson planning, record keeping, extracurricular activities, demonstrations, and handling laboratory work.

In the same survey, when asked to suggest improvements in the methods courses in physical and biological sciences, the following suggestions were made:

1. Put more emphasis on discipline problems, and on answering students' questions.
2. Have more discussion on techniques for handling slow and fast learners.
3. Do more demonstrations and experiments.
4. Emphasize methods of evaluation.
5. Provide opportunities to hear the experiences of recent student teachers.
6. Evaluate the texts and materials of the new secondary curriculum projects.
7. Provide more opportunities to speak in front of a group and do demonstration teaching.
8. Cover a greater variety of topics, including test construction, extra-credit work, interest development, grouping of students, policies regarding student failures, science fairs and exhibits, and so forth.
9. Provide opportunities to observe several teachers in one's field.
10. Acquire more information on specific sourcebooks of activities, demonstrations, and experiments.

Matters of concern to the beginning teacher were investigated by Adams and Krockover in 1997. Foremost among these were concerns about potential job assignments, teaching responsibilities and matters relating to curriculum development. Other more personal concerns were related to management of one's time, discipline control, and ways to present content information. In the same study, preservice teachers felt that content coursework for teachers was sometimes too specific and some of the pedagogical courses had limited usefulness. Also, the group surveyed believed that field experiences before graduation needed to be increased. To accomplish this, they felt that being an undergraduate teaching assistant helped to ease the transition to becoming a teacher.

PROFESSIONAL DEVELOPMENT STANDARDS

"Prospective teachers become active participants in schools through such activities as internships, clinical studies, and research."[1] This statement by the subcommittee on professional development standards of the *National Science Education Standards* (National Research Council) sets the tone for development of activities and experiences for prospective science teachers.

Professional Development Standard B—Learning to Teach Science—states that "professional development of teachers of science requires integrating knowledge of science, learning, pedagogy, and students, and applying that understanding to science teaching." A particularly appropriate suggestion in relation to student teaching is that "learning to teach science takes place in actual classrooms to illustrate and model effective science teaching and permit teachers to struggle with real situations, practice and expand knowledge and skills in an appropriate context."

The *National Science Education Standards* provide criteria for judging the opportunities and activities available for prospective and practicing teachers of science. Among these criteria is a recurring reference to the requirement of learning a breadth and depth of science content through the perspectives and methods of inquiry. Teachers must be actively involved in investigating scientific phenomena, interpreting results, and making sense of the findings. Problems should be organized around significant issues and events and should give opportunities to practice inquiry skills. There must also be opportunities to integrate science knowledge, pedagogy, and understanding of students.

A further interesting standard is that schools must become *Centers of Inquiry* that support the professional growth of science teachers. This includes involving teachers in leadership roles and providing an environment for support of new science teachers in their classroom responsibilities.

Visit http://www.prenhall.com/trowbridge and select Topic 6—Professional Development. Select "National Science Teaching Standards," then select the hot link for Professional Development Standards, and find the link to "Learning of Science Content Through Inquiry." Learn of the strategy of peer collaboration and how it can support professional development needs. Write your understanding of the concept and submit it to your instructor by using the Electronic Bluebook module.

LICENSURE OPTIONS

Some states require prospective teachers to take certain mandated tests before securing approval to teach in the state's schools. One example is the state of Colorado, which requires, as a result of the recent passage of the Educator Licensing Act, four assessments in the field of preservice education. Licensure requires four tests. An entry test in basic skills is followed by three exit tests in (a) liberal arts and sciences (general education), (b) professional knowledge, and (c) content knowledge. The tests are called the Program of Licensing Assessments for Colorado Educators (PLACE) exams. The tests are designed by the National Evaluation Systems of Amherst, Massachusetts, in contract with the state of Colorado. Other states have implemented or are considering implementation of similar preservice licensing procedures.

Each state has its own requirements for licensure. A list of requirements can usually be obtained by writing directly to the State Department of Education of the state for which you wish information. As an example of the requirements for certification and licensure at the Middle School Level in one state (which is quite representative of requirements in other states as well), there follows a complete listing of the requirements for the State of New Mexico:

Issuing Agency: Department of Education, Professional Licensure Unit [09-30-96]

Requirements:

- ◆ Bachelor's degree from a regionally accredited college or university and including, for those students first entering a college or university beginning in the fall of 1986, the following:
  a. twelve (12) semester hours of English;
  b. twelve (12) semester hours in history including American history and western civilization;
  c. six (6) semester hours in mathematics;

d. six (6) semester hours in government, economics, or sociology;

e. twelve (12) semester hours in science, including biology, chemistry, physics, geology, zoology, or botany;

f. six (6) semester hours in fine arts; and

◆ Thirty to thirty-six (30–36) semester hours of professional education in a middle school education program approved by the SBE, including completion of the SBE's New Mexico Middle Level Teacher Competencies and a mandatory student teaching experience; and

◆ Twenty-four (24) semester hours in at least one (1) teaching field such as mathematics, science(s), language arts, reading, and social studies (or other content related areas), twelve (12) semester hours of which must be in upper division courses as defined by the college or university. Individuals must also complete the SBE's approved competencies in the teaching field; and

Passage of the Core Battery of the National Teachers Examination (NTE), OR

◆ A valid and standard New Mexico license in early childhood education, elementary education, secondary education, K–12 education, or special education, and three (3) years of documented, successful teaching or administrative experience during the five-year period immediately preceding the date of application for middle level education licensure; and twelve (12) semester hours of coursework in middle level education to include representation in any combination of the New Mexico Middle Level Teacher Competencies; OR

◆ A valid certificate issued by the National Board for Professional Teaching Standards for the appropriate grade level and type.

The Middle Level Teacher competencies, mentioned above follow:

◆ *Teacher as Guide - Rationale:* Middle level teachers understand the developmental nature of young adolescents.

a. Knowledge of the physical, intellectual, emotional, and psychological changes that occur developmentally during early adolescence including the special needs of exceptional students.

b. Knowledge and understanding of the influence of linguistic, cultural, and sociological factors on the development of young adolescents.

c. Knowledge of specialized professional techniques used at the middle level including advisory programs, interdisciplinary team organizations, interdisciplinary planning and cooperative learning

◆ *Teacher as Instructional Leader - Rationale:* Middle level teachers work in ways which correspond to what they know about early adolescence.

a. Ability to develop middle level students' appreciation, enthusiasm, and skills as listeners, readers, speakers, writers, thinkers, problem-solvers, decision-makers, and researchers.

b. Ability to design and present instruction commensurate with the developmental needs and readiness of young adolescents.

c. Ability to plan, organize, manage, and evaluate student learning and classroom activities, including lesson planning, student discipline and classroom management, and the connectedness of knowledge by means of interdisciplinary and integrated instruction.

d. Knowledge of at least one content area appropriate to middle level curriculum. The content area knowledge base must be equivalent to the requirements for a teaching minor for other subject area endorsements.

e. Ability to interest and actively involve students in the study of issues related to their lives and the environment in which they live, drawing on the disciplined knowledge of mathematics, science, language arts, health, physical education, social studies, including history, the arts, and computer science.

◆ *Teacher as Person - Rationale:* Middle level teachers have a strong sense of self and foster the same in their students.

a. Ability to encourage students to express themselves creatively in a number of ways, including visual and performing arts.

b. Ability to provide an environment which encourages each student to become aware of himself or herself, to develop the ability to express, understand and control his or her feelings, and to develop a sense of trust and independence.

◆ *Teacher as Advisor - Rationale:* Middle level teachers exhibit strong interpersonal skills.

a. An understanding of each student in his or her family, school, and community context, and being cognizant of the variety of economic and cultural influences which affect each student's life.

b. Ability to provide an environment which encourages positive peer relations.

◆ *Teacher as Colleague - Rationale:* Middle level teachers establish and maintain collegial and collaborative relationships.

a. Ability to establish and maintain positive and productive relationships among professional colleagues, students, families, and the community.

Becoming a Professional

The science teacher today is a member of a dedicated group of professional educators that includes classroom teachers, supervisors, coordinators, administrators, and other educational specialists. This group has the responsibility for developing curriculum plans and effectively teaching the nation's youth.

Science teachers greatly influence our country's young people. Science courses are regarded as respectable academic subjects in any secondary curriculum, along with such courses as mathematics, English, foreign languages, and social sciences. The science teacher, by virtue of subject choice, is viewed with respect by other teachers and by laypeople of the community.

The young science teacher cannot help but feel pride in being a part of the science-teaching profession. Science holds the spotlight in many of our country's schools. It is an exciting time to be a science teacher, and the rewards are abundant. Along with a favorable focus of attention comes responsibility for dedication to the task and for self-improvement as a teacher. It is for this reason that in this chapter attention is directed to the preparation of the professional science educator.

Prospective science teachers in an undergraduate program at a college or university are nearing their goal of becoming qualified specialists in their subject. In most cases their decision to prepare themselves as teachers of a particular science subject was made early in their college career on the basis of interest, environmental background, previous training, and prospective rewards in the teaching field. As they approach the end of their training, prospective teachers look forward to an interesting and productive career as professional educators in a demanding field. They are concerned as to whether their training has been adequate for the task and whether they will be successful in meeting the challenges ahead.

Even if you obtain the best undergraduate preparation available to the prospective science teacher, it is a mistake to assume that your goal has been reached when you are granted your bachelor's degree. Because of the rapid and continuing pace of science achievements and the ever-changing pattern of teaching methods and curriculum organization, the science teacher must constantly be alert to new knowledge and new techniques. For this reason, conscientious science teachers will consider that their education is never finished as long as they wish to remain effective contributors to their profession.

SECURING A TEACHING POSITION

Recent years have shown a fluctuating job market for teachers. Currently, there is a severe shortage of science teachers. Even so, prospective teachers must work dili-gently at finding a suitable position. Competition is high, and they must use all available avenues to secure a satisfactory teaching job. Frequently, schools or departments of education set aside certain days in the spring of the year as "job fairs" at which prospective teachers and school administrators can meet and exchange information about job possibilities. Be sure to take advantage of these to become acquainted with school needs and to display your own qualifications.

Preparing to Look for a Job

As preparation to enter the job market, there are several necessary steps. As prospective employees of a school system, you will wish to secure several recommendations from your college instructors in your major and minor fields, your methods instructors, and perhaps others of your own choosing. Be sure to obtain permission to use an instructor's name for a reference and request the recommendation personally, either by letter or by personal conversation. Remember that instructors are asked to write many recommendations and that a thoughtful instructor will put in a reasonable amount of time toward writing a good one. To make the job as easy as possible, supply your instructor with specific information about yourself. For example, provide information on your hobbies and on your experiences in working with children, such as coaching, camp counseling, summer recreation programs, Sunday school teaching, and so forth. Relate any special competencies that you have, such as the ability to handle a photography club, or special knowledge of rocks and minerals, or model airplane building, or any other relevant experiences. Give specific evidence of the kinds of experiences that would qualify you to be a good science teacher. This kind of information will pay off and will secure for you the immediate attention of a thoughtful school administrator.

When requesting a recommendation, if the contact with the instructor is several months old, it is a good idea to supply a snapshot of yourself to refresh your instructor's memory. A sample recommendation request form is shown in Figure 24-1.

Using Placement Services

You will probably wish to use one or more teacher placement services to secure a satisfactory position. Most teacher-training institutions have placement offices. There may be an enrollment fee for this service. You would be well advised to get all your required materials submitted early, usually by January 1, because the placement offices begin to make appointments with school administrators early in the new year to interview applicants for positions. If you are conscientious about submitting all of your requirements, you will be eligible to meet with prospective employers.

FIGURE 24–1 Sample Recommendation Request Form

Personal Recommendation

Name _____

Classes from me _____

_____

Grades _____

Because many of you will be applying for teaching jobs (or other jobs in the near future), you will be required to obtain letters of recommendation for your files at the Office of Appointments. If requested to write such a recommendation, I shall be happy to oblige but I should like to have some further information about you to include in the recommendation. It is my belief that the following types of information can be very meaningful to a prospective employer and may take the difference between being hired and not being hired.
Please give information on the following points:

1. Any experience you have had working with young people in any capacity other than practice teaching, such as scout leader, Sunday school teacher, swimming instructor, camp counselor, or other. Give specific information.

2. Any scientific hobbies or specialties you may have (past or present), such as specimen collecting, lapidary, ham radio, model airplane building, amateur telescope making, special reading in a topic, expertise with computers, etc.

3. Any travel you have done that may have been scientifically broadening or educational, such as to Carlsbad Caverns, the Grand Canyon, Yellowstone Park, or any others.

4. Any other experimental information that may be important for a prospective employer to know.

Many state departments of education have placement bureaus. It is wise to contact them and give them the necessary information so they can assist you in locating vacancies within the state where you plan to teach.

Letters of Application

Once you have been notified of a suitable vacancy for which you wish to apply, you must prepare a letter of application that will be considered favorably by the recipient. If you plan to type your own application letter, it is a good idea to check with someone to refresh your memory on style and form. In many cases, your letter of application will merely elicit a standard application form from the school to which you apply. In this case, give the complete information required by the school.

If possible, have your letter of application typed by a professional. A professional letter adds quality and dignity to the correspondence and will impress the recipient. A poorly constructed letter with typographical errors, erasures, and other evidence of carelessness certainly will get tossed into the reject file.

In your letter of application, be sure to include all of the necessary information to give a clear picture of your qualifications for the job for which you are applying. Include your major and minor teaching areas, information on special competencies (such as ability to handle specific types of clubs), and information on your familiarity with new teaching trends (such as inquiry teaching, team teaching, individualized instruction, new curriculum projects, open-school concepts, and other current trends).

You might conclude the letter by volunteering your willingness to meet the superintendent for an interview at a mutually convenient time. A sample letter of application you might use as a guide is shown in Figure 24-2.

The Job Interview

If you are interviewed by the principal or superintendent of schools, you will wish to present yourself in the best possible manner. Be sure to arrive on time, dress appropriately, and be well groomed. Allow the employer to conduct the interview at her own pace and in her own manner. Supply information about yourself as requested. If asked, discuss your philosophy of teaching briefly, tell about your training and special competencies, and mention your professional memberships (such as the NSTA, Academies of Science, National Association of Biology Teachers [NABT], and other organizations to which you belong.)

You will have the opportunity to ask questions. You will want to know some of the details of the position, such as the level of the class, its probable size, the text materials that are used, and the availability of supplies. Perhaps you will want to ask questions about the community, such as the availability of housing, churches, and recreation facilities. Let the interviewer supply you with information on the prospective salary and other fringe benefits associated with the job.

FIGURE 24–2 Sample
Letter of Application

January 12, 2003
123 Hope Avenue
Caton, Missouri

Dr. Harold Oglesby
Superintendent of Schools
Wichita Falls, Missouri

Dear Dr. Ogelsby:

I wish to apply for the position as teacher of middle school science announced as a vacancy in your school system. The placement office at Webster State College, Webster, Kansas, will send my complete credentials.

My major teaching area is junior high school science and my minor is mathematics. In addition, I have secured a teacher's permit for driver education and am qualified to give the driver education course of the state of Missouri.

Photography has been a hobby and a vocation of mine for many years, and I would be interested in supervising a junior high school photography club.

I shall be happy to come for a personal interview at your convenience.

Sincerely yours,

John Tryst

After Obtaining the Job

Securing a position as a new teacher is a major accomplishment and may give you the feeling that your teaching career is set for all time. However, this would be a short-sighted view. Of course it should be your intention to remain on the job with the expectation of doing excellent work, but you should also recognize that you may want to move upward professionally. Therefore, it is a good idea to keep your placement file up to date. Keep in contact with the placement office by informing them of any new coursework you have taken, such as institutes or summer school attendance. Have updated transcripts supplied to the placement office, which may include the completion of a new degree or additional coursework. When you are ready to apply for a new position, be sure to get recommendations from your principal and supervisor.

MAKING THE TRANSITION TO A PRACTICING TEACHER

Up to this point, you have been a student preparing to meet the challenges of teaching science. You have studied your chosen subject(s) carefully, taking in volumes of factual knowledge with the expectation of using it at some time in the near future as a science teacher. You have been regaled with information about teaching methods and strategies and have observed other science teachers perform in the classroom. You have studied the psychology of adolescents and young adults to learn what makes them tick and what motivates them in and out of school. And you have gotten your feet wet in the science classroom by doing your student teaching under the supervision of an experienced science teacher.

Now you are approaching the end of this long process and are looking forward to being a science teacher in a classroom of your own. Perhaps you are a bit apprehensive at this point. Perhaps you have seen enough of the reality of teaching to feel intimidated by the thought of taking full charge of a class. Or, alternatively, perhaps you have gained confidence, through your student-teaching experience and with the guidance of sensitive science teachers, so that you are enthusiastically anticipating the real world of science teaching. The authors hope this is the case. To put this situation in a more concrete setting, we shall present four examples of prospective teachers as they move toward this final stage of their preparation.

JOSH

Josh is a student teacher in earth science at a medium-sized high school. He teaches five classes of ninth grade earth science under the tutelage of two different science teachers. His assignment of teaching was gradually increased from observing to teaching one class to ultimately taking over five classes. Although all classes were ninth grade level, there were perceptible differences in the nature and character of the five classes. The vagaries of grouping children and the dynamics that prevailed in different classes promoted a distinctive character obvious even to an outside observer. Josh found it necessary to make adjustments in his planning, teaching style, and handling of each of the classes.

As is common with new teachers, who have most recently sat through dozens of college classes in which lectures were the prevalent form of presenting material, Josh tended to emphasize lectures in his classes, too. While the topics under study were potentially interesting, the lecture format didn't capture the interest of the ninth graders. They were restless, somewhat noisy, and they carried out Josh's assigned tasks rather perfunctorily. The main emphasis for them seemed to be to memorize the factual information Josh presented to be ready to give it back on a factual test. While some of the students were comfortable with this teaching method, the majority of the class looked upon it as a rather onerous way to learn science. In fact, they did not clearly understand what the purpose of learning the facts was and did not perceive how the information would benefit them.

The experienced teachers under whom Josh was working talked with Josh and suggested he try an activity approach to teaching the topics. They gave him some concrete suggestions of materials he could use and procedures to follow. Josh tried out some of the suggestions in his next class periods and found that the students enjoyed them. To his surprise, Josh found that he had fun using activity labs and was actually less exhausted at the end of the day. The students did as well on the tests as they had in the former lecture approach. In addition, they seemed to have a better attitude toward their learning. There were no discipline problems.

BARBARA

Barbara is a student teacher in a junior high school in a medium-sized city. She teaches earth science to seventh graders three class periods a day and physical science to eighth graders two periods a day. She feels most comfortable with the seventh grade classes, mainly because they are less disruptive and easier to manage.

Barbara's supervising teacher has not had a student teacher before. He feels a bit intimidated by the new responsibility and has turned over much of the class management to her. While this is a challenge to Barbara, it is also a good experience because she is given considerable freedom to operate the classes as she wishes. Her teacher has operated his classes in a rather perfunctory manner and has not given much help to his student teacher other than to suggest that Barbara follow the standard format prevalent in the class.

Barbara has tried to provide a modicum of activity labs (at least once a week) in which the students participate in some type of investigation. These are followed by short postlab discussions. Students usually have some type of short write-up to turn in at the conclusion of the class period.

The discipline in the seventh grade classes is average. Most students are serious learners, but one or two give way to their adolescent urges to show off or distract their classmates. Barbara has learned infinite patience in dealing with these children and has good results without having to resort to authoritarian measures of discipline control. This is perhaps the best indicator of Barbara's potential success as a teacher of junior high school children in the future.

SAM

Student teaching for Sam took place in a modern high school under the tutelage of an experienced science teacher with a reputation for good teaching and control of his classes. Sam has two tenth grade physical science classes and one called global science, which is a class of students who have not taken a regular science sequence in high school but who need at least one science to graduate.

Although physical science was not Sam's major field in college, he had several courses in physics and chemistry that prepared him adequately for this assignment. He seemed to prefer teaching the physical science classes over the global science, mainly because of the quality and motivation of the physical science students. He has some very bright students in these classes, which lends challenge and satisfaction to his teaching. (It is not uncommon for beginning teachers to face two or three different subject assignments in their first year of teaching. A student-teaching assignment that gives varied experiences and responsibilities in different kinds of classes is an excellent preparation for this eventuality.)

Sam has a relaxed approach to his teaching and develops good rapport with the students. He is firm about tasks and requirements but is willing to listen to the students and is helpful in working with them. These traits, if carried over to his first job, will smooth the transition and raise considerably his chances of having a satisfying and productive teaching career in the sciences.

ERICA

Erica teaches biology and chemistry as her student-teaching assignment. She has three biology classes and two of chemistry. She is fortunate to have two highly qualified, experienced teachers as her supervisors in the classroom. They feel that she is doing an excellent job and are lavish in their praise of her teaching.

Two of Erica's classes are college-prep classes, with more than 80 percent of the students planning to go on to college. Consequently, Erica instructs them largely in a typical college manner, with much lecture, note taking, and factual emphasis on terminology, taxonomy, and high-level concepts in biology. The students seem to eat it up. They realize, it seems, that Erica knows what she is talking about when she informs them that they are getting excellent preparation for their upcoming experience in college. The small fraction of students in the classes who are not college-bound are not sure how the information they are getting will help them in their careers but are sure that somehow it represents science, which seems to be in the news quite often these days.

The examples described here represent four different sets of experiences by prospective teachers of science. A common thread is that each experience is unique and is the result of many factors coming together—individual natures of the students, varying traits and expertise of the supervising teachers, class makeup and objectives, and the subject matter of the class, among others. So it will be in your first employment opportunity as well. Perhaps the lesson to be learned is to be prepared for anything. A teacher needs to be flexible and adaptable. Of course this is what makes teaching exciting and rewarding as well!

Throughout this book we have emphasized *Becoming a Science Teacher* to bring unity and clarity to the organization and presentation of chapters. Here, we are switching to the theme *Being a Science Teacher*.

Becoming is the process of developing suitable or appropriate qualities needed for science teaching. Becoming, then, represents a change from that which you were to that which you are now. It is your coming to be all that you potentially can be as a science teacher, given the time and constraints of this textbook, your life, the methods course, and so forth.

Being is the existence of a particular state or condition—in this case, that of a secondary school science teacher. The title of this chapter signifies that you are one step closer to actually being a science teacher. In many ways you have probably already developed many qualities and attitudes of science teachers. Paradoxically, you will always be at some degree of both becoming and being a science teacher. For example, during the science methods course you have been involved with a variety of experiences, all contributing toward your becoming a science teacher. Simultaneously, you have developed a set of interests and attitudes similar to those of science teachers. Perhaps you imagined yourself as a science teacher and, on occasion, actually experienced this position through teaching a class and working with students. We are referring to your own attitudes and values and your own interest and desire to be a science teacher. These are the most significant variables in the becoming-being equation.

If we had to identify one symbolic point at which the percentage of becoming and being shifted in favor of being, it would be the first day of your first job. Throughout the practice-teaching experience, becoming and being will probably be about equal. However, there has been some degree of being a science teacher from the moment of your career decision, and there will be some degree of continually becoming a better science teacher throughout your career.

These two situations, summarized in "Fulfillments and Frustrations" at the end of this chapter, are two ends of an emotional continuum for science teachers. There are indeed frustrations and fulfillment, and both are a part of becoming and being a science teacher. For some reason, more time is devoted to the frustrating aspects of science teaching than to the fulfillments; yet, without a doubt, the latter occur each day and in many ways. Science teaching is a source of personal fulfillment because it contributes to the development of students and ultimately to society. Occasionally, we lose sight of this simple fact because of the daily frustrations, dissatisfactions, and challenges.

SCIENCE-TEACHING STANDARDS

The current teaching standards of the *National Science Education Standards* provide criteria to be used in making judgments about the quality of teaching in science classrooms. They set forth a vision of good science teaching to be used as a model for prospective and practicing teachers of science. Several roles and responsibilities are outlined in the following areas:

1. Teachers of science should plan inquiry-based programs for their students. This means selecting science content and curriculum directions to meet student interests, knowledge, skills, and experiences. It also means using teaching strategies that develop understanding and skills for doing inquiry science.
2. Teachers should interact with students to focus and support their inquiries, recognize diversity and provide opportunities for all children to participate fully in science learning, and challenge students to take responsibility for individual as well as collaborative learning.
3. Teachers should engage in ongoing assessment of their teaching and of resulting student learning. There should be formal assessment activities, as well as guidance, for students to do meaningful self-assessment.
4. Conditions for learning should provide students with time, space, and resources needed for successful science learning. These conditions include adequate tools and materials, as well as a safe working environment.
5. Teachers should foster habits of mind, attitudes, and values of science by being good role models for these attributes.
6. It is important for teachers to become active participants in ongoing planning and development of the school science program. This includes taking leadership roles and developing their own professional growth potential.

CHARACTERISTICS OF A GOOD SCIENCE TEACHER

Administrators and supervisors constantly evaluate teachers for salary increments, promotions to department chair, differentiated staffing, and other reasons. Unfortunately, many evaluations are made on the basis of superficial characteristics or personal qualities that happen to please or displease the evaluator, rather than on more basic characteristics that exemplify good teaching. Following is a question checklist that can be used by an administrator or supervisor, or by the science teacher for self-evaluation.[3]

Question Checklist

1. Is the teacher enthusiastic about what he is doing and does he show it?
2. Is the teacher dynamic and does she use her voice and facial expression for emphasis and to hold attention?
3. Does the teacher use gadgets or other illustrative devices extensively to make each new learning experience as concrete as possible?
4. Does the teacher show originality in making teaching materials from simple or discarded objects?
5. Does the teacher have a functional knowledge of her subject so that she can apply what she knows to everyday living?
6. Does the teacher possess the ability to explain ideas in simple terms regardless of the extent of his knowledge?
7. Does the teacher stimulate actual thought on the part of his students, or does he make parrots out of them?
8. Is the teacher a have-to-finish-the-book type of teacher, or does she teach thoroughly?
9. Does the teacher maintain calm and poise in the most trying of classroom circumstances?
10. Does the teacher use a variety of teaching techniques, or is it the same thing day after day?
11. Does the teacher exhibit confidence, and are the students confident about his ability?
12. Does the teacher encourage class participation and questions, and does he conscientiously plan for them?
13. Does the teacher maintain a good instructional tempo so that the period does not drag?
14. Does the teacher use techniques to stimulate interest at the beginning of new material, or does he treat it merely as something new to be learned?
15. Does the teacher concentrate on key ideas and use facts as a means to an end?

Of a more formal nature is the Stanford Teacher Competence Appraisal Guide.[4] It may be used to assist the individual teacher in assessing her strengths and weaknesses, or it may be used for formal evaluation purposes. For rating, each item may be evaluated on the basis of eight points and totaled for a cumulative score. The ratings are

0	Unable to observe
1	Weak
2	Below average
3	Average
4	Strong
5	Superior
6	Outstanding
7	Truly exceptional

Stanford Teacher Competence Appraisal Guide

Aims

1. *Clarity of aims.* The purposes of the lesson are clear.
2. *Appropriateness of aims.* The aims are neither too easy nor too difficult for the pupils. They are appropriate and are accepted by the pupils.

Planning

3. *Organization of the lesson.* The individual parts of the lesson are clearly related to each other in an appropriate way. The total organization facilitates what is to be learned.
4. *Selection of content.* The content is appropriate for the aims of the lesson, the level of the class, and the teaching method.
5. *Selection of materials.* The specific instructional materials and human resources used are clearly related to the content of the lesson and complement the selected method of instruction.

Performance

6. *Beginning the lesson.* Students come quickly to attention. They direct themselves to the tasks to be accomplished.
7. *Clarity of presentation.* The content of the lesson is presented so that it is understandable to the pupils. Different points of view and specific illustrations are used when appropriate.
8. *Pacing of the lesson.* The movement from one part of the lesson to the next is governed by the students' achievement. In pacing, the teacher stays with the class and adjusts the tempo accordingly.
9. *Pupil participation and attention.* The class is attentive. When appropriate, students actively participate in the lesson.
10. *Ending the lesson.* The lesson is ended when the students have achieved the aims of instruction. The teacher ties together chance and planned events and relates them to long-range aims of instruction.
11. *Teacher-student rapport.* The personal relationships between students and teacher are harmonious.

Evaluation

12. *Variety of evaluative procedures.* The teacher devises and uses an adequate variety of procedures, both formal and informal, to evaluate progress in all of the aims of instruction.

13. *Use of evaluation to provide improvement of teaching and learning.* The results of evaluation are carefully reviewed by teacher and students to improve teaching and learning.

Professional

14. *Concern for professional standards and growth.* The teacher helps, particularly in her specialty, to define and enforce standards for (1) selecting, training, and licensing teachers; and (2) working conditions.

15. *Effectiveness in school staff relationships.* The teacher is respectful and considerate of colleagues, and demonstrates awareness of their personal concerns and professional development.

16. *Concern for the total school program.* The teacher's concern is not simply for her courses and her students. She works with other teachers, students, and administrators to bring about the program's success.

17. *Constructive participation in community affairs.* The teacher understands the particular community context in which she works and helps to translate the purposes of the school's program to the community.

PERSONAL FULFILLMENT

This discussion of Maslow's hierarchy of needs emphasizes teachers' needs. The fulfillment of your needs can lead to your personal growth as a science teacher.

Safety and Security

Some teachers have a very real need for safety. Recent occurrences in which middle school and high school students have been found carrying weapons such as knives and guns to school have increased this perceived need. Fortunately, the numbers are still small. However, the numbers of incidents are growing, and school systems are working hard to change this situation. In Chapter 23, we offered suggestions for alleviating concerns about safety and control in the science classroom.

Science teaching is generally a secure career. From time to time, however, budget cuts and other economic problems make it difficult; there are also occasional reductions in the teaching force. These are short-term problems; our society always needs good teachers. Moreover, science teachers will be important as long as science and technology have a central role in society.

Love and Belongingness

The need for love and belonging can also be fulfilled through science teaching. At the secondary level, however, students do not express their closeness as clearly and unabashedly as at the elementary level. Adolescents are in their quest for separation from authorities and for development of their own identity, which makes their closeness and expression of appreciation toward an authority figure, such as a science teacher, particularly difficult. Often the students who like you the most will demonstrate it the least. Still, the picture is not all gray. Science teachers can and do earn the respect and affection of their students. It is often subtle, oblique, and obtuse. But it is there. You can contribute to the feelings of belonging by

Science teaching is both personally and professionally fulfilling.

establishing a climate of caring in your science classroom, thus fulfilling both your needs and those of the students.

Self-Esteem

What about the self-esteem of the science teacher? If self-esteem is equated with having material possessions, which in turn relates to a high salary, then the prospects for fulfilling this need are not very encouraging. There is, however, prestige within the educational community for science teachers, and there is a long tradition of respect for teachers in our society. Although education is frequently criticized, it is also looked to as a source of remedy for many problems. There is deserved, earned esteem in knowing you have helped young people understand more about the world in which they live, thus helping their personal development and improving society.

It would be nice if we could simply state that all of your needs would be met through science teaching and you would experience continued growth as a professional and as a person. Such is not the case. We can say that this is possible, in fact even probable, but part of the task will be your own contribution. For everything that Maslow did say about motivation and personal growth, he never said that it was easy.

Fulfilling Needs

How does an individual know which needs are important? Knowing this, how does one proceed to fulfill personal needs in the context of a science classroom? The first question is most directly answered by you. Our contribution to the answer has been to provide activities that direct you to reflect on various aspects of science teaching. If you wish to know more about your needs and possible ways to fulfill them, self-awareness is essential.

Once you have some insights concerning your personal needs as a science teacher, there are many ways to fulfill them. Here are a few suggestions listed under Maslow's categories.

Safety

1. Establish rules for the science classroom.
2. Clarify consequences of rule violation.

Security

1. Talk to your principal or personnel director about future goals, budgets, etc.
2. Work to develop a strong science program.

Belongingness

1. Have personal conferences with students.
2. Evaluate the class to see how it might be improved.
3. Have the students work on cooperative projects.
4. Spend more time talking to the students on a personal level during class.

Esteem

1. Conduct a workshop on a topic of interest to the rest of your school staff (e.g., energy, pollution, nutrition).
2. Attend a local or national meeting of science teachers.
3. Present a talk on science to a community group.
4. Join a local committee that is working on a science-related problem.

These are a few simple suggestions that can stimulate your thoughts about change and growth as a science teacher. The list is not unique; most of the ideas are simply a part of being a science teacher.

RESEARCH ON SCIENCE TEACHER CHARACTERISTICS

In 1980, using the principles of meta-analysis of research, Cynthia Druva and Ronald Anderson carried out a research project that focused on science teacher characteristics.[5] The results were reported by displaying correlations between these identified teacher characteristics, teacher behavior, and student outcomes. The meta-analysis was conducted of research studies that used characteristics of gender, course work, IQ, and so forth, as independent variables; and as dependent variables, (1) teaching behavior in the classroom, such as questioning behavior and teaching orientation, and (2) student outcome characteristics, such as achievement and attitudes toward science. The subject population was chosen from teachers and students in science classes throughout the United States from kindergarten through twelfth grade.

With respect to the relationships between teacher characteristics and teacher behavior, the following outcomes were reported:

1. Teaching effectiveness is positively related to training and experience as evidenced by the number of education courses, student-teaching grade, and teaching experience.
2. Teachers with a more positive attitude toward the curriculum that they are teaching tend to be those with a higher grade-point average and more teaching experience.
3. Better classroom discipline is associated with the teacher characteristics of restraint and reflectivity.
4. Higher level, more complex questions were employed more often by teachers with greater knowledge and less experience in teaching.

With respect to the relationships between teacher characteristics and student outcomes, several relationships were discovered:

1. Student achievement is positively related to teacher characteristics of self-actualization, heterosexuality, and masculinity. It is also related positively to

the number of science courses taken and attendance at academic institutes.

2. The process-skill outcomes of students are positively related to the number of science courses taken by teachers.

3. The outcome of a positive attitude toward science was positively associated with the number of science courses taken by teachers and the number of years of teaching experience.

One of the implications of the study is that there is a relationship between teacher preparation programs and what their graduates do as teachers. Science courses, education courses, and overall academic performance are positively associated with successful teaching.

For student teachers, the research reported above is significant because it gives direction and guidance to their career and goal preparation. While the results may seem to be natural, common-sense results, it is significant that data now show that teachers with better preparation in science, as well as in the pedagogical areas, do a better job of teaching. Also significant is the finding that a positive attitude toward their task relates to better results for the students in their charge.

One of the difficulties brought about by the daily routine of hard, laborious work in teaching—the incessant planning, paper grading, and all such work—is that this often has a debilitating effect on young teachers. It may cause them to become cynical and skeptical of the results they are achieving. Many times they will tend to blame the students or the system, when in fact it may be the negative attitude they themselves bring to the teaching task that is at least partially responsible for their poor results.

It is very important to maintain zest for teaching. In no other profession is it as important to exhibit a positive and enthusiastic relationship with individuals. Young minds in your charge are vulnerable to your attitudes and enthusiasm as well as to your obvious background of preparation and experience. A caring teacher is able to overcome many shortcomings in background and preparation, but an uncaring teacher cannot be successful, though he may have excellent preparation in terms of subject matter and teaching techniques.

PROFESSIONAL CHALLENGES

Helping Students to Become Science Teachers

After you have secured a teaching position and have settled into the routines of teaching classes, you may be asked to take on a "student teacher" for a semester. This probably won't happen for a few years and only after you have had an opportunity to demonstrate to the principal and other experienced teachers in your school that you are a competent teacher, know your subject, get along well with students and colleagues, enjoy your work, and wish to help other young people to enter the teaching profession.

Your first reaction may be "Wow!" "Why me?" "Am I good enough to be a role model for a prospective teacher?" This would be a natural concern for any new teacher. Consider that this also may be an opportunity to improve your own teaching skills. You know the old maxim "I never really learned the subject until I had to teach it." This applies to the art and skill of teaching as well. Think of the joy and responsibilities of conveying what you have learned about teaching to a new and enthusiastic student teacher.

Much has been learned about the task of being a "cooperative teacher," a "mentor teacher," or perhaps a "master teacher." Since teaching represents the epitome of people-oriented tasks, much of what has been learned concerns having good communication skills, willingness to listen, and empathy with the learner. Below are a few points that experts have found are important in developing a successful mentor-student teacher relationship.

1. The selection of mentor-student teacher pairs should be voluntary, if at all possible. Compatibility of personalities should be considered an important criterion.

2. There must be ample time provided for the mentor and student teacher to discuss methods, strategies, problems, objectives, and materials for the classes being taught.

3. Student teachers should be led gradually to increasing responsibilities in the classroom. Such things as observing classes being taught, learning names of pupils, working with small groups, reading essays, grading papers, and any other routine tasks should precede actual teaching of the class. Under no circumstances should the student teacher be thrown into a "sink or swim" situation, as this can have serious and adverse outcomes, both for the student teacher and the mentor, and even for the school in general.

4. A fair amount of time should be devoted to acquainting the student teacher with the community, the goals of the school, teaching colleagues, and parents of the pupils (in evaluation conferences, etc.). The student teacher should be encouraged to see the pupils in activities other than classroom functions, such as sports, dramatic events, assemblies, and honors programs. This will impress upon the student teacher the need to look at secondary education as a "whole-life" experience, rather than hold a narrow view only based upon the science subjects taught.

There are many other additional points that bear on the mentor-student teacher relationship. You will find, if you choose to embark on this experience, that you have grown and assumed a more mature view of teaching yourself. Grasp the situation when it presents itself and take repeated opportunities through the years. These experiences constitute the very best of professional development.

It is hard to identify all of the trends and issues that will affect science teaching in the years to come. We can assure you there will be new challenges. Here we discuss a few challenges that will face science teachers in the first decade of the new millenium.

Enrollments

Enrollments in secondary schools increased during the 1950s, 1960s, and 1970s. However, in the 1980s, they declined. Beginning about 1990, enrollments again began to increase, growing nearly 10 percent between 1994 and 1998. The children of the "baby-boomers" of the the '60's were arriving in the secondary schools. Currently, we see slowly increasing enrollments trending toward stability. At the same time, enrollments in the sciences at the secondary schools are increasing. Thus the opportunities for science teachers are improving at the present time. It is an opportune time to consider becoming a science teacher.

Curriculum

In the early 1980s, a number of reports on education recommended increasing graduation requirements by adding another year of science. While most applaud such requirements, there are implications not generally recognized by those making the recommendations. Who will take the extra courses? What are the curricular implications? Who will teach the courses? To answer the first question, students who have decided not to take any more science will now be required to take at least another course. The cur-

ricular implication is related to the inappropriateness of existing courses for the group of students now required to take another year of science. The result will be a need for new curriculum materials. Finally, increasing the requirements will increase the need for science teachers. There is the possibility of unqualified teachers teaching the newly required courses, and the need for inservice programs to better qualify these science teachers.

Disruptive Students

Student discipline and classroom management are concerns of science teachers. Junior high science teachers think their students are not well behaved. An estimated 5 percent of science teachers indicated that maintaining discipline was a serious problem, and 24 percent indicated that it was somewhat of a problem. These data are consistent with a National Institute of Education (NIE) report, Violent Schools—Safe Schools.[6] There are higher levels of violence (in intensity and numbers) at the junior high level than at elementary levels. Approximately 8 to 10 percent of schools see violence and disruption as a serious problem. Interestingly, one study showed that less than 10 percent of teachers, principals, and district program respondents indicated that maintaining discipline was a serious problem.

Careers

Science teachers should be aware of the continuing need for scientists and engineers. They should also be aware that career choices are often made based on experiences in science classes. We think most science teachers understand these two points. A more difficult issue is the fact that science teachers contribute to a filtering process that eliminates significant numbers of individuals from

In making decisions, the effective teacher takes into account spontaneous happenings in the classroom as well as instructional theory.

the talent pool of scientists and engineers. The imbalance is one of historical record and one that eliminates not on the basis of intelligence and ability but in large measure on the basis of gender, race, handicap, and cultural advantage.

Preparation

In the early 1980s, an estimated 30 percent of all teachers currently teaching science and math in secondary schools were either completely unqualified or severely underqualified to teach those subjects.[7,8]

When asked about the areas of greatest need, science teachers listed several items directly related to instruction. Approximately 66 percent of all teachers surveyed (science, mathematics, and social studies) indicated that they needed information about instructional media. Sixty-one percent indicated a need for assistance in learning new teaching methods. Fewer than 50 percent of teachers surveyed felt they were not competent enough to implement the discovery/inquiry approach. They felt they needed the assistance of a coordinator or other resource person. Forty-eight percent of all science, mathematics, and social studies teachers indicated they would like assistance in the use of manipulative materials. This need may relate to the fact that manipulative materials are generally used less than once a week in most science, mathematics, and social studies classes.

DECISION MAKING

During any single class period, a science teacher makes many decisions about students and the lesson. Often science teachers are unaware of these decisions. "Shall I tell John to be quiet?" "What is Pat doing?" "Do the students understand density?" "Should I use a different example of convection currents?" "Would it be best for the students to work in groups of two or three on this laboratory project?" The decisions may not seem that important, but they all add up to effective instruction and classroom management.

Teaching science is simultaneously directed and flexible. Decision making in science teaching is the process of synthesizing your planned direction with the instantaneous and spontaneous factors in the classroom.

Direction in teaching science is provided in two ways: first, through the organization of textbooks, curriculum guides, lesson plans, and objectives; and, second, from the science teacher's own instructional theory. When a situation emerges in the classroom, the teacher evaluates the situation, goals, curriculum, and consequences of choices and then decides on a course of action. One important, though seldom considered, variable in the decision-making process is the direction suggested by the science teacher's own instructional theory.

An instructional theory helps establish a frame of reference for decisions, gives consistency of responses, and provides a general direction as science teachers encounter different classroom situations. With the aid of an instructional theory, science teachers are in a better position to make instruction effective and fulfilling. In the final analysis, the individual science teacher is the one who can best relate the possible solutions to the actual situations as they present themselves to different students, classrooms, and schools. An instructional theory provides an underlying direction that transcends immediate classroom problems. Being able to go beyond the immediate situation affirms one's ability as a science teacher. Clarifying one's long-term goals and intentions helps provide an organizational pattern that slowly becomes a personal style of teaching. The power of an instructional theory is in the direction it provides. There must be another component, however: the freedom to deviate from the direct path in response to different classroom scenarios. This is the spontaneity and flexibility required in science teaching. Look at "Developing an Instructional Theory" at the end of this chapter.

Effective science teachers are able to deviate from the lesson. The degree of flexibility varies with the teacher's goals, students' needs, and environmental contingencies. The problems described in "What Would You Do—Now?" at the end of this chapter are similar to those presented earlier. This time, however, no solutions, directions, or ideas are suggested—you must resolve the incident on your own.

When confronted with problem situations such as those described in "What Would You Do—Now?" science teachers usually respond: "I would have to know more," "I would have to be in the situation," or "It depends; every teacher would probably do something different." This is precisely the point. The individual science teacher must decide the course of action in response to the classroom situation. Science teachers intuitively know that they are the primary source for effective education when they ask such questions as, "When should I answer the student's question if I am teaching by inquiry?" There is usually an implicit tone of voice that says, "There is no direct answer except as the individual teacher responds to the situation."

Science teachers enter the classroom with knowledge, techniques, plans, textbooks, and curriculum materials. It is also the teacher who combines all of these and builds a helping relationship with the students. In the classroom, the helping relationship is characterized by situations requiring the teacher to react spontaneously. Science teachers must think critically, diagnose, decide, and respond to conditions in the teaching environment. The creative, insightful, and perceptive science teacher does react effectively to the instantaneous needs and demands of the children, classroom, or school.

Developing a consistent direction through an instructional theory and flexibility in classroom situations will evolve into a personal teaching style that can help overcome frustrations and contribute to your fulfillment as a science teacher.

OPPORTUNITIES FOR PROFESSIONAL GROWTH

Among the opportunities for professional growth while on the job are completing graduate work during the summer or at night, depending on the available opportunities; participating in in-service workshops and institutes; attending government- or industry-sponsored summer institutes; doing committee work on curriculum revision or evaluation; maintaining membership in professional organizations, with accompanying attendance at regular meetings and participation in committee work; reading professional journals, scientific publications, and current books in science and teaching; writing for professional publications; and keeping up-to-date on new materials, teaching resources, and education aids.

Graduate Work

The NSF reported that 39 percent of science and mathematics teachers in the United States have master's degrees and that over 75 percent hold credits for at least ten semester hours of graduate work.[9] Twenty percent had completed at least one NSF summer institute. There are many opportunities for graduate work. The usual requirement for completion of a master's degree in education is one year

or four summers of coursework. Theses are generally not required, but comprehensive examinations in a major and minor field usually are. The monetary rewards for science teachers with master's degrees are well worth the time and expense involved in obtaining the degree. Most school systems have a salary differential of a thousand dollars or more for holders of master's degrees; furthermore, opportunities for higher-paying jobs are greater, and a better selection of teaching positions is available for the applicant who holds a master's degree.

In-Service Training and Institutes

In-service workshops and institutes are usually sponsored by public school systems for improvement of the teachers within that system. Degree credit may or may not be offered, depending on the arrangements with the colleges or universities from which consultant services are obtained. Such workshops and institutes often have objectives designed to stimulate curriculum improvement or to improve teacher competencies in subject-matter understanding and teaching techniques. New teachers are encouraged to avail themselves of these opportunities to familiarize themselves with broad problems of curriculum improvements and to benefit from the experience of older teachers in the system.

Government- or industry-sponsored summer and in-service institutes provide excellent opportunities to grow professionally. Although fewer of these institutes are available now than before, the usual requirement is three years of teaching experience; however, this rule is frequently relaxed for one reason or another.

Hands-on workshops provide confidence and expertise in preparing for science instruction.

GUEST EDITORIAL ◆ MICHAEL URBAN

Earth Sciences Graduate Student
University of Northern Colorado

TEACHING: IDEOLOGY VERSUS REALITY

In the Fall of 1999, I began what amounted to a three-year adventure as an eighth-grade earth science teacher in the small town of Detroit Lakes, Minnesota. I look back on my first year of teaching through rose-colored glasses at a blur of memories, and wonder how I ever managed to survive. There was so much to do that first year: prepare lessons, research topics, write worksheets, laboratory exercises, and tests, meet and work with new colleagues, learn how to deal with and develop rapport with students, creatively and resourcefully utilize the lab equipment I had, and muster every bit of restraint I could to refrain from stooping to the level of misbehaving students. Overall, though, the experience I gained from my first year made it well worth enduring.

We all know the adage that you learn more in your first year of teaching than in all of your previous years of schooling combined. This is true because you need to thoroughly understand a concept before you can effectively teach it, and also because you are constantly quizzed by your students when they ask questions (in many cases, the likes of which you have never heard before). We all leave college with at least some understanding of our subject area, but it is never enough. I spent a lot of time researching "simple" concepts; college was great at providing an advanced education, but I needed to bring it down to the *eighth-grade* level. Two sources of information I found invaluable were older textbooks (geared for the level I was teaching) and the "ask the expert" e-mail links found on many web sites. You may think it strange to refer to out-of-date textbooks from the 60's, 70's, and 80's, but they can be a wealth of information because they tend, generally speaking, to go into more detail on explanations of *why* than do most of their modern counterparts (and in most cases, in the field of earth science, the information they provide has changed little).

I consider myself fortunate to have worked in a very progressive school where there existed an ample supply of both technology and expertise in effectively utilizing it. All schools possess some state-of-the-art equipment, but many have such limited quantities that teachers must share it heavily and so can use it only sporadically. Familiarity with overheads, film-strips, and slide projectors is helpful as they still make up the bulk of most school AV departments. While it would be more efficient (and colorful) to project a computer-generated slide show onto the screen, an overhead projector can be just as effective. Teachers become experts at making the most of what they have.

Field trips, internet research projects, phenology journals, creative writing assignments, brief excursions outdoors to make observations, and science fairs are good ways to break up any monotony that may be taking place in the classroom. They can be undertaken with teachers of other subject areas both inside and out of the science disciplines. One of the most appealing aspects of a science class is its ability to be so diverse; math, reading, writing, and art can all be easily combined with studies of nature, making science the epitome of the interdisciplinary model. As long as he or she is well-rounded, there seems to be no limit to the extent of a science teacher's ability to flex his or her creative muscles.

Science affords the perfect opportunity to unite learning with imagination and discovery. Like the early explorers of centuries ago, our students have a chance to voyage into a land filled with mystery and splendor. The teacher is charged with the responsibility of bringing this journey to life by providing students with a launching platform (concepts), a means to carry out exploration (scientific method, critical thinking skills), and a challenging voyage (hands-on activities). Students can become frustrated by problem-solving exercises, especially if they are not well grounded in the related fundamental concepts. Therefore, it is vital to realize that our students need constant encouragement and facilitation. As science teachers, we need to introduce our students to nature by actively engaging them in the *process* of science, while at the same time stimulating creativity, promoting critical thinking, and providing a physically and emotionally safe environment in which to have fun while learning.

If we are brave enough to expose our inner selves and let our passion and love for our subject shine through, we can truly captivate students. A student who sees the relevance, importance, and excitement of science will have meaningful learning experiences and might one day devote his or her life to science or teaching. Perhaps one day a student will look at you the way you once looked at an inspirational teacher. Can you imagine what it must feel like to ignite the spark of passion for science in someone else?

Improving Your Use of Educational Technology in the Classroom

Technology

Link

It is important for teachers to feel at ease with equipment, software, and information resources and be able to effectively integrate technology in instruction to improve student motivation and learning. One way of learning about available new technologies is to attend the annual national and area conventions of the NSTA and to spend considerable time in the exhibit area. Virtually every supplier of educational technology for science will have a booth and a helpful staff to demonstrate products and to help you feel comfortable in working with them. Workshops, summer institutes, and college courses are also often available to help you learn to use new technologies. Another unique resource is the VideoPaper Builder developed by TERC. This tool allows teachers to create multimedia documents of best practices incorporating text, digital video, still photographs, and hyperlinks to web pages. [This tool can be downloaded free from the TERC website (www.TERC.org).] Nothing, however, can substitute for extended hands-on, trial-and-error exploration of computer-based materials individually or in a small group. You will find the Internet an excellent resource for learning more about what is available.

> **Companion Website**
>
> Visit http://www.prenhall.com/trowbridge and select Topic 2—Constructivism and Learning in Science. Select "Activities and Lesson Plans" and find the link for "TOPS." This will have many ideas for constructible projects that require work space to function. From this survey, write a brief paper on what it takes to facilitate project building in a science area. Submit this paper to your instructor for discussion using the Electronic Bluebook module.

To check your own understanding of technology education as it relates to teaching science, consider the following list. Ask yourself how well you are able to use each skill—do you function at a beginning, proficient, or advanced level? You can base decisions about further professional growth on your assessment.

- Demonstrate an awareness of the major types and applications of technology, such as information storage and retrieval, simulation and modeling, and process control and decision making.
- Communicate effectively to students and other teachers about technological equipment.
- Respond appropriately to common error messages when using software.
- Load and run a variety of software packages.
- Demonstrate an awareness of technology usage and assistance in the field of education.

- Describe appropriate uses for technology in education, including
  - computer-assisted instruction (simulation, tutorial, drill and practice),
  - computer-managed instruction,
  - microcomputer-based laboratory,
  - problem solving,
  - word processing,
  - equipment management, and
  - record keeping.
- Use technology to individualize instruction and increase student learning.
- Demonstrate appropriate uses of technology for basic skills instruction.
- Demonstrate ways to integrate the use of technology-related materials with other educational materials, including textbooks.
- Respond appropriately to changes in curriculum and teaching methodology caused by new technological developments.
- Plan for effective technology interaction activities for students (for example, debriefing after a simulation).
- Locate commercial and public domain software for a specific topic and application.
- Use an evaluative process to appraise and determine the instructional worth of a variety of computer software.
- Voluntarily choose to integrate technology in instructional plans and activities.

Committee Work

Committee activity is an excellent way to develop a professional attitude and become aware of the many problems facing the science teacher. Active school systems frequently have a curriculum committee, a professional committee, a salary and grievance committee, a textbook-selection committee, or other committees of temporary nature as needed. Participating on one or more of these committees can be enlightening and can contribute to the professional growth of the new teacher; however, committee responsibilities mean extra work, and the new science teacher should consider the total workload and weigh carefully the ultimate benefits of participation.

Professional Organizations

There are many professional organizations serving the science teacher. They are listed here along with their respective journals.

1. American Association of Physics Teachers, One Physics Ellipse, College Park, MD 20740-3845 —the *American Journal of Physics* and the *Physics Teacher*

Exchanging ideas with other teachers while participating in committee work stimulates professional growth.

2. The American Chemical Society, 1155 16th St. NW, Washington, DC 20036
   —the *Journal of Chemical Education*

3. The National Association of Biology Teachers, 12030 Sunrise Valley Dr., STE 110, Reston, VA 20191
   —the *American Biology Teacher*

4. The National Science Teachers Association, 1840 Wilson Blvd., Arlington, VA 22201-3000
   —the *Science Teacher, Science and Children, Science Scope,* and the *Journal of College Science Teaching*

5. The School Science and Mathematics Association, Curriculum and Foundations, Bloomsburg University, 400 East Second Street, Bloomsburg, PA 17815-1301
   —*School Science and Mathematics*

6. The National Association for Research in Science Teaching, c/o Arthur L. White, The Ohio State University, 1929 Kenny Rd., Rm. 200E, Columbus, OH 43210
   —*Journal of Research in Science Teaching*

7. The American Association for the Advancement of Science, 1200 New York Ave., NW, Washington, DC 20005
   —*Science*

8. Council for Elementary Science, International, University of Nevada-Reno, College of Education, M/S 282, Reno, Nevada 89557—*Science Education*

Membership in a professional organization carries benefits proportional to the member's active participation in the organization. Attendance at periodic meetings contributes to a sense of cohesiveness and shared objectives, the stimulation of meeting professional coworkers, and the absorption of new ideas. Voluntary participation as a panel member or speaker at a discussion session is a highly beneficial experience. It is not necessarily true that a teacher must have many years of experience before being considered worthy of a presentation at a professional meeting. A young, enthusiastic science teacher with a fresh approach to a problem can make a definite contribution to a meeting of this type.

Professional journals provide another source of teaching ideas. A science teacher should personally subscribe to one or two and make it a habit to regularly read others that may be purchased by the school library. Occasional contribution of teaching ideas for publication in a professional journal is highly motivating and is encouraged. The professional benefits of such a practice are unlimited because it helps one to become known in science-teaching circles and to make valuable contacts.

Professional journals usually contain feature articles on subject matter topics of current interest; ideas for improvement of classroom teaching techniques; information on professional meetings; book reviews; information on teaching materials, apparatus, and resource books; information on career opportunities for secondary school students in science; and information on scholarships and contests for students and teachers.

BECOMING A BETTER SCIENCE TEACHER

As discussed in the Introduction to this text, part of being a science teacher is engaging in the process of becoming a better science teacher. In this chapter, we will use a self-evaluation inventory to examine some of the immediate concerns of science teachers. (See "Improving My Science Teaching" at the end of this chapter.) Although this activity concentrates on improving various aspects of science teaching, the feedback will also contribute to your becoming a better educator and a more fulfilled person.

Remember, you do not have to be a bad science teacher to become a better one. Science teachers want to improve, as is shown by their continued involvement in workshops, college courses, attendance at conventions, and so forth. The responsibility for improving is yours; moreover, the means of developing as a science teacher are unique to your preferences, problems, and potential. Based on the categories in the self-evaluation inventory, several possible means are suggested.

GUEST EDITORIAL ◆ *MELINDA BELL*

Student Teacher
Northfield Senior High School
Northfield, Minnesota

STUDENT TEACHING IN SCIENCE

"We never learn as much with a student teacher."

"The student teachers are always nervous, lack confidence, and can't keep the classes under control."

"The student teachers expect us to be like college students because that is what they are most familiar with."

These comments were generated by high school students in the school where I am doing my student teaching. I think it is important to take them seriously, although I will rapidly deny that they characterize each and every student teacher. Sure, we're all bound to be a little nervous and to be somewhat unsure of how to discipline or how to present material so it is clear, understandable, and interesting to the students. But that doesn't mean we have to be bogged down by those things!

There is so much else that we, as student teachers, have going for us. We are well-armed with a knowledge of our subject and a delightful artillery of methods in which we can present our material. We are bright and enthusiastic and willing to try things in new, innovative ways. We have taken a science teaching methods course that has hopefully prepared us in some other ways. We even have students who will see advantages in our being there!

"Student teachers are young and don't seem as fuddy-duddy as the regular teacher."

"Student teachers are more on our level so they are easier to approach."

"Sometimes the student teacher can explain things in a different way than the regular teacher so more students understand it."

All of these things don't make student teaching easy; rather, they make it an exciting challenge and an opportunity for you to practice your skills—accepting the lesson plans that don't work, as well as feeling accomplishment and pride when your lesson goes over well, and the students get excited about something that you taught them! Not all of your students are going to enjoy you as a teacher, but some will welcome you openly, along with the fresh change and enthusiasm you bring to the classroom.

Some of my friends are amazed by the amount of enjoyment I get out of student teaching.

"Don't you get bored teaching the same material over and over?" is a question commonly asked. Once I've recovered from the shock of picturing myself bored, I reply that I can teach the same or similar materials in such a variety of ways that it remains interesting to me. In fact, the personalities of each class are generally so varied that the best way of presenting the material to one class might be the worst method for another. Gauging the class correctly and presenting the material in a suitable manner for that class is the challenge in making the lesson a successful one.

My friends also worry that teaching will not be intellectually satisfying enough for me. After all, it is only high school material! That is the least of my worries! I really learned about DNA when I had to understand it thoroughly enough to answer the students' questions on it, and when I had to be able to explain what newspaper articles meant when they talked about genetic engineering. To make DNA relevant, I had to ensure that it touched something that they are conscious of as happening in the world today. That holds for whether we are talking about DNA and test-tube babies or about photosynthesis and the greenhouse effect. If it doesn't make sense to them and if they don't find it relevant, it will be rapidly forgotten.

The intellectual challenge for me is to keep up on the recent advances in different areas of science and understand how these advances are applicable to the students' world today. Some people are curious as to why I am going into education when I could go on into research or a medical profession. Selfishly, it is because I hope that I will be an influence through teaching and other aspects of my life in helping people to understand that every decision they make is a reflection on how they look at the world. And science to me has an important message for everyone. Science is a way of looking at the world and dealing with the world on a physical level. Science gives us a method we can use for finding solutions to problems that come up in everyday life. It is unfortunate that science, for many people, is an object to be feared or held in mystified awe. Science is not magic. It is merely a way of putting curiosity and creativity together to come up with reasonable explanations for unanswered questions.

Not everyone has the capacity to become a nuclear physicist, but everyone can learn what processes a scientist goes through in his or her thinking and can apply these same methods to areas of his or her own life. If I can get that across to my students, I will feel that I have accomplished something.

Because I believe in science and because I am excited about the things we can learn from it, I want to share that with others. My own interest in it causes me to be enthusiastic and to remain involved myself.

The *National Science Education Standards,* previously referred to in this book, have outlined several assumptions concerning the desired relationships between science teachers and their students. Among these are:

1. What people learn is greatly influenced by how they are taught.
2. The actions of teachers are deeply influenced by their visions of science as an enterprise and as a subject to be taught and learned in school.
3. Cognitive research indicates that knowledge is actively constructed by a student through a process that is individual and social.
4. Actions of teachers are deeply influenced by their understanding of their students and the relationships they have with them.
5. Teachers are continuous learners, inquiring into the understanding of science, their students, and their teaching practice.[12]

Scientific Knowledge

There are a number of relatively easy ways to update and/or keep abreast of scientific developments:

1. Read an introductory textbook in an area in which you need improvement.
2. Enroll in science courses at a local college or university.
3. Contact the district or state science supervisor and see whether a workshop can be organized.
4. Join the American Association for the Advancement of Science and read their journal, *Science* (the figure changes with year of publication). The editorials will keep you up-to-date on social concerns and scientific developments.
5. Read *Scientific American* or purchase offprints of articles or the monographs of accumulated articles on important topics.
6. Join the National Science Teachers Association and read one of their journals: *Science and Children,* the *Science Teacher, Science Scope,* or *Journal of College Science Teaching.*

7. Subscribe to and read *Science News* or *Science World.*
8. Attend local, state, regional, and national conventions of scientific societies, and academies of science, science teachers, and teachers.
9. Make a point of watching television programs on scientific issues. *Nova* is a science program sponsored by the National Science Foundation and is shown on the Public Broadcasting System.
10. Read the science sections of weekly magazines, such as *Time* or *Newsweek.*
11. Go to local museums and planetariums.

Planning and Organization

If this is a concern, part of the problem can be improved through personal effort toward better lesson planning and classroom organization. We suggest that you:

1. Read the chapters on planning in any teaching-methods textbook.
2. Find a colleague who is well organized and ask if the two of you could spend some time planning classes together.
3. Ask the science supervisor to look over your science program and suggest ways to improve the organization.
4. Have a colleague observe your teaching and make suggestions concerning your lesson plans and class management.

The *National Science Education Standards* give considerable help in the planning and organization responsibilities of science teachers. Foremost in their suggestions is that teachers of science should plan and execute an inquiry-based science program for their students. (Refer to the examples of inquiry lessons in chapters 11, 12, 13, and 16).

A further suggestion is that teachers develop strategies that support the development of student understanding and comprehension of science topics rather than mere memorization and rote learning. "Inquiry into real questions generated from student experiences is the central strategy for teaching science."[10]

Teaching Methods

Teachers often find it difficult to break old teaching habits and try new methods of teaching, but you can do it. Here are some suggestions:

1. Read chapters on different methods in any science methods textbook and then imagine how the different approaches could work in your classroom.
2. Look over journals—such as *Science and Children,* the *Science Teacher,* the *American Biology Teacher,* the *Physics Teacher,* and *Journal of Geological Education*—for new approaches to science teaching.
3. Take a professional day and observe several science teachers who use methods that you are interested in adopting.
4. Read professional books on science and education.
5. Team-teach with another science teacher who uses different methods.
6. Request a student teacher—student teachers often have new and different approaches to science teaching.

Interpersonal Relations

This is an area that is essential to effective science teaching, yet it is one that often is neglected in the education of science teachers. Some suggestions that may help include the following:

1. Practice active listening when students talk.
2. Use questions that encourage students to express their ideas on certain issues.
3. Attend a workshop or course on human relations.
4. Read and apply ideas from *Human Relations and Your Career: A Guide to Interpersonal Skills* by David Johnson.

Personal Enthusiasm

If you lack enthusiasm for teaching science, the problem is difficult, but not impossible, to resolve. The reason for the difficulty is that the problem involves a very personal dimension of your teaching. We can recommend an introspective route to improvement:

1. Think about your original interest and excitement in science and teaching. What made you choose science teaching? Now, think about what you know about yourself and teaching science. What is lacking? Where did the spark of enthusiasm go?
2. List your frustrations with teaching. What are the problems you have encountered as a science teacher? What caused a burnout or your change of interest in science teaching?
3. Attend meetings of science teachers such as NSTA or NABT. These meetings often can inspire enthusiasm through new ideas and new colleagues.
4. Form a group to improve teaching in your school. You will probably find others who share your problem, and the discussion and support can certainly assist you in developing your enthusiasm for teaching.
5. Take a professional day and visit other science teachers who are dynamic and enthusiastic.
6. Request a sabbatical.

BEING A PERSON, EDUCATOR, AND SCIENCE TEACHER

Young children are often surprised to find that their teacher does not live at school. Older students think it is funny to meet their teacher shopping or on a picnic. Students often perceive the science teacher and not the person. We are all, however, first and foremost, people. What does this mean? Being a person means we share qualities with all other people: we struggle with decisions, we are sad and happy, we succeed and fail, we make mistakes and get things right, we are frustrated and fulfilled. Too often, students do not see us as people. Students should understand that we belong to the community and have hobbies, interests, and ideas that go beyond science teaching.

As an educator, science teachers are in the helping professions. Their identity is with people more than objects. Their goal is to help people improve their health, education, and welfare. There are aspects of science teaching that are shared with other helping professionals, such as doctors, counselors, social workers, nurses, and psychologists. The shared qualities have to do primarily with the interpersonal relations—the personal dimension of science teaching, those qualities that contribute to effective interactions among people, and that eventually contribute to someone facilitating another's personal development.

The science teacher has elected to help others through a better understanding of the physical and biological world, the methods of gaining knowledge about this world, and the role of science in society. Here the qualities of the person, the educator, and the science teacher should unite to achieve the dual goal of furthering the personal development of students and society through science education.

Much time, money, and effort have been expended on improving the science curriculum. Most science curricula have carefully structured texts and materials so the science teacher will have the maximum opportunity for a good teaching experience. The contribution of new programs and textbooks has been invaluable. But although curriculum materials are necessary and can account for some success in the classroom, they are not sufficient; they cannot account for effective and successful science teaching. The science teacher is still the crucial variable and the one person who must pull all the pieces together for effective teaching.

A review of the research literature on good, ideal, effective, or successful teaching reveals that it is impossible to identify any particular set of variables that amounts to being a good teacher. Yet, we all have had good science teachers, we know good science teachers, and, most important, we want to be good science teachers. Rather than looking at the research and concluding that we can't identify the characteristics of good science teaching, perhaps we can take a different view and thus form a different conclusion. Perhaps good science teachers have developed their potential, their talents, and their attributes, all of which give them an identifying teaching style. It is understandable then that our research efforts cannot find common characteristics, for the answer is to be found in uniqueness, not commonality.

Being a science teacher means improving. Science teachers want to improve and can improve. Even an especially good science teacher can become a better one. Often science teachers complain, "I just didn't seem to be effective today; the students seemed confused and frustrated. I didn't get the concept across." However, they never finish the statement with, "and if you think I was bad today—wait until tomorrow. I'll really be much worse!" Unfortunately, just the desire to improve is not enough; there must be a commitment to becoming a better science teacher through changing or altering one's personal teaching style.

Critics of education have done much to point out the wrongs of education and little to give direction. One result of this critical confrontation has been defensiveness by many teachers and administrators. Displacing blame is one manifestation of this defensiveness, the "let's blame somebody or something else" syndrome: "We would if we had money." "I have thirty-five children in my class." "Well, what do you expect?" and "The home has more influence than the short time students are in my classroom." The "let's try something new" syndrome is another manifestation. Teaching machines, contract performance, accountability, competency-based programs, and the open classroom are examples of this approach. The ideas presented in this chapter center on the science teacher developing as a person and as an educator. Our theme might be "Let's get with it as people and perform as professionals." You can be in any classroom, with any children, and with any curriculum to develop your competency as a science teacher. The ideas presented are not easy; for the most part, they deal with personal improvement and fulfillment.

Start being a science teacher by looking at your potential and not at your limitations. Becoming aware of the importance of the suggestions for improvement and translating them into actual practice can result in your development as a science teacher. The process of becoming a better science teacher is long, and it takes courage to overcome the many small barriers to personal and professional growth. It is not something that can occur through the purchase of a new set of science materials, a single workshop, or reading one methods textbook. Being a science teacher requires continuous personal development aimed toward the ideal of being a great educator; and for those who say, "I can't be a great science teacher," we reply, "If not you—then who?" We all have much more potential than we use. It is the actualization of this potential that will help you become a better science teacher, educator, and person.

SELF-INVENTORY FOR SCIENCE TEACHERS

The NSTA Commission on Professional Standards and Practices has published a Self-Inventory for Science Teachers.[11] The NSTA has summarized its beliefs concerning the professionalism of science teachers in this way:

> The professional science teacher: (a) is well educated in science and the liberal arts, (b) possesses a functional philosophy of education and the technical skills, (c) continues to grow in knowledge and skill throughout his career, (d) insists on a sound educational environment in which to work, (e) maintains his professional status, (f) contributes to the improvement of science teaching, (g) takes a vital interest in the quality of future science teachers.

This is the first time that a science teachers' organization has developed a set of standards against which science teachers can measure themselves and which provides stimulation and motivation for improving their professional practices.

EVALUATION OF TEACHERS

Increasingly, teachers are faced with periodic evaluations by their principals, peers, and students. Such evaluations are for the purpose of comparisons, retention, merit pay, salary increments, promotion, and/or tenure. Teacher evaluation is defined as "the process of an external observer (administrator or supervisor) gathering information regarding a teacher's instructional performance to determine the value and worth of that teacher."[12]

In 1987, a study of a teacher evaluation was reported by two researchers at McGill University, William Searles and Naile Kudeki. From the results of their study, it was possible to develop a profile of an outstanding science teacher as follows:

> The profile of an outstanding science teacher obtained from this study describes a person who is able to maintain a classroom with a pleasant atmosphere where learning can occur, one who is sure of the subject matter being taught, and presents the material to be learned in a clear and effective manner. This person is concerned about the students and ensures that they understand the concepts of science they are being taught by relating new knowledge to that which they already know. This instructor's

teaching shows evidence of creativity and resourcefulness by utilizing various materials and methods of teaching as deemed necessary. The teaching is definitely "pupil-centered" for an outstanding science teacher is able to perceive then make provisions for the needs and abilities of the individual student. The teacher is a person who is available after school for those students who need extra help. As an interested, enthusiastic science teacher, the instructor tries to develop the students' interest in science by varying instructional methods to keep up-to-date with contemporary developments in the teaching of science. An outstanding science teacher presents thought-provoking laboratory activities and encourages the students to develop hypotheses and theories. As a self-confident person, the science teacher attempts to develop the attributes of self confidence and motivation in the students. Such an individual is consistently fair and emotionally calm when enforcing the rules of the school, has a good sense of humor, and is respected by the students.

Outside of the classroom, the outstanding science teacher cooperates with colleagues, consults with them in case of difficulties, is interested in academic self-improvement, and keeps up-to-date with scientific developments by reading journals and taking refresher courses.[13]

SUMMARY

Student teaching is the most important phase of the prospective teacher's training. Entered into with enthusiasm and a willingness to learn, the experience will be a valuable culmination of college preparation for teaching.

The selection of subject, school, and supervising teacher is enhanced by visits to schools before the semester or quarter of student teaching. It is advisable to do one's student teaching in the major field of preparation to capitalize on one's strength of subject-matter competency.

The usual pattern of preparation is to spend several days or a week observing the class one is going to teach. Such observation can be done on a systematic basis and promotes real insight into the individual differences present in the class. Student teachers can be assistant teachers in the truest sense if they are alert to developing problems, anticipate future activities of the class, and prepare themselves accordingly.

Taking over the class to teach a lesson or a unit will be completely successful if student teachers plan adequately in consultation with their supervising teachers and make their preparations carefully. Advance rehearsal for the first day of teaching is an advisable procedure, particularly if the time budget is questionable or if class questions are anticipated. An immediate follow-up of a day of teaching with a brief conference with the supervising teacher is advisable. Necessary changes in lesson plans can be made at this time.

A desirable arrangement is to follow the student-teaching quarter with a final quarter on the college campus before graduation. At this time, seminars in special

problems of teaching can be most profitable, and the student teacher can reflect on the teaching experience. This affords the opportunity to give maximum attention to the important choice of a first teaching position in the light of the recent experience in student teaching.

Being a science teacher has its professional frustrations and motivational needs: safety, security, love and belongingness, and self-esteem are ways of thinking about levels of fulfillment in your job. Some of the professional challenges of the new millenium are competency and accountability, facilities and equipment, curriculum and instruction, funding, disruptive students, and career education.

Today's science teacher is in a position of respect and responsibility. The demand for well-prepared science teachers has never been greater, and the rewards are exceptional.

Decision making is a crucial aspect of being a science teacher. The particular focus of decision making is on two seemingly paradoxical aspects of teaching—that one must maintain a direction and that one must demonstrate flexibility. The balance between these variables is set by the science teacher's decisions. A personal theory of instruction will help guide the science teacher's decisions and develop a consistent pattern of responses to the instantaneous demands of the classroom.

Proper education of the science teacher in this fast-moving scientific age is a matter of increasing concern. A suitable balance of general education, subject-matter preparation, and professional training must be achieved. The current trend is toward strengthening all of these areas, particularly subject-matter preparation. Attainment of a bachelor's degree does not end the science teacher's education. More and more, graduate work, up to and beyond the master's level, is being demanded. From a financial standpoint, it is generally to the teacher's advantage to obtain this advanced training as soon as possible. Better-paying jobs with other attractive features frequently await the applicant who has additional training.

The science teacher can grow professionally in many ways. Graduate coursework, in-service institutes and workshops, summer institutes, committee involvement, membership in professional organizations, a program of reading, participation in meetings, and writing for professional journals are but a few possibilities. It is important to realize that continual growth and experience are necessary if one is to be an enthusiastic, productive science teacher.

Being a science teacher is more than signing your first contract or teaching your first class. It is more than your knowledge of science, capacity to plan, ability to use different methods, and your enthusiasm for teaching. Although these attributes are included, being a science teacher means

1. courage to continue your professional growth;
2. commitment to doing a better job tomorrow;

3. competence to fulfill your professional duties;
4. compassion toward your students; and
5. caring for your own dignity, integrity, and worth and for the dignity, integrity, and worth of those in your care.

The professional educator of today faces a challenging future. Investment in superior preparation and recognition of the need for continual professional growth can provide rich rewards: a citizenry better educated in the area of science.

◆
———

REFERENCES

1. National Research Council, *National Science Education Standards* (Washington, DC: National Academy Press, 1996).
2. Checklist from Lawrence A. Conrey, University School, University of Michigan, Ann Arbor, 1960.
3. Paul E. Adams and Gerald H. Krockover, "Concerns and Perceptions of Beginning Secondary Science and Mathematics Teachers," *Science Education*, 81(1) (1997): 29–50.
4. *Stanford Teacher Competence Appraisal Guide* (Stanford, CA: Stanford Center for Development in Teaching 1963).
5. Cynthia Ann Druva and Ronald D. Anderson, "Science Teachers' Characteristics by Teacher Behavior and by Student Outcome: A Meta-Analysis of Research," *Journal of Research in Science Teaching*, 20 (5) (1983): 467–479.
6. David Boesel, *Violent Schools—Safe Schools,* vol. 1 (Washington, DC: National Institute of Education, 1978).
7. Bill G. Aldridge and Karen L. Johnston, "Trends and Issues in Science Education," in *Redesigning Science and Technology Education*, 1984 NSTA Yearbook, R. Bybee, J. Carlson, and A. McCormack, eds. (Washington DC: National Science Teachers Association, 1984).

8. James A. Shymansky and Bill G. Aldridge, "The Teacher Crisis in Secondary School Science and Mathematics," *Educational Leadership*, 40 (November 1982).
9. National Science Teachers Association, "Secondary School Science and Mathematics Teachers," *NSF Bulletin* 63–10 (Washington, DC: U.S. Government Printing Office, 1963), p. 4.
10. National Research Council, *National Science Education Standards* (Washington, DC: National Academy Press, 1996).
11. National Science Teachers Association, "Annual Self-Inventory for Science Teachers in Secondary Schools," *Science Teacher*, 37 (9) (December 1970): 37.
12. G. D. Bailey, "Teacher Self-Assessment: In Search of a Philosophical Foundation," *National Association of Secondary School Principals Bulletin*, 62 (422) (1978): 64–70.
13. William E. Searles and Naile Kudeki, "A Comparison of Teacher and Principal Perception of an Outstanding Science Teacher," *Journal of Research in Science Teaching*, 24 (1) (1987): 1–13.

◆ ———————————— **INVESTIGATING SCIENCE TEACHING** ———————————— ◆

ACTIVITY 24–1
INDIVIDUAL DIFFERENCES

1. In your observation of a science class, use the checklist like the one on page 343 to discover the individual differences present in the class. At the end of a week, discuss your observations with the teacher. How does the student's achievement appear to correlate with your observations of study habits and classroom behavior?

2. List the traits you would like to see in the supervising teacher with whom you wish to do your practice teaching. Using this list as a guide, objectively analyze your own traits and compare them. Do you think similar or opposite traits are preferable, or that a judicious blend of both is preferable?

ACTIVITY 24–2
APPLYING FOR A JOB

1. Write a letter of application for a teaching position.

2. Briefly describe your qualifications, special areas of interest, and teaching field.

3. Volunteer to make an appointment for an interview at a mutually convenient time.

4. Write a short description of your philosophy of education. This need not be included in the letter of application but should be held in reserve for an appropriate time when called for.

ACTIVITY 24–3
BEING A PROFESSIONAL SCIENCE TEACHER

1. Write to the department of education in your state and obtain a summary of the current salary schedule in the major cities. Compare the starting salaries for teachers with bachelor's degrees and master's degrees. Compare the annual salary increase and the number of years required to reach maximum salary.

2. Obtain a copy of *Guidelines for Preparation Programs of Teachers of Secondary School Science and Mathematics* from the American Association for the Advancement of Science, Washington, DC. Compare the training you have received with that recommended by this group.

3. Prepare a critical analysis of two professional journals, such as the *Science Teacher, School Science and Mathematics*, the *American Biology Teacher*, and the *Physics Teacher*. Examine the feature articles, the classroom teaching tips, the articles contributed by teachers in the field, the book reviews, and other parts of the publications.

4. Prepare a critical review of two research-oriented professional science teaching journals, such as *Science Education* and *Journal of Research for Science Teaching*. Report on the results of one research study published in each of the journals reviewed.

ACTIVITY 24–4
FULFILLMENTS AND FRUSTRATIONS

Joan is approaching your desk, "Look, I solved the chemistry problem. It was easy after you explained the difference between ionic and covalent bonding." Then, with a warm smile, she said, "I really appreciate the extra time you spend helping me; you are a good teacher and I'm glad I decided to take chemistry." What would you do?

1. Ask her if she solved the other chemistry problems.
2. Say nothing, smile, and go on with your work.
3. Tell her that it is just part of your job.
4. Smile and thank her for the compliment.
5. Tell her you are glad she asked you about the problem.

You have just sat through one more insufferable faculty meeting. The results of the meeting: your clerical work will increase due to a new grading system; your budget has been reduced by 50 percent (and the price of science materials, equipment, and textbooks has gone up 25 percent); your new duty is to supervise the cafeteria; your new class will be a "difficult, but small" group of students; your salary increase for next year will be 3 percent below the present rate of inflation. What would you do?

1. Quit.
2. Go to the next NEA or AFT meeting and demand a change in contracts.
3. Ignore the situation because one-fourth of the problems will be changed in the next two weeks; one-fourth of the changes will never be implemented; you can ignore one-fourth of the problems, and the remaining one-fourth are "part of the territory."
4. Make an appointment with the principal and politely, but firmly, inform her that she has asked too much of you.
5. Talk over the problems with several colleagues.
6. Go to a psychotherapist to see if you or the school system is sick.

Once you have selected the option closest to what you think, you might discuss it with a partner. What else would you do?

ACTIVITY 24–5
DEVELOPING AN INSTRUCTIONAL THEORY

The idea of an instructional theory was introduced in Chapter 2. Now it might be a good idea to return to this idea. To help you develop your instructional theory, complete the following exercise.

1. What is the aim of your science teaching? What is the broad goal you would hope to achieve through your interaction with students in the science classroom?
   a. What is your primary goal?
   b. What are your secondary aims?
2. Based on your understanding of yourself, students, science, and society, what are your justifications for the goal and aims cited above?
   a. Why are these and not other aims to be the focus of science education?
   b. In a broad sense, what is to be done or not done to achieve these aims?

3. What are your conclusions about what to do, and how and when to achieve these aims?

   a. By what specific instructional methods or processes are the aims developed?

   b. What is your science curriculum?

   c. Is there any sequence in your instructional theory?

In sum, you should first state what your aims are, second, justify why these aims are important, and third, explain how you plan to achieve these aims through your science curriculum and instruction.

ACTIVITY 24–6
WHAT WOULD YOU DO—NOW?

Based on your sense of direction and flexibility, what would you do as a science teacher in these situations?

1. You are introducing a biology lesson on predator/prey relationships. The chameleons and crickets you ordered for the students to observe have not arrived. What would you do?

2. You are teaching a physical science lesson on energy. The class was supposed to read the chapter on energy in the book. You suddenly realize that several of the students cannot read at the level of your textbook. What would you do?

3. During an earth science lesson on the planets, a student informs you that he has talked with a visitor from another planet—called Xerob. He describes the visitor in detail. The class is interested and starts asking the student questions. What would you do?

4. The unit is on health, the lesson on smoking. A student tells about a person she knows who is 85 years old and very healthy. This person has smoked two packages of cigarettes a day for over 60 years. In addition, the person drinks, eats candy, and does not watch his diet. What would you do?

ACTIVITY 24–7
IMPROVING MY SCIENCE TEACHING

What are your strengths and weaknesses? How do you think you should improve as a science teacher? Following is a self-evaluation inventory designed to provide answers to these questions. We don't know how you would like to become more effective as a science teacher. Of course, the answers to these questions vary from person to person. The inventory will provide you with insights concerning some of your own characteristics as a science teacher. The self-evaluation inventory is based on items used in a study of teacher effectiveness and later modified for the study of science teaching. Only selected items are used here.

The following statements are descriptions of various facets of science teaching. Read each of the statements carefully. Using the scale, indicate how each statement presently characterizes you as a science teacher.

5   Very characteristic of me. This is a real strength of my teaching.
4   Frequently characteristic of me. This is a good aspect of my science teaching.
3   Sometimes characteristic of me. I should evaluate this aspect of my science teaching.
2   Seldom characteristic of me. I should improve this aspect of my science teaching.
1   Never characteristic of me. I really need to improve.

As a science teacher, I

_____ 1. am well read in science.

_____ 2. have a well-organized science course.

_____ 3. adjust my teaching to the class situation.

_____ 4. have a good rapport with my science students.

_____ 5. enjoy teaching science to students.

_____ 6. have a thorough knowledge of science.

_____ 7. have always planned and am prepared for science class.

_____ 8. use a variety of techniques in teaching science.

_____ 9. recognize the unique needs of my science students.

_____ 10. am enthusiastic about teaching science.

_____ 11. present science concepts that are current and relevant.

_____ 12. recognize the need to modify daily and unit plans.

_____ 13. facilitate different types of student activities in science.

_____ 14. relate well with students on the individual and group level.

_____ 15. become excited when students learn science.

_____ 16. am well informed in science-related fields.

_____ 17. have thought about the long-range goals of my science class.

_____ 18. use different curriculum materials and instructional approaches to teach science.

_____ 19. am sincere while helping my science students.

_____ 20. make an extra effort to help students learn science.

_____ 21. am knowledgeable concerning science-related social issues.

_____ 22. have a continuity of course material in science.

_____ 23. provide adequate opportunity for active work by science students.

_____ 24. listen to student questions and ideas.

_____ 25. am excited and energetic when teaching science.

Now go back and add up your responses for the items listed below in the left column. Divide the total by 5. The result should be a number between 1 and 5 for each of the categories listed. Refer back to the five-point scale for your evaluation.

Items	Average		Category
1, 6, 11, 16, 21	÷ 5	_____	Knowledge of science
2, 7, 12, 17, 22	÷ 5	_____	Planning and organization
3, 8, 13, 18, 23	÷ 5	_____	Teaching methods
4, 9, 14, 19, 24	÷ 5	_____	Personal relations
5, 10, 15, 20, 25	÷ 5	_____	Enthusiasm

APPENDIX

A

ADDITIONAL TEACHING SCIENCE ACTIVITIES

Biology

Evaluating Food Choices

The Evolution Simulation Game

Using an Identification Key

Effects of Acid Rain on Seed Germination

Chemistry

Quickies: A Collection of Classroom Demonstrations and Devices for Teaching Chemistry

Earth Sciences

Evaluating Laboratory Work: Experiment—Why Is the Sky Blue? Why Is the Sunset Red?

Weather: Air Masses and Fronts

The Moon

Astronomic Distances

Activity for Middle-level Students: How Can Hardness Be Used to Identify Minerals?

Geologic Time

Lab: Determining the Depth and Shape of the Ocean Floor

Gifted Students

Activities in Science for Gifted Students

Challenges to Thinking for Gifted Students Discovery Demonstration: Bottle and Key—Put the Key in the Bottle

Physics

Evaluation of Student Understanding of a Basic Physical Principle

Discovery Demonstration: Inquiring into Falling Bodies

How Long Can You Boil Water in a Paper Cup?

Problem Solving

Teaching Inquiry Skills

Small-Group Problem Solving

Science Fair Projects

Finding Local Variations in Relative Humidity

Measuring Cloud Direction and Speed

Technology

Mathematics

Population Growth and Energy Usage

Stimulating Mathematics Usage in Science Classes

Mathematics in Science: How Will Specific Gravity Help to Identify Minerals?

BIOLOGY

This is a fairly straightforward activity suitable for average students in middle school or junior high school life sciences. Its purpose is to develop consciousness of the importance of healthy diets and of the various nutrients that constitute such a diet. A small amount of record keeping is required and some practice in graphing is provided.

Evaluating Food Choices

OVERVIEW

For one day, students keep a record of the food they eat. By means of a graph, the students evaluate their food choices. This activity is designed for middle/junior high school.

SCIENCE BACKGROUND

Nutrients can be defined as the different substances in foods that function specifically to keep the body healthy, active, and growing. Some of the major nutrients needed by the body include proteins, fats, carbohydrates, vitamins, and minerals.

Protein is the body's building material. It contains nitrogen, which is necessary for all tissue building. Protein is essential for maintaining body structure, for providing substances that act as body regulators, and for producing compounds necessary for normal body functions. Milk products, meat, fish, poultry, eggs, legumes, and nuts are good sources of protein.

While protein also can provide energy for the body, *fats* and *carbohydrates* are the major food substances that provide the body with calories for heat and energy. If the body lacks sufficient amounts of fats and carbohydrates, or if there is an excess of protein in the diet, the body will use protein for heat and energy. Fats are normally consumed from margarine, butter, mayonnaise, salad dressings, and meat. Carbohydrates are found in grain products, fruit, and sugar-sweetened foods.

Although vitamins and minerals are needed in smaller quantities than are protein, fats, and carbohydrates, they remain essential to normal body functioning. Our discussion is limited to those often lacking in the diets of adolescents.

Vitamin A is important for vision. Night blindness, an inability of the eye to adjust to dim light, can result from a lack of vitamin A in the diet. Yellow, orange, and dark green vegetables, and fruits contain vitamin A (sweet potatoes, carrots, squash, spinach, broccoli, melon, apricots, and peaches).

Vitamin C contributes to the formation of a substance called collagen, which holds body tissue together and encourages healing. Vitamin C also strengthens blood vessel walls and helps the body utilize calcium in making bones and teeth. Scurvy, a disease characterized by swelling and tenderness of joints and gums, loosening of teeth, hemorrhaging, and puffiness can result from a severe lack of vitamin C. Citrus fruits, broccoli, spinach, greens, potatoes, tomatoes, melon, cabbage, and strawberries contain this vitamin.

Iron is a mineral that is essential to hemoglobin, the substance of the blood that carries oxygen. Oxygen is necessary for all cells. A diet that fails to supply a sufficient amount of iron may lead to anemia. This condition is characterized by a tired and listless feeling due to a lack of energy. Although liver is a major source of iron, greens, beans, beef, pork, prunes, and raisins are also good sources.

Calcium is the bone- and tooth-building mineral. It forms the structure of teeth and bones and helps keep them strong. Milk products are good sources for calcium.

MAJOR CONCEPT

Individuals should develop eating patterns that contribute to wellness.

STUDENT OBJECTIVES

By the end of this activity, the students should be able to:

◆ Analyze and evaluate food choices in terms of the Recommended Daily Allowance (RDA) of protein, energy, and selected vitamins and minerals.

MATERIALS

Comprehensive List of Foods booklet with nutritive values and percent of U.S. RDA for 139 foods, available from the National Dairy Council. Contact the office serving your area or write: National Dairy Council, 630 North River Road, Rosemont, IL 60018.

VOCABULARY

anemia	minerals	Recommended
calories	night	Daily Allowance
carbohydrates	blindness	(RDA)
fats	nutrient	scurvy
	proteins	vitamins

PROCEDURES

1. Have the students keep a complete record of all foods eaten for one day.

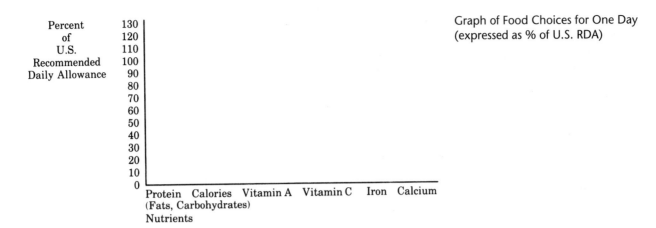

Graph of Food Choices for One Day
(expressed as % of U.S. RDA)

2. Using the "Comprehensive List of Foods," the students should then determine the nutritive values and graph the percent of RDA that chosen foods contained. (See sample graph.)

3. Upon completion of the bar graphs, invite the students to answer the following questions:

Is the percentage of calories (energy) in your daily diet too low, about right, or too high?

Nutrients I need more of are _____

Which foods could provide these nutrients?

Foods I ate that had a lot of calories (energy) but not many other nutrients are _____

How can I improve my diet?

The Evolution Simulation Game*

Information on the purpose, objectives, and function of the game is given in the description. Games such as this usually elicit considerable class interest and form an effective method of presenting abstract concepts to a class.

OVERVIEW

The following game simulates the process of evolution. It clearly demonstrates the role of mutations, adaptations, and chance in this process. The game also can be used as an introduction to food chains, the effects of competition within an environment, the effects of pollution, or man's role in relation to environmental issues. It is designed for high school students, but with some modifications it could be played with junior high school students.

SCIENCE BACKGROUND

Charles Darwin's theory of evolution states that every species on the earth is undergoing constant, gradual change controlled by natural selection. Today it is generally accepted that these changes are caused by genetic mutations. Those mutations that are harmful are weeded out by the low survival rate of their carriers. Conversely, those mutations that are beneficial gradually become more common due to the high survival rate of their carriers. Whether a given mutation is beneficial or detrimental is determined by the organism's environment: temperature, precipitation, competition, predators, and pollution.

ADDITIONAL SOURCES

Charles Darwin, *On the Origin of Species* (Cambridge, MA: Harvard University Press, 1964).

Charles Darwin, *The Illustrated Origin of Species*, abridged and introduction by Richard E. Leakey (New York: Hill and Wang, 1979).

Paul Amos Moody, *Introduction to Evolution* (New York: Harper and Row, 1970).

Ruth E. Moore, *Evolution* (New York: Time, Inc., 1964).

MAJOR CONCEPTS

- Mutations occur at random and their results cannot be predicted; organisms do not choose to mutate.
- Some mutations help a species adapt and survive in its environment.

*This activity was developed and field tested by Ms. Kathy James, Carleton College, Northfield, Minnesota. It is used with her permission.

◆ Just how helpful a mutation will be depends on the environment.

◆ Organisms with characteristics well suited to the environment in which they live will be able to adapt and survive.

STUDENT OBJECTIVES

After this activity, students should be able to:

◆ Describe the relationship between mutations and adaptations.

◆ Explain how natural mutations facilitate evolution.

◆ Describe the role the environment plays in evolution.

◆ Identify ways in which evolution is continuing today.

VOCABULARY

Mutation

Adaptation

MATERIALS

Handout stating rules of the game and describing the original organism

Overheads listing the mutation for each round (1–41)

Cards stating the environmental changes (1–19)

A map of the region (described as follows)

RULES OF THE GAME

All players begin as the same organism (described as follows) in the same geographic location (square K).

The game will be organized into rounds that represent periods of roughly 1 million years. These rounds will be organized as follows:

◆ At the beginning of each round, each player picks up to 2 mutations from a list prepared by the teacher. The mutations for each round should be displayed on an overhead. Suggested rounds are listed as follows.

◆ Do not allow students to see the list of mutations for future rounds. Most mutations will appear in more than one round. New mutations will be added each round.

◆ Each mutation is permanent to the player's species and will be effective in all the following rounds.

◆ Any new mutation replaces any contradicting traits. These contradictions are explained in brackets [ ] after the mutation.

◆ Some mutations require previous mutations, which are listed in parentheses ( ) after the mutation.

◆ In any round, any student may choose to migrate one square in any direction as one of his mutations, but the species must have adapted to survive any changes in climate caused by the

migration. (See "The Region" for a more detailed explanation.)

◆ After all mutations have been chosen, an environmental change is selected. This can be done by randomly drawing from a hat, thereby emphasizing the role of chance in evolution, or the sequence of mutations can be chosen by the teacher, allowing for the emphasis to be on the effects of specific environmental changes.

◆ The environmental changes only have an effect in the round in which they are chosen; no points will be gained or lost for past environmental changes.

◆ Students can be allowed to debate whether an environmental change was beneficial to their organism. Guidelines are as follows, but these are only guidelines.

SCORING

Each student begins with 5 points. A score of zero (0) represents extinction and the player is out of the game. Players attempt to survive and to increase their scores.

If an environmental change is beneficial, + 1

If an environmental change is detrimental, − 1

OPTION

After the first four rounds, competition may become a factor in scoring. If competition is included, see "The Region" for an explanation of the scoring.

The Original Species: A Salamander

Color: red

Skin: moist, soft

Size: 6 inches long

Body temperature: cold blooded

Diet: algae, swallowed whole

Reproduction:	Attracts mate by smell
	Mates on land
	Lays eggs in shallow pools of water
	Does not care for young in any way
Behavior:	Does not hibernate
	Low endurance—must rest after running or swimming 150 yards
	Poor swimmer—is carried away by a current flowing faster than half a mile per hour
	Poor jumper—can jump only 1 inch vertically
	Moderate runner—runs at the speed of the average house cat

Rests at night in holes in the ground, under logs, or wherever it can find some shelter

General: Mute
Body and eggs absorb salts from salt water so it cannot survive in a saltwater environment

THE REGION

The map and descriptions of the various regions on the map allow the teacher to include competition as a factor influencing the course of evolution. After the first five rounds, if there are 3 or more players in a given square, each player loses a point. If 2 players are in a square and another player then moves in that square, making a total of 3 players in the square, only the player moving into the square loses a point. (The maximum limit per square will need to be increased to 3 if more than 15 students are playing.)

These migrations will force players into new environments, which are described below. Players must have adapted to survive the conditions they will encounter before moving into an environment. For example, a player cannot migrate away from the river until he can reproduce on dry land.

This aspect of the game is optional. If it is included, tell the students about the environments they will encounter in each square, and discuss the adaptations necessary to survive in each environment before the game begins.

A	E	I	M
B	F	J	N
C	G	K	O
D	H	L	P

Square A is a northern region. It is well forested, with a wide variety of trees, plants, and animals. But six months a year the ground is covered with snow, making plant life very hard to find and a fur coat a necessity. Cold-blooded animals cannot survive here, nor can those who lay their eggs in water, since pools of water are scarce. Seasonal coloring, allowing an animal to be white in the winter but brown or green in the summer, is necessary here. Hibernation is also beneficial and would eliminate the need for seasonal coloring.

Squares B, E, and F are similar, but the winters are less severe. A fur coat and seasonal coloring will be helpful, but they are not a necessity.

Squares C and G are open prairie. There is little or no tree cover, but a wide variety of plants grow here. Many small birds and animals live in the grasses. Winters are cool, but snow rarely accumulates.

Square D is a desert. Days are hot and dry, but nights can be very cool. It never snows here. Water is sometimes hard to find, but desert plants are common. Some desert animals can be found here.

Squares L and P are saltwater regions. Those animals whose skin is permeable to salt cannot survive here.

Squares O and N are cut off from the rest of the region by the river, so only flying predators will affect species living there. To live in this region, species must develop the ability to cross the river, which requires increased endurance and webbed feet (or three times the original endurance if webbed feet are not added).

All other squares, H, I, J, and K, represent forested regions bordered by a large river. There is plenty of plant and animal life to support other forms of life. Winters are not severe; snow rarely accumulates.

MUTATIONS

1. dryer skin
2. develops scales (1)
3. develops hair (1, 2) [cancels 4]
4. develops shell-like exterior (2) [cancels 3, 36]
5. develops brown pigment, producing reddish brown color [cancels 8, 10]
6. increases brown pigment, producing solid brown (5)
7. develops white pigment, producing spotted white [cancels 6, 10]
8. increases white pigment, producing solid white color (7)
9. develops green pigment, producing spotted green [cancels 6, 8]
10. increases green pigment, producing solid green color (9)
11. seasonal color changes (5, 7, or 9) [cancels 12]
12. variety in pigment allowing color to change to fit environment, chameleon coloring (5, 9) [cancels 11]
13. variety in pigment so that mates are attracted by coloring (5, 7, or 9) [replaces use of scent to attract a mate so scent is lost]
14. skin becomes impermeable to salts found in salt water

CHANGES IN DIET

15. develops small molars, allowing organism to chew plants
16. adds enzyme in the digestive tract, allowing digestion of insects swallowed with the water

17. adds small canines, allowing organism to eat mice-sized rodents (16)
18. develops larger canines, allowing the organism to eat larger prey (17)
19. develops claws
20. develops a frog-like tongue, which allows the organism to catch flying insects (16)

CHANGES IN BODY TEMPERATURE AND HABITAT

21. becomes warm blooded (1)
22. becomes nocturnal (21)
23. builds a den/nest
24. spends part of its waking hours in trees (19)
25. nests in trees (23, 24)
26. burrows, nesting under ground (19)

CHANGES IN MEANS OF REPRODUCTION

27. develops a protective covering on eggs
28. lays eggs on land (27)
29. develops pigment in egg shell, which acts as a camouflage (27)
30. cares for young after eggs hatch
31. becomes a marsupial (30)
32. carries young to term (30)
33. uses voice to attract mates [replaces scent used to attract a mate]

CHANGES IN LOCOMOTION

34. changes in circulatory system increase endurance
35. develops webbed feet
36. leg length doubles, producing longer legs in proportion to body size, and allowing for swifter running—twice as fast as before
37. develops stronger leg muscles, allowing for greater jumping ability—twice as high as before [initial jumping ability was 1 inch]
38. loses limbs [cancels 35, 36, 37, 39]
39. develops fins (35) [cancels 37, 38]

OTHER CHANGES

40. increases size 50 percent (34)
41. lives in water continually (34, 35)

ENVIRONMENTAL CHANGES

1. Flies begin to be seen in the area [helps 16 + 20].
2. Temperatures drop; only severe in region A, where temperatures are now consistently below freezing and snow accumulates [little effect].
3. Small green land plants become common [helps 15].
4. Worms and slugs become common [helps 16].
5. Drought: small pools dry up and the river level drops 2 feet [hurts those without 28, 31, 32].
6. A herbivorous turtle moves into the region by the river [hurts those without 15, 16, 17, or 20].

7. Rabbits begin to populate the region [helps those with 18; hurts those with 15].
8. The population of songbirds in the region increases [little effect].
9. A population of freshwater carnivorous turtles moves into the river [hurts those without 28 and those with 41].
10. A population of freshwater fish that eats eggs laid in the water moves into the river [hurts those without 28 unless they also have 30; helps those with 18 that still live in or near the river].
11. A snake similar to a rattlesnake develops in the region; snakes locate their prey by warmer body temperatures [hurts those with 21 unless they have 40].
12. Hawks migrate into the region [hurts those without some form of protective coloring].
13. A weasel moves into the region; weasels locate their prey by scent [hurts those without 13 or 33; helps those with 18 and 40 four times].
14. A flood washes away regions near the river [hurts those in squares I, J, K, L, M, N, O who are without 24].
15. Sewage dumped into the river contaminates the river downstream from square J [hurts all in squares, J, K, N, O, L, P].
16. An oil spill contaminates the saltwater sea [hurts all those in squares L, O, P].
17. Prairie fire sweeps across square C [hurts those in square C without 16 and 17; helps those in square C with 16 and 17].
18. People begin to hunt species over 15 inches long [hurts those with 40 four or more times].
19. Squares I and M become a game refuge [helps all in those squares].

TIPS FOR PLAYING THE GAME

1. Keep a simplified copy of the rules and a description of the original species where it will be visible to all the students throughout the time that the game is played. The easiest way to do this will probably be to give each student a copy.
2. Have students individually record their species' evolutions by writing down their choices on mutations, and the environmental changes of each round.
3. After the first three or four rounds have been played, stop to discuss how the students' species have evolved to this point. What do they look like now? What advantages do they have that help them survive? Where can they best survive? Is there anywhere they could not survive? What additional changes might help them even more? Is it possible that evolution really happened this way?

4. Spend one full class period introducing and playing the game. Additional games/rounds can be played later with less preparation time. One round a day can be played, using the environmental changes as a means of focusing attention on the lesson topic. Or it may be useful on those days when the film you planned to show fails to come in or you did not have time to write up a lesson plan for the substitute teacher.

5. There is no limit to the number of rounds that can be played. Listed are 19 environmental changes, but these can be repeated or the list can be expanded.

6. Currently, the mutations will not allow a species to fly or walk erect. These advances involve an incredible number of mutations. It might be a good idea to tell this to students when the game begins.

7. There are no predators other than those introduced as environmental changes. Do not tell the students what types of predators these will be.

SUGGESTED MUTATION CHOICES

Round 1: 1, 5, 9, 15, 16, 17, 21, 27, 28, 34, 35, 40
Round 2: 7, 10, 14, 15, 16, 19, 21, 27, 29, 30, 36, 40
Round 3: 2, 3, 12, 15, 20, 22, 26, 28, 30, 33, 34, 39
Round 4: 6, 8, 11, 18, 19, 23, 29, 31, 36, 38, 39, 41
Round 5: 1, 3, 4, 5, 13, 15, 16, 24, 32, 34, 35, 36
Round 6: 2, 14, 19, 20, 21, 26, 28, 30, 33, 37, 39, 40
Round 7: 6, 7, 10, 11, 17, 18, 22, 23, 24, 32, 36, 38
Round 8: 4, 8, 9, 19, 29, 31, 34, 36, 37, 39, 40, 41
Round 9: 2, 3, 5, 13, 22, 33
Round 10: 13, 14, 35, 36, 39, 40
Round 11: 11, 14, 23, 32, 38, 39
Round 12: 3, 4, 27, 29, 40, 41
Round 13: 15, 24, 26, 30, 37, 39
Round 14: 13, 16, 22, 29, 36, 40
Round 15: 23, 26, 32, 33, 35, 41
Round 16: 4, 18, 22, 26, 40, 42
Round 17: 1, 12, 16, 34, 35, 41

Using an Identification Key

This activity provides an opportunity for pupils to work in groups and gives practice in classification of organisms using standard methods. As indicated in the description, the exercise may be programmed for use on a computer as an alternative or supplemental activity.

OVERVIEW

In this activity, students use a simple identification key to classify several animals. The activity is designed for middle/junior high school levels. This activity can be adapted and programmed for use on a computer.

STUDENT OBJECTIVES

At the completion of this activity, students should be able to:

◆ Use a simple identification key.
◆ Describe the usefulness of classifying organisms.
◆ Apply the identification key to identify an unknown organism.

MATERIALS

A variety of common organisms. The organisms should represent different phyla in the animal kingdom (see key for examples). In general, organisms commonly found in life science classrooms can be used.

A key for each student or group of students (see the following information).

Common references for information about organisms of different phyla.

PROCEDURES

1. Divide the class into groups of students. The size of groups should be determined by the number and variety of organisms available.
2. Provide 3–4 organisms for each group of students.
3. Distribute and introduce the key to the students. Some of the points to make are:
   ◆ The key is made up of a series of questions that can be answered by either YES or NO.
   ◆ The answer leads to the next question or identification of the organism.
   ◆ Go through the key and identify one organism at a time.
4. Have the students proceed to identify their organisms.
5. The students should look up information about the organisms they have identified.
6. As a follow-up evaluation, have the students go out of doors and identify an "unknown" organism.

A CLASSIFICATION KEY

1. Does the animal have a backbone? If your answer is YES go to 1a. If it is NO, go to 2.
   1a. Does the animal have hair or fur on its body? If YES, it is a MAMMAL. If NO, go to 1b.
   1b. Does the animal have feathers? If YES, its scientific name is AVES. If NO, go to 1c.
   1c. Does the animal have smooth skin and lay its eggs in water? If YES, it is an AMPHIBIAN. If NO, go to 1d.

1d. Does the animal have scaly skin and lay its eggs on land? If YES, it is a REPTILE. If NO, go to 1e.

1e. Does the animal have scaly skin and lay its eggs in water? If YES, it is an OSTEICHTHYES. If NO, return to question 1 and check to be sure the animal has a backbone.

2. If the animal does not have a backbone, begin here. Does the animal have a hard, outside covering and jointed legs? If YES, it is an ARTHROPOD—go to 2a. If NO, go to 3.

2a. Does the animal have three pairs of legs? If YES, it is an INSECT. If NO, go to 2b.

2b. Does the animal have four pairs of legs and two body sections? If YES, it is an ARACHNID. If NO, go to 2c.

2c. Does the animal have at least 5 pairs of legs and a hard covering? If YES, it is a CRUSTACEAN. If NO, go to 2d.

2d. Does the animal have many body sections with a pair of legs on each section? If YES, it is a CENTIPEDE. If NO, go to 2e.

2e. Does the animal have many body sections with 2 pairs of legs on each section? If YES, it is a MILLIPEDE. If NO, return to 2.

3. Does the animal have spines covering its skin? If YES, it is an ECHINODERM. If NO, go to 4.

4. Does the animal have a hard shell covering a soft body? If YES, it is a MOLLUSK. If NO, go to 5.

5. Does the animal have a long, wormlike body with many sections? If YES, it is an ANNELID. If NO go to 6.

6. Is your animal wormlike with a smooth tapered body? If YES, it is a NEMATODA. If NO, go to 7.

7. Does the animal have a flat ribbonlike body? If YES, it is PLATYHELMINTHES. If NO, go to 8.

8. Does the animal have tentacles around the mouth opening and a soft body? If YES, it is a COELENTERATE. If NO, go to 9.

9. Does the animal have openings, called pores, all over its body? If YES, it is a PORIFERA. If NO, go back to question 1, 2, or 3.

Effects of Acid Rain on Seed Germination

This activity can be used in a regular high school biology class (grade 10) to demonstrate inquiry techniques in an open-ended experiment. Data collection, graphing, and analysis are employed, and the results are tabulated. A further extension could be the writing of a complete report of the experiment to give practice in organization and communication.

OVERVIEW

Students investigate the effects of acid rain on seed germination by conducting an experiment with bean seeds, or locally available seed, under varying pH conditions. The estimated time for this activity is one class period to organize groups and set up the experiment, then, a few minutes at the start of every other class for approximately two weeks to water and measure seed growth and to record data on individual and class graphs.

MAJOR CONCEPTS

♦ Seed germination is dependent upon proper conditions of pH.
♦ Increases of acidity due to acid rain may inhibit seed germination and plant growth.

STUDENT OBJECTIVES

After the activity, students should be able to:

♦ Measure the growth of a bean seed.
♦ Record data on an individual graph and on a class graph.
♦ Draw the bean seed before seed germination and each day that growth measurements are taken.
♦ Make a summary graph of individual graphs.
♦ Compare data to establish the optimum pH for the germination of a bean seed.

MATERIALS

Petri dish

4 bean seeds (preferably seeds grown locally: alfalfa, pea, bean, etc.)

Water solutions ranging in pH from 2–7 (boiling will be necessary to drive off CO_2 and raise pH to 7)

Rain water (optional)

Absorbent paper towels

Transparent metric ruler

Graph paper

Colored chalk or magic markers

PROCEDURES

Preparation of bean seed:

1. Assign each student a pH solution to "water" the bean seeds. A couple of students should be assigned distilled or rain water for a control. The class as a whole should represent increments on a pH scale ranging from 2–7.

2. Cut 4 paper discs the size of a petri dish from the absorbent paper towel.

3. Dampen the paper discs with appropriate pH or rain water solution.

4. Place 2 discs at the bottom of the petri dish.

5. Measure the seeds and average them.

6. Arrange seeds in the petri dish and cover with the 2 remaining paper discs.

7. Replace lid on petri dish and label with student name.

8. Students should hypothesize on a piece of paper what they believe will be the ideal pH.

PREPARATION OF GRAPH

1. Obtain a piece of 8 × 11 in. graph paper.
2. Set up graph as follows: horizontal axis, age of seed in days; vertical axis, length of seed in millimeters (mm).

PROCEDURES FOR ALTERNATE DAYS

The students will be taking measurements of seed growth and recording data on individual and class graphs.

- Take measurements and plot data on individual graphs.
- Remove lid from petri dish.
- Sketch the shapes of the 4 seeds. Note the color of the seeds.
- Use transparent ruler to measure the straight length of seeds.

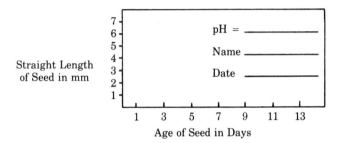

- Take the average straight-line length increase and plot it on your graph. (It is important to plot the increase of seed growth because seeds are different lengths before germination takes place.)
- Make sure paper towel is still moist. If not, add more pH solution (be sure pH solutions are not mixed).
- Replace lid on petri dish.
- Construct class graph on chalkboard or large piece of white construction paper on visible wall or board

to be saved throughout experiment. The graph should use same layout as individual graphs.
- Assign each pH a particular color (chalk or magic marker).
- More than one student may be experimenting with the same pH solution. These students should average their results of seed length.
- Have one student representing each pH record data on the board using the code color that represents pH used. (For example, a pH of 3 is represented by the color green; a pH of 7 is represented by the color purple.)
- After a few recordings have been plotted, students should draw a line connecting points of same pH.

DISCUSSION QUESTIONS

1. What appears to be the optimal pH solution for successful seed germination and growth? The least ideal?
2. How does the local rainwater used compare to the other pH solutions used?
3. From the data expressed on the class graph, what pH do you think the rainwater has?

EVALUATION

Each student should prepare a report that includes:

- brief description and purpose of experiment
- data collected, individual graphs, and seed drawings
- analysis of individual class results:
  1. Ideal pH
  2. Least-ideal pH
  3. Comparison of rainwater to other pH solutions
- discussion questions: What impact on local crops might an increased acidity have? Do you think there is a reason for concern?
- a concrete example of how acid rain and its effect on seed germination could affect food crops grown in the nearest agricultural area.

CHEMISTRY

Quickies: A Collection of Classroom Demonstrations and Devices for Teaching Chemistry

Chemistry teachers often have a need for quick, spectacular, attention-demanding illustrations or demonstrations to enhance their presentations, emphasize a principle, fix a fact, or condition the class for further learning. The following list of "Quickies" may serve these needs. They might form the nucleus for an interesting educational show before your student body, stimulating interest in chemistry through your school.

All these Quickies are suitable for eleventh grade chemistry students, either for demonstrations or for individual or class presentations. The activities will provide science methods students with ideas for generating interest or motivating chemistry students to learn basic principles of chemistry. Each of the Quickies can be done in a few minutes—none requiring more than 50 minutes of class time. The materials required can be found in most high school chemistry stockrooms and require no more than usual care in storage or usage. Common safety precautions must be observed. Further information on safety in the laboratory can be found in Chapter 14.

An interesting demonstration of science "magic" can be made with the "Magic Pitcher." An opaque pitcher is filled with distilled water. The contents of the pitcher are poured into a series of beakers containing a few drops of the following chemicals:

1. NH_4OH
2. Phenolphthalein solution
3. H_2SO_46N
4. $BaCl_2$ supersaturated

The four beakers are filled from the pitcher, then the first two are poured back into the pitcher. The first two glasses then are refilled with "wine." The first three beakers are then poured back into the pitcher, and then all three refilled from the pitcher with "water." The four beakers are then all poured back into the pitcher, and the beakers refilled with "milk." A good line of patter with several assistants can be worked up for this.

Surface tension phenomena may be demonstrated with simple objects. Razor blades, pins, and needles may be floated on the top of water. A small loop of thread (nylon works best) dropped on the surface of water will assume no definite shape, but a drop of detergent or soap solution dropped into the center of the loop will immediately cause it to form a circle. A matchstick floating on the surface of water will move rapidly away from a drop of soap or detergent placed near one end.

A graduated cylinder is filled about half full of water, and a cork disc is floated carefully on top of the water. The cylinder is then filled carefully with alcohol, taking care not to mix the two liquids, and the cork disc is fished off the top. A few drops of viscous lubricating oil are then dropped into the cylinder. The oil, being heavier than alcohol, drops through until it comes to the boundary of the water layer, where the drops become almost perfectly spherical. Careful observation can also show how slowly two liquids diffuse into each other if undisturbed.

Show that the wetting property of water is increased with the addition of detergents by filling two cylinders with water, one having a detergent added. Place a piece of wool yarn on each surface and observe the time required for the wool to sink.

Water filled above the rim of a glass, being held by surface tension, will float a cork in its center. In a glass only partly filled with water, the cork will be pulled to the glass.

Using a fine-nozzle blowpipe prepared from a glass tube, blow small bubbles in a pan of water containing a laundry detergent or dish soap, such as Tide or Joy. The bubbles will arrange themselves in patterns somewhat like molecules as they form crystals.

Light gases diffuse downward. Fill a wide-mouth bottle with hydrogen. Invert it over a like bottle filled with air. While waiting for the diffusion to take place, be democratic and allow the class to vote for what they think is most likely to happen. These possibilities exist: (a) the hydrogen being lighter will remain in the top bottle, (b) the gases will mix together, (c) all the hydro-gen will go to the bottom bottle, (d) most of the hydro-gen will remain in the top bottle, (e) nonvoters admit they do not know what will happen. Many persons vote based on too few facts and too little information.

Spontaneous ignition can be effected with a half teaspoon of sodium peroxide placed on a 2-inch cone of starch, sawdust, or finely-chopped paper. Lay a small chip of ice on the cone. Sufficient heat and oxygen will be released by the reaction of water (from the ice) with the sodium peroxide to ignite the material. Kindling temperature and oxidation can be discussed following the demonstration.

Graham's law of diffusion may be demonstrated by pinning a piece of absorbent cotton to each of two corks that are fitted to an 18 to 20 mm glass tube about 44 mm long. Concentrated HCl and concentrated NH_3 solutions are placed on the respective pieces of cotton and the corks inserted in opposite ends of the tube at the same time. A ring will shortly appear in the tube at the spot where the two gases meet. If the molecular weight of one of the gases is known, the other can be calculated from the respective distances the gases have traveled.

Boyle's law can be vividly demonstrated by connecting 4 one-liter spherical flasks with short L-tubes connected by short pieces of rubber tubing. One of the flasks is attached to an open-end mercury manometer, and the flask at the other end of the series may be attached to a vacuum pump, a water aspirator, or a water faucet, as desired. The flasks are evacuated and the difference in levels of the mercury column noted. If one flask is clamped off from the rest of the system, allowed to fill with air, closed off, and then opened to the rest of the system, it will be noted that the height of the mercury column is only three-fourths the original height, and that therefore the pressure drop is one-fourth atmosphere. This can be continued to pressures above atmospheric by connecting the tube and flask to a water tap and forcing one flask full of water, at which time it will be noted that the pressure is now four-thirds atmosphere. Unless you are prepared for a shower, it is not advisable to force more water than this into the system.

Gay-Lussac's law of the effect of temperature on the pressure of a gas in a closed system may be demonstrated by closing a 500 ml flask with a two-hole stopper. A thermometer that extends to near the center of the flask is pushed through one of the holes. A short piece of glass tubing connected to an open-end mercury manometer is pushed through the other hole. (It may sometimes be advisable to use a three-hole stopper with the third hole closed by a short piece of glass tubing, a piece of rubber tubing, and a pinch clamp. This setup aids in leveling the mercury in the manometer before starting.) The temperature of the gas may be changed by immersing the flasks in a large container of hot water or ice water, and noting the difference in pressure exerted by the gas. You may also note that air is a very poor conductor of heat by observing how slowly the temperature changes when the temperature of the surrounding bath is changed.

Dalton's law of partial pressure may be vividly demonstrated by fitting the top of a fair-sized distilling flask with a one-hole stopper through which extends a dropping funnel. A U-tube manometer with some colored liquid in it is connected to the side-arm of the distilling flask. Some volatile liquid such as ether or chloroform is placed in the dropping funnel and a few ml of the liquid run into the flask. Since the liquid occupied only a slight part of the volume, it cannot account for the considerable rise in the manometer liquid in the U-tube. If you have equipment for sealing the volatile liquid into a thin-walled ampule, to be placed in the flask and broken after it is closed off, the demonstration can be somewhat more dramatic.

In connection with the previous experiment, you can measure rather roughly the vapor pressure of various volatile liquids by closing one end of a 12 mm × 100 cm tube and filling it with mercury. When the tube is filled, it is inverted into a shallow pan partially filled with mercury. If you now wrap a cloth dipped into hot water around the top of the tube, you will note that the level of mercury changes very little—if it has been properly filled with mercury. With a curved-end dropper, now introduce a few drops of the liquid into the bottom of the tube and measure its vapor pressure. The liquid will rise to the top of the tube, and the mercury level will take a considerable drop. If the hot cloth is now wrapped around the top, you will note that the mercury drops much more than it did before the liquid was introduced. A cooled cloth may also be used to show an effect in the opposite direction.

EARTH SCIENCES

Evaluating Laboratory Work: Experiment—Why Is the Sky Blue? Why Is the Sunset Red?

Pupils in eighth and ninth grade classes will be interested in attempting to duplicate the conditions that produce a blue sky or a red sunset. This activity will give pupils an opportunity to work in small groups and to experience many of the key ingredients of any scientific investigation, such as keeping records, forming hypotheses, making predictions, and drawing conclusions. Materials required are common ones found in a chemistry lab and require only usual care in their use.

1. Have students form groups of 4 for this experiment.
2. Have each group follow the suggested procedure for doing the experiment.
3. As the experiment progresses, circulate among the groups and note the following:
   a. Ability to follow directions
   b. Ability to use proper safety precautions
   c. Keeping a record of observations
   d. Working cooperatively with other members of the group
   e. Ability to form hypotheses
   f. Ability to make predictions
   g. Ability to draw conclusions from the observations and data
   h. Care in using the materials, assembly, cleanup, and storage.
4. What kinds of process objectives were realized in having students do this experiment? What cognitive objectives were achieved? What affective objectives?

MATERIALS

Each group should have the following materials:

> 12- or 14-inch rectangular aquarium (clear glass)
> Flashlight
> Concentrated sulfuric acid (H_2SO_4)
> Sodium thiosulfate; may use sodium hyposulfite (photographic fix)
> Water
> White screen or white sheet of paper

PURPOSE

To demonstrate the effect of the atmosphere on the sun's rays. As white light passes through the atmosphere, various colors are removed by scattering and show up in the color of the sky. Violet is removed with smallest particles; blue, with next smallest; green, with next; and so on for yellow, orange, red, etc.

PROCEDURE

Figure A-1 clarifies the procedure. Mix thiosulfate, 10 g per liter of water (not critical), in the aquarium. Project light through aquarium to screen. Add a few drops of concentrated sulfuric acid and stir with glass rod.

DISCUSSION QUESTIONS

1. At the beginning, what color is the water when the flashlight shines through it? What color is the light of the flashlight when looked at directly?
2. How does the color of the water change as time goes on? How does the color of the light from the flashlight change? To what is this analogous in nature?

FIGURE A–1

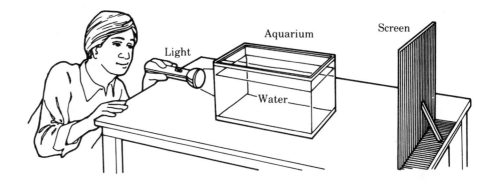

3. What causes the water to change color?
4. What causes the light source to change color?
5. What is the final color of the water? Why?
6. What is the final color of the light source? Why?
7. To what natural sky condition is this analogous?

EXPLANATION

Reaction of the acid on the sodium thiosulfate releases very fine particles. Only very fine particles in the atmosphere cause the rays to scatter. This phenomenon can be shown by the fact that smoke blown across a beam of light appears bluish, but chalk dust gives no coloration at all because the chalk particles are too large.

The scattering effect first removes the violet and blue end of the spectrum, and later the red end as the particles grow larger. Observe the color of the "sky" (water) and also the color of the "sun" (flashlight) that remains. The color of the sun goes from white to yellow to orange to red to blackness, where it is not visible at all.

In nature, the sunlight becomes redder near the horizon because the light passes through more atmosphere with larger particles when the sun is about to set.

TEACHING CONCEPTS

- ◆ Light travels in waves.
- ◆ White light contains all colors.
- ◆ Short waves are scattered more than long waves.
- ◆ Short waves are scattered by smaller particles than are long waves.
- ◆ Scattering subtracts colors from a beam of white light.
- ◆ Subtracting blue from white leaves yellow; therefore, the sun appears yellow.

ADDITIONAL PRINCIPLE

Use a Polaroid sheet and look at the beam from the side and turn your sheet through a 90-degree angle. Observe the fact that scattered light is polarized.

Weather: Air Masses and Fronts

This activity is suitable for ninth grade students and may be used with seventh and eighth grade students as well. It is a straightforward teaching exercise that requires only a few special materials such as old newspaper weather maps. It will be necessary for the teacher to present some additional information concerning weather concepts or to assign supplementary reading on the topics to be discussed.

OVERVIEW

Students observe weather reports on television over a period of a week. The concepts of air masses and fronts are then presented in a lecture-discussion format by the teacher. Weather maps are studied for the final section of the activity.

SCIENCE BACKGROUND

The movement of large air masses and the influence of more localized fronts determine the majority of daily weather. An air mass is a large body of air that originates in a particular location and then moves across the earth's surface. The important characteristic of air masses is that they acquire the properties (temperature and humidity) of the region in which they originate. Air masses are either tropical or polar and either continental or maritime. The major air masses and their origins are shown in Figure A-2.

Continental polar air masses are cold and dry. Maritime tropical air masses are warm and moist. Continental tropical air masses are warm and dry. Maritime polar air masses are cold and moist. The different characteristics of the air masses greatly influence local weather.

A *cold front* is the phrase applied to the leading edge of a cold dense air mass. Since the air is cold and dense, it wedges under lighter, warmer air and forces some air up into the atmosphere. As the warm air is lifted it cools and has a reduced capacity to hold moisture. As this occurs clouds form and precipitation falls. Cold fronts are often identified by a line of storm clouds (see Figure A-3).

A *warm front* results when warmer, lighter air pushes behind colder, denser air. The result is that

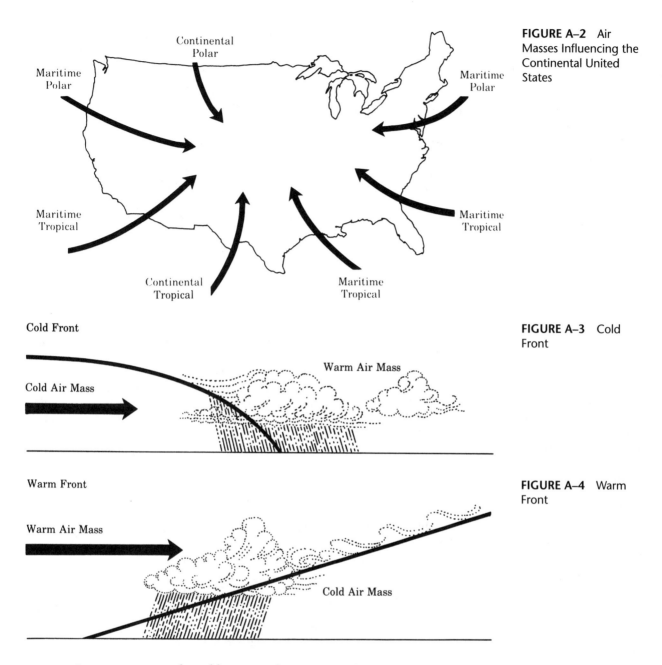

FIGURE A–2 Air Masses Influencing the Continental United States

FIGURE A–3 Cold Front

FIGURE A–4 Warm Front

warmer air moves up over the colder air producing a long area of precipitation as the warm air rises and cools. High cirrus clouds can precede the front by several days (see Figure A-4).

We are influenced daily by the weather. Yet, many know little about the dynamics of this daily phenomenon. The implications of weather range from moisture for agriculture to severe weather that threatens human life.

MAJOR CONCEPTS

Atmospheric motion occurs on many scales.

Air masses have characteristics of the place of origin.

The interaction of warm and cold air results in different patterns of weather called *fronts*.

STUDENT OBJECTIVES

At the completion of this activity, the student should be able to:

- Identify a warm front
- Identify a cold front
- Describe the characteristics and influences of different air masses

MATERIALS

Prepare overhead transparencies for Figures A-2, A-3, and A-4.

Chalkboard

Old weather maps (from the newspaper or weather station)

VOCABULARY

Cold front   Weather
Warm front   Air masses

PROCEDURES

1. Present the concepts of air masses and fronts in a formal manner (15–20 minutes).
2. Have the students apply their observations to the presentation during a discussion period.
3. In the final section of the activity, have the students look at weather maps and see whether they can discover the concepts of air masses and fronts as they have actually been recorded.

EVALUATION TASKS

Use Figures A-2, A-3, and A-4 without labels and have the students identify air masses and fronts.

Tell the students to observe weather forecasts for the next week and summarize their observations in terms of air masses and fronts.

EXTENDING THE ACTIVITY

Have the students look up occluded fronts and report on their characteristics.

Have a meteorologist (a local TV weather person) visit the class and tell about predicting the weather.

The students can study the instruments used in recording atmospheric conditions.

The Moon

Middle school pupils will enjoy and profit from this activity. Many people have misconceptions about how the moon presents various phases during each month. Be sure to provide adequate time to demonstrate how the moon's phases are formed by placing a lightbulb in a darkened room and having the pupils rotate themselves while holding a meterstick with a three-inch styrofoam ball representing the moon attached to the end of it. They can then observe how much of the "moon" is lighted.

OVERVIEW

Students make observations of the changing phases of the moon over a two-month period. After a summary of their observations, the phases of the moon are demonstrated using a simple classroom demonstration.

SCIENCE BACKGROUND

The moon travels around the earth in an elliptical orbit. The moon travels from west to east around the earth. (Due to the earth's rotation, the moon appears to rise in the east and move toward the west.) The average distance of the moon from the earth is 384,000 km (240,000 mi.). The lunar month is actually 27 1/2 days; but, the earth is traveling through space in its orbit around the sun, so the time from one full moon to the next is just over 29 days. The moon rotates on its axis west to east, the same direction that it revolves around the earth. The period of rotation is exactly the period of revolution for the moon.

The moon appears larger when rising because we see it in comparison to other objects such as buildings and trees. It also appears yellow or orange when rising or setting. This is because the reflected light from the moon must pass through longer sections of the earth's atmosphere; in doing so, the blue rays are reflected and scattered by dust particles. This is the same phenomenon that causes red sunsets.

As the moon travels around the earth, we see different amounts of the half of the moon that is in sunlight. During the lunar month, the moon goes through a continuous change from complete darkness (*new moon*) to complete light (*full moon*) and then back to complete darkness. As the moon goes from new moon to full moon, we term the phase *waxing*. The moon's change from full to new is called *waning*.

Outside of the romantic, aesthetic, and mythic qualities of the moon, one of the important societal implications is that the moon causes tides on the earth. Tides result because the moon's pull of gravity makes a bulge in the water on the earth's side facing the moon. Tides have been proposed as one potential source of energy.

MAJOR CONCEPTS

Phases of the moon and lunar eclipses depend on the relative positions of the sun and moon as viewed from the earth.

The earth and moon can be thought of as a system.

STUDENT OBJECTIVES

At the completion of this activity, the student should be able to:

◆ Identify the phases of the moon
◆ Describe the phases of the moon as a relationship among the earth-moon-sun system
◆ Describe the cycle of lunar phases

MATERIALS

Bulletin board calendar of two months
Duplicate of bulletin board calendar for students' notebooks
Globe
Styrofoam ball
Light source

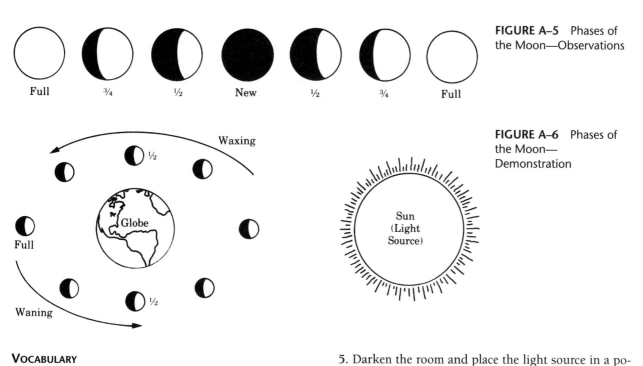

FIGURE A–5 Phases of the Moon—Observations

FIGURE A–6 Phases of the Moon—Demonstration

VOCABULARY

Lunar	Waning
Phases	Crescent
Waxing	

PROCEDURES

1. Place a calendar on the bulletin board. Each day on the calendar should have a space available for one student to draw in a record of the moon as it was observed that day/night. The students should record similar observations on a daily calendar in their notebooks. Starting with a full moon is strongly recommended.
2. Continue the calendars for two full cycles of the moon. (There are 29 days from one full moon to the next.)
3. After continuing the observations for about two months, plan on a period of discussion in which the students summarize their observations. Use Figure A-5 for the summary after the students have given their observations.
4. On a class period after the discussion of student observations, plan on completing a demonstration using a light source, globe, and styrofoam ball.

5. Darken the room and place the light source in a position where it will shine on the globe. Move the styrofoam ball around the globe in such a way as to demonstrate the moon's phases (Figure A-6).

EVALUATION TASKS

Give the students figures similar to Figure A-6, without the phases of the moon completed. Have them fill in the phases and label the diagram.

Set up different sun-earth-moon configurations, and have the students predict the moon's phase.

EXTENDING THE ACTIVITY

This activity can be extended to show how lunar and solar eclipses occur. Usually the moon passes above or below the earth's shadow so there is not a lunar eclipse. Likewise, the shadow projected by the moon does not usually cross the earth, but when it does, there is a solar eclipse along the shadow's path. These eclipses can be demonstrated and discussed with the materials and procedures of this activity. Students can also complete reports on the moon.

Astronomic Distances

This is a good activity for seventh, eighth, or ninth grade students to practice scaling and to develop a visual representation of astronomical distances. A small hand-held calculator may be used to reduce the labor involved in calculations. Because of the vast distances involved, a scale model may be laid out on a long corridor of the school, which will provide adequate room to measure off large distances.

OVERVIEW

In this activity, the students complete a scale model of astronomic distances. The goal is to have the students conceptualize the vastness of space. This activity should take two class periods.

SCIENCE BACKGROUND

A light year is an astronomic measure of distance. The words "light-year" as said quickly may not capture the immensity of the distance involved. So you will have an understanding of the astronomic distance, try completing the following exercise. You can have the students do the same activity. Light travels about 298,000 km per sec (186,000 mi. per sec).

$$
\begin{array}{rl}
298{,}000 \text{ km per sec} & .. \\
\times\ 60 & \text{sec per-min} \\
\times\ 60 & \text{min per hr} \\
\times\ 24 & \text{hr per day} \\
\times 365 & \text{days per yr}
\end{array}
$$

There are some terms and symbols in the activity (see Table A-1) about which students may ask. Some of these are defined for you:

Cluster—a group of stars or galaxies often identified by the constellation in which they are located

Galaxy—a group of stars

M—this stands for Messier number, a way astronomers catalogue stars

Milky Way—the galaxy in which our solar system is located

Nebula—a cloud of dust and gas

TABLE A–1 Distances to Selected Objects in the Celestial Sphere

Celestial Object	Distance in Light-Years
Quasar—3c 295	4.5 billion
Hydra Cluster of Galaxies	3.9 billion
Quasar—3c 273	1.5 billion
Gemini Cluster of Galaxies	980 million
Ursa Major 1 Cluster of Galaxies	720 million
Cygenus A—radio source	500 million
Pegasus II Cluster of Galaxies	470 million
Hercules Cluster of Galaxies	340 million
Coma Cluster of Galaxies	190 million
Perseus Cluster of Galaxies	173 million
Pegasus I Cluster of Galaxies	124 million
Fornox A—radio source	60 million
Virgo cluster of Galaxies	38 million
M49 in Virgo	11.4 million
M81	4.8 million
M31 in Andromeda	2 million
Leo II Galaxy	710 thousand
Fornox Galaxy	390 thousand
Megellanic Clouds	170 thousand
Center of Milky Way	30 thousand
Owl Nebula	12 thousand
Ring Nebula	4.5 thousand
Deneb—star	1.6 thousand
Regil—star	900
Polaris—star	680
Vega—star	26.5
Sirius—star	8.7
Alpha Centauri—star	4.3
Sol—our sun	8 light-minutes

This activity should give students a new perspective relative to the earth in time and space. Our earth is small and insignificant in the scale of astronomic time and distance. Yet, our earth is the most important astronomic object as far as our existence is concerned.

MAJOR CONCEPTS

The average distance between stars in space is incredibly large. Stars are made of hot gases, but they differ in temperature, mass, size, luminosity, and density.

STUDENT OBJECTIVES

At the completion of this lesson, the student should be able to:

◆ Describe the immensity of astronomic distance
◆ Indicate that stars have different distances from earth
◆ Identify her location in the scale of stellar space
◆ Define a light-year (lt-yr) as the distance light travels in a year

MATERIALS

Meterstick
Colored pencils
Adding machine tape (6 m strips for each group of 2)

VOCABULARY

Astronomic	Quasar
Stellar	Star
Distance	Nebula
Galaxy	

PROCEDURES

1. Divide the students into groups of 2–3.
2. Each group should have a piece of adding machine tape, 6 m long; a meterstick; and pencils.
3. Mark off a line about 5 cm from one end of the tape. Label this line EARTH.
4. Using the meterstick and the distances given in Table A-1, plot the distances to the various stellar objects on the adding machine tape. Tell the students they should start by using the scale 1 m = 1 billion lt-yr. (Note: When the students start plotting distances closer to the earth, millions of miles, they will find it impossible to use the scale of 1 m = 1 billion lt-yr. Frustration will be evident as they try to figure out how far a million is on their scale and finally how to get so many stellar objects located in such a small distance. This is the realization that is essential to the lesson. They will have to change the scale to 1 m = 1 million lt-yr, and then they will still have difficulty with the last few distances.)
5. Discuss the problems students had with the scale 1 m = 1 billion lt-yr. Ask them "How did you resolve this problem?" "How does this distance make you feel in the scale of the universe?"

EVALUATION TASKS

The students can use their tapes to explain the immensity of space.

EXTENDING THE ACTIVITY

The students can report on some of the stellar objects named in Table A-1.

Activity for Middle-Level Students: How Can Hardness Be Used to Identify Minerals?

This activity is suitable for middle school pupils as well as for ninth graders. If possible, obtain as many representative minerals as you can from the Moh's hardness scale. Have pupils test one another on their ability to identify minerals on the basis of hardness.

MATERIALS

Steel file
Copper penny
Table knife
Piece of glass
Collection of minerals

DISCUSSION

1. What will scratch glass? Wood? A penny?
2. How can hardness be used to identify minerals?
3. A substance's resistance to scratching is called its *hardness*. If calcite scratches gypsum, which is harder? If calcite scratches both talc and gypsum, which is harder, talc or gypsum? How could you find out?

PROCEDURE

1. Obtain a collection of minerals from a geology department. Make a list of minerals a fingernail will scratch, a file will scratch, a knife will scratch, and a copper penny will scratch. Which minerals are hardest?
2. Find out about Moh's hardness scale. What is the hardness of a knife blade on Moh's scale? A penny? A steel file? A fingernail?
3. Using the hardness number of the knife blade, penny, file, and fingernail, determine the Moh number for each mineral in your collection. Record your results. Obtain a mineral from your classmate without finding out the mineral's name. Using your new knowledge, can you identify the mineral from its hardness?

TEACHER'S INFORMATION

Moh's Hardness Scale	
1. Talc	1. Fingernail scratches it easily
2. Gypsum	2. Fingernail scratches it
3. Calcite	3. Penny scratches it
4. Fluorite	4. Knife scratches it
5. Apatite	5. Knife scratches it
6. Feldspar	6. It scratches glass
7. Quartz	7. It scratches glass
8. Topaz	8. It scratches most minerals
9. Corundum	9. It scratches topaz and most all minerals
10. Diamond	10. It scratches all other minerals

Geologic Time

This activity is similar to a previous one on astronomic distances and will provide practice in scaling. A calculator will come in handy. The model can be laid out on a school corridor as before to develop the concept of the enormity of geologic time.

OVERVIEW

Students complete a scale model of geologic time. The primary goal of the activity is to give them a concept of the immensity of geologic time. Secondary to this, they are introduced to geologic periods and the record of life as recorded in rocks. The activity should last for two class periods.

SCIENCE BACKGROUND

There are two primary methods of determining the age of materials and thus establishing a time scale. The first is an ordering of events, simply determining what happened first, second, third, and so on. In this method the dating is *relative*. The second method establishes a specific time of an organism, event, or rock stratum. This is an *absolute* method of dating materials. Geologists have used the relative method of dating materials for years. It is represented classically in the time scale constructed in this activity.

William Smith, working in the nineteenth century, is credited with formally establishing the practice of ordering geologic events. He observed that rocks revealed an orderly succession of life; that is, older species were represented in older rocks (bottom layers), and as these species disappeared from the rock record, fossils of new species appeared. This is called *faunal succession*—groups of fossils succeed each other in sedimentary rock layers in such a way that the sequences of rocks are predictable. It should be noted that Smith did not develop the idea of evolution—the biological implication of his observations. He was only concerned with the fossils as chronological indicators. The method used by Smith also allowed him to correlate groups of rocks that were some distance apart. The assumption here is that finding similar fossils in rocks at two different locations means the rocks were deposited in the same period.

Nineteenth-century geologists succeeded in ordering many formations of the world's rocks. The order was based on relative dates, since absolute dating methods had not been developed. Though there are inconsistencies and problems with this method of dating rocks, it does represent a good introduction to geologic time and the record of past life and events in the rocks.

Understanding the immensity of geologic time gives students some perspective relative to our time and influence on earth. Compared to other organisms, our time has been short and our impact can be viewed with mixed reactions: we probably represent the highest, most complex form of life and we have done the most to endanger our own existence and the existence of other species. For these reasons, as well as for the knowledge contained about the earth's history in the rock record, it is important for students to understand the perspective of geologic time.

MAJOR CONCEPTS

- ◆ Environments can change and conserve their identities.
- ◆ Environments change because living and nonliving matter interact.
- ◆ The earth is very old; geologic time is immense.
- ◆ Interpretation of rocks and fossils provides a record of the earth's history.
- ◆ Geologic time is subdivided on the basis of natural events in the evolution of life.

STUDENT OBJECTIVES

At the completion of this activity, the student should be able to:

- ◆ Describe the immensity of geologic time.
- ◆ Relate the relative ages of some geologic events.
- ◆ Identify his location in the scale of geologic time.

MATERIALS

Meterstick

Colored pencils

Adding machine tape (6 m strips for each group of 2)

VOCABULARY

Geologic time (you may wish to include the names of geologic eras)

PROCEDURES

1. Divide the students into groups of 2.
2. Each group should have a piece of adding machine tape 6 m long, a meterstick, and a pencil.

TABLE A–2   Approximate Age in the Earth's History

1. Earth's beginning	4.5 billion years ago
2. Oldest rocks	3.3 billion years ago
3. First plants (algae)	2.0 billion years ago
4. First animal (jellyfish)	1.2 billion years ago
5. Cambrian Period (abundant fossils)	600 million years ago
6. Ordovician Period	500 million years ago
7. Silurian Period	440 million years ago
8. Devonian Period	400 million years ago
9. Mississippian Period	350 million years ago
10. Pennsylvanian Period	305 million years ago
11. First reptiles	290 million years ago
12. Permian Period	270 million years ago
13. Triassic Period	225 million years ago
14. First mammals	200 million years ago
15. Jurassic Period	180 million years ago
16. First birds	160 million years ago
17. Cretaceious Period	135 million years ago
18. Paleocene	70 million years ago
19. Eocene	60 million years ago
20. Oligocene	40 million years ago
21. Miocene	25 million years ago
22. Pliocene	11 million years ago
23. First humanlike mammals	2 million years ago
24. Pleistocene	1 million years ago
25. Humans make tools	.5 million years ago
26. Last Ice Age	10,000 years ago
27. Calendars used in Egypt	4234 B.C.
28. Pythagoras proposes theory of mountain origin	580 B.C.
29. Eratosthenes measures Earth circumference	200 B.C.
30. Mount Vesuvius eruption at Pompeii	A.D. 79
31. First U.S. satellite	A.D. 1958
32. Mount St. Helens eruption	A.D. 1980
33. Asteroid	revealed A.D. 2000

3. Mark off a line about 5 cm from one end of the tape. Label this line NOW (today's date).
4. Using the meterstick and the ages given in Table A-2, plot the different times on the adding machine tape. Indicate that the students should start with the scale 1 m = 1 billion years.

   (NOTE: As the activity progresses the students will have difficulty with the scale of 1 m = 1 billion years. They will have to change the scale in order to include recent events on their tape. The frustration of this change and the realization of the difference between 1 year, 100 years, 1,000 years, 1 million years, and 1 billion years is as much a part of the lesson as the geological periods. Let students struggle with the new scale. It may help to point out that 1 mm equals a million years on a scale where 1 m equals a billion. Or, 1 billion = 1,000 million.)
5. After the activity, discuss the problem of scale and how the students resolved it. Usually they decide to change the scale for the last meter and make 1 m

equal to 1 million. Still, recent events are very hard to plot. Again, this is part of the realization of the immensity of geologic time.

EVALUATION TASKS

The students can use their tapes to explain some of the earth's history. Ask the students to explain why they had trouble plotting recent events. How did they overcome the problem?

EXTENDING THE ACTIVITY

The students can do a report on one geologic period.

Lab: Determining the Depth and Shape of the Ocean Floor

This activity, good for a ninth grade class in earth sciences, will give pupils an idea of a practical way to determine the contour of an inaccessible part of the earth's surface.

OBJECTIVE

To determine the contour of a plastic ocean floor model without seeing it, using other means of observation.

MATERIALS

1 box containing a sealed model of the ocean floor
1 metal probe
1 sheet of graph paper
5 sheets of white paper
Scissors and glue

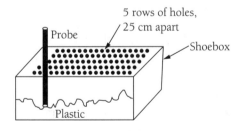

PROCEDURES

1. With all 5 sheets of white paper, measure down 10 cm from one long edge and fold the paper at your mark.
2. a. Place one sheet of the folded white paper on the long side of the box containing the holes in the lid, with the 10 cm section flush with the top edge of the box lid and the excess paper under the box.
   b. Slide the paper so it is also flush with the corner of the box in which the holes begin.
   c. Lightly tape the paper in place.
3. Notice the 5 rows of 10 holes in the lid of the box top.
   a. Starting with the row closest to the paper, place the metal probe in the hole until it hits something directly below. (Make sure with each probe that the rod stays straight up and down.)
   b. Note the depth of the rod with your finger.
   c. Withdraw the probe while keeping your finger in position and line it up on the paper 2.5 cm in from the corner of the box, and mark your depth of the probe on the paper by lining your finger up with the top edge of the paper. (Continue in the same way with the other 9 holes, each 2.5 cm apart.)
4. Once all the depths of a row are marked, take off the paper and connect your depth marks to make a contour for the ocean floor below that row.
5. Attach another sheet of paper in the same way as before and follow the same steps for the other 4 rows.
6. Once all 5 rows have been marked on their respective pieces of paper, cut out the contours on each of the 5 sheets of paper.
7. Now, on the flap of paper that was under the box, measure back 2 cm on each of the 5 sheets of paper and cut off the excess.
8. The rows on the box top are approximately 2 cm apart. To create your model, glue the 5 contours in order, 2 cm apart, onto the graph paper.
9. When finished, show the teacher and have your model checked against an actual plastic seafloor model to see how close you were.

GIFTED STUDENTS

Activities in Science for Gifted Students

Development of various talents among students requires providing for opportunities to practice these talents and abilities. Gifted students usually are quite self-reliant and resourceful. Following are several examples of activities a teacher can provide for gifted students to give practice in self-development.

To Develop Organizing Abilities:

◆ List the ways you can use a specific fact to help you.

To Develop Fluency and Flexibility:

◆ Have students discuss why being fluent and flexible would be an advantage for a scientist.

To Develop Use of Similes:

◆ Discuss a scientific field such as biology. Analyze science specialties in terms of similarities and differences.

To Develop Perception:

◆ Compare human sensations to animal sensations by analyzing the nervous system of each. Describe how signals are transmitted.

To Develop Abilities to Analyze Codes:

◆ Ask students to make a code. What codes are used in science? Why? Are there any international scientific codes?

To Develop Convergent Production:

◆ Have students bring in objects of nature such as leaves, pine needles, pebbles, shells, etc., and categorize them.

To Develop the Ability to See Trends:

◆ Write an invitation to inquiry.

To Develop the Ability to Give and Follow Directions:

◆ Have students write their own directions for doing an experiment:
  ◆ Plan a terrarium
  ◆ Plan a garden
  ◆ Plan a vegetable party
  ◆ Plan a unit of study on seeds
  ◆ Plan a landscaping project for trees, shrubs, and lawns

To Develop Divergent Production:

◆ Have one group give oral directions to another group for performing a science experiment, testing a theory, or showing a cause-and-effect relationship.

To Develop the Ability to Hypothesize:

◆ Answer the question, "What would happen if—?"

  ◆ There were no gravity?
  ◆ There was no action-reaction principle?
  ◆ Instead of discrete particles, matter was continuous?

To Develop the Ability to Compare and Contrast:

◆ Have students plan a zoo. What animals would be put together and why? What animals would definitely be kept apart and why?

To Develop the Ability to Make Decisions:

◆ Answer the questions:

  ◆ What was the world's most important discovery and why?
  ◆ What is the best way to test a principle? Give your reasons.
  ◆ Consider different climates. Which do you prefer and why? What type of soil and crops do you prefer? Why?

To Develop Creativity:

◆ Invent new words for common objects.
◆ Invent new names of plants and animals. Give reasons for your choices.

Challenges to Thinking for Gifted Students Discovery Demonstration: Bottle and Key—Put the Key in the Bottle

This activity will challenge the students to reason analytically by observing certain effects as the teacher manipulates the trapdoors on the box and asks the students to report what they see. Students will need to employ their previous knowledge of light, reflection, and vision to produce a hypothesis to explain what is happening. The activity is useful for grades 5–8, or above.

PROCEDURE

1. Prepare a box as shown in Figure A-7. The materials needed are listed below.
2. Demonstrate the device. Have each student look into the peephole while the teacher opens the trapdoors on the top alternately. Have students go back to their desks and try to draw a diagram of the outside and inside of the box, so that the images they see would be formed properly and in the right locations.

MATERIALS

2 shoe boxes, cut diagonally on one end at 45° angle

Piece of window glass, cut to fit the diagonal cut of the shoe boxes

Masking tape

Black rubber tape for light seal around trapdoors

Bottle of red-colored liquid

Red rubber stopper of same color as the liquid

25-watt light bulb mounted above trapdoor B

Small key suspended by tape from edge of opening A

DISCUSSION

1. What is the problem (or problems)? Is it a real problem to the students? What makes the device work? How is it built? What parts does it have?
2. What might be some explanations? It has mirrors. It is built like this (draw diagrams on the board). It has glass. (Try to select the most reasonable explanation after logical thinking.)

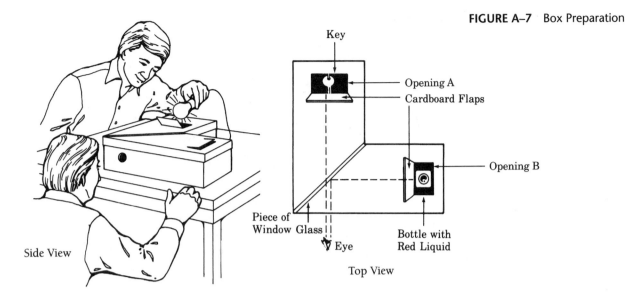

Key

Opening A
Cardboard Flaps

Opening B

Piece of
Window Glass

Eye

Bottle with
Red Liquid

Side View

Top View

3. We need more information. (Let one student look the device over carefully and report the data to the class. We need accurate observations here.)
4. Draw conclusions about construction of the device. Draw conclusions about its operation.
5. Test the conclusion with something else (piece of mirror, piece of window glass, piece of one-way glass).

EXPLANATION

The eye responds to the light having the strongest intensity.

OTHER APPLICATIONS:

- Why do you cup your hands around your eyes to look outside at night from a lighted room?
- Some sunglasses are partially silvered mirrors. Why?
- Some rearview mirrors on cars can be adjusted when the lights from a car behind cause too much glare.
- Using what you have learned from this demonstration, can you devise a way for such a mirror to work?

PHYSICS

Evaluation of Student Understanding of a Basic Physical Principle*

This activity should be preceded by a discussion of how a normal siphon works, and the role of atmospheric pressure and water pressure in its operation. With this understanding, students should have little difficulty in figuring out how the "Heron's Siphon" works. Conceptualizing

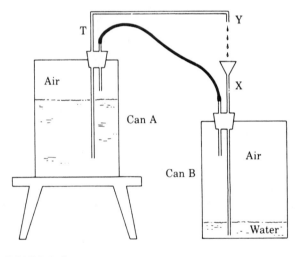

T   Y

Air

Can A   X

Can B   Air

Water

FIGURE A–8

how the interior of the two cans is constructed, and what principles are employed to make a *continuous siphon* operate, will provide a suitable challenge for grades 8–10.

Each student is to be given a mimeographed sheet containing the following information:

PROCEDURE FOR PART I

1. The demonstration material is set up as indicated in Figure A-8. A beaker of water is filled, and when the instructor is ready to start the demonstration,

*This demonstration and evaluation guide was prepared by Dr. Gene F. Craven, Department of Science Education, Oregon State University, Corvallis.

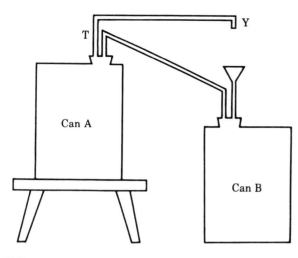

FIGURE A–9

he pours water in the thistle tube labeled X. The water will then flow from tube Y.

2. The students are next given a mimeographed sheet resembling Figure A-9 and asked to describe what they think the apparatus looks like within the can.
3. In a few sentences, students are to explain why the water started to run and why it continues.
4. They are also asked to write the basic principles involved in the demonstration and how long they think the water will continue to run.

PROCEDURE FOR PART II

After students have answered the questions, they are given a copy of Figure A-8 and asked to take the following test. They are to assume (1) that can A and can B are identical and (2) that all parts of the apparatus remain unchanged unless a change is specified in the statement they are considering.

DIRECTIONS

In the blank to the right of each statement, place a check mark in the column indicating the effect that the given change would have on the rate of flow.

How would the rate at which the liquid flows from the glass tube be affected if:

	No Flow	Slower	Same Rate	Faster
1. The top of the funnel was only one-half as far above can B as it was in the diagram?	___	___	___	___
2. Can B was lowered until the top of				

	No Flow	Slower	Same Rate	Faster
can B was level with the bottom of can A?				
3. The glass tube T was lengthened so that it extended twice as far above can A?	___	___	___	___
4. The funnel was replaced by a thistle tube extending to the same height above can B but having a bulb volume three times as great?	___	___	___	___

	No Flow	Slower	Same Rate	Faster
5. The tip Y of the glass tube from which the water is flowing was lengthened until it was level with the top of the funnel?	___	___	___	___
6. Kerosene, which is less dense than water, was used instead of water? (Neglect differences in viscosity and vapor pressure.)	___	___	___	___
7. The volume of can B was doubled while its height H remained constant?	___	___	___	___
8. The bottom of can A and can B were at the same level?	___	___	___	___
9. The funnel tube was cut off at X and did not extend below the stopper in can B?	___	___	___	___
10. The glass tube in can B to which the hose is fastened was extended to the bottom of the can?	___	___	___	___

PROCEDURE FOR PART III

After students have marked their papers, the instructor leads the class in discussing their answers. What types of process thinking are required in this type of demonstration?

Discovery Demonstration: Inquiring into Falling Bodies

The critical question in this activity is one that most students do not recognize: "Can objects in free fall under the force of gravity on the surface of the earth accelerate faster than 9.8 meters per second per second?" The answer to this question may come as a surprise to many students. Careful observation of the falling ball and stick, plus some critical reasoning, will bring forth the answer.

Construct the apparatus as shown in Figure A-10. Demonstrate it several times. Let several students try to demonstrate it.

MATERIALS

3 ft. piece of board (1 × 2 in.)
2 small plastic cups (1 in. diameter)
Bearing ball (1 in. diameter)

PROCEDURE

Put the ball in the cup at the end of the stick. Raise the stick to an angle of about 30 degrees. Drop the stick. The ball transfers to the other cup.

QUESTIONS

1. Why does the ball transfer to the other cup?
2. Is there a problem here? Is there anything out of the ordinary? Is there an easy answer?
3. How did the ball get out of the first cup? Don't the ball and cup fall at the same rate of acceleration?
4. Something must be accelerating faster than gravity here. What is it? How can this happen?
5. Suppose you tossed a tumbling board over a cliff. Would all parts of it be accelerating downward at the same rate? What part of it accelerates at 9.8 m/sec^2?
6. What part of the stick in this demonstration accelerates at 9.8 m/sec^2? Where is this point?

EXPLANATION

The cup at the end accelerates faster than 9.8 m/sec^2. The ball accelerates only at 9.8 m/sec^2. The point on the stick that accelerates at 9.8 m/sec^2 is the "center of percussion," which is two-thirds of the way from the pivot end to the end with the cup.

1. What parts of the inquiry demonstration represented problem identification?
2. What part involved making hypotheses?
3. What part represented data gathering?
4. What part was concerned with drawing conclusions

How Long Can You Boil Water in a Paper Cup?

The very question itself may raise the specter of absurdity, especially when pupils realize the demonstration is going to be done with the cup of water over an open flame! After all, doesn't paper burn when it is exposed to an open flame? This activity will generate interest and wonderment among middle school children as well as high school students.

Teacher's note: this is a junior high-level inquiry lesson. Sections I through III are for the teachers only, and Sections IV and V are to be duplicated for the student.

I. CONCEPTS

◆ A flame is a source of radiant heat.
◆ Water, when heated, expands and gives off water vapor.
◆ Water can absorb a considerable amount of heat.
◆ Before a substance will burn, its kindling temperature must be reached.
◆ The kindling temperature is the temperature at which a substance will first start to burn.

FIGURE A–10

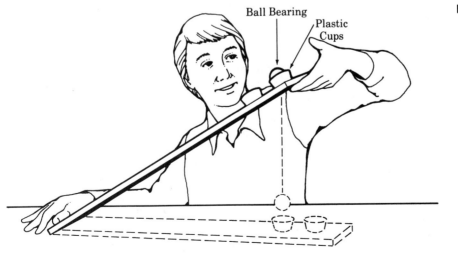

Ball Bearing
Plastic Cups

II. MATERIALS

Nonwaxed paper cup
Bunsen burner, propane torch, or alcohol burner
Ring stand
Ring clamp
Wire screen

III. PRELABORATORY DISCUSSION

Processes

Hypothesizing	1. What do you think will happen to a paper cup when you try to boil water in it?
Hypothesizing	2. What do you think will happen first, the water boiling or the cup burning?
Hypothesizing	3. How do you think you could get a paper cup containing water to burn?
Designing an investigation	4. What should you do to find out?

IV. PUPIL DISCOVERY ACTIVITY

Processes

Collecting materials	1. Obtain the following equipment: A nonwaxed paper cup, torch or burner, ring stand, ring clamp, and screen.
Designing an investigation	2. How could you use this equipment to find out whether you can boil water in a paper cup?

Teacher's note: Draw a diagram on the chalkboard showing a paper cup sitting on a wire screen on a ring stand placed over a burner. The students should place the paper cup, containing not more than 5 cm³ of water, on the wire screen and heat it from below with the burner.

Following directions	3. If you can think of no other ways to test your hypothesis, set up the equipment as indicated by your teacher's diagram.

Observing	4. What happens when you try to heat the water in the cup?
Inferring	5. What do you think the ring clamp and screen do to the heat from the flame?
Inferring	6. What can you say about the heat energy entering and leaving the water as you try to heat it to the boiling point?
	7. Why does the water level in the cup change?
	8. What effect does water in the cup have on the cup's temperature as it is being heated?
	9. Keep heating the cup until all the water is evaporated. Record your observations and conclusions.

V. OPEN-ENDED QUESTIONS

Processes

Hypothesizing	1. If you took paper, cloth, wood, and charcoal and heated them, in what order would they start to burn? Why?
Criticizing	2. If you were going to repeat the preceding experiment, what would you do to obtain better data?
Hypothesizing	3. How would the results be affected if you used a styrofoam cup?
Hypothesizing	4. How would varying the amount of heat energy applied to the cup change the results?
Hypothesizing	5. How would the results vary if there were a different liquid in the cup such as cola, syrup, etc.?
Hypothesizing	6. In what way would the results vary if the cup were supported by a ring clamp and screen?
Designing an investigation	7. What other experiments does this investigation suggest?

PROBLEM SOLVING

Teaching Inquiry Skills

Simple equipment is used in this activity to give pupils practice in observation, measurement, record keeping, graphing, and drawing conclusions. You can extend the activity by duplicating the experiment with rubber bands, but be prepared for a totally different result and a different set of conclusions from those obtained with springs. The activity is good for junior high or middle school classes.

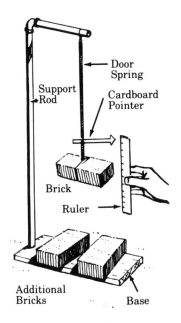

FIGURE A–11   Demonstration Setup

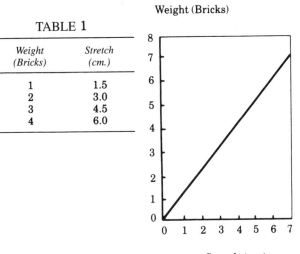

TABLE 1	
Weight (Bricks)	*Stretch (cm.)*
1	1.5
2	3.0
3	4.5
4	6.0

FIGURE A–12   Results Recorded in Table and Graph Form

STUDENT OBJECTIVES

To gain practice in the skills of (1) measurement, (2) record keeping, and (3) graphing

SUBJECT

Forces produced by springs

PROBLEM

How does the length of spring depend on the force exerted on it?

PROCEDURE

Work in pairs, or do as a student demonstration with all students recording the data and drawing the graph. Set up the spring and weights as shown in Figure A-11. Add weights one at a time and check the readings each time.

Record the results as shown in Figure A-12. Graph the results as shown.

MATERIALS

>   Door springs
>   Several bricks
>   Ruler
>   String

CONCLUSION

The change in length of a spring is directly proportional to the change in the force exerted on it—if the spring is not stretched beyond its elastic limit.

PROBABLE SKILLS DEVELOPED

1. Setup and adjustment of apparatus (manipulative)

2. Observation of initial conditions and changes due to experimental factors (acquisitive)
3. Recording of data (organizational)
4. Graphing and analysis of data (organizational and communicative)
5. Drawing conclusions (organizational)

EVALUATION

Can the student:

1. Set up the apparatus for use?
2. Devise a plan of procedure?
3. Read a scale to the limits of its accuracy?
4. Record data in a tabular form?
5. Plot a graph?
6. Interpret a graph?
7. Draw conclusions from the experiment?
8. Recognize sources of error?
9. Report the results lucidly?

Small-Group Problem Solving

Research has shown that having junior high students work in small groups is a very effective method of learning in science. The interactions that occur in small groups, questioning and probing, as well as sharing of knowledge, help to solve problems better than working alone. In addition, shy pupils may be encouraged to participate and develop sharing skills that they might not otherwise accomplish. The setting is less threatening, and the topics may be more easily controlled. Some guidelines for this variation of the discussion method follow:

1. Form groups of 3–5 persons
2. Present a problem. (For example, how could you determine what factors control the rate of swing

[vibration] of a pendulum?) What different factors would you try? What measurement tools would you need?

   a. Demonstration (Conduct a silent or oral demonstration using different lengths, weights of bob, amplitude of swing, heights above the ground, etc. Have students keep careful notes of what changes each new factor produced. Discuss these factors and experimental conditions.

   b. Story (find information and relate the story of how Galileo observed a swinging chandelier in a cathedral and used it to get some impression of time elapsed for each swing.)

   c. Social issue (Discuss what common misconceptions with respect to swinging pendulums are held by students and adults. How could these misconceptions be aired and compared with what scientists have found with respect to vibrating pendulums?)

   d. Dilemma

3. Each group appoints a spokesperson.
4. Allow discussion to continue 5–10 minutes.
   a. Clarify the problem
   b. Suggest hypotheses for solution
   c. Discuss hypotheses
   d. Obtain consensus in the group
   e. Draw conclusions
5. Assemble as a large group.
6. Spokespeople present the group conclusions.
7. Discuss as a large group using guidelines discussed earlier.

SCIENCE FAIR PROJECTS

Finding Local Variations in Relative Humidity

This is a long-term project (perhaps a month in length) that makes a good science fair project. The daily fluctuations in relative humidity may not be common knowledge to students. The representation of relative humidity in local areas by use of isolines is good experience for those interested in going on to study meteorology, where such representations are used frequently to display barometric pressures, temperature distributions, and other weather factors.

MATERIALS

Materials for sling psychrometer:

   2 Fahrenheit thermometers (210° to 1110° F range)
   Plywood block, 10 in. by 4 in. by 1/2 in.
   6 small screws, 1/2 in. long
   Wooden dowel, 1 in. diameter, 6 in. length
   2 small washers
   1 screw, 2 in. long
   Small square of cheesecloth, 2 in. by 2 in.

If you construct the sling psychrometer described in the experiment on measuring cloud height later in this section, you will have a useful device for measuring relative humidity. If you have access to a varied topography—hills, a body of water, perhaps—you have all the raw materials for an interesting investigation in relative humidity variations. Relative humidity can be measured accurately by use of the sling psychrometer.

To study relative humidity systematically, obtain a map of the area you wish to study—or draw your own simple map—and mark on it the specific locations you can reach conveniently on a regular basis. Select a variety of sites such as a hilltop, the shore of a small body of water, a wooded area, a grassy field, a playground, an asphalt parking lot—whatever locations offer as much variety in topography, exposure, and nearness to water as possible within a workable area.

Make your observations using the sling psychrometer on a regular basis, such as at 8:00 a.m., 12:00 noon, 4:00 p.m., and 8:00 p.m., every day in each of the selected locations. Take all readings in the shade to avoid the effects of direct sunlight on the psychrometer. Note the exact time for each observation, and repeat the observations at the same times for at least 10 days. At each observation, record the following information on a data sheet: location, time, date, wet-bulb degrees in Fahrenheit, dry-bulb degrees in Fahrenheit, relative humidity percent, wind direction, wind speed (est. mph), cloud cover (0 to .9), comments (precipitation, etc.).

Wind speed can be estimated accurately enough by using the Beaufort Wind Scale (Table A-3).

When you have obtained data for the period of study, you can tabulate it in a variety of ways for analysis. For example, you might wish to find the average relative humidity at each location at the time of observation. Plotting these data on a graph of relative humidity versus time of day will show the daily changes that occur on a regular basis. Such a graph might look like the one in Figure A-13. Or you might want to see how much fluctuation occurs in the relative humidity at a particular location over the period studied.

TABLE A–3 The Beaufort Scale of Wind Force with Specifications and Velocity Equivalents

			Velocity	
Beaufort Number	General Description	Specifications	Meters per Sec.	Miles per Hour
0	Calm	Smoke rises vertically	Under 0.6	Under 1
1	Light air	Wind direction shown by smoke drift but not by vanes	0.6–0.7	1–3
2	Slight	Wind felt on face; leaves rustle; ordinary vane moved by wind	0.8–3.3	4–7
3	Gentle breeze	Leaves and twigs in constant motion; wind extends light flag	3.4–5.2	8–11
4	Moderate breeze	Dust, loose paper, and small branches are moved	5.3–7.4	12–16
5	Fresh breeze	Small trees in leaf begin to sway	7.5–9.8	17–22
6	Strong breeze	Large branches in motion; whistling in wires	9.9–12.42	23–27
7	Moderate gale	Whole trees in motion	12.5–15.2	28–34
8	Fresh gale	Twigs broken off trees; progress generally impeded	15.3–18.2	35–41
9	Strong gale	Slight structural damage occurs; chimney damage	18.3–21.5	42–48
10	Whole gale	Trees uprooted; considerable structural damage	21.6–25.4	49–56
11	Storm	Very rarely experienced; widespread damage	25.5–29.0	57–67
12	Hurricane		Above 29.0	Above 67

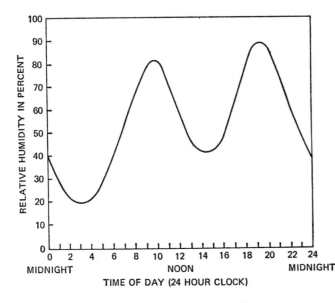

FIGURE A–13 Graph Showing Possible Daily Fluctuations in Relative Humidity

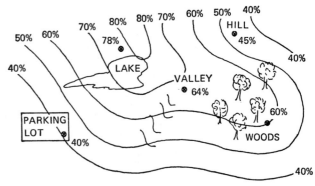

FIGURE A–14 Map Showing Lines of Equal Relative Humidity over Varied Terrain

After you have obtained the average relative humidity at each location, plot the information on a detailed map of the area, recording the average values obtained at each of the observation points. Draw lines of equal relative humidity on the map, as shown in Figure A-14, positioning them so the individual data points fit the lines. What can you learn from such a map? Can you give any reasons for the variations in relative humidity from point to point?

Study the data obtained with respect to other factors recorded at each observation, such as cloud cover, wind speed and direction, and precipitation. Can you discover any relationships between these factors and the relative humidity? For example, in Figure A-14, there is quite a difference in the relative humidity between one end of the lake and the other—from 50 percent to 80 percent. By comparing the map with a hypothetical data sheet, it might become apparent that the wind direction at the time of observation was from west to east. The air would thus pick up moisture and become more humid as it passed over the surface of the lake, explaining why the relative humidity is so much higher at the other end of the lake. Through careful coordination of all information on the contour maps and data sheets, try to obtain as much information as possible about variations in relative humidity and their causes.

Relative humidity, percent—Fahrenheit temperatures
[Pressure = 30.0 inches]

Air temperature t	Depression of wet-bulb thermometer $(t - t')$																				
	0.5	1.0	1.5	2.0	2.5	3.0	3.5	4.0	4.5	5.0	5.5	6.0	6.5	7.0	7.5	8.0	8.5	9.0	9.5	10.0	10.5
20	92	85	77	70	62	55	48	40	33	26	19	12	5								
21	92	85	78	71	63	56	49	42	35	28	21	15	8	1							
22	93	86	78	71	65	58	51	44	37	31	24	17	11	4							
23	93	86	79	72	66	59	52	46	39	33	26	20	14	7	1						
24	93	87	80	73	67	60	54	47	41	35	29	22	16	10	4						
25	94	87	81	74	68	62	55	49	43	37	31	25	19	13	7	1					
26	94	87	81	75	69	63	57	51	45	39	33	27	21	16	10	4					
27	94	88	82	76	70	64	58	52	47	41	35	29	24	18	13	7	2				
28	94	88	82	76	71	65	59	54	48	43	37	32	26	21	15	10	5				
29	94	88	83	77	72	66	60	55	50	44	39	34	28	23	18	13	8	3			
30	94	89	83	78	73	67	62	56	51	46	41	36	31	26	21	16	11	6	1		
31	94	89	84	78	73	68	63	58	52	47	42	37	33	28	23	18	13	8	4		
32	95	89	84	79	74	69	64	59	54	49	44	39	35	30	25	20	16	11	7	2	
33	95	90	85	80	75	70	65	60	56	51	46	41	37	32	27	23	18	14	9	5	0
34	95	90	86	81	76	71	66	62	57	52	48	43	38	34	29	25	21	16	12	8	3
35	95	91	86	81	77	72	67	63	58	54	49	45	40	36	32	27	23	19	14	10	6
36	95	91	86	82	77	73	68	64	60	55	51	46	42	38	34	29	25	21	17	13	9
37	95	91	87	83	78	74	69	65	61	57	53	48	44	40	36	31	27	23	19	15	11
38	96	91	87	83	79	75	70	66	62	58	54	50	46	42	37	33	29	25	21	17	14
39	96	92	87	83	79	75	71	67	63	59	55	51	47	43	39	35	31	27	24	20	16
40	96	92	87	83	79	75	71	68	64	60	56	52	48	45	41	37	33	29	26	22	18
41	96	92	88	84	80	76	72	69	65	61	57	54	50	46	42	39	35	31	28	24	20
42	96	92	88	85	81	77	73	69	65	62	58	55	51	47	44	40	36	33	30	26	23
43	96	92	88	85	81	77	73	70	66	63	59	55	52	48	45	42	38	35	31	28	25
44	96	93	89	85	81	78	74	71	67	63	60	56	53	49	46	43	39	36	33	30	26
45	96	93	89	86	82	78	74	71	67	64	61	57	54	51	47	44	41	38	34	31	28
46	96	93	89	86	82	79	75	72	68	65	61	58	55	52	48	45	42	39	35	32	29
47	96	93	89	86	82	79	75	72	69	66	62	59	56	53	49	46	43	40	37	34	31
48	96	93	90	86	83	79	76	73	69	66	63	60	57	54	50	47	44	41	38	35	32
49	96	93	90	86	83	80	76	73	70	67	64	61	57	54	51	48	45	42	39	36	34
50	96	93	90	87	83	80	77	74	71	67	64	61	58	55	52	49	46	43	41	38	35
51	97	94	90	87	84	81	78	75	71	68	65	62	59	56	53	50	47	45	42	39	36
52	97	94	90	87	84	81	78	75	72	69	66	63	60	57	54	51	49	46	43	40	37
53	97	94	90	87	84	81	78	75	72	69	66	63	61	58	55	52	50	47	44	41	39
54	97	94	91	88	85	82	79	76	73	70	67	64	61	59	56	53	50	48	45	42	40
55	97	94	91	88	85	82	79	76	73	70	68	65	62	59	57	54	51	49	46	43	41
56	97	94	91	88	85	82	79	76	73	71	68	65	63	60	57	55	52	50	47	44	42
57	97	94	91	88	85	82	80	77	74	71	69	66	63	61	58	55	53	50	48	45	43
58	97	94	91	88	85	83	80	77	74	72	69	66	64	61	59	56	54	51	49	46	44
59	97	94	91	89	86	83	80	78	75	72	70	67	65	62	59	57	55	52	49	47	45
60	97	94	91	89	86	83	81	78	75	73	70	68	65	63	60	58	55	53	50	48	46
61	97	94	92	89	86	84	81	78	76	73	71	68	65	63	61	58	56	54	51	49	47
62	97	94	92	89	86	84	81	79	76	74	71	69	66	64	61	59	57	54	52	50	47
63	97	95	92	89	87	84	82	79	77	74	71	69	67	64	62	60	57	55	53	50	48
64	97	95	92	90	87	84	82	79	77	74	72	70	67	65	63	60	58	56	53	51	49
65	97	95	92	90	87	85	82	80	77	75	72	70	68	66	63	61	59	56	54	52	50
66	97	95	92	90	87	85	82	80	78	75	73	71	68	66	64	61	59	57	55	53	51
67	97	95	92	90	87	85	83	80	78	75	73	71	69	66	64	62	60	58	56	53	51
68	97	95	92	90	88	85	83	80	78	76	74	71	69	67	65	62	60	58	56	54	52
69	97	95	93	90	88	85	83	81	79	76	74	72	70	67	65	63	61	59	57	55	53
70	98	95	93	90	88	86	83	81	79	77	74	72	70	68	66	64	61	59	57	55	53
71	98	95	93	90	88	86	84	81	79	77	75	72	70	68	66	64	62	60	58	56	54
72	98	95	93	91	88	86	84	82	79	77	75	73	71	69	67	65	63	61	59	57	55
73	98	95	93	91	88	86	84	82	80	78	75	73	71	69	67	65	63	61	59	57	55
74	98	95	93	91	89	86	84	82	80	78	76	74	71	69	67	65	63	61	60	58	56
75	98	96	93	91	89	86	84	82	80	78	76	74	72	70	68	66	64	62	60	58	56
76	98	96	93	91	89	87	84	82	80	78	76	74	72	70	68	66	64	62	61	59	57
77	98	96	93	91	89	87	85	83	81	79	77	74	72	71	69	67	65	63	61	59	57
78	98	96	93	91	89	87	85	83	81	79	77	75	73	71	69	67	65	63	62	60	58
79	98	96	93	91	89	87	85	83	81	79	77	75	73	71	69	68	66	64	62	60	58
80	98	96	94	91	89	87	85	83	81	79	77	75	74	72	70	68	66	64	62	61	59

Measuring Cloud Direction and Speed

The level of mathematics required in this activity is within the capabilities of junior high school students or tenth grade physical science students. As a science fair project, the activity will require several steps in the construction of a simple nephoscope for viewing movement of low clouds, and several measurements that can provide the necessary data to calculate cloud heights by triangulation methods. The time requirement for this project is about two or three weeks.

MATERIALS

Small table or stool, 18–24 in. high

Magnetic compass

Circular mirror, 6 in. in diameter

Plywood, 9 in. by 9 in. by 3/4 in.

3 screws, 2 in. long

Wooden dowel, 1/4 in. by 3 in.

Paper circle, 9 in. in diameter.

A weather observer is interested in cloud direction and speed because of the information they give him about winds aloft. And frequently this information is rather surprising. For example, would you expect winds a thousand feet above the ground to be exactly opposite in direction and at twice the speed of those at the ground? In fact, the average velocity of the wind does increase with height above the ground. This effect is most noticeable in the first 100 ft., the velocity generally doubling between a height of 1 1/2 ft. and 33 ft., and increasing an additional 20 percent to a height of 100 ft. Such a large variation is mainly due to the reduction in frictional *drag* with increased height above the ground. Along with the increased velocity, there is usually a decrease in turbulence also, although some surface eddies can affect the air several thousands of feet above the ground, particularly in mountainous areas.

On a day when noticeable winds are present at the ground, pay particular attention to their speed and direction. Then observe the clouds drifting above you. Are they traveling in the same direction as the winds at the ground? How can you obtain a reasonably accurate measurement of their direction and speed?

An instrument used for such measurements is called a *nephoscope*. You can construct a simple version following the directions given here. As you will see, the formula for calculating speed includes cloud height. If you have become proficient in the use of the height measurer or sling psychrometer, add the nephoscope to your bag of equipment to make a complete analysis.

Obtain a circular mirror about 6 in. in diameter. Mount it on a flat piece of plywood about 9 in. in diameter, or 9 in. square if you don't have a circular piece of wood. Glue a paper circle around the mirror, flat on the plywood surface. The circle should have a diameter of 7 1/2 in. and should be carefully marked off into 360 degrees. In other words, the calibrated paper border should be about 1 1/2 in. wide.

Glue or screw a sighting point, made of a 1/4 in. dowel, 3 in. long, to the plywood at the mirror's edge, as shown in Figure A-15. Mark with a felt-tip pen or lipstick a small dot in the center of the mirror. Finally, screw three 1/4 in. screws at three points around the plywood border. These should be long enough to extend through the base and will be used as leveling devices when you are ready to work.

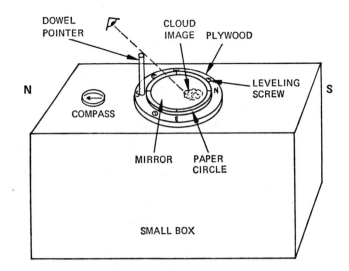

FIGURE A–15 Nephoscope Construction

Set up the nephoscope outside on a box on reasonably level ground, and, using a small pocket compass, orient the instrument so that south on the paper circle is pointing north (see Figure A-15). Bring the nephoscope to approximate level by the three adjusting screws.

To determine cloud direction, locate a cloud image at the dot in the center of the mirror. Continue watching the cloud image by sighting over the sighting point, and note the angle at which the image disappears from the edge of the mirror. This represents the wind direction at the height of the cloud observed.

To determine speed, you'll need a stopwatch or a friend who has a watch with a second hand who will do the timing as you watch the image. Without either, you can always count off seconds. Time the movement of the image from the center dot to disappearance at the mirror's edge. The formula for the calculation of cloud speed is

$$Speed = \frac{cloud\ height\ (ft.)\ \times\ mirror\ radius\ (in.)}{height\ of\ dowel\ (in.)\ \times\ time\ (sec.)}$$

NOTE: If the mirror radius and dowel height are the same, the equation reduces to

$$Speed = \frac{cloud\ height\ (ft.)}{time\ (sec.)}$$

Another way of applying the same technique to determine the speed and direction of winds at cloud level is called the *direct vision nephoscope*. In this case, you—the observer—move to keep the cloud sighted relative to a fixed point. Broken clouds at night may be sighted against the stars or moon; in the daytime, use a flagpole, light pole, or a prominent part of a building. To determine cloud direction alone, simply keep the eye stationary and watch the cloud with reference to the flagpole, or whatever you are using as your fixed point. To measure cloud velocity, it will be necessary to ascertain the amount of time the cloud took to move through a certain angle with reference to the fixed point. Keeping the cloud sighted over the flagpole, move your position so as to keep a point on the cloud in line with the top of the pole. Drop a marker at the beginning of the observation and another at the end of a known time interval. Measure the distance you have moved during the observation, and note the exact direction of movement. You will be moving in a direction opposite to that of the cloud, and you will be forming two similar triangles of which the angle points are eye level (at positions beginning and end) and pole, and cloud (at positions beginning and end) and pole (see Figure A-16). Therefore,

$$\frac{D}{H} = \frac{d}{h}$$

The speed of movement of the cloud is $V = D/t$. Substituting this in the proportion, we get

$$V = \frac{dH}{ht}$$

where d is the distance moved by the observer in feet,
h is the height in feet of the pole (measured or estimated) from above the observer's eye level,

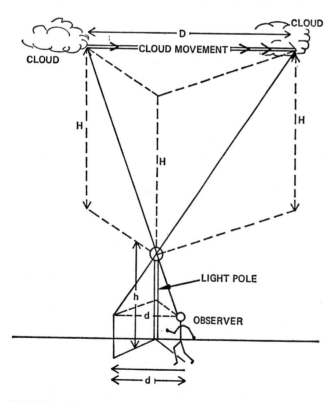

FIGURE A–16   Measurements Needed in Direct Vision Nephoscope

t is the time in seconds, and

H is the height of the clouds being measured from the top of the light pole. Because the height of the light pole is extremely small in comparison with the height of the clouds being measured, it is satisfactory to call H the height of the clouds above the ground.

Using your estimation of cloud height from the measuring techniques described in the previous section, feed your data into the formula and come up with how fast the winds at cloud level are traveling.

Some questions you might try to answer as you take measurements of speed and direction on moving clouds are:

1. Which types of clouds seem to move faster, high clouds or low clouds?
2. Can you use the nephoscope methods to obtain the rate of growth of a cumulonimbus cloud? Try it.
3. Determine the cloud direction and speed for two levels of clouds on the same day, and compute the wind shear between the two levels. Wind shear is the variation of wind speed and direction over a given vertical distance. If, for example, the lower layer of clouds had a velocity of 20 feet per second (fps) from the west, and the upper layer of clouds (say, 5,000 ft. higher) had a velocity of 60 fps from the northwest, the wind shear could be described as 60 fps − 20 fps = 40 fps per 5,000 ft., or 8 fps per 1,000 ft., clockwise, between the lower and the upper layers of clouds. In this case, wind shear is due to the shifts in wind direction from west to northwest (clockwise), with the vertical ascent from the lower level to the upper level.
4. Observe some lenticularis clouds, such as stratocumulus lenticularis, or altocumulus lenticularis, and compute their height, speed, and direction of movement. How does the speed differ from ordinary stratocumulus or altocumulus clouds present on the same day? The lenticularis cloud is caused when air is set into vertical oscillatory motion and travels in a series of waves. If conditions are right, condensation of water vapor occurs on the rising portion of the wave, and re-evaporation occurs on the falling portion of the wave (Figure A-17). As a result, a lenticular cloud may appear to remain stationary in the sky for a period of several hours. Lenticular clouds are not uncommon in mountainous areas, where the wind currents over the mountaintops are set into wavy motion. The clouds have a distinctive appearance, resembling flat wafers or thin lenses. Frequently, several may be seen at one time, extending in a line leeward from the mountain range, or even stacked vertically, one above the other.

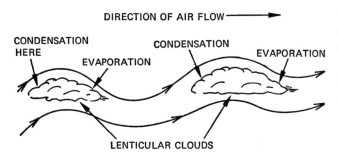

FIGURE A–17 Diagram Showing Formation of Lenticular Clouds

MATHEMATICS

Population Growth and Energy Usage

Students must absorb the ideas of population growth and the accompanying effects on life that accompany it. Important in this consideration is an understanding of the mathematical concept of exponential growth and doubling time. For example, if the rate of increase in a particular dynamic, such as rate of inflation, is 5% per year, the doubling time is 14 years. This means that something that costs $100 in 1996, an inflation rate of 5% will cost $200 in the year 2010. If the inflation rate is 7%, the doubling time is 10 years, so the item will double in cost by 2006. This is a fundamental relationship and is unaffected by other factors. To obtain the number of years for a particular item to double in value or cost, divide 70 by the rate of inflation during that period. For example, if the rate of inflation is just 3%, 70 divided by 3 equals 23.3 years. Or if the rate of inflation is 10%, the doubling time is 70 divided by 10, or 7 years.

To apply this concept to population growth, let us say the rate of population growth in the United States is 1.5% per year. Dividing 70 by 1.5 gives 46.7 years. That is the same as saying that the population of the United States, if determined to be 250 million persons in the year 2000, will have doubled to 500 million persons by 2047, which is well within the projected life span of persons born in 2000. Assuming the rate of population growth in the United States continues at 1.5% per year during their long lifetime, by the time these persons have reached the age of 94, a very real possibility considering the increasing life spans of humans in the United States, the population of the United States will be one billion persons! (The present rate of population growth in the United States is close to 1.5% per year)

Because the rate of growth of energy consumption is closely related to the rate of population growth, consider what will be the situation with respect to oil resources, coal resources, electrical demands, food consumption, and living space in the year 2094? Under the most liberal projections, it is believed we have about a 30-year supply of oil remaining in the United States and perhaps a 50-year supply of oil worldwide.

To bring home the seriousness of the problems, calculate the population of the United States after just two generations for children born in 2000 (Estimated time for these children to grow to adulthood, have children, and live to see their first born grandchildren might be 50 years.)

Let us suppose by some fortunate combination of factors, the rate of population growth in the United States decreases to just 1% per year. How would this change the answer to the previous question?

What do you consider to be viable alternatives to the dismal projections of the previous paragraphs?

Stimulating Mathematics Usage in Science Classes

This activity requires pupils to observe an action, gather data, draw a graph, analyze the data, and produce a mathematical expression that can be used to make a prediction of the time required to empty a water-filled can of known volume. The activity is suitable for middle school or junior high students.

The laboratory provides the opportunity for many data-gathering problems. The student may practice measuring, keeping records, and graphing. Analysis of experiments gives additional practice in using mathematics. The PSSC exercise entitled Analysis of an Experiment is an example. The data given in the exercise show a record of the time required to empty a can of water through a hole punched in the bottom.

Students are told to plot graphs of the data to analyze the relationships between emptying times and two other variables, diameter of the hold (d) and height of water in the can (h). Types of graphs suggested are one showing time versus diameter for a constant height and one showing time versus square of diameter. Graphs for different heights are also suggested. Typical questions asked in this exercise are:

1. From your curve, how accurately can you predict the time it would take to empty the same container if the diameter of the opening was 4 cm? 8 cm?
2. Can you write the algebraic relation between t and d for the particular height of water used?
3. Can you find the general expression for time of flow as a function of both h and d?[*]

---

[*]Physical Science Study Committee, *Laboratory Guide for Physics* (Boston: D.C. Heath).

This exercise illustrates clearly how using mathematics gives a student practice in analyzing the results of an experiment and demonstrates the integral nature of mathematics in science.

Senior high school science students should learn the limitations of measurement, the sources of quantitative errors, and standards of accuracy. How accurate is a meterstick? To how many significant figures can a measurement be made? Of what value are estimated units?

How accurate is a volume computation made from linear measurements that have estimated units? What are possible sources of error in an experiment? To what degree of precision are certain measurements made? How does one express the degree of precision in recording data?

Knowledge of significant figures is particularly important in chemistry and physics, where physical measurements are made frequently in laboratory experiments.

Mathematics in Science: How Will Specific Gravity Help to Identify Minerals?

Using specific gravity is a common method of identifying minerals and emphasizes the application of a simple procedure for determining specific gravity. Since the specific gravity of pure substances is a property of the material, this activity makes an excellent method of mineral identification in an earth science class. This activity is suitable for ninth or tenth grade students.

1. Obtain the following materials: Spring balance, string, can or jar of water, small iron object, small aluminum object, piece of glass, collection of minerals
2. Discussion:
   a. State the following: "Mary had a rock that weighed different amounts at different times. The rock has not changed in any way."
   b. What ideas do you have about how this may happen?
   c. Have you ever picked up a large rock under water and then carried it out of the water? Was it heavier in water or out of water?
   d. How could we make sure of our answer?
3. Suspend a rock on a spring balance with a length of string. Record its weight. Immerse the rock in water. Record its weight under water. How much more or less does it weigh now?
4. Specific gravity is a way to help identify minerals. Specific gravity is found by comparing the weight of a mineral in air to the amount of weight the mineral loses in water. Specific gravity may be found as illustrated in the following example:

Weight of rock in air	35g
Weight of rock in water	15g (subtract)
Loss of weight in water	20g

TEACHER INFORMATION
The following table lists average specific gravities for common minerals.

Material	Average Specific Gravity
Pyrite	5.0
Halite	2.2 (dissolves in water)
Fluorite	3.2
Quartz	2.7
Calcite	2.7
Graphite	2.3
Galena	7.5
Hematite	5.3
Magnetite	5.2
Limonite	4.3
Talc	2.7
Mica	2.8
Gypsum	2.3
Glass	2.13–2.99
Feldspar (orthoclase)	2.6
Feldspar (plagioclase)	2.7

Weight of rock in air	35g
Weight of rock in water	15 g (subtract)
Loss off of weight in water	20g
Loss of weight in water	Specific gravity / Weight of rock in air

```
      1.75
20)35.00
   20
   150
   140
    100
    100
```

The specific gravity of the rock is 1.75. How can specific gravity be used to identify minerals?

5. What is the specific gravity of the rock you weighed in and out of water? Record your answer and show how you obtained it.
6. Obtain pieces of iron, aluminum, glass, and other objects. Using the method above, find their specific gravities. Compare your results with those of your classmates.
7. Make a list of the minerals in your collection and find the specific gravity of each. Record the specific gravity of each in a column beside the name of the mineral.

B

DAILY LESSON PLANS

DAILY LESSON PLAN 1

Physical Science—Instructional Model

TOPIC: AIR IN MOTION

Engagement:

What is air in motion called? Wind? Storm? Gust? Jet?

How do we know air has mass? (It exerts force when moving.)

Which air has more pressure—still or moving air? (Still!)

Are you surprised? How can we find out?

Exploration:

Blow between two flat sheets of paper. What happens?

Where is the air still? Where is the air moving?

Where is the air pressure greater? How do you know?

Place a fan so it blows upward. Put a balloon above the fan. What does it do? Why does it stay above the fan and not fall off to the side?

Where is the air moving? Where is the air still?

Where is the air pressure smaller? Where is it greater?

Put a pingpong ball in a funnel. Try to blow it out.

Put the pingpong ball under the funnel. Try to blow it out. What happens?

Where is the air moving fastest? Where is the air still?

Wind a thread around a tissue roll. Fasten a rubber band to the end of the string. Snap the tissue roll forward. What does it do? Try different positions when you snap the roll (e.g., under, over, sideways).

Where is the air still? Where is it moving faster?

Explanation:

You have demonstrated Bernoulli's principle—whenever the speed of a moving fluid is increased, its pressure is decreased.

(Teacher—simulate Bernoulii's principle by using chalkboard and desk in front. Walk slowly in the space between board and desk—marks close together. Walk fast—chalk marks far apart).

Elaboration:

Two buses meeting one another will notice an inward sway when they pass. The faster air is between the buses and has less pressure than the air on the outside.

Two canoes floating side by side will tend to come together. Why?

Can you think of any other examples?

Evaluation:

Could you explain Bernoulli's principle to someone else?

If you blow between three sheets of paper, what happens?

Two apples are hung on strings next to each other. If you put a vacuum cleaner hose between them, what happens?

Two water faucets next to each other have water running from them. What happens to the streams of water?

DAILY LESSON PLAN 2

Physical Science—Instructional Model

TOPIC: MAGNETISM

Engagement:

What is a magnet?

What is a magnet used for?

Does a magnet pull or push?

What kinds of materials does a magnet pull or push on?

Exploration:

Tie a thread to a paper clip.

Tape one end of the thread to your desk or table top.

Lay a small magnet near the end of the paper clip without touching the paper clip.

What kind of reaction does the paper clip show?

Slowly raise the magnet up from the table. Do not let the magnet touch the paper clip. What does the paper clip do?

Continue raising the magnet until it is straight above the table. What does the paper clip do?

Measure the distance from the magnet to the paper clip in centimeters. What is the greatest distance you can raise the magnet off the table before the paper clip falls?

Have a contest with your classmate to see who can get the greatest distance.

Use a different magnet and do the experiment again.

Explanation:

The force of magnetism extends into the space around the magnet.

It is not necessary to touch the magnet to feel this force.

Not all metals are magnetic. The most powerful magnetic metals are iron, nickel, and cobalt. There are also some metal alloys that are magnetic.

Elaboration:

Make a written record of what you learned about magnets.

The earth is a magnet.

All magnets have poles, where the magnetic force is concentrated. These are called north-seeking and south-seeking poles.

The north-seeking pole of the earth is near Hudson Bay.

The south-seeking pole is in the Antarctic.

A compass is a small magnet mounted so it can turn. Similar poles repel; unlike poles attract each other.

Evaluation:

Explain to a classmate what you have learned about magnets.

DAILY LESSON PLAN 3

Physical Science—Instructional Model

TOPIC: BROWNIAN MOTION

Engagement:

What are molecules? (Smallest particles of elements or compounds that retain the characteristics of the material.)

Are molecules gas, liquid, or solid? (Could be any of these.)

Do molecules move? How do we know? How could we find out?

Can we see molecules? (Yes and no. Some molecules are very small, some are very large.)

Exploration:

We need a microscope, a strong light, a special chamber in which to observe molecules, and smoke particles.

Set up the apparatus and look through the microscope. What do you see? (Tiny dots of light?) What are they doing? (Describe their motion.)

What is making the dots move? Are they alive?

Are you looking at molecules? What do you think you are looking at? Why did we put smoke in the chamber?

Explanation:

Smoke is made of particles of unburned carbon.

They are very small but not as small as molecules.

Molecules of air may be oxygen, nitrogen, argon, water vapor, or other gases. All are too small to see in a microscope. What you are seeing are smoke particles that are reflecting the bright light of the lamp.

Why are they moving? (We assume they are being hit by molecules that are moving very fast, causing the smoke particles to jiggle this way and that randomly.)

Elaboration:

Why is it important for us that molecules are moving? (We can breathe only because molecules move into our lungs. We have clouds because molecules of water vapor move together to form cloud droplets. We have air pressure and water pressure because molecules of air and water are moving very fast. Sound travels through materials because molecules move fast.)

Life on earth is possible only because molecules move.

Molecules of different materials move at different speeds. Molecules of gases move fastest—for example, molecules of hydrogen move more than 7 miles a second.

Molecules get their energy to move from radiation from the sun and stars.

Evaluation:

Describe what a molecule is.

Tell where molecules get their energy to move.

We did not see molecules. What did we see?

What do we assume caused the smoke particles to move?

DAILY LESSON PLAN 4

Physical Science—Instructional Model

TOPIC: SOUND

Engagement:

What makes sound? Can you see sound? How does sound travel? Can sound travel in a vacuum?

How do sounds differ? (loudness, pitch, intensity, speed of travel) In what other ways do they differ?

Exploration:

We would like to make a sound we can see. How might we do this?

Cut both ends out of a small tin can, such as a juice can. Stretch a rubber membrane across one end of the can. Glue a small fragment of a broken mirror on the membrane, slightly off center.

In a darkened room, have a classmate shine a flashlight on the mirror fragment so the light reflects on to a wall or chalkboard.

Sing a note very loudly into the open end of the can. Observe what the light reflection does. Have you seen a sound? This is a simple *sound visualizer*. What do scientists sometimes use to see a sound wave? (an electronic tool—an oscilloscope) What are its advantages?

Explanation:

Individual voices have their own characteristics.

These are called *voice prints*. How might they be used?

Sounds always originate in vibrations—of air or other gases, of liquids, or of solids.

Sounds must have a medium to originate and travel through. No medium—no sound!

The sound visualizer you made uses the idea of a *light lever*, a small beam of light that has no weight, so the mirror can move easily when sound strikes the membrane.

Elaboration:

Can you measure the speed of sound in air?

There is a simple way to do this that gives a good result. It uses *resonance*. You need a tuning fork of 264

or 330 or 440 vibrations per second (middle C, E above middle C, or A above middle C).

Your results should be within 5 percent of the accepted value, which is 1087 fps at 0°C.

Evaluation:

How is sound produced?

Why are molecules important for sound to travel?

Describe how you could measure the speed of sound by a method different from the one we used.

In sound waves, how are speed, frequency, and wavelength related?

DAILY LESSON PLAN 5

Physical Science—Instructional Model

TOPIC: LIGHT

Engagement:

What kinds of light are there? (visible, ultraviolet, infrared)

The electromagnetic spectrum contains all the forms of light as well as radio waves, x-rays, and gamma rays.

How do the wavelengths differ in the forms of radiations in the electromagnetic spectrum? (They range from long to short in the following order: radio-infrared-visible-ultraviolet-x-rays-gamma rays).

What are the colors in visible light from long to short? (red-orange-yellow-green-blue-indigo-violet)

Exploration:

Hold a glass prism up to an incandescent light. What do you see? Make a narrow slit in a piece of paper.

Have the light go through the slit before going to the prism. Does this improve the spectrum you see?

Hold a diffraction grating up to an incandescent light. What do you see? How does the image compare with that seen using the prism? What is the order of colors seen with the prism or diffraction grating?

Explanation:

White light from an incandescent bulb has in it seven basic colors of light. When white light hits a glass prism, the short-wavelength light (violet) refracts, or bends, the most. Long-wavelength light (red) refracts the least. Other colors such as orange, yellow, green, blue, and indigo refract intermediate amounts. These varying amounts of refraction produce a spectrum of seven colors that looks like a rainbow.

White light passing through a diffraction grating (a piece of glass or plastic that has had thousands of parallel lines scratched onto its surface) is diffracted and produces a spectrum like that made by a prism. Each device breaks white light up into its respective colors.

Elaboration:

How could we find the wavelength of different colors of light? One way is to use a diffraction grating and a source of light like that from a showcase bulb. (The filament in a showcase bulb is a single tungsten wire.)

Use the description of the method provided for you to do this experiment. You should be able to obtain a value for red light of about 7000 Angstroms and for violet light of about 4500 Angstroms. (One Angstrom is equal to 10^{-8} centimeters). It is interesting that using simple materials, it is possible to get an acceptable wavelength for red and violet light.

How is a rainbow formed? Teacher: draw a diagram showing students how this can happen.

Evaluation:

What is the order of colors of light produced by a prism or diffraction grating from long to short wavelength?

What is meant by wavelength? What other things besides light have wavelengths?

Study of the stars using wavelengths of light can tell us what the stars are made of and whether they are moving toward us or away from us (Doppler effect).

Procedure for measuring wavelength of light:

1. Use diffraction grating (5000 lines per cm).
2. Use showcase bulb (single-line filament).
3. Hold grating near the eye.
4. Sight the showcase bulb and spectrum produced while viewing through the diffraction grating.
5. Aim one sight line at the bulb.
6. Aim one sight line at the color whose wavelength you wish to measure.
7. Using a protractor, measure the angle between the sight lines.
8. Find the sine of this angle.
9. Use the equation wavelength = d sine of angle between sight lines.
10. Calculate the wavelength in centimeters. Convert to Angstroms by the relationship one Angstrom = 10^{-8} cm.
11. Red light should approximate 7000 Angstroms.
12. Violet light should approximate 4500 Angstroms.

DAILY LESSON PLAN 6

Earth and Environmental Science— Instructional Model

TOPIC: AIR AND MOISTURE—CLOUD FORMATION

Engagement:

Is moisture part of the air? (Yes, water vapor.)

Are water droplets part of the air? (No, they are suspended in air but are not part of the air.)

Can you see water droplets? (Yes, enough of them together are called fog or clouds.)

Can you see water vapor? (No, because they are individual molecules and are too small to be seen.)

Exploration:

Can we make a cloud? What do we need? (We need water vapor, particles, and cooling. We also need a glass jar with a one-hole rubber stopper and a rubber tube in the hole.)

Put a small bit of water in a glass jar that has a tight stopper in the top. This is liquid water. How can you get water vapor from it? (Shake it.)

How can we cool it quickly? (Take a sudden breath from the jar. The air cools by expansion.) Do you get a cloud? Perhaps you need some particles. Put some smoke in the jar.

Now cool it by expansion again. Do you get a cloud this time? What made the difference?

Explanation:

Particles are needed for water molecules to gather (condense) on. These can be smoke, dust, ions, or pollen.

There are millions of water molecules in a single droplet of water. You can see water droplets when there are thousands of them in a group.

The motion of water molecules is necessary to let them come together to form a droplet. (Remember the demonstration of Brownian motion?)

Fog and clouds are made in the same way.

In nature, water vapor is always present in the air.

Dust or smoke particles are always present.

Cooling is caused by air expanding as it rises into lower pressures (adiabatic cooling). These conditions make clouds.

Fog can be caused by radiational cooling.

Elaboration:

Clouds form over mountains as air rises and cools.

Fog forms along seacoasts as air meets cold water.

Water vapor comes from evaporating oceans and lakes, and from transpiration from forests.

Heating from sunlight evaporates clouds and fog back into water vapor.

Evaluation:

What things are needed to form clouds or fog? Explain this concept to a classmate.

DAILY LESSON PLAN 7

Earth and Environmental Science

TOPIC: AIR AND MOISTURE—MEASURING RELATIVE HUMIDITY

Engagement:

What does it mean to be humid?

Can you feel humidity? Can you feel dryness?

Which do you prefer?

How can you measure humidity?

Does water evaporate from your skin when it is humid?

Exploration:

To measure humidity, we need a thermometer, a cloth wick, some water, and a way to swing the thermometer through the air. Psychrometric tables will be needed.

You can make your own device. It is called a sling psychrometer.

We will measure relative humidity with a sling psychrometer.

Find the dry-bulb temperature.

Find the wet-bulb temperature using the thermometer with the moistened wick.

Find the difference between the two temperatures. From the psychrometric tables, find the relative humidity.

Find the relative humidity in different locations at different times of the day.

Explanation:

Relative humidity is the ratio of the amount of moisture (water vapor) in the air to the amount the air could hold at a given temperature.

Warm air can hold more water vapor than cold air.

If the air temperature goes up, the relative humidity goes down.

Elaboration:

Relative humidity is usually the highest in the morning.

Relative humidity falls at midday, then rises in the evening, and reaches its highest point just before dawn.

Why does the sling psychrometer work as it does?

In dry air, there is a large difference between the dry-bulb and wet-bulb readings, which means low relative humidity.

In moist air, there is a small difference between the dry-bulb and wet-bulb readings, which means high relative humidity.

If the dry-bulb and wet-bulb readings are the same, the relative humidity is 100 percent.

Evaluation:

What is the meaning of relative humidity?

What temperature air can hold the most water vapor? The least water vapor?

Why does relative humidity decrease at midday?

Explain how a sling psychrometer works.

DAILY LESSON PLAN 8

Earth and Environmental Science

TOPIC: AIR AND MOISTURE—MEASURING CLOUD MOVEMENT

Engagement:

What does cloud movement tell you?

Do different layers of clouds all move in the same direction?

How fast do clouds move? How could we find out?

Exploration:

To find the direction and speed of cloud movement, we need a compass, a stop watch, a tape measure, and a sighting point.

Find a tall pole such as a telephone pole. To begin, try to find the direction of movement of low clouds, such as cumulus.

Sight over the very tip of the tall pole so that you can see the front edge of the moving cloud. With a small rock, mark the position of your feet on the ground where you stand. Also note the exact time with your stopwatch.

While watching the cloud, slowly walk so that you keep the same point on the cloud in sight over the tip of the tall pole.

Continue this procedure for at least 15 minutes.

When you stop, again note the exact position and time.

Estimate the height of the tall pole in meters.

Estimate the height of the cloud in meters. Most low clouds are between 1,000 m and 2,000 m high at their bases. For your experiment, assume the height is 1,500 m.

Explanation:

The proportion to use in the calculation is

$$\frac{H \text{ (height of cloud)}}{h \text{ (height of pole)}} = \frac{S \text{ (speed of cloud)}}{s \text{ (speed of walking)}}$$

If you walked 20 m in 15 minutes (900 seconds), your speed s was 1/45 m/sec (0.022 m/sec).

Suppose the pole height was 20 m and cloud height was 1,500 m. The proportion becomes

$$\frac{1500 \ m}{20 \ m} = \frac{S}{0.022 \ m/sec}$$
$$20 \ S \ m = 33 \ m^2/sec$$
$$S = 33/20 \ m/sec = 1.65 \ m/sec$$

To obtain the direction of cloud movement, use your compass to determine the direction of the walk line. If the direction of the walk line is 90 degrees (east), the cloud direction of movement is 270 degrees (west), in other words, toward the west (or from the east). Thus the wind carrying the cloud is an easterly wind.

Elaboration:

Wind directions at high elevations are important for airplane pilots and meteorologists because they may indicate the kind of weather that is approaching.

Wind speeds aloft are also important to pilots and meteorologists.

Speeds and directions of middle clouds (2–6,000 m) and high clouds (above 6,000 m) can also be found by this method, but its accuracy decreases with height.

Airplanes in flight can measure cloud height, direction, and speed more accurately than from the ground.

Evaluation:

Could you describe to a classmate how to measure cloud directions and speeds?

What kinds of errors might there be in the measurement of directions and speeds of clouds by the methods you used?

DAILY LESSON PLAN 9

Earth and Environmental Science— Instructional Model

TOPIC: MINERALS AND ROCKS—MINERALS

Engagement:

What are minerals? (Minerals have a definite chemical composition, shape, and structure.)

What are some examples of minerals? (Some are quartz [silicon dioxide], Halite [sodium chloride], Pyrite [ferrous sulfide], Calcite [calcium carbonate], Galena [lead sulfide].)

Minerals are made up of elements.

Some minerals are ores of metals, such as lead.

Where would you look for minerals?

How can you get valuable metals from their mineral ores?

Exploration:

Many minerals can be identified by hardness.

Moh's scale of hardness is often used to identify minerals.

Moh's scale of hardness is as follows:

1.	Talc	Fingernail scratches it
2.	Gypsum	Fingernail barely scratches it
3.	Calcite	Copper penny just scratches it
4.	Fluorite	Steel knife scratches it easily
5.	Apatite	Steel knife scratches it
6.	Feldspar	It scratches window glass easily

7.	Quartz	Hardest common mineral; scratches steel and hard glass easily
8.	Topaz	Harder than any common mineral (semiprecious stone)
9.	Corundum	Scratches topaz
10.	Diamond	Hardest of all minerals

Using the minerals and materials given to you, put the minerals in order of hardness from hardest to softest. Scrape some talc off the talc mineral. Rub it on your hands and face. How does it feel? What could it be used for?

Explanation:

The physical structure and the closeness of packing of the atoms and molecules may determine how hard the mineral is.

In addition to their beauty and demand as jewelry, diamonds are very important in industry because of their extreme hardness. They can be used in cutting and polishing tools.

The softest mineral, talc, is used for marking pencils in carpentry, for making talcum powder, and for heat resistance.

Elaboration:

In Wisconsin, there was a talc mine. The talc ore was sold to companies that made useful products.

What do you think is the most desirable quality of diamonds? Why?

Small crystals of quartz are used in watches to control vibration rates needed in keeping accurate time.

Evaluation:

Recall Moh's scale of hardness. Try to write down in order from softest to hardest the minerals used in Moh's scale.

DAILY LESSON PLAN 10

Earth and Environmental Science— Instructional Model

TOPIC: MINERALS AND ROCKS—ROCKS

Engagement:

What are rocks? (Rocks are mixtures of minerals and do not have a fixed composition.)

Teacher: Show some samples of rocks such as basalt, sandstone, and granite.

What are some rocks in your location?

What are mountains made of—rocks or minerals?

Some rocks are made deep underground from molten material called magma. These are igneous rocks.

Some rocks are made on the surface of the earth by accumulations of small particles worn off of other rocks. When these particles are packed together, they form sedimentary rocks.

Some rocks are formed underground from other rocks by heat and pressure. These are called metamorphic rocks.

What are some examples of the three kinds of rocks?

Exploration:

Get some sand grains and look at them carefully with a magnifying glass. How are the grains different from each other? (color, shape, shininess)

Use a sharp toothpick to separate the sand grains into several piles. How many different kinds of piles do you find? Describe the difference in appearance of the grains in each pile.

Explanation:

You may find examples of igneous rocks, sedimentary rocks, and metamorphic rocks.

Grains of sand differ in color because of different metallic impurities in them.

Which sand grains might have come from once living things? How can you tell?

What kinds of forces may have acted on rocks and minerals to break them up into small grains of sand? (gravity, heating, cooling, rubbing together, water)

Elaboration:

Rocks are often used for building materials.

Some rocks have layers and can be used for pavements.

Rocks of different colors can be used to make designs. The earliest buildings were made of rocks because they were abundant and durable. Some buildings are thousands of years old.

Evaluation

What are the three kinds of rocks?

How is each kind of rock made?

Why can you not list rocks by their definite chemical composition?

Name several uses for rocks (in construction and other purposes).

Daily Lesson Plan 11

Life Science—Instructional Model

TOPIC: HUMAN BODY CAPACITY

Measurement of lung capacity

Engagement:

What is meant by *lung capacity*? (It is the average volume of air inhaled by and exhaled from the lungs.)

What do you think your lung capacity is in liters?

Why is large lung capacity important?

How can you increase your lung capacity?

Where would large lung capacity be an advantage?

Exploration:

Test your lung capacity by taking a deep breath and exhaling into the apparatus set up for this purpose. (See Chapter 16, pp. 228–240)

Measure the change in water level and calculate your lung capacity when exhaling.

Check your capacity by inhalation. Again measure the change in water level and calculate your capacity.

Explanation:

Why does water leave the chamber when you exhale?

Why does water return to the chamber when you inhale?

Air exerts pressure on the water. A scientific principle is that "no two objects can occupy the same space at the same time."

Recalling the demonstration on Brownian motion, you may remember that molecules of air are in constant motion. How does that finding apply here?

Elaboration:

Some divers for oysters need to stay under water for several minutes. They need very large lung capacity. People who live at high altitudes in the mountains develop large lung capacity. Why is this so?

Athletes who live at sea level and compete at high altitudes sometimes are at a disadvantage because of insufficient lung capacity. Why might this be so?

Evaluation:

What is the average lung capacity of members of your class? For boys? For girls?

How could you increase your lung capacity?

What animals might have the largest lung capacity? What about whales who dive thousands of feet?

Daily Lesson Plan 12

Physical Science—Instructional Model

TOPIC: CARTESIAN DIVER

Engagement:

Have you watched a goldfish swim? How does it change depth? (it changes its volume) How does it do this?

What is a swim bladder? (small membrane filled with air)

How does a fish take in air? (gills)

How does a submarine rise and sink? (changes its weight)

How does it do that?

Exploration:

Make a Cartesian Diver. Teacher: show the students how.

What things are needed? (tall container for water, small vial or medicine dropper, rubber membrane)

Make the diver sink. Make the diver stay at one level. Make the diver rise to the surface.

Explanation:

Push on the membrane. What happens to water level in the vial? What happens to the diver?

Release the membrane pressure. What happens to the water level in the vial? What happens to the diver?

If water enters the vial, the vial gets heavier and sinks.

Fluid Pressure Principle: A force applied to an enclosed fluid is distributed equally in all directions, with equal force on equal areas.

Archimedes' principle: The buoyant force on a submerged object is equal to the weight of the fluid displaced.

Elaboration:

To rise, fish put air in their swim bladder, making themselves larger and displacing more water. Buoyancy pushes them upward.

To submerge, a submarine takes seawater into its tanks, making itself heavier than the water it displaces, so it sinks. To rise, the submarine forces water out of its tanks with compressed air, making itself lighter, and buoyancy forces it upward.

Evaluation:

State a rule that says why objects sink in water.

State a rule that says why objects float at the surface of water, partly above the surface.

State a rule that explains why a submerged object may stay at one level, neither rising nor sinking.

What is a deadhead? (An object staying at one level below the surface of the water.) This is called *equilibrium*. How does a person float on the surface of water—by increasing his volume or by decreasing his weight?

DAILY LESSON PLAN 13

Life Science—Instructional Model

TOPIC: HUMAN BODY CAPACITY

Measurement of horsepower

Engagement:

Horsepower is a common expression for power. It is a rate of doing work equal to 550 ft. lbs/second. A foot-pound is a pound of force exerted through a distance of 1 foot.

For example, if a person could lift 550 pounds 1 foot in 1 second, he would be working at the rate of 1 horsepower.

Of course, this is impossible, because few people can lift 550 pounds. But what if a person lifted 55 pounds 10 feet in 1 second. Would this be a horse-power? Do you think a person could do this?

Exploration:

We are going to see if you can work at the rate of a horsepower.

To do this, we need a stopwatch, a flight of stairs whose height can be measured, and persons whose weight in pounds is known. If you know your weight in kilograms, multiply that weight by 2.2 and you will have your weight in pounds.

Have the timer say "Go," and begin the stopwatch Race up the stairs as fast as you can. When you reach the top, the timer will stop the watch and announce your time.

Explanation:

To calculate your horsepower, use the equation

$$P \text{ (in horsepower)} = \frac{\text{height (ft.)} \times \text{weight (lbs.)}}{(550 \text{ ft. lbs/sec}) \times \text{sec}}$$

Each person figures his/her own horsepower. What was your result? Were you disappointed? Was it lower than you thought it would be?

A healthy horse has difficulty working continuously at the rate of one horsepower. This unit of doing work is quite large.

What is the horsepower rating of a small car? (100 hp) What is the horsepower of an airplane engine? (500 hp)

Elaboration:

In electrical terms, power is measured in watts. One thousand watts is a kilowatt. An electric bulb is about 100 watts.

Sometimes it is necessary to convert electrical power units (watts) into mechanical power units (horsepower). One horsepower equals 746 watts. In other words, 746 watts of electrical power could produce one horsepower if it were 100 percent efficient. This level of efficiency is impossible, however.

Evaluation:

What is the definition of power? (rate of doing work)

What is one horsepower? (550 ft. lbs per second)

What is the electrical equivalent of one horsepower? (746 watts)

Why do drivers often want a car with many horsepower? Do they want to do work faster?

DAILY LESSON PLAN 14

Life Science—Instructional Model

TOPIC: PLANTS AND ANIMALS

Diversity of organisms

Engagement:

There are organisms all around us, everywhere.

Can we make an estimate of the number of animal species we might find inhabiting the ground surface? (probably thousands)

Life is abundant in all its forms.

How could we make a count of the number of organisms in a square meter of earth's surface?

Exploration:

We will need a metric ruler, a piece of string 4 meters in length, a magnifying glass, and a small container for collecting specimens.

Find an open area on a lawn or yard.

Lay out a square meter of area on the lawn.

Using the magnifying glass and careful observation, collect all the animal specimens you can in a period of 15 minutes. Put the organisms in your collecting container.

Classify your collection in several categories by size, by color, by number of legs, by winged or wingless, or by any other classification system you wish to use. Keep a record of the specimens collected.

Explanation:

You may find many different species living in the same area of the lawn or yard.

Describe some characteristics of your collection.

Which do you think are predators and which are prey? Which organisms are useful to humans? Which are harmful?

Elaboration:

What is the total count of specimens collected in your square meter of area?

Multiply your number by 10,000, which gives you the number of organisms in an area approximately the size of a city block.

Estimate how many organisms you might have missed in your search. What is your percentage of error in this experiment?

Evaluation:

What might be the purpose of this exercise? There are about 5 billion people on the earth. How does this number compare with your estimate of the number of nonhuman organisms on the earth? Which do you think is the dominant species?

DAILY LESSON PLAN 15

Life Science—Instructional Model

TOPIC: PLANTS AND ANIMALS

Seed dispersal methods

Engagement:

There are many ways plants spread their seeds.

Why is seed dispersal necessary?

What are some methods of seed dispersal that you know of? List them.

Some plants produce millions of seeds. Why is this necessary?

Teacher: Show the handout picturing many different kinds of seed dispersal methods.

Teacher: Show the maple seeds and spruce cones.

Exploration:

Drop the maple seeds from a height of 3 m. What do you notice?

Make a paper whirlybird. How does it resemble a maple seed? Drop it from a height of 3 m. What do you notice?

Explanation:

Many seed dispersal methods depend upon animals or humans for success. Which methods require help from animals or humans?

Successful growth of new seedlings depends on good soil, water, sunlight, and proper temperature for growth. How does successful seed dispersal relate to those necessary conditions?

Elaboration:

What are the most exotic or unusual methods of seed dispersal you have seen or read about?

Some seeds may remain healthy for years until they reach the proper conditions for growth.

What are some examples of those?

Evaluation:

Write a short paragraph of what you have learned about seed dispersal.

DAILY LESSON PLAN 16

Earth and Environmental Science— Instructional Model

TOPIC: THE SUN'S DIAMETER

How can you measure the diameter of the sun?

Materials:

Meter stick or yard stick

Small metric or English ruler

Two 3 × 5 cards

Engagement:

What is the diameter of the earth? (about 13,000 kilometers, or about 8000 miles)

Is the sun smaller or larger than the earth?

In this activity, you will be able to get an approximate diameter of the sun with your own simple measurements.

Exploration:

Cut a narrow slit in one end of each of the 3 × 5 cards as shown in the diagram. The size of the slits should allow you to slide the cards over the meter stick or yard stick as shown.

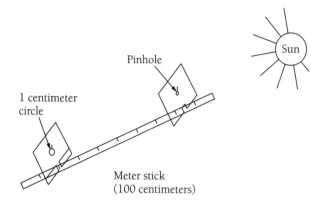

A rainbow is produced by refraction, reflection, and dispersion of light.

Draw a one centimeter (1/2 inch) diameter circle in the middle of the lower card as shown in the picture. Make a small pinhole in the middle of the upper card as shown. Enlarge the pinhole with the tip of your pencil lead.

The Experiment:

On a bright, sunny day, point your meter stick or yard stick directly toward the sun.

TO AVOID INJURING YOUR EYES, DO NOT LOOK DIRECTLY AT THE SUN.

An image of the sun will appear on the lower card. Slide the cards toward or away from each other until the sun's image exactly fills the circle on the lower card. Measure the distance between the two cards in centimeters or inches, depending on the kind of stick you are using. The distance from the earth to the sun is about 93 million miles. This is about 93,000,000 miles $\times$ 5280 feet per mile

6×12 inches per foot = $5,892,480 \times 10$ inches

The distance from the earth to the sun is about 149 million kilometers. This is about 149,000,000 kilometers $\times$ 1000 meters per kilometer $\times$ 100 centimeters per meter = $149 \times 11 \times 10$ centimeters.

To calculate the diameter of the sun, use the proportion

$$\frac{\text{Distance to the sun}}{\text{Distance between cards}} = \frac{\text{Diameter of the sun}}{\text{Diameter of the image}}$$

Thus,

$$\text{Diameter of the sun} = \frac{\text{Distance to sun} \times \text{Diameter of image}}{\text{Distance between cards}}$$

Explanation:

As an illustration, suppose the distance to the sun was taken as 150 million kilometers, the diameter of the image was one centimeter, and the distance between the cards was 100 centimeters. Then the diameter of the sun using these measurements would be 1.5 million kilometers.

The actual diameter of the sun has been estimated as 1.38 million kilometers.

How close to this figure was the result of your measurements?

(Principle: Light travels in straight lines in any given medium)

Elaboration:

The method you have used could also be used to measure the diameter of the moon. You would need to make your observations on a night when the sky is very clear and there is a bright full moon.

This experiment illustrates how scientists can use mathematics and indirect methods to measure many astronomical objects that might seem impossible to measure.

There is a book entitled, *Measuring the Universe* by Kitty Ferguson, published by Walker and Company, New York, 1999, that you might obtain from a library. It explains how indirect methods have been used throughout history to obtain information about the universe.

Evaluation:

What is the estimated value for the diameter of the sun?

The moon appears about the same size as the sun when you view it. Does this mean the moon is about the same size as the sun? Why or why not?

Can you think of any way your method of measurement could be used to measure other objects that are a great distance away? Could you measure the diameter of other stars this way?

(No, because the stars are so distant, they are only points)

DAILY LESSON PLAN 17

Earth and Environmental Science— Instructional Model

TOPIC: FORMATION OF A RAINBOW

What makes a rainbow?

Materials:

Small mirror, 10 centimeters by 15 centimeters (4 inches by 6 inches)

Small prism, 5 centimeters (2 inches) long

Flat pan with sides about 5 centimeters (2 inches) high

Piece of white cardboard about 15 centimeters by 20 centimeters (6 inches by 8 inches)

Water

Engagement:

Most of you have probably seen a rainbow during or after a rain shower. Can you name the colors seen in the rainbow?

What is the order of the colors you see?

Where was the sun when you saw the rainbow—in front of you, behind you, or directly above you?

Where was the rainbow you saw in relation to the sun—same direction as the sun or opposite the sun?

Where was the rain shower when you saw the rainbow—in front of you or behind you?

Do you think you can make a rainbow of your own? How would you do it?

Exploration:

Hold a small prism in direct sunlight coming through a window. Look for rainbow colors on a wall or ceiling.

What is the order of colors you see?

Another way to make a rainbow is to put a mirror in a flat pan of water in front of direct sunlight shining through a window.

A third way to make a rainbow is to spray water from a hose outdoors while the sun is shining.

Can you answer the question, "Is the order of colors in a rainbow always the same?"

What is that order?

Explanation:

Rainbows are caused when light *refracts* or bends when it goes through transparent materials. Water and glass are transparent materials.

White light can be separated into colors when it passes through water or glass. This is because each color has a wavelength and bends a different amount. The colors that can be seen in a rainbow are red, orange, yellow, green, blue, indigo, and violet. Red has the longest wavelength and bends the least. Violet has the shortest wavelength and bends the most. The other colors have wavelengths ranging from long to short as you go from orange to indigo.

When white light passes through a transparent material at an angle other than 90 degrees, the different wavelengths bend different amounts and produce a colored rainbow you can see in the sky or on a sheet of white paper. (See the following diagram to understand how these colors make a rainbow.)

(Principles: 1. Visible light consists of a range of waves designated as red, orange, yellow, green, blue, indigo, and violet. 2. Varying wavelengths of light travelling from a medium of one density to another transparent medium of a different density, refract or bend different amounts, depending on their wavelength.)

Elaboration:

When you see a rainbow outdoors, the sun is behind you and the falling raindrops are in front of you. It is

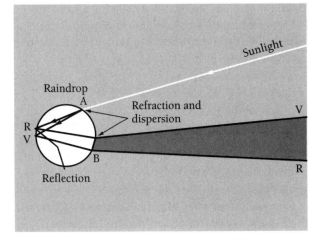

A rainbow is produced by refraction, reflection, and dispersion of light.

as if you were at the apex of a cone with the rainbow being at the base of the cone.

Because the angles at which each color leaves the raindrop are very exact, if you move to the right or left, you will see colors from different raindrops—so you will see a "different" rainbow than before.

If a companion stands beside you watching the rainbow, your companion sees a "different" rainbow than you do. So each person has his own rainbow! Isn't that a beautiful concept?

Evaluation:

Write down the order in which the colors appear in a rainbow.

Which wavelengths of light refract the most when white light passes at an angle through a transparent material? Which wavelengths refract the least? To what colors do these wavelengths correspond?

Explain to your parents or a friend how the rainbow is formed. What questions do you think they will ask you?

DAILY LESSON PLAN 18

Life Science—Instructional Model

TOPIC: CLASSIFYING OBJECTS OR EVENTS

How can you make a classification key?

Materials:

Population of your class

Pencil and paper

Ruler

Engagement:

Learning about organisms involves classifying them for purposes of observation and comparison.

There are many kinds of classification systems.

In the animal world, classification allows us to identify known varieties and species and also to identify new and previously unknown varieties and species.

Exploration:

Suppose we wish to classify our classmates into several categories so we can quickly identify or describe them.

We need to set up several criteria to classify the individuals. Such criteria might include gender, weight, height, eye color, hair color, complexion, type of ear lobes, hair type, and so forth.

Our task is to arrange the previous criteria in some form of system where one can designate specific individuals possessing the characteristics listed.

Try to develop a system to classify ten class members. Show the chart you construct to do this task.

Explanation

To illustrate the process, imagine there are 10 class members. Let us suppose that there are 9 categories of characteristics that are found among the classmates. A chart might look like the following sample shown. (Principle: Properties and characteristics of materials determine their placement in categories within a classification system)

Elaboration:

You might use the pertinent characteristics of each person for identification. Only one person would have that particular set of characteristics; therefore, recognition of that set of characteristics would identify the individual specifically.

Conversely, if you knew the name of the person, you would know that person's identifying characteristics.

Evaluation:

Of what use would such a chart be?

How could this method be used to identify leaves or rocks or minerals or automobiles? Try to make a key such as above to identify a favorite rock star or trees in a forest.

Using the following chart, what is the name of the female who weighs 151 pounds, is 5'6", has hazel eyes and blonde, straight hair?

How many girls in the class have blonde hair?

How many boys in the class weigh over 150 pounds?

How many boys with brown eyes have "blond" hair?

From the chart, can you predict how many boys with brown eyes have a fair complexion?

DAILY LESSON PLAN 19

Physical Science—Instructional Model

TOPIC: MAKING ELECTRICAL CIRCUITS WORK

How can you make a circuit that will turn a light off and on from two locations?

Materials:

1 1/2 volt dry cell with terminals

Insulated copper wire, 1 meter (1 yard) in length

Two on-off switches (You can make these)

Small flashlight bulb and socket

Engagement:

Most of you have seen lighting circuits in your homes where a light can be turned on or off from two locations, such as at the bottom and at the top of a flight of stairs.

Why would this be an advantage?

How could you arrange wiring to accomplish this task?

Exploration:

You will need a 1 1/2 volt dry cell with terminal connections on it, a flashlight bulb with socket, and about a meter of fine insulated copper wire.

For switches, you may be able to construct two of them from short (five-centimeter) pieces of copper wire.

Try several different arrangements of wiring a bulb, a self-made switch, and a dry cell to solve the problem. Keep a record, using diagrams, of the various methods you have tried.

Explanation:

See the diagram and explanations on the next page. Do not look there until you have tried several circuits of your own.

Classification System

name	gender	weight	height	eye color	hair color	complexion	ear lobes	hair type
Sam	m	150	5'8"	blue	black	dark	attached	curly
Ava	f	120	5'4"	brown	brown	dark	unattached	straight
Fran	f	151	5'6"	hazel	blonde	fair	attached	straight
Mike	m	160	6'1"	brown	black	dark	attached	wavy
Carl	m	136	5'8"	green	red	light	unattached	straight
Mary	f	124	5'9"	blue	brown	fair	attached	curly
Leslie	m	169	5'8"	hazel	brown	dark	unattached	straight
John	m	140	5'11"	brown	black	dark	attached	curly
Sue	f	119	5'3"	blue	blonde	fair	unattached	straight
Alice	f	131	5'6"	brown	brown	dark	attached	wavy

It is convenient to have a light that can be turned on or off from two locations, such as at the bottom and at the top of a stairs. How can a circuit be arranged to accomplish this?

Making a Three-way Light Switch

Step 1   Bottom of Stairs   A is right
                                             B is right
                                             Move A to Left
                                             Light goes on

Step 2   Top of stairs   A is left
                                             B is right
                                             Move B to left
                                             Light goes off

Step 3   Bottom of stairs
              Visitor wishes to come up   A is left
                                             B is left
                                             Move A to right
                                             Light goes on

Step 4   Top of stairs   A is left
                                             B is right
                                             Move B to left
                                             Light goes off

Step 5   Top of stairs
              Both wish to descend   A is left
                                             B is left
                                             Move B to right
                                             Light goes on

Step 6   Bottom of stairs   A is left
                                             B is right
                                             Move A to right
                                             Light goes off

(Principles: 1. An electrical current requires a complete circuit. 2. An electrical current in a divided circuit divides inversely proportional to the resistance in the circuit.

Elaboration:

Remember, each time you cause a bulb to light, there is a complete circuit for current to flow. Each time the light goes off, there must be an incomplete circuit.

After you have tried your own circuits, study the circuit diagram in the first column. Connect your bulbs, dry cell, and wiring as shown in the diagram and try to light the bulbs.

Did you succeed? This may be a hard problem to solve. If you were successful, congratulations!

Evaluation:

Summarize the main points you learned in making a three-way circuit.

What situations in your home are similar to the circuit you made in this experiment?

DAILY LESSON PLAN 20

Physical Science—Instructional Model

TOPIC: SERIES AND PARALLEL CIRCUITS

What is the difference between a series and a parallel circuit?

Materials:

Three flashlight bulbs, screw-in type

Three sockets to hold the three bulbs

One "D" flashlight cell

Several short pieces of fine insulated copper wire

Small screwdriver to tighten connections

Engagement:

Perhaps you have heard of 'series' and 'parallel' circuits.

These refer to two different ways to connect bulbs and dry cells or "batteries" together for different purposes.

In a Parallel Circuit, Every Bulb (or Appliance) Gets the Same Voltage.

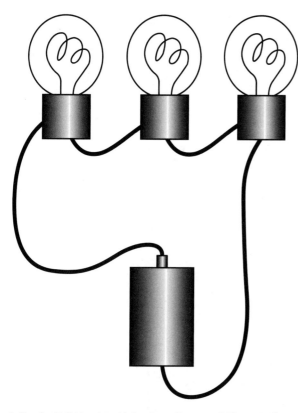

A Single Cell Used to Light One, Two, and Three Bulbs.

The most important principle is that there must be a complete circuit for electric current to flow.

Exploration:

Connecting in Series

Connect three bulbs together, one after the other in a line, and connect a wire from each end bulb to opposite ends of a dry cell (top and bottom). See the diagram. How many complete circuits do you have in each diagram?

Do the bulbs light up? Are they very bright?

Disconnect one bulb in the circuit. What happens?

Remove one bulb completely so that there are just two bulbs in the circuit. Again make a connection to the dry cell. Are the bulbs brighter or dimmer than with three bulbs? Why might this be so?

Finally, remove two bulbs from the circuit, leaving just one bulb remaining. Connect to the dry cell again. Is the bulb brighter or dimmer than before? Why might this be so?

Connecting in Parallel

Look at the diagram to see how to connect the bulbs in parallel. Each bulb has two connecting points. Connect all similar points together. Connect all the points on the opposite side of the bulbs together. Connect to the dry cell as shown.

Observe the bulbs. Are they all lit? Are they all bright? How do they differ from the situation with the series circuit?

Disconnect one bulb in the system. What happens to the other bulbs? Why might this be so?

How many complete circuits are there when all bulbs are connected to the dry cell? (Remember you can count some of the wires more than once.)

Explanation:

In the series circuit, there is only one complete circuit. The electric current has only one path to travel. If one bulb is disconnected, the circuit is broken and all lights go out.

Each bulb in a series circuit adds more *resistance* to the circuit, so less current flows through the circuit and the lights may be dim.

In the parallel circuit, there are three complete circuits.

Current from the dry cell can travel on three different paths to the dry cell.

If one bulb is disconnected, there are still two other circuits to travel on, so two lights stay on.

All the bulbs stay equally bright in a parallel circuit.

(Principle: Electric current travelling in a divided circuit divides inversely according to the resistance in the circuit)

Elaboration:

If you need light bulbs in a house that you can turn on and off without affecting other lights, what kind of circuit do you think would be best to use?

It is possible with parallel circuits to use lights and other appliances, even though each may need a different amount of current. Each appliance gets sufficient current to operate successfully.

Evaluation:

How many complete circuits are there in a series circuit?

How many complete circuits are there in a parallel circuit? (This depends on how many bulbs or appliances are in use.)

List all the things you learned from this experiment.

DAILY LESSON PLAN 21

Physical Science—Instructional Model

TOPIC: MEASURING THE SPEED OF SOUND

How can the speed of sound be measured?

Materials:

Tuning fork (Middle C 256 vps or G 384 vps)

Glass or plastic tube, about 3 cm in diameter and about 40 cm long

Deep container for water, such as a tall bottle or pail

Engagement:

This activity will let you measure the speed of sound quite accurately.

Do you think the speed of sound is quite slow or quite fast?

Have you ever seen someone pound on something quite far away and then noticed the sound arriving a fraction of a second later? What does this tell you about sound?

In this activity, you will use a concept that may be new to you called *resonance*.

Resonance happens when energy is added periodically to a vibrating object, making it vibrate even more vigorously.

Exploration:

Obtain a tuning fork with the number of vibrations per second marked on it. (Note: a tuning fork between 256 vps and 512 vps will work best for this activity.)

Obtain a glass or plastic tube about 40 cm. long and 3 cm. in diameter. Hold the tube upright with the lower end in a tall container of water.

Strike the tuning fork a sharp blow (using a rubber hammer or mallet) and hold the tuning fork over the open end of the tube.

Slowly move the tube up and down, keeping the vibrating tuning fork close to the open end of the tube until you find a place where the sound of the tuning fork is greatly magnified.

Measure the length of the tube from the water surface to the top of the tube in centimeters.

Explanation:

Why does the sound of the tuning fork become louder at a certain length of the tube? (A point of resonance is found, where the sound waves reflect from the water surface and reinforce the vibrations of the tuning fork.)

To calculate the speed of sound, know that speed equals wave length times frequency (This relationship is true of all kinds of wave motion, such as water waves, light waves, and other kinds of waves.)

Multiply by four the length of the tube that you measured. This product is the wavelength of the sound in centimeters. (The reason you multiply by four is because the sound wave travels the length of the tube four times for each vibration—condensation travels down and up, rarefaction travels down and up) Convert the wavelength to meters instead of centimeters by dividing by 100.

Now multiply the wavelength by the frequency (e.g., 256 vps) and this will be the speed of sound in meters per second. (Principle: Resonance is produced in vibrating objects when energy is added periodically to the vibrating object at a rate that matches the natural vibration rate of the object.)

Elaboration:

The established speed of sound is about 330 meters per second. How close to this was your result? If you were within 20 meters per second, your result was very good.

Speed of sound depends greatly on the temperature. At higher temperatures, the speed is greater than at lower temperatures.

In the English system, the speed of sound is about 1087 feet per second at 32 or "°F", the freezing point of water.

Evaluation:

Give some examples of resonance (e.g., a child pushing a swing).

Tell how you think the speed of sound is different in materials other than air. (in water, about 1300 meters per second; in steel about 5000 meters per second)

DAILY LESSON PLAN 22

Physical Science—Instructional Model

TOPIC: MEASURING THE WAVELENGTH OF LIGHT

How can you measure the wavelength of light?

Materials:

Plastic diffraction grating, transmission type—5000 lines per centimeter. (Obtainable from Edmund Scientific Co., 101 Gloucester Pike, Barrington, NJ 08007-1380)

Two meter sticks

Showcase bulb

Protractor

Sine tables

Engagement:

Do you think the wavelength of visible light is long or short?

What information do you have that would permit you to answer this question?

Are there forms of light that are shorter or longer than visible light? What kinds can you name?

In what units would it be appropriate to measure the wavelength of visible light?

Why would a person want to know the wavelength of visible light? Refer to Daily Lesson Plan 17, "Formation of a Rainbow".

Exploration:

Obtain a plastic diffraction grating. Look through it at a bright light. What do you see? (On either side of the light source, you will see a brilliant spectrum, consisting of seven colors of light arranged in order: red, orange, yellow, green, blue, indigo, and violet.)

Arrange a showcase bulb in a socket at the end of a long table, or if a table is not handy, perform the experiment on the floor.

From a distance of about two meters, arrange two meter sticks, one of which points directly at the lighted showcase bulb the other pointed to the right or left at an angle of approximately 20 degrees from the first meter stick. The exact angle will be determined after you sight the bulb through your diffraction, which you are holding close to your eye.

Decide which color is the one for which you want to find the wavelength. If you want to find the wavelength of blue light, point the second meter stick directly at the most intense area of blue light. If you want to measure the wavelength of red light, point the second meter stick at the most intensely red light. View the spectrum through your grating.

Carefully measure with a protractor the angle between the two meter sticks.

Using the sine tables, find the sine of the angle between the two meter sticks.

Calculations

Using the equation: Wavelength $= d$ sine alpha, where d is the distance between lines on your diffraction grating and alpha is the angle you measured between the meter sticks. (for the diffraction gratings described above, the distance between lines is 1/5000 centimeter, or in decimal notation, it is .0002 centimeters.)

Multiply the two numbers together to get the wavelength of light in centimeters. This will be a very small number. Wavelength of light is frequently expressed in Angstroms. To convert centimeters to Angstroms, divide the number in centimeters by .00000001 (one hundred millionth), or multiply the number in centimeters by 10^{-8}.

For example, if the angle you measured was 20 degrees, the sine of 20 degrees is .3420. To get the wavelength, use the equation: Wavelength $=$ d $\times$ sine of 20 degrees. This becomes

$$W = (.0002 \text{ cm.}) \times 3420.$$
$$\text{This is } W = (2^{-4} \times 10 \text{ cm.}) (3420 \times 10^{-4}$$

or $W = 6840 \times 10^{-8}$ centimeters or 6840 Angstroms.

The established wavelength for red light is 7000 Angstroms, so the result in this example is very close.

Explanation:

If you wish to obtain the wavelength of any of the other colors of light in the spectrum, perform the same experiment by pointing your second meter stick directly at the color for which you wish to measure the wavelength. Colors of the spectrum range from blue-violet (about 4000 Angstroms) to red (about 7000 Angstroms).

Elaboration:

It is quite remarkable that we are able to measure the wavelengths of colors of visible light with simple equipment such as a diffraction grating, two meter sticks, a showcase bulb, and a protractor. Consider that we are measuring something that is smaller than the human eye can resolve, yet we are able to get a reasonably accurate result.

Knowing the wavelengths of visible light is very important in astronomy, where it is used to determine the composition of stars and other astronomical objects. Most of the information astronomers have been able to obtain with telescopes and other earth-based equipment has been made possible due to knowing the wavelengths of light coming from the heavens.

Evaluation:

Explain to a classmate the procedure for finding the wavelength of a particular color of the spectrum.

Diffraction gratings are made by very precise machines called *ruling engines* that draw very closely spaced straight lines on glass, metal, or plastic. Why can you not see the lines on a diffraction grating?

Sometimes you may see a spectrum appear on CD or even on an oil slick on the floor of a garage. How might the spectrum you see through a diffraction grating be related to what you see on an oil slick?

INDEX